understanding
ADVANCED
HUMAN BIOLOGY

Jane Vellacott and Sarah Side

Hodder & Stoughton

A MEMBER OF THE HODDER HEADLINE GROUP

British Library Cataloguing in Publication Data
A catalogue record for this title is available from The British Library
ISBN 0340 679115

First published 1998
Impression number   10   9   8   7   6   5   4   3   2   1
Year   2002   2001   2000   1999   1998

Typeset by Wearset, Boldon, Tyne and Wear.
Printed in Great Britain for Hodder & Stoughton Educational, a division of Hodder Headline
Plc, 338 Euston Road, London NW1 3BH by Redwood Books, Trowbridge, Wiltshire.

Contents

Acknowledgements

The authors gratefully thank their families for their support and Dr Chris Side and Dr Colin Ryall for their help with research.

The publishers would like to thank the following artists who drew the illustrations: Maggie Brand, Tom Cross, Richard Duszczak, Jeff Edwards, Phil Ford, Ian Foulis, David Graham and Tech Type.

We are grateful to the following companies, institutions and individuals who have given permission to reproduce photographs in this book. Every effort has been made to trace and acknowledge ownership of copyright. The publishers will be glad to make arrangements with any copyright holders whom it has not been possible to contact.

Key:
Page references in italic refer to photographs which are repeated in the colour section.
l = left, r = right, t = top, b = bottom, m = middle

Action-Plus/Steve Bardens (325 b); /Glyn Kirk (63, 197 b); /P. Tarry (245, 316); Agence France Presse (396); Antiquités nationale/J.G. Berizzi (419); /Jean Schormans (418); R.D. Battersby (221, 237 t, 264 r); BBC Natural History Unit/Premaphotos (462); Biocompatibles Limited (102 t); Biophotos Associates (9, 11 both, 13 b, 14, 17, 18, 19, 65 m, 111 b l, 140 l, 196, 197 t, *215*, 224, 386, 424 b); C.D. Side (249 both, *390*); Bruce Coleman/Jane Burton (398 r b); /Alain Compost (409); /Peter Davey (408); /Jose Luis Gonzalez Grande (387 t, 425 b); /Stephen J. Krasemann (397 r); /Andrew J. Purcell (*425 t m*); /Hans Reinhard (198, 397 l); /John Shaw (397 m); Corbis UK Ltd (420 b); FLPA/David Hosking (424 t r); Robert Harding (*35 b*); Hodder and Stoughton Educational (*378*, 398 r t, 422); Hoechst Marion Roussel (3); Holt Studios/Nigel Cattlin (305, 325 t); /P. Peacock (21 r, 385); The Hutchison Library (206); /Audrey Zvoznikov (156 b); Life File/Emma Lee (43, 324, 389 both); /Nigel Sitwell (*392 m and r*); /John Woodhouse (271 r); National History Museum (*415, 416 b*); Oxford Scientific Films/Kathie Atkinson (463); /C.G. Gardener (65 b); /London Scientific Films (2 t); /Colin Milkins (*373*); Tim Page (222 b); Panos Pictures/L. Taylor (156 t); Philip Harris (434 t l and r); Renunion des Musée Nationaux/Musée de L'Homme (*420 t*); /St Germain-en-Laye (418, 419, *421*); Royal Botanical Gardens Kew (387 b); RSPCA Photo Library/E.A. Janes (102 b); St Mary's Hospital Medical School, London, Audio Visual Department (229 r); Science Photo Library (36 both, 51 t, 138, 186, *209 b*, 363, 405 l); /Michael Abbey (92, 111 t r); /Jim Amos (158); /A. Barrington Brown (328); /Alex Bartel (71); /Biology Media (118); /Biophoto Associates (2 b, 82, 90, *134, 137*, 229 l, 324/325 background, 368, *384 r*); /CDC (246);
/Chris Bjornberg (113); /Martin Bond (456); /Michael Bond (424 t l); /O. Bradfute/Peter Arnold Inc. (22 r); /BSIP/VEM (*162 b*, 209 t); /Dr Jeremy Burgess (3 t r, 446); /Tony Buxton (222 t); /Mark Clark (21 l); CNRI (33 all, *108*, 207); /Tony Craddock (51 b, 196/197 background); /Russel D. Curtis (404/405 background); /Deep Light Productions (184); /Department of Nuclear Medicine, Charing Cross Hospital (*70*); /Eye of Science (22 l, 174, *183*); /Don Fawcett (*179*); /Dr Gene Feldman, NASA GSFC (*459*); /Simon Fraser (398 l, 405 r, *452*); /G.F. Gennaro (145 b); /Eric Grave (140 r); /John Greim (121); /Nancy Hamilton (*368*); /John Heseltine (237 b); /Jan Hinsch (*425 t r*); /James Holmes/Cellmark Diagnostic (341); /Manfred Kage (264 l); /Dr Kari Lounatmaa (*199*); /King's College School of Medicine, Breast Screening Unit (293 both); /Mehau Kulyk (62/63 background); /Astrid and Hanns-Frieder Michler (111 t l and b r, 164); /Microfield Scientific (7); /Professor P. Motta, University 'La Sapienza' Rome (2/3 background); /Professor P. Motta and M.Castelucci (145 t); /Professor P. Motta/G. Macchiarelli University 'La Sapienza' Rome (75); /Larry Mulvehill (37); /Dr Gopal Murti (13 t, *382*); /National Library of Medicine (392 l) /Claude Nuridsany and Marie Perennou (4 b, *394, 425 t l*); /Alfred Pasieka (4 t, *16*, 65 t, *330*); /Petit Format/CSI (*283*); /D. Phillips (*298*); /Philippe Plailly/Eurelios (3 t r); /K.R. Porter (15); /John Reader (411, *412 t*, 412 b, *416 t*, 417); /John Radcliffe Hospital (93); /J.C. Revy (52); /P. Saada/Eurelios (289); /St Bartholemew's Hospital, London (150, 250); /Carl Schmidt-Luchs (225); /Jim Selby (135); /Dr Chris Somerville (*450*) /James Stevenson (*35 t*); /Erica Stone/Peter Arnold Inc. (271 l); /Andrew Syred (278); /Tek Images (252); /Science Source (329); /Sheila Terry and Anne Sheasby, Home Economist (239); /USDA (20); /Jerry Wachter (128/129 background); /Wellcome Department of Cognitive Neurology (*100*); /Munoz-Yague/Eurelios (444); /Hattie Young (384 l); Sealand Aerial Photography Ltd (448); South West News Service (404); Suntech Medical Instruments (162 t l and r); Telegraph Colour Library (270/271 background, 471); Tony Stone Images/RNHRD NHS Trust (*112*); Topham Picture Point (86); University of Nottingham (343); Wildlife Trust for Cambridge (434 b l and r); Zoological Society of London (407)

We would also like to thank the following examinations boards for permission to reproduce questions: The Associated Examining Board, University of Cambridge Local Examinations Board/the Midland Examining Group and London Examinations, A division of the Edexcel Foundation

Introduction

There is no doubt that the high standards demanded at advanced level challenge even the brightest amongst us. We hope that this text will help you in your studies by providing clear explanations, relevant information on current issues and an opportunity to test your knowledge and skills.

What can you expect from this book? The content is divided into seven sections, and is well focused to cover the core material required by the main A level syllabuses for Human Biology and much of the syllabuses for Biology. We have especially included **articles** and **case studies** demonstrating how the principles of biological science are applied, giving a vocational slant which is important for a variety of pre-university access courses as well as GNVQ Health and Social Care. Brief **summary points** in the margins could be used as triggers for making revision notes on key points. **Cross-references** will help you recognise links between the different sections when researching particular topics. The **short questions** are useful to test your knowledge and understanding while working through the sections and you can gain a better understanding of what will be required at examination by practising the **past and specimen A level questions** at the end of each section. Finally the **Colour Gallery** repeats those Figures from the text that need to be seen in colour to be fully appreciated or understood. The Figures that are repeated in this manner are highlighted by the symbol **C1** and a page reference given.

While no text can ever be totally complete, we think you will find that this comprehensive volume provides thorough, up-to-date and stimulating coverage of the material required for your studies at advanced level. Above all, we hope that you enjoy it.

Jane Vellacott and Sarah Side, 1998

SECTION 1

Cells and Molecules

in brief — The building blocks of life

The first section of this book provides the ground work for the chapters that follow, by describing cells and how they work.

The smallest functional unit of all living organisms is a cell. Here, the metabolic reactions take place which allow the organism to exist. Human cells and those of other animals and plants are eukaryotic, meaning that they are more highly organised than the prokaryotic cells of bacteria. Every cell is contained inside a cell membrane which is a selective barrier to molecules and ions passing in and out of it. Particles may move by an active (energy-requiring) process, or by one which is passive such as diffusion or osmosis.

All cells are built to a basic plan, but have modifications so that they can carry out their specialised function.

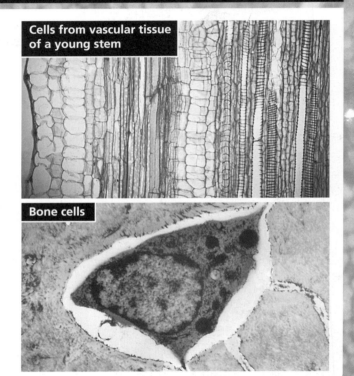

Cells from vascular tissue of a young stem

Bone cells

The way cells work

The existence of cells has been known for over 300 years. With the invention in the 1930s of the electron microscope our understanding has become very much more detailed. Sophisticated techniques such as x-ray crystallography and cell fractionation have also been developed that help us to understand how the cell works at a molecular level.

The cell's activities are ultimately controlled by the nucleus, within which the genetic material, the chromosomes, are found. The chromosomes consist mainly of DNA (deoxyribonucleic acid), a code directing which proteins the cell is able to make, and which should be made at any particular time. As a result of its particular proteins, the cell has individual characteristics and functions. Enzymes are especially important proteins as they determine which chemical reactions can take place in the cell. The cell's chemistry is called metabolism. Cytoplasm containing organelles fills the rest of the cell. Each organelle is surrounded by a membrane and is a highly specialised structure, with one or more particular metabolic roles.

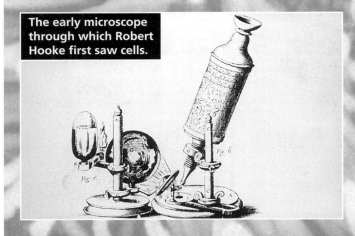

The early microscope through which Robert Hooke first saw cells.

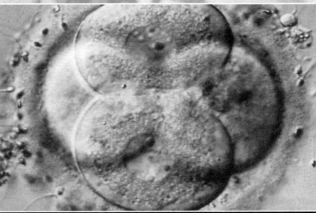

This fertilised egg will be transplanted into a woman's uterus. It has begun the first of the millions of mitotic divisions that will take place as it develops into a baby.

Increasing in complexity

Cells are grouped in to tissues which may have specialised functions. Tissues combine to form structures called organs, with important roles in the body. One or more organs with related body function forms a body system. A human is an organism with many integrated body systems. Some work throughout life; others such as the female reproductive system, work only for part of the normal life span.

▶ *Section 2* **covers body systems in more detail**

Increasing in number

Cells increase in number by a type of cell division called mitosis. The resulting daughter cells are genetically identical to their parents. This process allows the human body to grow, to repair damage and to replace cells lost through wear and tear, as happens from the skin epidermis. If mitosis becomes chaotic and out of control an enlarged group of cells called a tumour can develop; if the tumour is malignant it is able to spread damaging normal cells. This is cancer. An enormous amount of research is taking place to find ways of preventing tumours from spreading.

Biological molecules

In order to understand the way in which cells function we must be clear about the structure and behaviour of the molecules that build cells

and play a part in their metabolism.

Water is essential for life and accounts for a high proportion of human tissue. Other chemical compounds which make up cells are called organic compounds, because their structure is based on carbon. These are carbohydrates, proteins, lipids and nucleic acids.

Chemical reactions in the human body are catalysed by enzymes, types of proteins. They speed up metabolic reactions allowing them to occur rapidly at body temperature. Humans learnt long ago to apply the use of enzymes to their advantage, for example in brewing, baking and cheese-making. More recently, ways of using enzymes in other areas, such as the chemical, pharmaceutical and agricultural industries, have been discovered.

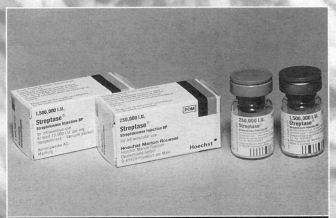

The drug streptokinase, developed from an enzyme, can be given after a heart attack – it is used to improve the chance of recovery

CHAPTER 1 The Discovery of Cells and Their Structures

1.1 The structure of cells

A cell is a self contained unit. During development it is able to adapt its structure appropriately to its function. It is the basic unit of all organisms, carrying out the essential chemical processes that keep the organism alive.

Cells were first seen with a light microscope by Robert Hooke in 1665. A talented scientist, he had designed one of the first optical (light) microscopes and was observing the appearance of thin sections of cork from the bark of a tree. He saw and drew numerous empty structures which he called 'cells'. Over the years, tissues from many other sources of plant and animal materials were examined and it became clear that organisms consist of cells. In 1839 T. Schwann, a zoologist, and M. Schleiden, a botanist, proposed the **cell theory**, that cells occur universally and are the basic units of a living organism.

Scientists using the light microscope discovered the major structures of cells. A typical animal cell is shown in Figure 1.1.

The cell is usually 10–30 μm in diameter and is enclosed within a **cell surface (plasma) membrane**. The cell contains a nucleus and cytoplasm. The **nucleus** is surrounded by a nuclear envelope (membrane) and when stained shows a dense area, the nucleolus, and chromatin, the material which makes up the chromosomes. The **cytoplasm** has a granular appearance. It contains numerous inclusions, for example deposits of the animal carbohydrate glycogen, and **organelles** which are the sites of the metabolic reactions of the living cell.

Plant cells are usually larger than animal cells and are surrounded by a permeable **cell wall** which is located outside the cell membrane. This consists of a thick deposit of the polysaccharide **cellulose** which is secreted by the cytoplasm. Cellulose is a tough material but is also slightly elastic and plays a vital role in the support of plants. The wall contains other materials such as **hemicellulose** and **pectins**. Some cells require extra thickening to give additional strength, in which case **lignin** is deposited. Cell walls are highly lignified in **xylem** tissue, the cells found throughout plants for the transport of water. Any lignified cell becomes impermeable to water and its living contents die. The cement between one plant cell and the next is the middle lamella which is made of calcium pectate.

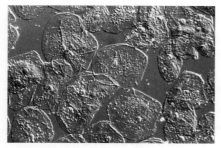

Figure 1.1 The appearance of human cheek cells under a light microscope (magnification ×99)

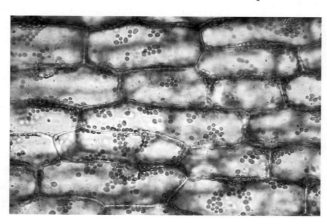

Figure 1.2 Cells from a leaf of *Elodea canadensis*, Canadian pondweed, as they appear under a light microscope (magnification ×60)

The organelles in the cytoplasm include colourless **plastids**. An example of such plastids are **leucoplasts**. They contain deposits of the carbohydrate starch which is a major food store of plants. Many plant cells carry out photosynthesis and their cytoplasm contains numerous green plastids called **chloroplasts**. Plastids are not found in animal cells.

Much of the plant cell is occupied by a large cell **vacuole** which contains watery **cell sap**. The membrane that separates the contents of the vacuole from the cytoplasm is the **tonoplast** or vacuolar membrane.

▶ *Chapter 21 describes the structure of chloroplasts in detail*

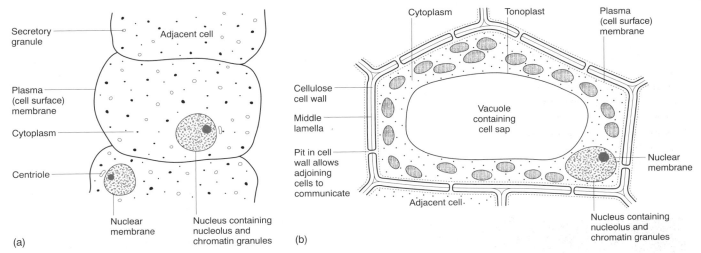

Figure 1.3 Typical structure of (a) an animal cell and (b) a plant cell as seen with a light microscope

1.2 Microscopy

The **light microscope** is the instrument with which scientists discovered cells and their major features. Progress was limited, however, by the lack of sophistication of the instruments that were available to them. Our understanding of the detailed fine structure of cells has been revolutionised in the last 50 years by the development of the **electron microscope**. Cell organelles and tiny particles such as viruses and molecules can now be viewed and their detailed organisation made clear. Before looking at the ultrastructure of the cell it is useful to consider the different kinds of microscope which can be used.

The light (optical) microscope

▶ *Chapter 21 Figure 21.6 shows the position of light in the electromagnetic spectrum*

For a light microscope the source of radiation is visible light, which may be built into the microscope or come from a bench lamp. The light passes through the specimen on the microscope stage. The image is magnified and focused by the lens in the objective and the lens in the eyepiece.

The total magnification of the specimen is calculated by multiplying the magnification of the two lenses. (If the magnification of the eyepiece lens is ×6 and the objective lens is ×40, the total magnification will be 6 × 40 or ×240.) The maximum magnification that is possible with a light microscope is around ×1500. However, the detail that can be seen with the light microscope depends not on magnification, but on the **resolution** or **resolving power** of the instrument. This means how well the microscope is able to distinguish two small objects that are very close together. If it has high resolution then close points can be seen separately, but if the microscope has low resolution they will merge as one.

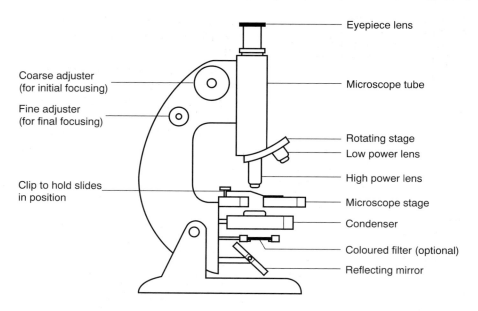

Figure 1.4 The light microscope

Resolution is inversely proportional to the wavelength of light illuminating the object being viewed. This means that high wavelengths of light give low resolution and shorter wavelengths give higher resolution. Because visible light has a fixed range of wavelength (average 550 nm) there is a limit to the resolving power of the light microscope. The best light microscope can distinguish two points about 200 nm (200×10^{-9} m) apart, but many cell structures are smaller than this.

Electron microscopes

In an effort to increase the resolution of the microscope, scientists tried using a source of radiation of shorter wavelength than light. As a result, the first **transmission electron microscope (TEM)** was developed during the 1930s. Nowadays, a TEM uses a beam of electrons which have wavelengths of about 0.004 nm and so the resolution is many times higher than that of a light microscope (0.1 nm) and it can magnify up to ×1 000 000.

The specimen is not viewed directly, but as an image produced on a fluorescent screen or photographic plate (an **electron micrograph**). The source of electrons is a tungsten filament electron gun at the top of the column. Electrons are emitted when a high voltage is applied; they are focused on to the specimen by powerful electromagnets. The vacuum inside the instrument prevents the scattering of electrons that would occur if they were fired through air.

The specimen can only be examined when dead because it is embedded in resin and cut using an ultra-microtome in to very thin sections (10–100 nm). Thin sections allow the electrons to pass through without being scattered or absorbed. A section is mounted on to a copper grid. Salts of lead or uranium may be used as 'stains' to give contrast in the final image because they are absorbed by some structures in the cell. These parts are electron dense, that is they do not allow electrons to pass through them.

A limitation of the TEM lies in the preparation of the specimen being observed. The fixing, sectioning and staining of a dead specimen may alter the material. Sometimes these changes produce an **artefact**, something which does not really exist in a living cell. This means that the interpretation of images and electron micrographs takes experience. In addition, the only

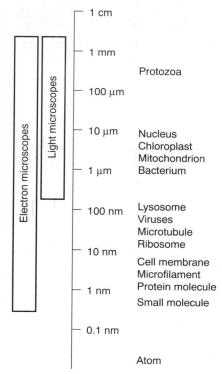

Figure 1.5 Comparison of the resolution of light and electron microscopes

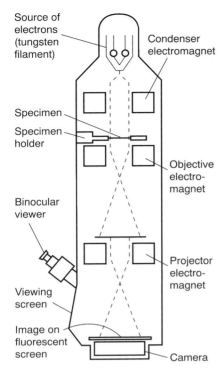

Source of electrons (tungsten filament)

Condenser electromagnet

Specimen

Specimen holder

Objective electro-magnet

Binocular viewer

Projector electro-magnet

Viewing screen

Image on fluorescent screen

Camera

Figure 1.6 The important features of a transmission electron microscope

Figure 1.7 Scanning electron micrograph showing mammalian sperm (magnification ×2700)

way to obtain a three-dimensional image is by reconstructing it from a series of two-dimensional images, and this requires a great deal of patience and skill.

The **scanning electron microscope (SEM)** was first produced commercially in 1965 and is used to bounce electrons off the surface of a specimen. It produces a detailed three-dimensional image as you can see in Figure 1.7.

As in the TEM, an electron beam controlled by electromagnets is used, but in a SEM electromagnetic coils make the electrons scan the surface of the specimen. Electrons reflected from the surface of the specimen form an image on the viewing screen. The resolution of the SEM is about 1.0 nm and its magnification ×800 000.

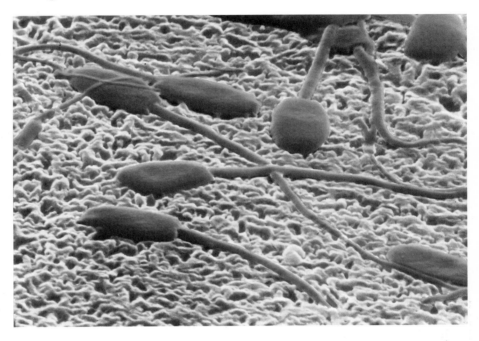

Questions

1 Why are the specimens examined with electron microscopes always dead?

2 Why is there a vacuum inside the electron microscope?

3 Would parts of a cell structure that have absorbed a lead salt appear light or dark in a black and white electron micrograph? Explain your answer.

4 List the advantages and disadvantages of both light and electron microscopes.

CHAPTER 2 The Detailed Structure of the Eukaryotic Cell

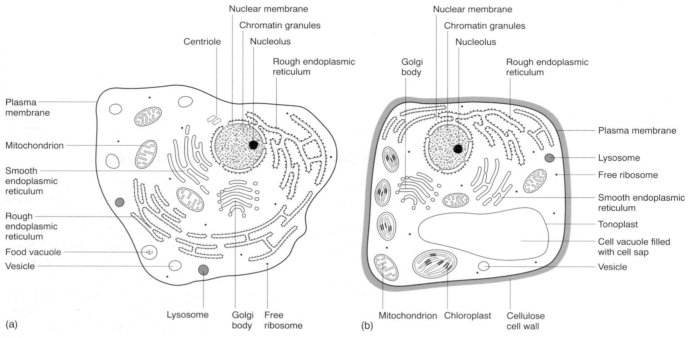

Labels for (a) animal cell: Nuclear membrane, Chromatin granules, Nucleolus, Centriole, Rough endoplasmic reticulum, Plasma membrane, Mitochondrion, Smooth endoplasmic reticulum, Rough endoplasmic reticulum, Food vacuole, Vesicle, Lysosome, Golgi body, Free ribosome

(a)

Labels for (b) plant cell: Nuclear membrane, Chromatin granules, Nucleolus, Golgi body, Rough endoplasmic reticulum, Plasma membrane, Lysosome, Free ribosome, Smooth endoplasmic reticulum, Tonoplast, Cell vacuole filled with cell sap, Vesicle, Mitochondrion, Chloroplast, Cellulose cell wall

(b)

Figure 2.1 Features of the ultrastructure of eukaryotic cells visible with an electron microscope (a) animal cell (b) plant cell. Electronmicrographs are shown on pages 18 and 19.

2.1 The cell surface membrane

The cell surface membrane has the same basic structure and properties in all cells. It controls the passage of molecules and ions in and out of cells as described in Chapter 4.

An experiment to investigate the chemical nature of the cell membrane

Beetroot cells contain cell sap which is coloured by dark red pigment molecules (xanthocyanin). If the tonoplast and cell membrane are damaged this red pigment escapes.

In an experiment some cylinders were cut from a fresh beetroot with a cork borer and trimmed so that they were all exactly 3 cm long. They were washed under running water for at least 1 hour to wash away the sap from cells damaged during cutting. A water-bath was prepared at 25°C and used to bring solutions in two test tubes to temperature. One tube (A) contained 20 ml of distilled water and the other (B) an equal volume of ethanol. A beetroot cylinder was placed in each tube for 10 minutes. It was then removed and discarded. The

liquid remaining in the test tubes was kept for comparison. The procedure was repeated exactly but using distilled water heated to 75°C (tube C). You can see the results of the experiment in Figure 2.2.

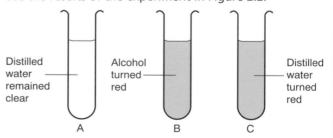

A — Distilled water remained clear

B — Alcohol turned red

C — Distilled water turned red

Figure 2.2 The appearance of the liquid in tubes A, B and C at the end of the experiment

Questions

1 In which tube did pigment remain in the beetroot cylinder?

2 Which cylinders lost pigment from their cells?

3 Which membranes separate the red pigment in the beetroot cell sap from the external surroundings?

4 Lipids (fats) dissolve in alcohol. How might this explain what happened in tube B?

5 Protein molecules are denatured (destroyed) at temperatures above 60°C. How could this be related to the result in tube C?

6 From your answers suggest two materials that might be important components of cell membranes.

You could extend this experiment in to an investigation to find out whether there is a critical temperature at which the membrane is destroyed. It is possible to take quantitative measurements of the density of pigment released from the beetroot if you have access to a colorimeter. Discuss your ideas with your teacher.

The structure of the cell membrane

In biology a **model** is a set of ideas used to describe the structure or function of a body component. It is constantly updated as new techniques bring more information to light. An early model of the cell membrane, proposed in 1935, suggested that it was rather like a sandwich of protein enclosing a double layer of lipid (a bi-layer). The membrane is universally 7–8 nm wide. When cell membranes from both animals and plants could be examined with the electron microscope they showed a similar three-layered appearance.

Further evidence came from other techniques, especially freeze-fracture. The main constituents of the cell membrane are protein and lipid and there are also small amounts of carbohydrate and cholesterol. However, the proteins were found to actually penetrate the lipid bi-layer, sometimes passing right through it.

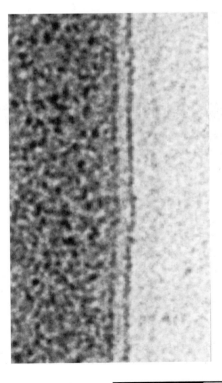

Figure 2.3 An electron micrograph of a cell membrane

Freeze fracture techniques

Freeze fracture is one method of preparing materials for examination under an electron microscope. It is of particular value in examining **membranes** because the tissue is killed rapidly and not treated with chemicals that are likely to distort its structure.

The cells are rapidly frozen in liquid nitrogen at −100°C to −196°C and then pushed in a precise way against a sharp metal blade. The cells tend to fracture along lines of weakness, often the middle of the cell membrane. The tissue is kept cold and in a vacuum. The ice sublimes leaving an etched surface over which a layer of carbon is deposited to make a replica. This is then sprayed with a heavy metal and finally the specimen is treated with a strong acid to destroy any cells remaining below the replica. It is then ready for examination under the electron microscope.

The current model for membrane structure is the **fluid mosaic model** proposed by two Americans, S. J. Singer and G. L. Nicholson, in 1972. It is shown in Figure 2.4.

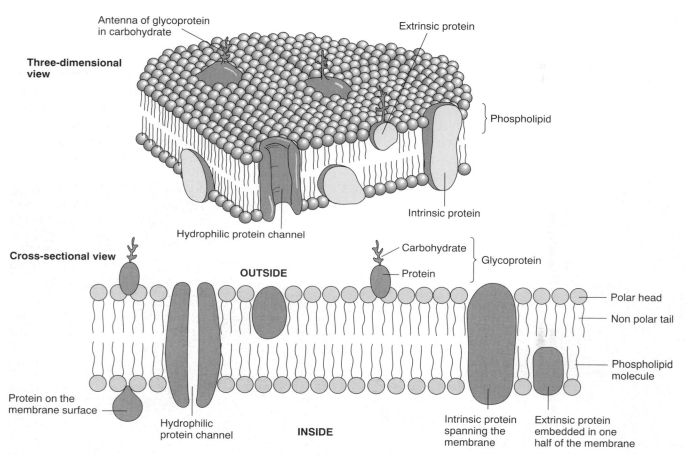

Figure 2.4 The fluid mosaic model to explain cell membrane structure

The name describes the viscous fluid nature of the membrane while the proteins occurring at random through it are the 'mosaic' part. The membrane is not rigid or fixed, but a dynamic structure which is continually changing. The movement is greatest in membranes with the highest cholesterol content. Analysis of cell membranes has shown that the proportion of lipid and protein varies. Cell membranes that have a high protein content surround cells with higher metabolic activity than membranes with less protein.

hydrophilic:
hydro = water,
philic = loving
hydrophobic:
hydro = water,
phobic = hating

▶ *Chapter 6.3 covers lipids in detail*

▶ *Chapter 30.3 describes the immune response*

All cells are surrounded by a cell membrane composed mainly of phospholipids and proteins. The cell membrane allows materials in and out of the cell. It is also involved in cell communication and the immune response.

The lipids in cell membranes are called **phospholipids** which are a type of **triglyceride**. Each phospholipid molecule has a part that will mix with water, the **hydrophilic** head, and a part which repels and does not mix with water, the **hydrophobic** tail. The lipids are not fixed and can move in the membrane.

The proteins that pass through one layer of the lipid bi-layer are called **extrinsic** proteins. On the outer membrane they may form a complex with a carbohydrate forming a **glycoprotein**. These structures are thought to play a part in communication between cells. They may act as receptors for hormones reaching the outer cell membrane or as antigens which are necessary in the immune response.

The **intrinsic** proteins span the membrane, some of them forming hydrophilic channels through which ions and water-soluble molecules can enter or leave the cell. They also act as carriers by actively pumping molecules across the membrane. Some proteins are enzymes, catalysing chemical reactions at the cell membrane.

2.2 The nucleus

The nucleus is the largest organelle found in almost all eukaryotic cells. An exception is mature mammalian red blood cells. A red cell loses its nucleus during development in the bone marrow. It only survives for about 12 weeks without a nucleus before being broken down. The nucleus is spherical or ovoid in shape and about 10 μm in diameter by 20 μm in length.

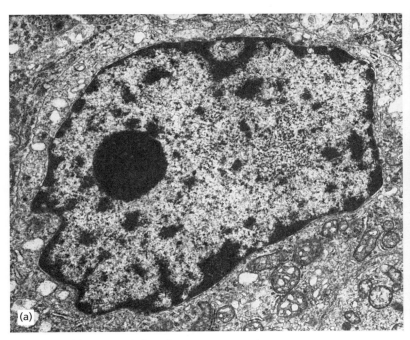

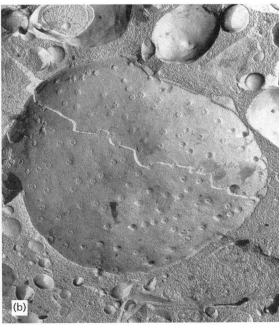

Figure 2.5 (a) A transmission electron micrograph of a section through a nucleus (magnification ×16000) (b) A scanning electron micrograph of the surface of the nucleus showing the nuclear pores

Surrounding the nucleus is the **nuclear envelope** consisting of a double membrane, the outer of which is continuous with the endoplasmic reticulum (ER) that runs through the cell. The envelope is perforated by **nuclear pores** which control the passage of molecules between the nucleus and cytoplasm. These pores are partially blocked by proteins and RNA. The contents of the nucleus are called the **nucleoplasm** (or **nuclear sap**) and consist of one or more nucleoli, chromatin, ions, proteins and nucleotides.

nucleolus = singular
nucleoli = plural

▶ *Chapter 5.3 describes cell division in detail*

The **nucleolus** looks darkly stained when seen with a light microscope. Its function is to manufacture ribosomal RNA (rRNA). During cell division the nucleolus breaks down, re-forming in the new cells. **Chromatin** is the DNA and histones (proteins) which form the chromosomes. In a non-dividing cell the chromatin is diffuse and has no obvious structure. It is readily stained and appears granular. During the first stage of cell division the chromatin becomes increasingly tightly coiled and denser to form chromosomes.

The nucleus is vitally important because it controls the activities of the cell. It contains the DNA which determines which enzymes can be operative in the cell; these control metabolism.

2.3 The cytoplasm, cytoskeleton and endoplasmic reticulum

The term **cytoplasm** describes all the cell contents inside the cell membrane except the nucleus. It consists of a watery material (matrix) called the **cytosol** which contains ions, sugars, amino acids, salts and larger molecules, such as nucleotides, proteins and fatty acids. Within the cytosol are the cell organelles.

The TEM revealed that the cytosol is highly organised and supported by a system of protein fibres called the cytoskeleton. The **cytoskeleton** contains solid **microfilaments** and larger hollow **microtubules**.

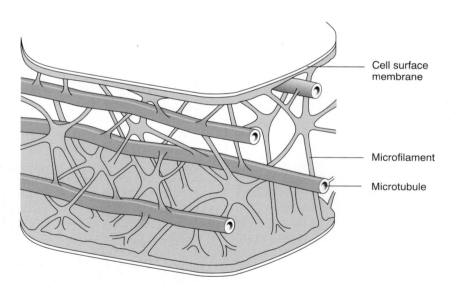

Cell surface membrane

Microfilament

Microtubule

Figure 2.6 Microtubules and microfilaments, important constituents of the cytoskeleton

The cytoplasm is all the cell contents except the nucleus. The fluid part is the cytosol. Throughout the cytosol are temporary protein structures called microtubules and microfilaments which form the cytoskeleton.

The cytoskeleton is not a permanent structure but appears to break down readily only to re-assemble in another part of the cell. Microfilaments are thought to be involved with cell movement, cytoplasmic streaming and muscle contraction. Microtubules are found in **cilia**, extensions of the cell surface that line some of the body's ducts and passages, beating rhythmically to move certain materials. In a cross-section of a cilium (Figure 2.7) the microtubules show a characteristic **9 + 2 arrangement**. This means that there are two central microtubules surrounded by another nine pairs; all are enclosed in a membrane which is an extension of the cell membrane. At the base of the cilium is the basal body consisting of nine triplets of tubules only, and other fibres extending deeper into the cytoplasm.

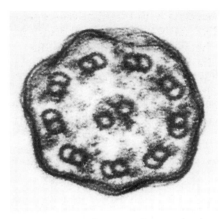

Figure 2.7 An electron micrograph of the structure of a cilium (plural: cilia) in cross section

> Rough ER synthesises and distributes proteins.
> Smooth ER synthesises and distributes lipids and steroids.

Triplets of nine microtubules are also seen in the walls of the two **centrioles** found at right angles to one another close to the nucleus of animal cells. It seems likely that centrioles are centres which organise all the microtubules in animal cells, forming cilia, and constructing the spindle during cell division.

Running through the soluble cytosol is the **endoplasmic reticulum (ER)** a series of flattened, hollow membranous sacs called **cisternae**. These extensive membranes provide a large surface area where metabolic reactions may occur. The system of cavities are connected and the membrane is continuous with the nuclear envelope as we have seen. The outer surface of the ER membrane may be covered with ribosomes and is then called **rough ER**. Rough ER is involved with the transport of proteins (for example enzymes) away from the cell where they have been manufactured in the ribosomes, to a site elsewhere in the organism where they are to be used. The protein may be chemically modified while it is being transported. Where ribosomes are absent, the ER is called **smooth ER**. Its cavities are more tubular in form and its purpose is the synthesis and distribution of lipids and steroids.

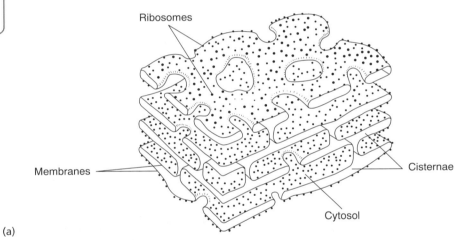

(a)

Figure 2.8 (a) Illustration and (b) transmission electron micrograph of the endoplasmic reticulum (shown here covered with ribosomes). Magnification ×20 000

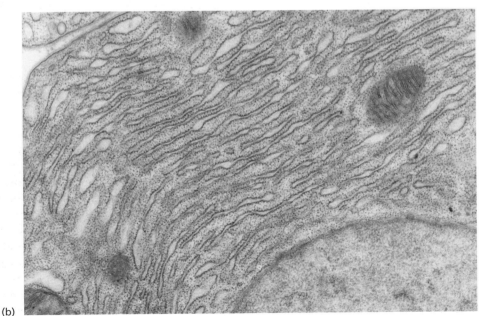

(b)

Cell fractionation and ultra-centrifugation techniques

The electron microscope has allowed scientists to determine the structure of cell organelles but other advanced techniques have been used to gain information about their functions. Organelles must be isolated from the cell before they can be studied.

The cells are first broken open by grinding with a pestle and mortar or are homogenised in a blender. They are mixed with an isotonic solution of sugar or salts (that is a solution with the same concentration of solute as the cells) and are kept very cold to reduce damage to the organelles by cellular enzymes. The resulting suspension of nuclei, organelles, pieces of cell membrane and whole cells is then poured into tubes which are spun at high speed in a centrifuge. A centrifugal force many times greater than gravity pulls the heaviest particles, such as nuclei, to the base of the tube, where they form a sediment. Lighter organelles remain in the supernatant (the liquid above the sediment). The supernatant is removed to another tube and spun at a higher speed.

Further organelles such as mitochondria are collected from this sediment. Some of the supernatant is removed and re-spun at even higher speeds to harvest the lightest organelles such as fragments of endoplasmic reticulum. In this way the organelles of the cell can be collected separately and investigated further to determine their functions.

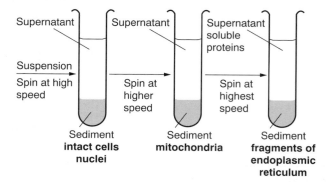

Figure 2.9

2.4 The Golgi body

The Golgi body (or Golgi apparatus) was first discovered by an Italian scientist called Camillo Golgi at the end of the nineteenth century while he was working with a special silver staining technique. At first his observations were not accepted by other people, who believed that he had seen an artefact.

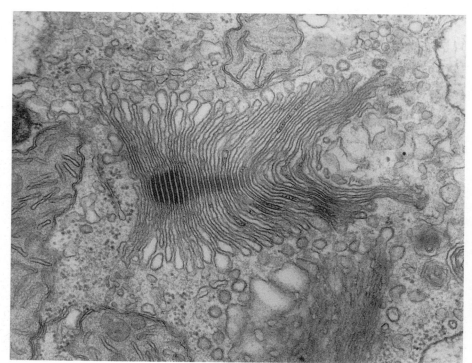

Figure 2.10 Transmission electron micrograph of the Golgi body (magnification ×44 000)

As you can see from the electron micrograph in Figure 2.10 this organelle consists of stacks of flattened sacs bound by smooth ER. The size of a Golgi body varies from cell to cell, but they are more conspicuous in metabolically active cells. The cavities are formed from vesicles pinched off from ER which fuse together. Proteins reach the Golgi body from the rough ER. They are converted in to glycoproteins such as mucus by the addition of polysaccharide carbohydrate, and are then pinched off in to other vesicles. These move to the surface of the cell, fuse with the cell membrane and release their contents outside the cell. In a similar way lipids from smooth ER are also reorganised.

Lysosomes

Lysosomes are vesicles budded off from the Golgi body or the rough ER which contain hydrolytic enzymes capable of digesting cell contents in the process of intracellular digestion. The surrounding membrane prevents the enzymes from breaking down organelles required by the cell. The enzymes are used for the digestion of damaged or redundant cell structures. When a cell dies its lysosomes release their contents and digest the cell in a process called **autolysis**. When an animal dies changes happen in its body tissues. These occur as the result of the action of enzymes from lysosomes which break open the dead cells. Animals slaughtered for their meat may be left to hang to improve texture and flavour.

> Intracellular = within cells
> intercellular = between cells
> extracellular = outside cells

2.5 Mitochondria

Mitochondria are found in every cell and are very numerous in cells such as liver or muscle cells that have high metabolic activity. These organelles are very important because:

> mitochondrion = singular
> mitochondria = plural

▶ **Chapter 25** *explains what happens in the mitochondria*

- they provide the site for the Kreb's Cycle which is an important part of cell respiration;
- they are involved in the formation of ATP;
- they are involved in fatty acid metabolism.

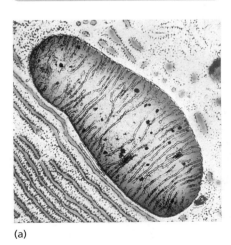

(a)

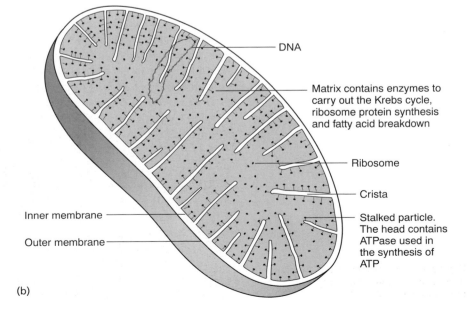

DNA

Matrix contains enzymes to carry out the Krebs cycle, ribosome protein synthesis and fatty acid breakdown

Ribosome

Crista

Inner membrane

Stalked particle. The head contains ATPase used in the synthesis of ATP

Outer membrane

(b)

Figure 2.11 (a) Transmission electron micrograph and (b) illustration of mitochondria, the site of respiration and other anabolic reactions in the cell

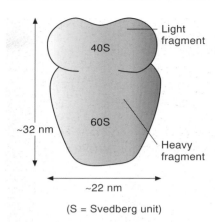

Figure 2.12 A ribosome consists of two extremely small sub-units

Each mitochondrion is cylindrical to spherical in shape and is on average 1.0 μm in diameter and 3.0–10 μm in length. It is surrounded by a double membrane, the inner one being folded to form **cristae** which increase the internal surface area. The cristae project into a matrix containing numerous chemical compounds including a small circular strand of DNA. Attached to the inner surface of the cristae are tiny **stalked particles** where ATP is synthesised. Small ribosomes resembling those found in bacterial (prokaryotic) cells occur in mitochondria and chloroplasts. This has led to the **endosymbiotic theory** which suggests that the ancestors of mitochondria might originally have been small prokaryotes preyed upon by a larger type. Having escaped digestion they then evolved inside the larger prokaryote which itself evolved into a eukaryotic cell.

2.6 Ribosomes

Ribosomes are very small organelles consisting of two unequally sized sub-units. They contain roughly equal proportions of protein and ribosomal RNA (rRNA). Ribosomes which occur free in the cytoplasm are the site for the synthesis of the cell's own proteins such as enzymes. The ribosomes that lie along the rough ER manufacture proteins for use outside the cell. Many ribosomes may be found together along a strand of messenger RNA (mRNA) forming a **polysome**.

▶ *Chapter 31.8 covers protein synthesis*

2.7 Cell walls

Cell walls are only found in plant cells, fungal hyphae and some bacterial cells. A cell wall is produced by the cell it surrounds and lies outside the cell membrane. A **cellulose** cell wall is characteristic of a plant cell. The cell wall is laid down at the end of mitotic cell division.

▶ *Chapter 5.3 describes the type of cell division called mitosis*

Vesicles from the Golgi apparatus collect across the equator of the spindle and form the **cell plate**. These fuse. Their membranes become the new cell membranes and their contents form the **middle lamella**, mainly calcium pectate. In each cell the **primary cell wall** is secreted between the middle lamella and the cell membrane. It consists of bundles of **cellulose microfibrils** laid down in all directions and held together by a matrix of hemicelluloses and pectates. This produces a strong structure to support the cell, but it is also capable of stretching as the cell grows. In places, ER becomes trapped across the middle lamella. These cytoplasmic strands form the connections between adjacent plant cells and are called **plasmodesmata**.

In many types of plant cell the **secondary cell wall** is laid down to give extra strength to the plant. Initially, it is a further layer of cellulose in which the microfibrils are packed more tightly together and lie in the same direction. Each additional sheet of microfibrils has a different orientation giving extra strength. The cellulose wall may be impregnated with additional substances. For example xylem vessels, which are found in stems and roots and transport water through the plant, are thickened by lignin which is extremely strong; the bark of trees is formed from cork cells waterproofed by deposits of waxy suberin.

Figure 2.13 Cross section of a tree stump. The vessels have lignin impregnating the cellulose walls which give a very rigid supporting structure and also allows the transport of water through the tree. (*See Colour Gallery page 347*)

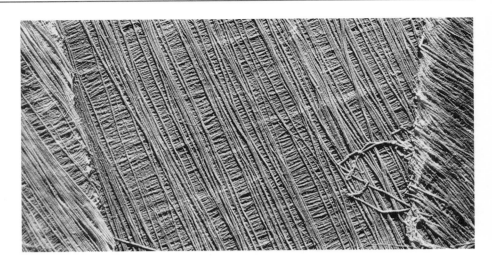

Figure 2.14 An electron micrograph showing how the microfibrils of cellulose are laid down in different directions, giving strength to the cell wall

2.8 Levels of organisation

Most organisms are **multicellular**, that is they consist of many cells. Apart from a very few organisms the cells are not all the same, they vary because they are required to perform different functions in the body. A group of cells and their intercellular substance which work together to carry out a particular function is called a **tissue**. The cells of a tissue may all be similar, as in the squamous epithelium tissue lining the human cheek, or they may differ, as do the red and white blood cells.

Humans (and other higher animals) have four main groups of tissues:

- **Epithelial tissues** which line all the interior and exterior surfaces of the body e.g. stratified epithelium of the skin, ciliated epithelium, glandular epithelium.
- **Connective tissues** which consist of cells embedded in a large amount of intercellular material – the **matrix** e.g. cartilage, bone, blood and adipose tissue. (Blood is a liquid tissue, its matrix is the plasma.)
- **Muscular tissues** which are all able to contract e.g. skeletal, smooth and cardiac muscle.
- **Nervous tissues** which are composed of specialised cells or neurones bound together by connective tissue.

At the next level of organisation, tissues work together to form the **organs** of the body which have specialised functions to perform. The brain, heart, skin and liver are all organs. Organs do not work in isolation, however, they are part of one of the **body systems** that carry out the major functions to keep the body alive. Failure of a system or vital organ causes ill-health, disability or death. Most systems in the human body are self-regulating and co-ordinated by the nervous and endocrine systems. You will learn more about body systems in Sections 2–5.

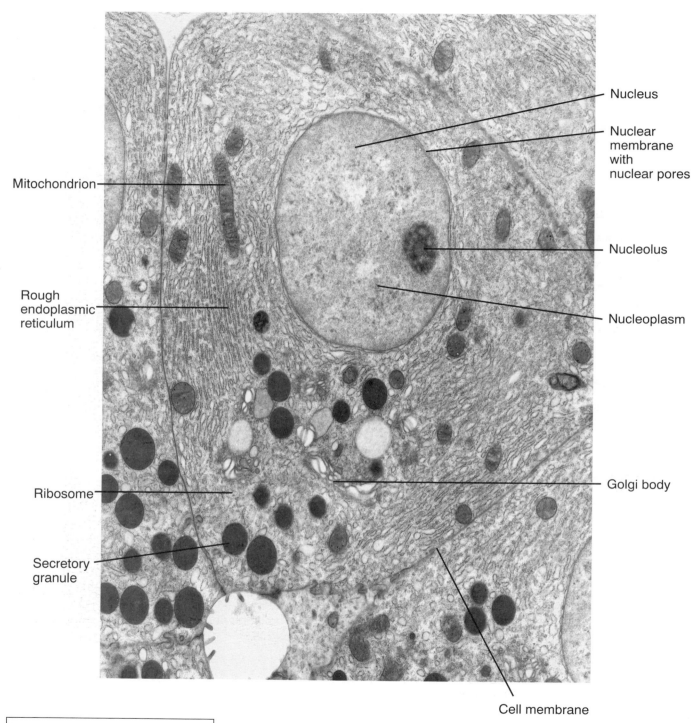

Nucleus

Nuclear membrane with nuclear pores

Mitochondrion

Nucleolus

Rough endoplasmic reticulum

Nucleoplasm

Ribosome

Golgi body

Secretory granule

Cell membrane

Figure 2.15 The detailed structure of a pancreatic cell viewed with an electron microscope

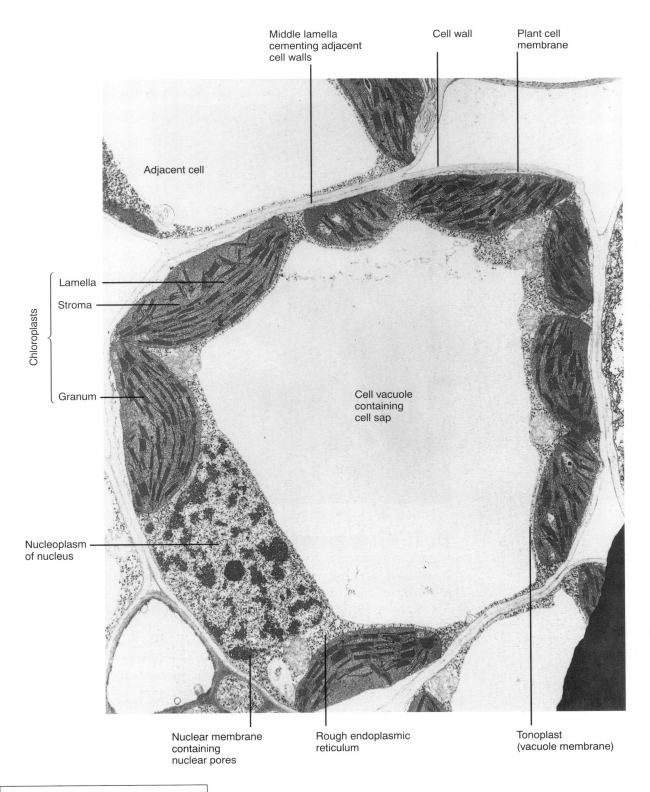

Middle lamella cementing adjacent cell walls

Cell wall

Plant cell membrane

Adjacent cell

Lamella

Stroma

Chloroplasts

Granum

Cell vacuole containing cell sap

Nucleoplasm of nucleus

Nuclear membrane containing nuclear pores

Rough endoplasmic reticulum

Tonoplast (vacuole membrane)

Figure 2.16 The detail that can be seen in a plant cell using an electron microscope

CHAPTER 3 Bacteria and Viruses

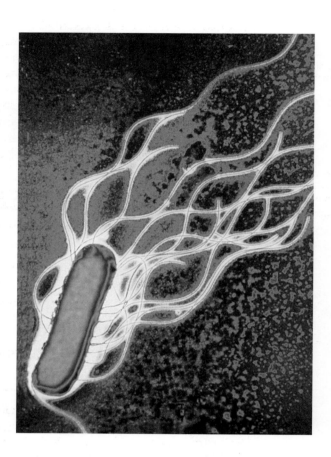

Figure 3.1 A bacterial cell is an example of a prokaryotic cell. This transmission electron micrograph shows *Salmonella* spp. that live in the gut of many animals.

3.1 The prokaryotic cell

As research in to cells continued, it became clear that there are two levels of cell structure. In Chapters 1 and 2 we have described the **eukaryotic** type of cell structure found in the majority of organisms, including all animals and plants. The main distinguishing feature of eukaryotic cells is the clearly defined nucleus and complex organisation of membranes and membrane-bound organelles. All other cells are said to be **prokaryotic** and have no distinct nucleus. These are the bacterial cells, probably the first cells to evolve some 3.7 billion years ago, and are far simpler in structure than the eukaryotic type.

An example of a typical prokaryotic cell is a bacterium. The cell is most commonly rod shaped or spherical, and is much smaller than a eukaryotic cell, being only 1.0 μm (1 × 10^{-6} m) in diameter. It is surrounded by a cell wall made of a mucopolysaccharide and amino acid complex. The cell wall may be covered with a **slime capsule**. This is only found in **pathogenic organisms**, where it protects them from their host's defence system and may also prevent dehydration. One or more **flagella**, similar in structure to the eukaryotic microfilament, may be present in motile species.

A pathogenic organism or 'pathogen' is one which causes disease

flagellum = singular
flagella = plural

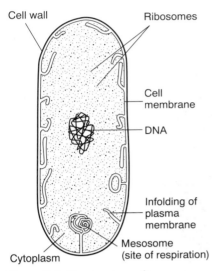

▶ *Chapter 32.4 describes the use of plasmids in genetic engineering*

Cell wall

Ribosomes

Cell membrane

DNA

Infolding of plasma membrane

Mesosome (site of respiration)

Cytoplasm

Figure 3.2 The structure of a prokaryotic cell

Inside the cell wall is the cell membrane. The cell is filled with cytoplasm containing numerous particles including stored food, such as glycogen and lipids, enzymes and ribosomes. The **ribosomes** are similar to those in eukaryotic cells but are smaller. There is no nucleus, but a **circular strand** of DNA. Smaller rings of DNA, **plasmids**, also occur. Infoldings of the plasma membrane form **mesosomes** which are the site of respiration. Some bacteria are photosynthetic and contain simple membrane-bound sacs in which photosynthetic pigment, **bacteriochlorophyll**, is found. Chemically this is similar to the chlorophyll found in plants, but is simpler in structure.

Bacteria multiply by simple asexual cell division, although a very simple form of sexual reproduction is recognised in some species. Bacteria divide quickly, as often as every 20 minutes provided that they have warmth, suitable nutrients and oxygen. From a single cell, millions of others can arise within a few hours. The bacterial cells stay together as a **colony** which can be seen with the naked eye. Because of this rapid capability for growth and relative ease of culture, bacteria are used as laboratory tools in many areas of research.

Questions

1 Draw up a table of the differences between a prokaryotic cell and a eukaryotic cell.

2 What do you consider to be the most significant advance in the evolution of the eukaryotic cell?

3.2 Viruses – an exception to the cell theory?

Viruses are parasites of plants, animals or bacteria, in which they reproduce. They are pathogenic, causing disease in the living cells of their host. Viral diseases of humans include influenza, measles, rabies and AIDS. However, viruses show no signs of life when they are outside living cells; they are unable to grow or move or to reproduce and they cannot respire or utilise food material. Viruses can be isolated in crystalline form but show no sign of being alive.

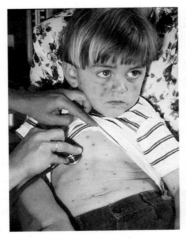

(a)

(b)

Figure 3.3 The child pictured in (a) has the rash caused by the chicken pox virus *Herpes zoster*. Other viruses cause symptoms in plants. The streaks on the tulip petals shown in (b) are considered desirable but are actually the symptoms of a viral infection.

Viral particles are very small, being in the order of 20–3000 nm in diameter. They were first discovered at the beginning of the twentieth century by biologists studying a plant disease now known as tobacco mosaic virus (TMV). When sap from an infected plant was filtered with a filter fine enough to remove bacteria, it remained infectious. Evidently, the disease agent was smaller than bacteria! Viruses were first viewed with an electron microscope in the early 1930s.

A viral particle is now called a **virion**. It consists of a variable mass of nucleic acid surrounded and protected by a protein coat called a **capsid**.

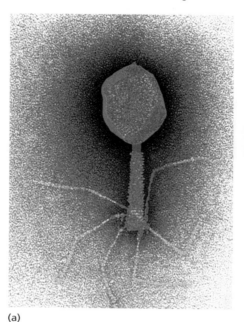

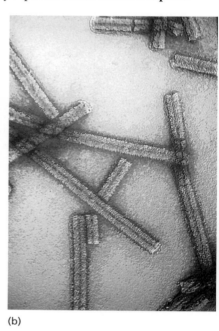

Figure 3.4 (a) A bacteriophage is a virus that attacks bacteria (magnification ×170 000) (b) Tobacco mosaic virus (TMV) one of the first viruses to be seen with the electron microscope shown here in its crystalline form (magnification ×345 000)

(a)

(b)

In many viruses the nucleic acid is DNA but in the group known as **retroviruses** the nucleic acid is RNA. HIV, the virus which causes AIDS, is a retrovirus. One of the most researched viruses is one which parasitises the bacterium *Escherichia coli*. This type of virus is called a **bacteriophage** (or **phage**). Figure 3.6 shows you the events that occur when the phage infects a bacterium and utilises the host's DNA to replicate hundreds of virus particles. These are released as the host cell bursts.

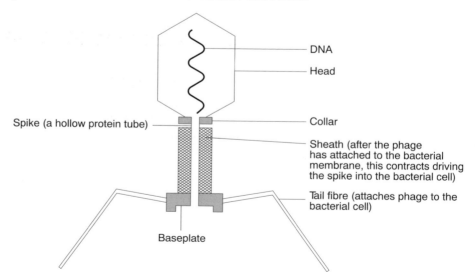

DNA

Head

Spike (a hollow protein tube)

Collar

Sheath (after the phage has attached to the bacterial membrane, this contracts driving the spike into the bacterial cell)

Tail fibre (attaches phage to the bacterial cell)

Baseplate

Figure 3.5 A cross section of a phage that infects *E. coli*

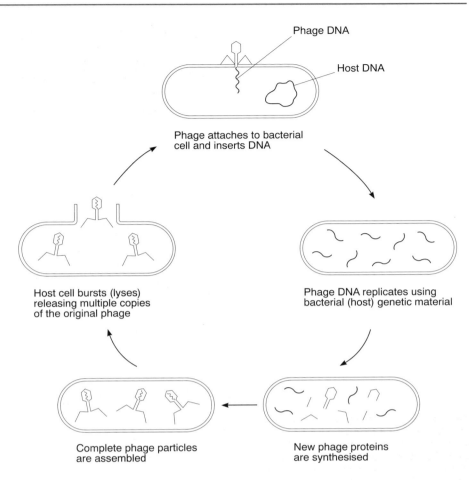

Figure 3.6 The replication of a viral particle inside the host bacterial cell. The complete cycle takes about 30 minutes.

Viruses frequently mutate and new forms are constantly appearing. This is a mechanism which protects viruses against the defence systems of their hosts – they are always 'one step ahead'. You probably know that each winter we are exposed to slightly different strains of the influenza virus. The World Health Organisation (WHO) monitors the progress of strains of the flu virus as they cross the continents. On the basis of their observations the WHO predict which type of flu is likely to be here each winter. This information is used by pharmaceutical companies to manufacture vaccines which they hope will be effective against the flu virus.

Questions

1 Why do you think it has so far proved difficult to manufacture drugs and vaccines that are effective against viruses?

2 Do you consider viruses to be living? Write a paragraph to explain the reasons for your answer.

CHAPTER 4 How Molecules and Ions Move Across Cell Membranes

Although cell membranes are only about 8.0 nm wide they are an effective barrier against ions and molecules moving in and out of cells. The movement of particles is vital to the cell because:

- this is the means by which a suitable pH and concentration of ions are maintained inside and outside the cell;
- food and oxygen are taken in since they are required for energy;
- hormones and enzymes may be secreted for use elsewhere in the organism;
- waste substances are excreted.

There are different ways by which particles can enter or leave a cell; **diffusion** and **osmosis** are *passive* processes which do not require energy to be expended, whereas **active transport**, **endocytosis** and **exocytosis** are energy consuming or *active* processes.

4.1 Diffusion

Diffusion is the process by which there is an overall (or net) movement of ions or molecules from an area where they are in high concentration to an area where they are in lower concentration, until the concentrations are equal. We say that movement is down a **concentration gradient** because particles move from high to low concentration.

Diffusion happens all the time in our surroundings. If someone lights a cigarette, the smoke can soon be smelt some distance away because the smoke particles have diffused from around the cigarette (high concentration) to the rest of the room (low concentration). When diffusion stops the particles still move, but equally in all directions (i.e. random movement).

Gases diffuse rapidly in solution through membranes as you will see when you study the exchange of oxygen and carbon dioxide between the lungs and the blood. Fat soluble molecules also diffuse quickly through cell membranes; they dissolve in the lipids in the cell membrane and move down the concentration gradient to the other side of the membrane.

In contrast, ions and charged (polar) molecules such as glucose and amino acids diffuse more slowly through the cell membrane. The charge on their molecule stops them from dissolving in the lipid part of the membrane. Charged particles are water soluble, and they can only move through the passages formed by the intrinsic proteins embedded in the membrane called **channel proteins**. These channel proteins form special hydrophilic passages through the membrane. The water soluble molecules and ions dissolve and are able to diffuse through. **Gated channels** are selective, allowing only ions which they recognise to cross the membrane. Some of the intrinsic proteins are called **carrier proteins**. They have specific receptor sites with which to recognise a particular polar molecule. When the polar molecule attaches to

▶ *Chapter 9 describes the process of gaseous exchange*

its receptor, the intrinsic protein changes its shape and deposits the polar molecule on the other side of the cell membrane. This type of diffusion, where assistance is given to the particles crossing the membrane, is called **facilitated diffusion**; it does not use energy and is reversible so that molecules and ions can be moved either in or out of the cell provided that there is a concentration gradient.

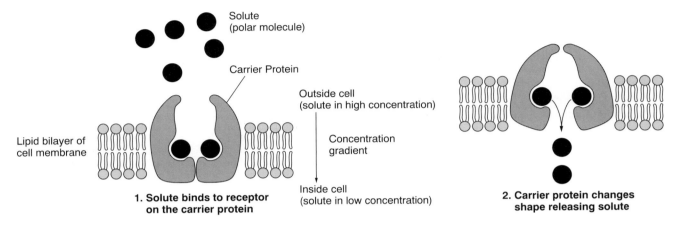

1. Solute binds to receptor on the carrier protein

2. Carrier protein changes shape releasing solute

Figure 4.1 Facilitated diffusion across a cell membrane

The speed of diffusion of a molecule depends on:

- the size of the molecule (small molecules diffuse more quickly than large ones);
- whether the molecule is fat soluble or charged;
- the thickness of the membrane;
- the concentration gradient (diffusion is more rapid if the concentration gradient is steep);
- temperature (diffusion is faster at warmer temperatures);
- the area over which diffusion is taking place – many cells where diffusion occurs all or much of the time, have some adaptation for increasing surface area, as we see in the alveoli of the lungs and in the villi in the ileum;
- the distance that the molecule has to move – the shorter the distance the greater the rate of diffusion.

Fick's Law combines some of these facts and states that the rate of diffusion is proportional to:

$$\frac{\text{surface area} \times \text{difference in concentration}}{\text{thickness of the membrane}}$$

Partially permeable membrane

Dilute sucrose solution | Concentrated sucrose solution

Sucrose molecule

Water molecule

HYPOTONIC SOLUTION | HYPERTONIC SOLUTION

Low concentration of solute molecules | High concentration of solute molecules

High concentration of water molecules | Low concentration of water molecules

Net movement of water molecules

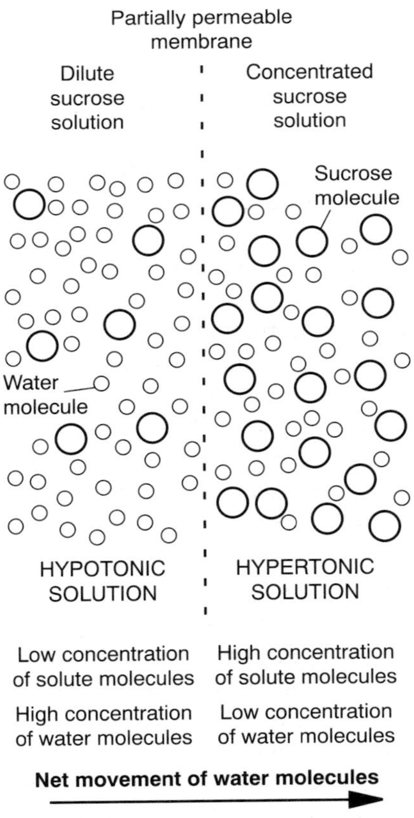

Figure 4.2 Osmosis – the net movement of water through a partially permeable membrane from a hypotonic to a hypertonic solution

4.2 Osmosis

A solution consists of **solute** molecules dissolved in a **solvent**. In living organisms the solvent is water. **Water** moves in and out of cells by **osmosis**, a special case of diffusion. It must pass through the cell membrane. The cell membrane is permeable to water but not to molecules which are too large to pass through the channels formed by the intrinsic proteins; it is called a **partially permeable** membrane.

If you look at Figure 4.2 you can see what happens when an aqueous solution is separated from pure water by a partially permeable membrane. The pores of the membrane are too small to allow the passage of solute through, though water can pass through easily. Osmosis will occur; water molecules will move from the water (a high concentration of water molecules) to the solution (a lower concentration of water molecules) through the partially permeable membrane.

Imagine two adjacent cells with different aqueous concentrations separated from one another by a cell membrane. Again osmosis will occur; water will move from the **hypotonic** solution (which has a higher concentration of water) to the **hypertonic** solution (the one which has a lower concentration of water). This will continue until the solutions are of the same concentration, that is they are **isotonic**. Figure 4.3 shows what happens to red blood cells placed in water or in a strong saline solution. Water is hypotonic to the red blood cells. The red blood cells gain water by osmosis and burst (**haemolysis**). When placed in the hypertonic salt solution the red cells lose water by osmosis and appear crinkled (or crenated). Compare this with the effects on plant cells given similar treatment (Figure 4.4).

> A *hypertonic* solution has a high concentration of solute and a lower concentration of water. A *hypotonic* solution has a low concentration of solute and a higher concentration of water. *Isotonic* solutions have the same concentrations of solute and water as one another.

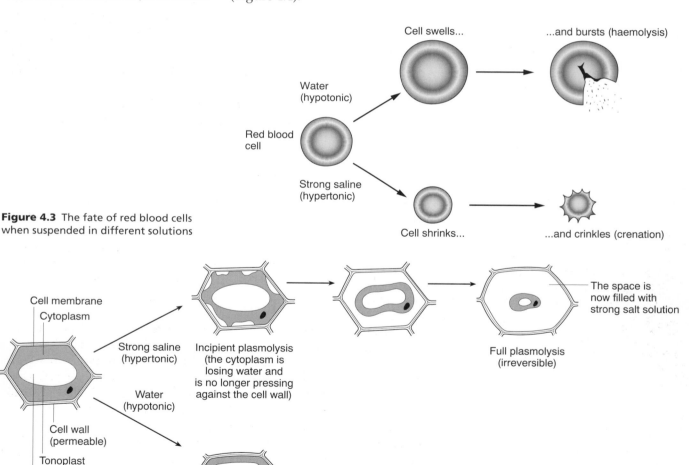

Figure 4.3 The fate of red blood cells when suspended in different solutions

Figure 4.4 Onion cells in water and in a strong salt solution

Water potential

A solution which has a high concentration of water may also be said to have a high water potential. **Water potential**, represented by the Greek letter psi, ψ, is the tendency for water molecules to enter or leave a solution by osmosis. In cells it is a measure of the pressure that is exerted by water molecules as they collide with the cell membrane. The more collisions per unit of time the greater the water potential because there is more likelihood of particles leaving the cell. The units used to measure water potential are kilopascals (kPa). The water potential of pure water (ψ_w) at standard atmospheric pressure (101.32 kPa) and temperature is 0 kPa. *Pure water has the greatest value of any water potential.*

The water potential of a solution is always a *negative* value. This is because the dissolved particles in the solution attract water and hold it in the system, as well as physically getting in the way. So solutes lower the water potential below zero. A hypertonic solution will have a more negative water potential than one which is hypotonic to it. We can now define osmosis in terms of water potential.

> Osmosis is the net movement of water molecules from a solution of less negative water potential, through a partially permeable membrane to a solution of more negative water potential.

This is in line with our model of a diffusion gradient, since water moves from where there is more of it to an area where its concentration is less.

Plant water relations

In order to understand the water relations of plant cells we need to understand two additional pressures that are involved solute potential and pressure potential. For the reasons already explained, solute molecules present in the cell vacuole of plant cells lower the water potential (i.e. make it more negative). The greater the concentration of solutes the more negative the water potential of the vacuole. This lowering of water potential due to solute molecules is the **solute potential** (ψ_s), which always has a negative value.

When an animal cell is immersed in water it takes up water by osmosis. Its volume increases and consequently pressure inside the cell membrane increases. Eventually, the pressure is so great that the cell bursts. However, plant cells are different because they are surrounded by a cellulose cell wall. As water is taken in, the cell membrane pushes against the cell wall. The cell wall in turn exerts a pressure against the expanding cell contents. This is **pressure potential** (ψ_p) and it always has a positive value. Eventually, the point is reached where there is no further net uptake of water into the cell. The cell is then described as being **turgid**. *In a turgid cell solute potential and pressure potential are equal.*

If the plant cells are then placed in a solution which is hypertonic to the cell contents (and so has a more negative solute potential than the cell sap) they will lose water by osmosis. The cell contents shrink and pressure potential decreases. It reaches zero as the cell contents no longer push against the cell wall. This is **incipient plasmolysis**. Further water loss causes

---

kPa is the abbreviation for kilopascals. Pascals are a unit of pressure (see Basics in Brief). 1000 pascals = 1 kilopascal

---

Water potential always has a negative value.

Solute potential always has a negative value.

Pressure potential always has a positive value.

more shrinkage of the cell contents and the cell becomes **plasmolysed** and **flaccid**. You can see the effects of this in a plant that has wilted. *In a plasmolysed cell, water potential and solute potential are equal.*

The water relations of a plant cell are summarised by the graph in Figure 4.5 and the following equation:

$$\text{water potential} = \text{solute potential} + \text{pressure potential}$$
$$\psi = \psi_s + \psi_p$$

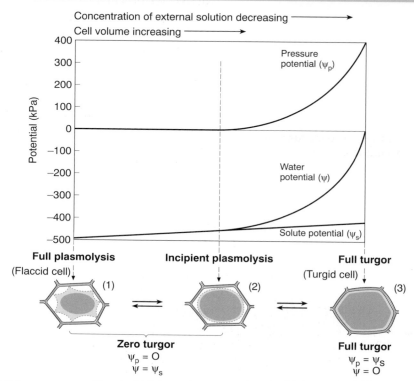

Figure 4.5 The relationship between water potential, solute potential and pressure potential in a plant cell at the different stages between being turgid and plasmolysed

Questions

1   Look again at Figures 4.3 and 4.4. Why did the red blood cells burst when put in water, whereas the onion epidermis cells did not?

2   Put the following water potentials of cells A–D in order, starting with the one that has the greatest value.

(A) $\psi = -500$ kPa   (C) $\psi = -300$ kPa

(B) $\psi = 0$ kPa   (D) $\psi = -600$ kPA

3   Cell F which has $\psi = -550$ kPa is separated from cell G which has $\psi = -450$ kPa. Will water move from one to the other by osmosis? If so in which direction?

Choose one answer from (a) to (c) and explain your reasoning.

(a) F to G

(b) G to F

(c) There will be no net movement of water.

4.3 Active transport

Active transport is very important because it is the means by which ions and molecules are moved across a cell membrane *against* the concentration gradient, that is from where they are in low concentration to where their concentration is higher. This means that a cell can take up nutrients even when they are in low concentration outside the cell, or rid itself of waste products which have accumulated inside the cell. This requires *energy* from the breakdown of ATP and so is an active process. If the tissues are deprived of oxygen, or a metabolic poison such as cyanide is applied, active transport will stop because ATP cannot be formed.

The mechanism of transporting ions or molecules across a membrane using energy is called a **biological** or **protein pump**. It appears that the intrinsic proteins once again act as specific protein carriers across the membrane. The mechanism is shown in Figure 4.6. Note that the proteins bind with their specific molecule or ion on one side of the membrane only. A molecule of ATP attaches itself to the protein and undergoes a hydrolysis reaction releasing energy. The protein changes its shape (conformation) and transports the molecule or ion to the other side of the membrane. It then returns to its original shape.

► *Chapter 25 describes the formation of ATP*

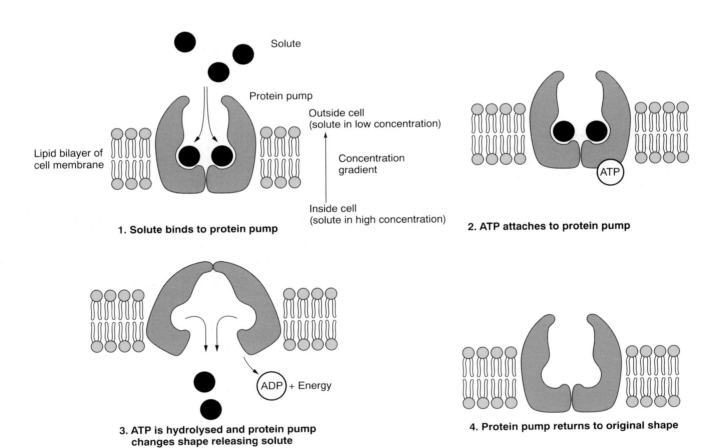

Figure 4.6 Active transport across a cell membrane

You will come across active transport again when you study the **sodium–potassium pump** and its importance in the functioning of nerve cells in Chapter 20.2.

4.4 Endocytosis

Endocytosis is the way in which quantities of material which are too large to be transported by protein carriers can be taken into the cell across the membrane. The cell membrane encloses the material in a vacuole which becomes pinched off and enters the cytoplasm. Lysosomes fuse with the vacuole and their enzymes are used to digest the material. Useful metabolites can then be absorbed into the cytoplasm.

Phagocytosis is the ingestion of solid material that we see when neutrophils (a type of white blood cell) engulf pathogenic bacteria; **pinocytosis** describes the intake of liquid or suspensions.

Figure 4.7 Endocytosis – another way into a cell. A neutrophil ingests bacteria as part of the body's defence system.

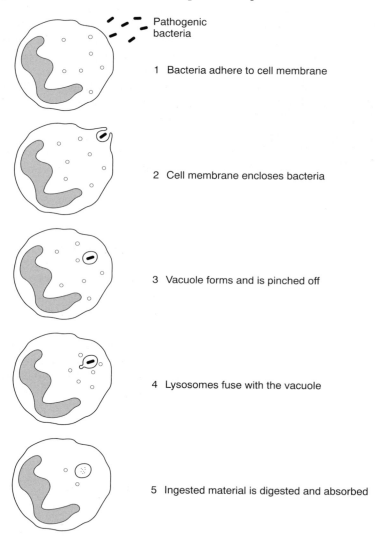

Pathogenic bacteria

1 Bacteria adhere to cell membrane

2 Cell membrane encloses bacteria

3 Vacuole forms and is pinched off

4 Lysosomes fuse with the vacuole

5 Ingested material is digested and absorbed

4.5 Exocytosis

Exocytosis is the reverse process to endocytosis. It allows ions, simple molecules, proteins such as enzymes, polysaccharides and lipids or hormones manufactured in the cell to be secreted for use elsewhere in the organism. The secretion of milk by the mammary glands of humans and other mammals is an example of exocytosis.

▶ *Chapter 28.5 describes lactation (milk secretion)*

CHAPTER 5
How Cells Replicate Themselves

5.1 The importance of mitosis

Protoplasm is the term that describes all the living material inside the cell membrane

▶ Chapter 29.2 gives details on the subject of growth

▶ Chapter 27.1 describes meiosis in detail

Cells in all living organisms may be replaced from time to time because of damage or because they have come to the end of their life. In humans the red blood cells are replaced about every three months; epithelial cells on the skin's surface and those lining the gut are continually worn away and must be renewed. In addition, **growth** can only occur if there is an increase in protoplasm and this means an increase in cell size and number. **Mitosis** is the process by which the cells of living organisms divide, allowing growth and replacement or repair of old or damaged tissues. The daughter cells resulting from mitosis are *identical* to one another (and to the parent cell that they originated from) because there is no change in the genetic material. Only when gametes are formed in the gonads (the ovaries and testes) is a different method of cell division called **meiosis** employed .

5.2 The cell cycle

Cells do not necessarily divide continuously by mitosis. They exist for much of the time in a state called **interphase**. Interphase and mitosis together can be described as the **cell cycle**. You can see from Figure 5.1 that mitosis occupies only about 5% of the cell cycle.

Following a mitotic division the cell is in interphase and enters the first growth phase (G1) in which it manufactures new cell components. The G1 phase varies in length from one cell to another, lasting from just a few hours to a number of years. This is followed by the synthesis or S phase, during which the chromatids synthesise a complementary strand of DNA and each centriole replicates. Finally there is another short phase of growth (G2).

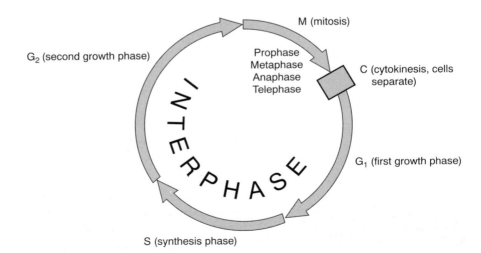

Figure 5.1 The cell cycle

5.3 Mitosis

Examination by a light microscope shows that a cell in interphase has a granular nucleus, but the chromosomes are not visible as separate structures. The first stage of mitosis is **prophase**. Activity in the nucleus begins with the contents becoming darker and denser, as the material of the chromosomes progressively condenses, twists and becomes shorter and fatter.

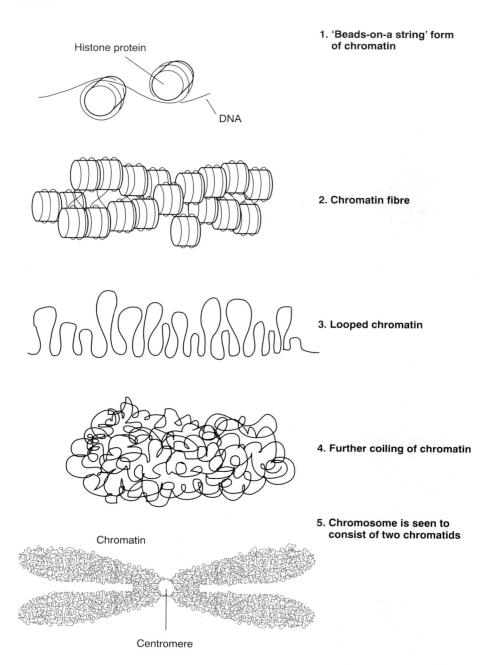

1. 'Beads-on-a string' form of chromatin

Histone protein

DNA

2. Chromatin fibre

3. Looped chromatin

4. Further coiling of chromatin

5. Chromosome is seen to consist of two chromatids

Chromatin

Centromere

Figure 5.2 Prophase – the chromatin becomes dense and the chromosomes reform

Across the middle of the cell, the centrioles organise the microtubules from the cytoskeleton into a **spindle**. By the end of this stage the nuclear material can be seen as definite chromosomes each consisting of two chromatids held together by the centromere. The chromosomes lie randomly around the spindle. One of each pair of centrioles lies at opposite ends or poles of the spindle. The nuclear membrane breaks down and the chromosomes move and lie across the equator of the spindle. Their centromeres attach to the spindle. This is **metaphase**.

Anaphase is marked by the centromeres splitting in to two halves. This is followed by the chromatids of each chromosome being pulled apart by some of the filaments of the spindle which shorten, while at the same time being pushed apart by other fibres which apparently lengthen. They move towards the spindle poles. By the end of anaphase one chromatid from each chromosome will lie at opposite poles of the spindle.

Telophase is the final stage of mitosis. The spindle begins to break down. A new nuclear membrane forms around the chromatids at each pole. The chromatids begin to unravel themselves and once again become indistinct structures. One or more nucleoli form in each nucleus.

Figure 5.3 The different stages of mitosis

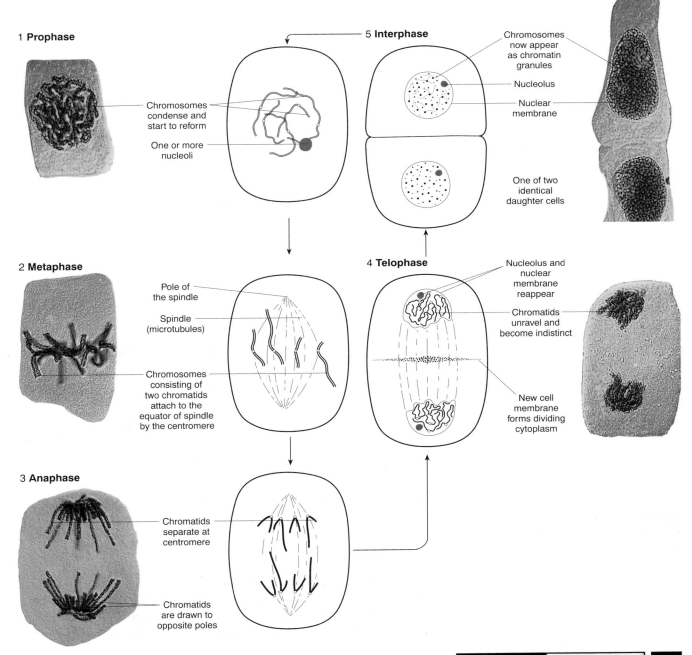

1 **Prophase**

Chromosomes condense and start to reform

One or more nucleoli

5 **Interphase**

Chromosomes now appear as chromatin granules

Nucleolus

Nuclear membrane

One of two identical daughter cells

2 **Metaphase**

Pole of the spindle

Spindle (microtubules)

Chromosomes consisting of two chromatids attach to the equator of spindle by the centromere

4 **Telophase**

Nucleolus and nuclear membrane reappear

Chromatids unravel and become indistinct

New cell membrane forms dividing cytoplasm

3 **Anaphase**

Chromatids separate at centromere

Chromatids are drawn to opposite poles

To complete the division of the two daughter cells there must be cytoplasmic division or **cytokinesis**. In animal cells the cell organelles distribute themselves evenly through the cytoplasm. The cell membrane is then drawn in to form a furrow (or cleavage). This deepens until eventually the two cells are separated. Each cell now enters interphase of the cell cycle. It will increase in size and must replicate a new chromatid for each chromosome and more cell organelles before it can undergo another mitotic division.

5.4 Cancer – mitosis out of control

Cancer is the name given to a group of over 200 diseases which result from a loss in control of cell division. Often a solid mass of cells forms which is called a **tumour**. Primary tumours may be benign or malignant. **Benign** tumours do not spread to other organs but can grow to be quite large and cause problems by starving normal cells nearby of essential nutrients; they might also press on blood vessels and nerves. A **malignant** tumour poses more of a medical problem since it gives rise to cells which travel (usually via the lymph and/or blood vessels) to distant organs of the body where they start to grow in to secondary tumours. This process is called **metastasis**. In the Western world the most common cancers are in the lung, breast, skin, gut and prostate gland.

Causes of cancer

There are very many different causes of cancer but they all result in a mutation in the DNA which causes uncontrolled mitosis.

A *chemical* which causes such a mutation is called a **carcinogen**. As early as 1775 Percival Pott, a surgeon in London, noticed that there was a high incidence of scrotal cancer amongst young chimney sweeps. In Denmark laws were passed that required the sweeps to wear protective clothing and to wash more frequently, following which there was a drop in the incidence of these cancers. In Britain the chemicals responsible for most cancers are those found in cigarette smoke. At present the biggest killer of males in the UK is lung cancer, although due to increased smoking by women, it is predicted that by the year 2007 deaths caused by lung cancer in women will overtake the number in men.

Environmental factors are sometimes implicated in the development of cancers. For example in Australia skin cancer is 200 times more common than in India. It is thought that long exposure of pale Caucasian skin to strong sunlight is a major factor.

There is evidence that diet is responsible for some cancers. In countries where the diet is rich in fibre, there is a low incidence of bowel cancer for example. A well balanced diet provides the antioxidant vitamins A, C and E which may give some protection against cancer and indeed other diseases by combining with free radicals that are present in the cells. **Free radicals** are very reactive particles that can disrupt chemical pathways, which is why they are dangerous to cells.

Lifestyle is probably an important factor in the development of cancer too. A report in *New Scientist* in April 1996 offers an explanation as to why heavy alcohol users suffer more than twice the rate of breast, liver and digestive

▶ *Chapter 34 **explains about mutations***

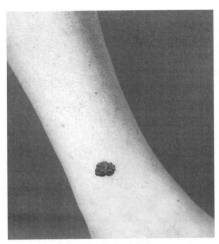

Figure 5.4 (a) Melanoma is a form of skin cancer which readily forms secondary tumours
(See Colour Gallery page 347)

Figure 5.4 (b) Over exposure to the sun increases the risk of skin cancer
(See Colour Gallery page 347)

Figure 5.5 One form of breast cancer has been found to run in families

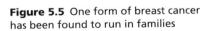
▶ *Chapter 27.2 covers cervical smears*

cancers compared with non-drinkers. It was found that in rats given alcohol equivalent to twice the legal limit for driving in Britain, there was a 40-fold increase in cancerous cells that became lodged in the lungs. In the absence of alcohol the body's immune system would destroy the tumour cells before they reached the lungs, but when alcohol levels were high this protective mechanism did not function. This effect of alcohol seems to be temporary as the immune system was only disabled while there was a high alcohol level in the blood.

It is recognised that there are some *chronic viral diseases* that are associated with cancers. Hepatitis B and hepatitis C for example may lead to the development of liver cancer in some cases.

Other cancers have a *genetic* basis. All humans have genes called **oncogenes** which are concerned with the regulation of cell division. They do not cause cancer unless they are activated by a trigger. A second type of gene called a **suppressor** normally prevents cells from dividing. However, if the suppressor gene mutates, the trigger is activated and cell division may proceed out of control.

A major advance in the understanding of cancers with a genetic basis was the discovery of two genes (BRCA1 and BRCA2) which cause a type of breast cancer that runs in families. It is now possible to offer genetic screening and counselling to women who belong to families where there is a history of breast cancer. At present, there is no way of preventing the disease from developing in women carrying the cancer gene except by an operation to remove the healthy breasts (mastectomy). It may be possible in the future to 'switch off' the genes for breast cancer and so avoid this drastic treatment.

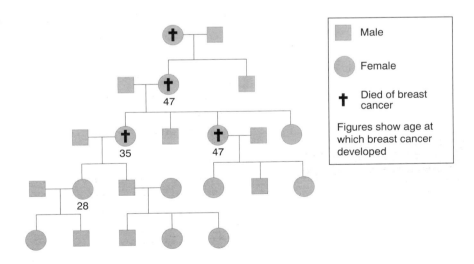

■	Male
●	Female
†	Died of breast cancer

Figures show age at which breast cancer developed

Diagnosis and treatment

Cancers that are diagnosed early have a better **prognosis** (chance of a cure). Screening is available for age groups at risk to detect cancer of the cervix, breast, prostate gland and large bowel and some tumours are found this way. Self-examination of the breasts and testicles may result in the early discovery of changes in the tissues such as small lumps.

Primary tumours can become quite large before they cause any symptoms. Diagnosis may include:

- blood tests to look for tumour markers or abnormal cells;
- examination by X-ray, CT scans or MRI scans;
- tagging the tumour with radioactive tracers so that they can then be detected by a scanner.

Figure 5.6 The results of two cervical smear tests. Malignant cells from the cervix (a) have large nuclei in comparison with those from a healthy cervix (b). The malignant cells are also larger

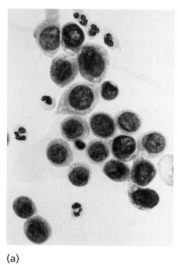
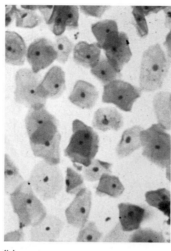

(a)   (b)

Seeing inside the human body

Scans and X-rays are used for obtaining images of structures inside the body.

The first pictures of human anatomy were obtained by taking X-ray photographs or **radiographs**. X-rays affect photographic plates in the same way as light does and so the developed radiograph is just like a black and white photographic negative. Body materials absorb X-rays to differing degrees depending on their density. Therefore bones which are dense absorb more radiation than soft tissues and so on the radiograph bone shows up lighter compared to soft tissue. Initially, X-rays were used to locate foreign bodies such as bullets in the body, but soon it was found that X-rays give excellent images of the lungs and so were used to diagnose TB. Mammograms (X-rays to detect breast cancer) are radiographs in common use today. Patients can be given dyes by mouth or injection allowing sharper images to be obtained in kidney and blood vessel investigations. A barium meal (barium sulphate) can be given before an X-ray is taken of the stomach and upper intestinal tract. You can see the results in Figure 24.5 (page 250).

A **body scanner** (CAT or CT scanner), a British invention, uses X-rays to obtain clear images of the anatomy including soft tissues. The scanning head rotates in an arc around the body sending out a thin beam of X-rays. These are detected by crystals which record the absorption rates of the different tissues. The data is converted by a computer into a picture on a monitor. As the scanner moves down the body a series of cross sections (slices) of the body are recorded. Bones

appear distinct and bright in the image but soft tissues such as blood vessels, muscle or tumours show up as varying shades of grey. Digital processing may add false colour to the scan which then allows different tissues to be identified. Any tumour shown can be studied to see whether it has spread to surrounding tissue. The data obtained may be used to make diagnosis of cancer and indicate the best treatment of the condition, be it surgery, chemotherapy or radiotherapy.

Nuclear magnetic resonance (NMR) is the basis of the **MRI scan** (magnetic resonance imaging). It does not subject the patient to radioactivity or any other form of ionising radiation but to a very strong magnetic field. The patient lies on a scanning table and a magnetic coil is put around the relevant part of the body. The table moves into a narrow but light tunnel housing a very powerful magnet. An intercom keeps the patient in contact with the radiographer. The scan can be noisy and earplugs are supplied; it takes on average 25 minutes to complete the scan.

The MRI scan begins when the magnetic field is switched on. It affects the spin of the atomic nuclei of some of the common elements of the body. They are re-orientated when a radiowave is passed through the tissues. Energy is released as the radiowave is turned off and so converted into an image on a computer screen. The quality of such images is superb. MRI scans repeated over a period of time can show the progression of a tumour, or may confirm that a tumour has been destroyed following a course of treatment.

Treatment involves surgery to remove the tumour in about half of all cases. This may be followed by radiotherapy or chemotherapy aimed at destroying any remaining cancer cells. **Radiotherapy** involves treating the diseased area with X-rays or gamma rays from cobalt or caesium. **Chemotherapy** is a technique using a drug, or combination of drugs to treat the cancer. It has the advantage of being able to treat a tumour that has spread from its primary site. Meanwhile, research continues to find new treatments. One line of enquiry includes the development of **magic bullets** which consist of an antibody specific to the surface receptors on the cancer cells combined with a toxic drug to kill them. The antibody binds with the cancer cell and the drug kills it but healthy cells are not affected. **Monoclonal antibodies** which can stimulate the lymphocytes to act against tumour cells may prove promising. The synthesis of drugs using recombinant DNA technology is also important.

▶ **Chapter 30** *explains about monoclonal antibodies*

▶ **Chapter 32.4** *gives details on recombinant DNA technology*

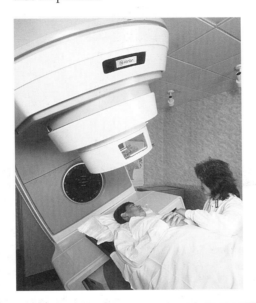

Figure 5.7 This patient is receiving radiotherapy for the treatment of a brain tumour *(See Colour Gallery page 348)*

Cell suicide – apoptosis

Programmed cell death or **apoptosis** is a mechanism used by the body to rid itself of damaged cells. Sometimes perfectly healthy cells are destroyed by the same mechanism, for no apparent reason, resulting in the development of serious **autoimmune diseases** such as multiple sclerosis or insulin-dependent diabetes.

Papers published in the journal *Scientific American* in 1996 by two teams of researchers claim that an enzyme has been identified which plays a crucial part in triggering the process. It seems that there are two receptor molecules found on a cell surface which receive the instructions for the cell to self-destruct. Once they have been switched on they bind to an adaptor protein inside the cell. This activates the newly discovered enzyme, which is the suicide weapon. It sets off a series of chemical reactions which breaks down DNA and vital proteins and so causes cell death. As the cell dies, parts of it are pinched off enclosed within a cell membrane and are engulfed by nearby cells.

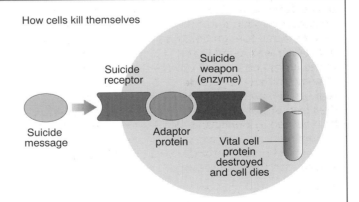

Figure 5.8 How cells self-destruct

Understanding of the process of apoptosis is important because it may hold a key to the control of some cancers and other diseases. It is necessary to find out how the process can be programmed so that only damaged and diseased cells self-destruct.

Questions

1 Make a table to summarise the main events in each stage of mitosis.

2 Which cell organelles contribute to the construction of the spindle during mitosis and meiosis?

3 Why are mature red blood cells unable to divide by mitosis?

4 a) What is cancer?

b) List different causes of cancer and give an example of the type of cancer resulting from each one.

c) What are the differences between

i) radiotherapy and chemotherapy?

ii) X-ray and MRI imaging?

5 What is apoptosis and why is it important?

CHAPTER 6 The Molecules of Life

Chapter 6 considers the structure and functions of compounds which are of vital importance to humans and other living organisms. These include water, carbohydrates, lipids and proteins. The chemical structure of the nucleic acids is described in Chapter 31.

The study of the compounds found in living organisms is called **biochemistry**, while the study of the structure and behaviour of individual molecules is termed **molecular biology**. Biological molecules are based on a small number of chemical elements, particularly carbon, hydrogen, oxygen and nitrogen. They frequently consist of monomers combined to form polymers. Complex compounds of carbon are called **organic** molecules and all others are termed **inorganic**. A carbon atom has a valency of four, meaning that each carbon atom can make four bonds with other atoms. The bonds are covalent and atoms, including more carbon atoms, can be added on in each direction. It is possible to build many different complex molecules.

You may need to refer to the section *Basics in Brief* at the back of this book for definitions of basic chemical terms.

6.1 Water

Water is the most common compound on our planet and in living organisms. The human body contains around 60 per cent water, as you can see from Table 6.1. The unusual molecular structure of the water molecule results in special properties which make it of great biological importance.

A molecule of water consists of two hydrogen atoms and one oxygen atom. There is a small uneven distribution of charge, the oxygen atom being slightly negative and the hydrogen atoms being slightly positive. The molecule is therefore described as being **dipolar** (two charges). This property means that water is an excellent **solvent** for other polar molecules such as sugars and amino acids, and for ionic compounds such as sodium chloride. **Non-polar** molecules like lipids are not soluble in water. In addition, although water molecules are very small, they are in a liquid state

Table 6.1 The approximate percentage composition of body mass for males and females

	Percentage of body mass	
Substance	Woman	Man
water	57	64
fat	23	15
protein	16	17
carbohydrate	2	2
other organic	1	1
inorganic	1	1

δ^- = Slight negative charge

δ^+ = Slight positive charge

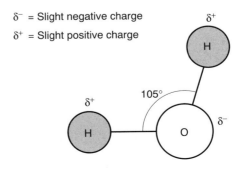

Figure 6.1 The water molecule, H_2O, has a slightly positive charge at each hydrogen atom, but the oxygen atom has a small negative charge

Some molecules and all ions have a charge, and are described as polar. They are soluble in water.
Non-polar molecules are not charged. They are insoluble in water but are soluble in lipids.

at normal atmospheric pressure in the temperature range 0–100°C. This is because clusters of water molecules form due to attractions between the positive hydrogen atoms of one molecule and the negative oxygen atom of another. The link between an oxygen atom and a hydrogen atom is a **hydrogen bond**. A single hydrogen bond is not a particularly strong bond, but they are common and important in the structure of many biological molecules.

Water, being a liquid and a common solvent, is vitally important for all living organisms including humans. In the cells metabolic reactions take place in a water-based or **aqueous** medium. Here are some examples:

- Many materials are dissolved and transported in the aqueous plasma of blood.
- Water is used in hydrolysis reactions in the breaking down of polymers to smaller molecules.
- Metabolic waste such as urea is excreted in an aqueous solution of urine.
- Secretions from exocrine glands, such as digestive enzymes or tears are dissolved in water.
- Oxygen dissolves in the watery film lining the alveoli of the lungs before diffusing into the pulmonary capillaries.
- Sperm require a fluid medium in order to reach an ovum.
- Water is a raw material for photosynthesis.

6.2 Carbohydrates

Carbohydrates are a large group of organic compounds containing the elements carbon, hydrogen and oxygen. They include sugars, starch, glycogen and cellulose. The main function of sugars, and glycogen in humans and other animals, is to provide an accessible source and store of energy. In plants starch is a common food store while cellulose is the important structural material of cell walls. Cellulose also provides the fibre in the human diet.

Carbohydrates consist of carbon, hydrogen and oxygen.

Monosaccharides

Monosaccharides (single sugars) are the simplest carbohydrates. They are sweet, crystalline compounds which are soluble in water. They have the general formula $(CH_2O)_n$ where n stands for the number of carbon atoms in each molecule and is always between three and seven. The most common monosaccharides are the **hexose** sugars that have six carbon atoms per molecule and of these glucose is the best known.

Figure 6.2 The structural formulae of three hexose sugars; (a) for the sugar α-glucose and (b) β-glucose. The only difference is that the –H and –OH groups attached to the first carbon atom are reversed.

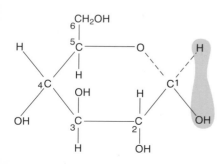

(a) α-Glucose

(b) β-Glucose

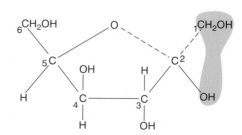

(c) α-Fructose

Glucose has the chemical formula $C_6H_{12}O_6$. All other hexose sugars such as fructose and galactose have this general formula. Compounds that share the same chemical formula but differ in structure are called **isomers**. So to identify the difference between these compounds we need to look at their structural or three-dimensional formulae. All hexoses exist as a ring structure. The ring consists of five carbon atoms and an oxygen atom and has side chains attached which end in either a hydrogen atom (–H) or a hydroxyl group (–OH), and has the sixth carbon atom in an alcohol group (–CH_2OH). By convention the carbon atoms are labelled from 1 to 6 in a clockwise direction starting from the right-hand side. The exact arrangement of the side arms determines the identity of the hexose sugar. Look carefully at Figure 6.2 which illustrates this important point.

Ribose ($C_5H_{10}O_5$) is an important **pentose** sugar, having five carbon atoms in each molecule. It is found in RNA (ribonucleic acid). Ribose also gives rise to the sugar deoxyribose ($C_5H_{10}O_4$) which is a constituent of DNA.

> Monosaccharides are simple sugars e.g. glucose and fructose.

▶ **Chapter 31.3** describes the structure of DNA

▶ **Chapter 31.4** describes the structure of RNA

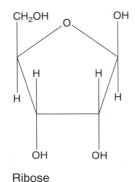

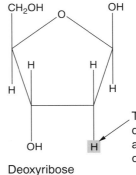

Ribose   Deoxyribose

This is where the loss of the single oxygen atom found in ribose occurs

Figure 6.3 The structural formulae of ribose and deoxyribose

Disaccharides

Disaccharides, or double sugars, are sweet, soluble in water and form crystals. They are synthesised from monosaccharide molecules which combine in pairs. All disaccharides have the general chemical formula $C_{12}H_{22}O_{11}$. The reaction that takes place when they are synthesised is called a **condensation** reaction because a molecule of water is removed from the two monosaccharide molecules. The covalent bond which links the monosaccharide molecules is called a **glycosidic bond**. When the bond forms between carbon 1 and carbon 4 of two monosaccharide molecules, it is

Figure 6.4 Two glucose molecules condense to form one molecule of maltose

α 1–4 Glycosidic bond

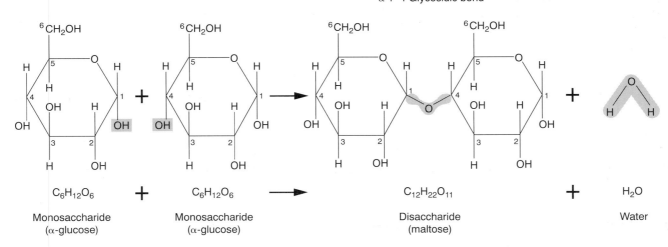

| Monosaccharide (α-glucose) | | Monosaccharide (α-glucose) | Disaccharide (maltose) | Water |

$C_6H_{12}O_6$ + $C_6H_{12}O_6$ ⟶ $C_{12}H_{22}O_{11}$ + H_2O

a 1–4 glycosidic **bond**. Figure 6.4 shows how maltose (malt sugar) is formed by the condensation of two α-glucose molecules. Other common disaccharides are **sucrose** (cane sugar), synthesised from glucose and fructose, and **lactose** (milk sugar) synthesised from glucose and galactose.

Under suitable conditions, disaccharide molecules can be broken down in to two monosaccharide monomers in a **hydrolysis** reaction (which is the *reverse* of condensation). The addition of a molecule of water results in breakage of the glycosidic bond.

> Disaccharides are built up in condensation reactions between two monosaccharide monomers.

> A monomer is a simple molecular unit used for building large molecules called polymers.

Polysaccharides

Many monosaccharide monomers may combine by numerous condensation reactions to form polymers called **polysaccharides**. The resulting chains may be branched or unbranched. They can be folded into compact shapes making ideal storage compounds, such as glycogen in the liver and muscles of humans and starch in plants. Other polysaccharides found in humans are the **mucopolysaccharides**, an example being hyaluronic acid found in the matrix of cartilage and bone. The anticoagulant heparin is also a polysaccharide. Polysaccharides are not sweet, are insoluble in water (because of their large molecular size) and do not form crystals.

> ▶ *Chapter 14 explains how blood sugar levels are controlled*

Glycogen

Glycogen is the storage carbohydrate found as granules in the cytoplasm of human and other animal cells. It is involved in maintaining normal levels of glucose in the blood. An average person has about 100 g of glycogen stored in their liver and more in the muscles, which would provide the energy needed for about an hour and a half of strenuous exercise.

The glycogen molecule is a polymer of α-glucose molecules joined by 1–4 and 1–6 glycosidic bonds. The chains are highly branched, each branch consisting of 10–20 glucose molecules.

> Glycosidic bonds link carbohydrate monomers.

Starch

Starch is a plant storage carbohydrate and is important to humans and other animals as a constituent of a balanced diet. It is synthesised from glucose made during photosynthesis. Using a light microscope it can be seen in the cell cytoplasm as granules, and is found particularly in seeds and storage organs such as potato tubers. In many Third World countries crops with a high starch content, such as rice and yam, provide the major constituent of the diet.

Starch is a mixture of two components, **amylose** (approximately 25 per cent) and **amylopectin** (approximately 75 per cent), packed together. Amylose is an unbranched chain of up to 300 molecules of α-glucose linked by 1–4 glycosidic bonds. The chain is twisted to form a helix. Amylopectin also has chains of α-glucose with 1–4 bonds, but there are branches from about 4 per cent of the glucose units where a bond forms between carbon 6 of the main chain and carbon 1 of the side branch. The molecule is like a helix with side helices coming off it. The –OH groups on the glucose monomers project to the inside of the helices and are unable to form hydrogen bonds with other parts of the molecule. This is why starch has no structural properties such as those of cellulose.

Cellulose

We have already seen in Chapter 2.7 that the polysaccharide cellulose is the major component of the plant cell wall. It is a structural material and looking at its molecular structure explains why this is so.

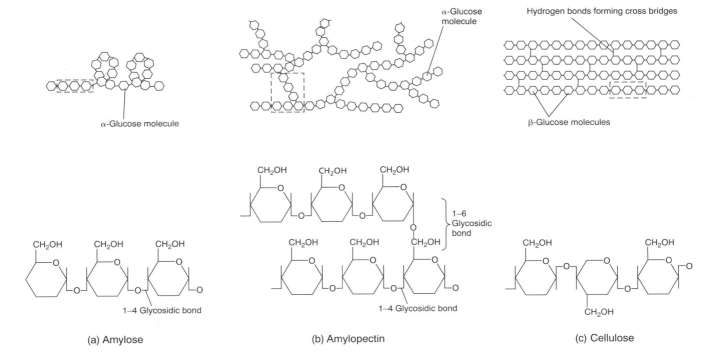

α-Glucose molecule

α-Glucose molecule

Hydrogen bonds forming cross bridges

β-Glucose molecules

CH₂OH   CH₂OH   CH₂OH

1–4 Glycosidic bond

(a) Amylose

1–6 Glycosidic bond

CH₂OH   CH₂OH   CH₂OH

1–4 Glycosidic bond

(b) Amylopectin

CH₂OH   CH₂OH

CH₂OH

(c) Cellulose

Figure 6.5 Amylose (a) has unbranched chains folded in to a helix. The chains of amylopectin (b) are branched. Compare these with the linear structure of cellulose (c) strengthened by hydrogen bonds.

> Polysaccharides are polymers of simple sugars. They are storage compounds (e.g. glycogen and starch) or have a structural function (e.g. cellulose).

▶ *Chapter 23.2 describes the importance of fibre in the diet*

The cellulose polymer is built of long straight chains of approximately 10 000 β-glucose units with 1–4 glycosidic bonds. Here, the –OH groups stick outwards from the glucose molecules and form hydrogen bonds linking neighbouring chains. In this way groups of 60–70 chains are held together and form the microfibrils shown in Figure 2.14 (page 17). This arrangement gives cellulose its strength and ensures that it is a very stable material.

The properties of cellulose make it an important material for humans. Fibres from flax are used to make linen, and cotton or cotton mixtures are used in the manufacture of many types of fabric. Paper is made from the cellulose in wood pulp. Derivatives of cellulose include cellophane used for packaging and celluloid for photographic film. Also, cellulose is the indigestible fibre component of our diet, and helps to keep food moving through the gut.

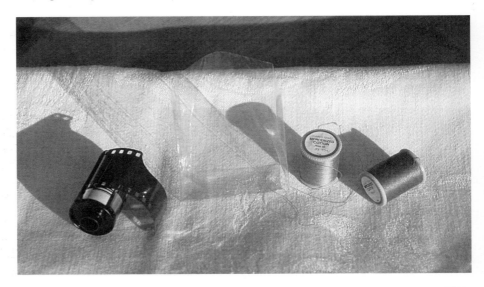

Figure 6.6 Some products from cellulose

Questions

1 Explain why glucose and salt (sodium chloride) can dissolve in water, but lipids cannot.

2 What is the chemical formula of the three hexose sugars shown in Figure 6.2?

3 Write (a) a word equation and (b) a chemical equation to summarise the condensation reaction shown in Figure 6.4.

4 Make a table to compare the properties and functions of monosaccharides, disaccharides and polysaccharides.

6.3 Lipids

Lipids are a large group of important organic molecules. Like carbohydrates, they contain the elements carbon, hydrogen and oxygen, although lipids contain proportionately less oxygen. Lipids are insoluble in water but will dissolve in organic solvents such as alcohol. Lipids can be divided into two groups: **fats and oils** and **steroids**.

Fats and oils

The difference between fats and oils is simply that fats are solid at room temperature (20°C), whereas oils are liquid. Their basic structure is the same as they are composed of **glycerol** and **fatty acids**.

Glycerol has the chemical formula $C_3H_8O_3$. It has three hydroxyl groups (–OH). Each group can combine, in a condensation reaction, with a fatty acid molecule to form a **triglyceride** and three molecules of water. The bonds between the glycerol and each of the three fatty acids is called an **ester** bond. If water is added to a triglyceride under suitable conditions, hydrolysis occurs and the reaction is reversed.

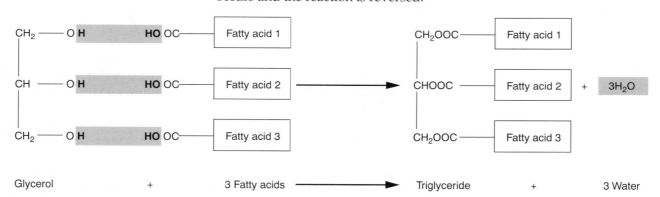

Figure 6.7 How a triglyceride is formed

Fatty acids vary considerably in structure and it is they that give a fat or oil its individual characteristics. Each fatty acid contains a **carboxyl** group (–COOH) and a chain of carbon and hydrogen atoms of varying length. There may be one or more double bonds between adjacent carbon atoms, and if so the fatty acid is **unsaturated**. Fatty acids with a single double bond are **monounsaturates**, while those with two or more double bonds per molecule are the **polyunsaturated** fats. Oleic acid, which occurs widely in plant and animal fats, is an unsaturated acid, as you can see in Figure 6.8.

Table 6.2 The structure of fatty acids is very varied

Name of fatty acid	General formula	Saturated/ unsaturated	Occurrence
butyric	C_3H_7COOH	saturated	butter fat
linoleic	$C_{17}H_{31}COOH$	unsaturated	linseed oil
oleic	$C_{17}H_{33}COOH$	unsaturated	all fats
palmitic	$C_{15}H_{31}COOH$	saturated	animal and vegetable fats
stearic	$C_{17}H_{35}COOH$	saturated	animal and vegetable fats
arachidonic	$C_{19}H_{39}COOH$	saturated	peanut oil
cerotic	$C_{25}H_{51}COOH$	saturated	wool oil

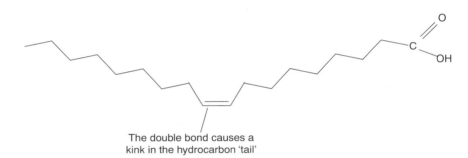

(a) Structural formula of oleic acid

The double bond causes a kink in the hydrocarbon 'tail'

Figure 6.8 Oleic acid is an unsaturated fatty acid – there is a double bond in the hydrocarbon chain of its molecule

(b) Simplified structure

Fatty acids without double bonds are described as **saturated** since no more atoms can be added to their molecule. They are solid at room temperature. The general chemical formula of a saturated fatty acid is $CH_3(CH_2)_nCOOH$.

Like carbohydrates, fats are a source of energy. Mass for mass they yield more than twice the energy from respiration than carbohydrates do when respired. Because of the body's need to use space economically, humans and many other animals store fat as a source of energy to be used as required. Fat stores around delicate organs such as the kidneys and the heart give a degree of protection from physical damage. Fat is also an excellent insulator and the layer of subcutaneous fat below the skin helps to maintain body temperature. Oily secretions over the surface of the skin and the hair keep it supple and waterproof.

▶ *Chapter 17.2 describes the structure of the skin in detail*

As we saw in Chapter 2.1, lipids are very important in the structure of the cell membrane. Many of the lipids found there are phospholipids, which are formed when glycerol reacts with phosphoric acid and two fatty acid molecules.

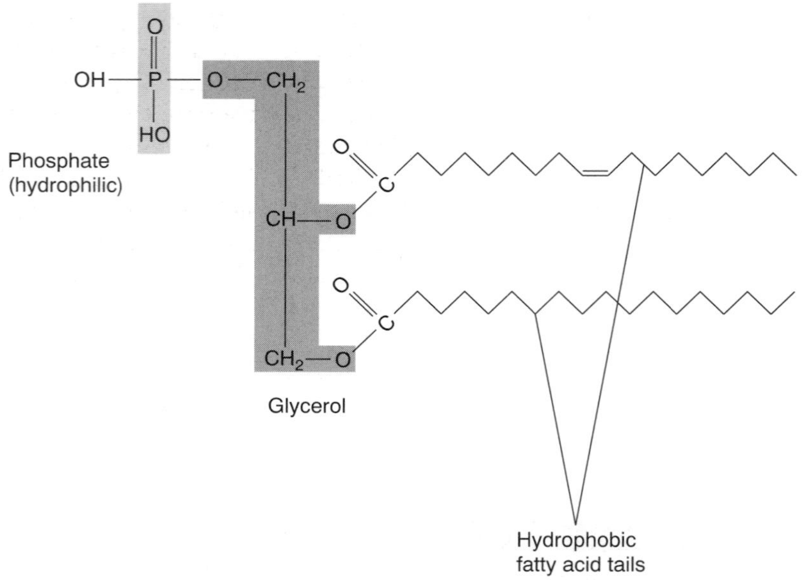

Figure 6.9 A simplified diagram of a phospholipid molecule

Steroids

Steroids are important lipids in humans. Their general structure is based on four rings of carbon atoms. Side chains are attached to these and give identity to the molecule. **Cholesterol** is probably the best known steroid because of its involvement in the health of the circulatory system. Around 10 per cent of the body's cholesterol comes from our diet; the rest is synthesised in the liver. Cholesterol is important in the structure of cell membranes since it is responsible for their fluidity. Cells lacking cholesterol tend to break open. Derivatives of cholesterol include the sex hormones testosterone and progesterone, and bile salts which emulsify fats during digestion. Recently published research suggests that cholesterol is essential for the healthy development of the fetus.

Some Man-made steroids are drugs that play an important role in the treatment of diseases including asthma and rheumatoid arthritis. Others, the anabolic steroids and testosterone, are body-building drugs which increase muscle mass. It is illegal to use these drugs in competitive sport and they can also be dangerous to health, potentially causing liver damage and sterility.

▶ *Chapter 11.3 describes the role of cholesterol in heart disease*

▶ *Chapter 19.3 explains problems involved with testing athletes for drug abuse*

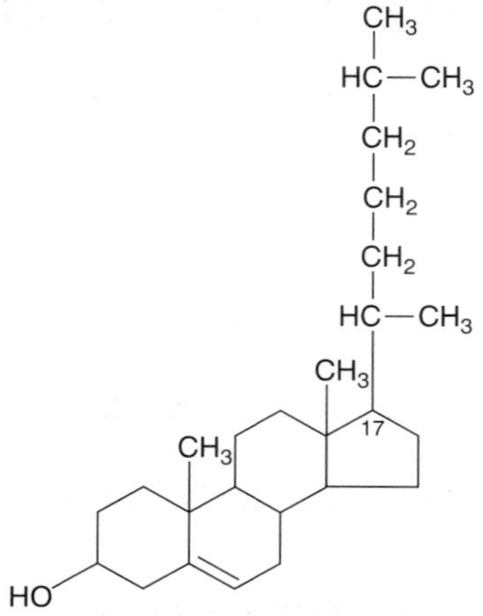

Figure 6.10 A molecule of cholesterol

Questions

1 Describe six functions of lipids in the human body.

2 Why do athletes consume glucose during exercise, but a high starch diet during training?

3 Give three similarities and three differences between lipids and carbohydrates.

4 What exactly is meant by the phrase 'High in polyunsaturates' found on some tubs of margarine?

6.4 Proteins

Proteins are a large group of organic molecules which are vital to the functioning of all living organisms. They all contain carbon, hydrogen, oxygen and nitrogen and, in addition, sometimes include sulphur and phosphorus. Their molecular mass is high (as shown by haemoglobin, 64 500) and so they cannot dissolve in water; instead they form **colloids**. As we shall see, their structure is complex and each protein has its own unique shape. If a protein is subjected to slight changes in the surrounding pH there is an alteration in the arrangement of charge along the polypeptide chains. This alters the bonds and causes the overall structure to change. When the change in pH is reversed, the protein reverts to its original **conformation**, (or shape). However, if a protein is heated to a temperature above 55°C the protein is **denatured**, which means that it undergoes an irreversible change in shape and is effectively destroyed.

Amino acids

Non-essential	Essential
alanine	isoleucine
arginine*	leucine
asparagine	lysine
aspartic acid	methionine
cysteine	phenylalanine
glutamic acid	threonine
glutamine	tryptophan
glycine	valine
histidine*	
proline	
serine	
tyrosine	

* essential in children

Table 6.3 Some amino acids can be synthesised in the human body – those that must be supplied in the diet are the essential amino acids

The units that proteins are made of are **amino acids**. These are crystalline solids which are soluble in water but insoluble in organic solvents. Twenty different amino acids are commonly used in the building of proteins. The names of these 20 amino acids are given in Table 6.3.

Those known as **essential** amino acids cannot be synthesised in the human body and must be obtained via the diet. The **non-essential** amino acids can be synthesised in the body and so are not required from the diet. Arginine and histidine are needed in growth and are essential amino acids for children but not for adults.

Each amino acid molecule has an amine group $-NH_2$ (*basic*) and a carboxyl group $-COOH$ (*acidic*). Additional amino groups are found in the basic amino acids (for example arginine) and additional carboxyl groups give rise to the acidic amino acids (such as aspartic acid). A substance that has both basic and acidic characteristics is described as **amphoteric**. In addition each amino acid has an R group which gives it its identity.

The R group may be a hydrogen atom (H) which occurs in the simplest amino acid, glycine; in alanine it is CH_3 and in methionine the R group is $CH_2CH_2SCH_3$.

The charge on an amino acid changes with pH.

- In a *neutral* solution the amino acid molecule is a **dipolar ion** or **zwitterion**, having both a positive and negative charge.
- In *acidic* conditions the amino acid gains hydrogen ions (H^+) from the medium and becomes positively charged.
- In an *alkaline* solution the amino acid loses hydrogen ions and becomes negatively charged.

The pH at which the amino acid molecule is electrically neutral is called the **isoelectric point**. This ability of amino acids to change their charge enables them to act as **buffers** and prevent changes in pH where small amounts of acid or alkali are added. Therefore, the pH of human blood remains between 7.35 and 7.45, in spite of very varied concentrations of carbon dioxide and carbonic acid levels, due to buffering by a mixture of proteins, hydrogencarbonate ions and phosphate ions.

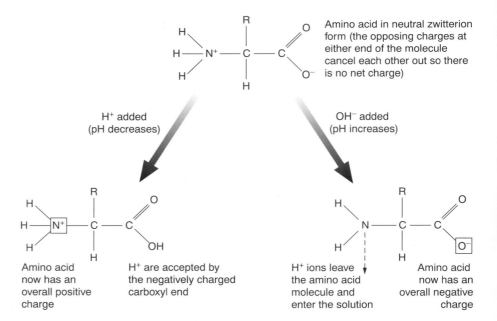

Figure 6.11 The acidic and basic properties of an amino acid allow it to act as a buffer preventing changes in pH if small amounts of acid or alkali are added

Two amino acids may join together in a condensation reaction occurring between the amino group of one amino acid and the carboxyl group of the second to form a **dipeptide**. A molecule of water is released. The covalent bond linking the amino acids is a **peptide bond**. Further amino acids can be added in additional condensation reactions leading to a long chain called a **polypeptide**. Hydrolysis reactions work in reverse to bring about the breaking of one or more peptide bonds and so shortening the polypeptide chain.

Protein structure

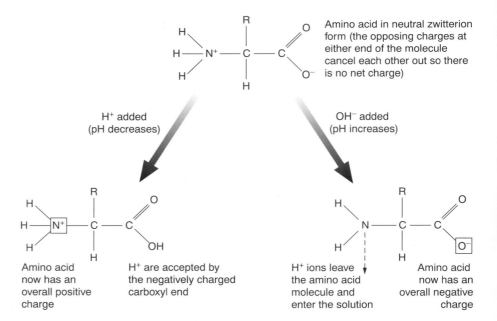
► *Chapter 31.8 explains protein synthesis*

Since there are 20 amino acids and an unlimited number of times that each may be used in the structure of any protein, it follows that an infinite number of different proteins may be built. The **primary** structure of a protein is the order in which its amino acids are linked together, and this is determined by DNA.

The protein chain folds up and is held in place mainly by weak bonds, such as hydrogen and ionic bonds. In some proteins stronger covalent disulphide bonds or sulphur bridges are found. This arrangement is called the **secondary** structure of the protein. The most common is where the protein coils to form a helix, called the **α-helix**. A protein containing a significant number of α-helices is keratin which is found in human skin, hair and nails. Enzymes and antibodies also contain α-helices. Alternatively, but less commonly, the protein may form **β-pleats** (also called sheets) which give strength to the protein. The protein in silk, fibroin, is very strong due to the high proportion of β-pleats in its structure. Many proteins have a mixture of α-helices and β-pleats.

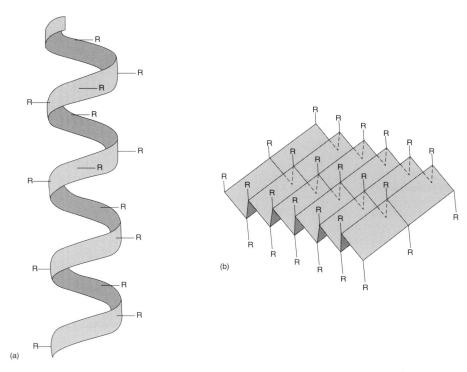

Figure 6.12 The secondary structure of proteins (a) α-helix and (b) β-pleat

Each protein has a unique molecular shape made by the polypeptide chains folding in a particular way. This is the **tertiary** structure of the protein. The three-dimensional structure of a protein can be worked out using the technique of X-ray diffraction or crystallography. The chains are held in shape by hydrogen bonds, ionic bonds and sulphur bridges. In complex proteins which have more than one polypeptide chain, the precise arrangement found is called the **quaternary** structure.

▶ *Chapter 31.2 covers X-ray diffraction in more detail*

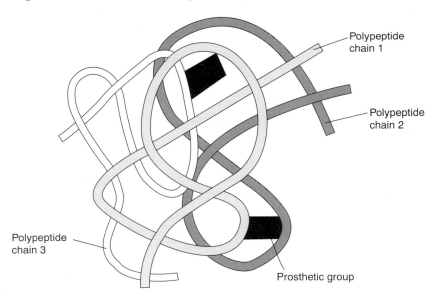

Polypeptide chain 1

Polypeptide chain 2

Polypeptide chain 3

Prosthetic group

Figure 6.13 The quaternary structure of a protein *(See Colour Gallery page 347)*

Haemoglobin, the pigment in red blood cells, has a quaternary structure since it consists of four polypeptide chains and four non-protein haem (iron-containing) groups which must be packed in a precise way for the proper functioning of the pigment. A protein containing a non-protein component in the molecule is a **conjugated** protein and the non-protein part is the **prosthetic** group.

▶ *Chapter 10.3 describes the structure and function of haemoglobin*

The *function* of a protein is related to the *shape* of its molecule. There are two main groups: globular and fibrous proteins.

Globular proteins are folded tightly in to spherical shapes. They are soluble in water, although because the molecules are large, they form colloidal suspensions rather than true solutions. They play a part in homeostasis acting as buffers which stabilise the pH in the body; insulin and glucagon regulate sugar level in the body. Enzymes are important globular proteins, as are the proteins of the cell membrane involved in the transport of materials in and out of the cell and the membranous organelles. Antibodies involved in the defence of the body against disease are another important class of globular protein. Finally, some globular proteins have important structural roles, for example actin in muscles and tubulin in microtubules.

Fibrous proteins are by contrast very tough and insoluble in water. They consist of long polypeptide chains strengthened by numerous cross links giving them the necessary strength for their structural function. Keratin in the skin, hair and nails is a fibrous protein. The most abundant fibrous protein in humans is collagen, which is very strong and occurs in bone, cartilage, tendons, ligaments, connective tissue and skin. It is often associated with elastin in connective tissue.

▶ *Chapter 2 describes the cell and its organelles*

▶ *Chapter 7 considers enzymes in detail*

▶ *Chapter 12.2 describes the distribution and function of connective tissues in the skeleton*

Questions

1 Aspartic acid is an amino acid with the R group $-CH_2-COOH$. Draw the structural formula of aspartic acid.

2 Explain what is meant by the *isoelectric point* of an amino acid or protein.

3 Explain the difference between

   a) the primary and secondary structure of a protein

   b) a globular protein and a fibrous protein

   c) a dipeptide and a disaccharide.

4 In a healthy person how do the proteins in blood help to maintain the pH of blood within the normal narrow range?

CHAPTER 7 Enzymes

Figure 7.1 Eduard Buchner, whose observations led to the discovery of enzymes

Enzymes were discovered at the end of the nineteenth century by Eduard Buchner, a German chemist. He observed that an extract from yeast was able to ferment sugar to alcohol. Previously, it had been thought that it was the yeast organism itself that carried out the fermentation. Buchner called the active ingredient in the yeast extract **'enzyme'**, which means 'in yeast'. Now we use the term to describe the hundreds of these organic compounds produced by living cells. Enzymes speed up and control metabolic reactions because they are **catalysts**. Almost all enzymes are proteins. They are usually specific in the reaction that they catalyse. They can be used many times over because they do not get used up during a reaction. Enzymes work within a narrow range of pH and are denatured by high temperatures.

7.1 The importance of enzymes

Usually, in the laboratory we use heat energy if we need to speed up a chemical reaction, or alternatively an inorganic catalyst. Most organisms live in a relatively narrow temperature range between just above 0°C and 45°C, at which reactions proceed too slowly to maintain life processes. Heating is not an option for living organisms because the temperatures necessary to increase reaction rates sufficiently would kill cells. Instead, cells produce enzymes which are organic catalysts, speeding up their metabolic reactions by a million (10^6) to a trillion (10^9) times, allowing living organisms to exist at quite low temperatures.

Secondly, enzymes are important in controlling metabolism. Over 1000 chemical reactions occur in a living cell. Many take place in a specific order as one compound is converted to other products in a chain reaction or **metabolic pathway**. Each reaction in the chain is catalysed by a specific enzyme. Enzymes ensure that the reactions in the cell proceed in an ordered fashion. DNA in the genes is responsible for determining which enzymes are functional in a cell. Some human illnesses are caused by a genetic fault which prevents an enzyme from functioning or even being produced. Cystic fibrosis is one of these diseases.

Thirdly, enzymes are important to humans because they have been exploited for thousands of years to make useful products such as beer, bread and cheese and, more recently, new commodities such as biological washing powders have been developed. This is part of a branch of science called **biotechnology**, which is described in more detail towards the end of this chapter.

► **Chapter 33.1 gives more information about cystic fibrosis**

Figure 7.2 The bread, cheese and beer in this Ploughman's lunch are all the products of enzyme action

7.2 How enzymes work – lowering activation energy

Liquids and gases consist of molecules which are constantly on the move. If they collide, they may react together. However, a chemical reaction between

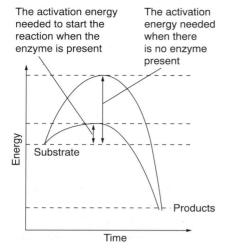

The activation energy needed to start the reaction when the enzyme is present

The activation energy needed when there is no enzyme present

Energy

Substrate

Products

Time

Figure 7.3 Enzymes lower activation energy so reactions proceed faster at lower temperatures

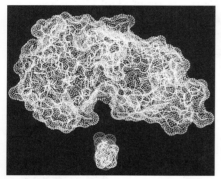

Figure 7.4 The enzyme molecule is considerably larger than the substrate that it reacts with
(See Colour Gallery page 348)

C6

two reactants can only take place if they collide at the right angle to one another and with enough energy. If the alignment of the two molecules is incorrect the molecules will just bounce off one another. If the molecules collide too gently there will not be enough energy to make or break chemical bonds and the reaction will not occur. The energy that is needed before a chemical reaction can take place is called the **activation energy**.

Look at Figure 7.3. In any chemical reaction before two molecules react their energy levels must be raised so that they can form a temporary complex. This energy (activation energy) might be transferred to the reactants by heating. The complex then quickly breaks down to form the products of the reaction. However, when an enzyme is present it *lowers the activation energy required* for the reaction to proceed and so many more molecules have enough energy to react and the whole process speeds up.

The reaction in which a substrate (S) releases end-products (P_1 and P_2) is catalysed by an enzyme (E). The progress of the reaction, including the formation of an intermediate enzyme substrate complex (E–S) can be expressed as:

(1) $E + S \rightarrow E\text{–}S$
(2) $E\text{–}S \rightarrow E + P_1 + P_2$

The overall reaction is $S \rightarrow P_1 + P_2$

The lock and key hypothesis

As we have said, almost all enzymes are globular proteins. (A very few have been described, called ribozymes, which consist of RNA.) Enzymes are usually much larger than the substrate molecule which they react with.

Scientists proposed that in an enzyme-controlled reaction the enzyme and substrate react forming a temporary enzyme–substrate complex. The complex then reacts to form the end-products of the reaction. The position on the surface of the enzyme molecule where the substrate fits precisely is called the **active site**. It can be thought of as a special pocket opening in the enzyme's surface. It contains chemical groups which *attract* and bind the substrate and others to *catalyse* the reaction.

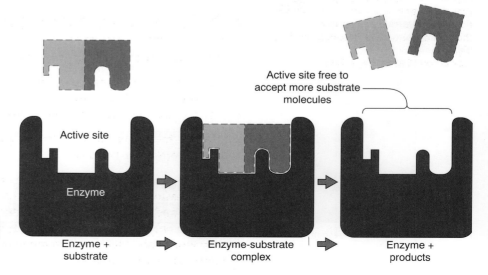

Active site free to accept more substrate molecules

Active site

Enzyme

Enzyme + substrate

Enzyme-substrate complex

Enzyme + products

Figure 7.5 A highly simplified and stylised diagram showing the lock and key hypothesis of enzyme action

C7

The enzyme was therefore thought to be like a lock into which the substrate fits, providing a model called the **lock and key hypothesis**. This model explains why an enzyme is specific in its action, for only the reactant(s) of one reaction will be a suitable shape to bind to the active site on each enzyme.

Induced fit

The lock and key model suggested that enzymes were rigid structures and did not explain all the behaviour of enzymes that had been observed. For example it did not explain **allosteric** effects (Chapter 7.4) which occur when other molecules bind to a site on an enzyme well away from the active site and yet still interfere with the enzyme's activity. It appeared that an enzyme is a *flexible* molecule with two possible **conformations** (or shapes) and so the idea of **induced fit** was proposed. Firstly, we recognise the **binding conformation** where the enzyme wraps around the substrate so that it joins with the active site. This disturbs the structure of the enzyme molecule causing a slight change in shape or *inducing fit*. This re-arrangement of shape (to the **active conformation**) brings catalytic enzymes in to contact with the substrate. The now distorted enzyme deforms the substrate, causing bonds within the molecule to break. In this way, activation energy is lowered and the end-products of the reaction are rapidly produced. The products do not fit within the active site of the enzyme and they diffuse away. The enzyme, being flexible, returns to its original shape and is able to catalyse the next reaction.

> The shape of a protein, including the active site of an enzyme, is called its conformation. If the conformation is changed the protein cannot react.

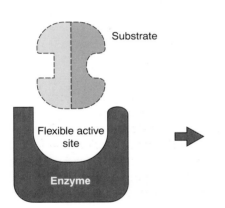

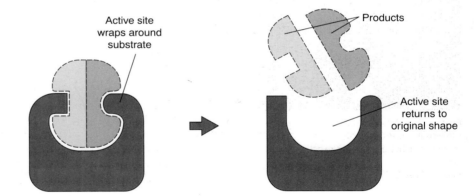

Figure 7.6 Induced fit suggests that enzymes have a more flexible structure than was once thought as shown in this very simplified diagram
(See Colour Gallery page 348)

7.3 The properties of enzymes

Enzymes share the following properties with inorganic catalysts:

- they speed up chemical reactions;
- they are not used up in the reaction that they catalyse;
- they are not chemically changed during the reaction they catalyse.

In addition, they have other unique properties which are related to the fact that they are *globular proteins*:

- they are specific in the reaction that they catalyse because of the conformation (or shape) of their active site (look back at the sections on the lock and key hypothesis and induced fit);
- they can only function within a fairly narrow range of pH;
- they work only over a certain range of temperature and are denatured by temperatures above 55°C.

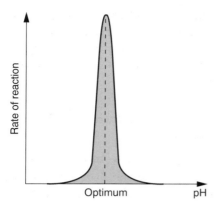

Figure 7.7 This graph shows how enzyme activity varies with changing pH

How pH affects enzymes

Enzymes have their own specific range of pH within which they can function. The pH at which they are most efficient is the **optimum** pH. For most intracellular enzymes this is around neutral, pH 7.0. The enzymes of the digestive system (Chapter 22) work in acidic or alkaline environments. For example pepsin is a **protease** (protein-digesting enzyme) in the stomach that has an optimum pH of 2.0. In contrast, the protease trypsin found in the duodenum where conditions are alkaline has an optimum pH of 8.5.

If an enzyme is subjected to even slight changes in pH it will become much less efficient. Changes in pH can alter the charge on the amino acids at the active site so that substrate molecules are unable to bind. The process is reversible for a small change in pH. Large changes in pH will permanently denature enzymes.

How temperature affects enzymes

Increases in temperature increase the rate at which molecules collide. As temperature rises enzyme and substrate molecules collide with more energy and so more product is formed. The temperature at which the enzyme catalyses a specific reaction most rapidly is called the **optimum temperature**. Optimum temperature is 35–40°C for most animals.

Between 4°C and optimum temperature, an increase in temperature of 10°C doubles the rate of reaction. This is called the **temperature coefficient (Q$_{10}$)** and is calculated using the following equation:

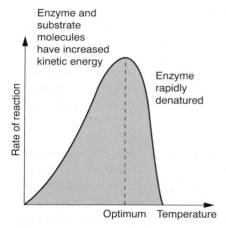

Figure 7.8 The progress of an enzyme-catalysed reaction as temperature increases

$$Q_{10} = \frac{\text{rate of reaction at } (x°C + 10°C)}{\text{rate of reaction at } x°C}$$

$$Q_{10} \sim 2$$

x°C is a temperature between 1 and 40°C

Once temperature rises very much above the optimum enzymes are rapidly denatured. The increased temperature causes the bonds holding the protein's structure together to break, destroying the tertiary shape. The change is irreversible.

Substrate concentration and the rate of an enzyme-controlled reaction

If the concentration of an enzyme remains constant but the substrate concentration is increased, the rate of reaction will rise and eventually remain stationary. This is shown in Figure 7.9. Initially, the number of substrate molecules itself limits the rate of reaction. As substrate concentration increases there are more molecular collisions between substrate and enzyme molecules so the reaction rate is faster (Y). Increasing substrate concentration further fails to increase reaction rate (Z). This is because all the active sites on the enzyme molecules present are being used at any one time and some substrate molecules have no enzyme to react with. In this case, the concentration of an enzyme is *limiting* the rate of the reaction.

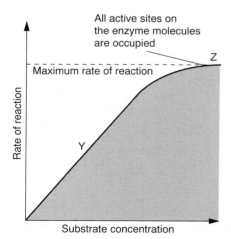

Figure 7.9 The effect of increasing the concentration of substrate while enzyme concentration remains constant

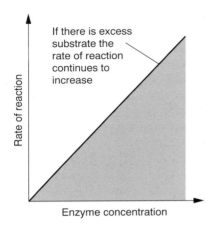

Figure 7.10 The rate of an enzyme-controlled reaction will continue to rise if temperature and pH are within normal range and substrate is in excess – there are no limiting factors

If there is excess substrate the rate of reaction continues to increase

Rate of reaction

Enzyme concentration

The **Michaelis constant** is the concentration of substrate needed to make a reaction proceed at half its maximum rate. Each enzyme has its own Michaelis constant. Its value gives an indication of the *affinity* of the enzyme for its substrate. Therefore, if the constant has a low value the enzyme has a high affinity for its substrate and vice versa.

Enzyme concentration and the rate of an enzyme-controlled reaction

Enzymes work efficiently even in low concentration. Their active site can be used time and time again. Providing that temperature and pH are within the normal range and there is an excess of substrate molecules, increasing the enzyme concentration will result in a directly proportional rise in the rate of reaction.

7.4 Enzyme inhibition

Enzyme action can be reduced by various substances, which may originate inside the cell or outside in the external surroundings. The enzyme combines with the inhibitor and so cannot bind with its normal substrate. The action may be reversible or irreversible. Understanding of enzyme inhibition has led to the development of drugs and insecticides which act on the enzyme systems of pathogens and pests and so stop them from working properly. Reversible inhibitors bind loosely to the enzyme causing a change which is temporary.

Competitive inhibitors often occur naturally in cells. They are compounds which have a structure close to that of the normal substrate and so they are able to bind to the enzyme's active site. The inhibitor occupies the active site of the enzyme and prevents binding by the normal substrate. This slows down or stops the reaction that the enzyme usually catalyses (depending on the number of active sites occupied by inhibitor molecules). Malonate is a competitive inhibitor of succinate, competing against it for the respiratory enzyme succinate dehydrogenase which takes part in the Krebs cycle.

▶ *Chapter 25.5 covers the Krebs cycle*

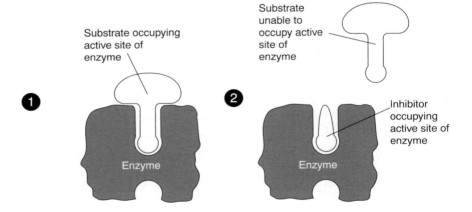

1 Substrate occupying active site of enzyme

2 Substrate unable to occupy active site of enzyme

Inhibitor occupying active site of enzyme

Enzyme

Enzyme

Figure 7.11 Competitive inhibition

Non-competitive inhibitors bind to the enzyme close to the active site. The shape of the active site changes so that the substrate cannot bind to it and this slows down the rate of reaction. The action may be reversible. Irreversible non-competitive inhibitors will bind to the enzyme molecule very tightly and permanently at a position away from the active site. This alters the enzyme's shape so that its substrate can no longer fit into the active site. The enzyme loses its ability to catalyse the reaction. Ions of heavy metals such as mercury and silver function in this way. Their poisonous action occurs quickly and at low concentrations, but the results are irreversible. Cyanide is a poison which is a non-competitive inhibitor. It inhibits the action of the enzyme cytochrome oxidase which catalyses the final reaction of respiration. Respiration is halted with a fatal result.

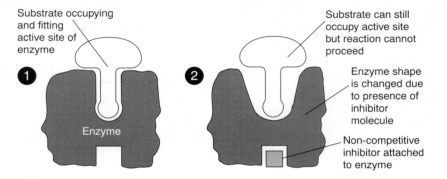

Figure 7.12 The action of a non-competitive inhibitor

Allosteric inhibition

Some enzymes are **allosteric**, which means that they exist in two forms *active* and *inactive*. In the active form they catalyse reactions but in the inactive form they are unable to bind with their substrate. There are compounds in the cell called **allosteric effectors** which are able to change an allosteric enzyme from one form to the other, thereby controlling its activity. Also, an active form of the enzyme may combine with its allosteric inhibitor. This alters the shape of the active site, converts the enzyme to the inactive form and prevents it from reacting. If the inactive enzyme molecule later combines with an allosteric activator, its conformation (shape) changes so that it can accept a substrate molecule at its active site and catalyse the reaction once more.

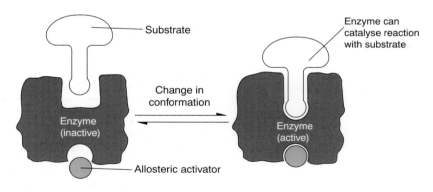

Figure 7.13 Allosteric enzymes have two shapes; in one conformation they are active and in the other they are inactive

End-product inhibition

We have already come across the idea that many metabolic pathways consist of a number of enzyme-catalysed reactions. Commonly, when the end-product of a pathway accumulates, it acts as an allosteric inhibitor on the enzyme catalysing the first reaction in the chain. Reactions in the metabolic pathway stop and prevent the accumulation of unnecessary end-product. This is an example of **negative feedback**. When the end-product is used up, inhibition stops and the chain reaction resumes.

▶ *Section 3 in brief* covers *negative feedback in depth*

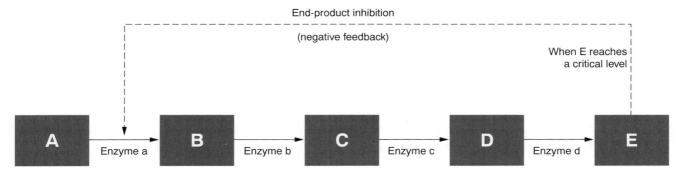

Figure 7.14 This metabolic pathway shows end-product inhibition. When product E has accumulated it inhibits the action of enzyme a and there will be no further synthesis of E until its concentration has dropped; enzyme a will then become active again.

Questions

1 Look at Figure 7.9. How would you increase the rate of reaction once the maximum rate has been reached?

2 How do enzymes allow humans to survive in the temperatures found on Earth?

3 List five important characteristics of all enzymes.

4 Explain the difference between the lock and key hypothesis and induced fit to explain how enzymes work.

5 Write a paragraph to explain the term 'enzyme inhibition'.

6 Find out which kind of chemical reactions are catalysed by

   a) hydrolases

   b) polymerases

   c) ligases

   d) synthetases

   e) oxidoreductases

   f) transferases

7.5 Enzymes in industry

Humans have used enzyme action in making alcohol, bread and cheeses for hundreds of years. Enzymes have been used commercially throughout the twentieth century, firstly in the tanning and textile industries. More recently, the large-scale production of enzymes from microbes has become possible, leading to the development of numerous innovative processes such as sensitive diagnostic tests.

The immobilisation of enzymes

As enzymes are used in solution when added to their substrate they can be diluted or even washed out of the commercial reactor and lost. The enzyme may need to be recovered once it has completed catalysing the substrate in the industrial process so that it can be used again. Enzymes can be stabilised by attaching them to the surface of inert materials such as resin beads

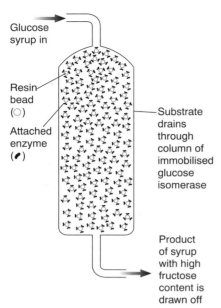

Glucose syrup in

Resin bead (○)

Attached enzyme (●)

Substrate drains through column of immobilised glucose isomerase

Product of syrup with high fructose content is drawn off

Figure 7.15 A simplified diagram to show the principle of using immobilised enzymes in an industrial reactor

► *Chapter 14.5 explains about diabetes*

packed into a column through which the substrate is allowed to pass. These enzymes are described as being **immobilised** and can be used more efficiently and economically in this form.

The production of fructose from starch

An example of a process that uses immobilised enzymes is found in the food industry. Many foods have added sugar to sweeten or improve their flavour. However, sucrose (cane sugar) is expensive and a method of making fructose from starch using microbial enzymes has been developed as a cheaper alternative. Since fructose is sweeter than sucrose, less of it has to be added to the food product.

The initial substrate is a cheap form of starch such as corn starch. It is heat-treated to convert the starch to a gelatinised form to which microbial enzymes are added. These enzymes, α-amylase and amyloglucosidase, are unusual in that they can tolerate high temperatures. They hydrolyse the starch to dextrins and then to glucose in syrup form. The glucose syrup is a useful product in its own right and may be added directly to drinks and other foods. Alternatively, the glucose syrup may be converted to fructose by adding it to an immobilised enzyme, glucose isomerase. The resulting product is a syrup high in fructose which is a common food additive.

The use of enzymes as analytical reagents

Diagnostic testing kits are now available over the counter for people to use at home. Previously, it was necessary to send off a sample (usually blood or urine) to a specialist laboratory, often in a hospital. Some of these kits make use of an immobilised enzyme which acts as a biosensor because it detects and reacts only with a specific substrate in the human sample.

The enzyme is very sensitive and capable of detecting very low concentrations of substrate. The reaction causes a change which can be converted in to an electrical signal that in turn, is converted in to a digital read out.

This principle is used in glucometers to monitor the level of blood glucose of diabetics. The immobilised enzyme used is glucose oxidase.

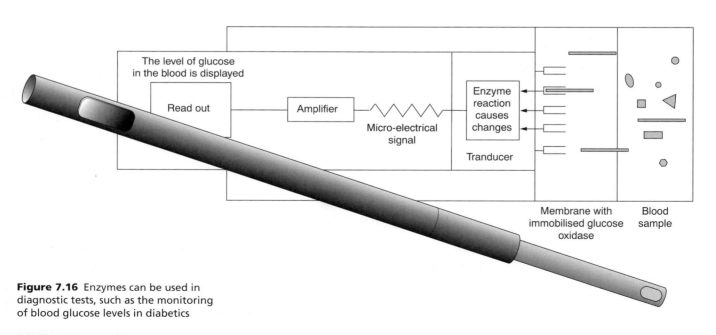

The level of glucose in the blood is displayed

Read out

Amplifier

Micro-electrical signal

Enzyme reaction causes changes

Tranducer

Membrane with immobilised glucose oxidase

Blood sample

Figure 7.16 Enzymes can be used in diagnostic tests, such as the monitoring of blood glucose levels in diabetics

1 Figure 1 (a) and (b) represent a phospholipid molecule.

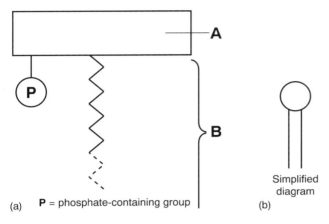

(a) **P** = phosphate-containing group

(b) Simplified diagram

Figure 1

a) i) Name the parts of the molecule labelled A and B. *(2 marks)*

ii) How do these two parts of the molecule differ in their properties with respect to water? *(1 mark)*

b) i) Use the simplified diagram of this molecule (Figure 1 (b)) to illustrate how phospholipid molecules are arranged in cell membranes. *(1 mark)*

ii) Explain *one* way in which evidence from electron micrographs would support the arrangement that you have shown. *(2 marks)*

AEB Specimen Question

2 An enzyme electrode can be used to measure the amount of a biochemical substance (analysate). The principle by which it works is that it contains an enzyme which converts the analysate into products which give rise to an electrical signal. The strength of the electrical signal may be measured with a suitable meter. Figure 2 shows a simple enzyme electrode.

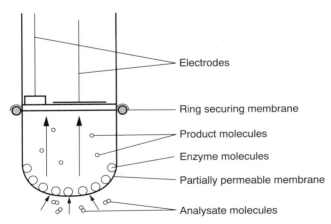

Electrodes

Ring securing membrane

Product molecules

Enzyme molecules

Partially permeable membrane

Analysate molecules

Figure 2

a) By what process do the molecules of analysate reach the enzyme? *(1 mark)*

b) From your knowledge of enzymes:

i) suggest how temperature might be expected to affect an enzyme electrode. *(2 marks)*

ii) suggest *two* advantages of using an enzyme electrode rather than a chemical test such as Benedict's test to determine the amount of glucose in a test sample. *(2 marks)*

AEB Specimen Question

3 Figure 3 shows the relationship between certain organelles in a phagocytic cell.

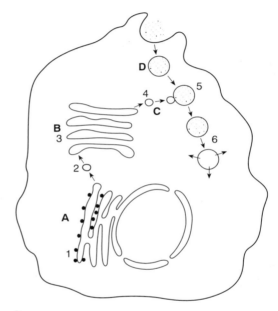

Figure 3

a) Identify organelles A to D. *(4 marks)*

Numbers 1 to 6 on Figure 3 represent a sequence of events occurring in the cells.

b) State what is occurring at 1 to 6. *(6 marks)*

UCLES

4 An experiment was carried out to determine the effect of temperature on the activity of an enzyme digesting the protein gelatin.

Gelatin was incubated with the enzyme at a range of temperatures from 5 to 60°C. The rate of amino acid production was measured over a 3 hour period.

The results are given in Table 1, expressed as rate of amino acid production in mg dm^{-3} h^{-1}.

Table 1

Temperature (°C)	Rate of production of amino acid (mg dm^{-3} h^{-1})
5	14
10	19
15	24
20	31
25	40
30	51
35	68
40	93
45	98
50	89
60	33

a) i) Plot the data on graph paper. *(4 marks)*

ii) Comment on the effect of temperature on the activity of the enzyme as shown in the graph. *(3 marks)*

b) The experiment was continued at 45°C for a further 7 hours. At the end of this time, an additional 292 mg dm^{-3} of amino acid had accumulated.

i) Calculate the mean rate of reaction during the 10 hours at 45°C. *(1 mark)*

ii) Give *two* possible reasons for the difference between the rate at the end of 10 hours and the rate after 3 hours incubation. *(2 marks)*

c) Protein-digesting enzymes can be used as an ingredient in biological washing powders.

i) Suggest how the results of this experiment could be used to design a suitable washing programme using a biological washing powder. *(2 marks)*

ii) Suggest possible advantages of using biological washing powders rather than non-biological detergents. *(2 marks)*

Edexcel

5 Table 2 refers to a liver cell, a palisade mesophyll cell and a bacterium (prokaryotic cell) and structures which may be found in them.

If the structure is present, place a (✓) in the appropriate box and if the structure is absent, place a cross (✗) in the appropriate box.

Table 2

Structure	Liver cell	Palisade cell	Bacterium
nuclear envelope			
cell wall			
microvilli			
chloroplasts			

(4 marks)

Edexcel

6 Figure 4 shows how an enzyme is thought to catalyse the breakdown of a substrate molecule to two product molecules.

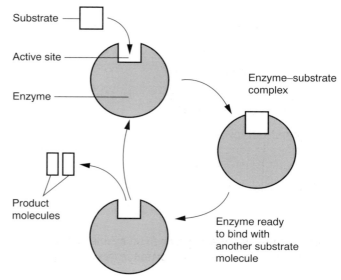

Figure 4

Use the diagram to help explain the following.

a) Peptidases will hydrolyse dipeptides but they will not hydrolyse maltose. *(3 marks)*

b) The rate of enzyme-controlled reactions varies with temperature. *(7 marks)*

c) The addition of inhibitors will affect the rates of enzyme-controlled reactions. *(7 marks)*

Quality of language *(3 marks)*

AEB Specimen Question

7 Figure 5 shows the relationship between the volume, water potential (ψ_{cell}) and solute potential (ψ_s) of a cell immersed in a series of sucrose solutions of increasing concentration. In each solution the cell was allowed to reach equilibrium with the bathing solution, so that water was being neither lost nor gained, before the measurements were made.

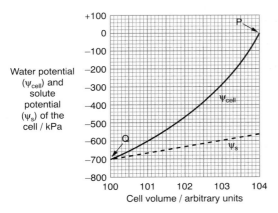

Figure 5

a) Explain what is meant by the following terms.

   i) Solute potential (ψ_s)   (2 marks)

   ii) Pressure potential (ψ_p)   (2 marks)

b) What terms are used to describe the condition of the cell at P and at Q?   (2 marks)

c) What is the volume of the cell (in arbitrary units) when in equilibrium with a sucrose solution of solute potential -400 kPa?   (1 mark)

d) Calculate the pressure potential (ψ_p) of the cell when its volume is 103 units. Show your working.   (2 marks)

e) Suggest *two* ways in which reversible changes in cell volume may be important in flowering plants.   (2 marks)

Edexcel

8 a) State what you understand by each of the following terms in relation to enzymes.

   i) Active site   (2 marks)

   ii) Denaturation   (2 marks)

b) In an investigation of enzyme inhibition, a student made mixtures of substrate and inhibitor in the following proportions (Table 3).

Table 3

Mixture	Substrate (units)	Inhibitor (units)
1	10	0
2	10	10
3	10	20

She added 20 cm³ of each mixture in turn to 20 cm³ of a standard enzyme solution, and measured the amount of product accumulating over a period of several minutes. The results are shown in Figure 6 below.

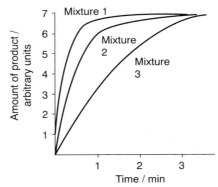

Figure 6

   i) What kind of enzyme inhibition is shown by these results? Explain your answer.   (3 marks)

   ii) Draw and label on a similar graph curves showing the expected results if the experiment were repeated with mixtures 4 and 5 as follows (Table 4).

Table 4

Mixture	Substrate (units)	Inhibitor (units)
4	10	5
5	5	10

(4 marks)

Edexcel

9 Lysozyme is an enzyme that can destroy certain bacteria by catalysing the breakdown of the polysaccharide chains that form part of their cell wall.

a) i) Name the bond between the adjacent sugar units of a polysaccharide.   (1 mark)

    ii) Explain how this bond may be broken. (1 mark)

b) Suggest how the substrate may be held in the active site of an enzyme while the reaction occurs.   (2 marks)

Lysozyme is made up of 129 amino acids. The active site is composed of two amino acids that are at positions 35 and 52 in the amino acid sequence.

c) Explain how these two amino acids are brought close together to form the active site.   (3 marks)

d) Explain the effect of increasing temperature on enzyme activity.   (3 marks)

UCLES

SECTION 2

Systems of Life

in brief — All systems go for life

Maintaining life involves a number of interacting systems, which supply living tissue with all the requirements of life. The integrated functioning of these systems is what makes biomass *alive*. Biomass is the mass of living material that makes up the body of an organism. Once body systems cease working, biomass is dead organic matter which begins to decompose.

Body mass is made of cells which are mainly grouped together as tissues. Different tissues make up specialised functional units called organs, which are uniquely designed for the jobs they perform. Therefore, within the body there is a high degree of division of labour which has the advantage of allowing a faster rate of cellular metabolism and effective performance of specialised organs. For example hepatocytes are cells in the liver that can detoxify potentially poisonous materials, but they are unable to contract like muscle fibres or transmit impulses like nerves. The size and complexity of an organism would be limited without this level of organisation and integration.

Integrated systems

The following table summarises some examples of how body systems work together. You may not be familiar with all the terms, but definitions and further details of each component are given in the appropriate chapters.

Function	Body system	Role
defence against disease	skin (Chapter 17)	provides a physical barrier preventing the entry of disease-causing organisms; repairs wounds by cell division
	cardiovascular (Chapters 10 and 11)	transports materials and cells vital in clotting, which assists wound healing; neutrophils and monocytes are phagocytic and engulf non-self particles; T-cells and B-cells are involved in the humoral immune response
	lymphatic (Chapters 10 and 30)	lymph glands contain T-cells and B-cells involved in immunity, and also filter out bacteria and other foreign particles by phagocytosis; the spleen produces T-cells and B-cells and destroys antigens by phagocytosis
excretion	skin	nitrogenous waste (as urea) is excreted in sweat
	kidneys (Chapter 16)	nitrogenous waste (as urea) and excess water and salts are excreted in urine
	lungs (Chapters 8 and 9)	remove carbon dioxide from the body
	gut (Chapter 22)	bile salts and pigments are removed in faeces
	liver (Chapter 15)	not an excretory organ as such, but has a role in removing nitrogen from excess amino acids and converting it to non-toxic urea
communication and control	nervous system (Chapter 20)	forms an extensive network of nerves which carry impulses; sense cells and organs detect changes internally and externally
	endocrine (Chapter 19)	glands produce hormones which circulate in blood and influence target cells
	cardiovascular	transports hormones

Exchanging materials

Some body systems exist to exchange materials with the environment. Substances such as food and oxygen are needed by the body and move into it from the environment. For example food is taken into the body within the digestive system, where it is broken down into particles which are small enough to move through the exchange surfaces. Oxygen exchange happens in the lungs at the alveolar surfaces. Other substances (mainly excretory products) pass out from the body to the environment. For example, carbon dioxide moves across the alveolar exchange surface and out of the lungs, while water moves from the body to the environment through the skin.

The features of exchange surfaces relate closely to their role in moving materials into and out of cells or the body itself.

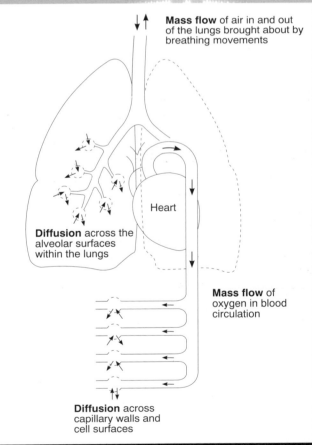

Mass flow of air in and out of the lungs brought about by breathing movements

Diffusion across the alveolar surfaces within the lungs

Heart

Mass flow of oxygen in blood circulation

Diffusion across capillary walls and cell surfaces

A model showing how particles are exchanged with the environment and are transported around the human body.

Moving and supporting the body

Working together within the body are systems which give support and bring about movement. These include the skeletal system consisting of bones and tissues such as ligaments, muscles and tendons, and the nerve networks. Muscles are distributed throughout the body, but where they are attached to bones they cause movement by contracting and pulling on them. They contract when they are triggered into action by impulses which reach them via nerve cells. We can cause the voluntary contraction of many muscles, choosing the movements we make. Some muscle contractions can become automatic once we have learnt them, for example those involved in maintaining body posture. Many muscle actions are involuntary and do not need to be learned, for example breathing movements.

The repeated use of muscles stimulates their development and our mastery in using them.

Completing the lifecycle

Reproduction is the life process which provides new individuals for the future of any population. The reproductive system is mainly controlled by hormones, for example by causing the developmental changes which happen at adolescence, and stimulating the production of sex cells. Once again there is an integrated functioning of body systems, e.g. the blood serves to transport hormones, while nervous tissue stimulates the contraction of the muscular uterus during birth.

CHAPTER 8 The Breathing System

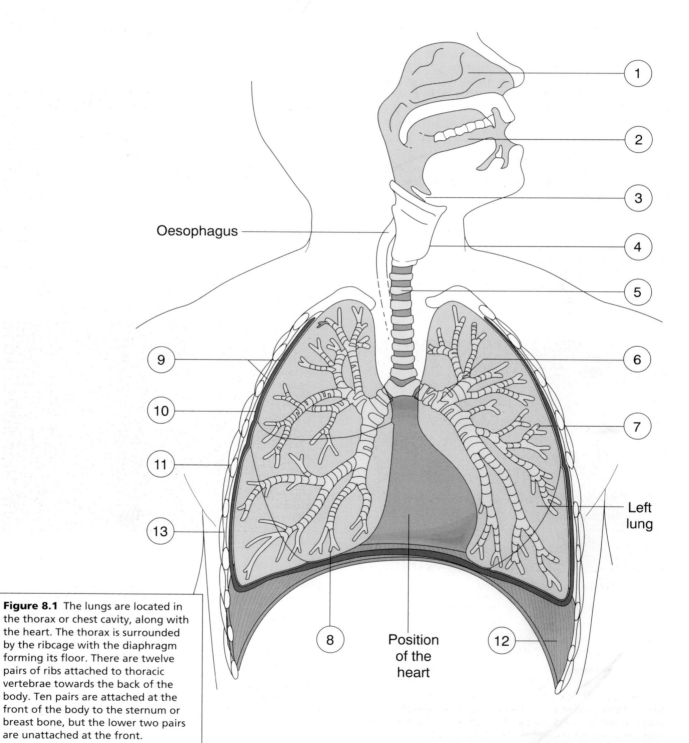

Oesophagus

Left lung

Position of the heart

Figure 8.1 The lungs are located in the thorax or chest cavity, along with the heart. The thorax is surrounded by the ribcage with the diaphragm forming its floor. There are twelve pairs of ribs attached to thoracic vertebrae towards the back of the body. Ten pairs are attached at the front of the body to the sternum or breast bone, but the lower two pairs are unattached at the front.

1 Nasal cavity – the lining of the nasal cavity is covered in hairs and secretes mucus, both of which help to clean dust and small particles such as bacteria out of the air we inhale. The air is moistened as it passes over these wet surfaces, and warmed by the rich blood supply. The nose also has an olfactory function, as it contains chemoreceptors to detect smell.

2 Mouth – air may enter the breathing system through the mouth, but is not as effectively cleaned or warmed via this route

3 Epiglottis and **glottis** – the epiglottis is a flap of cartilage which closes over the glottis in a reflex action during swallowing, preventing food entering the trachea

4 Larynx – the voicebox or larynx is composed mostly of cartilage and stretched across it are the fibrous and muscular vocal cords. Air moving in and out of the lungs may pass across the vocal cords, making sounds.

5 Trachea –the main airway leading to the lungs which is lined by ciliated columnar epithelium. The cilia beat towards the back of the mouth (the pharynx) moving mucus away from the lungs, so that trapped dirt or bacteria are swallowed. The air pressure inside the trachea fluctuates, but it remains open even when the pressure drops because of the incomplete rings of cartilage supporting it.

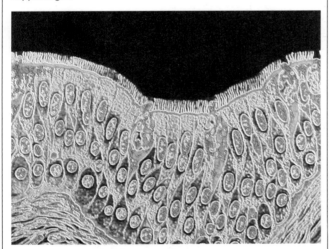

Ciliated epithelium cells in the trachea

6 Bronchus – the trachea divides into two tubes called the bronchi, one passing to each lung

13 Intercostal muscles – there are two main sets of muscles running between the ribs. Contraction of one set raises the ribs and increases the volume of the chest cavity. Contraction of the other set lowers the ribs and decreases lung capacity.

7 Bronchioles – there are many branching bronchioles which are smaller tubes than the bronchi, containing smooth muscle in their walls. Bronchioles over 1 mm in diameter are held open by rings of cartilage, but smaller ones are liable to collapse. The smallest bronchioles are lined by cuboidal epithelium which consists of fairly flattened cells that make diffusion more likely. However, most gaseous exchange happens in the alveoli.

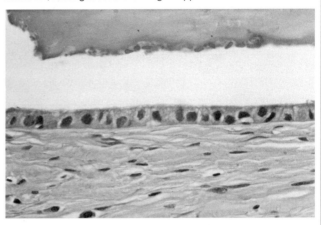

Cuboidal epithelium cells in the bronchioles

8 Alveoli – at the closed ends of the tiny bronchioles are clusters of microscopic air sacs called alveoli. A massive network of capillaries runs closely over the surface of the alveoli, with elastic connective tissue throughout. There are around 700 million alveoli which are the site of most gas exchange.

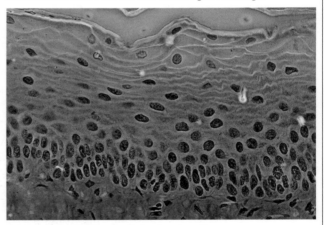

Squamous epithelium cells in the alveoli

9 Pleural membranes – these membranes are a continuous lining of the thorax, covering the outside surface of the lungs.

10 Pleural cavity – this space is filled with a lubricating fluid which allows the membranes to slide easily during breathing

11 Ribs – the ribs act as a protective bony cage around the lungs and heart

12 Diaphragm – this is a sheet of fibrous muscular tissue which is important in ventilation of the lungs

8.1 Introduction

▶ *Chapter 25 gives details of the process of aerobic respiration*

The body's energy requirements are mainly satisfied by the breakdown of glucose during respiration, and also of fatty acids and amino acids. **Aerobic respiration** happens when there is enough oxygen available. The importance of oxygen supply is clear, since aerobic breakdown has the advantage of transferring more energy than would happen in a lack of oxygen. To supply oxygen continuously to all body tissues, these events must occur:

- exchange of oxygen between the air in the lungs and the blood;
- sufficient oxygen distribution to all cells;
- oxygen exchange between blood and cells.

The breathing or respiratory system is designed to cope with the first of these events and its structure is shown in Figure 8.1.

8.2 The structure of the breathing system

The breathing system is essentially an internal space with an airway leading to it, which is richly supplied with blood. The surface area inside the system is hugely increased by dividing the space into an estimated 700 million smaller spaces, which are called alveoli. Air enters through the nose and mouth, and follows the route of the trachea, bronchi and bronchioles leading to the alveoli. Figure 8.1 shows that different epithelia occur in different places in the breathing system, depending on their function. The presence of the pleural cavity is important in allowing expansion of the lungs during inhalation and also in easing breathing movements.

8.3 Breathing mechanism

Breathing involves **inhalation** (or inspiration: taking air into the chest cavity) and **exhalation** (or expiration: moving air out of the chest cavity). Inhalation and exhalation require breathing movements to alter the volume of the chest cavity, which in turn creates air pressure differences between the thorax and the atmosphere outside (Figure 8.2). The air pressure differences involved here create a pressure gradient equivalent to a concentration gradient, and so the movement of air follows the general model: air moves from an area of higher pressure to one of a lower pressure, tending to equalise the pressure throughout. Note that there is a pressure gradient between the lungs and the pleural cavity, as well as between the lungs and the atmosphere outside.

> Breathing movements cause a change in the volume of the thorax and hence the air pressure inside it, resulting in airflow into or out of the lungs.

> **Boyle's Law** states that the pressure of a fixed mass of gas is inversely proportional to its volume. In other words, when volume decreases, pressure increases, and vice versa.
>
> $$P = 1/V$$

The lungs are not attached directly to the inside of the thorax. They lie against the pleural membranes and move as the thorax increases or decreases in volume.

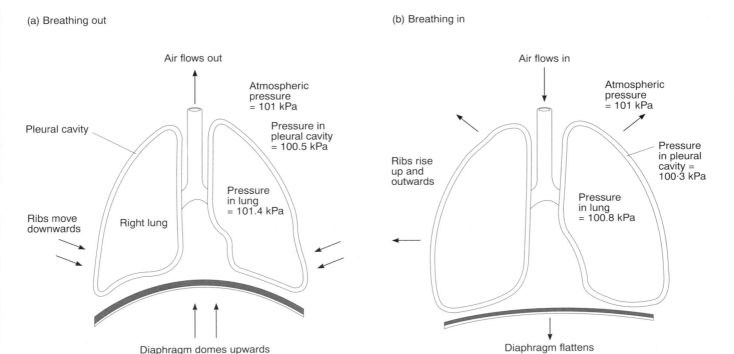

(a) Breathing out

Air flows out

Atmospheric pressure = 101 kPa

Pleural cavity

Pressure in pleural cavity = 100.5 kPa

Pressure in lung = 101.4 kPa

Ribs move downwards

Right lung

Diaphragm domes upwards

(b) Breathing in

Air flows in

Atmospheric pressure = 101 kPa

Pressure in pleural cavity = 100·3 kPa

Ribs rise up and outwards

Pressure in lung = 100.8 kPa

Diaphragm flattens

Figure 8.2 Breathing movements alter the volume of the chest cavity (or thorax) and hence the lungs, and in turn change the air pressure inside them

Inspiration is an active process, during which the external intercostal muscles contract and the internal intercostal muscles relax. The contraction of the external muscles pulls the ribs upwards and outwards, and at the same time the diaphragm contracts and flattens. These events expand the thorax and hence the lungs, increasing the volume inside. Since the lung volume increases, it follows that the pressure drops. Once the pressure inside the lungs is below that of the atmosphere, air moves into the lungs until the pressure equalises inside and outside.

When we breathe out, the external intercostal muscles relax while the internal muscles contract. Even so, exhalation is largely a passive process, partly because gravity assists in moving the ribs downwards and inwards. The diaphragm relaxes and domes upwards, helped by the elastic fibres between the alveoli. These were stretched during inhalation, but return to their normal length due to **elastic recoil**. These breathing movements reduce the volume of the thorax and so the pressure inside increases above that of the atmosphere outside. Air moves out of the lungs until the pressure is equal inside and outside. It is possible to force more air out of the lungs than would happen during normal exhalation, by the contraction of other abdominal muscles – as a musician might when playing the saxophone. This is called **forced exhalation**, and it also happens during rigorous exercise.

Injury may cause a 'punctured lung' which is a dangerous condition because it interferes with ventilation. A hole through the wall of the thorax and the pleural membranes allows air to move in between them and the lungs during inhalation. This means that the lungs do not expand with the thorax and inhalation is ineffective.

Surfactants and juvenile lungs

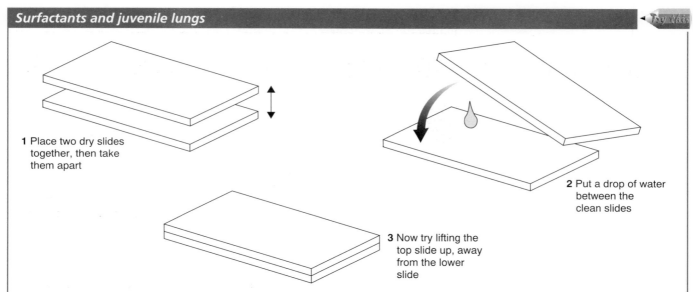

1 Place two dry slides together, then take them apart

2 Put a drop of water between the clean slides

3 Now try lifting the top slide up, away from the lower slide

Try this simple demonstration. Take two clean microscope slides and put one of the large flat surfaces on top of the other one. Now try pulling the two slides apart, noting the effort required. Then smear the same surfaces lightly with water. Place one on top of the other as before, and try to pull them apart again. This time it takes a lot more effort to separate the slides. What you experience mostly are the forces of attraction between the particles of water, known as **surface tension**.

The thin wet surfaces of alveoli come closely into contact with each other within the lungs. There is a danger that surface tension might cause the internal surfaces of the alveoli to stick together, hindering expansion during

Figure 8.3 Surfactant is not produced by a developing fetus until after week 24 of pregnancy, which means that the lungs of very premature babies are prone to collapse

inspiration, and preventing air moving in. However, epithelial cells produce a phospholipid which acts as a **surfactant**, lowering surface tension and preventing the collapse of the alveoli. Many more premature babies now survive due to the use of surfactant. A baby's first breath is stimulated by an increase in carbon dioxide concentration in the brain, once the placenta is no longer removing it.

> Surfactant is important in lung function because it reduces the surface tension of liquid inside the lungs, helping the alveoli to stay open.

Questions

1 a) Why is a breathing or respiratory system necessary in large organisms such as mammals?

b) What are the main functions of the following components of the breathing system: alveoli, ribs, cartilage rings around trachea, ciliated epithelium, squamous epithelium, intercostal muscles, epiglottis, pleural liquid?

2 a) How do breathing movements bring about

i) inhalation

ii) exhalation?

b) Comment on the air pressure gradient shown in Figure 8.2, which exists when someone is breathing in.

c) How and why is breathing affected by injury that results in a hole in the lung?

8.4 Lung capacities

Using a spirometer

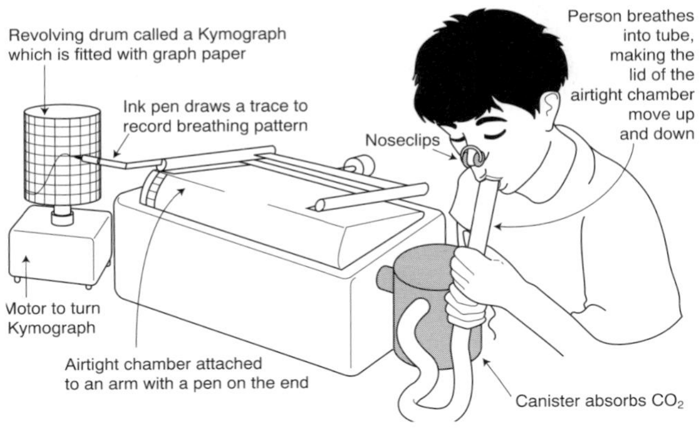

Revolving drum called a Kymograph which is fitted with graph paper

Ink pen draws a trace to record breathing pattern

Noseclips

Motor to turn Kymograph

Airtight chamber attached to an arm with a pen on the end

Person breathes into tube, making the lid of the airtight chamber move up and down

Canister absorbs CO_2

A spirometer is a machine for measuring the amount of air moving into and out of the lungs as we breathe. The basic design involves an airtight chamber which is filled with oxygen or air at the start of the experiment. Attached to the moveable lid is a pen which can mark paper on a revolving drum as the person breathes in and out and the lid rises and falls. Carbon dioxide is absorbed from the chamber by soda lime because it would otherwise accumulate and affect breathing rate.

Figure 8.4 A spirometer is used to measure lung volumes

> A spirometer is used to investigate lung capacities.

> ▶ *Chapter 18 describes the control of ventilation rate and the effects of exercise*

The human lungs of an adult male have a total possible capacity of about 5 dm³. Only about 450 cm³ of air is breathed in and out during each normal resting breath, and this is called the **tidal volume**. A person with healthy lungs can normally force at least 80 per cent of the tidal volume out in one second. This is useful in clinical diagnosis because it reflects resistance in the airways. The rate of breathing, or **ventilation rate**, is an indication of the amount of air breathed in one minute. It is calculated by multiplying the tidal volume with the number of breaths taken in one minute.

ventilation rate = tidal volume × frequency of inspiration (per minute)

Figure 8.5 Human lung capacity

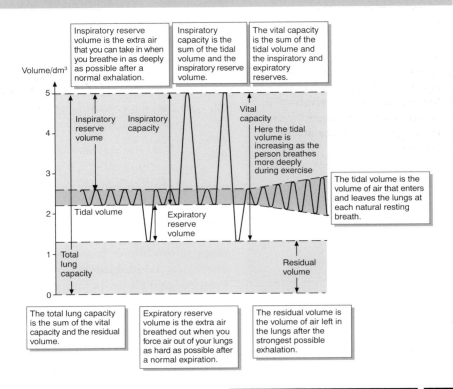

Volume/dm³

Inspiratory reserve volume is the extra air that you can take in when you breathe in as deeply as possible after a normal exhalation.

Inspiratory capacity is the sum of the tidal volume and the inspiratory reserve volume.

The vital capacity is the sum of the tidal volume and the inspiratory and expiratory reserves.

Inspiratory reserve volume

Inspiratory capacity

Vital capacity

Here the tidal volume is increasing as the person breathes more deeply during exercise

Tidal volume

Expiratory reserve volume

The tidal volume is the volume of air that enters and leaves the lungs at each natural resting breath.

Total lung capacity

Residual volume

The total lung capacity is the sum of the vital capacity and the residual volume.

Expiratory reserve volume is the extra air breathed out when you force air out of your lungs as hard as possible after a normal expiration.

The residual volume is the volume of air left in the lungs after the strongest possible exhalation.

Around 150 cm³ of the tidal volume of air is held in the air tubes such as the trachea and bronchi which lead to the lungs, and no gas exchange takes place here. This unchanged air which is breathed out from the air tubes during normal breathing is called the **dead space**.

By breathing in as hard as possible after a normal breath, a person can expand their lungs by about another 3.0 dm³. After breathing out normally, a person can expel around another 1.5 dm³ of air. But however deeply we breathe there is always some air left in the lungs called the **residual volume**. The relatively small amount of air which is exchanged at each breath mixes with this residual volume. Figure 8.5 is a summary of this information.

Questions

1 Why is there a difference between the total lung volume and the vital capacity in human lungs?

2 A doctor may measure how much of their tidal volume someone can forcibly expire. Why might this be a useful measurement?

3 Suggest conditions which would change the ventilation rate.

4 Use Figure 8.5 to answer this question.

   a) What is the tidal volume indicated by the spirometer trace?

   b) How much air is taken into the lungs during one breath?

   c) What is the ventilation rate?

8.5 Allergies and inflammation in the breathing system

Substances that cause an immune response by the body are called **allergens**. Allergens are not normally a constituent of the body, but are usually some substance, for example pollen, fur, dust or cells such as bacteria, which originate elsewhere. Hayfever is an example of the body's response to pollen allergens, which enter through the respiratory tract and result in excess mucus production and inflammation. The person usually suffers a blocked nose, sneezing and coughing, and may have itchy, swollen or streaming eyes.

Asthma is a common respiratory condition in which the air passages become inflamed and smooth muscles within them contract, causing narrowing of the airways. In asthma this is reversible. In some cases the condition it is known to be aggravated by allergens, including diesel residues, animal fur, pollen and dust in the air. The term 'asthma' covers a range of conditions from wheeziness to severe breathing difficulties. In every case the problem is that it is difficult to exhale. Other factors such as exercise, cold air temperature, viral infections, 'passive smoking' (breathing in other peoples' cigarette smoke) or anxiety contribute to the frequency and severity of attacks. In childhood, boys are roughly twice as likely to be affected as girls, although it is slightly more common in women than men. The most important factor in childhood asthma is probably 'dust' in the form of droppings from microscopic house dust mites. Millions of these tiny

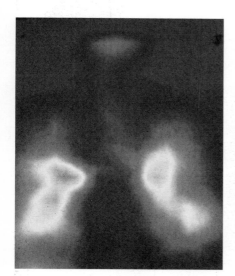

Figure 8.6 Asthmatics are breathless when they cannot clear their airways
(See Colour Gallery page 349)

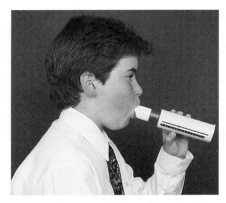

Figure 8.7 A peak flow meter is used regularly by someone with asthma to monitor resistance in the airways – the narrower the tubes, the slower the flow of air through them will be and the lower the readings

Figure 8.8 This trace was drawn using peak flow readings taken over six days from a 58 year old woman who was in hospital because of her difficulty in breathing. At A there is an area of consistently low readings. B is a dip in the flow rate which happens intermittently e.g. in the evening when she is tired. C shows that the flow rate has improved. However, it has still not reached the flow rate she achieves when feeling well.

animals live in carpets, mattresses and furry toys, excreting faeces which contain a protein allergen.

Continual exposure to the protein in house dust mite faeces causes an allergic reaction, triggering the contraction of smooth muscle fibres in the walls of the airways. These tubes then contract, constricting them and increasing the resistance to air movement through them. Added to this, the airways often become inflamed so there is increased mucus secretion which again obstructs airflow. The latter is also true of **bronchitis**, in which the bronchi become inflamed due to infection.

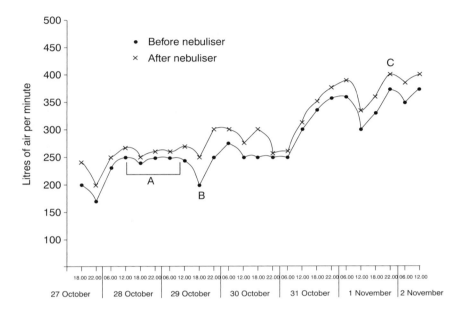

Managing asthma

The aim of a management plan for asthma is to help someone control their condition so that it does not interfere with their normal lifestyle. The first stage in managing asthma is to follow the self help code.

Self help
- Control the house dust mite by removing carpeting, substituting blinds for curtains, buying occlusive bedding (e.g. special mattresses in which mites cannot live) and freezing furry toys for 12 hours each week to kill the mites.
- Avoid central heating which involves air moving through the house in ducts, because of increased dust.
- Avoid food allergens e.g. peanuts or wheat.
- Avoid cigarette smoke.
- 'Warm up' gently before exercising, keep inhalers to hand, and possibly use an inhaler preventatively before exercise.
- Severe asthmatics may not be able to keep pets.
- Avoid aspirin and beta-blockers, which make the condition worse.

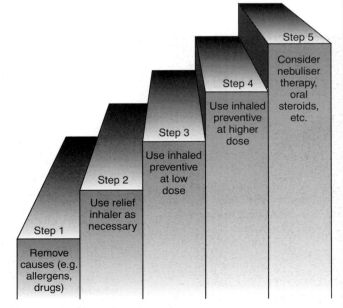

Figure 8.9 A stepwise approach to controlling asthma

Managing asthma – continued

Developing a plan

Together, a patient, a clinic nurse and a doctor can develop a plan for managing asthma using a set of guidelines (Figure 8.9). The plan may involve regularly recording symptoms or peak flow (Figure 8.10) and monitoring medication. The value of a management plan is that it involves the patient in an ongoing scheme, with the aim of avoiding emergency treatment.

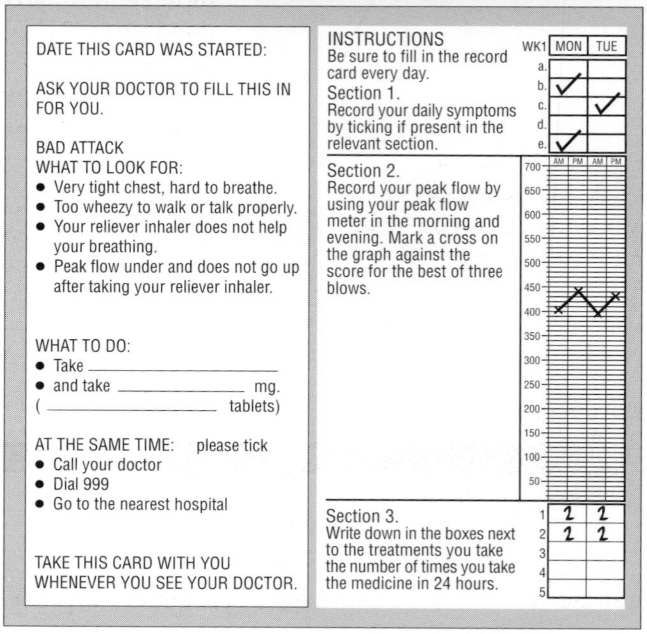
DATE THIS CARD WAS STARTED:
ASK YOUR DOCTOR TO FILL THIS IN FOR YOU.
BAD ATTACK
WHAT TO LOOK FOR:
• Very tight chest, hard to breathe.
• Too wheezy to walk or talk properly.
• Your reliever inhaler does not help your breathing.
• Peak flow under and does not go up after taking your reliever inhaler.
WHAT TO DO:
• Take
• and take mg.
(tablets)
AT THE SAME TIME: please tick
• Call your doctor
• Dial 999
• Go to the nearest hospital
TAKE THIS CARD WITH YOU WHENEVER YOU SEE YOUR DOCTOR.
INSTRUCTIONS
Be sure to fill in the record card every day.
Section 1.
Record your daily symptoms by ticking if present in the relevant section.
Section 2.
Record your peak flow by using your peak flow meter in the morning and evening. Mark a cross on the graph against the score for the best of three blows.
Section 3.
Write down in the boxes next to the treatments you take the number of times you take the medicine in 24 hours.
WK1
MON
TUE
a.
b.
c.
d.
e.
AM
PM
AM
PM
700
650
600
550
500
450
400
350
300
250
200
150
100
50
1
2
3
4
5
2
2
2
2

Figure 8.10 An example of a management plan based on recording peak flow

Asthma is an inflammation of the airways often following an allergic response to allergens in the environment. The airways become constricted.

News for asthmatics?

Scientists at the Johns Hopkins University in Baltimore have been testing asthmatics and non-asthmatics with a substance called methacholine, which makes the airways constrict. Here is what they did:

1. First, scientists gave a dose of methacholine to each volunteer. Then the volunteers were asked to take three deep breaths in, followed by three forceful breaths out.
   Results – only the asthmatics became wheezy.
2. Secondly, the volunteers repeated the dose of methacholine, but without taking any deep breaths afterwards.
   Results – both groups of volunteers became wheezy.
3. Finally, a few minutes after the second test, the volunteers were told to take deep breaths again.
   Results – both groups remained wheezy.

The researchers concluded that non-asthmatics can manage to re-open their constricted airways by deep breathing, *unless* they reach a critical point of airway constriction beyond which deep breathing cannot help. They now plan to research further, using scanning and imaging techniques to directly observe what happens to muscles in the airways. This 'deep breathing hypothesis' does not help to explain all the features of asthma, such as the build up of fluid in lung tissue which some asthmatics suffer, but it contributes to the data concerning airway contraction.

► *Chapter 19.3 describes how a medicine to treat asthma was developed*

8.6 The effects of smoking

Someone who smokes 20 cigarettes in a day probably inhales at least 200 dm^3 of smoke-laden air, and over many years this adds up to a huge volume.

Passive smoking is inhaling smoke from other peoples' cigarettes, cigars or pipes, and the effects of this are similar to being a smoker. It is no surprise that around 15–20 per cent of all deaths in the UK are related to tobacco smoking. In 1992 the Government published its Health of the Nation report, in which it targeted smoking as one of five main areas for improving public health. The chemical hazards in cigarette smoke are numerous and include:

> Smoking has a variety of damaging effects on health.

- nicotine: stimulates adrenaline production, and heart rate; increases the likelihood of clots developing; is addictive.
- carbon monoxide: has a high affinity for haemoglobin, combining with it rapidly and reduces the amount of oxygen the haemoglobin carries.
- tars: stop cilia working so that mucus, dirt and germs collect in the lungs, increasing the chances of infection; causes thickening of the epithelium of the airways leading to bronchitis; contains carcinogens which are substances that trigger cancer.

Table 8.1 Facts about smoking

Condition	Effects	Cause
cardiovascular disease	increased cholesterol deposits; increased incidence of stroke and heart attack	nicotine affects formation of low density lipids damaging the inside of arteries which initiates clotting
fetus size	low body mass ('birth weight')	reduction of blood flow in placenta; reduced metabolic rate in fetus due to carbon monoxide reducing oxygen tension in blood
cancer	tumours of the mouth, nose, lung, bladder, stomach, breast and cervix	tars/other carcinogens
emphysema	alveoli walls break down and they fill up with mucus, severe breathlessness	cilia stop working; reduced surface area for gaseous exchange
poor circulation	constriction of arterioles	nicotine affects smooth muscle

The original research

The following extracts are taken from one of the earliest and most significant studies carried out by Richard Doll and Bradford Hill, into the association between smoking and lung cancer. Their full report was published in the *British Medical Journal* in September 1950.

In England and Wales the phenomenal increase in the number of deaths attributed to cancer of the lung provides one of the most striking changes in the pattern of mortality recorded by the Registrar-General. For example, in the quarter of a century between 1922 and 1947 the annual number of deaths recorded increased from 612 to 9,287, or roughly fifteenfold. This remarkable increase is, of course, out of all proportion to the increase of population – both in total and, particularly, in its older age groups. ...

The method of the investigation was as follows. Twenty London hospitals were asked to co-operate by notifying all patients admitted to them with carcinoma of the lung, stomach, colon, or rectum. ...

As well, however, as interviewing the notified patients with cancer of one of the four specified sites, the almoners were

Table 8.2 Proportion of smokers and non-smokers in lung-carcinoma patients and in control patients with diseases other than cancer

Disease Group	No. of non-smokers	No. of smokers	Probability test
males			
lung-carcinoma patients (649)	2 (0.3%)	647	P (exact method) =0.00000064
control patients with diseases other than cancer (649)	27 (4.2%)	622	
females			
lung-carcinoma patients (60)	19 (31.7%)	41	$x^2 = 5.76$; n = 1 $0.01 < P < 0.02$
control patients with diseases other than cancer (60)	32 (53.3%)	28	

required to make similar inquiries of a group of 'non-cancer control' patients. These patients were of the same sex, within the same five-year age group, and in the same hospital at or about the same time. ...

Discussion
To summarise, it is not reasonable, in our view, to attribute the results to any special selection of cases or to bias in recording. In otherwords, it must be concluded that ➡

there is a real association between carcinoma of the lung and smoking. . . .

Our findings did not immediately convince cancer research workers, let alone the general public and the Department of Health, so that if any preventative action was to be taken, we needed to test that conclusion by some other means. . . .

The obvious way to test this was to get a large number of people to tell us about their smoking habits and to follow them up to see who died of the disease. With the help of the British Medical Association, questionnaires were mailed, at the end of October 1951, to around 60,000 doctors in the UK. Some 40,000

replied to a single mailing and we began a prospective study of the subsequent causes of death of this cohort of doctors that has now lasted for four decades. Within two and a half years, the early results confirmed the relationship between smoking and lung cancer, both qualitatively and quantitatively and, as the deaths accumulated they began to show that myocardial infarction, chronic obstructive lung disease and many other diseases were also related to smoking: some closely, as cancer of the lung, others less closely, but collectively contributing even more to the total number of deaths attributable to smoking because of the frequency with which the diseases occured.

Dead cool to smoke?

A study by the United States National Cancer Institute found that 86 per cent of children who smoke prefer the three most advertised brands, and that the introduction of a cartoon character by one brand hugely increased their market share amongst the youngest smokers. In both the UK and US, the percentage of teenagers who smoke regularly is on the increase. At the same time, more adults are giving up, and smoking is disappearing from many workplaces and other public places.

In Norway, advertising and sponsorship has been banned for over 20 years, and this led to a fall in tobacco sales – but only initially. Despite the fact that between a third to a half of all smokers end up dying from cancers or heart disease caused by their habit, discouraging people is not easy. In England and Wales the phenomenal increase in the number of deaths attributed to cancer of the lung provides one of the most striking changes in the pattern of martality recorded by the Registrar-General. For example, in the quarter of a century between 1922 and 1947 the annual number of deaths recorded increased from 612 to 9,287, or roughly fifteenfold. This remarkable increase is, of course, out of all proportion to the increase of population – both in total and, particularly, in its older age groups.

Questions

1 a) Why is suffering an asthma attack dangerous?

b) What are the main treatments for asthma?

c) Suggest reasons why asthma may become worse

   i) for someone living in an inner city.

   ii) for someone visiting a friend at their house.

   iii) before an examination.

   iv) when running to catch the bus on a frosty morning.

2 a) Who formed the control group of people in Doll and Hill's investigation?

b) Why did Doll and Hill use control groups?

c) How did Doll and Hill follow up their preliminary study?

d) Suggest a reason why some people were initially sceptical of their findings?

e) Suggest reasons why people continue to smoke despite the dangers to health.

CHAPTER 9

Gaseous Exchange in the Lungs and Body Tissues

9.1 Gaseous exchange in the lungs

In humans, **gaseous exchange** involves oxygen moving into the body and carbon dioxide moving out of it, and it is a process which happens throughout life. Gaseous exchange occurs in the lungs by diffusion through the **alveolar surface**, which is relatively enormous considering how compactly it is arranged within the thorax. Altogether the many millions of alveoli in the lungs provide around 70 m² of exchange surface.

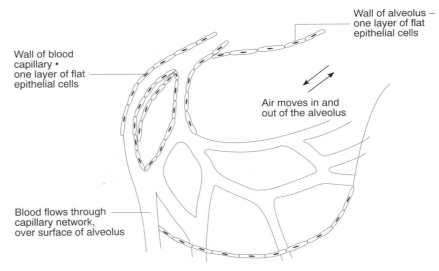

Wall of alveolus – one layer of flat epithelial cells

Wall of blood capillary • one layer of flat epithelial cells

Air moves in and out of the alveolus

Blood flows through capillary network, over surface of alveolus

Figure 9.1 Alveoli have important features which make them ideally suited for gaseous exchange

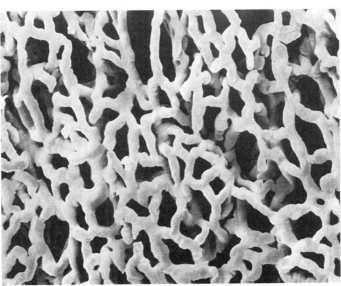

Figure 9.2 Micrograph of lung tissue, showing alveolar blood supply

Table 9.1 Percentages of gases in air

	O_2	CO_2
inspired air	20.8	0.04
alveolar air	13.1	5.2
expired air	15.3	4.2

▶ **Chapter 4.1 describes diffusion**

Table 9.1 shows the amount of oxygen and carbon dioxide in the air moving in and out of the lungs. Other gases such as nitrogen and water vapour are also present. The percentage of nitrogen hardly varies, but the amount of water vapour in exhaled air is usually greater than in inhaled air.

During inhalation or exhalation gases must diffuse across the squamous epithelial cells of the alveoli, through tissue fluid between the alveoli and the blood capillaries, and through the single layer of cuboidal cells which form the walls of blood capillaries. The direction and rate of diffusion is affected by the pressure gradient, and is facilitated by the short diffusing distances involved.

In the lungs, two important factors affecting diffusion of a gas are its solubility in water, and its pressure (dependent on the concentration). The solubility is important because a gas must dissolve in the water that exists in the cytosol of cells and in tissue fluid. The **partial pressure** of a gas is the pressure it exerts individually within the total pressure in a gas mixture. For example, if the percentage of oxygen in a gas mixture is 21 per cent and the total pressure of that mixture is 101 kPa, then the pressure which is due to oxygen alone is:

$$\frac{21}{100} \times 101 \text{ kPa} = 20.8 \text{ kPa}$$

The partial pressure is the driving force for the diffusion of individual gases and is particularly important for a gas such as oxygen which has a low solubility. The partial pressure gradient for oxygen between the alveolar air and the arterial blood is relatively high (compared to that for carbon dioxide), generally allowing diffusion to be fast enough to satisfy demand. Carbon dioxide has a greater solubility in water than oxygen, and there is a lower pressure gradient between alveolar air and venous blood.

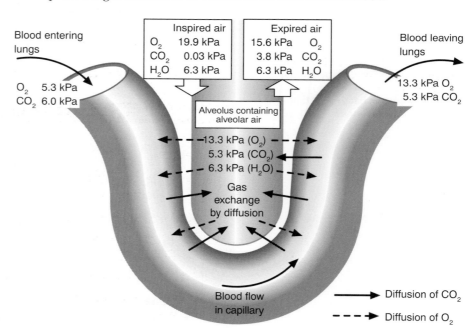

Figure 9.3 Partial pressures of gases in air and in blood in the breathing system

Blood enters the lungs in the pulmonary artery, which divides to form an extensive network of capillaries surrounding the alveoli. These blood capillaries collect together, finally forming the pulmonary vein which carries blood away from the lungs and towards the heart. Figure 9.3 shows the increase in oxygen content of blood in the pulmonary vein compared to the pulmonary artery. Notice that the partial pressures of oxygen and carbon dioxide are the same for blood in the pulmonary vein as in the alveoli. In other words, these gases are in equilibrium in the venous blood and alveolar blood.

9.2 Maintaining a gradient

Oxygen diffuses from the air into the blood within the lungs because of a partial pressure (or diffusion) gradient. Why doesn't equilibrium occur, which would tend to stop net oxygen diffusion? The answer is that the blood flows continuously, carrying the oxygen away towards body cells where it is used in respiration. The partial pressure of oxygen in the cells is around 5.3 kPa but it is being used rapidly for respiration. This maintains a sufficient partial pressure gradient for oxygen to exchange and supply the respiring cells.

The exchange of carbon dioxide happens in the reverse direction. The cells constantly generate carbon dioxide as a result of aerobic respiration, and so in the tissues there is a gradient between the cells and the venous blood supply. In addition, there is a gradient for carbon dioxide between the blood and the alveoli. This is maintained when we breathe out, expelling carbon dioxide from the body.

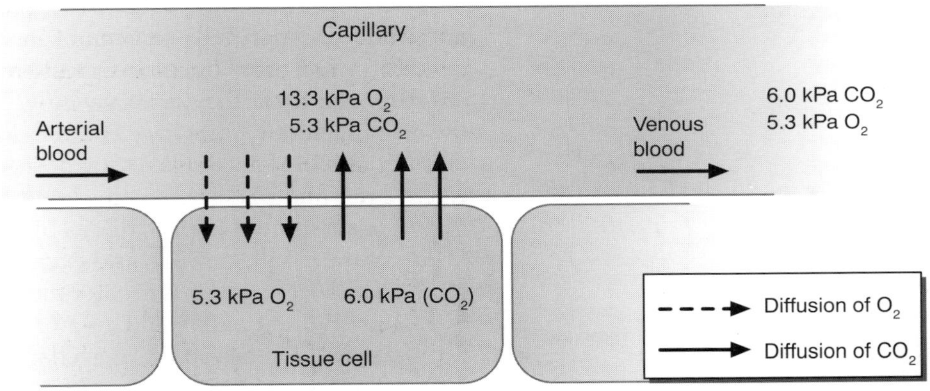

> Blood circulation and breathing movements help to maintain diffusion gradients at the alveolar surface and in the tissues.

> ▶ **Chapter 10.3 discusses the mechanism of oxygen and carbon dioxide transport**

Figure 9.4 Oxygen is used in the body cells and carbon dioxide is generated during respiration

Questions

1 a) Describe the route taken by gases diffusing into the blood from the alveoli.

   b) What features of the alveolus/blood exchange unit make it well adapted for its function?

   c) The rate of blood flow through capillary networks is around 0.5 cm/s, which is much slower than through other blood vessels. Suggest a reason for this.

   d) What factors might dictate the minimum size of a blood capillary?

2 a) Comment on the differences in partial pressures of carbon dioxide and oxygen between inspired air and expired air.

   b) How does the change in partial pressures of these gases relate to the change in partial pressures happening in the blood capillary?

   c) In what way does the continuous flow of blood help to maintain diffusion gradients?

CHAPTER 10

The Circulatory System – Transport and More

10.1 Transporting substances in body fluids

The heart and blood vessels make up the **cardiovascular** system. The main role of this system is transport, which is important in maintaining the conditions surrounding the cells that make up the body, and therefore within the body as a whole. Blood is an example of a body fluid. It is responsible for moving materials between exchange surfaces by mass flow, for example the respiratory gases between the lungs and the tissues. It carries a wide variety of other substances too, such as hormones from the glands that produce them to the target organs where they take effect. **Tissue fluid** is the body fluid which bathes the cells that make up the tissues.

Plasma is the liquid part of the blood which is comprised mainly of water and contains blood cells, plasma proteins, hormones and many ions (electrolytes). Diffusion, blood pressure and in some cases active transport are responsible for the necessary movement of materials out of the blood. At the arterial end of a capillary bed the diffusion gradient favours water moving into blood vessels (by osmosis) from tissue fluid. This is because the electrolytes and plasma proteins lower the water potential of plasma below that of tissue fluid. Despite this, as blood is circulating it presses on the inside of the capillary walls and exerts a hydrostatic pressure within the blood capillaries, which is greater than the forces driving the opposing diffusion gradient. As a result, water and electrolytes are forced out of the capillary, and the net outward exchange causes the formation of tissue fluid. At the venous end of a capillary bed the blood pressure is lower and therefore much of the water moves back into the blood supply by osmosis following a water potential gradient.

Tissue fluid is very close in composition to plasma, consisting of an aqueous solution of substances required by the cells, including oxygen, glucose, amino acids, fatty acids, inorganic ions and hormones. However, tissue fluid does not contain proteins as does plasma.

Of the liquid that originates in the blood which later forms tissue fluid, around 90 per cent eventually returns to the venous blood supply. The remainder re-joins the blood circulation via the lymphatic system, which can be considered to be an extension of the blood system. Figure 10.1 shows the blind-ending tubes called **lymphatic vessels**, which run between cells and have a similar structure to veins. The endothelial cells of the walls of the lymphatic vessels overlap and act as one-way valves through which tissue fluid drains, forming **lymph**. The lacteals in the villi lining part of the small intestines are also part of the lymph system. Tissue fluid collects in these vessels because the accumulation of the fluid causes a pressure differential between the tissue and the lymph capillaries. Cell debris and bacteria pass into lymph too. The lymphatic vessels collect together in to larger vessels which are squeezed by the muscles and tissues as the body moves, pushing the lymph in a unidirectional flow. At points there are collections of lymph

► *Chapter 4.2 covers osmosis in detail*

► *Chapter 22.4 describes the structure of the small intestine*

► *Chapter 30.3 describes the part played by the lymphatic system in immunity*

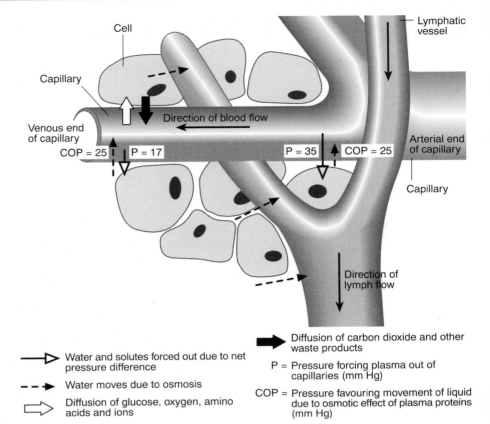

Figure 10.1 The relationship between plasma, tissue fluid and lymph

Key labels for Figure 10.1:

→▷ Water and solutes forced out due to net pressure difference

---▶ Water moves due to osmosis

⇨ Diffusion of glucose, oxygen, amino acids and ions

⬛▶ Diffusion of carbon dioxide and other waste products

P = Pressure forcing plasma out of capillaries (mm Hg)

COP = Pressure favouring movement of liquid due to osmotic effect of plasma proteins (mm Hg)

Image labels: Cell; Capillary; Venous end of capillary; COP = 25; P = 17; Direction of blood flow; Lymphatic vessel; P = 35; COP = 25; Arterial end of capillary; Capillary; Direction of lymph flow

> **Tissue fluid forms from plasma and recirculates to blood as lymph in the lymphatic system.**

tissue called **lymph glands**. As lymph flows through the lymph glands, cells remove suspended solids, such as cell debris, by phagocytosis. Finally, lymph drains into the blood circulation in the neck region through two large ducts.

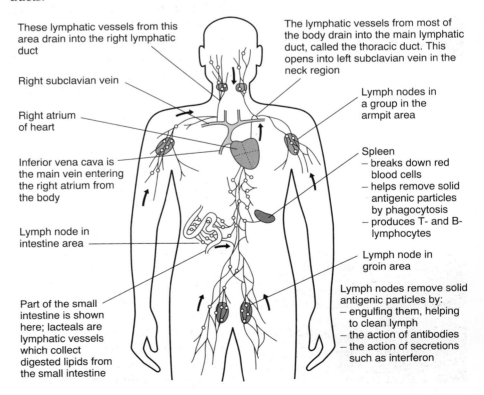

Image labels for Figure 10.2:

These lymphatic vessels from this area drain into the right lymphatic duct

Right subclavian vein

Right atrium of heart

Inferior vena cava is the main vein entering the right atrium from the body

Lymph node in intestine area

Part of the small intestine is shown here; lacteals are lymphatic vessels which collect digested lipids from the small intestine

The lymphatic vessels from most of the body drain into the main lymphatic duct, called the thoracic duct. This opens into left subclavian vein in the neck region

Lymph nodes in a group in the armpit area

Spleen
– breaks down red blood cells
– helps remove solid antigenic particles by phagocytosis
– produces T- and B-lymphocytes

Lymph node in groin area

Lymph nodes remove solid antigenic particles by:
– engulfing them, helping to clean lymph
– the action of antibodies
– the action of secretions such as interferon

Figure 10.2 Water and many dissolved substances circulate around the body in plasma, tissue fluid and lymph

Oedema

Sometimes tissue fluid collects in the tissues when it is not draining back into the lymphatic system as fast as it is collecting. This may be the case if blood pressure is abnormally high or if excess sodium and chloride ions, or other metabolites remain in the tissues. The collection of tissue fluid above the normal range is called **oedema**. Occasionally, oedema results after surgery, due to the removal of lymph glands.

Cellulite

Cellulite refers to the formation of fat-based tissue which gives a dimpled appearance to the skin, rather like the peel of an orange. Cellulite is common in the upper arms and thighs, mainly in women. The formation of cellulite begins when toxins which are by-products of metabolism collect in fat cells and as a result water is drawn into the tissue. Connective tissue fibres (made of collagen) which form a supporting network within the tissue become thickened, while the proportion of elastin fibres decreases. Gradually, fat cells become completely encased in connective tissue and form hard nodules, trapping fluid and toxins. At the same time there is weakening of blood capillaries which leak plasma and a widening of lymphatic vessels which slows the flow of lymph. Alongside this is a change in the biochemistry of the lipids in fatty tissue.

Cellulite formation is often but not necessarily related to obesity. It mainly reflects a poor lymphatic circulation and hence the build up of toxins. Reducing the intake of toxins such as those in tobacco smoke, coffee or highly processed foods, increasing exercise to increase circulation and massage (to help break down connective tissue nodules and stimulate circulation) help to reduce the formation of cellulite.

Questions

1   a)   What is plasma, and what is its important role in blood?

b)   What factors affect the formation of tissue fluid from blood?

c)   Why is there a difference in the passage of materials out of blood capillaries between the venous and arterial end?

d)   Why is the composition of plasma and tissue fluid critical for cells to function well?

e)   Why is it necessary for tissue fluid to drain constantly into the lymphatic capillaries?

2   Describe the role of the lymph glands.

10.2 The structure and functions of blood

Blood circulation is the main transport system in the body, but blood has other important functions such as defence against disease.

The human body contains approximately 4–5 litres of blood in females and 5–6 litres in males. Blood is a very complex mixture, which is the main medium of transport in the body. In transporting materials the blood plays a vital role in maintaining the internal environment within the body, helping to regulate the conditions around cells such that they do not fluctuate to

> ▶ *Chapter 30.3 deals with the immune response in more detail*

extremes which might cause cell damage. It carries a variety of cells and substances throughout the body.

The functions of blood are summarised below:

- Transport of digested food from the intestines (see page 130 and 218) and from storage areas to the cells (see page 132).
- Transport of excretory products such as urea (see page 139) and carbon dioxide (see pages 75–77).
- Transport of oxygen (see pages 75–77 and 83–85).
- Transport of hormones from glands to target organs (see page 166).
- Helping to maintain a steady state (homeostasis): control of body temperature or thermoregulation (see pages 156–157).
- Providing immunity by the phagocytic action of some white blood cells (see pages 307–308).
- Producing antibodies (see page 308).
- Clotting, to seal a wound and halt blood loss (see pages 87–88).
- Acting as a pH buffer.

The role of the cardiovascular system

About 55 per cent of blood volume is composed of red blood cells, around 44 per cent is plasma, and the remaining one per cent is mostly white cells and platelets. The structure and function of the components of blood are briefly summarised in Table 10.1 and Figure 10.3.

Table 10.1 Blood structure and function

Component of blood	Features
plasma	the liquid part of blood (see Figure 10.3)
erythrocytes (red blood cells)	disc-shaped cells with dented centres (biconcave discs) which lack a nucleus but have a large surface area; approximately five million per mm^3 of blood; made in the bone marrow of some bones; contain haemoglobin and transport oxygen and carbon dioxide
leucocytes (white blood cells)	larger than erythrocytes, but can leave blood vessels by changing shape to squeeze out through capillary walls; about 7000 per mm^3 of blood; made mostly in the white bone marrow of long bones or in the lymph glands and spleen; main function is in defence and immunity

granulocytes
  neutrophils
  eosinophils
 	
  basophils
	engulf bacteria or debris such as cell fragments in tissues
	antihistamine properties which combat allergies; can enter tissues and engulf material which is labelled with antigens
	produce histamine in damaged tissues, combat allergies; produce heparin

agranulocytes
  monocytes
  lymphocytes
	engulf bacteria or debris in tissues
	produce antibodies in the lymphatic system against specific antigens

platelets	fragments of large megakaryocyte cells which occur in the bone marrow; important in clotting; around 0.25 million per mm^3

How are new blood cells made?

> Blood cells are made in bone marrow.

Stem cells in bone marrow are thought to give rise to all types of blood cells. The stem cells differentiate in to other cells which then give rise to red blood cells, white blood cells or platelets. Approximately one per cent of

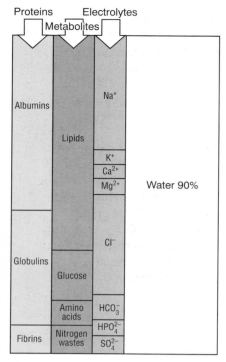

Proteins Electrolytes
Metabolites

Albumins

Lipids

Na⁺

K⁺
Ca²⁺
Mg²⁺

Water 90%

Cl⁻

Globulins

Glucose

Amino acids   HCO₃⁻
HPO₄²⁻
Fibrins   Nitrogen wastes   SO₄²⁻

Figure 10.3 The composition of plasma

Figure 10.4 This smear of human blood has been stained to show the nuclei of three neutrophils

erythrocytes in circulating blood are replaced daily, which means that around three million enter the circulation each second. Red blood cells last around 120 days, while leucocytes generally break down after four to five days (although neutrophils last only 12 hours or so). The spleen, liver and lymph nodes remove old red blood cells from circulation, and the iron is either stored or re-used immediately.

Electrolytes

Electrolytes are ions which have dissociated in the plasma solution. Ions are active in a variety of life processes and their concentration is controlled closely. Apart from the main electrolytes shown in Figure 10.3, there are some such as aluminium and zinc which are present in tiny amounts. These are called **trace electrolytes** and despite occurring in such minute quantities they have important roles, such as activating enzymes.

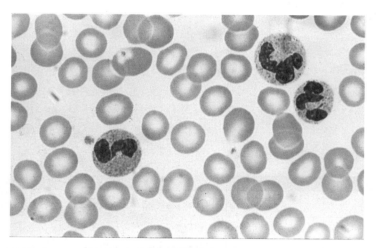

Blood as a health status indicator

As blood contains a variety of components, the specific concentrations or amounts of each of these may act as an indicator of health, since the values should lie within a normal range. Table 10.2 shows data from a blood sample taken from a five-year-old child with leukaemia, and a second sample taken some years later after treatment with radiotherapy and chemotherapy. The second sample shows values within the normal range for the indicators shown here. In practice, blood tests provide more detailed information than has been summarised in this table.

Questions

1 In 1989 the child was anaemic. How does the data support this statement?

2 What is the significance of the very reduced level of platelets in the blood sample taken in 1989?

3 Myelocytes and blast cells are immature stages in the production of white blood cells, and an indicator of leukaemia. Do these stages normally appear in blood?

4 What other abnormality is evident from this data?

Table 10.2 Data from two blood samples

Blood component tested	April 1989	February 1992
haemoglobin	10.4	12.9
nucleated red blood cells	2	0
platelets	11	232
total white cells	12.1	6.6
percentage of each:		
neutrophils	16	50
lymphocytes	46	38
monocytes	3	6
eosinophils	1	2
myelocytes	5	0
blast cells	29	0

10.3 Haemoglobin is a carrier

Red blood cells (erythrocytes) are different to all other human cells because they do not contain a nucleus. This limits the metabolic capability of the cell, as well as how long it can live. Erythrocytes are tiny biconcave discs with a diameter of approximately 7.2 μm and a maximum thickness of 2.2 μm, slimming to 0.8 μm at the centre. Even so, in one red blood cell there may be as many as 200–300 million molecules of haemoglobin. Figure 10.5 shows the structure of one haemoglobin molecule, which consists of four units of a globular protein called globin and four pigment units called haem. Each globin unit is a polypeptide composed of amino acids, but the four globin units are not identical because of slight differences in their amino acid composition. They are called α and β chains. The significance of this is reflected by the affinity of haemoglobin for oxygen, in other words, how easily it combines with it. In a fetus the haemoglobin contains a different proportion of the globin molecules which make up adult haemoglobin, because the conditions for oxygen exchange are different in the womb.

> Fetal haemoglobin and myoglobin are slightly different forms of haemoglobin.

▶ *Chapter 6.4 describes the structure of proteins*

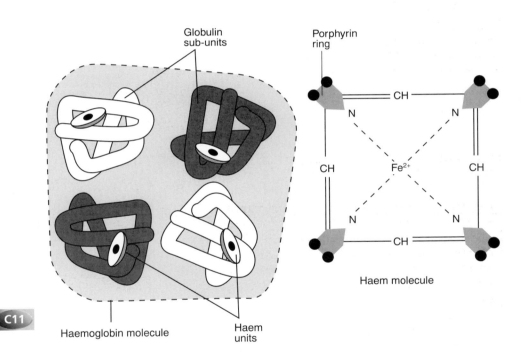

Figure 10.5 Haemoglobin structure
(See Colour Gallery page 349)

The **haem** unit is an organic molecule known as a porphyrin, which is associated with a metal ion. In haem, the metal ion is iron (Fe^{2+}) which can combine reversibly with an oxygen molecule (O_2). Since there are four haem groups, one haemoglobin molecule can combine with a total of four oxygen molecules, resulting in the formation of **oxyhaemoglobin**. When saturated with oxygen, 100 cm³ of blood will carry around 19 cm³ of oxygen. This is summarised by the equation:

$$Hb \quad + \quad 4O_2 \quad \rightleftharpoons \quad HbO_8$$
haemoglobin   oxygen   oxyhaemoglobin

Since oxygen is not very soluble in plasma, it is important that there is sufficient haemoglobin to carry enough oxygen for all of the requirements of the cells. Some carbon dioxide is carried by haemoglobin, but it is also directly soluble in plasma as well as being transported as hydrogencarbonate ions (HCO_3^-).

Equally important as the affinity of haemoglobin for oxygen, is its ability to dissociate from it. Clearly, the process of oxygen uptake by haemoglobin must be reversible to satisfy the oxygen demands of the tissues. What determines whether oxygen will load into erythrocytes or unload from them is the partial pressure of oxygen in the surrounding tissues. Where the partial pressure is high, such as in the lungs, the oxygen binds rapidly to haemoglobin so that the arterial blood (returning to the heart in the pulmonary vein) is fully saturated. However, in tissues where the cells are using oxygen in respiration, the partial pressure of oxygen is lower and it dissociates from haemoglobin. If a drop in oxygen partial pressure happens in a local area, for example due to muscle action, the oxygen unloads more in that area. Blood in the veins is considerably darker in colour than the bright red blood in the arteries, though it still may be around 70 per cent saturated with oxygen.

Figure 10.6 (a) Graph showing the loading and unloading of oxygen at different partial pressures of oxygen. This is called an oxygen dissociation curve. (b) Graph showing the effect of increased carbon dioxide on unloading of oxygen in the tissues. (c) Graph showing a typical loading and unloading curve for fetal haemoglobin, which is slightly different in composition to adult haemoglobin. (d) Graph showing how myoglobin, which is found in skeletal muscles, has a very high affinity for oxygen.

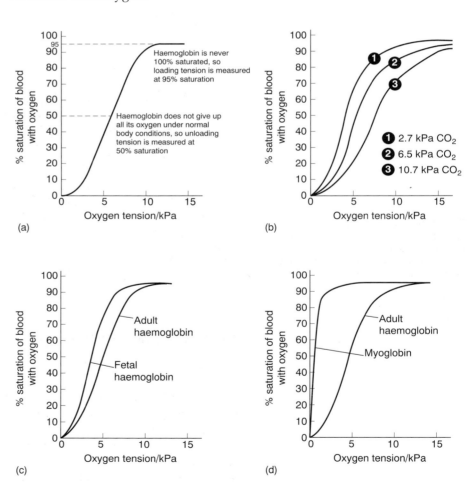

The oxygen dissociation curve in Figure 10.6 (a) is S-shaped. This is because the first oxygen molecule to bind to haemoglobin slightly changes the overall shape of the molecule. This allows each of the following oxygen molecules to load progressively more easily, and the process speeds up.

Haemoglobin carries oxygen and carbon dioxide. The affinity of haemoglobin for oxygen is affected by the partial pressure of carbon dioxide in blood.

▶ *Chapter 13.1 covers the role of myoglobin, which is a type of haemoglobin found in skeletal muscles*

When cells are actively respiring they produce carbon dioxide which increases the partial pressure in the blood circulating through the capillary beds in the tissues from around 5.26 kPa to 6.05 kPa. The haemoglobin has less affinity for oxygen under these conditions, so more oxygen unloads to the cells. This effect is called the **Bohr shift** after the scientist who discovered it (Figure 10.6 (b)).

Around seven per cent of the total carbon dioxide carried by the blood is dissolved in the plasma. Another 23 per cent combines with deoxygenated haemoglobin forming **carbaminohaemoglobin**, and the rest is carried as hydrogencarbonate ions. The partial pressure of carbon dioxide in an erythrocyte determines exactly how much combines with haemoglobin and how much forms hydrogencarbonate ions. The partial pressure gradient for carbon dioxide also drives the direction and amount of carbon dioxide diffusion out of cells into plasma. Figure 10.7 summarises how carbon dioxide is carried by the blood as it circulates through the tissues.

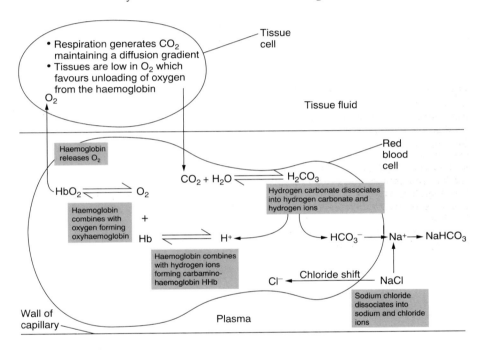

Figure 10.7 Carbon dioxide which is carried by the blood also has a role in the release of oxygen in the tissues – these reactions are reversible and occur in the reverse direction in the lungs

Carbon monoxide poisoning

Carbon monoxide forms from the incomplete oxidation of carbon, for example when fuels such as hydrocarbons burn in conditions of limited oxygen availability. This accounts for the carbon monoxide released in car exhaust fumes. Organic substances such as the tobacco in cigarettes contain carbon too, and carbon monoxide occurs in tobacco smoke. This gas is highly toxic to humans because of its very high affinity for haemoglobin – it combines with the iron(II) ion in haemoglobin several hundred times more easily than oxygen does. Haemoglobin combines irreversibly with carbon monoxide to form **carboxyhaemoglobin**. Therefore smokers lower the oxygen carrying capacity of their blood systems, which explains the link between smoking and circulatory diseases. In extreme situations, such as the production of carbon monoxide in high concentrations from a gas burning appliance which is not working correctly, the toxicity of this gas can be fatal.

Life in high places

The effects that Melanie talks about are called **mountain sickness**. They are a set of symptoms that someone may experience at high altitude, varying from incapacitating to life-threatening, particularly if the first signs are ignored. Most common is a condition called acute mountain sickness, and more rarely brain swelling and lung problems occur due to excess fluid collecting in these tissues. People who were born and continue to live at high altitude are mostly better adjusted and rarely suffer mountain sickness, but visitors usually do even though their bodies generally adapt to the new conditions. This is the process of **acclimatisation**.

Figure 10.8 'I was expecting some problems because this high up the air pressure is less so there is less oxygen. But I actually felt really ill with dizziness and sickness, a headache and I was very breathless. Although I felt really lethargic, I couldn't sleep very well.'

Table 10.3 Changes to the atmosphere and blood at different altitudes

Altitude (m above sea level)	Effects of sudden exposure to altitude	Atmospheric pressure (kPa)	Oxygen partial pressure (kPa)	Haematocrit – packed cell volume (%)	Human erythrocyte count (million/mm³)
0	–	101.3	21.2	45	5.0
5000	extreme breathlessness to unconsciousness	54.0	11.3	↓	5.95 (visitor)
10 000	unconsciousness	26.4	5.5	65	

The percentage of oxygen in air remains at around 20.9 per cent at any altitude, but the amount of oxygen changes because of the drop in air pressure with increasing altitude. This in turn affects the partial pressure of oxygen in alveolar air and makes it more difficult for haemoglobin to load fully with oxygen. Initially, the body detects the lack of oxygen and compensates with increased breathing, which has the effect of removing more carbon dioxide from the body. Removing carbon dioxide causes the pH of blood to rise slightly and the chemoreceptors may become less effective, initially upsetting the control of breathing rate.

A slow ascent means that the human body can acclimatise in other ways, such as removing more water from the blood to concentrate the red blood cells. Later still there is a period of increased production of erythrocytes stimulated by erythropoietin released by the kidneys. Finally, there may be more capillary formation to increase the amount of blood reaching the tissues. On a cellular level, the number of mitochondria may increase, to increase the rate of metabolism and energy transfer. However, there is a limit to how little oxygen the human body can cope with over an extended period of time, and the highest permanent human settlements are probably around 5500 m above sea level, e.g. La Paz in Ecuador.

Anaemia

When the amount of haemoglobin in blood drops below the normal range a person becomes **anaemic**. Whatever the cause, the effect on the body is a lack of oxygen supply to the tissues. This may be visibly noticeable in people with pale skin, but other symptoms are tiredness and increased pulse and breathing rate, as the body systems try to compensate.

There are a variety of causes of anaemia which include:

- lack of iron in the diet, so that haemoglobin production is limited;
- increased blood loss due to menstruation or injury;
- reduced red blood cell production because of bone marrow failure;
- inherited diseases such as sickle cell anaemia and thalassaemia.

▶ *Chapter 23.2 describes the symptoms of anaemia*

▶ *Chapter 34.3 covers inheritance of sickle cell anaemia*

Questions

1 a) What is the ratio of white blood cells to red blood cells?

   b) What other components apart from cells are not dissolved in plasma?

   c) Give examples of plasma proteins, and explain why they are an important component of blood.

2 Why is a lack of haemoglobin likely to have more impact on the transport of oxygen than carbon dioxide?

3 a) How does the affinity of haemoglobin change

      i)   as it progressively loads with oxygen?

      ii) in increasing concentrations of carbon dioxide?

   b) Suggest why fetal haemoglobin has a higher affinity for oxygen than maternal haemoglobin.

   c) What is myoglobin and where is it found?

   d) Comment on the affinity of myoglobin for oxygen compared to haemoglobin.

10.4 How blood clots

Blood capillaries run close to the surface of the skin. If the skin is injured, the capillaries are often damaged too, leading to blood loss. When arterioles are cut there is a more substantial blood loss than from a superficial wound. But more dangerous than this is bleeding from an artery since these vessels are at the highest blood pressure. Rapid blood loss can lead to unconsciousness and death. However, once bleeding has stopped, the volume of blood lost from the circulation is quickly made up by tissue fluid draining into the blood vessels, although the composition takes a longer time to adjust. Apart from the actual loss of blood which an injury may cause, a wound gives bacteria and other disease-causing agents the opportunity to enter the body. Blood clotting helps to stop bleeding and seal a wound, protecting against infection. The blood also has a role in defending the body against infection through the immune response.

▶ *Chapter 30.3 covers the immune response and immunity*

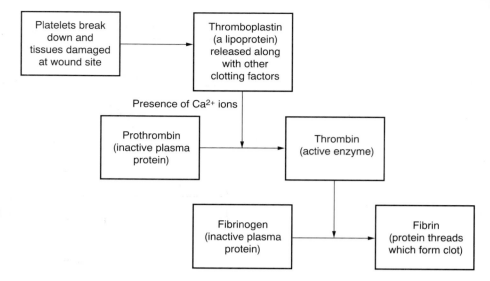

Figure 10.9 Only the main clotting factors are shown in this model of the clotting mechanism. The result of clotting is that damaged tissues are plugged and a scab develops. Tissues such as the skin repair and regrow beneath the scab which eventually drops off.

Rapid clotting is vital to stop dangerous blood loss following injury, yet clots in circulating blood are very damaging to life or even fatal. The clotting mechanism in human blood is a complex sequence of events called a **cascade**, because one event follows another. This sequence is normally only triggered by damage to tissues and the release of blood from vessels, which in turn affects the platelets. The inside of healthy blood vessels are smooth and unlikely to cause any platelet damage which might start the clotting process. As a further safeguard there are substances such as **heparin** present in low concentrations in circulating blood, which act as **anticoagulants** slowing or preventing the clotting process.

As the clotting mechanism relies on many different factors being produced in the correct amounts and sequence, a missing factor can interupt the whole process. **Haemophilia** is an inherited condition in which the blood clots slowly or not at all, because the sufferer (a **haemophiliac**) does not produce one or more of the clotting factors. About 2000 people in the UK are haemophiliacs. Treatment generally involves injecting clotting factors on a regular basis.

> Clotting involves a chain of reactions brought about by a series of clotting factors. Platelets are important in clotting because they mainly trigger the clotting mechanism.
>
> Haemophilia is an inherited disease in which a lack of clotting factor(s) slows or prevents clotting.

► *Chapter 33.9 explains more about haemophilia and how it is inherited*

10.5 The circulatory system

As blood circulates repeatedly around the body, substances move into it from the tissues and out of it to the tissues. This bulk flow of materials is essential in any organism for which diffusion alone would not supply material or remove wastes fast enough. The human blood circulation consists of a vast number of vessels, blood as the medium of transport and the heart which is the pump. The layout is called a **double circulation**. One side of the heart pumps blood through vessels which run to the tissues and most of the major organs of the body. This is called the **systemic circulation**, which delivers oxygen and food to the tissues. The other side of the heart pumps blood via the **pulmonary circulation** through the lungs, where it becomes oxygenated. Both the systemic and pulmonary circulations carry blood away from the heart in **arteries** and smaller **arterioles**, returning blood to the heart via small **venules** and larger **veins**. Between the arterioles and venules are **capillary beds** where exchange of materials between the tissues and blood occurs.

> The systemic circulation carries blood to most body tissues and back to the heart. The pulmonary circulation carries blood to the lungs and back to the heart.

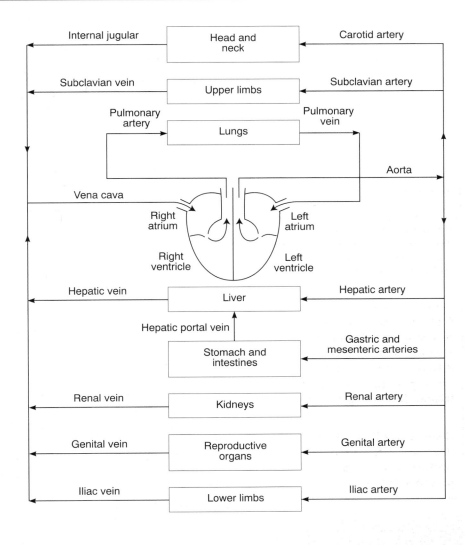

Figure 10.10 The circulatory system

Table 10.4 How is the blood distributed?

	Systemic circulation (%)	Pulmonary circulation (%)	Heart (%)
arterial	13	3	7
venous	64	4	–
capillaries	7	2	–

Blood vessels in different parts of the human circulation function in very differing conditions, such as the pressure of blood inside them and their relation to other tissues. For this reason the structure of blood vessels varies although the walls of all vessels (apart from the capillaries) show a similarity in the three layers they are composed of.

The inner layer called the **tunica intima** consists of endothelial cells supported by elastic connective tissue. The middle layer, the **tunica media**, varies most in composition but contains muscle supported by tough collagen fibres and elastic connective tissues. The **tunica externa** is a connective tissue sheath surrounding the vessel. Table 10.5 summarises the main differences between different types of blood vessels and Figure 10.11 shows their appearance using a light microscope.

Table 10.5 Comparing the structure and content of blood vessels

	Artery	Capillary	Vein
tunica externa	present as a thick layer	absent	present as a thin layer
tunica media	present as a thick layer	absent	present as a thin layer
tunica intima	present	present	present
pressure	high (10–16 kPa)	falling (1–4 kPa)	low (1 kPa)
pulse	none	none	present
valves	none	none	semilunar valves
speed	rapid	slowing	slow
other features	transports blood away from heart	site of exchange between blood and tissues	transports blood towards heart

Lumen · Tunica externa · Tunica intima · Tunica media · Endothelial cell · Lumen · Tunica externa · Tunica intima · Tunica media

Large arteries such as the aorta contain sufficient elastic fibres to allow them to stretch greatly each time blood is pumped into them by the heart and return to their original shape afterwards. This **elastic recoil** also helps push blood along the arteries leading from the heart while the ventricles are relaxed and the heart is refilling. In smaller arteries which distribute blood around the body, there is a greater proportion of muscle fibres in the tunica media compared to elastic fibres. These vessels cannot stretch as much as larger arteries, but if the muscle in their walls contracts, less blood passes through them, directing it elsewhere in the circulation. This is called **vasoconstriction** and is described in Chapter 17.4. Branches of the smallest arteries, called arterioles, have only an incomplete muscle layer in the tunica media but are still important in controlling blood distribution. Where capillary networks develop from these smallest arterioles there are **precapillary sphincters**. These are ring structures which can close a vessel leading into a capillary network, causing the blood to redistribute through another route.

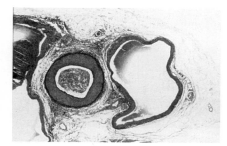

Figure 10.11 The appearance of blood vessels through a light microscope

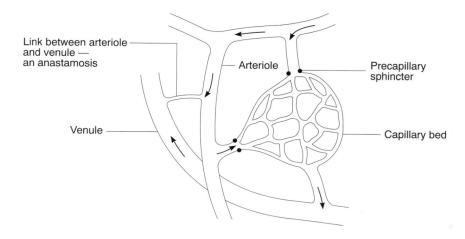

Link between arteriole and venule — an anastamosis · Arteriole · Precapillary sphincter · Venule · Capillary bed

Figure 10.12 Blood distribution in a capillary bed

Capillaries are the smallest blood vessels of all and run closely next to body cells exchanging metabolites with the tissue fluid that bathes them. They richly supply areas of high metabolic activity such as the liver. Other areas, such as the skin epidermis, lack capillaries and metabolise very slowly in comparison. However, there are capillaries in the dermis of the skin which are important in the control of body temperature. Capillary walls are thin, consisting of one layer of endothelial cells which are closely-packed, flattened cells. In some places, such as the start of a kidney tubule, large amounts of material exchange and the endothelial cells have gaps between them to facilitate this.

Tiny veins called venules are similar to capillaries in structure, but as they increase in size they have a tunica media and tunica externa. Even so, overall they have thinner walls than arteries and are not as elastic or muscular. Their large lumens have a low resistance to flow, which necessitates the presence of valves inside veins to prevent backflow of blood. Valves are essentially folds of endothelium which are pushed open by a forward flow of blood, but become filled by backflow of blood, blocking the lumen. A varicosed vein has faulty valves which do allow blood to leak backwards and it tends to collect, stretching the veins and giving them a 'knotty' appearance. Large veins run between panels of muscle in the limbs, and are squeezed by these muscles as the body moves, assisting blood flow.

> ▶ *Chapter 17.3 describes thermoregulation, which is the control of body temperature*

> Arteries, veins and capillaries are differently adapted for their functions.

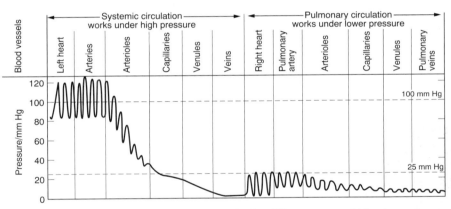

Figure 10.14 The nature of blood flow varies in the different types of blood vessels

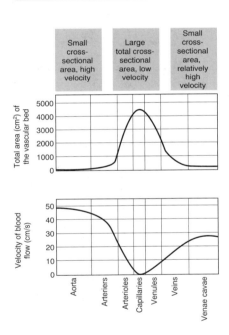

Figure 10.13 How fast blood flows depends on blood pressure and the resistance of the blood vessels to the flow

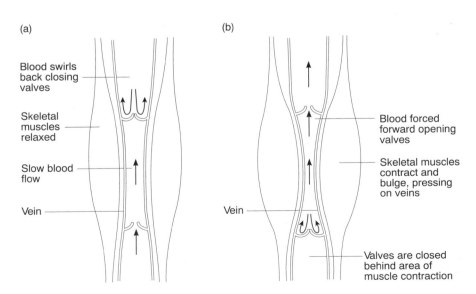

Figure 10.15 Blood flow in the veins is assisted by skeletal muscles

CHAPTER 11 The Human Heart

11.1 The structure of the heart

The heart is a muscular organ located in the chest cavity, between the spine at the back of the body and the sternum at the front, and embedded between the lungs at either side. The upper part is broader in shape and called the base, while the lower part is the narrower apex. The base is slightly tipped towards the right shoulder, so the heart lies obliquely, partly kept in position by the large blood vessels attached to it. Surrounding the heart is a double layer of membrane called the **pericardium**, with **pericardial fluid** between the two layers to provide lubrication as the apex of the heart moves continuously. Fibrous membranes also help to hold the heart in position, loosely anchoring it to the diaphragm and sternum. Running across the surface of the heart are **coronary arteries** supplying oxygen and food to the heart muscle itself. The heart is composed of specialised muscle tissue called **cardiac muscle**.

Cardiac muscle

The cells which make up cardiac muscle are similar in structure and in the way that contraction occurs to those of the skeletal muscles. However, cardiac muscle fibres have unique adaptations:

- they are smaller, fatter and branched cells, with only one nucleus;
- adjacent cells are interconnected by cross-bridges and **intercalated discs** which anchor them together as contraction occurs;
- they have many more mitochondria;
- they are myogenic, i.e. able to contract without any external stimulation.

This structure means that the tissue functions as an integrated whole because contraction occurs in all planes very rapidly, rather than in a linear fashion as happens in skeletal muscle.

> ► *Chapter 13 explains the structure and function of skeletal muscle*

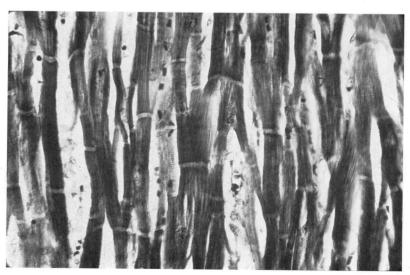

Figure 11.1 Cardiac muscle has a specialised structure for the conduction of impulses

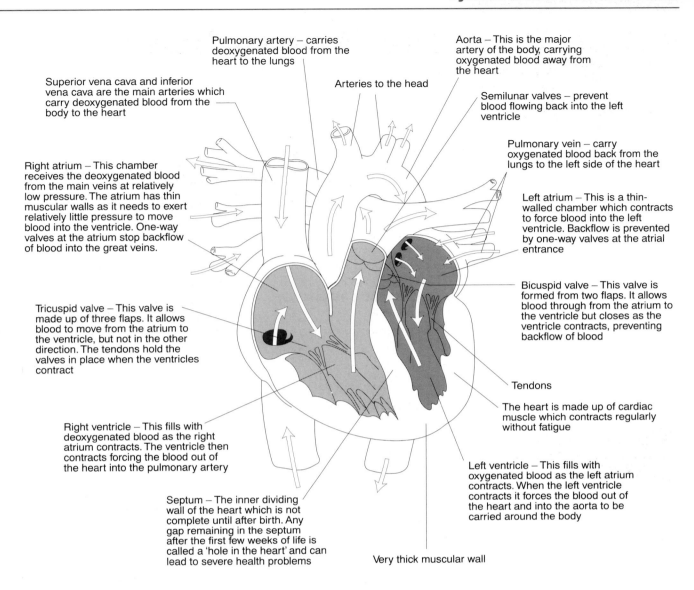

Pulmonary artery – carries deoxygenated blood from the heart to the lungs

Arteries to the head

Aorta – This is the major artery of the body, carrying oxygenated blood away from the heart

Superior vena cava and inferior vena cava are the main arteries which carry deoxygenated blood from the body to the heart

Semilunar valves – prevent blood flowing back into the left ventricle

Pulmonary vein – carry oxygenated blood back from the lungs to the left side of the heart

Right atrium – This chamber receives the deoxygenated blood from the main veins at relatively low pressure. The atrium has thin muscular walls as it needs to exert relatively little pressure to move blood into the ventricle. One-way valves at the atrium stop backflow of blood into the great veins.

Left atrium – This is a thin-walled chamber which contracts to force blood into the left ventricle. Backflow is prevented by one-way valves at the atrial entrance

Bicuspid valve – This valve is formed from two flaps. It allows blood through from the atrium to the ventricle but closes as the ventricle contracts, preventing backflow of blood

Tricuspid valve – This valve is made up of three flaps. It allows blood to move from the atrium to the ventricle, but not in the other direction. The tendons hold the valves in place when the ventricles contract

Tendons

The heart is made up of cardiac muscle which contracts regularly without fatigue

Right ventricle – This fills with deoxygenated blood as the right atrium contracts. The ventricle then contracts forcing the blood out of the heart into the pulmonary artery

Left ventricle – This fills with oxygenated blood as the left atrium contracts. When the left ventricle contracts it forces the blood out of the heart and into the aorta to be carried around the body

Septum – The inner dividing wall of the heart which is not complete until after birth. Any gap remaining in the septum after the first few weeks of life is called a 'hole in the heart' and can lead to severe health problems

Very thick muscular wall

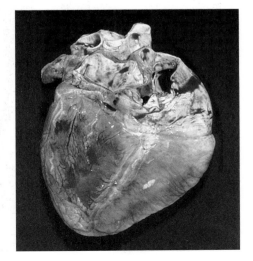

Figure 11.2 The human heart

The heart muscle, or **myocardium**, is lined by a smooth sheet endothelium which is continuous with the endothelium inside blood vessels. The heart is divided in to four chambers with walls or **septa** between them. In an adult the septum between the two sides of the heart is complete, preventing any mixing between the blood on either side. However, valves allow blood flow between the upper and lower chambers on each side and serve to prevent backflow of blood. The function of the upper chambers is to contract and pump the blood into the lower chambers. There is little resistance to this and gravity assists the process, so the muscle layer which makes up their walls is quite thin. It is really the two thick-walled lower chambers which act as a double pump, contracting simultaneously at each heart beat and pumping blood separately into the systemic and pulmonary circulations. The myocardium contains a network of nerve tissue which stimulates and coordinates contraction, first downwards and across the atria from the base, and then from the apex upwards.

The heart valves

There are four heart valves which open and close passively according to the pressure of blood on either side of them. The valves at the base of the aorta and the pulmonary artery are called **semilunar valves**, and are pocket-shaped. When the pressure of blood leaving the heart is higher than the pressure in the vessels themselves, they flatten against the inside of these vessels, opening and allowing blood to flow past. As the ventricles relax between each heart beat, the blood pressure drops on the side of the valve nearest to the heart. As some blood moves back towards the heart, the semilunar valves fill up and block the vessel.

The cusps of the tricuspid and bicuspid valves are made of fibrous connective tissue covered with endothelium. Attached to them are tiny tendons, sometimes known as the 'heart strings'. These tendons are attached at the other end to small papillary muscles which extend from the myocardium. As blood flows from the atria to the ventricles the cusps are pushed open by the higher blood pressure in the atria. When the atria have emptied and the ventricles begin to contract, the blood surges upwards so that it pushes the cusps upwards and they close against each other. The muscles attached to the tendons contract, pulling them taut and preventing the cusps from flapping upwards into the atria.

> septum = singular
> septa = plural

> The heart consists of four chambers. It functions as a double pump as the two sides function independently though simultaneously.

> Valves prevent backflow of blood.

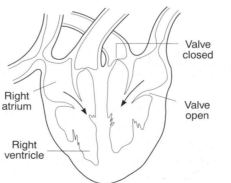

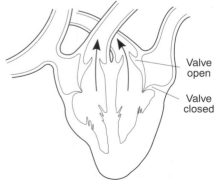

Figure 11.3 The role of valves is to ensure unidirectional flow

Diastole : the heart is relaxed and fills with blood

Systole : the heart contracts and forces blood out to the lungs and round the body

Some diseases such as rheumatic fever can result in damaged valves as the edges of the cusps become scarred. This means that some blood flows past the cusps when the valves are in the closed position. Sometimes the cusps might stick together, narrowing the opening which blood can flow through. In either case the heart has to work harder to pump the amount of blood required by the heart. In the long-term the heart can become weakened or even fail.

How does the heart sound?

A stethoscope is used to listen to the sounds made by the heart, which are actually the sounds of the valves closing. The closure of the valves between the atria and the ventricles is slower than that of the semilunar valves, and is described as a 'lub'. Following this is the second sound which happens as the semilunar valves snap shut. This shorter sound is called the 'dub'. If there is damage to heart valves, the heart makes extra noises as blood moves past them. This is known as a **heart murmur**.

▶ *Chapter 11.3 covers the heart and health*

Questions

1 a) In what way is the structure of an artery different to a vein?

   b) How do the differences in structure between an artery and a vein relate to their function in the circulatory system?

   c) Blood capillaries are very small in size, but their collective cross-sectional area is greater than that of arteries or veins. Explain why this is so.

   d) How does the cross-sectional area of capillaries affect the rate of flow through them?

   e) Which of the blood vessels has a pulsatile blood flow? How does this come about?

2 a) Why is there no direct connection between the circulation passing through the two sides of the heart?

   b) How do valves in the heart and in blood vessels assist in circulation?

   c) Why is there a difference between the thickness of the ventricle wall on either side of the heart?

11.2 How the heart beats

A single heart beat takes about 0.8 seconds and happens repeatedly throughout life without the owner of the heart having to think about it once. In every day terms, the heart is an amazingly trouble free pump for most people, for most of their lives. Figure 11.4 shows the key events in terms of blood circulation at each heart beat.

There is a cycle of contraction of the atria, called **atrial systole**, followed by contraction of the ventricles, called **ventricular systole**. Following each phase of contraction, the atria and the ventricles relax in order to return to a condition in which they can contract again. The heart chambers fill while

A heart beat consists of a relaxation phase called diastole followed by a wave of contraction called systole.

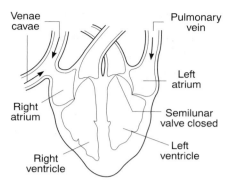

(a)

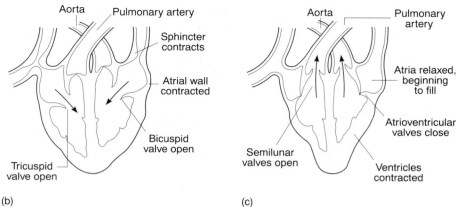

(b)

(c)

Figure 11.4 (a) The atria are relaxed and fill via the venae cavae and the pulmonary vein; the semilunar valves close (the **lub sound**). (b) The atria contract and squeeze blood into the relaxed ventricles; sphincter muscles at the base of the veins prevent backflow of blood. (c) As the ventricles fill up the valves between the atria and ventricles close (the **dub sound**); the ventricles contract from the apex upwards, forcing blood into the arteries.

▶ *Chapter 20 describes the nervous system*

Figure 11.5 The SA node, AV node and Purkyne tissue make up the special conducting system within the heart

The heart beat is initiated by the SA node causing atrial systole. The AV node directs the wave of excitation via the Purkyne fibres to the apex of the ventricles, so they contract from the apex upwards.

▶ *Chapter 18.2 discusses the control of heart rate*

relaxed. Phases of relaxation are called **diastole**. When an atrium or ventricle is contracted the blood pressure inside it is higher than when it is relaxed. This creates a pressure difference between the chamber itself, and the chamber or vessel it empties into, which maintains the flow in one direction.

This series of events is initiated rhythmically within the heart at the **sinoatrial node (SA node)**, which is situated close to the point where the venae cavae enters the right atrium. The SA node sets the heart rate and so it is known as the **pacemaker**. Since the stimulation for each heart beat comes from within the heart itself, it is said to have an **intrinsic rhythm**. A heart removed from the body but kept in an oxygenated solution will beat about 60 times per minute, without any nerve or hormone connection with the body. However, adjustments to the heart rate are brought about by nerves in the autonomic (or automatic) nervous system.

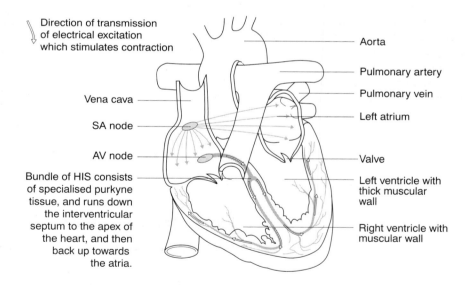

A wave of excitation similar to a nerve impulse starts at the SA node and moves down and across the atria as they contract. This is picked up by the **atrioventricular node (AV node)** which conducts more slowly, allowing the atria to finish contracting before the ventricles contract. From the AV node the excitation passes more rapidly along the fibres of the Purkyne (or Purkinje) tissue which pass through the septum between the two sides of the heart. This sets off contraction of the ventricles, spreading upwards from the apex.

(a) Electrical activity of the heart is recorded as it beats and is displayed on a chart or VDU as an electrocardiogram

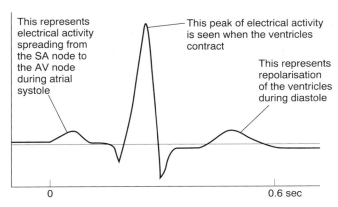

This represents electrical activity spreading from the SA node to the AV node during atrial systole

This peak of electrical activity is seen when the ventricles contract

This represents repolarisation of the ventricles during diastole

0   0.6 sec

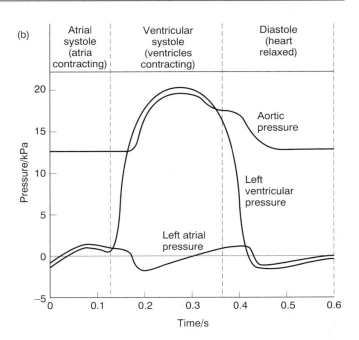

Figure 11.6 (a) An ECG trace (or electrocardiogram) which shows the periods of excitation and rest during the heart beat (b) Pressure changes associated with the heart beat

An irregular heart beat?

An electrocardiogram (ECG) is a picture produced by a machine which records the electrical activity of the heart as it is beating. In fact, an ECG is composed of 12 traces, which together give a three-dimensional picture of how the heart is beating. A full ECG takes knowledge and skill to interpret, and for simplicity only one trace is shown in each of Figure 11.7 parts a–c. Figure 11.7 (a) shows a trace for a normal heart beat, compared with Figure 11.7 (b) in which the frequency of the heart beat is different. The person in Figure 11.7 (b) has a condition called tachycardia. Figure 11.7 (c) shows a trace from a person with an abnormal heart beat in the atrial part of the cycle.

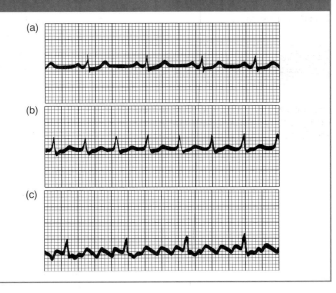

Figure 11.7 (a) Normal ECG (b) ECG for someone with tachycardia (c) abnormal ECG trace

Baby blood flow

While the fetus is still developing it receives oxygen and dissolved food and gets rid of waste substances via the mother's blood supply. A connecting organ called the **placenta** allows these two blood supplies to come into contact without actually mixing. The reason for this is that the blood group of the mother and fetus may not be the same, so mixing of the two might result in **agglutination**, which is a clumping of blood cells (see Chapter 11.4). The fetal heart pumps blood to the placenta via the umbilical artery, and it returns through the umbilical vein. Notice some of these important differences in the fetal circulation (Figure 11.8):

- The **foramen ovale** connects the right and left atria; this is to re-direct most of the deoxygenated blood to the placenta, via the aorta.

- The **ductus arteriosus** is a short vessel connecting the pulmonary artery to the aorta; this is to direct 90 per cent of the blood flow to the aorta and on to the body tissues, since the fetal lungs are not yet functional and there is a high resistance within them as they are filled with liquid.
- The **ductus venosus** carries oxygenated blood from the placenta and blood from the fetal gut, by-passing the liver, which only takes on a regulatory role after birth.

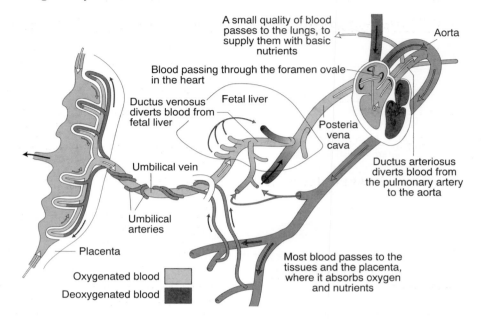

Figure 11.8 Fetal blood circulation maximises the flow of oxygenated blood to the fetal tissues *(See Colour Gallery page 349)*

The foramen ovale and ductus arteriosus quickly seal off after birth. A condition sometimes called 'hole in the heart' occurs if the foramen ovale does not close completely, which can be detected from abnormal heart sounds (heart murmurs). Many people live healthily with a small hole in the septum between the two sides of the heart, however a larger hole can be life-threatening and require surgery. Muscular contractions also seal off the ductus venosus and the baby's liver takes over the functions previously performed by the mother's.

Questions

1   a) Outline the events which occur during a heart beat.

b) How are these events co-ordinated?

c) How would the malfunction of the SA node affect the action of the heart?

2   Use Figure 11.7 (a–c) to answer this question.

a) What patterns in the heart beat can be seen from the ECG in Figure 11.7 (a)?

b) What differences are there between the pattern of events in Figure 11.7 parts (a) and (b)? How might these differences affect the person?

c) What differences are there between the pattern of events in Figures 11.7 parts (a) and (c)? How can you tell from the trace that the abnormality is in the atrial part of the cycle?

11.3 The heart and health issues

The main health issues concerning the cardiovascular system are: hypertension and stroke, coronary heart disease and circulatory disease.

Table 11.1 Coronary heart disease is a major health problem in some countries – apart from causing early death, it is responsible for loss of working days and a lowering of the quality of life for many people

Location	Data
Worldwide	• in both developed and developing countries deaths from cardiovascular diseases account for almost 50% of all deaths • globally, premature death due to cardiovascular disease is 2.5 times higher in men than in women
Europe	• cardiovascular diseases are the principal cause of death, accounting for more than 50% of all deaths in those aged over 65
Eastern Mediterranean	• the proportion of deaths from cardiovascular disease ranges from 25 to 45%
Africa, Western Asia and South-east Asia	• 15 to 20% of annual deaths are due to cardiovascular disease
India	• the proportion of deaths due to coronary heart disease has risen from 4 to 30% in the last 30 years
China	• in 1990 the mortality rate attributable to cardiovascular disease was 35.8% of total deaths in urban areas
Indonesia	• cardiovascular diseases have become the leading cause of death, accounting for 16.5% of all death
Africa	• cardiovascular death ranges from 20 to 45%

Source: Biostatistical Fact Sheets (http://www.amhrt.org/hs96/bioin.html)

An urgent concern in some countries, in particular industrially developed countries in the Western world such as the USA and those in Europe, is reducing the level of coronary heart disease (CHD) and high blood pressure (hypertension). In the UK this is reflected by a government report which was published in 1992, setting some targets for improving the average health across Britain (see also Table 11.2).

Targets:

• To reduce death rates for CHD and stroke in people under the age of 65 by at least 40 per cent by the year 2000.
• To reduce the death rate for CHD in people aged 65–74 by at least 30 per cent by the year 2000.
• To reduce the mean blood pressure in the adult population by at least 0.667 kPa (5 mmHg).

Table 11.2

Age	Cause of death	Deaths per 100 000	
		1990	2000 (proposed target)
>65	CHD stroke	58 12.5	35 7.5
65–74	CHD	899	629

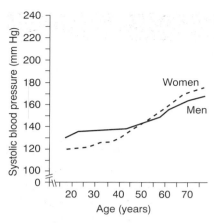

Figure 11.9 Systolic blood pressure in men and women (at the 50 percentile level i.e. 50 per cent of people of these ages will have this blood pressure)

Pulse pressure = systolic pressure − diastolic pressure

▶ *Chapter 16 deals with kidney function*

▶ *Chapter 8.5 describes the health risks of smoking*

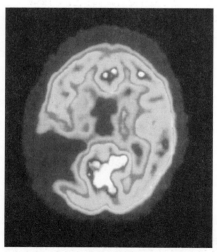

Figure 11.10 A thrombosis in the brain can have an almost instantaneous and often irreversible effect, which is why it is called a stroke.
(*See Colour Gallery page 349*)

Hypertension and stroke

In the vast majority of cases of hypertension, the cause is *multifactorial* because more than one factor brings about or contributes to the condition. Hypertension runs in families and so some factors are genetically determined. Other factors are environmental such as smoking, which causes constriction of blood vessels, and a high dietary intake of salt, which increases water retention. A stressful lifestyle may increase the production of adrenaline and so increase blood pressure in the short-term, but whether it causes hypertension in the long-term is unclear. Obesity is another factor which can raise blood pressure and puts a strain on the heart. One estimate suggests that for every 14 kg of excess body mass the body requires 40 km of extra blood vessels! The strain on the heart makes the likelihood of heart attack greater.

There is a tendency for blood vessels to lose their elasticity with age, and become more fibrous and rigid. The increased rigidity causes increased pulse pressure, which further disrupts the elastic tissue. At points where arteries divide in to two the pressure is greatest and so this is where there is maximum damage. The net effect is that there is increased resistance to blood flow and the heart has to work harder to sustain the necessary blood flow. If untreated, the heart muscle mass will increase and the enlarged heart finally fails. An important effect of untreated hypertension is kidney damage. The fine blood vessels in the kidneys are damaged by the high pressure and become less efficient at filtering waste products such as urea. High blood pressure may also lead to blood vessels bursting, especially in the eye or the brain (known as **cerebral haemorrhage**). In the brain this is one cause of a stroke.

Another effect of a high pulse pressure is damage to the lining or endothelium of arteries. Again this occurs, particularly where arteries divide, and a fatty deposit called an **atheroma** may develop. The problem with this is that the blood is more likely to clot where there is an atheroma, but also the clot may detach and pass into circulating blood. The clot, or **thrombus**, flows down the artery until it cannot travel any further, where it causes a blockage.

Smokers are more likely to develop atheromas because carbon monoxide encourages their formation. High levels of low density cholesterol also accelerate the formation of atheromas, although diet does affect the level of cholesterol in the blood, it is mostly genetically determined. These deposits can build up to such an extent that they block a vessel. However, regular and sensible aerobic exercise, such as walking or swimming, has a very beneficial effect in preventing the build-up of cholesterol and prolonging active life.

Where an organ or part of an organ is supplied by only one artery, blockage may be catastrophic; a heart attack if the coronary arteries are involved or a stroke if blood supply to the brain is interrupted. If the blockage is not complete, the blood flow may only be deficient at certain times and give rise to **angina** in the case of the heart, which results in a pain in the chest because the heart is not getting sufficient oxygen. In the brain, deficient blood flow may cause a **transient stroke**. This is less damaging than a stroke which results from cerebral haemorrhage or complete blockage of an artery.

Table 11.3 There are some factors which increase the risk of a heart attack. If more than one of these risk factors is present, the chance of a heart attack increases dramatically

Risk factors	Risk (average risk = 100)
none	77
cigarettes	120
cigarettes and cholesterol	236
cigarettes, cholesterol and high blood pressure	384

How hypertension is treated

If appropriate, the first treatment for hypertension is a change in lifestyle, by introducing more leisure and relaxation time and reducing stress. Also, diet is a feature of self-help; reducing fat intake and obesity, as well as salt intake. Alcohol should not exceed 21 units for females and 28 units for males.

However, the main approach to treating hypertension is with medicines:

- **Diuretics** work by increasing salt excretion, and have an unknown direct effect on the blood vessels.
- **Beta-blockers** work by reducing the output from the heart, partly by slowing the heart rate.
- **Calcium channel blockers** affect calcium transport in arteriole muscle cells causing dilation and lowering resistance to blood flow.
- **Alpha-blockers** also lower resistance by relaxing smooth muscle.
- **ACE inhibitors** affect substances secreted by the kidney, which affect the muscle tension in arterial walls.

Coronary heart disease

The treatments for coronary heart disease include **angioplasty** or **bypass surgery**. The first of these options involves stretching the coronary arteries which are most affected, by inserting a device with a balloon-like structure on the end. The balloon is inflated to expand the blocked area. Bypass surgery is both common and successful. It involves taking a piece of vein from the patient (usually from the leg) and grafting it onto a coronary artery, bypassing the blocked section. Figure 11.11 (a) and (b) show where a new piece of blood vessel might be placed and some new technology which makes the surgery easier. A heart transplant is also an option.

> Treating CHD could involve angioplasty or bypass surgery.

Figure 11.11 (a) A new section of blood vessel literally bypasses the blocked section, ensuring a good blood supply to the heart muscle. (b) Around 16 000 people have bypass surgery each year in the UK. Timing is crucial, since the surgeon must have enough time to work accurately and carefully, yet fast enough that damage to tissues does not occur. This new device provides a way of joining the healthy piece of vessel onto the diseased one. It is made of polyurethane tube, reinforced with an alloy which is imprinted with a shape that it 'remembers' or returns to when it reaches a threshold temperature. The device is easily inserted as it is flattened, but it springs back to shape opening the tube as it reaches body temperature.

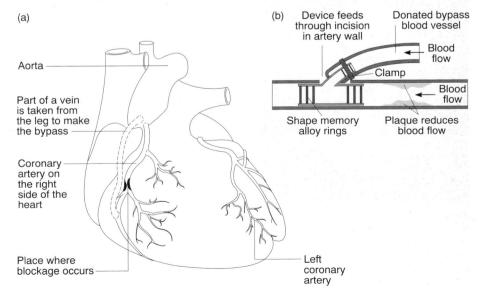

Figure 11.12 One way of dealing with blocked coronary arteries is to hold them open with a stainless steel basket. But up to now, blood clots have gathered around these implants, see photo (a), in about 25 per cent of patients, causing heart attacks. In the latest design, scientists have used a slippery polymer to coat the tubes, see photo (b), stopping blood clots accumulating.

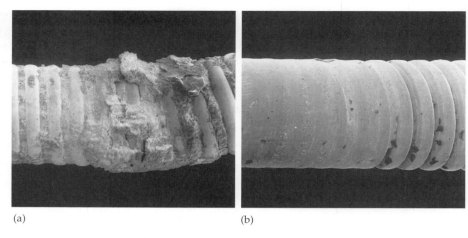

(a)
(b)

Heart transplants

A heart transplant is a complex operation, but is the only chance of extending life for people with very damaged hearts. One challenge with organ transplantation is that the recipient's immune system may reject the new organ. Despite the permanent need for **immunosuppressant** drugs which reduce the chance of rejection, heart transplant is very successful: 77 per cent of heart transplants are still functioning after five years. In the UK there are currently around 100 people waiting for heart transplants and the list is growing at 5 per cent per year. Only half the people receive the organs they need because of a shortage of donors.

Xenotransplantation involves using a heart from another animal species. Surgeons in the UK are currently considering xenotransplants from genetically engineered pigs. The main challenge with xenotransplants is overcoming immediate and complete rejection because of antibodies from the recipient attaching to the donor organ. However, the rejection response is regulated by molecules called RCAs. The idea behind using genetically engineered or **transgenic** pigs is to introduce a human gene for RCA which can reduce or prevent this rapid rejection. This approach had promising results when pig hearts were transplanted into monkeys. However, there are many challenges ahead, including the chance that virus diseases may spread between species (as HIV may have done). What is more, the response of the xenotransplant to human hormones and nervous control is not known. However, it should be remembered that pig heart valves have been used in human heart surgery for 15 years or so.

> Transplants are used when there are inherited deformities or rare conditions which make the heart useless as a pump.

> ▶ *Chapter 13.6 describes the benefits of keeping fit*

> ▶ *Chapter 30 considers various aspects of health and disease*

> ▶ *Chapter 11.1 mentions how damage to heart valves can happen*

Figure 11.13 Are transgenic pigs the organ donors of the future?

11.4 Blood groups

Losing a lot of blood is a threat to life which may require an immediate transfusion. A transfusion involves giving a donor's blood to the person who has lost blood. When this treatment first began it was not always successful because the **blood group** of the donor and recipient were not always compatible. Blood group refers to the antigens on the erythrocytes. Patients who received the incompatible blood developed an immune response which destroyed the red blood cells in the donated blood and caused death. Now, this immune challenge is virtually unheard of because all donated blood samples and all recipients are tested for blood group.

On the surface of red blood cells are mucopolysaccharides which act as markers or antigens (also known as agglutinogens). There are around 20 known blood group systems, but the **ABO system** and the **Rhesus system** are the most important. In the ABO system there are two antigens called A and B. Some people have antigen A on their erythrocytes, others have B, some have A and B and others have none at all. In the plasma there are antibodies (also known as agglutinins) which correspond to these antigens. People with blood group A have antibodies for B, and vice versa. If someone has antigens A and B then they do not have antibodies for either, but if they do not have either antigen then they do have both antibodies. Figure 11.14 summarises the antigens and antibodies for each blood group.

Agglutination is a clumping of red blood cells which happens when an antigen is in contact with the corresponding antibody. For example, agglutination would occur if someone with blood group B received blood from someone with blood group A.

> ▶ **Chapter 33.10 explains the inheritance of ABO blood groups**

> ▶ **Chapter 2.1 describes the structure of cell surface membranes with relation to cell recognition**

Figure 11.14 The ABO system of blood grouping

	RECIPIENT			
DONOR	O (Antibodies a and b)	A (Antigen A, antibody b)	B (Antigen B, antibody a)	AB (Antigens A and B)
O (Antibodies a and b)	✓	✓	✓	✓
A (Antigen A, antibody b)	✗	✓	✗	✓
B (Antigen B, antibody a)	✗	✗	✓	✓
AB (Antigens A and B)	✗	✗	✗	✓

The Rhesus system is also due to antigenic substances on the surface membrane of the red blood cells, mostly the D-antigen. About 75% of humans have the D-antigen and are Rhesus positive (Rh+). There is no antibody corresponding to this in plasma unless someone who is Rhesus negative (Rh−) has been exposed to the antigen. Then, the 'anti-D' antibody develops as in any immune response, although this occurs slowly after the first exposure to the antigen. The second exposure to the D-antigen causes a much faster and more dangerous response. Therefore, Rh− people must be given Rh− blood, although Rh+ people do not produce any rhesus antibodies so can receive either Rh+ or Rh− blood.

The Rhesus factor and mother and child

During pregnancy there is not normally any exchange of blood between a mother and the developing fetus. However, at birth the placenta separates from the uterus wall and a limited amount of mixing may occur. A Rh− mother may have a Rh+ child, and at birth she may receive some of the baby's blood and hence become sensitised to it. To stop an immune response developing because of this, she would be given an injection of anti-D antibodies to quickly destroy the red cells with the rhesus antigen. If a mother developed anti-D antibodies and later had another Rh+ child, her immune response to it could cause damage.

Blood transfusions

A **blood transfusion** involves using either whole blood or a component of blood from one person, and delivering it via a vein into another person. This might be done to help make up the volume of blood or to restore the correct balance of blood components, or to replace blood which contains some toxicity. Blood transfusions save thousands of lives every year, but they could go horribly wrong if the blood groups of donor and recipient were not taken into account. The ABO and Rhesus factor antigens are very important in deciding which blood type someone should receive. Within the ABO system people with blood group O are called **universal donors**, because their blood does not contain antigens. This means their blood can be given to anyone, irrespective of blood group. People with blood groups AB are the **universal recipients** who can receive any blood group, because they do not make antibodies to antigens A or B.

Questions

1 a) Why is blood pressure necessary?

  b) What trends are seen in the blood pressure data given in Figure 11.9 on page 100?

  c) Why does raised blood pressure occur and why is it dangerous to health?

  d) What factors contribute to the incidence of CHD?

  e) How can CHD be treated?

2 a) Why are immunosuppressant medicines needed by someone receiving a donated heart?

  b) What is meant by the terms *transgenic* and *xenotransplant*?

  c) Suggest reasons why both genetic engineering and transplantation of the type mentioned in part (b) are controversial.

3 a) Why are there different blood groups?

  b) Why is it important to match blood groups when giving blood transfusions?

  c) Why is the determination of Rhesus factor particularly important for women?

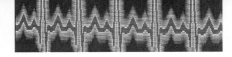

CHAPTER *12* Supporting and Moving the Human Body

12.1 Humans on the move

Locomotion means that we are able to move our whole body about from place to place. This has lots of advantages, because we can search for food or a more favourable place to live, escape dangers or enemies and find a reproductive partner. Mobility is an integral part of people's lives, and we extend this ability by using all forms of transport, such as cars, and mobility aids, such as wheelchairs. People with reduced mobility may depend on others for help, and in the long-term severely immobile people may develop breathing, cardiovascular and digestive challenges. Apart from physical health, immobility and dependency can affect self-image and psychological well-being. Clearly, our ability to move is important to us, and regular exercise and a sensible strategy for keeping fit can extend the healthy, active phase of life.

12.2 The human skeleton

> The skeleton provides a strong jointed framework which supports and protects the body.

> ▶ Chapter 10.2 describes erythrocyte production and Chapter 15.2 describes their destruction

> ▶ Chapter 37 describes the change in cranial shape during human evolution

The skeletal system is a rigid and jointed framework which supports our bodies so that a posture can be held against gravity. Internally, organs are attached by connective tissue to the skeleton, helping to locate their position. The human skeleton is inside the body since it is an **endoskeleton**, although some parts of it surround delicate organs and protect them from injury. For example, the cranium of the skull protects the brain and sense organs, such as the eyes, the ribcage and sternum protect the heart and lungs, and the spine protects the nervous tissue which makes up the spinal cord. The joints between bones along with complex musculature which is attached to bones, allow co-ordinated movement. Apart from this, erythrocytes and blood cells are produced by the bone marrow inside certain bones, and bone tissue acts as a reservoir of calcium (Ca^{2+}) and phosphate (PO_4^{3-}) ions.

The adult skull has an internal volume of about 1.5 litres, housing the brain, the eyes and the ears. It is made up of 22 bones which are firmly jointed together at the **sutures**. Notice in Figure 12.2 the way that the bones dovetail together along the sutures. As a fetus develops the skull is first formed of softer cartilage which is later replaced by bone. When a baby is born there are still some softer parts of the skull, called the **fontanelles**. These allow the head to change in shape as it passes down the birth canal (called **moulding**), as well as allowing for growth in the first year. Although they are quite easily visible at first, these areas become bony within one or two years. The lower jaw is held onto the skull by ligaments and moved by muscles, articulating with the cranium on both sides. On the lower surface are two knobs of bone which articulate with the first vertebra of the spine and a hole through which the spinal cord enters the brain.

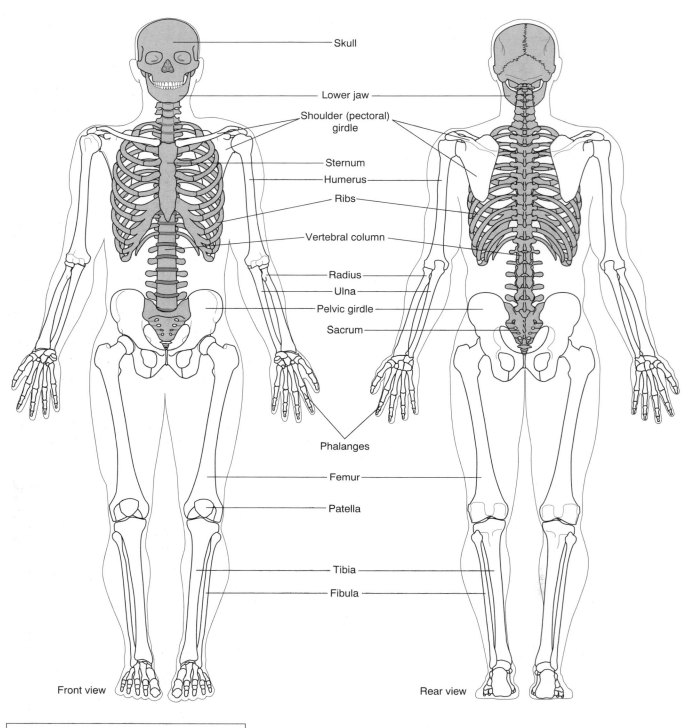

Skull

Lower jaw

Shoulder (pectoral) girdle

Sternum

Humerus

Ribs

Vertebral column

Radius

Ulna

Pelvic girdle

Sacrum

Phalanges

Femur

Patella

Tibia

Fibula

Front view

Rear view

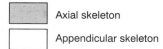

Axial skeleton

Appendicular skeleton

Figure 12.1 The general plan of the human skeleton, showing details of the main tissues which make it up. Altogether there are 206 bones in the body, most of which **articulate** or move against the surface of another bone. Some are arranged along the long axis of the body (shown here shaded) and make up the **axial skeleton**. The limb and limb girdles make up the **appendicular skeleton**, which literally means 'hanging on'.

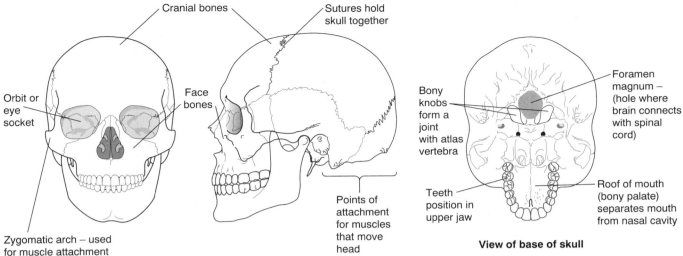

Figure 12.2 What a brainbox – the human skull protects this vital organ

vertebra = singular
vertebrae = plural

The **vertebral column** is a row of 33 bones which articulate with each other, and additionally in the chest region with the ribs. Together they form a strong and flexible system. The vertebrae vary in shape according to the part of the vertebral column they are found in, but the general plan is the same for most of them. There is a strong central piece of bone called the **centrum** which is the load-bearing part, above which is a pad of cartilage. These cartilage pads act as shock absorbers between the vertebrae, and are known as **intervertebral discs**. An arch of bone called the **neural arch** surrounds a hole called the **neural canal**, through which the spinal cord runs. Muscles are attached to bony spines called **processes** which project from the neural arch of a vertebra. One other feature is the holes through which the spinal nerves emerge on either side.

Figure 12.3 The vertebral column

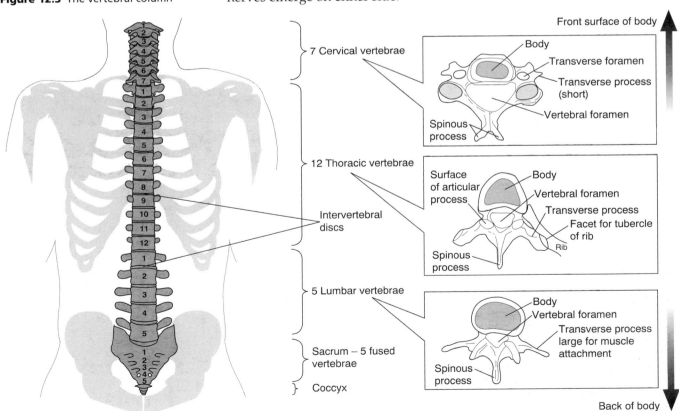

Why is posture important?

When the body is upright, the intervetebral discs are under high pressure because of the mass of the body pressing downwards. Even so, keeping the body in the correct posture helps to minimise the strain on the vertebrae, discs and muscles in the back (Figure 12.4). Some of the discs are in a more vulnerable part of the back than others, for example bending to lift heavy items increases the forces acting on the lumbar region of the back. Maintaining a position, such as stooping the head over a desk, can also be stressful for vertebrae in the neck and upper back.

The intervertebral discs may suffer from wear or damage. There is a fibrous coat around the outside of the disc of cartilage which normally helps it to keep in shape. If the coat is worn or broken, the softer inner core of cartilage bulges outwards at that point, and can press on a spinal nerve. This is why a 'slipped disc' is so painful. Muscles in the area are sensitised by the pressurised nerves and become tense and contracted, adding to the pain. The best remedy is to take painkillers initially, along with medicines to reduce the inflammation. Once the tissues become less sensitive the condition often rights itself unless there is an underlying cause such as injury, and assuming the person has good posture.

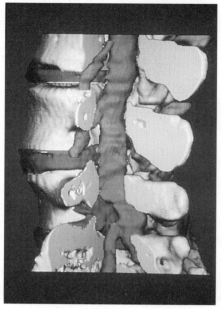

Figure 12.4 This is a three-dimensional computer tomography scan. The dark areas between the vertebrae are the disks: the lower one has slipped sideways and is pressing on the spinal cord *(See Colour Gallery page 350)*

Questions

1 a) What is the function of intervertebral discs?
   b) Suggest reasons why these discs may become damaged.
   c) Why is the use of painkillers and anti-inflammatory medicines recommended when someone 'slips' a disc?

2 The chair shown in Figure 12.5 is recommended by one manufacturer for use by people who have to sit at a desk for long periods of time.
   a) Suggest a reason why sitting at a desk for an extended period of time could trigger back problems.
   b) In what ways is the design of the chair shown in Figure 12.5 beneficial to posture?
   c) Can you suggest any disadvantages of this chair for use in an office environment?
   d) Why do some car manufacturers provide adjustable lumber support in the driver's car seat?

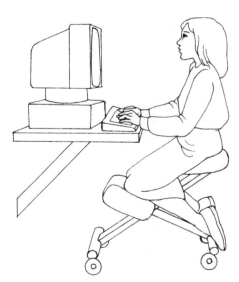

Figure 12.5 Remaining in one position for a long time puts a strain on the skeletal system

Limbs and limb girdles

Limbs are long in shape with bones running through the middle of them, and for this reason bones such as the humerus and femur are called long bones. The long bones are the main site of white blood cell production which occurs in the yellow bone marrow in the shaft. Red blood cells are produced in the red bone marrow found in shorter bones, such as the ribs and in the heads of long bones.

Figure 12.6 shows the bones of the **pectoral girdle** which consists of the arm and shoulder. There are two shoulder bones: the collar bone and the shoulder blade. The collar bone or clavicle is slender, articulating with the sternum at one end and the shoulder blade at the other. It helps to strengthen the shoulder area and some muscles are attached to it. The shoulder blade or scapula is broad, flat and triangular-shaped. It articulates at one end only with the clavicle and the humerus, but it has many muscles attached to it. The shoulder can be rotated quite fully because of the way the scapula articulates. The upper arm contains the humerus which articulates at the elbow joint with two bones: the radius and ulna. There are a number of wrist bones called carpels which articulate with the metacarpels in the palm of the hand, and the fingers and thumb are supported by bones which are called phalanges. In the forelimb are examples of different types of joints: **ball and socket joint** at the shoulder, **hinge joint** at the elbow and **gliding joints** in the wrist. Apart from these types of joints, there are others in the human body including the **pivot joint** between the skull and the spine (see Chapter 12.3).

Figure 12.6 (a) The pectoral girdle and forelimbs, with insert (b) The pentadactyl limb (c) The pelvic girdle and hindlimbs

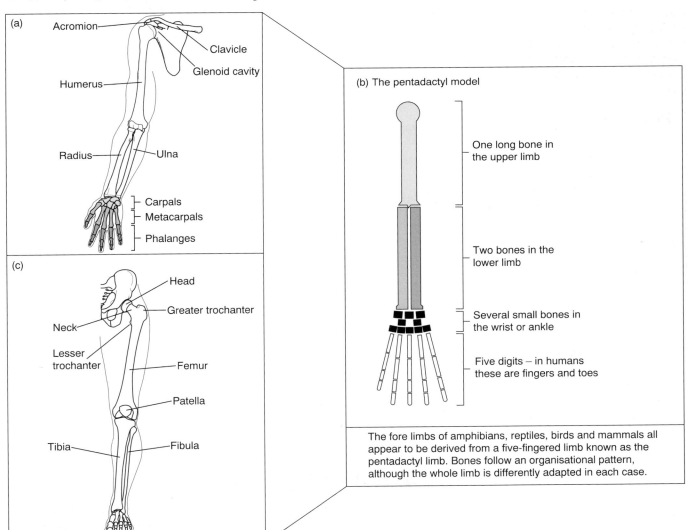

(a)
Acromion
Clavicle
Glenoid cavity
Humerus
Radius
Ulna
Carpals
Metacarpals
Phalanges

(b) The pentadactyl model

One long bone in the upper limb

Two bones in the lower limb

Several small bones in the wrist or ankle

Five digits – in humans these are fingers and toes

The fore limbs of amphibians, reptiles, birds and mammals all appear to be derived from a five-fingered limb known as the pentadactyl limb. Bones follow an organisational pattern, although the whole limb is differently adapted in each case.

(c)
Head
Greater trochanter
Neck
Lesser trochanter
Femur
Patella
Tibia
Fibula

Bone density and sport

Watching sports events gives cause for thought: why do the best sprinters often have African ancestry, while the best swimmers are usually Caucasian (meaning light or 'white' skinned people indigenous to Europe)? According to Professor Purdie of Hull University, it is all to do with bone density.

All the evidence, such as DNA analysis, confirms the suggestion that early humans evolved in The Great Rift Valley in Africa, and that many migrated north reaching Europe some 35 000 years ago. Amongst other changes, evolution saw the gradual lightening of skin coloration due to a reduction in melanin pigmentation, and a decrease in bone density. In the water, lighter people swim faster so lower bone density is an advantage. However, sprinters benefit from a heavier skeleton because they have a greater momentum propelling them forward.

Osteoporosis is a disease in which there is a loss of bone density, leading to very brittle bones. The following information about bone density and osteoporosis is from the Department of Health Advisory Group on Osteoporosis (November 1994):

- The incidence of bone fracture in the community peaks in the young (leg, arm) and very elderly (hip, spine and wrist).
- 90 per cent of hip fractures occur in people aged over 50.
- 80 per cent of hip fractures occur in women.
- Bone quality and density are affected by race.
- Hip fracture rates are generally higher in white than black or Asian populations.
- A survey in 1993 showed that 96 per cent of GPs felt that preventative measures should be taken to avert the onset of osteopososis.

▶ **Chapter 30.5** describes osteoporosis as an effect of ageing

▶ **Chapter 23.2** describes the effects of a lack of dietary calcium

Questions

1 a) Why do differences between races, such as bone density, exist?

b) Do you think there is a link between bone density and size of skeleton? How might this be investigated for humans?

2 Look at the information from the Advisory Group on Osteoporosis and Figure 12.7.

a) Explain why bone density and osteoporosis are linked.

b) What is the link between the prevalence of osteoporosis and (i) gender and (ii) age?

c) Suggest why there is a lower prevalence of osteoporosis in African people compared to Caucasian.

3 What environmental factors might contribute to osteoporosis developing?

(a)
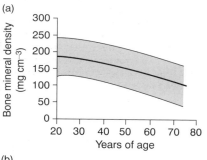

(b)
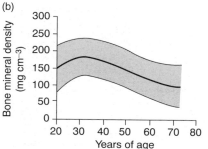

Figure 12.7 Osteoporosis and bone density in (a) men and (b) women

The main skeletal tissues are bone, cartilage and connective tissues.

12.3 Skeletal tissues

The main tissue making up the human skeleton is bone. Compact bone is very dense and hard and surrounds spongy bone with marrow. Compact bone provides more strength, while spongy bone lightens the skeleton and contains marrow which produces blood cells.

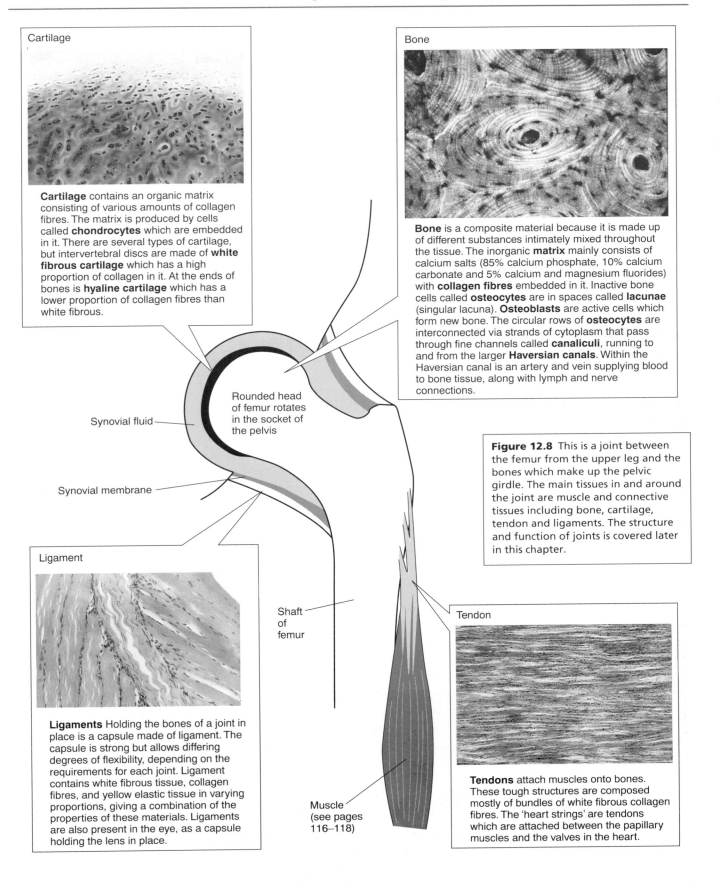

Cartilage

Cartilage contains an organic matrix consisting of various amounts of collagen fibres. The matrix is produced by cells called **chondrocytes** which are embedded in it. There are several types of cartilage, but intervertebral discs are made of **white fibrous cartilage** which has a high proportion of collagen in it. At the ends of bones is **hyaline cartilage** which has a lower proportion of collagen fibres than white fibrous.

Bone

Bone is a composite material because it is made up of different substances intimately mixed throughout the tissue. The inorganic **matrix** mainly consists of calcium salts (85% calcium phosphate, 10% calcium carbonate and 5% calcium and magnesium fluorides) with **collagen fibres** embedded in it. Inactive bone cells called **osteocytes** are in spaces called **lacunae** (singular lacuna). **Osteoblasts** are active cells which form new bone. The circular rows of **osteocytes** are interconnected via strands of cytoplasm that pass through fine channels called **canaliculi**, running to and from the larger **Haversian canals**. Within the Haversian canal is an artery and vein supplying blood to bone tissue, along with lymph and nerve connections.

Synovial fluid

Rounded head of femur rotates in the socket of the pelvis

Synovial membrane

Figure 12.8 This is a joint between the femur from the upper leg and the bones which make up the pelvic girdle. The main tissues in and around the joint are muscle and connective tissues including bone, cartilage, tendon and ligaments. The structure and function of joints is covered later in this chapter.

Ligament

Ligaments Holding the bones of a joint in place is a capsule made of ligament. The capsule is strong but allows differing degrees of flexibility, depending on the requirements for each joint. Ligament contains white fibrous tissue, collagen fibres, and yellow elastic tissue in varying proportions, giving a combination of the properties of these materials. Ligaments are also present in the eye, as a capsule holding the lens in place.

Shaft of femur

Muscle (see pages 116–118)

Tendon

Tendons attach muscles onto bones. These tough structures are composed mostly of bundles of white fibrous collagen fibres. The 'heart strings' are tendons which are attached between the papillary muscles and the valves in the heart.

Table 12.3 Connective tissues

Substance	Tissue/where it is found in the body	Properties
collagen	white fibrous cartilage in intervertebral discs, ligaments and tendons, and in hyaline cartilage at the ends of bones	hard-wearing, strong (especially under tension), non-stretchy but flexible
elastic fibres	yellow elastic tissue in cartilages of pharynx and in ligaments	elastic so returns to shape after compression

The properties of bone and cartilage are the combined properties of the matrix and fibrous material within them. The organic matrix of cartilage is not as hard as the matrix of bone, but both are strong and stand up to compression (squashing forces) well. Collagen is strong under tension (pulling forces), while elastic tissue gives both strength and elasticity.

Bone is a living tissue which responds to the mechanical stresses affecting it, and bone shape is modelled by these forces. During growth or repair of bone, cells give rise to active osteoblasts which lay down new bone matrix. Other cells break down and reabsorb bone tissue. Where bone is under constant pressure it tends to be reabsorbed, while intermittant stress stimulates bone production. Clearly, bone modelling is significant for children and will be affected by physical activities including sports. What's more, physical activity is important in keeping the bones strong, particularly as people become elderly. Extended periods of weightlessness experienced by astronauts in space are a concern because of the effect on bone structure. Bone is a store of calcium and phosphate which can be drawn on (e.g. if dietary supply is low). This release of minerals into the blood from bone is controlled by hormones.

▶ *Chapter 19 deals with the hormones as chemical co-ordinators*

Osteoarthritis

A joint has to be both strong and flexible to give good mobility. An inflammatory disease called osteoarthritis leads to:

- the destruction of the cartilage pads covering bone surfaces;
- the ligaments surrounding the joint becoming less flexible because of calcium deposits and as a result mobility is reduced;
- erosion of the bones which rub together;
- pain.

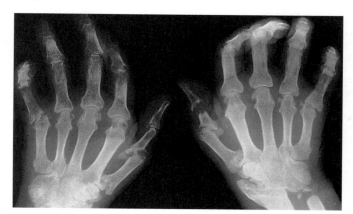

Figure 12.9 Osteoarthritic hands
(See Colour Gallery page 350)

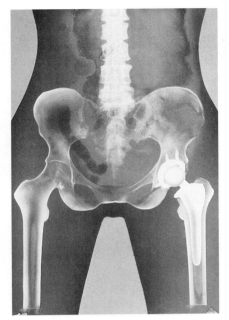

Figure 12.10 A 'hip replacement' involves removing the damaged head of the femur and cleaning the old socket, then replacing it with a stainless steel head and a new socket lining. Modern materials used in artificial joints are strong, hard-wearing and do not irritate inside the body. About 30 000 people each year in Britain have hip replacement surgery.

Questions

1 What are the properties of bone and cartilage, and how are they suited for their functions?

2 Why do tendons and ligaments consist of different types of connective tissue?

3 How is maintaining physical activity linked to skeletal health?

4 a) In what ways does osteoarthritis reduce the quality of life?

   b) Describe the features of a management plan that might make life more comfortable and raise the quality of life for someone with osteoarthritis.

12.4 Joints between bones

The skeleton is rigid and strong in order to support the body, but at the same time the design has to allow for movement. Joints are necessary points of weakness in this framework which give flexibility. A joint holds two bones close together, although not all joints allow movement.

The sutures in the skull, and the joint between the ulna and radius in the arm are examples of **fixed joints**. **Gliding joints** such as those between adjacent vertebrae and between the bones in the wrist and ankle are partly moveable. A specially adapted articulation between the first two vertebrae (the axis and atlas) is another example of a partly moveable joint which has a swivel action like a pivot. The fully **moveable joints** have a fluid lubricant in the cavity between them, as well as hard-wearing cartilage layers on the bone surfaces which move against each other. The fluid is viscous and originates from the blood plasma. The cartilage is rubbery and smooth, and can be replaced as it wears. Moveable joints are also known as **synovial joints** because of this structure, and an example is shown in Figure 12.11. In this case the head of the femur articulates in a socket in the pelvis, and so

Figure 12.11 The range of movement possible by different joints (a) ball and socket joint (b) hinge joint (c) pivot joint

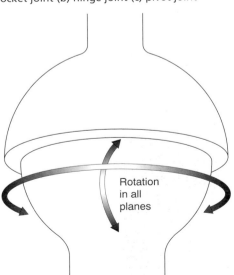

(a) Ball and socket joint

Rotation in all planes

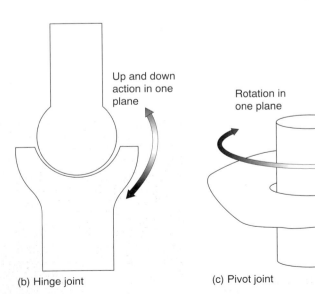

Up and down action in one plane

(b) Hinge joint

Rotation in one plane

(c) Pivot joint

> The different types of joints include fixed joints which are immoveable, gliding joints which are partly moveable and fully moveable joints which are synovial joints. Synovial joints contain a fluid lubricant.

this type is called **'ball and socket'**. Another example of a ball and socket joint is the humerus articulating at the shoulder. Both these joints are surrounded by a considerable number of muscles and allow the arm or leg to be rotated through a wide circle. At the knee and the elbow is another type of moveable joint called a **hinge joint**, because like a hinge it only has movement in one plane. This means that the lower arm or lower leg can only move up and down in one direction, and so involves less sets of muscles. Joints between the finger bones are also hinge joints, and likewise have much less mobility than ball and socket joints.

12.5 Muscle pairs

> Tendons join muscles to bone.

When muscles contract they pull on bones and bring about movement. A muscle is attached to at least two bones by tendons, and spans at least one joint. The **origin** of the muscle is where it is attached to the bone nearest to the heart. Generally, this bone does not move a lot, while at the other end the muscle is attached at the **insertion** to a bone which typically moves more. For example, a muscle in the top of the leg has its origin in the pelvis and its insertion in a bone of the lower leg. When a muscle is not contracted it is relaxed and can be pulled back into its original shape. This means that skeletal muscles are usually found in pairs, one to pull a bone in one direction while the other muscle is mainly relaxed. These pairs of muscles are called **antagonistic pairs** because when either contracts it pulls the bone in the opposite direction to the other muscle. However, they work together, usually with several pairs assisting co-ordinated movement.

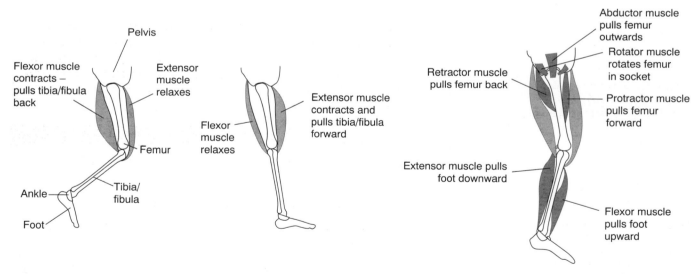

Figure 12.12 The main muscle movements

> ► *Chapter 13.4 also discusses how we adjust the use of our muscles in response to different tasks*

Moving on land, through air (which offers little resistance) or in water involves limbs acting as levers. A lever is a simple machine which does work by applying forces to a load. The joint is the pivot or **fulcrum** about which the limb moves, the bone is the lever and the muscle is the effort required to do the work (see Figure 12.13 (a)). When you are walking or running, you press your foot downwards and backwards, exerting forces in those directions. Equal and opposite forces act on your foot propelling you up and forwards (see Figure 12.13 (b)). When swimming, limbs can push upwards through the water, resulting in downwards movements.

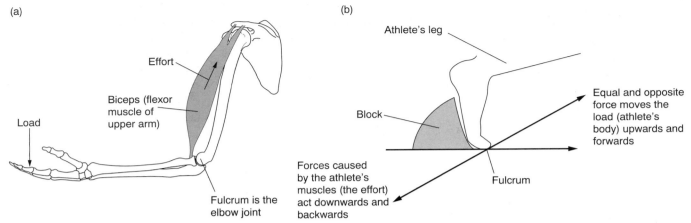

Figure 12.13 (a) The arm as a lever (b) A fast start involves pairs of forces acting on a foot at the starting block

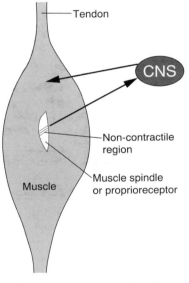

Figure 12.14 The stretch reflex allows the body to adjust contraction of one muscle in an antagonistic pair, and inhibit the contraction of the other muscle. Not all muscles work in antagonistic pairs, instead some work in co-ordinated groups called **synergists**.

The role of stretch receptors

There are **proprioreceptors** or stretch receptors called **muscle spindles** within skeletal muscles. They consist of specialised non-contractile fibres enclosed in a connective tissue sheath, which are connected to the central nervous system. When the muscle contracts, the muscle spindles send impulses via the central nervous system back to the muscle itself, stimulating further contraction. This is called the **stretch reflex** and it allows the strength of response to be increased to cope with increasing load on the muscle, while keeping the length of muscle fibres constant. For example imagine holding a watering can as it gradually fills with water from a tap. The amount that the biceps (at the front of the forelimb) has to work to hold the watering can increases as the can fills.

Muscle tone refers to the fact that skeletal muscles are not generally totally relaxed. Some muscle spindles will be under tension, and so some muscle cells within the whole muscle are contracted at any particular time. This type of action involves slow twitch muscle fibres (explained in Chapter 13) which generate a slower and more sustained contraction and use up less fuel than fast twitch muscle fibres.

Questions

1 a) Why is muscle tone important in activities such as maintaining posture?

b) What happens to muscle tone when people sleep?

c) How is the stretch reflex important in the action of an antagonistic pair of muscles?

2 Briefly describe the main tissues involved in the structure of a named joint, and explain how they help in locomotion.

CHAPTER 13 Muscles and Movement

13.1 Distribution and functions of different types of muscle

Muscle is widely spread throughout the body, making up to 40 per cent of body mass in mammals. All muscles contract to bring about movement providing they are supplied with oxygen and glucose (via the blood circulation). However, there are three types of muscle which are differently adapted in terms of structure and function according to their role. Table 13.1 summarises the main features of striated, smooth and cardiac muscle.

Skeletal muscles contain a mixture of two types of fibres: **slow twitch** and **fast twitch** fibres. Most people have roughly the same proportion of slow and fast twitch muscle fibres, depending partly on the type of physical activity in their lifestyle. Slow twitch fibres contract and fatigue slowly, and can remain contracted for some time. They have lots of mitochondria and a rich blood supply, and appear red because of the presence of myoglobin. Myoglobin is an oxygen carrier like haemoglobin, but it is only found in muscle tissue and it has a very high affinity for oxygen. It acts as an oxygen store because it only loses its oxygen to the tissues when the oxygen tension is very low indeed (and the carbon dioxide tension is correspondingly high). Slow twitch muscle fibres are more common where steady muscle action is required, for example in maintaining posture, or in muscles which are involved in long periods of activity. For example a high proportion of slow twitch muscle fibres may be found in the neck muscles which support the head. Fast twitch muscle fibres contract very rapidly but fatigue easily, operating in conditions of low oxygen availability. There is little or no myoglobin present. They respond well to sudden bursts of activity which is important during all types of movement, particularly sports and for animals which may need to escape dangers, such as predators, in order to survive.

> The three muscle types include cardiac muscle which is only found in the heart, striated or voluntary muscle which is joined to bones, and unstriated or involuntary muscle which is controlled by the autonomic nervous system.

> A muscle twitch refers to the contraction of a muscle fibre.

> ▶ *Chapter 10.3 gives more details about myoglobin*

13.2 The detailed structure of striated muscle

Table 13.1 includes a figure which shows the striped appearance of striated muscle. To see the details of this complex tissue, an electron microscope is needed. Notice that in Figure 13.1 you can see that the striped appearance is actually made up of wide dark bands (**A bands**) and narrow light bands (**I bands**) alternating across the width of a muscle fibre, and that the light bands have a dark line (**Z line**) running through the centre.

Each muscle fibre is made up of numerous parallel **myofibrils** which in turn consist of two protein myofilaments: **actin** and **myosin**. The light I bands consist of thinner actin filaments and the dark A bands of thicker myosin filaments overlapping with actin filaments at the sides, but not at the centre where there is just myosin. This is why the centre of an A band (called the **H zone**) looks lighter. From one Z line to another is a unit called the

> Striated muscle fibres show cross banding because of the overlapping myofilaments of actin and myosin.

Table 13.1

Feature	Description for each muscle type		
Name	smooth, unstriated, unstriped or involuntary	cardiac	striated, striped, voluntary
Appearance	*Nucleus*, *Spindle shaped cell*	*Nucleus*, *Striations*, *Cross bridge*, *Muscle cell*, *Intercalated disc*	*Myofibril of muscle fibre*, *Striations*, *Nucleus*
	individual, spindle-shaped cells are grouped together in bundles or sheets	cells are interconnected forming a three-dimensional functional unit (see Chapter 10.4)	elongated cells (up to 50 mm in length) called muscle fibres are bound into bundles by connective tissue
Cell contents	each cell has one elongated nucleus, many mitochondria	numerous large mitochondria in rows between cells	multinucleate, consist of many microfibrils made of smaller units called sarcomeres, with many mitochondria
Special features	least specialised type of muscle	very specialised since the structure allows the tissue to act as an integrated whole, the waves of contraction moving through the mass of tissue	conspicuous banding which results from the sarcomere structure
Activity	can sustain contraction and relaxation, and is slower to contract and fatigue	rapid, rhythmical contractions and relaxations, does not fatigue	rapid contraction, but fatigues relatively rapidly
Innervation from	controlled by the autonomic nervous system, which is why it is also called involuntary muscle	intrinsic, initiating the sino-atrial node (SA node); the control of heart rate is brought about by nerves from the autonomic system acting on the SA node	stimulated by motor nerve cells the central nervous system
Where it is found	in the wall of the gut, blood vessels, urinary and respiratory passages, ciliary muscle of the eye and iris	only in the heart	attached to the skeleton

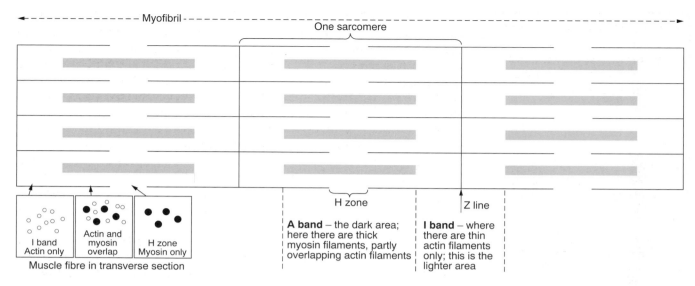

Muscle fibre in transverse section

A band – the dark area; here there are thick myosin filaments, partly overlapping actin filaments

I band – where there are thin actin filaments only; this is the lighter area

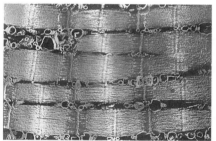

Figure 13.1 Muscle fibre structure

sarcomere. The cytoplasm inside the myofibrils is called **sarcoplasm**, and it has a network of membranes running through it called the **sarcoplasmic reticulum**. Between the fibrils and running transversely across the fibre are tubules called **T tubules**. These store and release calcium ions, affecting contraction. This structure of overlapping myofilaments is the key to the way that muscle fibres contract.

13.3 How muscles contract

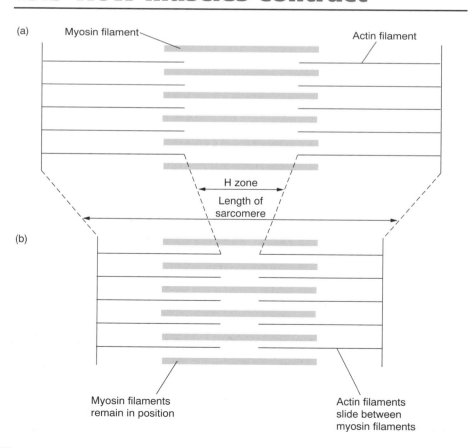

Figure 13.2 (a) A relaxed sarcomere
(b) A contracted sarcomere

Muscle contraction is thought to occur through a ratchet mechanism between actin and myosin filaments. This is called the sliding filament theory.

▶ *Chapter 20.4 describes how nerve impulse transmission stimulates muscle action, through the muscle end plates*

▶ *Chapter 25 describes respiration and the formation of ATP*

When scientists first started investigating muscle action with the help of electron microscopes, they discovered, as is shown in Figure 13.2 (a) and (b), that only one of the bands changes length during contraction. The light I bands get shorter, as does the H zone. This discovery and further research gave rise to the currently accepted theory called the **sliding filament theory**. As the name suggests, the main idea of this theory is that the actin filaments slide in between the myosin filaments, linked by bridges on the myosin filaments. During contraction these bridges attach, detach and re-attach up to 100 times per second, similar to a ratchet mechanism. Scientists know from mixing actin and myosin in the laboratory that this is an active process that uses energy transferred by ATP; if this is done without ATP nothing happens, but with ATP the actin and myosin form a new protein called **actomyosin**. Another feature of muscle contraction is that calcium ions must also be present.

The sliding filament theory is summarised in Figure 13.3. ATP is formed by oxidative phosphorylation of glucose. Glucose is supplied by converting the store of glycogen in muscle cells. In the presence of phosphocreatine, ATP re-forms from ADP and P.

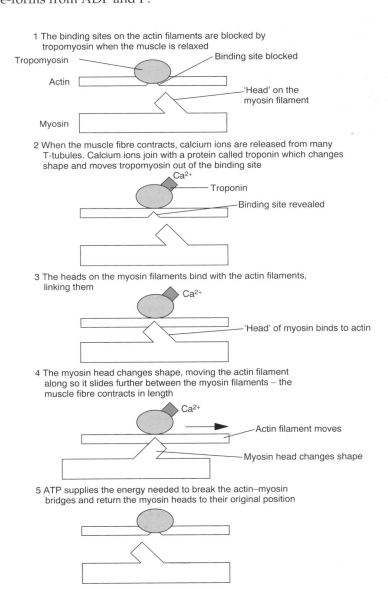

1 The binding sites on the actin filaments are blocked by tropomyosin when the muscle is relaxed

Tropomyosin — Binding site blocked

Actin — 'Head' on the myosin filament

Myosin

2 When the muscle fibre contracts, calcium ions are released from many T-tubules. Calcium ions join with a protein called troponin which changes shape and moves tropomyosin out of the binding site

Ca^{2+} — Troponin — Binding site revealed

3 The heads on the myosin filaments bind with the actin filaments, linking them

Ca^{2+} — 'Head' of myosin binds to actin

4 The myosin head changes shape, moving the actin filament along so it slides further between the myosin filaments – the muscle fibre contracts in length

Ca^{2+} — Actin filament moves — Myosin head changes shape

5 ATP supplies the energy needed to break the actin–myosin bridges and return the myosin heads to their original position

Figure 13.3 The sliding filament theory

(a)

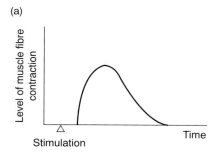

(b)

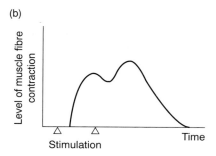

(c)

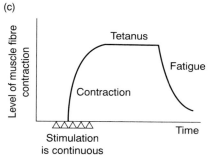

Figure 13.4 (a) A single twitch
(b) Summation of stimuli (c) Tetanus and
fatigue

Muscles can respire both
aerobically and anaerobically.
Muscle cramps happen because
of the accumulation of lactate
which is produced during
anaerobic respiration in muscle
fibres.

13.4 Adjusting muscular response

Carrying a tiny baby does not take as much effort as carrying some heavy
shopping and therefore does not require as much muscle action. How is the
amount of muscle action controlled? Logic tells us that both of the following
factors are important:

- the number of muscle fibres which are excited to contract;
- the frequency of stimulation of a muscle fibre.

A single muscle fibre can be investigated by stimulating it with a tiny
electric shock. The findings are summarised in Figure 13.4. A single
contraction is called a **twitch**. A small stimulus may be below a **threshold
level** which is needed to cause contraction, in which case nothing happens.
But if a stimulus is large enough it will cause a single twitch. However much
above the threshold a single stimulus is, the twitch is always the same size.
This is called the **all or nothing** rule. However, if a second stimulus is used
before the muscle fibre has completely relaxed it will twitch again, making it
even shorter. If the two stimuli are very close together their effect adds up
(known as **summation**), and it looks as if one large contraction has
happened. Many rapid stimuli make a muscle fibre completely contracted.
This condition is called **tetanus**, but cannot be sustained by a muscle fibre
which will eventually fatigue. Many of the muscles involved in maintaining
posture are in tetanus, but as we generally keep moving the activity keeps
changing between sets of fibres.

13.5 Exercise and oxygen debt

Working muscles require energy which is transferred during **respiration** of a
food substrate. Respiration is explained in more detail in Chapters 25 and 26,
but the main point is that food is broken down, transferring energy to **ATP**,
which can then be used as an energy source for other cellular processes. At
rest, humans expend about 0.36 MJ (megajoules) of energy per hour, but
during increased physical activity energy expenditure can rise by 25–75 per
cent. In other words, active muscles are actively respiring. An intense
sporting activity such as a 100 metre sprint demands a huge and rapid
energy supply. This is funded by respiring the glycogen stores in muscle.
The glycogen is easily converted to glucose and then, via a series of chemical
reactions, to pyruvate. What happens next depends on the amount of
oxygen available. If there is plenty of oxygen the pyruvate is fully oxidised
during **aerobic respiration**. If oxygen availability is limited (called **anaerobic**
conditions), the pyruvate changes to lactate. Lactate is toxic and accumulates
in the muscles causing pain, which is what usually persuades people to stop
what they are doing. When sufficient oxygen is available to pay back the
oxygen debt the lactate breaks down further, through aerobic respiration.
Carbohydrates are more readily respired than fats, because fat first has to be
taken out of fat stores. Also, fats can only be respired aerobically.

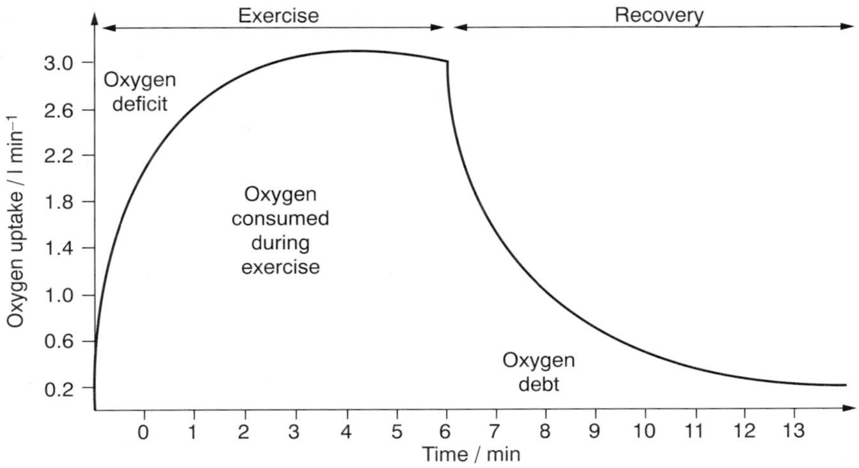

Figure 13.5 The breathing system responds rapidly at the start of a period of exercise, but is not able to keep up with increased demand for oxygen. This means that there is a lack of oxygen in the active tissues such as muscle, and they respire anaerobically, causing a build up of lactic acid. During the recovery phase the breathing rate remains raised until the lactic acid has been removed, by supplying enough oxygen to respire it fully. This is what is meant by an oxygen debt.

Figure 13.6 Lifting these heavy loads involves the action of slow twitch muscle fibres, and probably experiencing pain due to the accumulation of lactate, however, no pain – no gaining the prize!

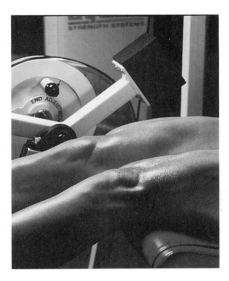

Table 13.2 Supplying energy, aerobically and anaerobically

Respiration	Oxygen supply	Substrate for respiration	Type of activity
aerobic	adequate	fats carbohydrates	low intensity and early stages of strenuous activity
anaerobic	limited	carbohydrates	intense, and late stages of low intensity

Questions

1 What type of muscle tissue:

   a) is found between the ribs?

   b) makes up the heart?

   c) is in the walls of arterioles?

   d) forms the iris of the eye?

   e) moves the fingers?

   f) pushes food through the gut?

2 Explain why the distribution of fast and slow twitch muscle fibres depends on the type of activity a muscle is involved in.

3 What are the roles of each of the following in muscle contraction:

a) myosin?

b) actin?

c) tropomyosin?

d) troponin?

e) T-tubules and the sarcoplasmic reticulum?

f) calcium ions?

g) ATP?

h) phosphocreatine?

4 a) Why are fats slower to be metabolised than carbohydrates?

b) What is the main source of carbohydrate for respiration in muscle cells?

13.6 Get in training

Exercising has both immediate and long-term effects on body systems. For example the cardiovascular and respiratory systems (co-ordinated by the nervous system) respond to exercise in the short-term, by increasing heart rate and breathing rate. Section 3 covers the control of these processes as part of the concept of homeostasis. Longer term effects include an improvement in circulation and the possible reduction in the level of cholesterol in the blood plasma. A further effect of regular exercise is the increase in and maintenance of bone density, mentioned in Chapter 12. The skeletal system also experiences a general increase in mobility and flexibility.

Apart from this, muscle tone increases and also muscle strength, which is proportional to the cross-sectional area of a muscle. Exercise can increase muscle size by up to 60 per cent, mostly because of an increase in diameter of individual fibres, as well as an increase in their number. More glycogen, fat and phosphocreatine are stored, and the level of myoglobin increases so that more oxygen is stored. There is also an increase in the number and size of mitochondria within the fibres, so that respiration happens faster. Therefore an athlete relies less on anaerobic exercise and produces less lactate. Exercise increases the proportion of muscle to other tissues and hence increases energy usage. Fats are more easily mobilised from stores, so fit people use up more fat during exercise than unfit people. Muscles working at or close to their maximum contracting force will gain in strength very quickly. Just a few minutes exercise regularly is enough to maintain this strength.

Clearly, there are times when damage to the skeletal or nervous system can happen during exercise. But generally this is due to accidental injury in a contact sport or because there has been little preparation (called 'warming up'). If any activity is taken to extremes then stresses on certain areas of the body result. However, there is little doubt that moderate and regular exercise undertaken with a gradual build up to fitness has enormous benefits and prolongs the active phase of life.

Exam questions for Section 2

1 From the blood of cattle, which is readily available from slaughter houses, an American company has produced purified haemoglobin stored in the form of a frozen liquid. The company hopes its product will be given to humans who have lost blood. It will serve as a temporary blood substitute, allowing patients time to make more blood of their own.

a) Suggest *two* advantages of this treatment by comparison with transfusion of whole human blood. *(2 marks)*

b) Suggest *two* disadvantages of this treatment by comparison with transfusion of whole human blood. *(2 marks)*

AEB Specimen Question

2 The graph in Figure 1 shows the oxygen dissociation curve for the pigment haemoglobin in a human. The loading tension is the partial pressure of oxygen at which 95% of the pigment is saturated with oxygen. The unloading tension is the partial pressure at which 50% of the pigment is saturated with oxygen.

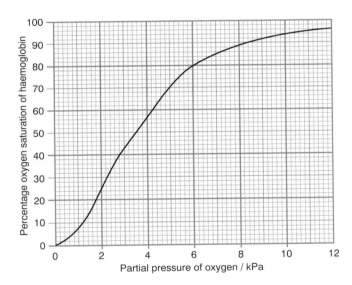

Figure 1

a) Explain why haemoglobin is an efficient respiratory pigment. *(2 marks)*

b) i) From the graph determine the difference between the loading and unloading tensions of the haemoglobin. Show your working. *(2 marks)*

ii) Give *one* location in the human body where partial pressures lower than the unloading tension may be reached. Give a reason for your answer. *(2 marks)*

c) Suggest what effects increasing concentrations of carbon dioxide in the blood would have on the loading and unloading tensions of human haemoglobin. Give reasons for your answers. *(4 marks)*

d) The oxygen dissociation curve for fetal haemoglobin lies to the left of the curve for adult haemoglobin. Suggest an explanation for this difference. *(2 marks)*

e) State *three* ways in which carbon dioxide is transported in the blood. *(3 marks)*

Edexcel

3 The drawing in Figure 2 has been made from a slide of skeletal muscle tissue seen with a light microscope at a magnification of 800 times. It shows part of two motor units.

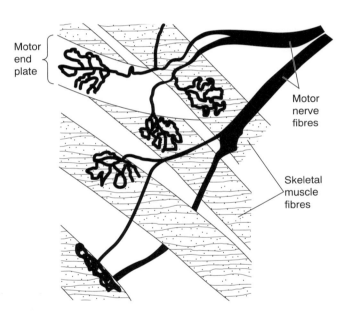

Figure 2

a) Use evidence from the drawing to suggest:

i) A meaning for the term *motor unit*. *(1 mark)*

ii) Why all the muscle fibres shown will not necessarily contract at the same time. *(1 mark)*

b) Briefly describe the sequence of events at the muscle end plate which leads to an action potential passing along the muscle fibre. *(3 marks)*

Figure 3 shows the pathways by which energy is produced for muscle contraction. Numbers 1 to 3 indicate the order in which the various pathways are called on to supply ATP as muscular effort increases.

Table 1

Characteristic	Slow twitch fibre	Fast twitch fibre
contraction time/milliseconds	110	50
mitochondria	many present	relatively few
glycogen store	low	high
myosin ATPase activity	low	high
capillaries	many present	fewer present
sarcoplasmic reticulum	poorly developed	well developed
rate of fatigue	slow	fast

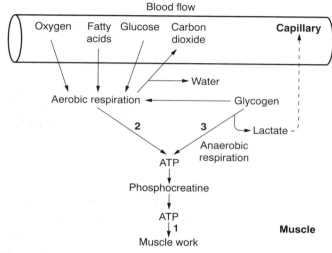

Figure 3

a) i) What happens to the lactate produced in pathway 3? *(3 marks)*

ii) Explain the part played by phosphocreatine in supplying energy to the muscle. *(2 marks)*

Most muscles contain both slow twitch and fast twitch fibres but the proportion of each depends on the function of the muscle as a whole. Table 1 lists some differences between slow twitch and fast twitch muscle fibres.

d) Suggest why muscles concerned with maintaining the posture of the body might be expected to have a large proportion of slow twitch fibres. *(2 marks)*

e) Explaining your answer in each case, give *two* pieces of evidence from Table 1 which:

i) suggest that fast twitch fibres may easily build up an oxygen debt. *(4 marks)*

ii) might account for the difference in speed of contraction of the two types of fibre. *(4 marks)*

AEB Specimen Question

4 In an investigation of the relationship between sodium intake and blood pressure, 537 hospital patients over the age of 39 were questioned about their salt intake.

Each patient's salt intake was assessed on a scale from 0 to 6. Patients who took no added salt with their meals were assessed as 0, those who took added salt with all meals at 6. Salt intake was then considered in relation to the patients' mean systolic blood pressure. The results are shown in Table 2.

Table 2

Salt intake	Mean systolic blood pressure (kPa)	Standard deviation
0	18.4	0.53
1.5	18.7	0.67
3.5	19.6	0.53
5.5	20.1	0.40

a) Describe and comment on the relationship between salt intake and systolic blood pressure in Table 2. *(3 marks)*

b) Comment on the significance of the standard deviation values. *(2 marks)*

c) i) Explain why the scale used as a measure of salt intake in this investigation gives only an approximate indication of each patient's sodium intake. *(3 marks)*

ii) Discuss how the nature of the population sampled in this investigation may affect the interpretation of the results. *(3 marks)*

Edexcel

Table 3

Rate of energy expenditure (J min⁻¹ kg⁻¹)	Rate of oxygen consumption (cm³ min⁻¹ kg⁻¹)		(mg min⁻¹ kg⁻¹)	Rate of lactic acid production	
	athletes	non-athletes		athletes	non-athletes
600	30	29		0	0
800	40	39		0	0
1000	50	44		0	185
1200	57	45		85	350
1400	58	45		305	590

Adapted from Margaria, Scientific American (226:3)

5 An investigation was carried out into the effects of athletic training on respiration in human muscle.

In the investigation, a group of trained athletes and a control group of non-athletes exercised at different levels. The levels of exercise were expressed as rates of energy expenditure in J min⁻¹ kg⁻¹ of body mass. At each level, oxygen consumption and lactic acid production were measured, and converted into rates per kg of body mass.

The results are shown in Table 3. Figures in Table 3 are the means of the measurements made for each group.

a) i) Compare and comment on the effects of increasing the levels of exercise on rates of oxygen consumption in athletes and non-athletes.

(3 marks)

ii) Compare and comment on the effects of increasing the levels of exercise on rates of lactic acid production in athletes and non-athletes.

(3 marks)

b) Suggest how training may alter the muscles of athletes to bring about these differences in muscle respiration.

(5 marks)

Edexcel

6 All the cells in the blood come from just one type of cell, the *multipotential stem cell*. When the stem cell divides one of the two daughter cells may go on to give rise to other types of cell, whereas the other daughter cell remains a stem cell.

Adapted from The Triumph of the Embryo, Wolpert 1991

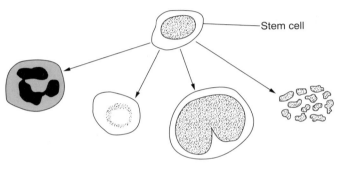

Stem cell

Figure 4

a) Suggest *one* region of the body where the stem cells referred to in the above extract are formed.

(1 mark)

b) Name *two* types of blood cells that are phagocytic.

(2 marks)

c) Which cellular component of blood begins the process of blood clotting? *(1 mark)*

d) Suggest why, when a stem cell divides, it is important that one daughter cell remains a stem cell. *(1 mark)*

Edexcel

7 Stem cells in the bone marrow divide to form reticulocytes, which are immature red blood cells. They have no nucleus, but retain the remains of some RNA in their cytoplasm. Some of these reticulocytes leave the bone marrow before becoming fully developed red blood cells.

a) State *two* consequences of red blood cells lacking a nucleus. *(2 marks)*

Samples of blood were taken from two Peruvians, one living at sea level and the other at high altitude (approximately 5000 metres). The number of all red blood cells, including reticulocytes, was counted in each sample of blood. The number of reticulocytes was also counted. The concentration of haemoglobin in the blood samples was measured in mg per 100 mm³ whole blood. The release of new red blood cells from the bone marrow of each person was estimated.

A small quantity of each blood sample was placed into a capillary tube and spun in a centrifuge to measure the percentage of the total blood volume occupied by red blood cells and reticulocytes (haematocrit). The results of this test are shown in Figure 5.

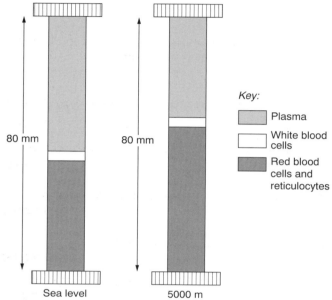

80 mm   80 mm

Key:

- Plasma
- White blood cells
- Red blood cells and reticulocytes

Sea level   5000 m

Figure 5

Table 4 compares the result for the blood samples from the two Peruvians.

b) Complete Table 4 by calculating the haematocrit of the blood sample for the Peruvian living at 5000 metres. *(1 mark)*

The percentage of reticulocytes among the red blood cells of the Peruvian living at sea level is 0.36%.

c) i) Calculate the percentage of reticulocytes among the red blood cells in the Peruvian living at 5000 metres. Show your working. *(2 marks)*

ii) With reference to the information given about the two blood samples, explain how the haemoglobin concentration is raised in people living at high altitude. *(4 marks)*

iii) Explain why this high concentration is necessary when living at high altitude. *(3 marks)*

d) Explain briefly how carbon dioxide is transported in the blood. *(3 marks)*

UCLES

8 Diagrams A, B and C in Figure 6 show cross sections of three different types of blood vessel. They are not drawn to the same scale.

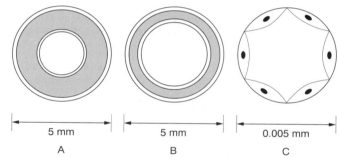

5 mm   5 mm   0.005 mm

A   B   C

Figure 6

a) Identify blood vessels A, B and C. *(3 marks)*

b) State *two* ways in which vessel A is adapted for its functions. *(2 marks)*

Edexcel

Table 4

	Peruvian at sea level	Peruvian at 5000 metres
red cell count/cells mm⁻³	5.0×10^6	6.4×10^6
reticulocytes/cells mm⁻³	1.8×10^4	4.5×10^4
red cell production/no. cells produced per day	2.0×10^{11}	2.6×10^{11}
concentration of haemoglobin/mg 100 mm⁻³ whole blood	15.0	20.0
haematocrit/%	45.0	

9 Figure 7 shows the oxygen dissociation curve of haemoglobin from a mammal at two different temperatures (38 °C and 43 °C).

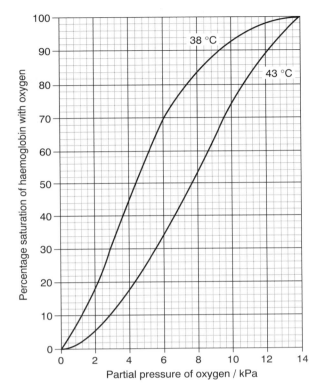

Figure 7

a) i) From the graph find the percentage saturation of haemoglobin in blood from an area of the body where the temperature is 43 °C and the partial pressure of oxygen is 4 kPa. *(1 mark)*

   ii) Blood that is fully (100%) saturated with oxygen carries 105 cm³ of oxygen in 1 dm³ (litre) of blood.

   Calculate the volume of oxygen released from 1 dm³ of blood when blood that has become 90% saturated at 38 °C reaches a part of the body where the temperature is 43°C and the partial pressure of oxygen is 4 kPa. Show your working.
   (3 marks)

b) Suggest how this effect of temperature on the oxygen dissociation curve of haemoglobin might be advantageous to the mammal. *(2 marks)*
   Edexcel

10 Give an account of the structure and functioning of cardiac muscle. *(10 marks)*
   Edexcel

11 a) Describe the features of a gaseous exchange surface. *(5 marks)*

   b) Explain the mechanism of ventilation in humans. *(10 marks)*

   c) Suggest reasons why a management plan for someone with asthma is an effective way of dealing with the condition. *(3 marks)*

12 Why is smoking an important health and social issue? Discuss this question, using scientific facts to support your opinions. *(10 marks)*

13 a) What is meant by the term **tidal volume**? *(1 mark)*

   b) How is ventilation rate calculated? *(1 mark)*

   c) Under what conditions might ventilation rate alter from resting rate? *(3 marks)*

14 Give an account of the functions of the vascular system in humans. *(20 marks)*

15 a) Why does exercise help to maintain health? *5 marks)*

   b) Under what conditions might exercise improve health? *(3 marks)*

   c) Under what conditions might exercise endanger health? *(3 marks)*

   d) Suggest what type of exercise or activity programme might be set up for:

   i) an office worker,

   ii) a six year old child

   iii) a 70 year old man,

   iv) a pregnant woman. *(12 marks)*

SECTION 3
Control and Balance

in brief — Life in a steady state

Living things, such as humans are enormously complex in terms of cellular biochemistry. Many millions of chemical reactions are continually and simultaneously operating. Control systems are the key to the smooth running of such complex beings, as they are needed to successfully integrate the functioning of cells within the whole organism. Section 3 introduces you to the idea of cells and organisms remaining in a steady or balanced state. There is also an opportunity to consider how some of the main life processes are controlled, and how communication happens within the human body.

The cell environment

In simple terms, a cell is the smallest functional unit of life. However, cells do not exist in isolation, they interact with their environment and are sensitive to changes within it. The conditions surrounding a cell are called the external cell environment. These conditions are important, since an external change can cause a change within the cell itself – to the internal cell environment. For example, to function properly cells require particular concentrations of glucose, but are damaged by the build up of toxins such as waste products. Fluctuations in pH and temperature directly affect how enzymes work, and therefore indirectly affect the chemical reactions which enzymes catalyse.

So to what extent can cells control conditions within their internal environment? A cell membrane partly controls which substances enter and leave a cell, because some substances move through the membrane more easily than others. Therefore membranes are said to be partially permeable. The permeability of cell membranes varies under the influence of hormones, or ion concentrations.

Since enzymes catalyse chemical reactions in a cell, the level of a particular metabolite depends on the production of the relevant enzymes. By 'switching on or off' the genes that act as a code for the production of certain enzymes, the level of metabolites can be controlled at the cellular level.

▶ *Section 1 describes cells and enzymes*

Regulating body conditions

In multicellular organisms such as humans, cells work together as tissues and organs, each part being affected by its immediate environment. However, it is also important to consider how any fluctuations in the external environment of an organism may affect its overall functioning. The ability to regulate the internal environment of the body despite fluctuations in the external environment is called homeostasis. Homeostasis gives a degree of independence from external factors such as climate, and extends the range of conditions in which the organisms can function and survive.

▶ *Section 6 considers human adaptation to the external environment*

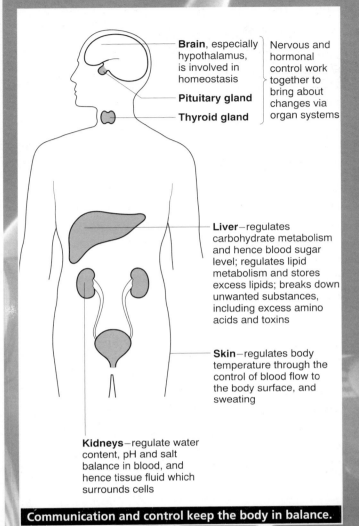

Communication and control keep the body in balance.

Chemical and nervous co-ordination

Two communication systems help to co-ordinate activities within the body and bring about control: chemical co-ordination and nervous co-ordination. Chemical co-ordination involves hormones. Hormones circulate in the blood and act as chemical messengers. They act where there are specific receptors on cell surfaces which they can lock into. Nervous co-ordination involves the movement of electrical signals called nerve impulses. Generally, chemical co-ordination provides a steady and longer term response to changes, while nervous co-ordination is important for a rapid response.

A model of negative feedback

The human body is a continuously dynamic system. Yet homeostatic mechanisms keep the conditions within the body remarkably constant, each factor controlled to within a very narrow range of values. Negative feedback plays a vital part in homeostasis. The key point is that the product of a series of chemical reactions (e.g. a hormone from a gland) 'feeds back' and reduces the production of the same substance. Chapter 14.3 gives an example of negative feedback in the control of blood sugar level, and other examples are covered elsewhere.

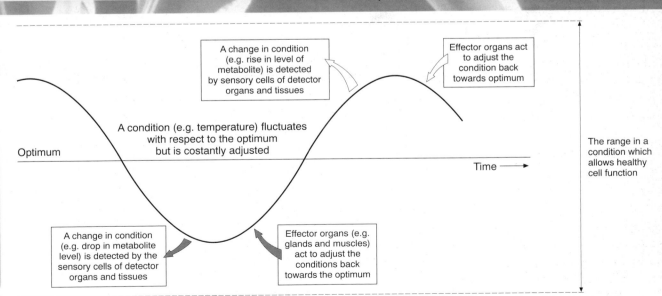

This model shows the basic principle of negative feedback.

CHAPTER 14

How Homeostasis Works – Controlling Blood Glucose Level

14.1 Blood glucose – supply and demand

> The input of glucose to the blood fluctuates continuously. The liver helps in regulating blood sugar level.

> ► *Section 4 describes nutrition and respiration*

> The rate of cellular respiration and demand for glucose fluctuates, which affects the blood glucose level.

Humans eat a variety of foods, which are sources of energy and raw materials. Digested foods are absorbed into the bloodstream and then move around the body in circulating blood. One of the digested foods contained in blood is glucose, which can be drawn upon as and when it is required to fund the body's energy needs. The liver is the main organ controlling the level of glucose in the blood, which involves the hormones insulin and glucagon. This is an example of homeostasis since the glucose level in blood is regulated close to a set point, from which it fluctuates continuously.

In the UK, on average about 45 per cent of our diet is carbohydrate. The carbohydrates we eat may include sugars, starch and cellulose. Carbohydrates such as maltose, fructose, starch, and to a very limited extent cellulose, are converted to glucose during digestion. Therefore the fluctuation in input of glucose to the blood is influenced by both the amount and type of carbohydrate we eat.

Glucose is oxidised during **cellular respiration** and broken down into carbon dioxide and water. During this complex series of chemical reactions, energy transfers from glucose to ATP. Some body activities, for example rigorous exercise such as rowing, demand a greater energy supply than other activities, such as watching television. This means that the rate of cellular respiration varies, affecting how fast cells take up glucose from the blood. The liver has to cope with the fluctuation in demand for glucose, as well as supply.

Questions

1 In what way is the effect on blood sugar level likely to be different for someone who eats a piece of toast compared to if they eat a chocolate bar?

2 Why are starchy snacks such as a baked potato more sustaining as an energy source than sugary foods such as biscuits or sweets?

3 What other main food type, apart from carbohydrate, provides energy in the foods shown in Table 14.1?

Table 14.1 Analysis of some fast foods (Source: Bender and Bender Food Tables)

Fast food	Energy (kJ)	Fat (g)	Sodium (mg)	Fibre (g)
Burger King hamburger	1220	13	525	n/a
Burger King regular French fries	880	11	230	n/a
Kentucky Fried Chicken, one piece	920	14	n/a	n/a
Kentucky Fried Chicken jacket potato (200 g)	630	0.8	n/a	n/a
Little Chef's chef's grill	4330	67	n/a	n/a
McDonald's hamburger	1090	9.8	400	n/a
McDonald's Big Mac	2270	28	1000	n/a
McDonald's regular fries	1220	16	290	n/a
Pizzaland deep pan cheese and tomato pizza	4870	6.3	n/a	n/a
Wendy hamburger, single	1970	26	770	n/a
Wendy French fries	1390	16	110	n/a
Wimpy hamburger	1010	9.4	600	1.8
Wimpy fish and chips	2060	23	240	3.2

Note: all amounts given are contained in one standard portion of the fast food. n/a indicates that data for these contents were unavailable.

14.2 Blood glucose level and cellular function

> **Chapter 4.2** deals with osmosis and water potential

> **Chapter 16** describes the processes involved in osmoregulation

Regulating blood glucose level is vital, because glucose in blood plasma and tissue fluid affects the water relations of cells.

Blood plasma moves out of blood capillaries forming the liquid around cells, which is called **tissue fluid**. Glucose is dissolved in blood plasma and in tissue fluid, lowering the water potential of these liquids. As the level of glucose in tissue fluid rises above a certain level, the water potential outside cells becomes *lower* than the water potential inside them. At this stage, water is lost from cells into the tissue fluid surrounding them, and then into the blood capillaries by osmosis. This can result in cellular damage.

When the blood glucose level is too high, the condition is called **hyperglycaemia**. **Hypoglycaemia** is the condition in which blood glucose level is too low. Body tissues and the brain in particular are very intolerant of a low blood glucose level. If there is insufficient energy supply to the brain in the form of glucose, a person becomes unconscious, passing into a coma. Unless treatment is rapid, death follows. Equally, a high blood glucose level can be dangerous.

14.3 The liver as a regulator

The liver has a vital role to play in controlling the blood glucose level to within 80–100 mg per 100 ml (equivalent to 4–6 mmol dm^{-3}), and ultimately in maintaining life. How does it keep such a close control on blood glucose level, when the supply and demand varies tremendously? A simple model is that the blood acts as a reserve or a pool of glucose, and that glucose is added to or drawn out of this pool as necessary. Insulin and glucagon are chemical co-ordinators in this process, necessary for the liver cells to bring about the regulation of glucose in the blood. Both these hormones are produced by the pancreas. Keeping the level of glucose within a narrow range mainly involves:

- converting excess glucose in the blood to a store (glycogen or lipid) when the level rises *above* the optimum;
- converting stored glycogen or lipid to glucose when the level of glucose in the blood drops *below* the optimum.

Proteins make up much of every cell in the body. When blood glucose and glycogen reserves are used up, proteins may be broken down and respired. This process is called **protein catabolism**, which is a strategy for surviving starvation but leads to a breakdown of the tissues themselves.

> Glucose and glycogen are interconvertible. The rate and direction of interconversion depends on the supply of glucose, and the demand for it created by respiring cells.

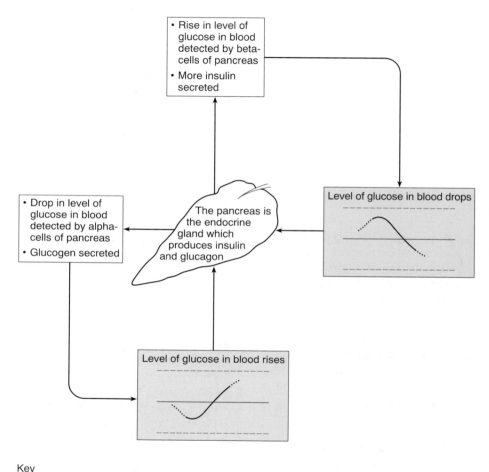

Figure 14.1 Negative feedback systems allow the blood glucose level to be adjusted continuously, maintaining the level close to the optimum

The liver maintains glucose in the blood at a steady level through negative feedback systems involving two hormones: glucagon and insulin (see Figure 14.1). Insulin has the overall effect of causing blood sugar level to decrease, while glucagon has the overall effect of causing an increase. Table 14.2 shows how these effects are brought about by insulin and glucagon.

> ► *Chapter 15.2 gives details of other functions of the liver*

Table 14.2 The effects of insulin and glucagon

Effects	Insulin	Glucagon
rate of cellular respiration	increases	–
conversion of glycogen to glucose	–	increases
conversion of glucose to glycogen	increases	–
uptake of glucose by cells (particularly muscle)	increases	–
rate of conversion of glucose to fat	increases	–
rate of conversion of amino acids to glucose	–	increases

Cortisol is a steroid hormone produced by the outer layer of the adrenal gland. It has a wide variety of functions, some of which influence the level of glucose in blood plasma, generally causing an increase. Cortisol stimulates the production of glucose from amino acids and glycogen production in the liver, as well as inhibiting uptake of glucose by the cells of some tissues.

14.4 Receptors and hormone action

In order to have an effect on a cell, a hormone has to bind to a receptor site on the cell surface membrane. The cells of different tissues and organs have specific receptor sites. For example, only cells in the liver have receptor sites for glucagon. This means that the liver is a **target organ** for glucagon. On the other hand, most body cells have receptors for insulin. So insulin acts on most cells, binding with the surface membrane and making it more permeable to glucose. It is important to remember that chemical reactions such as those involved in the conversion of glucose to glycogen are catalysed by enzymes. The biochemical pathway that converts glucose to glycogen is activated in the presence of insulin, whereas the enzymes involved in the conversion of glycogen to glucose are activated in the presence of glucagon.

A target organ has receptors for a particular hormone. Processes within the target organ are initiated or altered in the presence of the hormone.

The islet cells within the pancreas produce insulin and glucagon as required to regulate blood glucose level.

▶ *Chapter 19 covers the endocrine system and chemical co-ordination*

▶ *Chapter 22.3 describes the role of the pancreas*

The pancreas

The pancreas contains cells which are sensitive to blood glucose levels, and produce insulin or glucagon accordingly. These special groups of cells are called the **islets of Langerhans** (see Figure 14.2). There are two types of islet cells. Glucagon is produced by α-islet cells and insulin is produced by β-islet cells. The islet cells are surrounded by other pancreatic cells which produce digestive enzymes.

14.5 Diabetes mellitus

A **diabetic** is a person whose body does not control blood sugar level sufficiently. After a carbohydrate-containing meal the level rises to a point at which the kidneys cannot cope with reabsorbing all the glucose which has been filtered out of the blood plasma. Therefore glucose is lost from the body in urine. In some people diabetes mellitus develops when they are young because the pancreatic cells are not producing insulin, or are not producing enough. This condition is **insulin-dependent** diabetes mellitus, and it occurs because of a genetic mutation, which can be inherited. In this case the usual

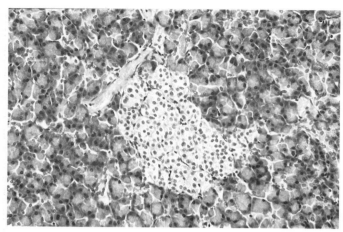

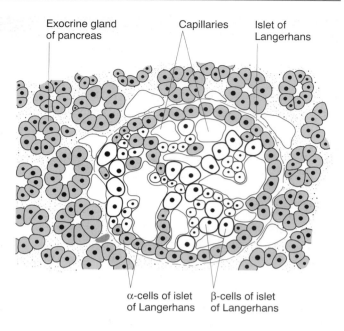

Exocrine gland of pancreas Capillaries Islet of Langerhans

α-cells of islet of Langerhans β-cells of islet of Langerhans

Figure 14.2 The pancreas produces many secretions. It acts as an **endocrine gland** in producing insulin and glucagon which pass directly into blood. It acts as an **exocrine gland** when digestive secretions are discharged through the pancreatic duct into the duodenum. *(See Colour Gallery page 350)*

C15

treatment is to give insulin by regular injection into the bloodstream since insulin would be destroyed by digestive enzymes if taken orally. A diabetic learns to inject themselves and regulates how much insulin is needed according to their diet and activities each day. Some long-term effects are as yet unavoidable, even so, a diabetic can lead a perfectly normal, active life. Diabetes mellitus can also develop in adults if there is insufficient secretion of insulin due to ageing. Controlling diet, mostly by avoiding sugary foods, is usually sufficient to deal with diabetes which starts late in life.

In some people, body cells seem to lack insulin receptors and they fail to 'recognise' insulin, so although insulin is produced it does not have the desired effect. This is called **insulin-independent** diabetes. Again, dietary control may form part of the treatment, but medicines may also be used to increase tissue function and the uptake of glucose by cells. Some of the symptoms of diabetes mellitus include thirst, the production of a large volume of dilute urine and loss of body mass.

Diabetes in pregnancy

During pregnancy, glucose may appear in a woman's urine, even though its level in her blood is within the normal range. The reason for this seems to be that the kidneys are not as efficient at absorbing glucose from the glomerular filtrate. This is a temporary condition which is not a health hazard, and glucose disappears from the mother's urine soon after the birth of her baby.

However, **gestational diabetes** (meaning diabetes in pregnancy) is true diabetes, since the woman has a raised level of glucose in her urine *and* in her blood. The condition is treated either with insulin or by a change of diet. Gestational diabetes does not remain after the birth of the baby, and the mother's blood glucose level returns to normal. The baby may have a larger than average mass at birth and occasionally may be hypoglycaemic. Later, the baby's own homeostatic mechanisms restore its blood glucose level to normal.

Insulin patches might save the daily needle

The chemical structure of insulin (Figure 14.3) was determined in 1950 by Frederick Sanger. It is a short chain polypeptide containing 51 amino acids. If it enters the body by mouth it is digested in the same way as other proteins in the diet. This means that the only way of using insulin at present is to inject it directly into the body. This is a straightforward procedure, but not pleasant – particularly for children or for people with a needle phobia. What's more, it requires hygienic handling of a daily supply of syringes and the medication itself.

Now there may be a better alternative for getting insulin into the body. Scientists have been experimenting with the use of ultrasound and skin patches. A skin area is first treated with ultrasound to disrupt underlying fat tissue. This is necessary because insulin is water soluble, so disrupting the fat tissue allows it to move in through the skin more easily. The patch containing insulin is then applied to the area, and can supply insulin for several days.

Source: *New Scientist*, 19 August 1996

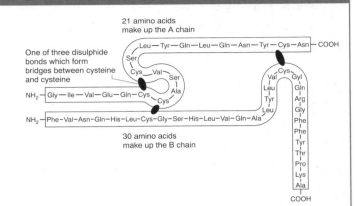

Figure 14.3

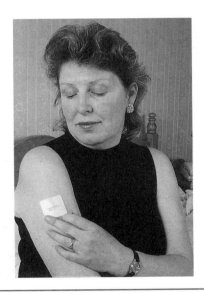

Figure 14.4 Applying a patch may soon replace the need for daily injections for diabetics

14.6 Adrenaline – the 'fight, fright or flight' hormone

Adrenaline is another hormone which raises blood sugar level. It is produced by the adrenal glands and by some nerve endings. Adrenaline is usually produced in response to stress, such as fear or aggression. The biological significance is that a surge of adrenaline releases glucose into the blood which can be rapidly taken up by cells and respired. This provides a boost of energy which makes instant activity (such as fighting or running away) more easily possible.

CHAPTER 15 The Liver

15.1 Structure of the liver

The liver is a large and very important organ involved in regulating many metabolic activities, particularly those which help to maintain the blood composition in a steady state. It is richly supplied with blood directly from the systemic circulation through the hepatic artery, as well as from the gut via the hepatic portal vein (Figure 15.1). It makes up a substantial proportion of human body mass at birth, and three to five per cent in adults (because other parts of the body grow more in relation to the liver). It is attached by ligaments below the diaphragm to the right hand side of the upper abdomen. The liver has several lobes surrounded by a two-layered capsule. The outer layer is smooth and moist which allows the liver to change position slightly within the abdomen as the body moves, without frictional damage occurring. The inner layer is fibrous and helps to support the liver tissues.

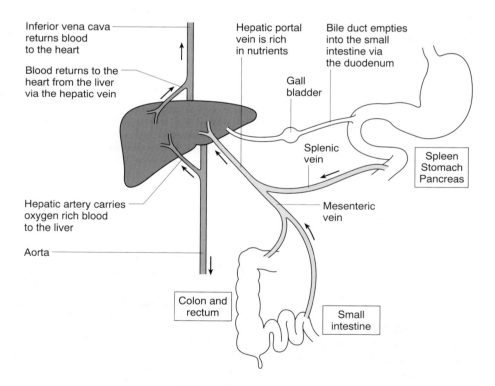

Figure 15.1 The position and blood supply of the human liver

Liver cells are called **hepatocytes** and they are arranged in sheets like vertical walls, often only one cell thick. Seen through the microscope, the hepatocytes look like strings of cells radiating out from a central vein. They lie between **sinusoids** containing the blood supply and channels called **bile canaliculi**, which collect the bile as it forms. These blocks of cells make up many **lobules**, which are each about 1 mm in diameter. Lymph capillaries and nerve fibres run alongside the blood supply.

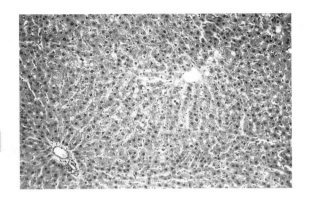

Figure 15.2 Rows of hepatocytes within the liver lobules can be seen clearly using a light microscope (*See Colour Gallery page 351*)

C16

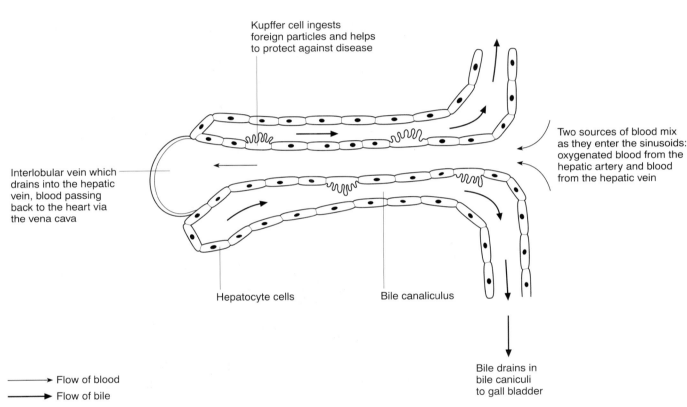

Kupffer cell ingests foreign particles and helps to protect against disease

Two sources of blood mix as they enter the sinusoids: oxygenated blood from the hepatic artery and blood from the hepatic vein

Interlobular vein which drains into the hepatic vein, blood passing back to the heart via the vena cava

Hepatocyte cells

Bile canaliculus

Bile drains in bile caniculi to gall bladder

Flow of blood
Flow of bile

Figure 15.3 The layout of cells within a liver lobule

> Liver cells are called hepatocytes. They are very active metabolically and have numerous mitochondria. Kupfer cells are phagocytic and engulf bacteria and debris.

Liver cells are very active, and their structure reflects this, as every cell is packed with mitochondria and has prominent Golgi bodies and a large nucleus. The faces of the hepatocytes in contact with the blood in the sinusoids are folded into many microvilli, providing a relatively enormous surface area. Within the cytoplasm are numerous glycogen granules, fat droplets and lysosomes. There are more specialised cells called **Kupfer cells** in the lining of the sinusoids. These are phagocytic cells which change shape as they ingest debris and bacteria, and help to defend against disease.

The blood mixes as it enters the sinusoids from branches of the hepatic artery and hepatic portal vein. The direction of flow of blood in the sinusoids and the bile in the canaliculi is opposite, the blood flowing inwards towards the centre of a lobule. This type of counter flow system helps to maintain a diffusion gradient, because materials that diffuse into the blood are rapidly carried away. The blood in the hepatic portal vein carries soluble food substances such as glucose and amino acids from the alimentary canal, while the hepatic artery brings the oxygen supply needed by such active cells. The lymph capillaries carry lipids from the intestines to the liver. Materials exchange between the blood and hepatocytes as the blood flows through the liver lobules. The liver cells take up oxygen and food substances as well as other metabolites and toxins. Substances such as heparin which are made by the hepatocytes but destined for use elsewhere in the body, pass into the blood from the cells. Apart from the large surface area, the cell membranes have pores up to 10 nm in diameter, which facilitate this exchange. **Bile** which is produced by hepatocytes passes into the bile canaliculi and finally drains into the gall bladder, which is a temporary storage area. From here the bile empties into the duodenum via the bile duct.

15.2 Functions of the liver

> **The liver has numerous functions and is very important in homeostasis.**

The liver has many important functions, and the main ones are summarised in Table 15.1. Its major roles are involved with homeostasis (maintaining many substances at levels which are not harmful to the body), storage, secretion and excretion.

The regulatory or homeostatic role of the liver in carbohydrate metabolism is discussed in detail in Chapter 14. However, the functions of the liver in the metabolism of lipid and carbohydrate are closely linked. Initially, excess glucose is converted to glycogen and stored in liver cells. But the liver only has a certain capacity to store glycogen (about 100 g), and once this has been reached, any further glucose absorbed from the small intestine is converted to lipid. Both glycogen granules and lipid droplets are common in liver cells, which can chemically process lipids for transport to other storage areas, such as under the skin.

The liver also makes cholesterol if required. Cholesterol is needed by the body for the formation of cell membranes and in the production of hormones. However, too much cholesterol in the body can cause problems. Cholesterol in the blood stream may deposit on the inside of blood vessels, eventually leading to circulatory problems including hypertension and stroke. Cholesterol may also crystallise in the gall bladder, where bile is temporarily stored, forming gall stones which can block the bile duct and cause a lot of pain.

> ► *Chapter 11.3 describes the link between disease of the cardiovascular system and cholesterol*

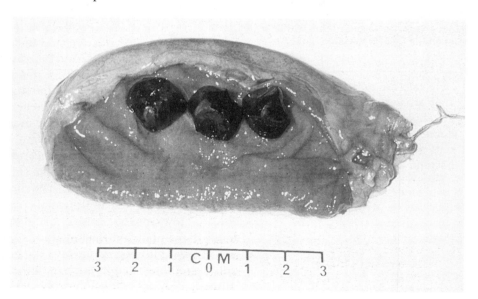

Figure 15.4 These gall stones are quite large enough to block the bile duct

Table 15.1 The main functions of the liver

Function	Comments
carbohydrate metabolism	interconverts glucose and glycogen to regulate blood sugar level and the supply of glucose to the cells; stores glycogen; converts excess carbohydrate to lipid
lipid metabolism	breaks down excess lipid, or modifies it for transport; excretes excess cholesterol in bile and can synthesise it as needed
protein metabolism	breaks down excess amino acids during a process called deamination; changes one type of non-essential amino acid into another (transamination); produces plasma proteins such as albumens, globulins and clotting factors e.g. fibrinogen
bile production	bile contains excretory products from the breakdown of old red blood cells and has a digestive function because it helps to emulsify lipids
storage	minerals such as iron and zinc, and vitamins (A, D, E, K); about 1.5 litres of blood are contained in the liver, but much of it can be diverted into the systemic circulation if there is sudden blood loss
breakdown of hormones	hormones are broken down preventing accumulation; some are excreted in bile, others by the kidneys
detoxification	toxic chemicals such as ethanol and nicotine are broken down and made harmless by chemical conversion; Kupfer cells remove bacteria and cell debris
heat production	metabolic activity in the liver (which has a heating effect) is triggered by the hypothalamus if the body temperature falls

Breaking down and making harmless

A major role of the liver in keeping us alive, is to break down substances which are potentially harmful and toxic. This process is called **detoxification**. Examples of toxins include:

- drugs such as nicotine, alcohol and medicinal drugs
- toxins that are made by the body itself, e.g. hydrogen peroxide a by-product of many metabolic processes
- toxins made by bacteria
- toxins taken into the body with food

▶ *Chapter 7 deals with enzymes*

These toxins are all chemically altered by the liver so that they become harmless. For example, hepatocytes contain the enzyme **catalase**, which breaks down hydrogen peroxide into water and oxygen.

However, hepatocytes are sensitive to toxic substances in the same way that all other body cells are, and exposure to continuous or high levels of some toxins does result in liver damage. For example, paracetamol is a very popular painkiller but it can cause fatal damage to the liver. **Cirrhosis** is an example of such damage in which liver cells are replaced by connective tissue, causing scarring and a reduction in function. Chemical substances such as ethanol and also infection by some viruses and parasites may cause cirrhosis.

Breaking down excess proteins

▶ *Chapter 6 describes biochemicals including proteins*

Proteins are nitrogen-containing compounds composed of sub-units called amino acids. During digestion, proteins are broken down into amino acids which pass from the gut into the bloodstream, and on to the liver via the hepatic portal vein. The body does not store amino acids that are in excess to

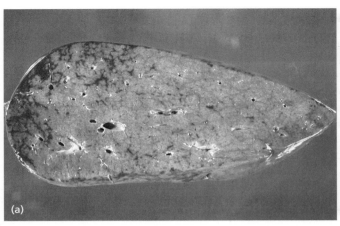

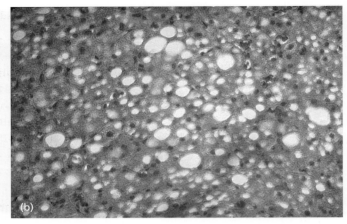

(a)

(b)

Figure 15.5 (a) A bisected normal human liver. (b) A micrograph of a section of liver in which areas of cells have been damaged by severe alcohol abuse

its immediate needs. Instead, the amino group (–NH$_2$) is split from each amino acid and along with a hydrogen atom, forms ammonia (NH$_3$). This oxidative process is called **deamination**.

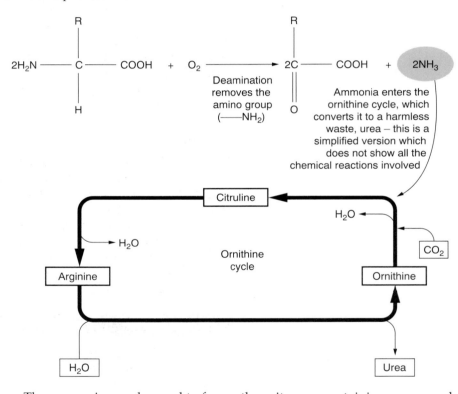

Figure 15.6 Deamination is the removal of an amino group – the ammonia may enter the ornithine cycle

Deamination is the removal of the amino group from excess amino acids, forming ammonia. Excess ammonia is quickly converted to urea and is excreted in urine.

▶ *Chapter 23.2 considers the role of essential amino acids*

The ammonia may be used to form other nitrogen-containing compounds such as bases, which may later become part of nucleotides, or to make different amino acids. However, if the level of ammonia is above the required range it is toxic to cells, and so excess is converted into urea by a cyclic chemical pathway called the **ornithine cycle**.

The urea passes in the bloodstream to the kidney and is filtered out and excreted from the body in urine. The part of the amino acid molecule left once the amino group has been removed is called a **keto acid**. The keto acid is either respired or converted into glycogen. Depending on which amino acids are required, the liver can transfer the amino group from one amino acid to a keto group, producing a different amino acid. This process is called **transamination**. However, there are some essential amino acids which can only be obtained from the diet.

The liver and red blood cells

Red blood cells are made in the liver of a developing fetus, but by the time the baby is born they are being produced in the bone marrow. At the end of their lifespan, erythrocytes are engulfed by the phagocytic Kupfer cells and are broken down. Haemoglobin is split into the haem group and the protein part (globin). Iron from the haem part of the haemoglobin molecule is retained and re-used by the body, and the remainder passes into bile as bile pigments (**bilirubin** and **biliverdin**) and excreted. The globin part of haemoglobin is split into amino acids, which are then processed (see page 139).

Secretion of bile

Bile is an alkaline fluid containing mucus, bile pigments and bile salts. The liver produces about 0.5–1.0 litres of bile per day. Bile, cholesterol and phospholipids are secreted into the region of the small intestine called the duodenum, as particles called **micelles**. Within the micelles, the polar molecules of the bile salts are orientated such that the hydrophilic ends of the molecules face the same direction and attract water. Meanwhile, the hydrophobic ends attract lipid particles. This lowers the surface tension of lipid droplets and they split into smaller droplets. Therefore the essential function of bile is to help cause the formation of an emulsion of soluble lipid droplets with the watery contents of the small intestine, facilitating lipid absorption.

Jaundice

After birth the baby's liver has to deal with an increased workload, including the removal of bile pigments such as bilirubin from the blood. Unless the liver is immediately effective at this, the bilirubin level in the blood increases. This shows as a yellow coloration of the skin and the whites of the eyes, a condition known as jaundice. Jaundice is very common in newly born babies, but generally disappears within the first few days. Excessive bilirubin levels in the blood can cause brain damage, so jaundice is carefully monitored. If necessary, the baby is treated with a broad spectrum light source for a number of hours each day, and the light breaks down the bilirubin.

Questions

1 Glucose is always present in the bloodstream and liver of a carnivorous animal such as a dog, although it does not eat sugar.
   a) Explain why this happens.
   b) What other food stores are found in hepatocytes?
   c) Suggest why hepatocytes might be lacking in food stores?
   d) What happens to glycogen which the liver cannot store?
2 Someone with diabetes mellitus usually injects themselves regularly with the hormone insulin.
   a) Why is insulin injected rather than swallowed?
   b) What other possible treatments might be used for diabetes mellitis?
3 What is the difference between deamination and transamination?
4 A person who accidentally swallowed a toxic substance was treated in hospital. One of their symptoms was jaundice.
   a) What is jaundice?
   b) Suggest why the person was jaundiced after the accident.

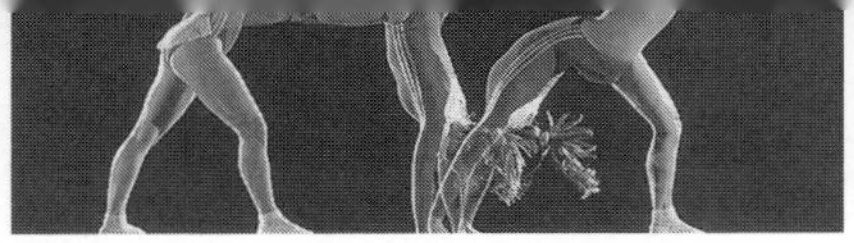

CHAPTER 16

How Homeostasis Works – Controlling Water and Salt Balance

16.1 Water and the body fluids

Water makes up much of the cytoplasm inside cells (**intracellular water**), as well as body fluids such as the tissue fluid around cells, blood plasma and lymph (**extracellular or intercellular water**). Figure 16.1 shows the exchanges that can occur between intracellular water, extracellular water, and the external environment of the body. The extracellular fluid is mostly influenced by exchanges with the external environment, for example at the alveolar surface of the lungs. In turn, the extracellular fluids influence intracellular water content. Receptor cells called **osmoreceptors** detect changes in the composition of extracellular fluid such as blood plasma. They stimulate homeostatic mechanisms to regulate the water and electrolyte content, so that the cell environment does not fluctuate to a damaging extent. The processes that bring about this balance are called **osmoregulation**. Osmoregulation involves changing the rate of output relative to input, for example by increasing urine production or drinking more fluids. The kidneys are mainly responsible for osmoregulation, but they also excrete the urea which is formed in the liver and eliminate other substances from the body such as medicines (e.g. penicillin).

> ► *Chapter 10.1 describes exchanges between plasma, tissue fluid and lymph*

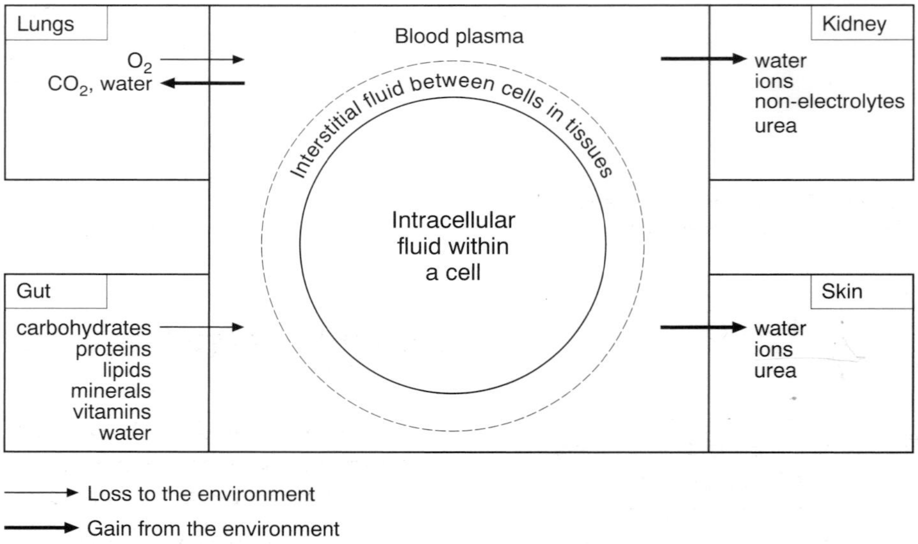

Figure 16.1 Exchanges between intracellular and extracellular fluids and the external body environment

Lungs: O_2; CO_2, water

Blood plasma

Kidney: water, ions, non-electrolytes, urea

Interstitial fluid between cells in tissues

Intracellular fluid within a cell

Gut: carbohydrates, proteins, lipids, minerals, vitamins, water

Skin: water, ions, urea

→ Loss to the environment
➜ Gain from the environment

16.2 The structure of the kidneys

The two kidneys are positioned towards the top of the abdomen, one on either side of the vertebral column. Often they are embedded in fat for protection. The right kidney is a little lower than the left because the liver displaces it slightly. A human kidney weighs around 140 g and receives blood from a branch of the aorta called the renal artery. Blood leaves the kidney via the renal vein which drains into the vena cava from the lower part of the body. The kidney has a nerve supply from the autonomic nervous system. The ureter carries urine from the kidney to the bladder. Figure 16.2 shows the external and overall internal appearance of a kidney. A kidney is comprised of about a million tiny tubules called **nephrons** and many blood capillaries. Notice the clearly defined outer **cortex** region which contains the start of each nephron: the **Bowman's capsule** with **glomerulus**, and sections called **convoluted tubules**. The inner medulla contains longer lengths of tubules called the **loop of Henle** and **collecting ducts** and more blood capillaries. The medulla tissue projects like several pyramids into the part of the kidney where the ureter arises, which is called the **pelvis**.

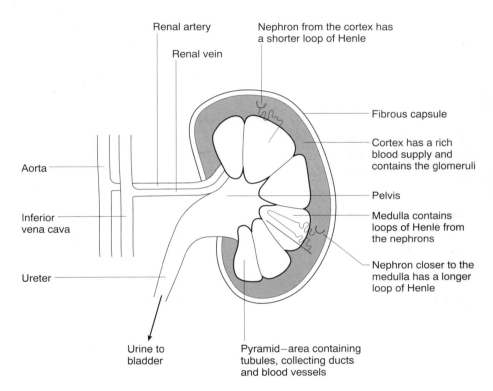

Figure 16.2 The human kidney is 7–10 cm long and 2.5–4 cm wide

The ultrastructure of the kidney related to function

To understand how the kidney works, it is important to know a little about the structure of a nephron and its blood supply, which is shown in Figure 16.3. The main stages in osmoregulation are:

- **ultrafiltration** which happens in the glomerulus and Bowman's capsule;
- **selective reabsorption** which happens in the proximal convoluted tubule;
- **tubular secretion** by the distal convoluted tubule.

The loop of Henle is vital in osmoregulation because it concentrates the urine, conserving water. The mechanism for concentration of the filtrate is called the **countercurrent multiplier hypothesis**, and is described further on in this chapter.

> Ultrafiltration is due to blood pressure forcing substances out of blood plasma into the Bowman's capsule. Selective reabsorption is the reabsorption of useful substances back into blood plasma in the proximal convoluted tubule. Tubular secretion is the active transport of other unwanted material into the distal convoluted tubule.

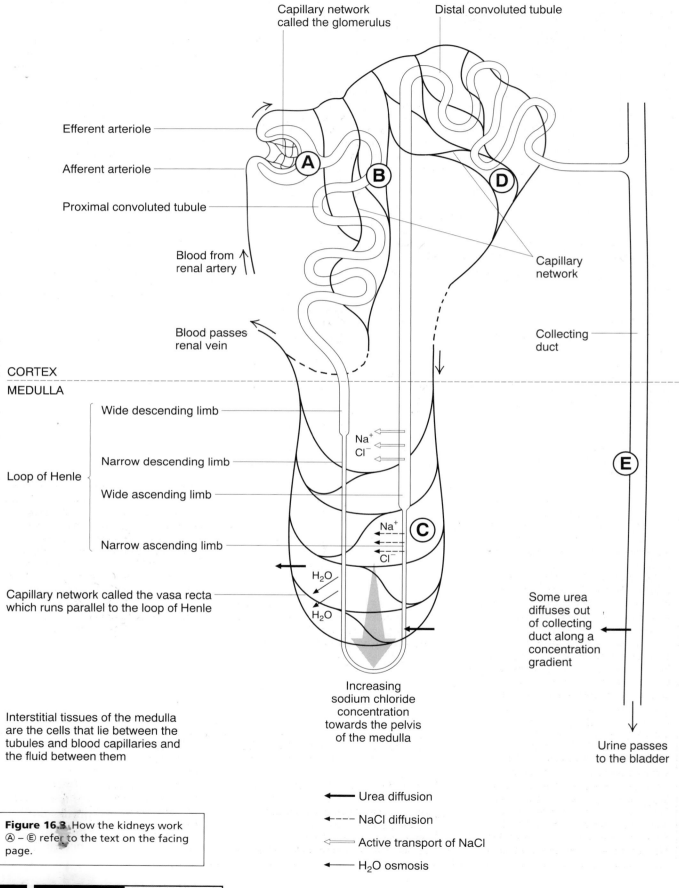

Capillary network called the glomerulus

Distal convoluted tubule

Efferent arteriole

Afferent arteriole

(A)

(B)

(D)

Proximal convoluted tubule

Capillary network

Blood from renal artery

Blood passes renal vein

Collecting duct

CORTEX

MEDULLA

Wide descending limb

Na⁺
Cl⁻

Narrow descending limb

(E)

Loop of Henle

Wide ascending limb

Na⁺

(C)

Narrow ascending limb

Cl⁻

H_2O

Capillary network called the vasa recta which runs parallel to the loop of Henle

H_2O

Some urea diffuses out of collecting duct along a concentration gradient

Increasing sodium chloride concentration towards the pelvis of the medulla

Interstitial tissues of the medulla are the cells that lie between the tubules and blood capillaries and the fluid between them

Urine passes to the bladder

Urea diffusion

NaCl diffusion

Active transport of NaCl

H_2O osmosis

Figure 16.3 How the kidneys work Ⓐ – Ⓔ refer to the text on the facing page.

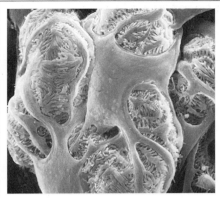

Podocyte cells

A **Ultrafiltration** – Blood enters the capillary network called the glomerulus within the Bowman's capsule from the afferent arteriole and leaves it via the efferent arteriole. Since the afferent arteriole branches into smaller capillaries and the efferent arteriole is narrower than the afferent, there is an increase in blood pressure which forces materials out from the blood capillaries into the Bowman's capsule. The endothelial wall of the capillaries in the glomerulus has large pores; it rests on a basement membrane and is closely pressed against the inner wall of the Bowman's capsule. This wall is composed of special cells called **podocytes** with numerous processes called **slit pores**. Together these structures act as a filter, allowing smaller molecules to pass through. Molecules with a molecular mass greater than 68 000, such as platelets and plasma protein and all blood cells, are retained. Most of the water, glucose, amino acids, urea, vitamins, hormones, ions and other simple nitrogen-containing compounds pass into the tubule forming the **filtrate**. Altogether around 125 ml of filtrate pass through the Bowman's capsule every minute, a total of 180 litres of filtrate every day.

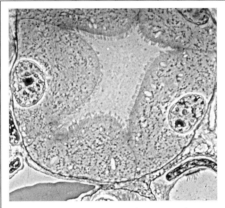

Microvilli increase the surface area for selective reabsorption in the proximal convoluted tubule.

B **Selective reabsorption** – The epithelial cells of the proximal convoluted tubules have many mitochondria, and also microvilli on the faces which line the tubule. There are spaces between the bases of adjacent epithelial cells, and between these cells and the capillary basement membrane. As the filtrate moves through this region of the tubule, over 80% of it is absorbed back into the blood capillaries nearby. The reabsorbed materials include glucose, amino acids, vitamins, hormones and around 85% of sodium chloride and water. Selective reabsorption happens in this way: firstly these substances diffuse into the epithelial cells of the proximal tubule and then they are actively transported into the intercellular spaces. From here they diffuse into the blood capillary, where the continuous flow of blood maintains the diffusion gradient. Water follows the dissolved materials, moving by osmosis.

C **The role of the loop of Henle** – The loop of Henle and the blood capillaries called the vasa recta create an increasing concentration gradient of sodium chloride towards the medulla, which draws water out of the filtrate in the descending limb by osmosis. The wide part of the descending limb is impermeable to water and carries the filtrate to the narrow descending limb. Water passes by osmosis from the narrow descending limb out into the interstitial tissues of the medulla, and into the vasa recta. This happens because the water potential within the descending limb is greater than that of the interstitial tissue, which has a high salt concentration. By the time the filtrate reaches the hairpin bend it is a lot more concentrated than it was at the start. Even so, some of the sodium chloride diffuses along the concentration gradient back into the descending limb. The ascending limb is impermeable to water along its entire length. Sodium and chloride ions are pumped out of the ascending limb by active transport, increasing the concentration in the medulla and decreasing it in the filtrate.

D **Tubular secretion** – The distal convoluted tubule and its blood supply are very close to each other within the cortex. Cells in this part of the tubule have microvilli and can actively secrete substances into blood or into filtrate. For example creatinine (a nitrogen-containing waste) and potassium ions are actively secreted into the tubule from the nearby blood capillaries. Particularly important is the role of this part of the tubule in balancing pH. If the pH of the blood falls hydrogen ions are secreted from the blood into the filtrate in the tubule. If the pH rises, hydrogencarbonate ions are secreted into the filtrate from the blood. This means that the pH of the blood does not significantly vary, whilst that of the filtrate does. The hormone **ADH (antidiuretic hormone)** affects the permeability of this part of the tubule.

E **The collecting ducts** – As the filtrate moves along the collecting duct it becomes more concentrated because water passes out of it by osmosis into the medulla, down a water potential gradient. Again, it is the high sodium chloride concentration in the medulla that causes water to move out of this part of the tubule. The permeability of the collecting duct is also affected by the hormone ADH. The concentration of urea increases as the filtrate passes along the tubule because the reabsorption of water reduces the volume. However, about 50% of the urea passes out of the filtrate into the interstitial tissue, and finally into either the base of the loop of Henle or the vasa recta.

The countercurrent multiplier theory

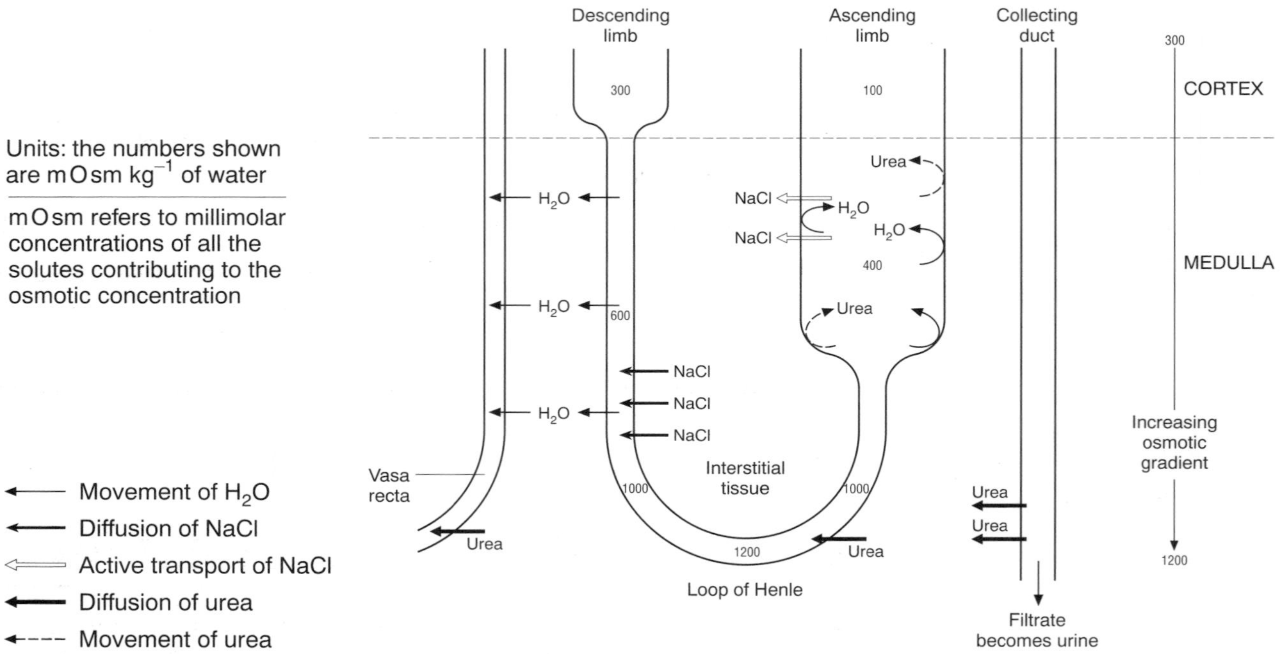

Units: the numbers shown are $mOsm\ kg^{-1}$ of water

$mOsm$ refers to millimolar concentrations of all the solutes contributing to the osmotic concentration

←——— Movement of H_2O

←——— Diffusion of NaCl

⇐==== Active transport of NaCl

←——— Diffusion of urea

←---- Movement of urea

Figure 16.4 This is a complex model which suggests how the loop of Henle works. However, it is not the whole picture. Adjacent lengths of vasa recta capillaries also help to maintain an increasing concentration gradient in the interstitial tissues via a countercurrent exchange mechanism.

The term countercurrent refers to the fact that the filtrate in the two limbs of the loop of Henle is flowing in opposite directions. The cells of the ascending loop actively transport sodium and chloride ions out into the interstitial tissue. This creates a gradient which allows sodium and chloride ions to diffuse into the descending limb, and water to pass out by osmosis. This effect is happening continuously, and as the filtrate 'rounds the bend' it is very concentrated. The concentration difference between the descending and ascending limbs is only slight at any point, but the longer the loop of Henle is the more this effect multiplies. Therefore in animals which are adapted to dry climates the loop on Henle is longer proportionately than in humans.

Questions

1 a) In what ways is the glomerulus adapted as an effective filtration unit?

b) What features determine which components of blood will be filtered out?

2 Look at Table 16.1 below.

Table 16.1 Analysis of fluids in the kidney (units = g/100 cm³)

Substance	Blood plasma entering the glomerulus	Filtrate in Bowman's capsule	Urine in collecting duct
water	90–93	97–99	96
blood proteins	7–9	some	0.0
glucose	0.10	0.10	0.0
urea	0.03	0.03	2.0
sodium ions	0.32	0.32	0.30–0.35
chloride ions	0.37	0.37	0.60
other ions	0.038	0.038	0.475
pH	7.35–7.45		4.7–6.0 (average 5.0)

a) Compare the concentration of components in the blood plasma with that of the substances in the glomerular filtrate (Table 16.1).

   i) From this data, how can you tell which substances are not filtered out of the blood?

   ii) For those substances which are filtered out of blood plasma, what pattern is there between their concentration in the plasma and glomerular filtrate?

Now compare the glomerular filtrate with the data for urine (Table 16.1).

b) Which substances are more concentrated in the urine than they are in the filtrate? Suggest why these substances are excreted from the body.

c) Suggest a reason why there is a difference in pH between plasma and urine.

16.3 Adjusting osmoregulation

Osmoregulation involves balancing the body's intake of water with its output. This involves sensitivity to both solute potential of blood plasma (i.e. how concentrated it is) and blood pressure.

    There are osmoreceptors in the hypothalamus of the brain which are sensitive to the solute potential of blood plasma. If there has been very little intake of water, or water loss has been high (usually because of sweating) or a lot of salty food has been eaten, the solute potential of blood plasma will increase. The osmoreceptors are sensory nerve cells, and impulses pass along them to the pituitary gland. The pituitary gland produces ADH which affects the permeability of the distal convoluted tubules and collecting ducts (Figure 16.5). Increased permeability of the tubules allows water and urea to

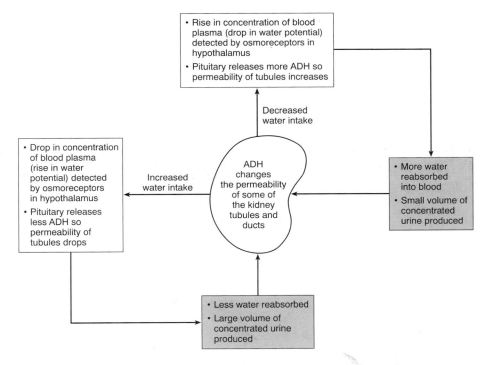

Figure 16.5 ADH affects the distal convoluted tubules and collecting ducts making them more permeable to water and urea. The mechanism of osmoregulation involves negative feedback, maintaining optimum water and solute potential in blood plasma, and therefore in tissue fluid

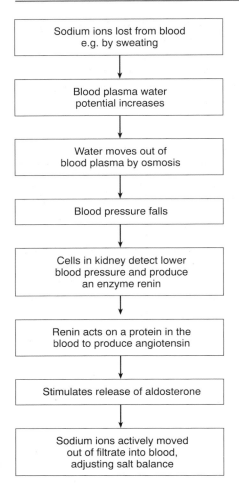

Sodium ions lost from blood e.g. by sweating
Blood plasma water potential increases
Water moves out of blood plasma by osmosis
Blood pressure falls
Cells in kidney detect lower blood pressure and produce an enzyme renin
Renin acts on a protein in the blood to produce angiotensin
Stimulates release of aldosterone
Sodium ions actively moved out of filtrate into blood, adjusting salt balance

Figure 16.6 Events leading to the release of aldosterone

move out of them along concentration gradients and back into the blood plasma. The urea helps to maintain the concentration gradient in the medulla, and the water helps to lower the solute concentration in the blood plasma. The reverse of this regulatory mechanism occurs if the solute potential of blood plasma decreases, as might happen if someone drinks a large volume of dilute liquid in a short time.

The solute concentration of blood plasma affects blood pressure by influencing how much water moves in or out of the blood by osmosis. For example, if the solute concentration in plasma increases, more water is drawn into the blood vessels from the tissue fluid and so the blood pressure increases. There are groups of cells in certain blood vessels which are sensitive to blood pressure, which can also trigger the release of ADH.

Aldosterone is another hormone which has an effect on the solute potential of blood plasma. It is produced by the adrenal glands and causes active uptake of sodium ions from the filtrate in the distal convoluted tubule, into blood plasma. The events which trigger the release of aldosterone are complex but allow the fine tuning of salt balance in this part of the tubule (see Figure 16.6).

16.4 Micturition – controlling the loss of urine from the body

Urine passes from the kidneys along tubes called **ureters** to the bladder, partly because of gravity and partly because of peristaltic movements of the muscular ureter walls. The bladder wall is mostly made of muscle, with an epithelial lining. When it is almost empty the inner surface of the wall is folded which allows considerable stretching as the bladder fills. At the neck of the bladder are two rings of muscle or **sphincters**. The internal sphincter is under the control of the autonomic nervous system, but the outer sphincter can be controlled voluntarily, up to a point.

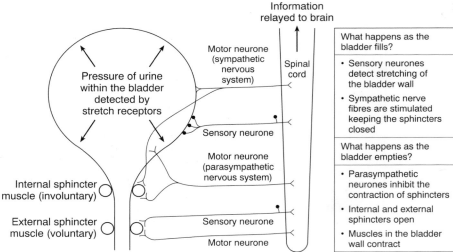

Figure 16.7 The nerve supply involved in bladder control

As the bladder fills to around 200 ml the pressure inside it rises. Further filling to around 400 ml does not cause further increase in pressure because the muscle layer relaxes and is stretched. As urine continues to enter the bladder there is an increase in pressure and the sensation of a 'full bladder' becomes more intense. Once the bladder contains around 600–700 ml of urine, the emptying response cannot be voluntarily suppressed any longer.

Stretch receptors of sensory neurones in the sympathetic nervous system transmit impulses increasingly as the bladder fills. This stimulates parasympathetic motor nerve fibres to the bladder wall which contracts, and at the same time the internal sphincter opens. As the external sphincter relaxes at this stage urine passes out of the body. Normally, we learn to control this sphincter at about the age of two years.

▶ *Chapter 20 describes the nervous system*

16.5 Kidney failure

Kidney failure happens when the kidneys are not able to regulate body fluid and salts to within the range which is appropriate for the human body. They fail to excrete urea and it accumulates in the blood. Sometimes plasma proteins may get through the glomerular filter if there is damage to the nephrons. Generally, kidney failure is a slow, progressive condition either because of ageing or prolonged infection. Sudden and acute renal failure may be due to damaged nephrons or interstitial tissue caused by certain toxins (including some drugs), by infection, by high blood pressure, or by an injury. Obstruction of the ureter can cause problems too.

Kidney failure can be treated by:

- careful regulation of fluid and salt intake
- reduced protein intake
- dialysis
- transplant

Dialysis

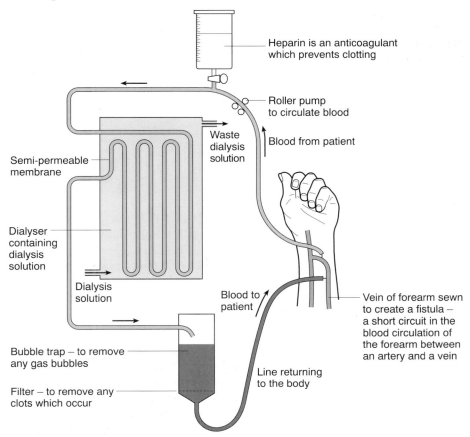

Figure 16.8 A kidney machine takes over the role of the kidneys

A kidney machine or 'artificial kidney' can keep someone with kidney failure healthy over a long period of time, by taking over the filtering role of the kidneys. The principle is straightforward: the person's blood passes on one side of a special membrane and a solution called the **dialysate** passes on the other side. The membrane allows some materials to pass through but not others, which is similar to the filtering action of the glomerulus. Materials which are small enough in size exchange across the membrane by diffusion, according to concentration gradients. This process is called **dialysis**.

Notice in Figure 16.8 that a direct connection is made between an artery and a vein in the wrist, near the point where the patient is linked to the machine. This connection is made prior to treatment, since it avoids the risk involved in linking the machine directly to an artery. An anticoagulant is added to prevent blood clots as the blood flows through the machine. The blood and dialysate flow in opposite directions (a countercurrent system), maximising diffusion gradients. Clearly, the composition of the dialysate is very important. It contains the same level of glucose and solutes as normal tissue fluid, and these exchange in both directions. Urea and excess solutes diffuse out of blood and into the dialysate. This treatment takes a few hours and is usually required three times a week, which does interfere with the person's normal routine. However, there are alternatives to hospital-based dialysis, such as using a machine at home or a technique called continuous ambulatory peritoneal dialysis (CAPD). Clearly, both of these options are only sensible when someone feels confident about taking over control of dialysis themselves. To reach such a point, a patient would need nursing assistance at home, at least initially.

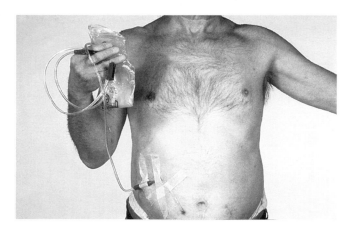

Figure 16.9 Stuart prefers CAPD to the dialysis he used to have in hospital, because he finds it more convenient

Using CAPD to deal with kidney failure is a slightly different approach that uses the body's own peritoneal membranes which line the abdomen, to filter the body's waste. Dialysate is periodically forced into the abdomen from a bag. Materials exchange across peritoneal membranes, removing unwanted wastes from the blood circulation as they diffuse into the dialysate solution in the abdomen. Then this solution is drained from the abdomen, removing waste substances.

Kidney transplant

In the long-term, a kidney transplant is an excellent solution for treating a person with kidney failure: dialysis through a machine is no longer needed and a better lifestyle is possible. A healthy person can survive with only one kidney, because there is enough renal capacity to filter the body's blood. If someone allows one of their healthy kidneys to be used for transplant, they are called a **donor**. Most donated kidneys come from people who have offered their organs for use after their death, say from an accident. The kidneys need to be removed very soon after death and packed on ice to lower the temperature to a point which slows deterioration of the tissues. Even so, kidneys need to be used within 12 hours or so of removal from the donor.

Around 2000 kidneys are transplanted each year in the UK, with about an 80 per cent success rate. In the early days in particular, the challenge with these transplants was that they were sometimes rejected by the recipient's immune system, which recognised the tissue as being foreign to the body. However, nowadays the success rate is good because kidneys are **tissue-typed** to check for matching immunological markers. Unless there is a high match a donor kidney is not transplanted. The tissue-typing database is international and if the transplant time is not too great, kidneys from one country may be received by people in another.

There are around 5000 people in the UK who are on a waiting list for a kidney transplant, because there is a shortage of donated kidneys which match potential recipients.

Bladder infection

Cystitis is a painful inflammation of the bladder, which is not serious in itself and can be successfully treated with antibiotics, and improved by drinking large volumes of dilute fluids. It is not normally associated with kidney problems. However, the concern is that the infection might move back up the ureters to the kidney, so seeking immediate medical advice is important.

CHAPTER 17

How Homeostasis Works – Controlling Body Temperature

17.1 Human body temperature

Temperature has an important effect on the rate of chemical reactions in living cells. In humans the optimum body temperature for metabolism is 36–37°C. You might expect that an increase in temperature above this would increase the rate of metabolism. In fact this is not true because the additional heating can cause changes to the chemical structure of proteins, including enzymes. High temperatures can denature enzymes with the loss of active sites, decreasing their catalytic effect.

At a cellular level, an organism functions best when the internal conditions of the body do not fluctuate far from the optimum. However, conditions within the surroundings do fluctuate, and some organisms have developed homeostatic mechanisms to overcome this challenge. These processes bring about **thermoregulation**. **Endotherms** are animals that gain more heating from processes which happen within the body than they do from the environment. Due to this and their ability to thermoregulate, they can, to an extent, control body temperature to within the homeostatic range, independent of the temperature of the environment. The advantage of this is that humans colonise almost all climatic regions of the world. However, this homeostatic strategy is more energy-demanding than allowing body temperature to fluctuate with the ambient temperature, and so requires a higher level of feeding.

> ▶ **Chapter 7 is about enzymes and their functioning**

> ▶ **Chapter 34.7 considers variation in the human form related to environment**

An endotherm is an animal that gains more heating from internal processes than the environment. Thermoregulation is the ability to control body temperature to within a homeostatic range, independent of environmental temperature fluctuations.

A warm core

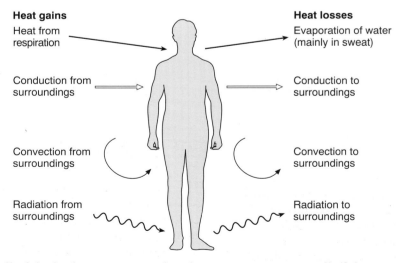

Figure 17.1 Heat inputs and outputs

Not all of the body is maintained at the same temperature all of the time. The **core** of the body is considered to be the brain and the organs within the chest and abdomen. Around 70–75 per cent of the body's heat is generated by the core, reflecting the high metabolic activity of this area. This is the

> The body core stays warmer than its surface or the limbs.

region of the body which is normally maintained at an optimum of 36.8°C and within the maximum range of 25–43°C.

Heat transfers from the body surfaces to the environment along a temperature gradient, cooling the skin. The limbs have a relatively high surface area in comparison to their volume, and so cool faster than the body core.

Variations in body temperature

It is normal for the activity of the body to vary due to natural rhythms, collectively called **circadian rhythms**. Some cells of the body are more active in the morning when we are 'wide awake' and others are more active when we are asleep. These natural rhythms are disturbed if we are ill, travel across time zones, work shifts or stay up late at weekends. There is slight variation between individuals, some people claiming to be more alert earlier in the day and others waking up towards the evening.

One well documented circadian rhythm is the change in body temperature, which is a diurnal rhythm because it happens over a 24 hour period. Figure 17.3 shows that the lowest body temperatures tend to be recorded between 2 a.m. and 5 a.m. Variation in body temperature is linked to how active a person is, because both brain activity and using our muscles transfers heat to the body. It has been established that there is a correlation between body temperature and performance, for example at mathematical calculation. The peak performance corresponds to the time when the body temperature is rising mostly steeply. The lowest performance time happens after lunch in the mid-afternoon, when there is a natural dip in activity level. The 'post-lunch dip' has not been satisfactorily explained and cannot be attributed directly to the fact that a proportion of the cardiac blood circulation is diverted to the gut area. Many environmental factors influence body temperature, such as eating hot or cold food, dressing warmly and access to a heating source.

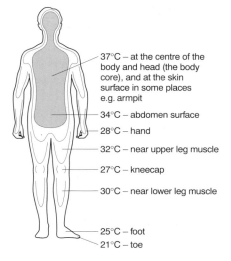

37°C – at the centre of the body and head (the body core), and at the skin surface in some places e.g. armpit

34°C – abdomen surface

28°C – hand

32°C – near upper leg muscle

27°C – kneecap

30°C – near lower leg muscle

25°C – foot

21°C – toe

Figure 17.2 Approximate temperature, recorded after a person has remained at about 20°C for some time

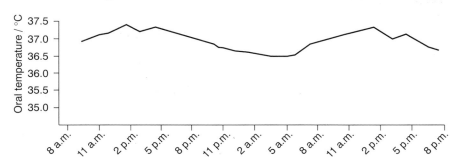

Figure 17.3 Body temperature fluctuation is an example of a diurnal rhythm

17.2 The skin

> The skin consists of many layers of cells, organised into the hypodermis, dermis and epidermis. The epidermis is where new cells are produced. Cells work their way towards the surface, gradually become filled with keratin, die and flake off.

The skin is an organ and the tissues it contains function together. The part nearest the skin surface is called the **epidermis** and consists of 10–20 layers of stratified epithelial cells. The innermost layer of the epidermis is the **Malpighian layer** containing mostly **keratinocytes** which divide repeatedly by mitosis. New cells successively work their way towards the surface, becoming flattened and impregnated with a fibrous protein called **keratin**. Eventually, the cells die and are known as **squames**, which either flake off or get worn off at a rate of around 30 000 per day. The process of making new cells and losing dead ones continues constantly. There are more layers of

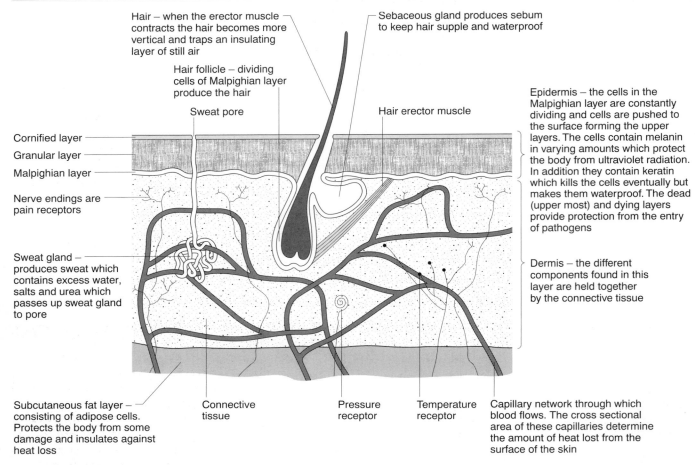

Hair – when the erector muscle contracts the hair becomes more vertical and traps an insulating layer of still air

Hair follicle – dividing cells of Malpighian layer produce the hair

Sweat pore

Sebaceous gland produces sebum to keep hair supple and waterproof

Hair erector muscle

Cornified layer

Granular layer

Malpighian layer

Nerve endings are pain receptors

Sweat gland – produces sweat which contains excess water, salts and urea which passes up sweat gland to pore

Epidermis – the cells in the Malpighian layer are constantly dividing and cells are pushed to the surface forming the upper layers. The cells contain melanin in varying amounts which protect the body from ultraviolet radiation. In addition they contain keratin which kills the cells eventually but makes them waterproof. The dead (upper most) and dying layers provide protection from the entry of pathogens

Dermis – the different components found in this layer are held together by the connective tissue

Subcutaneous fat layer – consisting of adipose cells. Protects the body from some damage and insulates against heat loss

Connective tissue

Pressure receptor

Temperature receptor

Capillary network through which blood flows. The cross sectional area of these capillaries determine the amount of heat lost from the surface of the skin

Figure 17.4 The human body is covered by around 1.5–2.0 m² of skin, which is the interface between the internal tissues and the environment. As such, it is the point at which exchanges happen, such as evaporation of sweat and heat transfer.

keratinised cells where there is most friction between the body and other surfaces. This is why some parts of the soles of the feet tend to build up thick pads of hardened skin. Lipids fill the spaces between squames, and along with the keratin, give the skin its waterproof properties. Ten per cent or so of the cells in the Malpighian layer are **melanocytes**, which produce the dark pigment called **melanin**. The melanin transfers to other cells in the Malpighian layer, giving an overall coloration. Exposure to the Sun increases the level of melanin, deepening the skin colour and giving added protection against harmful ultraviolet rays. It is interesting to note that racial variations in skin colour depend on the *rate* of melanin production, since everyone has roughly the same number of melanocytes.

The **dermis** is much thicker than the epidermis. It gives the skin some elasticity, because it consists of connective tissue with fibrous collagen fibres and elastic fibres. With age, the amount of collagen tends to decrease and the skin wrinkles. This natural process can be accelerated in some skin types by excessive exposure to ultraviolet light. Following injury, collagen forms at the site of the repairing wound, forming **scar tissue**. Within the dermis are hair follicles, muscles, sebaceous glands and sweat glands, blood capillaries and nerve receptors. A hair follicle is a fold in the Malpighian layer of the epidermis. Cells divide at the base of the follicle to form a hair, and attached to it is a muscle which runs to the base of the epidermis. When the muscle contracts it pulls the hair into the upright position, which is why is it known as the **erector pili muscle**. Dark hairs contain more melanin pigment than lighter hairs. The hairs are kept supple and waterproof by **sebum** which is a lipid based substance made in the **sebaceous gland** at the side of each hair. There are no sebaceous glands on the soles of the feet or the palms of the hands.

Sweat is a dilute solution containing solutes, usually including urea. Urea is a waste product and so the skin has an excretory role in removing it from the body, although the majority of it is lost in urine. Sweat is produced by around two to four million sweat glands. It moves along the ducts on to the surface of the skin, from where it evaporates. This transfers heat from the body to water particles, and has a cooling effect on the skin and the blood within it. The evaporation of sweat is a major factor in thermoregulation, the rate of sweat production increasing with body temperature.

Below the epidermis and dermis is a layer called the **hypodermis**, consisting mainly of a layer of fat tissue known as **subcutaneous fat**. This layer varies in thickness according to its position in the body, and according to body mass. Fat reduces mechanical wear on underlying tissues and acts as an insulating layer, as well as being a food store. Arteries arise in the hypodermis, which branch as smaller arterioles and form extensive capillary networks in the dermis. Venules return blood from the capillary beds via the hypodermis, and then re-join to form veins. These capillary beds are very important in thermoregulation, because the blood flow through them can be altered. The significance of this is explained in Chapter 18.3.

▶ **Chapter 6.3 describes the structure of lipids**

Too much Sun?

Exposing your skin to the ultraviolet light radiating from the Sun is harmful. Over a period of years constant exposure to the Sun causes premature ageing or **photoageing**, and the skin becomes very wrinkled, dry and has a yellowy-brown colour. The three types of ultraviolet radiation are summarised in Table 17.1.

UVB is the most dangerous source of ultraviolet radiation to humans because it can severely burn the epidermis causing inflammation. What's more, capillaries may be damaged so they become constantly dilated showing as reddened vessels. The collagen fibres break down and the skin becomes less elastic, so it stretches and wrinkles more. More dangerous still is the ability of ultraviolet radiation to cause changes in the DNA of skin cells, leading to the development of skin cancers. Melanoma is a very dangerous form of skin cancer which develops rapidly and is often fatal. However, there are many other forms of skin cancer and they are mostly treatable, especially if caught early. (see C3 and C4 on page 347)

Table 17.1 Ultraviolet electromagnetic radiation

Waveband	Wavelength (nm)	Characteristics
UVA	320–400	passes through glass and water; reflected by light surfaces; tans skin slowly
UVB	290–320	passes through water; reflected by light surfaces; damaging to skin
UVC	100–290	absorbed by ozone in the atmosphere

▶ **Chapter 5.4 mentions other mutagenic factors which bring about cancer due to damaged DNA**

Questions

1 a) What are the main layers forming the skin?

   b) Which structures in the skin are associated with sensitivity?

   c) Why does skin 'tan'?

   d) Why is UV radiation damaging to skin?

   e) In what way is skin different to other epithelia in the body?

2 Suggest reasons why skin is considered to be an organ rather than a tissue.

Figure 17.5 The human body form has evolved slightly differently in climatic regions of the world. Which of these people has the greatest surface area in relation to volume? How are they both well adapted for the climates they live in?

▶ *Chapter 23.3 gives more information about BMR*

17.3 How thermoregulation works

Humans cope with external temperatures which vary from extreme heat to extreme cold. There are various ways in which people deal with temperature variation:

- types of behaviour
- how they are physically adapted
- changes in body function

Many aspects of lifestyle depend on the climate, for example housing, transport, clothing and eating habits. These are **behavioural adaptations** which help us to cope with extremes of temperature. **Structural adaptations** include physical differences in body type, which occur because humans have evolved differently. Look at the people in Figure 17.7 who have differently adapted body types. Their limb shape and the thickness of the layer of subcutaneous fat are very different. Alongside this are **physiological adaptations**. For example exothermic chemical reactions such as the breakdown of carbohydrates and fats have a heating effect on the body. The amount of heating in a resting and fasting animal is known as the **basal metabolic rate (BMR)**. The BMR alters with temperature changes, the faster the rate, the greater the heating effect. Occasional muscle action such as 'shivering' generates warmth, while more persistent rhythmic contractions occur at very low external temperatures. The other major physiological responses to changes in body temperature are changes in the rate of sweat production and changes in the distribution of blood.

The change in blood distribution towards or away from the skin surface, is probably the main way in which thermoregulation is achieved. Energy is transferred from the skin surface by radiation, convection and conduction. Since blood circulation continually distributes heat towards the skin surface, it follows that heat transferred to the surroundings is proportional to the amount of blood flowing through the capillary networks of the dermis.

17.4 Vasoconstriction and vasodilation

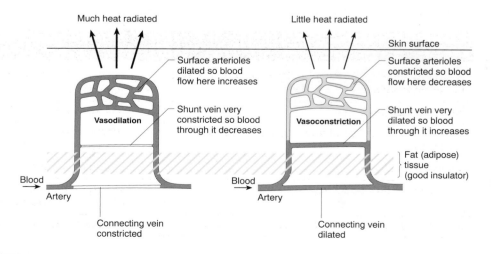

Figure 17.6 Controlling the distribution of blood is important in thermoregulation

> Vasoconstriction is the narrowing of arterioles supplying the capillary networks in the dermis of the skin. Vasodilation is the widening of these arterioles.

▶ *Chapter 10.4 also mentions vasoconstriction*

Capillaries have thin walls with no muscular fibres. Their walls stretch, so the size is determined by the amount of blood flowing through them. The arterioles supplying blood to the capillary networks are able to change shape because of muscular walls. If the muscle in their walls contracts, they become narrower in diameter and less blood flows through them. This is called **vasoconstriction** and it reduces the amount of blood flowing through the dermis. Alternatively, the muscles may relax and the arterioles dilate so that more blood flows through them. This is called **vasodilation**, and is the reason why pale skins can look pinker or 'flushed' when someone feels hot.

A **shunt** is a small vessel that links the arteriole and venous supply to a capillary network. **Precapillary sphincters** constrict the entrance of a shunt, causing more blood to flow through deeper blood vessels, so less reaches the skin surface. However, dilation of the shunt vessels increases blood flow to the surface. The rate of flow through the skin in humans can vary from less than 1 cm^3 min^{-1} 100 g^{-1} in cold conditions to around 100 cm^3 min^{-1} 100 g^{-1} in warm conditions.

17.5 How thermoregulation is controlled

How is the body sensitive to its own temperature and to the external temperature? Clearly, the sensory nervous system is involved in detecting temperature fluctuations. There are **temperature receptors** in the skin which detect changes in the external conditions, triggering impulses to the **hypothalamus** in the hindbrain. At the same time, the hypothalamus detects the temperature of the blood which flows through it. The hypothalamus is most important in co-ordinating many homeostatic mechanisms, and in this case acts as the body's thermostat. The hypothalamus triggers responses which are brought about by effector organs. These responses (listed in Table 17.2) depend on whether the body is too hot or too cold. Negative feedback is a feature of homeostatic control systems, as explained in the *in brief* at the start of Section 3.

Table 17.2 Co-ordination of thermoregulation involves the nervous system

Anterior hypothalamus (heat loss centre)	Posterior hypothalamus (heat gain centre)
triggered by an increase in the temperature of blood flowing through it	activated by impulses from cold receptors in the skin or temperature of the hypothalamus
increases vasolidation	increases vasoconstriction
increases heat loss by radiation, convection and conduction	decreases heat loss by radiation, convection and conduction
increases sweating	inhibits sweating
decreases metabolic activity	increases metabolic activity through shivering and release of thyroxine and adrenaline
decreases thickness of air layer by flattening hair	increases thickness of air layer by action of hair muscles

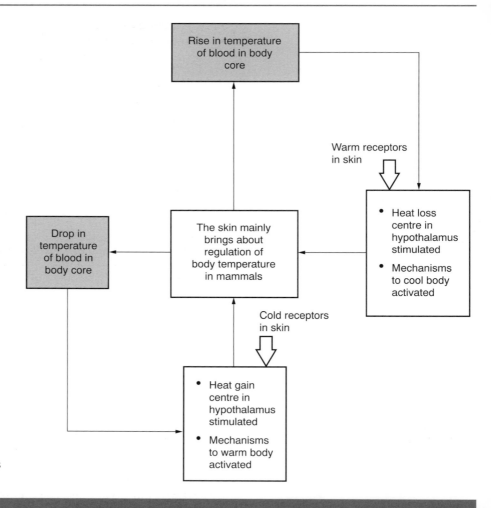

Figure 17.7 Negative feedback operates in any homeostatic control system

Feeling chilly?

If the body temperature falls much below 35°C, the hypothalamus effectively stops functioning as a thermostat, and the body's temperature gets lower and lower. This condition is called **hypothermia**, and the person may themselves be unaware of what is happening. If no action is taken a person becomes unconscious and finally dies. Elderly people are particularly vulnerable to hypothermia for a variety of reasons. A combination of these reasons could be lethal:

the elderly are not usually very physically active, they may have less fat to insulate the body, they do not always bother to eat hot meals regularly and may not be able to afford sufficient heating. Environmental conditions have a lot to do with hypothermia. For example, hikers and pot-holers can get hypothermia because of exposure to wet clothing or cold winds. Even trained soldiers may be unaware of the onset of hypothermia, which is why it is a dangerous condition.

Figure 17.8 A premature baby has not developed the appropriate control systems to regulate body temperature sufficiently, which up to birth is controlled by the mother's womb. Also, a baby has a high surface area to volume ratio which maximises heat transfer. It is vital to reduce heat loss because the baby's energy expenditure should be used in building new cells, for example by wrapping the baby warmly, perhaps using a reflective material. As the baby grows it develops more insulating subcutaneous fat and control systems start to function efficiently.

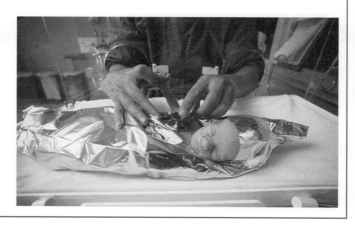

Questions

1 a) Why is thermoregulation significant in biological terms?

b) Why is thermoregulation more energy-demanding than allowing body temperature to fluctuate with ambient temperature?

c) What behavioural mechanisms for thermoregulation might humans employ?

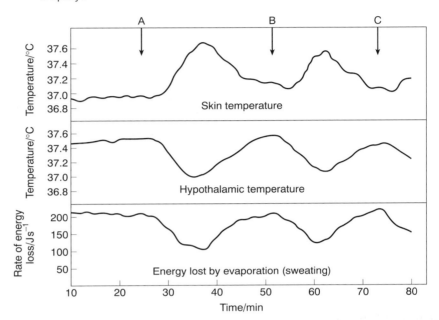

Figure 17.9 Relationship between skin and hypothalamic temperature and rate of sweating

2 The data in Figure 17.9 was obtained from someone in a warm chamber (45°C) who swallowed iced water at points A, B and C as indicated on the graph.

a) Why do the three graphs remain fairly constant in the first 20 minutes?

b) What is the link between the temperature of the hypothalamus and the rate of sweating?

c) Suggest why skin temperature rises after the person swallows iced water.

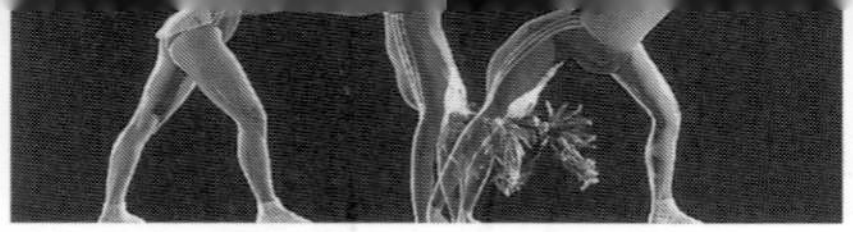

CHAPTER 18 Adapting to Exercise

18.1 Adjusting the supply

When we are resting, our organ systems are set to provide just the right amount of the essential requirements, such as food and oxygen, to support the body's basal metabolism. Once we start exercising, the body systems have very different demands placed on them. The muscle fibres in particular have greater requirements for energy. This energy is transferred from ATP, which is made during respiration. This means that the cells need extra supplies of glucose and oxygen, and so the cardiovascular and breathing systems must increase their response in order to deliver these substances. If the body systems did not respond to increased needs during exercise, it would not be possible to sustain an increased level of activity. Equally, the body must react to a decrease in physical activity, or it would be oversupplying tissues and placing a strain on the organ systems.

As we start a period of exercise, the increased rate of metabolism causes chemical changes in cells. These changes are constantly monitored by sensory cells, which relay the information via the central nervous system to effector organs. The effector organs, for example the muscles involved in ventilation movements, do whatever is necessary to supply the body during exercise. Since changes are monitored constantly, this information feeds back and adjusts the level of response on an ongoing basis. Clearly, the cardiovascular system and the breathing system are very important in the body's response to exercise, and the control of these systems is closely linked.

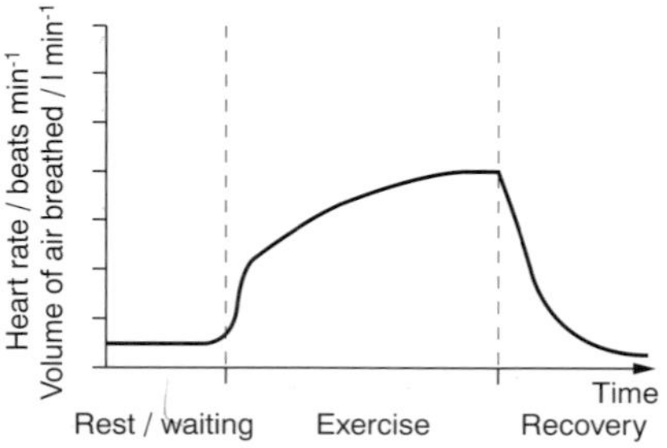

> ▶ **Chapter 25 describes the process of respiration and the formation of ATP**

> **Exercise increases the heart rate and the breathing rate.**

> ▶ **Chapter 12 describes the action of skeletal muscles, and the benefits of regular exercise to health**

Figure 18.1 The cardiovascular and breathing systems respond fast to exercise. The volume of blood pumped by the heart can increase from around five litres per minute to 30 litres per minute. This happens because the heart beats faster and more forcefully. The recovery period depends on the fitness of the individual, tending to be shorter for people who exercise regularly. Similarly, the amount of air breathed at rest is around six litres per minute, but this can increase to between 45–80 litres in females and 80–100 litres in males.

18.2 Controlling heart rate and output

The control of cardiac output involves reflex actions brought about by the autonomic nervous system. There are several inputs to this system which allow finely tuned control. The components of this control system are:

- **Sensory** – Stretch receptors (which respond to increased blood pressure) in the walls of the aortic arch, the sinuses of the carotid arteries and walls of the vena cava. Sensory nerves from these receptors carry impulses to the cardiovascular control centre in the hindbrain.

  Receptors in the carotid artery are also sensitive to changes in pH, which result from changes in carbon dioxide concentration in the blood. If the level of CO_2 rises during exercise, the pH falls and the receptors send impulses to the acceleratory area of the cardiovascular centre. The reverse happens if blood pH rises due to a fall in the concentration of CO_2.

- **Processing** – Acceleratory and inhibitory areas in the cardiovascular control centre process the information received via sensory nerves and send impulses to effector organs via motor nerves.

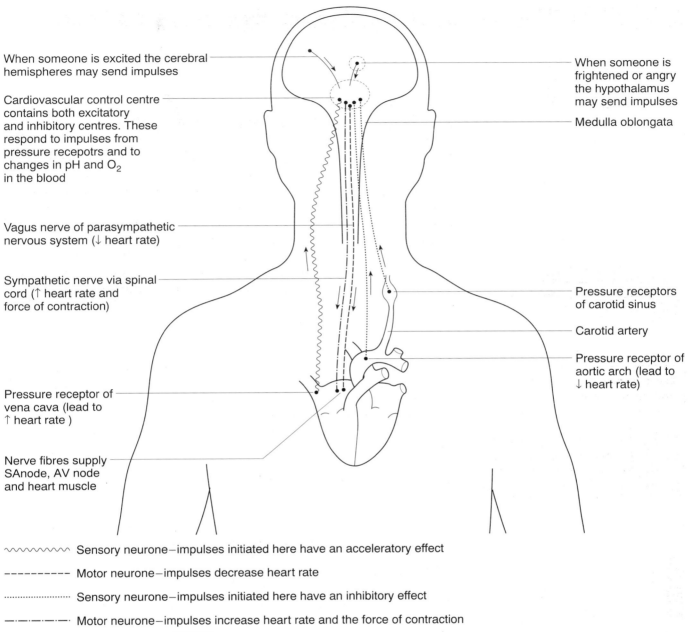

When someone is excited the cerebral hemispheres may send impulses

Cardiovascular control centre contains both excitatory and inhibitory centres. These respond to impulses from pressure recepotrs and to changes in pH and O_2 in the blood

Vagus nerve of parasympathetic nervous system (↓ heart rate)

Sympathetic nerve via spinal cord (↑ heart rate and force of contraction)

Pressure receptor of vena cava (lead to ↑ heart rate)

Nerve fibres supply SAnode, AV node and heart muscle

When someone is frightened or angry the hypothalamus may send impulses

Medulla oblongata

Pressure receptors of carotid sinus

Carotid artery

Pressure receptor of aortic arch (lead to ↓ heart rate)

〜〜〜〜〜 Sensory neurone–impulses initiated here have an acceleratory effect

– – – – – – Motor neurone–impulses decrease heart rate

·············· Sensory neurone–impulses initiated here have an inhibitory effect

—·—·—·— Motor neurone–impulses increase heart rate and the force of contraction

Figure 18.2 The nervous system mainly controls the heart rate
(See Colour Gallery page 351)

- **Effectors** – A sympathetic nerve links the acceleratory centre to the SA node, and it stimulates an increase in heart rate. As the heart beats faster, stretch receptors in the cardiac muscle make it contract more forcefully, increasing stroke volume. Parasympathetic nerve fibres link the inhibitory centre to the SA node, AV node and the bundle of His, and the heart rate is decreased.

The distribution of blood flow does depend on the priority to the body of its activities: for example, after a meal there is an increased blood flow to the alimentary canal, while during exercise there is increased flow to the skeletal muscles. Hormonal influence (such as the effect of adrenaline) on the heart rate mimics that of the sympathetic nervous system, increasing heart rate. Increased levels of thyroxine have a longer term and more sustained effect in increasing heart rate.

▶ *Chapter 20 outlines chemical control which involves hormones*

Data-logging blood pressure during activity and rest

An ambulatory blood pressure monitor takes accurate readings as the person moves about during their normal daily activities. These readings are stored by the monitor, which later may be linked through a computer to a printer, so that a copy of the results can be obtained.

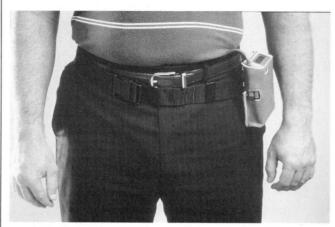

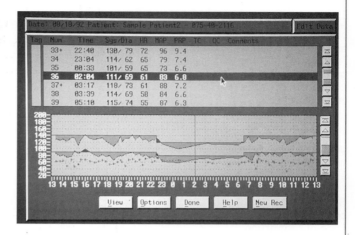

Figure 18.3

Setting the pace

What happens if the control system for cardiac output is not working properly? If the coronary arteries are blocked there may be a lack of blood supply to the conducting fibres of the Purkyne tissue within the heart. For this reason, or because of infection, the conducting tissue may be damaged. If so, it may not relay the wave of electrical activity that normally spreads across the atria, and later upwards across the ventricles during a heart beat. This is potentially fatal, but can be solved with the use of an artificial pacemaker. These may be installed temporarily in an emergency, or can be permanent. Permanent pacemakers have a battery power source which can transmit electrical stimulation through a pacing wire. There are different designs, depending on the exact reason for the person's problem. The latest generation of artificial pacemakers are called rate responsive, as they sense physiological changes in the body and respond by setting an appropriate heart rate. Pacemakers require regular 'service checks' but are a useful solution to the failure of the natural control system.

18.3 Controlling breathing rate

The respiratory centre in the hindbrain is responsible for controlling the breathing rate. Within the respiratory centre are the inspiratory and expiratory centres. The following are the main components of the control system for breathing:

- **Sensory** – Chemoreceptors in the hindbrain and in the carotid arteries and aorta are sensitive to carbon dioxide concentration. Sensory nerves transmit impulses from these receptors to the inspiratory centre. Stretch receptors in the lungs transmit impulses to the expiratory centre.

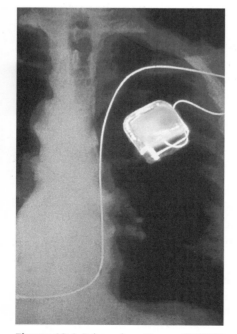

Figure 18.4 False-colour X-ray of a heart pacemaker in position
(See Colour Gallery page 351)

- **Processing** – The respiratory centre relays the information received from the receptors to the effectors, via motor nerves. These nerves run from the respiratory centre to the intercostal muscles and diaphragm.

- **Effectors** – The diaphragm and the intercostal muscles attached to the ribs bring about changes in ventilation rate. If the inspiratory centre is stimulated, the intercostal muscles cause the rib movements needed for inspiration and the diaphragm lowers. As the stretch receptors stimulate the expiratory centre, this has the effect of inhibiting the inspiratory centre so that exhalation occurs.

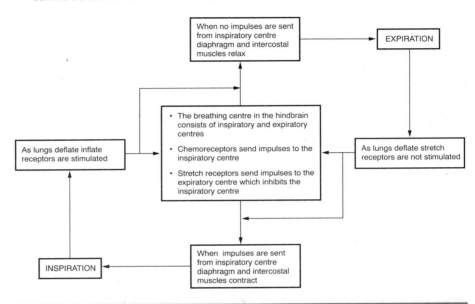

Figure 18.5 The nervous control of breathing rate involves negative feedback

Questions

1   Why are breathing rate and heart rate controlled by the autonomic nervous system?

2   The chemical co-ordination system and nervous system work in an integrated fashion. Use (a) the control of breathing rate and (b) the control of heart rate, to demonstrate this.

CHAPTER 19

Chemical Co-ordination

Hormones are chemicals produced in one part of the body which have an effect on target cells elsewhere. They are carried by the blood circulation.

19.1 Chemicals as messengers

The opening pages of Section 3 mentioned two communication systems which help to co-ordinate processes within the human body. This chapter develops ideas about chemical co-ordination, which involves the production of **hormones** by glands. Hormones are carried to all parts of the body in extracellular fluid, most commonly blood plasma, but also to a lesser extent by diffusion through tissue fluid. Hormones only cause specific responses in the cells of **target organs and tissues**, because these cells have the appropriate receptor sites for particular hormones. Chemical co-ordination is effective in certain circumstances, often those which require a long-term response. This is the case during a growth phase or reproductive development, as well as in some control systems such as the control of blood glucose level. The chemical control system and nervous system interact in co-ordinating body processes.

Figure 19.1 Microscope photo of thyroid tissue. The gland is composed of irregular follicles bound by cuboidal epithelial cells which rest on a basement membrane. The dark patches contain thyroid secretions

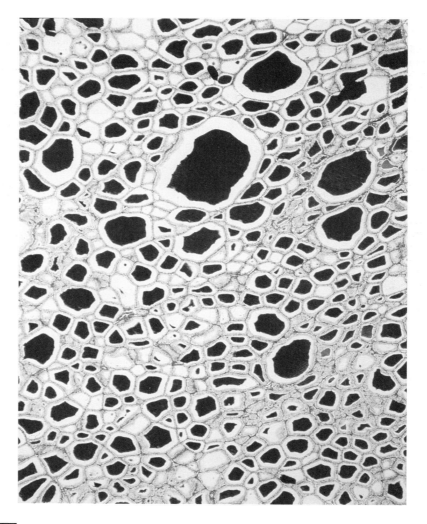

Types of hormones

Hormones vary widely in chemical composition but basically fall into four main types as summarised in Table 19.1.

Table 19.1 The main types of hormones

Type	Chemical nature	Solubility	Need for receptor sites	Examples
peptide	chains of amino acids with specific 3-D shape	water soluble, stored in vesicles	target cells have specific receptors	insulin, oxytocin
catecholamine	derived from the amino acid tyrosine	water soluble, stored in vesicles	target cells have receptors	adrenaline, noradrenaline, thyroxine
steroid	derived from cholesterol	lipid soluble, so not stored	intracellular receptors	testosterone, oestrogens, cortisol, aldosterone
prostaglandin	derived from fatty acids	lipid soluble, so not stored	intracellular receptors	prostaglandin

How do hormones affect cells?

Hormones are secreted into extracellular fluid such as blood plasma, but despite their low concentration they produce the desired effect on target cells. Outlined below are two of the ways this is thought to happen:

Figure 19.2 Hormones affect cell processes

1 Once a hormone interacts with receptor sites an enzyme is activated and a **'second messenger'** substance is produced within the cytoplasm of target cells. The second messenger activates other enzymes within the cells, so influencing their chemical processes. Adrenaline is thought to act like this, causing the second messenger cyclic AMP to form from ATP, which in turn activates enzymes.

In fact, there may be a series of stages involving the activation of enzymes, giving a **cascade** effect. For example, one molecule of the hormone glucagon acts on liver and muscle cells through a cascade of chemical events, causing the breakdown of glycogen, and the formation of many molecules of glucose. In other words, there is a multiplying effect.

2 In some cases the hormone linked with the receptor moves within a cell and acts as an internal messenger. Lipid soluble steroid hormones such as oestrogen and testosterone work this way. They have a direct effect by triggering the process of transcription of the DNA within a cell. This 'switching on or off' of sections of DNA affects protein synthesis and determines which enzymes are made within the cell.

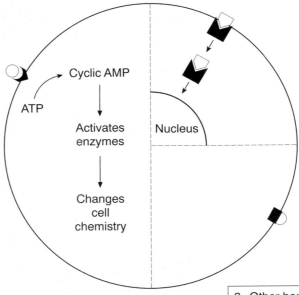

3 Other hormones bind to receptor sites on the cell surface membrane, altering permeability.

Questions

1 Why can the body store water soluble hormones in membrane-bound vesicles, but not lipid soluble ones?

2

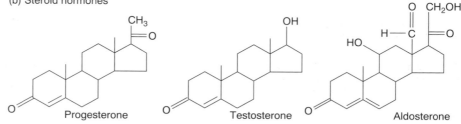

(a) Precursor molecule

Cholesterol

(b) Steroid hormones

Progesterone   Testosterone   Aldosterone

Figure 19.3 The molecular structure of some steroid hormones

▶ *Chapter 31.8* **explains** *protein synthesis*

▶ *Chapter 32.2* **describes how** *genes are switched on and off*

a) In Figure 19.3 what is the main difference in structure between the derivative of cholesterol shown in part (a) and the steroid hormones shown in part (b)?

b) Suggest a reason why the influence of oestradiol on fluid balance during the menstrual cycle can include a stimulation of the aldosterone receptors in the kidney.

19.2 Human glands and hormones

Glands such as sweat glands, which release their secretions outside the body, are called **exocrine glands**. Other exocrine glands release substances into the lumen of the gut, which is actually an external space although it is located at the centre of the body. Therefore salivary glands and the pancreas are exocrine glands that have ducts through which they release their secretions. Digestive glands which produce digestive enzymes are examples of ductless exocrine glands. However, the secretions of these exocrine glands are not considered to be hormones.

The main hormones affecting the body are produced by **endocrine glands** which release their secretions directly into body fluids such as blood plasma. Glands release hormones because of stimulation by nerve cells, or in response to other hormones in the blood. Figure 19.4 summarises the position, secretion and functions of the main endocrine glands.

The hypothalamus has a role in overseeing many important conditions which affect living cells. For example, it monitors many metabolite and hormone levels in the blood, as well as the body temperature. As a result of this, the hypothalamus is involved in most control systems. The hypothalamus and the pituitary gland are intimately connected in terms of their origin and physical position, their nerve and blood links, and therefore their functioning. The hypothalamus largely controls the pituitary gland which in turn controls many other glands in the body.

The hypothalamus and pituitary glands oversee chemical co-ordination.

Hypothalamus – This is situated in the hind brain and produces: ADH or antidiuretic hormone (see pages 147–148), which decreases the amount of urine produced and causes constriction of blood vessels after injury which helps to stop bleeding; and oxytocin (see page 290), which stimulates the uterine muscle to contract during labour, and stimulates mammary tissue to squeeze out milk during suckling

Thyroid gland – This is situated at the base of the neck and produces: T4 or thyroxine and T3 or triiodothyronine (see page 294), which are both involved in controlling the rate of metabolism; and calcitonin, which is involved in the absorption of calcium ions by bones

Parathyroid glands – These are behind the thyroid gland and produce parathormone

Thymus gland – This is situated around the base of the trachea and produces thymus hormone (see pages 307 and 319), which has a role in the development of immunity

Glands in the wall of the duodenum – These produce secretin (see page 170), which increases the secretion of digestive enzymes by the pancreas

Stomach

Duodenum

Small intestine

Kidneys – These are situated on the back wall of the abdomen and produce renin and angiotensin (see page 148), which are involved in a cascade of events, resulting in the fine tuning of sodium concentration and volume of blood

Ovaries – These are located in the lower abdomen and produce: oestrogen (see page 296), which causes body changes at puberty in females and stimulates thickening of the uterine lining during the menstrual cycle; and progesterone (see page 297), which is important in the menstrual cycle

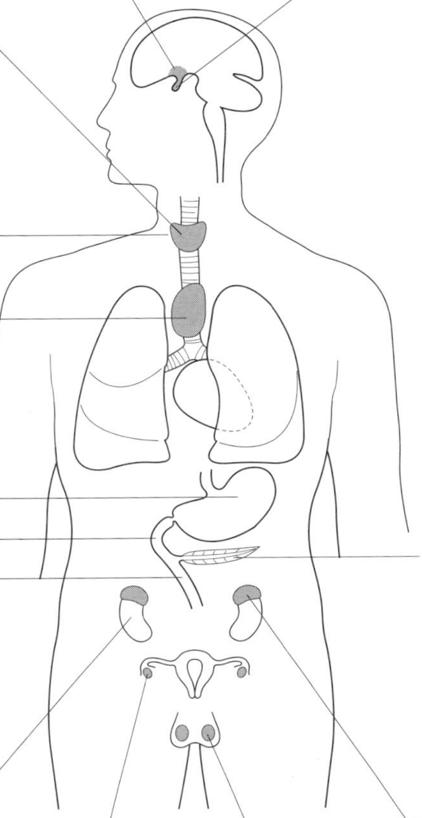

Pituitary gland – This is situated directly below the hypothalamus and produces: ACTH or adrenocorticotrophic hormone (see page 294) which controls the secretion of some hormones by the adrenal glands; FSH or follicle stimulating hormone (see page 297), which in females stimulates the ovaries to produce oestrogen and promotes the maturation of ova, and in males it stimulates sperm production in the testes; LH or luteinising hormone (see page 297), which in females stimulates ovulation, the formation of the corpus luteum and the thickening of the lining of the womb, and in males it stimulates the testes to produce testosterone; prolactin (see pages 291–292), which stimulates milk production in females; growth hormone (see page 294), which has a long-term effect by stimulating growth; and TSH or thyroid stimulating hormone (see page 294), which controls secretion of hormones produced by the thyroid

Pancreas – This is both an exocrine and an endocrine gland. As an exocrine gland it produces digestive enzymes which are released via the pancreatic duct into the lumen of the gut. As an endocrine gland it produces insulin and glucagon (see pages 131–132), which are both important in controlling the level of glucose in blood plasma

Adrenal glands – These are situated above the kidneys and produce: glucocorticoids, which have diverse effects including anti-inflammatory and anti-allergy effects; aldosterone (see page 148), which affects sodium regulation by the kidneys and the balance of sodium and potassium in extracellular fluids; adrenaline (see page 135), which increases the rate and force of the heart beat, dilates the arterioles of the heart and muscles, constricts skin arterioles and raises blood glucose levels; and noradrenaline (see page 170), which constricts arterioles in body tissues, raising blood pressure

Testes – These are held in the scrotum, and produce testosterone (see page 296), which causes body changes at puberty in males and stimulates sperm production

Figure 19.4 The hormones produced by endocrine glands have a powerful effect on the processes of life

All nerve fibres secrete a chemical substance (a neurotransmitter) from their terminal nerve endings. But these **neurosecretory cells** are able to secrete to a greater extent than other nerve cells. The substances they produce are called **releasing factors** which pass either:

- directly into the blood supply within the posterior lobe of the pituitary or;
- indirectly via the blood supply which leads to the anterior lobe.

Figure 19.5 Substances made by neurosecretory cells are the link between the hypothalamus and the pituitary gland

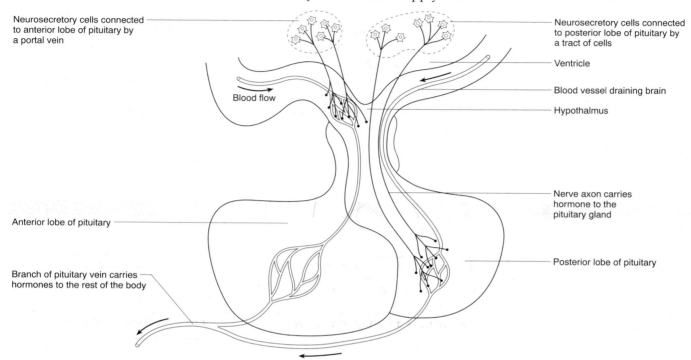

Neurosecretory cells connected to anterior lobe of pituitary by a portal vein

Neurosecretory cells connected to posterior lobe of pituitary by a tract of cells

Ventricle

Blood vessel draining brain

Hypothalmus

Blood flow

Nerve axon carries hormone to the pituitary gland

Anterior lobe of pituitary

Posterior lobe of pituitary

Branch of pituitary vein carries hormones to the rest of the body

Hypothalamus

Inhibits production of releasing factor

Releasing factor

Inhibits TSH release

Anterior pituitary gland

Thyroid-stimulating hormone (TSH)

Thyroid gland

Thyroxine in bloodstream

Figure 19.6 (left) The hypothalamus is sensitive to the level of thyroxine in the blood. If the level falls below a certain level, the hypothalamus produces more releasing factor. This stimulates the anterior lobe of the pituitary to release more thyroid stimulating hormone, which in turn stimulates the thyroid gland to produce thyroxine. Thyroxine has an effect on both the anterior lobe of the pituitary and the hypothalamus, which leads to a reduction in the production of more thyroxine. This is an example of a negative feedback loop, which are so common in control systems.

Figure 19.7 (right) The cascade effect initiated by the hypothalamus means that a small amount of initial hormone can cause a larger end effect

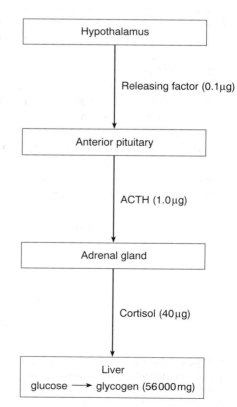

Hypothalamus

Releasing factor (0.1 μg)

Anterior pituitary

ACTH (1.0 μg)

Adrenal gland

Cortisol (40 μg)

Liver
glucose ⟶ glycogen (56 000 mg)

19.3 Two systems of communication

The chemical and nervous systems act differently, yet they complement each other and interact. In the nervous system impulses moving along the neurones are responsible for transmitting information. However, there are gaps between nerve cells called **synapses** which an impulse must cross. Chemical substances called **neurotransmitters** link the synapses by moving from one nerve cell across the gap, and interacting at receptor sites on the next. In this respect, both systems use the release of a chemical and its interaction with receptors. This provides a useful approach when designing medicines. Many medicines fit into the receptors sites on cells, and either increase or block the effect of a hormone or a neurotransmitter from a nerve cell.

▶ *Chapter 20 describes the nervous system in detail*

Table 19.2 General differences in the mode of operation between chemical and nervous co-ordination

Feature	Chemical co-ordination	Nervous co-ordination
how the system transmits information	chemicals (hormones)	impulses (electrical changes)
speed of transmission	not usually rapid, takes longer to have effect	travel fast and act rapidly
area affected	widespread effect, specific response relies on siting of receptors	very localised as individual effector cells are stimulated
substances involved	each hormone is different in structure	neurotransmitters at synapses between neurones

Modifying hormones to make medicines

Noradrenaline is a hormone made in the adrenal gland. It is also made at the ends of some nerve cells. It acts as a **neurotransmitter** by helping nerve impulses cross the gap between two nerve cells, or between nerves and cells such as muscle fibres within an organ. In humans, noradrenaline causes an increase in heart rate, dilation of the air tubes (bronchioles) in the lungs and increases sweating. To have an effect on cells, a hormone has to bind to a receptor site on the surface membrane. Figure 19.8 shows the part of the noradrenaline molecule which exactly fits and binds to the receptor.

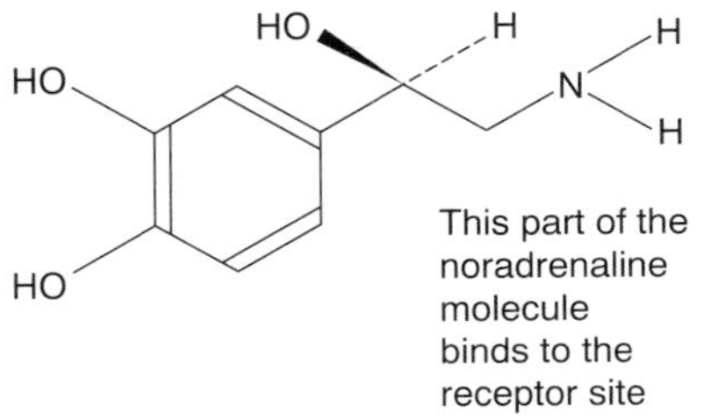

In recent years, noradrenaline has been modified to make medicines for treating two common conditions: asthma and heart disorders such as angina. People with asthma have difficulty breathing when their air tubes become constricted. Heart disorders are generally aggravated when the heart muscle is stimulated, making it work harder.

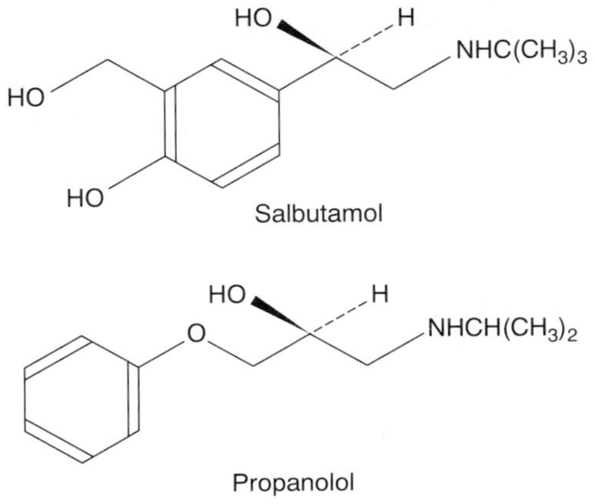

Salbutamol

Propanolol

Figure 19.9 Molecules that mimic noradrenaline

This part of the noradrenaline molecule binds to the receptor site

Figure 19.8 Part of a molecule exactly fitting a receptor is called **molecular recognition**

Modifying hormones to make medicines – contd.

New substances can be made from noradrenaline by keeping the part of the molecule which recognises and binds to a receptor, but changing other parts of the noradrenaline molecule. Figure 19.9 shows salbutamol and propanolol, two medicines made by modifying noradrenaline.

The interesting thing is that these new substances act in opposite ways. Salbutamol is an **agonist** because it binds to the same receptor sites as noradrenaline in the heart and causes the same effect – a widening of the air tubes in the lungs. But it does not affect receptor sites on muscle cells in the heart, so does not speed up heart rate which could be dangerous. Propanolol is an **antagonist** because it binds to the same receptor sites as noradrenaline, but does not have the same effect. It blocks the receptor sites so that noradrenaline cannot bind with them, and so heart rate is slowed.

Questions

1 a) In what ways are the three molecules shown in Figure 19.9 similar, and in what ways are they different?

   b) Why are some parts of the original molecule retained?

2 Suggest reasons why the scientists who develop these medicines start with a molecule which is already present in the body.

3 Find out about the testing and licensing procedures which are required before a new medicine can be used in general practice in the UK.

How do the nervous system and hormonal system interact in the alimentary canal?

The control of most body systems involves both chemical and nervous co-ordination. An example of this is in the alimentary canal (Figure 19.10). Many secretions are produced within the alimentary canal and the associated organs such as the liver. The most efficient use of resources is to get the correct amount of each of these secretions to the right part of the alimentary canal at the right time. How is this level of control brought about?

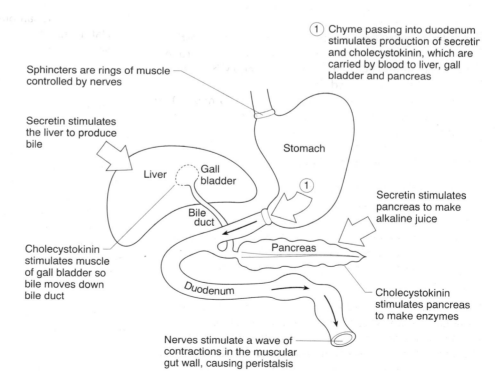

Sphincters are rings of muscle controlled by nerves

Secretin stimulates the liver to produce bile

Cholecystokinin stimulates muscle of gall bladder so bile moves down bile duct

① Chyme passing into duodenum stimulates production of secretir and cholecystokinin, which are carried by blood to liver, gall bladder and pancreas

Liver — Gall bladder

Bile duct

Stomach

Secretin stimulates pancreas to make alkaline juice

Pancreas

Duodenum

Cholecystokinin stimulates pancreas to make enzymes

Nerves stimulate a wave of contractions in the muscular gut wall, causing peristalsis

Figure 19.10 Luckily for us, all of these events go on automatically, so all we have to do is enjoy the meal

The sight, smell and taste of food is an immediate stimulus for the nervous system which brings about reflex responses – the secretion of bile from the liver and pancreatic juice from the pancreas. When chyme passes from the stomach into the duodenum, the epithelial cells lining this area of the gut are stimulated to produce both digestive enzymes and hormones. The hormones (mainly secretin and cholecystokinin) then stimulate the other events shown in Figure 19.10.

Another role of the nervous system in the alimentary canal is in bringing about peristalsis. Between the inner circular muscle layer and the outer longitudinal layer of smooth muscle is a network of autonomic nerve fibres forming the Auerbach's plexus. This stimulates the smooth muscle to contract regularly, pushing food through the gut. There is another nerve network between the circular muscle layer and the submucosal layer, which affects secretion from glands in the gut wall. There are also rings of muscle called sphincters at either end of the stomach, which are controlled by the nervous system, so that they only open periodically to let some of the contents move along the gut.

Hormones and athletes

In 1994 British Olympic hopeful runner Diane Modhal was banned by the British Athletic Federation from competition, as a result of a test which showed unusually high levels of the hormone testosterone in her urine. Testosterone is a steroid hormone which has the effect of promoting the growth of muscle tissue. Right from the start, Diane denied taking the steroid.

The evidence against Diane

This came from a urine sample taken in June 1994 in Lisbon. The sample was immediately divided into two: sample A and sample B, which were sent off for testing. Two months later Diane was told that the testosterone level in sample A was abnormally high and when sample B was tested it confirmed the results: over 120 nanograms per millilitre, compared to the norm of 10 ng ml^{-1}. The laboratory compared the level of testosterone with that of another hormone (a test that compensates for the concentration of urine), giving what is known as a T/E ratio. This also proved higher than the norm.

The evidence for Diane

The urine sample taken in Lisbon was kept unrefrigerated for two hot nights and a summer day. The smell of ammonia from sample B was very strong and the pH was 8.85 which is generally thought to be a sign that bacteria have begun to break down some substances.

Modhal consulted a specialist in endocrinology to see if she had a medical condition which could affect the level of testosterone in the analysis. His answer was no but he noticed that the original analysis showed extremely low levels of two other hormones which are normally present. He suggested that bacteria may have converted these hormones into testosterone.

An experiment at Manchester University

Scientist Simon Gaskell took a urine sample from two women under the same conditions that Diane's sample had been taken. He split each sample into two and stored one at −20°C and the other at 37°C for three days. The T/E ratio was analysed and had risen to above the norm in the sample stored at 37°C. This experiment was later repeated by Rod Bilton of John Moore's University in Liverpool, where recorded levels of testosterone in female urine after storage at 30°C were between 120 and 150 ng ml^{-1}.

Christine Ayotte of Montreal's accredited laboratory has tested poorly stored urine samples from athletic competitors over the last five years, and claims she has not recorded high testosterone levels or T/E ratios but has actually found the reverse: that testosterone can break down. Ayotte has also stated that testosterone made in humans or injected by them is usually bound to sugar molecules. Testosterone made by bacteria is in its free form and is gradually oxidised. She suggests that it is possible to test for unbound testosterone and discard the sample if the level is too high.

Faced with the doubt caused by these latest tests, an appeal panel ruled that Diane's ban should be lifted. However, the debate continues as other facts and ideas are considered.

Source: *New Scientist*, 23 March 1996

CHAPTER 20 Nervous Co-ordination

20.1 Sensitivity and the nervous system

Neurones and neuroglial cells make up nerve tissue. Sensitivity involves detection of a stimulus, processing the information and a response.

The nervous system is composed of highly specialised cells called **neurones**, which transmit information very rapidly in the form of electrical events known as **impulses**. Grouped together, these neurones form nerves which are conducting pathways that spread throughout the body. Within nerve tissue are other cells which are not neurones. These **neuroglial cells** help in providing nutrients and support to neurones, form a covering around some nerves, and may have other specific functions.

The simplest nervous response is a **reflex** which can involve as few as two or three neurones. Yet some areas of the nervous system such as the sense organs and the brain are highly developed for more specific functions. Broadly speaking, the organisation of the nervous system falls into two parts: the **peripheral nervous system** which conducts impulses to and from the tissues, and the **central nervous system (CNS)** which processes the information. The components of these systems are described in Chapter 20.5.

Many changes happen constantly in our environment. The chance of survival is improved for any living organism which can detect and respond to these changes. Not only is sensitivity important in avoiding immediate danger, but it also becomes possible to search for the most favourable set of living conditions. A **stimulus** is a change in the environment which the body can detect. Stimuli are detected by a **receptor** of a **sensory cell**. Sensory cells link either directly or via interconnecting neurones in the spinal cord or brain, to effector cells. **Effector cells** link with a part of the body that brings about a change. The overall chain of events involves detection, processing and response to a stimulus in the environment. Remember though, many impulses originate in the brain rather than in a receptor, but are still conducted to an effector.

stimulus = singular
stimuli = plural

Neurones

Like other cells, neurones consist of cytoplasm containing organelles such as a nucleus, many mitochondria and rough endoplasmic reticulum. Most of the cytoplasm is in the **cell body**, and the remainder is in the fine cytoplasmic threads which extend from the cell. Impulses move towards the cell body via a single **dendron** or finer **dendrites**. The **axon** is the strand of cytoplasm which takes the impulse away from the cell body.

Types of nerves

Neurones are specialised cells. The exact structure of a neurone depends on its function (Figure 20.1). Sensory neurones conduct impulses from receptors towards the central nervous system. Relay neurones, also called intermediate or bipolar neurones, interconnect sensory and motor neurones in the CNS. Cells which conduct impulses from the CNS to effector organs or tissues (e.g. muscles and glands) are motor neurones.

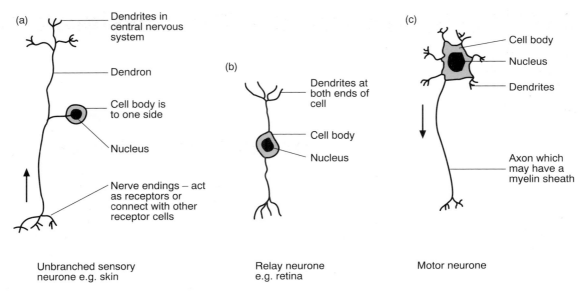

Figure 20.1 (a) A sensory neurone (b) A relay neurone (c) A motor neurone

Schwann cells are a type of neuroglial cell which form an insulating covering to some neurones by growing spirally round the axon many times, as if the axon was 'rolled up' in a blanket. The cell membranes of Schwann cells are rich in phospholipid and another fatty substance, which is why many layers insulate the neurone. The covering they form is called the **myelin sheath**, which is protective and has the effect of speeding up the rate that impulses move along neurones. There are minute gaps between two adjacent Schwann cells, so that the myelin sheath is not complete. Spinal and cranial nerves are **myelinated nerves**. Schwann cells do associate with unmyelinated nerves, but the arrangement is such that there is no myelin sheath, and their function is mainly support.

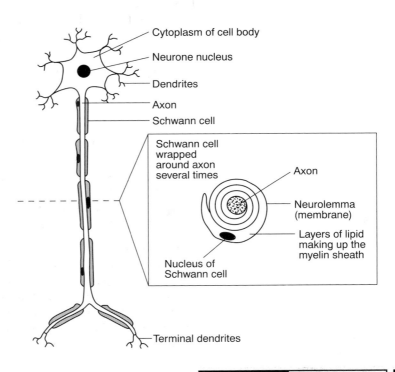

Figure 20.2 Schwann cells are important in the functioning of myelinated neurones

Brain cell circuits

Scientists have succeeded in growing circuits of neurones on a silicon base outside the body. The problem they faced was getting the cells to grow normally on a non-biological material. First they coated the silicon base with one type of molecule which attracts to silicon, forming a bristle-like layer sticking out from the surface. Then they attached a second type of molecule to the free ends of the molecules in the first layer. The second type of molecule was a protein which forms the active site of a nerve growth factor, known to promote the growth of neurones in the body.

The nerve cells grew normally, forming axons and dendrites, and interconnecting by way of synapses. The direction of growth was controlled by removing some areas of the growth promoting layer and substituting an inhibiting layer. This left a pattern of paths along which neurones grew.

What are the possible applications for this technique? The scientists working on this project hope to use neurone circuit boards for testing the toxicity of drugs and chemicals, and therefore to avoid unnecessary

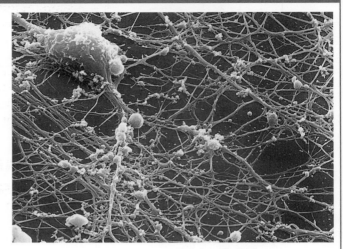

Figure 20.3 Neurones form numerous interconnections in the brain

animal testing. Looking ahead, could this pave the way to brain cell computers, benefiting from the learning ability of living neurones?

Source: *New Scientist*, 30 March 1996

Receptors

The human body contains receptors of various levels of complexity. The simplest receptors consist of one cell: a sensory neurone, with dendrites which are sensitive to a particular stimulus. This is a **primary receptor**. Examples are pressure receptors and touch receptors found in the skin. **Secondary receptors** are formed from more than one cell. Taste buds and olfactory receptors (which give the sense of smell) are secondary receptors. In both cases, a special epithelial cell called a receptor cell is sensitive to chemical stimuli. This is close to a sensory cell which carries the impulse to the central nervous system. A further level of development occurs when many sensory receptors are grouped within a **sense organ**. For example, in the eye there are millions of secondary receptors making up the light-sensitive layer called the **retina**. The eye is described in detail later in this chapter.

(a) A pressure receptor

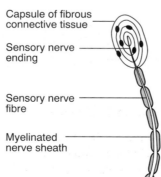

Capsule of fibrous connective tissue

Sensory nerve ending

Sensory nerve fibre

Myelinated nerve sheath

(b) A taste bud

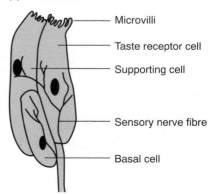

Microvilli

Taste receptor cell

Supporting cell

Sensory nerve fibre

Basal cell

Figure 20.4 (a) A primary receptor
(b) A secondary receptor

Types of receptors

- **Chemoreceptors** are sensitive to chemical stimuli, e.g. pH, all types of dissolved substances (giving sense of taste and smell).
- **Photoreceptors** are sensitive to visible light, e.g. rods and cones in the eye.
- **Thermoreceptors** are sensitive to temperature.
- **Mechanoreceptors** are sensitive to mechanical stimuli such as pressure, tension, gravity (according to body position) and movement. The term proprioreceptor is used in relation to muscles detecting contraction.

20.2 How do neurones transmit impulses?

Much of the evidence for the current model of how the neurone works has been gained by investigating 'giant axons' of squid. These axons form part of the nervous system of the mantle of a squid which is used for rapid escape movements. Their large size (1 mm diameter) means they conduct impulses faster than smaller axons and so allow a fast response. The model is based on the fact that there is a difference in charge across the neurone membrane, which can be measured using the specially developed equipment shown in Figure 20.5. A momentary change in the electrical or potential difference across the neurone surface membrane is an electrical event (an impulse).

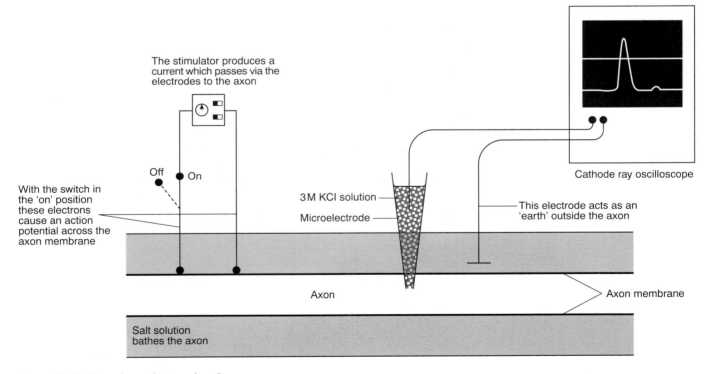

The stimulator produces a current which passes via the electrodes to the axon

Off ● ● On

With the switch in the 'on' position these electrons cause an action potential across the axon membrane

3 M KCl solution
Microelectrode

Cathode ray oscilloscope

This electrode acts as an 'earth' outside the axon

Axon

Axon membrane

Salt solution bathes the axon

Figure 20.5 Micro-electrodes are placed on the outside and into giant axons of squid. Electrical potentials recorded outside and inside enable the potential difference across the membrane to be calculated.

A resting neurone

The cell membrane of the axon of a neurone is partially permeable, giving control over what substances can enter and leave the cell. The membrane is relatively impermeable to sodium (Na^+) but relatively permeable to potassium (K^+). There are active transport channels in the plasma proteins of the membrane, which pump Na⁺ ions out of the cytoplasm of the neurone and pump K⁺ ions in. This requires energy in the form of ATP gained from respiration. As the membrane is only partially permeable to Na⁺ ions, there is an accumulation of Na⁺ ions outside the neurone, relative to the inside. However, K⁺ ions which are pumped in, diffuse back out along a concentration gradient. For these reasons, the neurone membrane is relatively positive outside compared to inside.

In this condition there is a charge or potential difference across the membrane of around -70 mV, which is called the **resting potential**, although it clearly takes energy to maintain this situation. The term refers more to the fact that the neurone is not conducting an impulse. The neurone remains at the resting potential unless stimulated, and at this stage it is **polarised**.

> ▶ **Chapter 4.3 describes the mechanism of sodium and potassium active transport**

Figure 20.6 The resting potential is maintained by sodium pumps

How does the potential difference across the membrane develop?

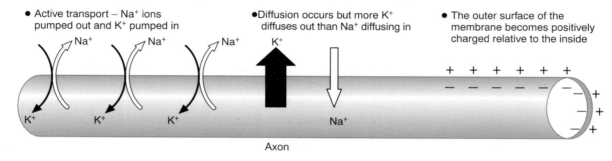

- Active transport – Na⁺ ions pumped out and K⁺ pumped in
- Diffusion occurs but more K⁺ diffuses out than Na⁺ diffusing in
- The outer surface of the membrane becomes positively charged relative to the inside

Axon

An active neurone

When a neurone is stimulated a series of events result in a change in the potential difference across the surface membrane of the cell. The mechanism of this hinges on the fact that when stimulated, the membrane permeability momentarily alters. Channels in the membrane called **sodium gates** open and Na⁺ ions rapidly move in along concentration and electrochemical gradients. The potential difference across the membrane briefly reverses and the inside of the membrane becomes relatively more positive than negative, around $+40$ mV. This is called the **action potential** because it occurs when the cell is stimulated and an impulse is transmitted. The neurone is now said to be **depolarised**.

Figure 20.7 An impulse is the temporary reversal of the electrical potential difference across the neurone membrane, in which the membrane is depolarised

- Sodium pumps working
- Sodium gates closed

- Sodium gates open Na⁺ ions move in
- K⁺ ions move out along electrochemical gradient as membrane permeability changes

- Sodium pumps working
- Sodium gates closed

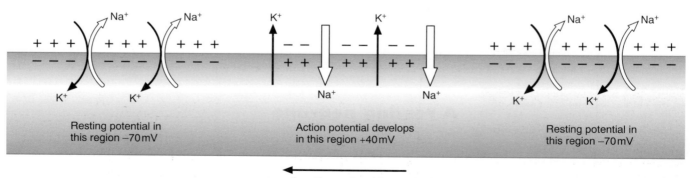

Resting potential in this region -70 mV

Action potential develops in this region $+40$ mV

Resting potential in this region -70 mV

Impulse moving this way

Returning to resting potential

At the tail end of an impulse, the sodium gates close and the sodium pumps again actively move Na$^+$ ions out of the neurone and move K$^+$ ions in. Na$^+$ ions again accumulate outside the cell. The membrane becomes slightly more permeable to K$^+$ so it diffuses out along the electrochemical gradient. After a short while the resting potential is restored. The time taken for this to happen is the **refractory period**. During the initial part of this time (the **absolute refractory period**) the neurone cannot be stimulated to depolarise again. During the **relative refractory period** only a high intensity stimulus can lead to further depolarisation. This means that an impulse can only move forward during the refractory period, so the neurone transmits unidirectionally.

The impulse timescale

> An action potential occurs when the neurone membrane is depolarised, and there is a membrane potential of +40 mV. A resting potential occurs when the neurone membrane is repolarised, and the membrane potential is −70 mV.

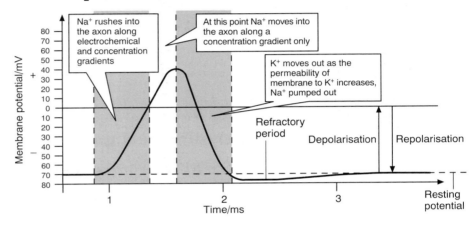

Figure 20.8 Depolarisation takes around 0.5 ms to reach a maximum, after which repolarisation begins. The refractory period lasts another few milliseconds. Altogether this is a very brief electrical event. Neurones may conduct 500–1000 impulses per second.

The **threshold** is the point at which depolarisation and an action potential can happen again. Exactly when the threshold occurs depends on sufficient sodium channels being open to allow Na$^+$ ions in, and for sufficient repolarisation to have occurred. If a neurone is being stimulated an action potential occurs once the threshold is reached. The size of the stimulus does *not* affect the size of the action potential, which is always the same. The neurone either conducts an impulse or does not. This is called the **all or nothing** rule. However, the effect of constant stimulation on a whole nerve is different, because individual neurones have different thresholds. Those with a low threshold will be depolarised first and others will follow suit as their threshold is reached. Even so, each neurone obeys the all or nothing rule once it reaches its threshold.

> The threshold is reached when there is a sufficiently negative membrane potential for an action potential to occur. Neurones obey an 'all or nothing' rule: the size of the action potential is always the same, despite the size of stimulation.

(a)

(b)

Figure 20.9 (a) Stimulation of a single neurone: no response until the threshold is reached, then the same strength of response each time (b) Repeated stimulation of a whole nerve: no response until the threshold is reached, then increasing response as the threshold for more and more neurones is reached

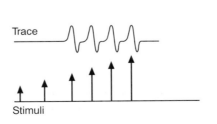

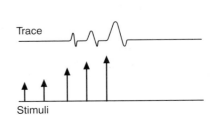

Starting and continuing

An impulse is initiated by stimulation of the receptor, causing a change in membrane permeability and subsequent depolarisation. What makes an impulse continue along the axon? This process, called the **propagation** of the impulse, is due to ion attractions across either side of the membrane. Figure 20.10 shows how minute local circuits develop, both ahead and behind the action potential. As already noted, the refractory period ensures one-way travel.

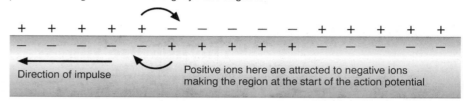

Sodium ions (Na⁺) are attracted to negative ions at the start of the action potential leaving the membrane slightly more negative

Direction of impulse

Positive ions here are attracted to negative ions making the region at the start of the action potential

Figure 20.10 The wave of depolarisation moves along the axon

Area ahead of action potential

Action potential propogates in this region

Area behind action potential

Myelinated nerves conduct faster

Myelinated nerves contain neurones with an insulating myelin sheath. The ions can only pass in and out of the gaps between Schwann cells at the **nodes of Ranvier**, which are about 1 mm apart. Propagation in myelinated cells is more complex than previously described, however, it is sufficient here to note that action potentials jump from node to node, and so their speed along the axon is faster. This 'jumping' from node to node is called **saltatory conduction**. The diameter of an axon is also important in determining the speed an impulse travels at: the bigger the diameter of the axon the faster impulses travel. Scientists have recorded impulses moving at speeds of 0.5–100 metres msec⁻¹.

Questions

1 a) What is the difference in polarity of the axon membrane when a neurone is stimulated and when it is not stimulated?

   b) About how long does depolarisation last?

   c) What is the refractory period, and why is it of benefit?

   d) Why is there a different response to continual stimulation by an individual neurone and a whole muscle?

2 Experiments have shown that using an ATP-inhibitor prevents a resting potential developing within an axon. Explain the link between ATP and the resting potential.

3 Explain these statements:

   a) The resting potential is mainly determined by K⁺ ions.

   b) The action potential is mainly determined by Na⁺ ions.

20.3 Synapses link up the system

A synapse is a gap between the dendrites of two nerve cells.

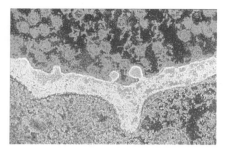

Figure 20.11 The synaptic cleft is around 20 nm wide, across which neurotransmitters must pass in order to trigger an action potential in the adjoining neurone *(See Colour Gallery page 352)*

C19

The junction between two neurones is called a **synapse**. They occur as tiny gaps where the dendrites of different neurones almost meet. There are usually numerous synapses on any particular neurone. For example, up to 100 synapses may occur on the cell body and dendrites of a motor neurone in a spinal nerve. The mechanism in most nerves has a chemical basis, although there are some in which it is an electrical event.

We need to consider some of the structural details of a synapse to understand how it works. The end of the neurone conducting an impulse towards a synapse is called the **presynaptic knob**. Within it are numerous mitochondria, microtubules and special presynaptic vesicles which are bound by membrane. These vesicles contain the vital chemical ingredient: a **neurotransmitter**. The gap between the presynaptic neurone and the postsynaptic neurone is called the **synaptic cleft**. After crossing the cleft, an impulse reaches the postsynaptic neurone. The membrane of the postsynaptic neurone which borders the cleft has receptor molecules on its surface which are also vital in allowing an impulse to cross the synapse. How this happens is described in Figure 20.12.

(a) An impulse moves along the presynaptic cell, reaching the presynaptic knob. This causes an increase in the permeability of the membrane to calcium ions.

(b) There is an influx of calcium ions, which causes the vesicles to fuse with membrane so that neurotransmitter is released into cleft.

(c) The neurotransmitter binds with receptor molecules on the postsynaptic cell membrane.

(d) The permeability of the postsynaptic membrane changes and Na+ ions rush in, initiating depolarisation and an action potential.

(e) Once the impulse has moved on, the neurotransmitter molecules are split by an enzyme produced by the postsynaptic knob. The components diffuse back into the presynaptic neurone along a concentration gradient.

(f) The mitochondria within the presynaptic knob generate ATP, which is the energy source for the synthesis of more neurotransmitter.

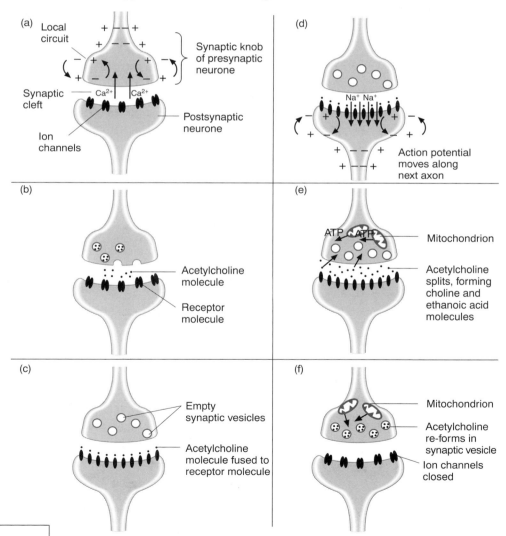

Figure 20.12 Neurotransmission

Neurotransmitters

> Neurotransmitters are chemicals that affect the permeability of the postsynaptic membrane, triggering depolarisation.

A neurotransmitter may be produced in the cell body and pass along the axon by cytoplasmic streaming through the microtubules. Other neurones make neurotransmitter in the presynaptic knobs. The two main neurotransmitters in humans are acetylcholine and noradrenaline. Acetylcholine is produced by cholinergic neurones and noradrenaline by adrenergic neurones.

The sequence of events at inhibitory synapses is different to that described by Figure 20.12. At inhibitory synapses the neurotransmitter causes the postsynaptic membrane to become more negative inside, therefore making it more difficult to reach threshold potential, and impulses are not transmitted. A neurotransmitter may have an excitatory effect at one synapse but an inhibitory one at another. This is the case with acetylcholine, which has an excitatory effect on most synapses and muscle fibres, but inhibits the action potential developing in cardiac muscle and smooth muscle, e.g. in the gut wall.

What is the role of a synapse?

- To pass information between neurones (and receptor cells), or to inhibit its progress.
- To ensure that impulses always travel unidirectionally.
- To adapt to intense stimuli. There is a limit to how quickly neurotransmitter can be resynthesised. If it is not made as fast as it is released into the cleft, the cell becomes 'fatigued' and stops making neurotransmitter. As a result, action potentials are not triggered in the postsynaptic neurone. The importance of this is that it prevents overstimulation that might otherwise cause damage to an effector.
- To adapt to and screen out continual stimuli.

You will have noted a common effect which occurs when there is a continual stimulus present in the environment. For example, you may notice a particular smell of say a furniture polish when you enter a building, or the feel of a collar touching your neck when you first put on a shirt. However, after a short while you do not notice the smell as much, or feel the collar – you have become used to these stimuli. This is called **adaptation** or **accommodation** and can affect receptor cells and neurones. In receptor cells, the generator potentials gradually decrease, triggering less impulses as time goes by. Exactly how this happens is not known. The significance of this is that the nervous system is not reacting unnecessarily to every stimulus that occurs, but can screen out information which is not important, leaving the system free to deal with important events.

Synapses sum up

Receptor cells are closely linked to neurones, often in sense organs. Like neurones they develop a potential difference across their membranes, which is set up by the presence of a stimulus. This is called the **generator potential**. However, unlike a neurone, the generator potential alters in size, depending on the size of the stimulus. The more a receptor cell is stimulated, the greater the generator potential. If the generator potential reaches the threshold for a sensory cell it synapses with, it triggers an action potential. On the other hand, it may take the added generator potentials of several receptor cells to

> Convergence of the impulses from several sensory neurones increases sensitivity to differing intensities of a stimulus.

trigger the action potential in a sensory cell. This summing of generator potentials is known as **convergence**, and it is useful for the body because it increases sensitivity to differing intensities of stimulation.

At a synapse there is often more than one presynaptic neurone. Some of these may be excitatory while others may be inhibitory. By summing up or integrating the effects of each of the presynaptic neurones, the synapse allows a greater degree of control of the response.

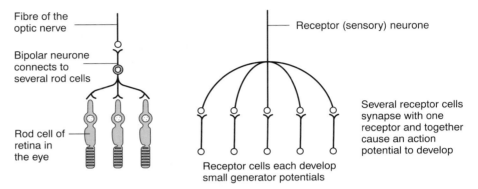

Figure 20.13 Humans are aware of varying levels of lightness and darkness

How do drugs affect the synapse?

Drugs are substances that alter the body's physiology, i.e. how it works. Drugs are used in medicines to promote, improve or sustain health. However, drugs of abuse are used to alter mood, or to experience a particular sensation. No safety testing has been completed on drugs of abuse, and many have unknown and harmful effects.

Agonist drugs affect the body by mimicking the effect of a neurotransmitter, increasing stimulation of the postsynaptic neurone.
This may be because the drug:

- acts on receptor molecules in the same way as a neurotransmitter, e.g. 'speed' or amphetamine, nicotine;
- stimulates the release of more transmitter, e.g. caffeine;
- might not be broken down, i.e. stays in place and maintains stimulation, e.g. Prozac – a tranquilliser.

Antagonist drugs have inhibitory effects, reducing stimulation of the postsynaptic neurone.
This may be because the drug:

- blocks the receptors on the postsynaptic membrane, e.g. beta-blockers;
- prevents the release of neurotransmitter, e.g. botulin – a bacterial toxin that stops the release of acetylcholine.

Some drugs may have both agonistic and antagonistic effects in different parts of the body.

How alcohol affects the nervous system

Although people may think that alcohol (ethanol) livens them up, in fact it does the opposite! Alcohol actually makes it harder for impulses to pass along nerve cells, so it has a slowing or depressant effect. This makes people feel relaxed, sometimes so relaxed they get drowsy, which is one reason why 'drink driving' is so dangerous. What is the scientific basis of the effect of drinking alcohol?

When the axon is polarised it is more positive on the outer surface and there is a resting potential of around −70 mV. For a neurone to transmit an impulse, the polarity of the axon must change, and it must become more negative on the outside and more positive on the inside.

There is a substance called gamma amino butanoic acid (GABA) which is a neurotransmitter that has the effect of switching off neurones – or making it harder for action potentials to develop. GABA binds to receptors on the axon membrane, altering the shape of the receptor so that a channel opens up in the membrane. This is a **chloride channel**, which allows chloride ions to flood into the axon. Since chloride ions are negative they make the inside of the axon more negative, so it is harder for the cell to depolarise and for an action potential to develop. How does this relate to alcohol?

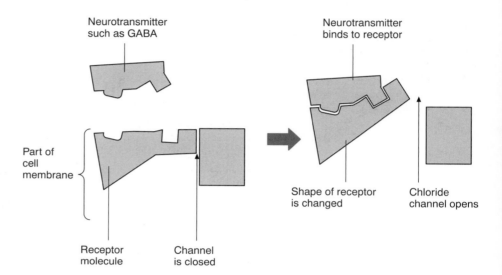

Neurotransmitter such as GABA

Neurotransmitter binds to receptor

Part of cell membrane

Receptor molecule

Channel is closed

Shape of receptor is changed

Chloride channel opens

Figure 20.14 A model of how GABA binds to a receptor and opens the chloride channel

Ethanol is thought to bind to the axon membrane close to the GABA receptors and to enhance their effect, because nerve cells are more inhibited and less likely to transmit impulses if alcohol is present. Some depressant drugs are used in medicines to treat anxiety (for example valium, containing benzodiazepine). It is very dangerous to drink alcohol if you are taking this type of medicine, because the effect of both of these drugs together can be very much greater than taking one on its own.

20.4 Where neurones meet muscles

Motor neurones carry information from the central nervous system and link with effectors. If the effector is a muscle, the point where the neurones branch and supply a group of muscle fibres is called the **motor unit**. The **neuromuscular junction** is the point where an individual neurone and a muscle fibre meet. At this junction the muscle cell membrane (called the **sarcolemma**) is folded, forming an area called the **end plate**. Within the motor neurone are many mitochondria and vesicles containing the neurotransmitter acetylcholine. The arrival of an impulse causes acetylcholine to be discharged into the cleft, which affects the sarcolemma. As a result, an end plate potential sets up and spreads via the T-tubules of the muscle fibre, causing the fibre to contract.

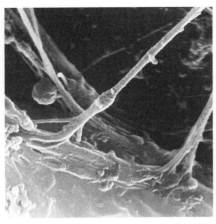

Figure 20.15 At the neuromuscular junction the impulse passes to the muscle causing contraction
(See Colour Gallery page 352)

C21

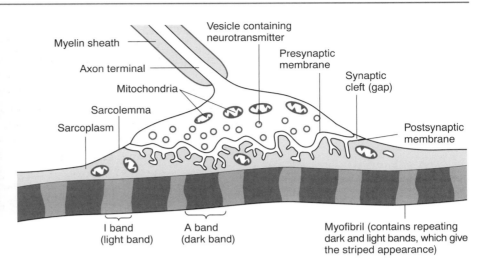

- Myelin sheath
- Axon terminal
- Mitochondria
- Sarcolemma
- Sarcoplasm
- Vesicle containing neurotransmitter
- Presynaptic membrane
- Synaptic cleft (gap)
- Postsynaptic membrane
- I band (light band)
- A band (dark band)
- Myofibril (contains repeating dark and light bands, which give the striped appearance)

20.5 The organisation of the nervous system

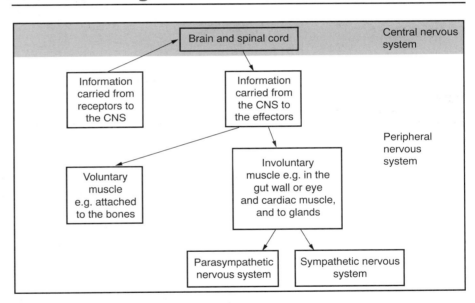

Figure 20.16 An outline of the nervous system

The central nervous system is the part concerned with processing the information which is detected by receptors and transmitted by sensory nerves. Interpreting the information involves deciding on what actions, if any, are required in response to stimuli. This processing may be both conscious and subconscious, the latter meaning that it occurs without our awareness. Subconscious processing is vital because it maintains life processes such as breathing and heart function. The **peripheral nervous system** is the system of nerves which carries information from the CNS to the effector organs. A major component of this system is the **autonomic nervous system** which brings about automatic responses, via the **sympathetic** and **parasympathetic** nervous systems. The advantage of having an autonomic system is that the conscious brain is then free to deal with other information. However, much of the peripheral nervous system is under voluntary control, such as the innervation of skeletal muscles.

The brain

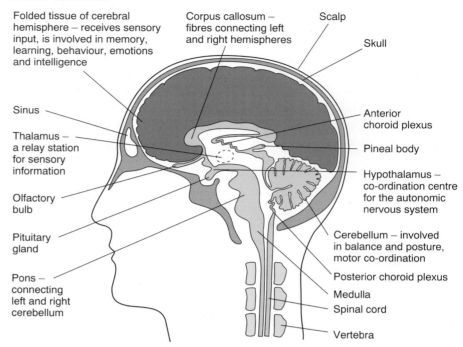

Folded tissue of cerebral hemisphere – receives sensory input, is involved in memory, learning, behaviour, emotions and intelligence

Corpus callosum – fibres connecting left and right hemispheres

Scalp

Skull

Sinus

Thalamus – a relay station for sensory information

Olfactory bulb

Pituitary gland

Pons – connecting left and right cerebellum

Anterior choroid plexus

Pineal body

Hypothalamus – co-ordination centre for the autonomic nervous system

Cerebellum – involved in balance and posture, motor co-ordination

Posterior choroid plexus

Medulla

Spinal cord

Vertebra

Figure 20.17 The human brain is a mass of nerve tissue which is a development of the end of the spinal cord. Structurally, it is organised into the forebrain, midbrain and hindbrain, the latter extending as the spine. In humans the forebrain is well developed and folded back over the midbrain and hindbrain. Despite the large amount of information known about the brain, there are many unknown aspects of its functioning. Our understanding of the human brain has come from studying the brains of other animals, experiments with human volunteers, cases of brain damage through injury, and from abnormal brain development in the fetus.

Brain waves

Some aspects of brain activity can be studied and recorded by using an **electroencephalogram (EEG)**. Electrodes are in contact with the scalp and electrical changes within the cerebral hemispheres are recorded using a pen and rotating drum with paper attached. These electrical changes are recorded as waves:

- alpha waves which are recorded when the person is relaxed with their eyes closed;
- beta waves which are present at all times, unless the brain stem is 'dead';
- gamma waves which occur when someone is asleep.

Information about where brain activity is happening can be determined with this type of investigation.

Figure 20.18 Electrode gel is used to establish a good contact between the electrodes and the scalp – the doctor can interpret the brain waves seen on a trace

The forebrain consists of two halves called the left and right **cerebral hemispheres**, or collectively the **cerebrum**. The outer layer or **cortex** is about 3 mm deep and its large surface area is heavily folded. It is composed of the cell bodies of neurones, which is why it looks darker in colour than other brain tissue, and is called **grey matter**. Since the cell bodies are packed so closely and each can form hundreds of synapses, there is much interconnection throughout the cortex of the cerebrum. The two hemispheres are connected by bundle of axons. The cerebrum has a variety of functions, yet it appears that the left side is to do with the ability to be analytical, giving skills in mathematics and logic. The right hemisphere is utilised in the analysis of shape, form and space, skills which are considered to be more developed in artistic people. The nerve tracts cross over as they enter and leave the brain, so that the left hemisphere controls some functions of the right side of the body and vice versa. Some people believe that the hand used for writing indicates which side of the brain is most dominant, and hence personality traits. This lobed part of the brain is involved with receiving sensory input, interpreting information in the association areas and with memory, learning, behaviour and emotions, and the ability to reason. There are also motor areas which output information via nerve tracts which pass down the spine, connecting via the peripheral nervous system to voluntary muscles.

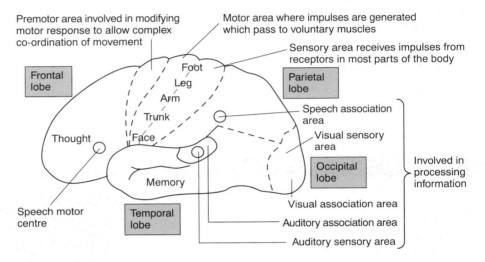

Figure 20.19 A brain map illustrates how different regions of the brain are involved in processing different types of information

The forebrain also includes the thalamus and the hypothalamus. The thalamus analyses and relays sensory input to the relevant areas of the cerebral cortex. The hypothalamus is a small structure at the base of the brain and much of the information reaching it is passed to the medulla of the hindbrain. In this way the hypothalamus acts as a co-ordination centre for the autonomic nervous system. Alongside this, secretion by neurosecretory cells in the hypothalamus controls the functioning of the pituitary gland, which in turn affects other endocrine glands. Overall, the hypothalamus has an important homeostatic role in the human body as it monitors metabolite and hormone levels and the temperature of the blood.

The midbrain contains visual and auditory reflex centres. It co-ordinates eye movements, for example in focusing, and the head movements involved in locating a sound. The midbrain relays sensory information to the thalamus, and motor information towards the muscles.

The hindbrain is composed mainly of the cerebellum and the medulla. The cerebellum receives information from the sensory centres in the brain, sensory receptors in muscles and tendons surrounding joints and the balance organs in the ears. This information is processed and then leads to routine maintenance of posture. The actions of the cerebellum are involuntary but are modified by learning. For example, learning to ride a bike takes a lot of concentration at first, until a new skill is mastered, after which the cerebellum takes over. The medulla contains important reflex

> The brain consists of the forebrain, midbrain and hindbrain.

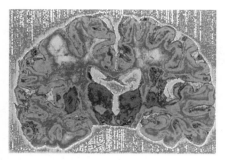

Figure 20.20 A section through a human brain. The vesicles (which are the lighter regions on this photo) are filled with fluid.

centres controlling the autonomic nervous system, which regulates automatic functions such as heart and ventilation rate, blood pressure, swallowing and peristalsis.

Brain membranes and fluid

Around the outside of the nerve tissue which makes up the central nervous system are three layers of membrane known as the **meninges**, which are themselves enclosed in the bone of the cranium and vertebrae. Between the outer and innermost layer of membrane is a second layer containing spaces which are filled with **cerebrospinal fluid (CSF).** This fluid also fills the central canal of the spine and spaces at the base of the brain. It bathes the brain, supplying nutrients and oxygen and removing wastes, as well as protecting against mechanical shock.

Meningitis is an inflammation of the membranes of the central nervous system. It can be caused by bacterial or viral infection. Nowadays there is a vaccination for the bacterial form so children are generally immunised. However, meningitis is life-threatening and it can be fatal at any age.

The spinal cord and reflex actions

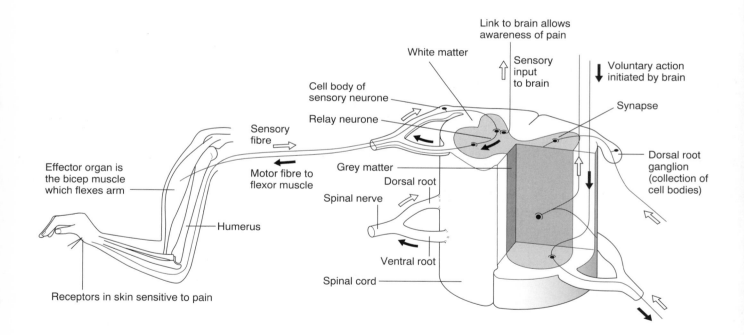

Figure 20.21 Damage limitation is afforded by a reflex arc, which allows very rapid response.

Reflex responses to specific stimuli are shown even by newborn babies illustrating the idea of responses which are 'programmed in' at the very start of life. Such reflexes are called **unconditioned reflexes** because they do not need to be learned. You have experienced many unconditioned reflexes such as swallowing food as it reaches the throat, blinking if something flies towards your eyes and moving your hand from a hot surface. The pathway taken by impulses during a reflex action is called the **reflex arc** (Figure 20.21). A **conditioned reflex** is a reflex which has been modified by experience. Pavlov carried out a well known experiment involving salivation in dogs, whom he trained to salivate at the sound of a bell by initially feeding the dogs at the same time as ringing the bell. Later, the bell alone was enough to stimulate the reflex because the dogs had been conditioned. The association of events is important in memory and learning which are well developed in humans.

Can the spinal cord be repaired?

Scientists researching in Sweden have stimulated the growth of nerve cells in rats whose spinal cords had been severed, using nerve grafts and doses of growth factor. Most of the nerve tissue in the spine produces an inhibitory factor, which is in part why axons of neurones in the spine do not regrow after injury. The Swedish scientists took nerve tissue from elsewhere in the body, which does not produce the inhibitory factor. They transplanted it into the spine, bridging the gap where the spinal cord was severed, and applied nerve growth factor. Three weeks later, axon growth had occurred and there were some signs of leg movements, which went on improving for up to a year. However, this technique needs a lot of development before it can be considered for trial in humans.

Source: *New Scientist*, 3 August 1996

The peripheral nervous system

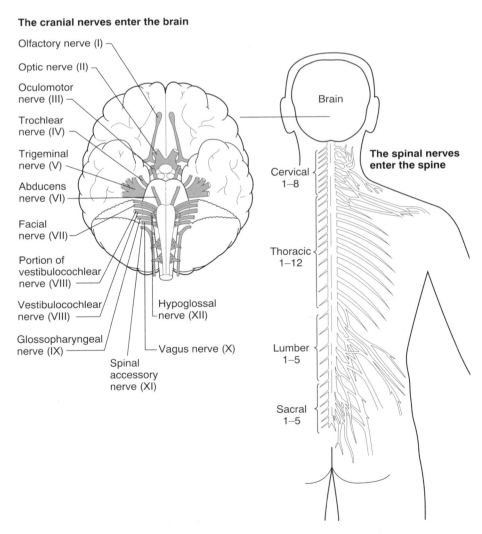

The cranial nerves enter the brain

Olfactory nerve (I)
Optic nerve (II)
Oculomotor nerve (III)
Trochlear nerve (IV)
Trigeminal nerve (V)
Abducens nerve (VI)
Facial nerve (VII)
Portion of vestibulocochlear nerve (VIII)
Vestibulocochlear nerve (VIII)
Glossopharyngeal nerve (IX)
Hypoglossal nerve (XII)
Vagus nerve (X)
Spinal accessory nerve (XI)

Brain

The spinal nerves enter the spine

Cervical 1–8
Thoracic 1–12
Lumber 1–5
Sacral 1–5

Figure 20.22 There are 31 pairs of spinal nerves which enter or exit the CNS via the spinal cord, and 12 pairs of cranial nerves which connect directly with the brain. The cranial nerves mostly innervate the head and neck area.

Spinal and cranial nerves make up the peripheral nervous system. Part of this system is under voluntary control and part is autonomic.

The nerves servicing the tissues of the body make up the **peripheral nervous system**. The part of the peripheral nervous system involved in autonomic activities can be further divided into the sympathetic and parasympathetic systems. There are both functional and structural differences between the tissues in these systems which are not described here. However, one notable difference is that the neurotransmitter produced by the sympathetic nervous system is noradrenaline, while that of the parasympathetic system is acetylcholine. In simple terms, the sympathetic system often has a stimulatory effect while the parasympathetic system is inhibitory, although this is not always the case.

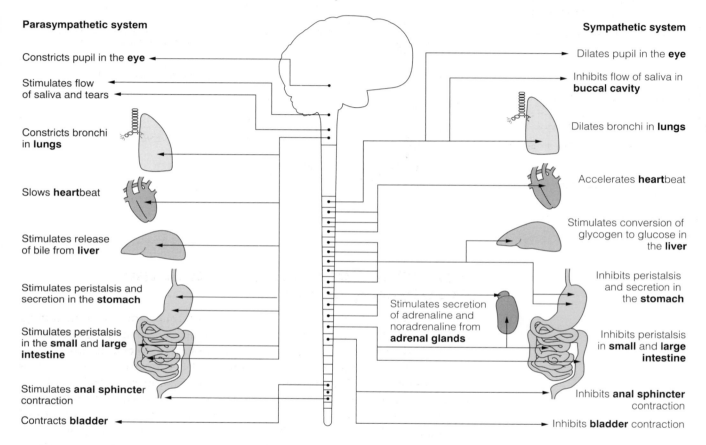

Parasympathetic system

Constricts pupil in the **eye**

Stimulates flow of saliva and tears

Constricts bronchi in **lungs**

Slows **heart**beat

Stimulates release of bile from **liver**

Stimulates peristalsis and secretion in the **stomach**

Stimulates peristalsis in the **small** and **large intestine**

Stimulates **anal sphincter** contraction

Contracts **bladder**

Sympathetic system

Dilates pupil in the **eye**

Inhibits flow of saliva in **buccal cavity**

Dilates bronchi in **lungs**

Accelerates **heart**beat

Stimulates conversion of glycogen to glucose in the **liver**

Inhibits peristalsis and secretion in the **stomach**

Inhibits peristalsis in **small** and **large intestine**

Inhibits **anal sphincter** contraction

Inhibits **bladder** contraction

Stimulates secretion of adrenaline and noradrenaline from **adrenal glands**

Figure 20.23 Most body systems are supplied with both sympathetic and parasympathetic nerves, and may also have some nerve fibres from the voluntary nervous system, giving a very sophisticated level of control and response

Questions

1 a) What is the resting potential of a cell?

   b) How is the resting potential maintained?

   c) How is the action potential propagated?

   d) Describe in outline why drugs affect the nervous system.

2 a) What is the difference between an unconditioned reflex action and a conditioned reflex?

   b) Why are reflexes useful?

   c) Which part of the nervous system is involved in a reflex action such as ducking to prevent hitting your head on a cupboard door which someone has left open?

20.6 The human eye

The human eye is an amazingly well developed optical organ, which can detect far more than light and dark or simple shapes or movement. The eye is capable of focusing throughout a large distance range, and can distinguish detail to 0.01 mm, as well as a vast tonal range of colours. However, all these functions are only possible in the presence of visible light, i.e. electromagnetic radiation of wavelength 400–700 nm.

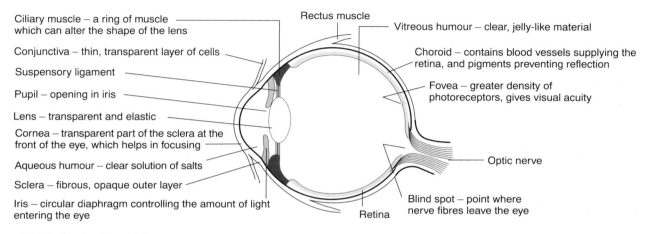

Ciliary muscle – a ring of muscle which can alter the shape of the lens

Conjunctiva – thin, transparent layer of cells

Suspensory ligament

Pupil – opening in iris

Lens – transparent and elastic

Cornea – transparent part of the sclera at the front of the eye, which helps in focusing

Aqueous humour – clear solution of salts

Sclera – fibrous, opaque outer layer

Iris – circular diaphragm controlling the amount of light entering the eye

Rectus muscle

Vitreous humour – clear, jelly-like material

Choroid – contains blood vessels supplying the retina, and pigments preventing reflection

Fovea – greater density of photoreceptors, gives visual acuity

Optic nerve

Blind spot – point where nerve fibres leave the eye

Retina

Figure 20.24 The structure of the human eye

Role of the nervous system in the functioning of the eye

The nerve supply to and from any organ is very important in its functioning. In the eye, the innervation of external muscles allows a wide range of movements such as rotation in the socket. Innervation to tear glands maintains their regular secretions and ensures the surface of the eye is swept by the automatic and regular blink reflex of the lid. The iris contains radial smooth muscle fibres which contract to widen the pupil, so more light enters. When they relax the iris widens, so reducing the size of the pupil and the amount of light getting in. The retina contains receptors which are sensitive to light and trigger impulses which pass along the optic nerve to the brain.

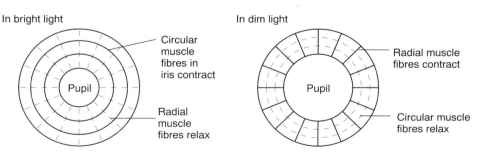

In bright light

Circular muscle fibres in iris contract

Pupil

Radial muscle fibres relax

Pupil decreases in diameter reducing amount of light entering the eye and thus preventing damage to the retina

In dim light

Radial muscle fibres contract

Pupil

Circular muscle fibres relax

Pupil increases in diameter, allowing more light into the eye thus facilitating clear vision at low light intensity

Figure 20.25 The iris controls the size of the pupil and hence the amount of light entering the eye

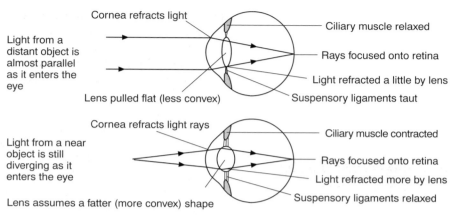

Figure 20.26 The ciliary muscle controls the size of the lens by tightening or slackening the tension on the suspensory ligaments which support the lens and hold it in position

In focusing, innervation to the ciliary muscle causes contraction of circular muscle fibres. These pull inwards and have the effect of lessening tension on the ligaments which hold the lens in place. When the ligaments slacken the lens flops back into a fatter or more convex shape, allowing closer objects to be observed in focus **(accommodated)**. The reverse set of events happen when looking at distant objects. The image of the object on the retina is in fact inverted, but we perceive images the right way up because the brain processes the information.

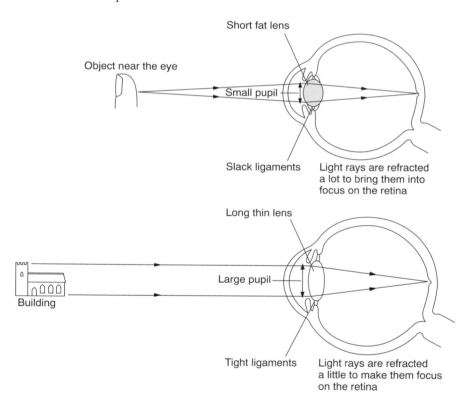

Figure 20.27 Accommodation brings viewed objects into focus. The brain interprets the series of electrical events occurring when the receptors in the retina are stimulated.

Photoreceptors in the retina

The retina contains about 100 million photoreceptors, as well as the sensory neurones with which they synapse. The photoreceptors are **rods** and **cones**; both of these are secondary receptors. Most of the receptors are rods, spread across the retina but not closely packed, which is why they do not give a very clear image. Several rods synapse with the same sensory neurone and so the impulses from them converge. The generator potentials from them summate or add up to cause an action potential in the sensory cell. This is useful in low light intensity because the summated generator potentials are big enough collectively to allow vision in dim light. The generator potentials of cones are not triggered so easily as rods, and so we need bright light to make them work. This is the reason why colours are not easy to distinguish at night. There are about six million cones closely packed at the fovea, giving greater accuracy of vision or **visual acuity**. Different cones are stimulated by different wavelengths of light, according to the visual pigment they contain. Since we can discriminate between different wavelengths we can see different colours. This is known as the **trichromatic theory**.

▶ *Chapter 33.9 explains the inheritance of colour blindness*

Photoreceptors in the retina synapse with sensory neurones. Note that in Figures 20.28 and 20.29 the light passes first through the synaptic region and inner segments of the photoreceptors, before reaching the outer segments containing visual pigments. The information in the form of nerve impulses passes out of the eye through the retina and along the optic nerves to the brain. These nerves cross over on their way to the visual cortex for processing.

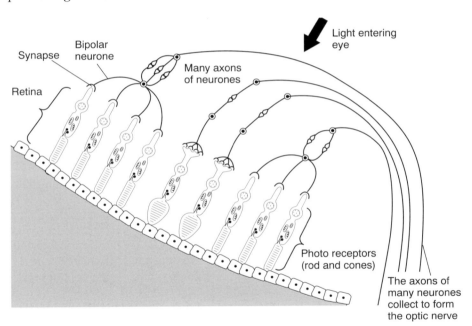

Figure 20.28 Rods and cones in the retina

How rods and cones work

Both these receptors work on the same principle which involves pigments. The pigment in a rod cell is **rhodopsin**, and in a cone is **iodopsin**, of which there are three forms. In the presence of UV light the pigment splits, altering the chemical balance within the sensory cell and causing a generator potential. This is propagated to a sensory neurone and if it reaches the required threshold, sets up an action potential. The splitting of the pigment is called **bleaching** and in normal light rods are almost entirely bleached. They are therefore unable to respond and are **light adapted**. It may take 30 minutes or so to totally re-form the rhodopsin and become adapted to the dark.

Figure 20.29 A rod cell: rhodopsin breaks down in low light intensity so that we can see in dim conditions. A cone cell: the three forms of iodopsin are sensitive to the different wavelengths of light corresponding to the three primary colours – red, green and blue. The brain interprets the number and frequency of stimulation of different cone cells as colour.

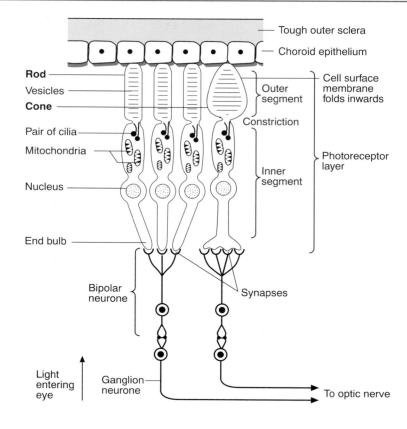

Testing eyesight

Good eyesight is a broad term, used to describe being able to see near and distant objects clearly and in focus, as well as to determine colour. How much detail we can see about objects is called **visual acuity**, and it is partly determined by the size and spacing of cone cells. Each cone cell is 2–3 μm in diameter, and a change of only a fraction of a degree in the angle of light reaching a cone is needed to ensure that a particular cone is stimulated – but its neighbour is not. It is this fine difference that gives definition to an outline.

The Snellen chart is the standard test for visual acuity. It has letters of particular sizes that should be visible to a person standing at the appropriate distance. For example, if someone standing 6 metres (20 feet) away can read a certain row of letters correctly, they are said to have 6/6 or 20/20 vision. If someone standing at 6 metres can only read letters which they should be able to read from 12 metres away, then they would have 6/12 vision and therefore a sight defect.

Questions

1 Suggest explanations for these events:

  a) when you go to bed and switch off the light at night the room seems very dark.

  b) if you wake up in the night it is possible to see your way around even though only very little light is present.

  c) you can distinguish between red and blue.

2 Make a summary table of the differences between rods and cones.

Exam questions for Section 3

1 Figure 1 shows a single rod from a mammalian retina.

Figure 1

a) Name the parts labelled A and B and give *one* function of each. *(4 marks)*

b) Draw an arrow next to the diagram to indicate the direction in which light passes through this cell. *(1 mark)*

c) State *two* ways in which vision using cones differs from vision using rods. *(2 marks)*

Edexcel

2 Table 1 shows the mean voluntary energy intake per day of soldiers stationed in climates with different local mean temperatures.

Table 1

Local mean temperature (°C)	Voluntary energy intake per day (kJ)
+35	13 000
+15	15 000
+5	16 800
−5	18 000
−20	20 000
−30	21 000

a) Discuss the physiological significance of the energy intake in relation to local mean temperature. *(4 marks)*

b) State *three* ways in which the body acclimatises to *high* temperatures. *(3 marks)*

c) i) Compare the body's tolerance to increases and decreases in core temperature. *(2 marks)*

   ii) Describe the effects of cold stress. *(2 marks)*

Edexcel

3 Figure 2 shows the simplified structure of a kidney tubule (nephron).

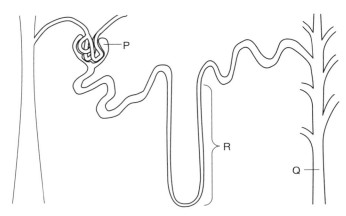

Figure 2

a) In Table 2, columns 1 and 2 show the quantities of water, glucose and urea passing through P and Q in a 24 hour period. Columns 3 and 4 show the quantities and percentages reabsorbed during the same period.

Complete Table 2 by writing the correct figures in the boxes labelled (i) to (iv). *(4 marks)*

b) Describe how R is involved in adjusting the concentration of the filtrate as it passes through the medulla of the kidney. *(3 marks)*

Edexcel

Table 2

Substance	Quantity passing through P	Quantity passing through Q	Quantity reabsorbed	Quantity percentage reabsorbed
water	180 dm³	1.5 dm³	178.5 dm³	(i)
glucose	180 g	(ii)	180 g	100
urea	53 g	25 g	(iii)	(iv)

4 Figure 3 shows a sarcomere from a myofibril of a striated muscle fibre.

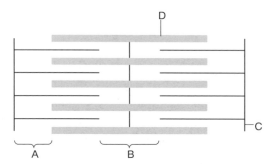

Figure 3

a) i) Name the regions labelled A, B and C. *(3 marks)*

ii) Name the material which makes up part D. *(1 mark)*

b) State the change in appearance of B when the muscle fibre contracts. *(1 mark)*

Edexcel

5 a) Describe the sequence of events that takes place when a nerve impulse arrives at a synapse. *(4 marks)*

b) Figure 4 (a) and (b) shows the changes in membrane potential in a presynaptic neurone and postsynaptic neurone when an impulse passes across a synapse.

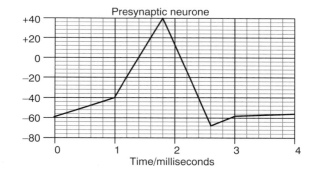

(a)

(b)

Figure 4

i) Explain how depolarisation occurs in the presynaptic neurone. *(3 marks)*

ii) The maximum depolarisation in the presynaptic neurone is +40 mV. What is the maximum depolarisation in the postsynaptic neurone? *(1 mark)*

iii) How long is the delay between the maximum depolarisation in the presynaptic and postsynaptic neurones? *(1 mark)*

iv) What is the cause of this delay? *(1 mark)*

c) Describe how nicotine affects synaptic transmission. *(2 marks)*

Edexcel

6 Figure 5 shows the relation between skin temperature, hypothalamus temperature and the rate of sweating in a human subject in a warm chamber at 45°C. Ice was swallowed by the subject at the time indicated.

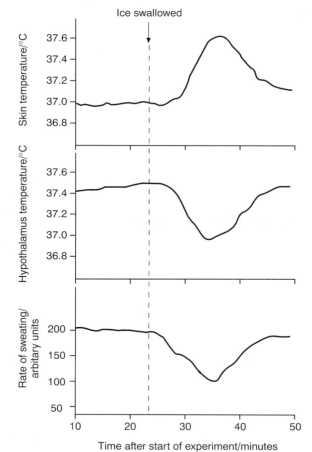

Figure 5

a) Explain how the fall in hypothalamus temperature that follows the swallowing of ice would be brought about. *(1 mark)*

b) Describe the mechanism by which the hypothalamus brings about the change in sweating rate after ice is swallowed. *(2 marks)*

c) Suggest a reason for the rise in skin temperature that follows the swallowing of ice. *(2 marks)*

AEB Specimen Question

7 Diabetes insipidus is a condition in which large volumes of dilute urine are produced.

The volume of urine produced each day by a patient with diabetes insipidus was recorded. On certain days the patient received an injection of pituitary extract. The results are shown in Table 3. The asterisks (*) indicate the days on which pituitary extract was injected.

Table 3

Day	Volume of urine (dm³)	Day	Volume of urine (dm³)
1	5.4	9	6.3
2	6.0	10	4.9
3	5.8	11	5.1
4	5.0	12	5.5
5	7.0	13*	1.5
6	5.7	14*	2.1
7*	1.9	15*	2.4
8	2.2	16*	1.7

a) Describe the effect of the injection of pituitary extract on the volume of urine produced each day. *(2 marks)*

b) Name the substance responsible for this effect. *(1 mark)*

c) Describe how this effect is brought about. *(2 marks)*
Edexcel

8 Figure 6 shows a synapse as seen with the electron microscope.

a) Explain the function of each of the following.

   i) The mitochondria *(2 marks)*

   ii) The synaptic vesicles *(2 marks)*

b) Figure 7 show the effect of adding acetylcholine to skeletal muscle and heart muscle.

   i) Describe the effect of acetylcholine on skeletal muscle. *(2 marks)*

   ii) State how the effects of acetylcholine on heart muscle differ from its effects on skeletal muscle. *(2 marks)*

   iii) Suggest how these differences may be related to the functions of the two types of muscle. *(2 marks)*

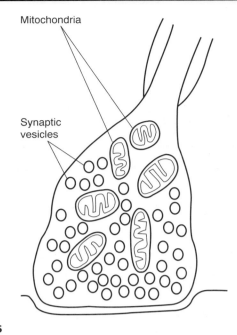

Figure 6

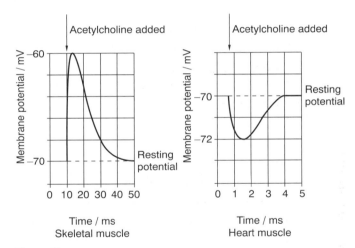

Figure 7

c) i) Suggest why it is important that acetylcholine is rapidly hydrolysed after its release. *(2 marks)*

   ii) Some organophosphate insecticides work by inhibiting the enzyme that catalyses the hydrolysis of acetylcholine. Suggest what effects this will have in the body of the insect. *(2 marks)*
   Edexcel

9 Explain what is meant by each of the following terms.

a) Action potential *(2 marks)*

b) Transmitter substance *(2 marks)*

c) Myelination *(2 marks)*
Edexcel

Food and Energy for Living

In this section we shall be exploring the energy relationships of living things. An energy source is used up when work is done. When it is used up, the energy gets spread out and is no longer easy to use. For example, a fuel is a concentrated source of energy, but once it has been burnt and heated up a room the energy is no longer as useful, even though the amount of energy is the same. Similarly, a food is a concentrated energy source, and once respired the energy becomes more spread out; some of it transfers to other molecules in cells, and some of it heats the body. The heat may help to keep an animal warm, but it will mostly radiate away from the body. Therefore only some energy from the original source will be available for use in important biological processes such as the synthesis of new materials. These examples illustrate both the first and the second laws of thermodynamics.

The first law (also known as the law of conservation of energy) states that energy is conserved, it is not created or destroyed. Although energy is transferred from food to our bodies and the surroundings, the total amount of energy has remained the same. However, the amount of *useful* or *free energy* has decreased – which is the second law.

The second law states that energy sources will spread out and become more disordered. A concentrated energy store such as food eventually ends up as heat and the temperature of the Earth's atmosphere increases a little. But the rise in temperature is too small to be useful, for example it couldn't boil a kettle. To remain in an ordered state, living things need a continuous input of energy – the Sun.

Getting a concentrated energy source

Simply by warming us up, the Sun does not supply living systems with a useful energy source for maintaining order. There has to be a mechanism for concentrating the Sun's energy.

During photosynthesis plants transfer energy from the Sun to organic molecules such as glucose, which is stored as starch. This energy source enables plants in a tropical rainforest to produce, on average, 2.2 kg m^{-2} year^{-1} of dry biomass, which is equivalent to 45 kg m^{-2} of standing plants.

This process is a type of autotrophic nutrition known as photosynthesis which is carried out mostly by plants, and by some bacteria. Other autotrophs include chemoautotrophs, such as the nitrifying bacteria living in soil, which can synthesise organic molecules using energy released from chemical reactions.

Heterotrophic nutrition

Animals are heterotrophs and are unable to synthesise their own food. They either directly rely on consuming organic molecules that have been synthesised by plants, or on other organic food sources such as those from animals which themselves fed on plants, or a mixture of both. Some heterotrophs are parasites (see page 000) feeding directly from a living host, while others are saprophytes, feeding on the decaying remains of an organism.

Good health partly depends upon the diet being balanced and the right amount of food being consumed so that the nutritional needs of the body are met, and the energy supply meets demand. Throughout life the specific dietary requirements of a human will change according to age, gender and level of activity, as well as health conditions such as diabetes. Eating disorders such as anorexia nervosa, bulimia or obesity may arise from distressed behaviour where food has become the focus. Some forms of disease such as bowel cancer and ulcers may be caused by dietary habits, and food may be the vehicle for transmission of infections.

Energy from food – respiration

During respiration, food (usually in the form of glucose) is oxidised within cells, liberating free energy. The universal energy carrier is the compound ATP (adenosine triphosphate) which stores the energy liberated during respiration until it is used in cell metabolism. If sufficient oxygen is not available, for example when muscle cells are metabolising during strenuous

A tapeworm is a parasite, living in the intestines of animals such as humans or pigs. Tapeworms absorb digested food from within the intestine, through their whole body surface.

exercise, glucose can be respired anaerobically. But the amount of free energy liberated from anaerobic respiration is not as great.

The energy stored in this banana that Boris Becker is eating must be converted to ATP in his body cells, before it can be used.

CHAPTER 21 Photosynthesis

All living organisms need food to provide the energy for anabolic reactions, active transport and other life processes. **Autotrophic** organisms are able to synthesise organic nutrients from simple inorganic raw materials and an energy source. By far the most important group of autotrophs are the green plants that photosynthesise carbon dioxide and water to manufacture glucose using energy from the Sun. This carbohydrate molecule forms the basis of many other materials such as starch and cellulose in plants, and glycogen in animals.

Photosynthesis is a process consisting of many chemical reactions which take place in the chloroplasts. Glucose that is formed is stored in the leaf as starch, and later transported away from the leaf to other parts of the plant in the form of sucrose. It can be converted to a wide range of organic nutrients using additional ions such as nitrates that are absorbed by roots from the soil.

The food produced by plants is passed either directly or indirectly to all living organisms via food chains. Plants are therefore called **producers** and animals are **consumers**. Primary consumers (herbivores) feed directly on plants and animals higher in the food chain, secondary and tertiary consumers, are carnivorous.

► *Chapter 38.4 considers food chains in more detail*

Figure 21.1 Plants convert an enormous amount of carbon dioxide into carbohydrate each year. Carbohydrate is an energy source for plants used to build biomass.

Equations that summarise the process of photosynthesis:

Word equation

$$\text{carbon dioxide} + \text{water} \xrightarrow[\text{LIGHT ENERGY}]{\text{chlorophyll}} \text{glucose} + \text{oxygen}$$

Chemical equation

$$6CO_2 + 6H_2O \xrightarrow[\text{LIGHT ENERGY}]{\text{chlorophyll}} C_6H_{12}O_6 + 6O_2$$

21.1 The chloroplast

► *Chapter 1.1 describes the structure of a plant cell*

Photosynthesis can only take place in cells which have chloroplasts. These are found mostly in the **mesophyll**, the tissue in the middle of leaves, and there are also some in the parenchyma cells just below the surface of non-woody stems.

The **chloroplast** is an organelle called a plastid which contains pigments such as chlorophylls a and b. As many as 50 chloroplasts may be found in a mesophyll cell. In common with most cell organelles, chloroplasts are bound by a double membrane. Internally there is a continuous and complex system of double membranes called **thylakoids**. They are extensions of the inner membrane of the chloroplast. In places the layers of membrane are stacked up rather like a pile of coins. Each of these structures is a **granum**. The space between the membranes is called the **stroma**. The thylakoids contain the chlorophyll molecules within the grana and function to trap the maximum amount of sunlight. Also within a chloroplast are starch grains and a very small length of DNA.

granum = singular
grana = plural

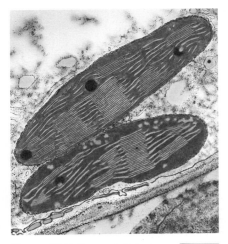

Figure 21.2 Transmission electron micrograph of a chloroplast
(See Colour Gallery page 352)

C20

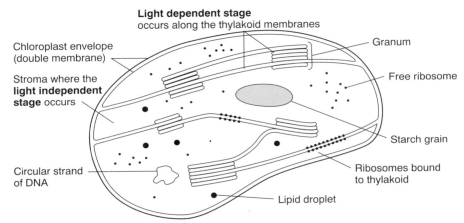

Figure 21.3 The structure of a chloroplast, the site of photosynthesis, where all the reactions of this process occur

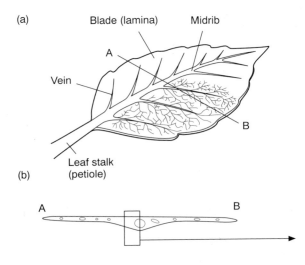

Figure 21.4 The structure of a leaf seen in transverse section

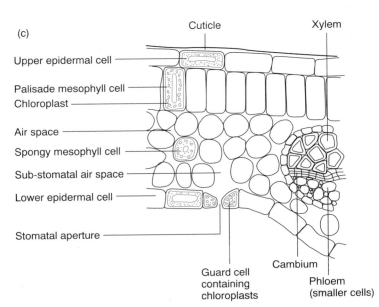

21.2 The chemistry of photosynthesis

Look carefully at Figure 21.5. This summarises the main events in photosynthesis which we can then examine in more detail.

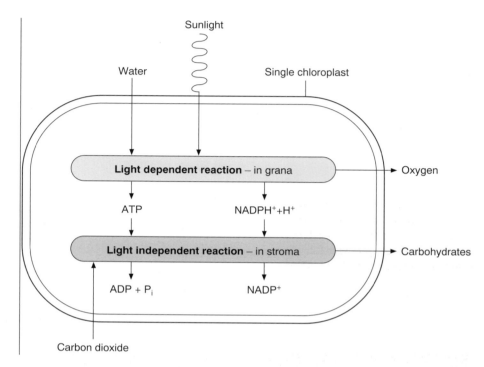

Figure 21.5 In the first stage of photosynthesis light energy from the Sun is absorbed by chlorophyll and converted into chemical energy in ATP molecules. At the same time water molecules are split into hydrogen ions (called protons), oxygen and electrons. NADP$^+$ is reduced to NADPH by some of the hydrogen ions. In the second stage, hydrogen from NADPH reduces carbon dioxide to glucose. The process is endergonic and uses ATP formed in the first stage as an energy source. During photosynthesis carbon dioxide is 'fixed' as carbohydrate.

Hydrogen ions (H$^+$) are called protons.

The energy source for photosynthesis is visible light. It is absorbed by the photosynthetic pigments found in plant cells.

Light – the energy source for photosynthesis

Visible light is a small part of the electromagnetic spectrum, with wavelengths between 400 nm and approximately 750 nm. Nevertheless, it is hugely important as the energy source for almost all forms of life on Earth.

The most common photosynthetic pigment is chlorophyll *a*, but chloroplasts contain other pigments too such as chlorophyll *b* and the orange and yellow carotenoid pigments. The reason why this is useful can be seen if we look at the **absorption spectrum** of different pigments (i.e. the wavelengths that they absorb).

Figure 21.6 Visible light is part of the electromagnetic spectrum
(See Colour Gallery page 352)

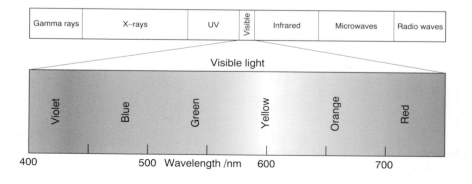

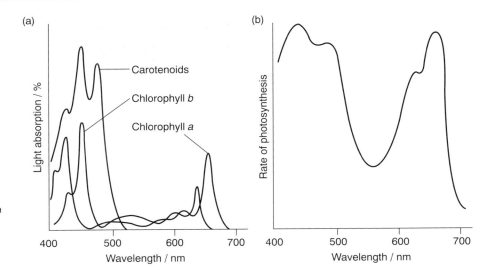

Figure 21.7 (a) The absorption spectra for chlorophylls *a* and *b* and carotenoids showing which wavelengths of light each pigment can absorb (b) The action spectrum showing the amount of photosynthesis that occurs at each wavelength

> The wavelength absorbed by each pigment is its absorption spectrum. The efficiency of each pigment at using a particular wavelength of light is its action spectrum.

Chlorophylls *a* and *b* mostly absorb light from the blue part of the spectrum, and some red light. Other pigments absorb other wavelengths. By having a variety of pigments the plant can make maximum use of the wavelengths of light that fall upon it. Very little green light is used in photosynthesis, most of it is reflected away from leaves which is why they look green.

Light intensity is also important. The greater the intensity of the light reaching a leaf, the greater the energy the pigment can absorb in a given time. How efficient each pigment is in using the light it has absorbed in photosynthesis is shown by its **action spectrum**.

Chromatography

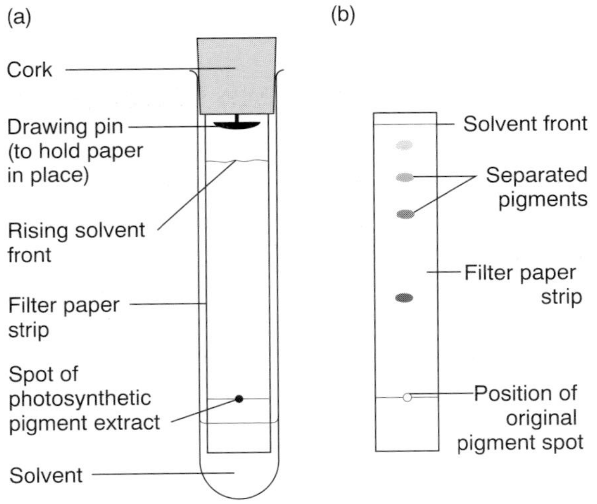

(a)

Cork

Drawing pin
(to hold paper
in place)

Rising solvent
front

Filter paper
strip

Spot of
photosynthetic
pigment extract

Solvent

(b)

Solvent front

Separated
pigments

Filter paper
strip

Position of
original
pigment spot

Chromatography is a process which can be used to separate the components in a solution. Leaf pigments can be separated in this way. The photosynthetic pigments in a leaf are extracted and a concentrated spot of the extract is put about 1 cm from the end of a strip of absorbent filter paper. The position of the spot is marked by a pencil line. The paper is then suspended in a glass tube so that it just touches a solvent in the bottom. As the solvent rises up the paper the pigments dissolve in it. They travel at different speeds according to factors such as their solubility in the solvent and thus become separated. Just before the solvent reaches the top of the paper strip, the paper is removed from the tube and the position of each pigment and of the solvent front is marked. A value called the Rf value can be calculated for each pigment.

Figure 21.8 (a) The apparatus used in leaf chromatography
(b) A chromatogram showing the separated pigments

$$Rf = \frac{\text{distance travelled by pigment}}{\text{distance travelled by solvent}}$$

The pigments are identified by comparing the Rf value obtained with standard values in a Rf table.

21.3 The light dependent stage of photosynthesis

> **NADP (nicotinamide adenine dinucleotide phosphate) is a hydrogen accepter. It exists in the cell as the ion NADP$^+$.**

Experiments have shown that only the first stage of photosynthesis must occur in the presence of visible light. This first stage is called the **light dependent stage**.

The main events of the light dependent stage are:

- sunlight is absorbed by the pigments in the grana and is converted to ATP (chemical energy);
- water molecules are split into electrons, protons and oxygen;
- NADPH (a reducing agent) is produced.

How does all this happen?

The photosynthetic pigments are organised with enzymes and electron acceptors into two slightly different photosystems called photosystem 1 and photosystem 2. When the photosynthetic ('antenna') pigments of the photosystem have absorbed light energy, it is channelled to a chlorophyll reaction centre. Here, electrons are excited to a higher energy level and pass to an electron acceptor and then along an **electron transport chain**. As the electrons travel along the chain they transfer energy to chemical reactions and so their energy level is lowered. Depending on which pathway is being followed, either ATP or NADPH + H$^+$ are produced. These are needed for the second stage of photosynthesis. The splitting, **photolysis**, of water uses the energy from sunlight and releases both protons and electrons. Look carefully at Figure 21.9 and follow the steps which happen in the reactions of the light dependent stage.

Figure 21.9 The steps that occur in the light dependent stage of photosynthesis

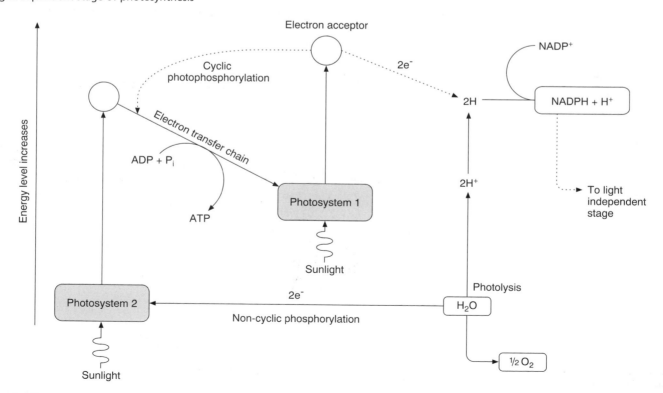

More about photosystems 1 and 2

Energy from sunlight is absorbed by photosystem 2. Each chlorophyll molecule loses two electrons which are boosted to a higher energy level and received by an electron acceptor. The excited electrons pass along an electron transfer chain to photosystem 1 which is at a lower energy level. As the electrons fall down the energy gradient they release energy. The energy is transferred to ADP as it bonds with more phosphorus, converting it to ATP. This is how light energy is converted to chemical energy. The process is known as **non-cyclic photophosphorylation**.

Photosystem 1 absorbs light energy which increases the energy level of the electrons further and they are transferred to a second electron acceptor. Some of them will return to the chlorophyll in photosystem 1 via the electron transport chain, allowing further synthesis of ATP. This is called **cyclic photophosphorylation**.

The electrons which were lost from the chlorophyll in photosystem 2 are replaced with electrons released by the photolysis of water molecules. This reaction also releases protons and oxygen gas which is given out from the leaf to the surroundings.

The remaining electrons from the second electron acceptor combine with the protons from the splitting of water to reduce NADP. NADP now becomes NADPH + H⁺ which plays an important role as a reducing agent in the second part of photosynthesis.

> In the light dependent stage the energy source, sunlight, is absorbed by photosynthetic pigments and converted to chemical energy, ATP. Water molecules are split by photolysis into oxygen, which diffuses out of the plant, and hydrogen ions. Some hydrogen ions and electrons reduce NADP to NADPH + H⁺.

21.4 The light independent stage of photosynthesis

This stage of photosynthesis does not require light and it follows the light dependent stage. The importance of this stage is that carbon dioxide is reduced to carbohydrate. The reactions involved were worked out by a scientist called Melvin Calvin.

The light independent stage requires:

- ATP as an energy source;
- NADPH + H⁺ to supply hydrogen to reduce carbon dioxide.

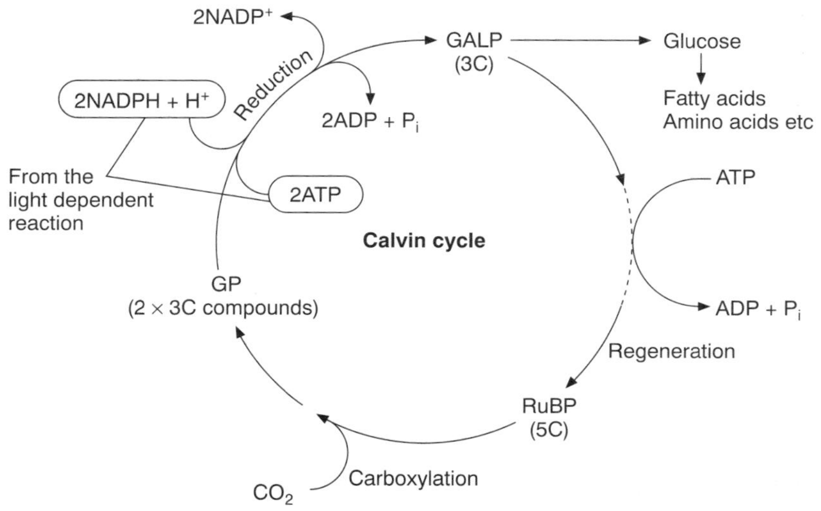

Figure 21.10 The light independent stage of photosynthesis

Carbon dioxide diffuses from the atmosphere (or from the surrounding water in an aquatic plant) into the leaf cells and then into the stroma of the chloroplasts. It combines with a carbon dioxide acceptor, a pentose (5-carbon) sugar called ribulose bisphosphate (RuBP). In this way an unstable 6-carbon sugar is formed which immediately breaks down into two molecules of the 3-carbon sugar glycerate 3-phosphate (GP). These reactions are called **carboxylation**, since carbon dioxide is added.

GP is then *reduced* to triose phosphate (glyceraldehyde-3-phosphate or GALP) by combining with hydrogen from the NADPH + H$^+$ using energy from ATP produced in the light dependent stage. NADP$^+$ and ADP are regenerated and are free once more to take part in the light stage.

Some of the triose phosphate molecules combine in pairs to form 6-carbon phosphate sugars which give rise to glucose. Glucose undergoes condensation reactions to synthesise sucrose and starch and the synthesis of lipids and amino acids may also follow. The plant can manufacture all the foods that it needs providing that it has the necessary raw materials and an energy source.

The remaining triose phosphate takes part in a cycle of reactions, the Calvin cycle, which regenerates the original carbon dioxide acceptor, RuBP. Three molecules of 5-carbon sugar are re-formed from five molecules of triose phosphate. Some of the ATP made in the light stage provides the necessary energy for the reactions.

> In the light independent stage carbon dioxide is reduced to carbohydrate using hydrogen from reduced NADP and energy from ATP. Glucose is formed which is converted into sucrose, starch and other carbohydrates.

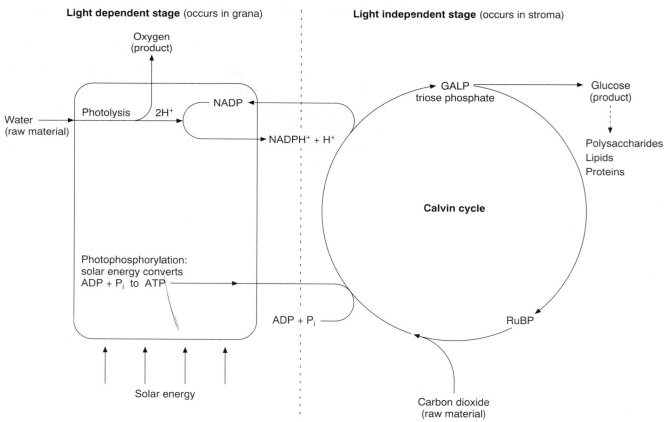

Figure 21.11 Overview of photosynthesis

21.5 The importance of photosynthesis

Photosynthesis is the means by which all green plants synthesise their nutritional requirements. It involves the transfer of solar energy to chemical substances within plants. Plants provide food and hence are an energy source either directly or indirectly for all other living organisms. They are eaten by heterotrophic organisms (herbivorous animals), which in turn are eaten by carnivores. Omnivores such as humans feed on both plants and animals. The dead remains of parts or of whole plants and animals are the food of the saprophytic decomposers. There is a flow of food and energy through food chains which always originates from plants.

Oxygen is a waste product of photosynthesis which is vital to animals and other living organisms that respire aerobically. Photosynthesis plays an important part of the carbon cycle, maintaining a balance of carbon dioxide and oxygen in our environment.

▶ *Chapter 38.5 considers the cycling of materials in more detail*

Questions

1 What are (a) the raw materials and (b) the end-products of photosynthesis?

2 Why do you think that seaweeds growing in fairly deep seawater are red?

3 Where does the light dependent reaction occur?

4 Explain how energy from the Sun is transferred to chemical energy in plants.

5 What is the photolysis of water? Why is it important?

6 Where does the light independent stage occur? Why is not all the triose phosphate (GALP) used in biosynthesis?

7 How are the light stage and the dark stage of photosynthesis dependent on one another?

CHAPTER 22 Heterotrophic Nutrition

▶ *Chapter 38.4 explains about food chains*

Humans and all other animals are unable to manufacture their own food and are dependent on plants to do this for them. The food materials made during photosynthesis are either the direct or indirect food sources for *all* animals. Animals that feed only on plant material are **herbivores**, or **primary consumers**; animals that feed on herbivores or other animals are **carnivores** and are **consumers**. Most humans eat both plants and animals and so are called **omnivores**. However, some people choose to have a completely vegetarian diet (see Chapter 23.8).

Figure 22.1 These Bushmen survive mainly on a vegetable diet similar to one gathered and eaten by early man 4.5 million years ago

Over the past four million years of human evolution, the available sources of food have played an important role in structuring the way of life. Our early ancestors such as *Homo erectus* were initially vegetarians and opportunistic scavengers for meat, but later also hunted for meat. Before farming was established the main dietary items were roots, nuts and fruits. Even today there are bushmen living in the Kalahari Desert who feed mainly on the mongongo nut (an excellent source of protein and polyunsaturated oil), small animals and game. Their diet is nutritionally healthy and the people have low cholesterol levels, low blood pressure and are not obese. The bushmen eat only small amounts of sugar and as a result have no tooth decay. Their living conditions are very harsh and yet their life expectancy is similar to people living in Britain.

22.1 Digestion in humans

The digestive system processes food to convert it into a useful form. The food that has been **ingested** (eaten) must first be **digested**. This means it must be converted into a soluble form so that it can be absorbed from the gut and transported to cells in all parts of the body where it can be **assimilated** (used) in a number of ways.

Digestion is of two types: physical and chemical. **Physical digestion** is mechanically breaking the food into smaller pieces and is carried out by the action of the teeth and tongue. It continues to a lesser extent as the food passes through the stomach and is constantly churned and mixed by **peristalsis**, the alternate contraction and relaxation of muscles in the gut wall. The smaller pieces of food have an increased surface area and are more efficiently broken down by enzymes during chemical digestion. **Chemical digestion** takes place as the food moves from the mouth to the stomach, duodenum and the first part of the small intestine. It is the hydrolysis of large molecules of carbohydrate, protein and fat which are broken down to soluble products (monosaccharides, amino acids, fatty acids and glycerol) which can be absorbed in the ileum.

22.2 Human dentition

Humans have a strongly fixed upper jaw and a moveable lower jaw. The teeth are embedded in the jaws and are used to chew food into small pieces. Humans have two sets of teeth, the set of 20 **deciduous** (or milk) teeth appear first, usually between the ages of six months and three years, to be replaced later by the **permanent** teeth. The last four molars or wisdom teeth usually appear in early adulthood. The teeth are different in shape and size depending on their different functions.

Adult humans have 32 permanent teeth which are represented by the following dental formula (i = incisor, c = canine, pm = premolar, m = molar)

$$2\left[\text{i}\,\frac{2}{2}\ \text{c}\,\frac{1}{1}\ \text{pm}\,\frac{2}{2}\ \text{m}\,\frac{3}{3} \right]$$

The upper numbers and letters show the number and types of teeth in the upper jaw and the lower numbers and letters those in the lower jaw. This arrangement represents one side of the face.

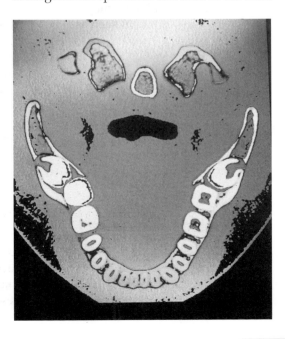

Figure 22.2 This is a CT scan which shows the permanent dentition of the lower jaw of an adult human

The incisors are at the front and are used for cutting or biting the food. The canines are the most pointed teeth. They are not well developed in humans and are much more important in carnivorous animals which use them to pierce, hold and kill prey. The premolars crush and grind food and may also tear it. The molars, which are not present in the milk dentition, also crush and grind food. The upper molars have three roots and the lower molars have two.

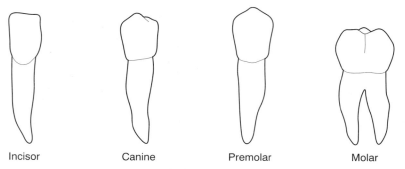

Figure 22.3 Humans have four different types of teeth

Incisor · Canine · Premolar · Molar

All types of teeth have the same basic structure. Above the gum the tooth is covered by **enamel**, the hardest material in the body. Beneath it is **dentine**, which is also tough. The **root** of the tooth is embedded in the gum and is covered by **cement**, a material similar to bone. **Periodontal fibres** hold the tooth in place but allow slight movement during eating. In the centre of the tooth is the **pulp cavity** which contains blood vessels and sensory nerve endings. The blood vessels bring oxygen and food materials to the tooth and remove waste products. When each tooth has reached a particular size the hole at the base of the pulp cavity narrows and the tooth stops growing.

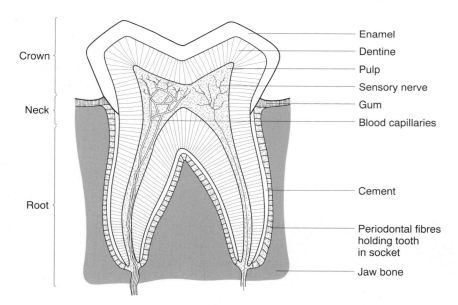

Crown · Neck · Root

Enamel · Dentine · Pulp · Sensory nerve · Gum · Blood capillaries · Cement · Periodontal fibres holding tooth in socket · Jaw bone

Figure 22.4 A vertical section through a molar tooth

Dental disease

A 'nice smile' is important to many people for not only does it display their looks, but it also reveals the health of their teeth and gums. Despite advances in dental technology there is still a high incidence of dental disease which often reflects the diet we eat. We all need to care actively for our teeth if they are to remain healthy.

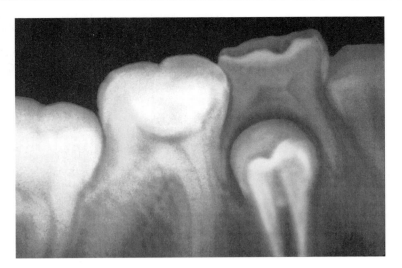

Figure 22.5 This shows a permanent tooth developing in the jaw – the milk teeth are still in place

The two most common forms of dental disease are **dental caries** (decay) and **periodontal disease** (gum disease). Both are caused by **plaque** which is a mixture of saliva, mucus and bacteria which live in the mouth. Plaque forms a coating over the teeth especially between the teeth and where the gums and tooth enamel meet. It is very important to brush teeth regularly and effectively so that plaque is removed. If it is not, minerals, such as salts of calcium and magnesium in the saliva, form hard deposits of tartar or **calculus** which cannot be removed by brushing.

Bacteria living in the plaque convert sugars left in the mouth to acids. This dissolves away calcium salts in the enamel causing tiny cavities in the surface. If the holes get bigger and are not filled by a dentist, they spread into the dentine and eventually the pulp cavity, exposing the nerve endings. The exposed nerve endings are sensitive to hot and cold foods and acids in the mouth, which can be very painful. The bacteria may then invade the pulp cavity and so infect the root of the tooth and cause an abscess. The only permanent way to cure an abscess is the removal of the decayed tooth.

The incidence of tooth decay is highest in developed countries where refined sugar is common in the diet as people regularly eat snacks, sweets and sugary drinks. Tooth decay can be reduced by limiting the amount of sugar in the diet, by brushing the teeth regularly and by increasing the intake of fluoride. Fluoride gets incorporated into enamel increasing its resistance to acids. Teeth can be treated with fluoride by a dentist, it can be taken in tablet form or it may be added to the drinking water supplies.

The British Dental Association recommends that infants and young children should be given supplements of fluoride to protect against dental decay if they live in an area where the fluoride concentration of the drinking water is less than 0.7 ppm. However, there is no value to be gained by giving more than the suggested dose, as too much fluoride can cause **fluorosis** (the teeth become mottled). The enamel becomes affected before the teeth erupt through the gum. The mottling may vary from being hardly detectable to obvious in direct proportion to the concentration of fluoride received. Mottled teeth are still resistant to decay.

Nowadays, gum disease is more of a problem than dental decay. If plaque is not brushed away properly when the teeth are cleaned it causes inflammation of the gums (**gingivitis**) and they bleed very easily. The gums recede exposing the roots. Eventually, the periodontal fibres that hold each tooth in place are destroyed and the teeth become loose and need to be extracted.

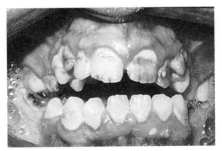

Figure 22.6 This shows cavities caused by decay and reddened patches, the telltale signs of gum disease
(See Colour Gallery page 353)

Question

1 Find out more about fluoride in drinking water. There is often controversy as to whether fluoride should be added to drinking water. List the points for and against this practice.

22.3 The human alimentary canal

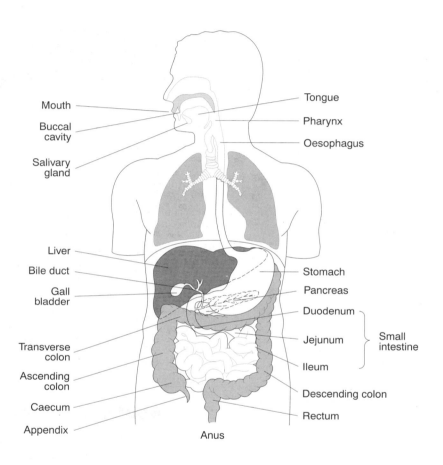

Figure 22.7 The human alimentary canal
(*See Colour Gallery page 353*)

The **alimentary canal** is also called the **digestive system** or **gut**. It is a continuous tube which runs from the mouth to the anus and is about 10 m in length. Although it runs centrally through the body, the **lumen** of the gut is really no more than a useful space which food moves through. Associated with it are organs such as the teeth, tongue and salivary glands, pancreas, liver and gall bladder, all of which play an important part in the proper functioning of the system. Some substances are secreted into the lumen and others are absorbed from it.

The gut lies mainly within the abdominal cavity. It has a basic structure of muscle and epithelial tissues which are adapted to the functioning of the different regions of the gut. However, it is possible to recognise a general design including four main layers of tissue. These (starting from the inside) are:

1 The **mucosa** which lines the gut and surrounds the lumen.

2 The **submucosa** which produces the secretions of digestive juices. Between the submucosa and muscular layers is **Meissner's complex** which controls the secretion from the glands.

3 The **muscular layers**, an inner layer of smooth circular muscle and an outer sheet of longitudinal smooth muscle. Between these is a network of nerves called **Auerbach's plexus** which co-ordinates the activity of the two muscular layers.

4 The **serosa** which is a layer of connective tissue and is part of the peritoneum. It forms a continuous low friction surface over the digestive system and abdominal wall. Sheets of this tissue hold the gut in position, suspending it within the abdomen.

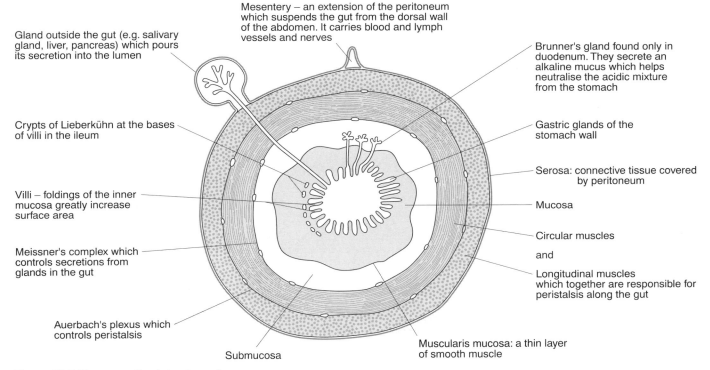

Figure 22.8 The generalised structure of the human gut

Labels:
- Mesentery – an extension of the peritoneum which suspends the gut from the dorsal wall of the abdomen. It carries blood and lymph vessels and nerves
- Gland outside the gut (e.g. salivary gland, liver, pancreas) which pours its secretion into the lumen
- Crypts of Lieberkühn at the bases of villi in the ileum
- Villi – foldings of the inner mucosa greatly increase surface area
- Meissner's complex which controls secretions from glands in the gut
- Auerbach's plexus which controls peristalsis
- Submucosa
- Brunner's gland found only in duodenum. They secrete an alkaline mucus which helps neutralise the acidic mixture from the stomach
- Gastric glands of the stomach wall
- Serosa: connective tissue covered by peritoneum
- Mucosa
- Circular muscles
- and
- Longitudinal muscles which together are responsible for peristalsis along the gut
- Muscularis mucosa: a thin layer of smooth muscle

The mouth is the start of the gut

The mouth is where digestion begins as the food is broken up by biting and chewing, a process called **mastication**. It is mixed with **saliva** secreted by the three pairs of salivary glands which open into the mouth. We make between 1.0 and 1.5 dm³ of saliva every day. Secretion is under the control of the parasympathetic nervous system and is stimulated by the sight, smell and taste of food. Even thinking about food may induce the secretion of saliva!

Saliva is composed of water (90–95 per cent) in which are dissolved ions (e.g. sodium, chloride, potassium, phosphate and bicarbonate), enzymes (salivary amylase and lysozymes), mucus, and organic substances such as antibodies. The pH of saliva is neutral to slightly alkaline. As the food is masticated the tongue works it into a soft ball or **bolus**, which is easily swallowed. Mucus in the saliva helps to bind the food and lubricate the inside of the mouth.

Salivary amylase catalyses the breakdown of starch to maltose. It is unlikely that there would be time for enzyme action to hydrolyse very much of the food that is swallowed, but the enzyme acts on any starchy debris left in the mouth and converts it to sugar.

Enzyme action in the mouth:

● Salivary amylase converts starch to maltose.

Swallowing is a reflex action. The mechanisms involved are designed in such a way as to ensure that the food goes into the oesophagus and not into the respiratory system. Firstly, the tongue contracts and forces the bolus against the soft palate, so closing off the opening to the nasal cavity. Then, when food reaches the back of the mouth, the glottis is covered by the epiglottis to prevent food from being taken into the airways.

(i)   (ii)

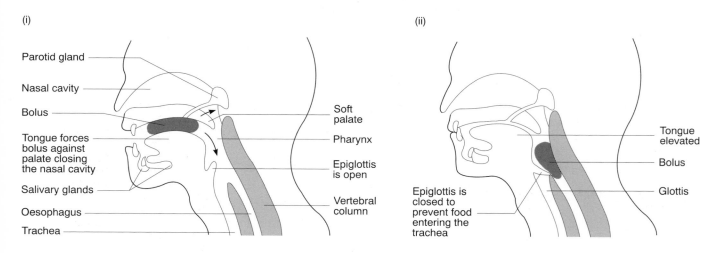

Figure 22.9 The action of swallowing – openings to the respiratory system are closed to direct food to the oesophagus

The oesophagus

Once the bolus has entered the oesophagus, it is transported to the stomach by waves of muscular movements called **peristalsis**. The bolus is pushed downwards as circular muscles in the oesophagus wall behind it contract, forcing it along by a squeezing action. When the bolus moves on, the circular muscles relax. Longitudinal muscles in front of the bolus contract, widening the oesophagus and allowing its passage.

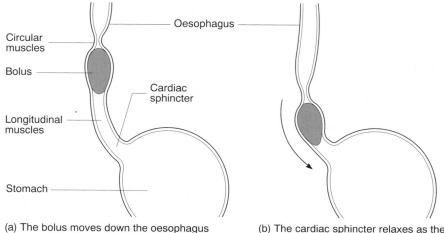

Figure 22.10 Peristalsis in the oesophagus

(a) The bolus moves down the oesophagus

(b) The cardiac sphincter relaxes as the bolus reaches the stomach

The stomach

A sphincter is the thickening of the muscle layer of a tube which forms a ring. It relaxes to open the tube and contracts to close it again.

When food reaches the lower part of the oesophagus the **cardiac sphincter** muscle relaxes and opens the sphincter to allow food into the stomach.

The stomach is a J-shaped muscular sac on the left of the abdomen, just below the diaphragm muscle. Its size changes depending upon how much food it contains. Food is usually in the stomach for one to four hours. During that time it is constantly churned and mixed with gastric juice. The semi-liquid contents of the stomach are then known as **chyme**. The folded gastric epithelium which lines the stomach consists of mucus-secreting cells and millions of tiny pits or gastric glands which secrete hydrochloric acid and gastric juice. Look at Figure 22.11 (b) and see the different types of cell making up the gastric gland.

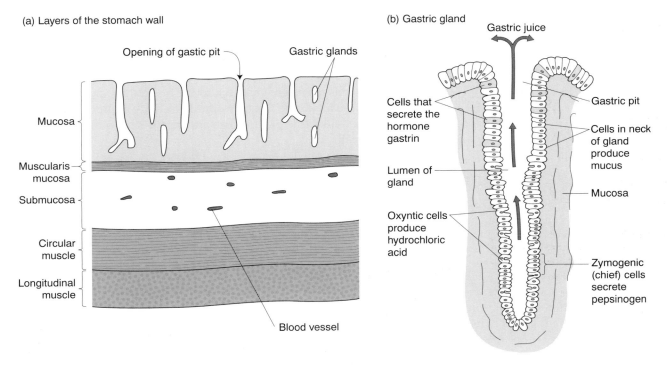

(a) Layers of the stomach wall

(b) Gastric gland

Figure 22.11 (a) A section through the layers of the stomach wall (b) The structure of a gastric gland in the lining of the stomach

Endopeptidases are enzymes which digest proteins to polypeptides by breaking the peptide bonds between amino acids in the protein chain. Exopeptidases split off amino acids from the ends of polypeptide chains.

Gastric juice consists of:

- water;
- hydrochloric acid, secreted by the **oxyntic cells** in the gastric glands;
- pepsinogen, a precursor (or inactive form) of the endopeptidase enzyme pepsin – this is secreted by the **zymogenic** or **chief cells** in the gastric glands;
- prorennin, a precursor of rennin is secreted by the chief cells in babies and very young children;
- mucus secreted by the **goblet cells** in the gastric mucosa and by cells in the gastric glands.

Hydrochloric acid produces a pH of 1–2 in the stomach which is the optimum pH for pepsin to work. It activates pepsinogen and prorennin, converting them to pepsin and rennin, respectively. Acid also kills bacteria that have been ingested with the food.

Mucus is secreted in large volumes by the gastric glands and by cells in the gastric epithelium. It forms a layer to protect the cells of the stomach lining against the action of pepsin and the strong hydrochloric acid in the gastric juice. Even so, the cells lining the stomach and those in the gastric glands live for only a few days and have to be replaced continually throughout life.

Enzyme action in the stomach:

- Pepsin (from pepsinogen) converts proteins to polypeptides.
- Rennin (from prorennin) coagulates milk to increase the time that it remains in the stomach where protein digestion occurs.

The secretion of gastric juice is a nervous response stimulated by the presence of food in the stomach. However, it is also controlled by a hormone called **gastrin**. In the pyloric region (the distal end) of the stomach, there is an additional type of cell in the gastric lining. Food in the stomach stimulates these cells to secrete gastrin into the blood system. This is an example of positive feedback. Gastrin stimulates the secretion of pepsinogen and hydrochloric acid in the gastric juice and also the peristaltic contractions of the stomach wall.

The small intestine

villus = singular
villi = plural

Intracellular digestion takes place within a cell.
Extracellular digestion takes place outside a cell.

The small intestine extends for about 6 m. A characteristic of the small intestine is that the mucosa is folded to form finger-like **villi** which increase the surface area. Deep folds found in the wall of the intestine at the bases of the villi are called the **crypts of Lieberkühn**. The epithelial cells of the villi have a brush border of up to 2000 **microvilli**. The microvilli are involved with intracellular digestion, but the cells die after a short time. The dead cells become mixed into the contents of the duodenum. Proteases digest the dislodged cells and release their enzymes extracellularly on to the food that is being digested.

Each villus has a rich blood supply and a lymph vessel or **lacteal**. The significance of this arrangement is considered in Chapter 22.4.

Below the crypts of Lieberkühn in the duodenum are the Brunner's glands which secrete a juice called the **succus entericus**. This is a viscous alkaline fluid which helps to protect the lining of the duodenum from the acidic chyme arriving from the stomach. Three different regions of the small intestine are recognised in humans, the duodenum, the jejunum and the ileum.

The duodenum

The **pyloric sphincter** controls the passage of chyme from the stomach to the first 25–30 cm of the small intestine, the duodenum. From time to time the sphincter alternately contracts and relaxes allowing small volumes of chyme through. Associated with the duodenum are the liver, the gall bladder and the pancreas.

The presence of the acidic chyme stimulates cells in the wall of the duodenum to secrete the two hormones **secretin** and **cholecystokinin-pancreozymin (CCK-PZ)** into the blood (see Figure 19.10 on page 170).

- Secretin is transported to the pancreas where it stimulates the secretion of the non-enzyme part of the pancreatic juice. Secretin also acts on the gall bladder which contracts and releases bile.
- CCK-PZ stimulates the secretion of pancreatic digestive enzymes into pancreatic juice.

The gall bladder stores the bile that has been secreted by the liver. Leading from the gall bladder is the bile duct which meets and fuses with the pancreatic duct. A mixture of pancreatic juice from the pancreas and bile are secreted into this tube and so into the duodenum.

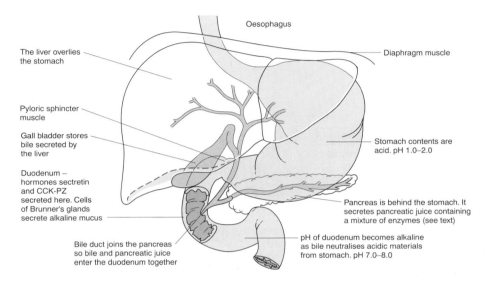

Oesophagus

The liver overlies the stomach

Diaphragm muscle

Pyloric sphincter muscle

Gall bladder stores bile secreted by the liver

Stomach contents are acid. pH 1.0–2.0

Duodenum – hormones sectretin and CCK-PZ secreted here. Cells of Brunner's glands secrete alkaline mucus

Pancreas is behind the stomach. It secretes pancreatic juice containing a mixture of enzymes (see text)

Bile duct joins the pancreas so bile and pancreatic juice enter the duodenum together

pH of duodenum becomes alkaline as bile neutralises acidic materials from stomach. pH 7.0–8.0

Figure 22.12 How the duodenum, liver and pancreas are connected

Demonstrating emulsification

You can see emulsification if you pour a small volume of water into a test tube. Add a thin layer of oil. To begin with the oil lies in a layer on top of the water but if you shake the tube hard you will break it up into a temporary milky emulsion of small fat droplets.

Bile is a yellow or green alkaline fluid with a pH of 7.6–8.6. It neutralises the acidic materials passing from the stomach by raising pH and so pepsin stops hydrolysing proteins. Bile is a watery mixture of ions, bile salts, bile pigments, cholesterol, lecithin and mucus. The bile salts are responsible for the **emulsification** of fats, that is they break down fats into small droplets. This increases the surface area available for enzymes involved in fat digestion.

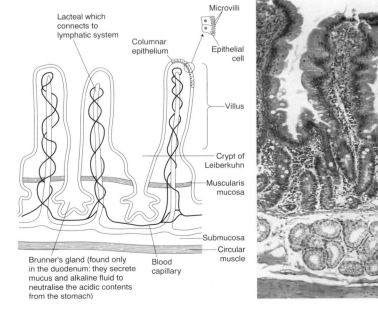

Microvilli

Lacteal which connects to lymphatic system

Columnar epithelium

Epithelial cell

Villus

Crypt of Leiberkuhn

Muscularis mucosa

Submucosa

Circular muscle

Blood capillary

Brunner's gland (found only in the duodenum: they secrete mucus and alkaline fluid to neutralise the acidic contents from the stomach)

Figure 22.13 Transverse section through the wall of the duodenum

(*See Colour Gallery page 353*)

► **Chapter 15.2** describes the secretion of bile by the liver

► **Chapter 14.4** provides more information about the pancreas

The bile pigments (red bilirubin and green biliverdin) are excretory products from haemoglobin released when red blood cells are destroyed. Bilirubin is absorbed from the gut and products from its breakdown are excreted by the kidneys; they colour urine. Biliverdin remains in the intestine and colours the faeces.

Pancreatic juice contains enzymes and enzyme precursors which are secreted by the exocrine glands of the pancreas, while other cells add salts such as sodium hydrogencarbonate which make the fluid alkaline. The enzyme precursors of proteases in pancreatic juice are trypsinogen and chymotrypsinogen. They are rapidly activated once they reach the duodenum.

Trypsinogen is converted to the endopeptidase trypsin, by an enzyme called enterokinase which is secreted by cells in the duodenal epithelium. In a positive feedback response, trypsin activates the conversion of more trypsinogen to trypsin; it also converts chymotrypsinogen to active chymotrypsin, another endopeptidase. Trypsin and chymotrypsin digest polypeptides to smaller chains called peptides.

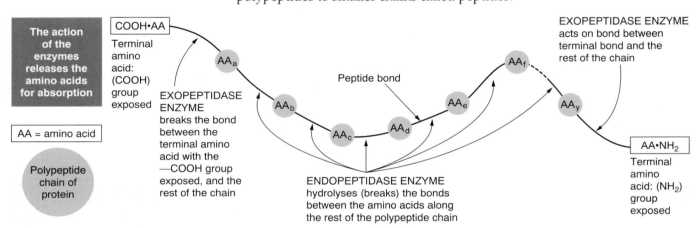

Figure 22.14 The action of endopeptidase and exopeptidase enzymes on proteins

Trypsin also activates the precursors of some exopeptidases, which are involved in breaking the terminal peptide bonds at the ends of peptide chains to release free amino acids.

Pancreatic amylase in the duodenum converts starch to maltose. Pancreatic lipase breaks down triglycerides. The fatty acids are removed one at a time until free fatty acids and glycerol remain. Finally, pancreatic juice contains nucleases which break down nucleic acids in cell fragments to nucleotides.

Enzyme action in the lumen of the duodenum:

- Enterokinase converts inactive trypsinogen to trypsin.
- Trypsin (endopeptidase) converts polypeptides to peptides.
- Chymotrypsin (endopeptidase) converts polypeptides to peptides.
- Carboxyexopeptidases break terminal peptide bonds where the amino acid has an exposed carboxyl group.
- Aminopeptidases break terminal peptide bonds where the amino acid has an exposed amino group.
- Lipase converts triglycerides to fatty acids and glycerol.
- Pancreatic amylase converts starch to maltose.
- Nucleases break down nucleic acids to nucleotides.

Digestion in the small intestine is also aided by intracellular enzymes produced in the cells originating in the crypts of Lieberkühn, which constantly migrate to the surface of the villi where they form short-lived microvilli. Mitosis in the base of the crypts of Lieberkühn ensures that the cells are continually replaced.

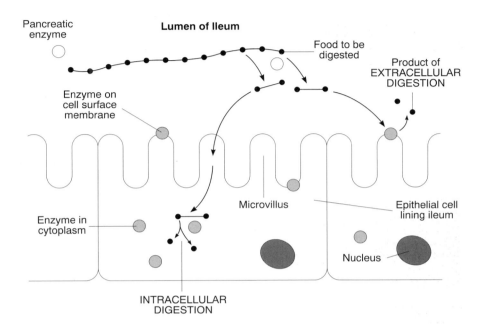

Figure 22.15 This shows how both intracellular digestion and extracellular digestion take place in the intestine

Enzymes bound to the cell membranes of the microvilli complete digestion:

- Peptidases hydrolyse short peptides to amino acids.
- Maltase hydrolyses maltose to glucose.
- Sucrase hydrolyses sucrose to glucose and fructose.
- Lactase hydrolyses lactose to glucose and galactose.

Lactose intolerance

Lactose is a disaccharide found in milk and is sometimes called 'milk sugar'. During digestion lactose is hydrolysed to the simple sugars glucose and galactose by the enzyme lactase (also called β-galactosidase). Glucose and galactose are absorbed by active transport in the small intestine. If someone does not make lactase they cannot digest lactose and any undigested lactose remains in the lumen of the small intestine and causes diarrhoea. Bacteria living in the gut ferment the undigested lactose and this leads to gaseous, acidic faeces. This condition is called **lactose intolerance**.

Lactase is secreted by all babies and young children but only by adults of northwest European origin. Lactase deficiency is very common in adults of other ethnic groups. It is found in about 90 per cent of orientals and 75 per cent of American blacks and Indians. There is also a high incidence of lactase deficiency amongst people from the Mediterranean.

The symptoms of lactose intolerance are:
- A child will have diarrhoea and fail to gain weight.
- An adult is likely to have diarrhoea, abdominal bloating and pain.
- The diarrhoea may prevent the absorption of other nutrients.
- The faeces are acidic.

Lactose intolerance – contd.

A **lactose tolerance test** gives a definitive diagnosis of lactase deficiency. The patient is given 50 g of lactose solution by mouth and if they develop diarrhoea and abdominal discomfort within 30 minutes and have a low blood glucose curve, lactose intolerance is proved.

The treatment for lactose intolerance is to follow a lactose-free diet. Products are available in which the lactose in milk has been predigested by the addition of a commercial preparation of lactase. Calcium supplements should also be given.

Questions

1 What type of chemical reaction is involved in the digestion of food?

2 What is bile? Why is it important?

3 Make a list of the hormones that help to control the process of digestion. Explain the function of each one.

4 How are the cells lining the stomach and those lining the duodenum protected from the action of proteases?

5 Why is peristalsis important in digestion?

22.4 Absorption in the small intestine

Alcohol molecules are absorbed directly through the cells of the epithelium lining the mouth and stomach, which is why the effects of drinking alcohol are felt quickly. GTN, the medicine taken as a spray or tablet under the tongue, is used to relieve the pain of angina. It is absorbed through the epithelium in the mouth and rapidly reaches the blood supply which transports it to the coronary arteries.

Most absorption, however, takes place in the small intestine. Absorption of the end-products of digestion, monosaccharides, amino acids, fatty acids and glycerol, and of soluble substances that are ingested (e.g. vitamins, minerals, water) occurs in the ileum. The water soluble products, glucose and amino acids, are taken into the epithelial cells of the ileum lining the enormous surface area presented by the villi and microvilli coupled to sodium ions. They leave the cells and enter the blood capillaries by facilitated diffusion. A sodium–potassium pump maintains the correct concentration of sodium ions for continued transport of the substrates out of the lumen of the ileum.

Fatty acids and glycerol and fat-soluble vitamins are not water soluble. They form tiny globules called **micelles** which dissolve in the cell membranes of the cells lining the villi, and diffuse into the cell cytoplasm. Here they are built up again into a milky-white emulsion of triglycerides and phospholipids which is shed into one of the lacteals found in the centre of each villus. The lacteals are part of the lymphatic system. The lymph carrying the lipids eventually empties into a large vein near the heart and the lipids are transported by the circulating blood to the hepatic artery which supplies the liver.

> Absorption through the ileum is efficient because there is a large surface area, the surface epithelium is very thin and there is a rich network of blood capillaries.

▶ *Chapter 10.1 describes the lymphatic system*

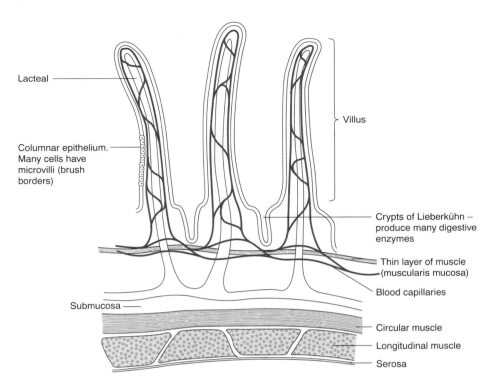

Lacteal

Columnar epithelium. Many cells have microvilli (brush borders)

Villus

Crypts of Lieberkühn – produce many digestive enzymes

Thin layer of muscle (muscularis mucosa)

Blood capillaries

Submucosa

Circular muscle

Longitudinal muscle

Serosa

Figure 22.16 The detailed structure of a small part of the wall of the ileum

Events in the colon

The ileum leads to the first part of the colon, a sac called the **caecum** and the **appendix** (a vestigial structure in humans). About 10 dm^3 of fluid is secreted into the human gut every day. It is mainly water, some of which is re-absorbed by the ileum but most of which is taken up by the cells lining the colon. The colon is inhabited by a rich natural flora of bacteria including *Escherichia coli*.

> A vestigial structure is one that has evolved so that it no longer has a function in the body.

Why do we need bacteria in the colon?

The colon is around 1.5 m long. It has a large population of bacteria which break down the **slow release starch** in the diet – starch which takes a long time to be broken down by pancreatic amylase. Slow release starch is found in whole grain cereals, pulses and pasta. It is better for health than rapidly digested starch like bread and potatoes because it causes a lower rise in glucose and insulin response after a meal. We also know that some foods, sweet corn and bananas for example, contain **resistant starch** which passes to the large intestine undigested and is fermented by bacteria. The bacteria may also synthesise vitamins K and B$_{12}$ which are absorbed by the colon.

Dietary fibre from plant cell walls is also fermented by bacteria inhabiting the colon. This releases energy, in some animals as much as 30 per cent of their daily requirement. However, humans living on Western style diets, which are low in starchy foods and fibre, may get only ten per cent of their daily energy this way.

Other benefits of fermentation in the colon are that the growth of beneficial bacteria in the colon is stimulated and the biomass of bacteria increases faecal bulk and protects the lining of the large intestine against cancer.

> Egestion is getting rid of undigested food that has passed through the gut and has never been part of the body.
> Excretion is getting rid of waste products formed by metabolic reactions in the cells of the body.

Egestion

The colon leads to the rectum where the undigested remains of the food mixed with mucus, dead cells and bacteria form the semi-solid **faeces**. These are expelled at regular intervals when the sphincter muscle around the anus relaxes.

CHAPTER 23 Dietary Matters

23.1 The human diet

Foods we eat supply the raw materials that are needed for growth and for the repair and replacement of cells and cell structures. They are also a source of energy needed to maintain metabolic functions. The nutritional requirements of an individual vary with their age, sex, size, their particular level of activity and lifestyle. It is necessary to alter the diet during pregnancy, or because of a health problem such as kidney disease, diabetes or obesity.

An ideal diet is one which has nutritional balance and maintains health, causing neither deficiency symptoms nor effects from an excess of any nutrient.

Figure 23.1 The exact nutritional requirements vary with the age and activity of the individual

► *Chapter 6 covers the biochemistry of carbohydrates, proteins and lipids*

The human diet has a number of important constituents necessary to maintain growth and health. The **macronutrients**, carbohydrates, proteins and lipids, make up the bulk of the diet. The **micronutrients**, vitamins and minerals, are essential for health but cannot be synthesised by the body. Even though they are required only in very small quantities they must be supplied by the diet. Essential amino acids must also be provided. Water is also important and its intake must balance the loss from the body through urination, sweating and use in metabolism.

23.2 Components of the diet

Carbohydrates

Carbohydrates are important sources of energy and of fibre. They are obtained from cereals, fruits and vegetables or from products made from them such as flour and sugar. The energy is usually stored as the polysaccharide starch or as a disaccharide such as sucrose.

Figure 23.2 Rice is said to be the staple food of one-third of the world's population

There is actually more to starch than we once thought; there are *three* types of starch in our diet:

1 rapidly digested starches – in cornflakes, bread and potatoes;
2 slowly digested starches – in raw oats, beans, peas, cold potatoes and cooled, cooked starchy foods;
3 resistant starch – in sweetcorn, bananas and cooled, heat-processed food.

Cereal crops, in particular rice and increasingly wheat, are enormously important since they feed large populations in many of the poorer countries in the world. Maize and traditional root crops such as yam and cassava are also important.

The carbohydrate glycogen, found in meat, may also contribute a relatively small amount of carbohydrate to the diet.

Global food: fair shares for everyone?

On our planet food production is successful. What is not so successful is the unequal distribution of the produce. In the Northern hemisphere there are large excesses of some foods, while in the developing countries (mainly in the Southern hemisphere) many people do not get enough food. The world's population is estimated to be approaching six billion and as many as 66 per cent of the population probably do not receive enough energy from their diet. Poor countries do not necessarily have malnutrition but very often poverty lies at the root of poor nutrition. It is closely linked to many other problems such as:

● little or no education;
● fast-growing populations or over-population;
● poor housing, shanty towns or slums;
● an insufficient and/or polluted water supply;
● little or no agricultural mechanisation;
● political instability, perhaps leading to wars.

In addition:

1 Climatic conditions such as drought or floods may lead to the loss of all or a major part of the crop.
2 Where forests are cut down to provide more agricultural land, the land does not prove to be fertile. It is readily eroded and quite quickly desertification occurs.
3 Some developing countries use their land to grow cash crops such as coffee, tea and chocolate which are sold to developed, industrialised countries. Basic food crops are not grown. Profits from the cash crops are used to buy imported manufactured goods or to pay off the interest on national debts, but the agricultural workers often have insufficient basic foods.

4 International aid given by wealthier countries to develop agriculture in poorer countries is shrinking. In 1980 $12 billion were given; this was reduced to $10 billion by 1990.

Drought and war frequently lead to failure of the basic crops causing famine on a huge scale. The results are a human tragedy as many people die. When someone has little or no food the human body will first metabolise its fat stores to supply energy, but once these reserves have been used up muscle is broken down to provide energy, and starvation and death follows.

Figure 23.3 This woman in Croatia used to farm land now devastated by war. For the time being she must rely on aid for survival.

► **Basics in Brief explains the units that are used for measurements of energy**

Carbohydrates are the most easily accessible sources of energy to the human body. One gram of pure carbohydrate provides 17.2 kiloJoules (kJ) of energy. Monosaccharides such as glucose can be respired most quickly because they do not have to be digested before being absorbed into the blood circulation.

Table 23.1 The daily estimated average requirement for energy (EAR) changes throughout life and differs for males and females

Age	EAR in MJ/day (Kcal/day)			
	Males		**Females**	
0–3 months	2.28	(545)	2.16	(515)
4–6 months	2.89	(690)	2.69	(645)
7–9 months	3.44	(825)	3.20	(765)
10–12 months	3.85	(920)	3.61	(865)
1–3 years	5.15	(1230)	4.86	(1165)
4–6 years	7.16	(1715)	6.46	(1545)
7–10 years	8.24	(1970)	7.28	(1740)
11–14 years	9.27	(2220)	7.72	(1845)
15–18 years	11.51	(2755)	8.83	(2110)
19–50 years	10.60	(2550)	8.10	(1940)
51–59 years	10.60	(2550)	8.00	(1900)
60–64 years	9.93	(2380)	7.99	(1900)
65–74 years	9.71	(2330)	7.96	(1900)
75+ years	8.77	(2100)	7.61	(1810)

A distinction is made between **intrinsic** sugars that occur naturally in fruit and vegetables and in milk, and refined (or **extrinsic** sugars) that are added to manufactured foods. There is no evidence that intrinsic sugars are harmful to health but an intake of over 200 g a day of extrinsic sugars is believed to contribute to obesity, diabetes and tooth decay. Artificial sweeteners such as saccharin and aspartame are added to sweeten foods without increasing the energy value of the food to any extent.

Fibre is made of cellulose, hemicellulose and pectins from plant cell walls. It cannot be digested by humans because we do not secrete enzymes such as cellulase which are necessary to break it down. Consequently, it passes through the digestive system and is egested in the faeces. The importance of fibre from fruit and vegetables in the diet is to promote peristalsis in the digestive system. This ensures regular removal of faeces from the bowel. In populations that are wholly or largely vegetarian, cancer of the large intestine is unknown. As a rule of thumb, four to six helpings of fruit and vegetables every day are good for health.

► **Chapter 22.4 covers starch and the large intestine**

Lipids

Lipids are high-energy foods and are the main energy store in animals. Plant cells sometimes store oils, and nuts and seeds are usually a rich source. Fats are important because when oxidised they will release over twice the amount of energy as an equal mass of carbohydrate. One gram of pure fat contains 38.5 kJ of energy. However, energy is more readily released from carbohydrate, so fats are only used as an energy source when the supply of carbohydrate is low or the demand for energy is great.

► **Chapter 25.8 has more information about the respiration of fat**

Our diet must supply the essential fatty acid linoleic acid, since it cannot be synthesised in the body. Rich food sources are sunflower and corn oils, nuts and wheatgerm. Linolenic and arachidonic acids are also considered to be essential to human health, but when they are absent from the diet they can be synthesised in the liver.

Fats are also important in the body as a constituent of cell membranes, and are used as a raw material for the synthesis of steroids, including some hormones. They are essential in the diet for the absorption of the fat-soluble vitamins A, D, E and K, and they prevent the skin and hair from becoming dry.

Figure 23.4 These foods are all rich sources of lipid

▶ *Chapter 6.3 explains about saturated and unsaturated fats*

cis and *trans* relate to the configuration of the fatty acid molecule.

Saturated fats are connected with raised levels of cholesterol in the blood, one of the factors increasing the risk of coronary heart disease. Many but not all animal fats are high in saturated fat; beef, lamb and pork are rich sources even when the visible fat has been cut off. Butter, lard, cheeses, cream and full-fat milk are further examples. Polyunsaturated fats appear to lower low-density lipoproteins and cholesterol. There is some debate about this, some scientists believing that the *cis* polyunsaturates are better for health than the *trans* forms.

Determining the energy content of food using a calorimeter

A bomb or food calorimeter measures the amount of energy transferred to the surroundings when a known mass of food is oxidised by burning. The apparatus is shown below.

A sample of food to be tested is dried, ground up and weighed. It is placed in the crucible. The sample is protected by a metal jacket filled with oxygen, which is surrounded by a known volume of water. Waste gases are sucked out of the calorimeter by a suction pump. The temperature of the water is taken.

The food is then ignited using an electric element. As the food burns the water is stirred to disperse heat from the heat exchange coil evenly through the water. When the food has finished burning the temperature of the water is taken again. The rise in temperature of the water is due to the transfer of energy from the burning food to the surrounding water.

The energy transferred from the food can be calculated in joules. 4.2 joules are needed to raise the temperature of 1 g of water by 1°C.

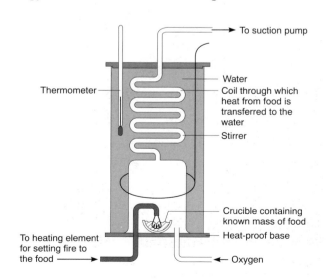

Figure 23.5 The calorimeter

Table 23.2 Daily requirement for protein depends on a person's age and sex

Age	Reference nutrient intake (g/day)
0–3 months	12.5 (approximate)
4–6 months	12.7
7–9 months	13.7
10–12 months	14.9
1–3 years	14.5
4–6 years	19.7
7–10 years	28.3
Males:	
11–14 years	42.1
15–18 years	55.2
19–50 years	55.5
50+ years	53.3
Females:	
11–14 years	41.2
15–18 years	45.0
19–50 years	45.0
50+ years	46.5
Pregnancy	adult requirement +6

Proteins

Proteins are required for growth and the replacement of cells. In the absence of any other energy source they may be respired to give energy. The diet must provide enough amino acids to maintain a positive nitrogen balance in the body, i.e. to prevent a net loss of body protein. The daily intake varies with age.

Protein foods may be either animal or plant in origin. Animal sources include meat, fish, eggs and milk products. Animal proteins include a wider range of amino acids than plant proteins and include all the essential amino acids. (Essential amino acids must be obtained from the diet because they cannot be synthesised in the body. Non-essential amino acids can be synthesised in the body). Plants do not contain as much protein as animal foods but nuts and legumes, such as beans and lentils, are useful sources. The soya bean is a particularly useful source. Plant proteins may be deficient in some of the essential amino acids that must be supplied in the diet. Sometimes a combination of two foods will fulfil a dietary requirement. For example, the proteins in beans do not contain the amino acid cysteine but some are rich in lysine; wheat protein is rich in cysteine but lacks lysine.

The soya bean

The soya plant has been cultivated in China for 5000 years. During the early nineteenth century the beans were used as ballast in ships sailing to the USA. It is probable that they were then cultivated merely for curiosity and it was not until the First World War (1914–18) that the beans were recognised as being a good source of oil.

During the 1940s when there was a shortage of food because of the Second World War, it was realised that the soya bean is an excellent source of protein, iron, calcium and some of the B vitamins. The main producers of the soya plant today are the USA, Brazil and China. The bushy plants grow best in a warm temperate climate and will produce mature pods within four months of germination.

The soya bean has many diverse uses including:
- roasting beans to make a coffee substitute;
- grinding beans to make flour (although this is not suitable for making bread as its fat content is too high);
- germinating beans to give a sprouting salad or using them to make bean salad;
- extracting soya milk which can be made into the cheese called 'tofu';
- adding to manufactured baby foods and slimming foods.

Figure 23.6 The beans of the soya plant are rich in protein and oil – they are incorporated into many different foods

Proteins that are ingested are hydrolysed during digestion to peptides and finally to amino acids. These are absorbed through the walls of the villi of the ileum and transported to the liver via the hepatic portal vein. The proteins that are essential for each cell are assembled from the amino acids absorbed from proteins digested in the diet. Any non-essential amino acids that are needed but which have not been obtained from the diet can be synthesised by the process of **transamination**. A transaminase enzyme catalyses the exchange of the amino acid group from an amino acid from the diet with a keto group from a carbohydrate. You can see how this happens in Figure 23.7.

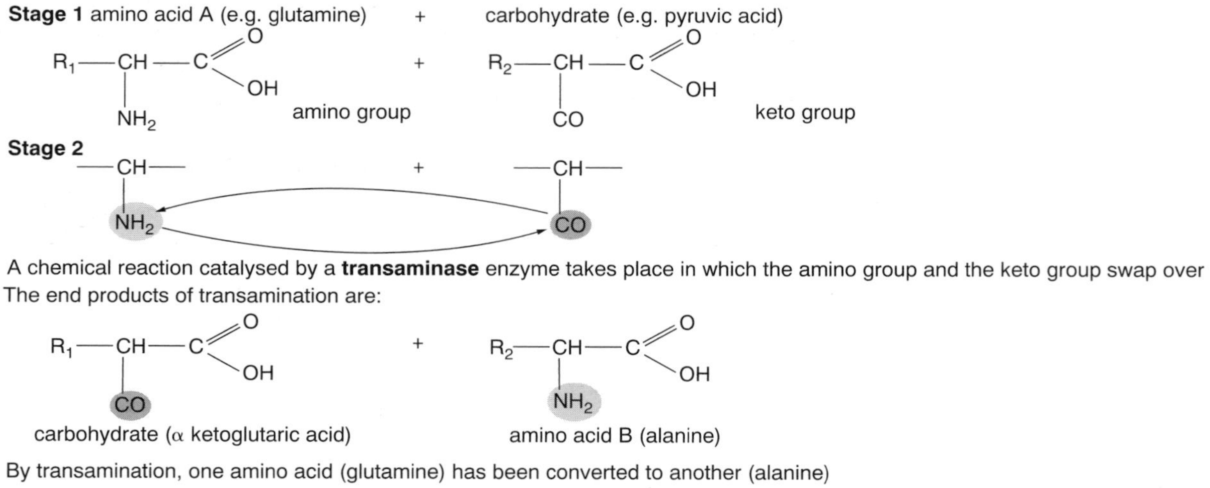

Stage 1 amino acid A (e.g. glutamine)   +   carbohydrate (e.g. pyruvic acid)

R_1—CH—C$\begin{smallmatrix}=O\\ \ \\ OH\end{smallmatrix}$ amino group   + R_2—CH—C$\begin{smallmatrix}=O\\ \ \\ OH\end{smallmatrix}$ keto group

     NH_2 CO

Stage 2

—CH—   +   —CH—

   NH_2 CO

A chemical reaction catalysed by a **transaminase** enzyme takes place in which the amino group and the keto group swap over
The end products of transamination are:

R_1—CH—C$\begin{smallmatrix}=O\\ \ \\ OH\end{smallmatrix}$ + R_2—CH—C$\begin{smallmatrix}=O\\ \ \\ OH\end{smallmatrix}$

   CO NH_2

carbohydrate (α ketoglutaric acid)   amino acid B (alanine)

By transamination, one amino acid (glutamine) has been converted to another (alanine)

Figure 23.7 Non-essential amino acids are synthesised in cells by transamination

▶ *Chapter 15.2 explains deamination in the liver*

Apart from the protein found in muscles, humans and other mammals are unable to store protein in their bodies. As a result they must get rid of any excess amino acids that they absorb. The process involved is called **deamination**. An amino group ($-NH_2$) is removed from each amino acid molecule and the remaining part of the molecule is converted to carbohydrate and respired, or to fat and stored. The amino groups are converted to ammonia (NH_3). Ammonia would be toxic if it accumulated in body tissues and so, along with carbon dioxide and the amino acid ornithine, it is converted to urea. This is called the **ornithine cycle** and is shown in Figure 23.8. The resulting urea is filtered from the blood by the kidneys and excreted in urine.

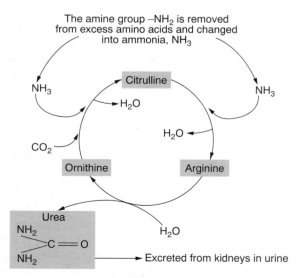

Figure 23.8 The ornithine cycle by which ammonia is converted to urea

Vitamins

The discovery of vitamins was made by the English biochemist Frederick Gowland Hopkins in 1912. He showed that rats fed on a diet of protein, carbohydrates, fats, minerals and water became ill and failed to grow. A control group of rats was given the same diet but a small volume of milk was added to it. Their growth was normal. If the diet of the groups of rats were swapped over their development was reversed.

The same year a Polish scientist discovered that an extract of an amine from rice husk could cure beri beri in sailors living on a diet of white rice. It looked as though the extra dietary ingredient needed for health was an amino acid, and so it was named 'vitamine' to mean 'vital amine'. In fact we now know that one vitamin, thiamine (vitamin B$_1$) is an amino acid, but the others are a variety of different kinds of compounds.

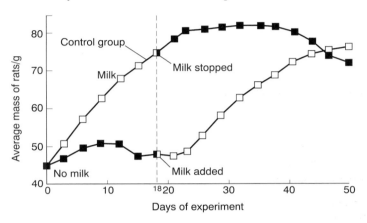

Figure 23.9 The results of the first scientific experiment to show that vitamins are essential in the diet

Vitamins are required in the diet in very small amounts and 13 different ones have been identified. They are organic compounds that have specific biochemical functions in humans. Many vitamins give rise to coenzymes that are essential for particular enzymes to work within the body. Deficiencies of vitamins cause diseases. Vitamins are found in some foods and, except for vitamin D, are not made in the body. Vitamin supplements are sold over the counter, however, a well balanced diet should provide the daily requirement of vitamins.

Vitamins can be classified according to whether they are soluble in water or in fat. Vitamins A, D, E and K are fat soluble whilst vitamins of the B group and vitamin C are water soluble.

Fat soluble vitamins that we have eaten may be stored in the body's fat deposits (the adipose tissue). An excessive intake of these vitamins can raise the levels of stored vitamins to a toxic level. For example an excess of vitamin D may lead to an excessive uptake of calcium from the gut, which is then deposited in the soft tissues. An excessive intake of vitamin A is also toxic and it can cause a condition called **carotenosis** which causes the skin to turn yellow. Liver damage occurs and may be fatal. However, the deficiency of a vitamin is *much more* likely to occur than an excess.

One form of vitamin D is synthesised by the action of sunlight on a compound related to cholesterol found in the skin. Vitamin D is the only vitamin that the human body can synthesise. For this reason a deficiency of vitamin D is rare unless the climate has very little natural sunlight, the atmosphere is very smoky or people spend little time out of doors. The result of vitamin D deficiency is the disease rickets. The bones are soft because they do not calcify as they develop and the legs bow.

Table 23.3 The sources and functions of vitamins

Vitamin	Source	Metabolic functions	Effects of deficiency	Effects of excess
Fat-soluble vitamins				
A	liver, green leafy vegetables; synthesised in gut from ß-carotene	maintain epithelia; provide visual pigment; bone/teeth growth	atrophy of epithelia, e.g. dry skin + cornea, increased susceptibility to respiratory/urinary/digestive tract infection, skin sores; 'night blindness'; slow bone/tooth growth	anorexia, dry skin, sparse hair, raised intracranial pressure in children; blurred vision, enlarged liver in adults; may be fatal
D	synthesised as provitamin D_3 in skin using UV light; also in fish liver, fish oils, egg yolk, milk	absorption of calcium and phosphate from gut	demineralisation of bone (rickets in children, osteomalacia in adults)	excess calcium absorption from gut; calcium deposition in soft tissues
E	nuts, wheatgerm, seed oils, green leafy vegetables	inhibits catabolism of membrane lipids; promotes wound healing and neural function	abnormal organelle/plasma membranes; oxidation of polyunsaturated fatty acids	
K	produced by intestinal bacteria; also in spinach, cauliflower, cabbage, liver	synthesis of blood clotting factors	delayed blood clotting	haemolysis and increased bilirubin in blood in children, otherwise toxic build-up unlikely
Water-soluble vitamins				
B_1 (thiamin)	whole grain, eggs, pork, liver, yeast	coenzyme in carbohydrate metabolism; essential for synthesis of acetylcholine (neurotransmitter)	build-up of pyruvic/lactic acids; energy deficient; partial paralysis of digestive tract/skeletal muscle (beri-beri); degeneration of myelin sheath	
B_2 (riboflavin)	yeast, liver, beef, lamb, eggs, whole grain, peas, peanuts; small quantities produced by gut bacteria	component of coenzymes in carbohydrate and protein metabolism, esp. in eye, blood, skin, intestinal mucosa	blurred vision, cataracts; lesions of intestinal mucosa; dermatitis; anaemia	
B_3 (niacin or nicotinamide)	yeast, meats, liver, fish, whole grain, peas, beans; also synthesised from amino acid tryptophan	component of coenzyme NAD in intracellular respiration; assists breakdown of cholesterol	hard, rough, blackish skin; dermatitis, diarrhoea (pellagra); psychological disturbance	burning sensation in hands/face, cardiac arrhythmias, increased glycogen utilisation
B_{12} (cyanocobalamin)	liver, kidney, milk, eggs, cheese, meats; requires intrinsic factor from stomach for absorption	coenzyme for haemoglobin synthesis; amino acid metabolism	pernicious anaemia; nerve axon degeneration	
Folate (folic acid)	green leafy vegetables, liver; synthesised by gut bacteria	synthesis of nucleotides; red/white blood cell production	macrocytic anaemia due to abnormally large red blood cells; neural tube abnormality in fetus	
C (ascorbic acid)	citrus fruits, tomatoes, green vegetables	promotes protein metabolism, formation of connective tissue and wound healing	retarded growth; poor connective tissue repair/growth (scurvy) including swollen gums, tooth loosening, fragile blood vessels; poor wound healing	

Figure 23.10 Deficiencies of vitamins cause diseases (a) A child with rickets (b) A lack of vitamin C causes sore, bleeding gums and loose teeth – symptoms of scurvey. Vitamin C helps to heal wounds and detoxify proteins. It also plays a part in protein metabolism and the synthesis of the connective tissue collagen.

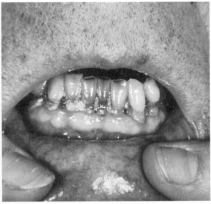

(b)

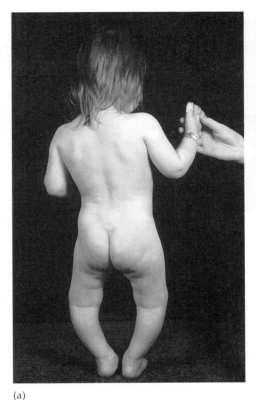

(a)

Anti-oxidant vitamins

Over the past 12 years researchers have been investigating the anti-oxidant vitamins A, C and E to see whether they are able to give protection against cancer. Cancers can develop from free radicals that damage the DNA in the cells, causing a mutation, and it was thought that anti-oxidants might neutralise their harmful action. However, latest published results are not encouraging. A study from Finland showed an *increase* in lung cancer amongst a group taking beta carotene (vitamin A) compared to a group not given the vitamin. Similar results were obtained from the CARET trial published in the USA early in 1996.

Nevertheless, many studies have shown that people who eat a lot of fresh fruit and vegetables are less likely to develop cancer or cardiovascular disease. It may be that these people simply eat a more healthy diet than others, but many scientists believe that there is a protective component in fruit and vegetables. Research continues to try and identify it.

Figure 23.11 The results of the studies in (a) Finland and (b) USA failed to show that beta carotene protected against lung cancer

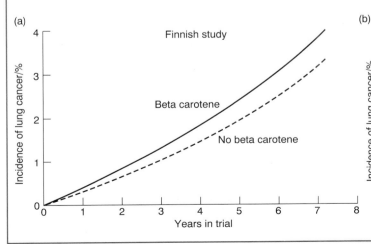

(a) Finnish study — Beta carotene — No beta carotene. Incidence of lung cancer/%. Years in trial.

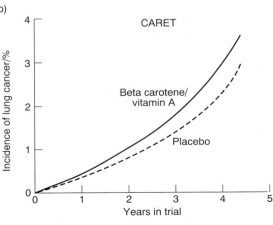

(b) CARET — Beta carotene/vitamin A — Placebo. Incidence of lung cancer/%. Years in trial.

Minerals

Minerals are elements other than carbon, hydrogen and oxygen that are required for health. The **macroelements**, which include iron and calcium, are present in relatively large amounts in the body; others needed in smaller amounts are the **trace elements** or **microelements**.

Mineral	Source	Function	Effects of deficiency
calcium	milk, egg yolk, shellfish, green leafy vegetables	formation of bones/teeth; blood clotting, muscle contraction; muscle/nerve action potentials; endo- and exocytosis; cell division	loss of bone density, e.g. osteomalacia/ rickets
phosphorus	milk, meat, fish, poultry, nuts	formation of bones/teeth; buffer chemical; muscle contraction/ nerve activity; component of ATP, DNA, RNA + many enzymes	deficiency rare
potassium	widespread – 'Lo-salt'	action potential of muscle/nerve cells	neuromuscular depression
sodium	widespread – table salt	major osmotic solute of extracellular fluids; action potential of muscle/nerve cells	
chlorine (chloride)	non-processed foods, usually found with sodium, e.g. table salt	involved in acid–base balance; major osmotic solute of extracellular fluids; formation of gastric acid	deficiency usually occurs with sodium
magnesium	beans, peanuts, bananas	constituent of many coenzymes; role in bone formation and muscle/nerve cell functions	muscle weakness; convulsions; hypertension
Trace minerals			
iron	widespread but esp. red meats, liver, beans, fruits, nuts, legumes	component of haemoglobin; component of chemicals involved in cell respiration	anaemia
iodine (iodide)	seafood, cod-liver oil, iodised table salt	component of thyroid hormones	thyroid hormone deficiency (induces thyroid goitre)
fluorine (fluoride)	tea, coffee, fluoridated water	component of bones/teeth	decreased bone/teeth density
zinc	widespread but esp. meats	component of some enzymes; promotes normal growth, spermatogenesis; involved in taste and appetite	dermatitis; growth retardation; diarrhoea
copper	eggs, wholewheat flour, liver, fish, spinach	haemoglobin synthesis; component of some enzymes or acts as cofactor	retarded growth; cerebral degeneration
chromium	yeast, beer, beef	involved in insulin synthesis; maintains HDL concentrations in plasma	

Table 23.4 Minerals essential for the health of the human body

Calcium

An adult human contains 1.0–1.5 kg of calcium. It is an important element being a constituent of bones and teeth, and playing an essential role in the clotting of the blood and the functioning of muscles and nerves. Calcium is present in dairy products and in tinned fish such as sardines and pilchards which contain bones that are softened and edible.

Vitamin D assists the uptake of calcium from the gut, although calcium is not absorbed easily. Probably at least half the calcium eaten in the diet is egested with the faeces. Wholemeal flour contains compounds which bind with calcium, preventing it from being taken into the blood circulation. Calcium supplements are not usually absorbed very efficiently.

If there is a deficiency of calcium in the body, calcium passes out from the bones of the skeleton, which weakens it, and into the blood. This may happen during pregnancy but mainly occurs in women after the age of 60. About 25 per cent of women develop this condition which is called **osteoporosis**. It appears that the drop in the levels of oestrogen after the menopause is directly related to the condition. People who drink high levels of alcohol, are underweight and take little exercise are also more at risk. As the vertebral column loses calcium it becomes bowed so that the posture is poor and bones break more easily. Fractures of the hip and spine are particularly serious. Osteoporosis also occurs in men, but is much less common.

> ▶ *Chapter 30.5 describes osteoporosis and ageing in general*

Iron

Most of the iron in the human body is present in the pigment haemoglobin found in the red blood cells. One millilitre of healthy blood contains 0.5 mg of iron. It is also a constituent of myoglobin in muscle cells. Every body cell contains some iron because it is needed as a cofactor for some enzymes involved in respiration and for others involved in the synthesis of DNA. In the spleen, the bone marrow and the liver iron is stored as ferritin, an iron–protein complex. A deficiency of iron in the body results in **anaemia** which is believed to affect over 500 million people world-wide. However, there are many causes of anaemia and not all are due to a lack of iron in the diet.

Normal loss of iron from the body in men, children and post-menopausal women is in cells sloughed off naturally from the surface of the skin and the epithelium lining the gut. Anaemia which is not due to a dietary deficiency arises from loss of blood which may have a simple cause such as regular nose-bleeds or piles; bleeding may be secondary to a tumour, or may be the result of an accident. Women of reproductive age lose on average 30 ml blood at each menstrual period, so they need more iron in their diet than men.

In anaemia there is a decrease in the *size* of red blood cells and so they carry less haemoglobin than usual. As a result, less oxygen can be transported by the blood and this reduces respiration, causing lethargy (a lack of energy). Often the skin is pale and there is a tendency to bruise and bleed more easily than normal.

The main sources of iron in the diet are red meat and some green, leafy vegetables, mushrooms, nuts, legumes and wholemeal bread. The absorption of iron is difficult, probably only 5–20 per cent of the total ingested iron is actually assimilated; it is more readily absorbed from meat than from plant foods. Iron absorption can be increased by the presence of foods rich in vitamin C or lactic acid, but is reduced by the presence of tannins, such as those which occur in tea.

> ▶ *Chapter 10.3 describes haemoglobin which contains most of the body's iron*

Water

The daily water balance of a human not engaged in heavy manual work (and so not sweating excessively) is shown in Table 23.5.

Process	Water intake (ml)	Water output (ml)
drinking	1450	–
food	800	–
from respiration	350	–
in urine	–	1500
in sweat	–	600
from lungs	–	400
in faeces	–	100
Total	2600	2600

Table 23.5 The human daily water balance – humans take in between two and three litres of water every day and lose a similar volume

Questions

1 Explain why (a) iron and (b) calcium are important in metabolism. Under what circumstances *might* they be deficient in a woman aged 50 years?

2 a) How is vitamin D different from the other vitamins in the human diet in the way that it is obtained?

 b) Suggest why it was not uncommon in the early twentieth century for children in the British Isles to suffer from vitamin D deficiency. What would have been wrong with them?

3 What are essential amino acids and essential fatty acids? Give two examples of both. How are they obtained by a human?

4 Why are some polyunsaturated fats said to lessen the risk of coronary heart disease?

5 Explain why different types of starch are important in the human diet.

23.3 Meeting energy needs

The balanced diet

Everyone needs a balanced diet providing the correct nutrients and energy content for their age and level of activity. The details of an individual's requirements vary with age, activity and health.

It would be impractical for everyone to consult food tables and calculate energy values for each meal, and so the general rules to be followed are:

- eat a wide variety of foods;
- eat mostly cereals, pasta, bread and potatoes;
- eat four to six portions of fruit and vegetables daily;

- eat milk, cheese, yoghurt, lean meat, poultry, eggs, legumes and nuts in moderation;
- eat butter, margarine and added sugar sparingly.

As much fresh food as possible should be included.

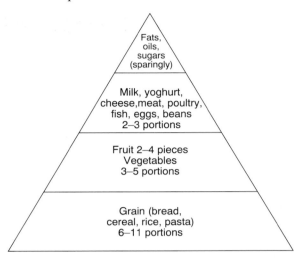

Figure 23.12 The healthy eating triangle – a quick rule of thumb to a balanced diet

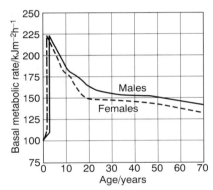

Figure 23.13 A graph to show that the BMR of human males and females varies with age

▶ *Chapter 17.3 describes the effect of temperature on BMR*

Basal metabolic rate (BMR)

Basal metabolic rate (BMR) is the minimum amount of energy that is required to maintain metabolism at a level sufficient for the body to survive. It is the energy needed to keep the heart beating, the ventilation of the lungs and keep the temperature at the normal level. It is measured when a person is awake, has fasted for 8–12 hours and has been resting at a comfortable temperature (e.g. 20°C).

The BMR changes throughout human life. In a new born baby it is low, around 100 kJ m^{-2} h^{-1}. The level then rises rapidly during the first year, when there is a rapid growth rate, to ~220 kJ m^{-2} h^{-1}. This then declines as growth rate ceases but throughout life males have a slightly higher BMR than females of the same age. (At age 20 the average BMR is 150 kJ m^{-2} h^{-1} for women and 167 kJ m^{-2} h^{-1} for men.) It becomes lower as the body ages.

BMR also changes in response to certain external factors:

1 In very hot or very cold climates it is reduced by five to ten per cent.
2 It rises after a meal has been eaten in proportion to the energy content of the food.
3 It rises after exercise as more energy is expended.

Activity	Energy expenditure (kJ min^{-1})	
	Woman	Man
sleeping	3.8	4.2
sitting	5.0	5.8
light work	15.0	17.0
sawing	34.0	38.0
maximum work	57.0	63.0

Table 23.6 The rate of energy expenditure depends on the type of activity a person is involved in

Physical activity level (PAL) gives some indication of lifestyle. It works out at a value of between 1.4 for someone who uses very little energy and 1.9 for a very active person.

BMR can be used to calculate the energy requirement of an individual by applying the expression:

$$\text{BMR} \times \text{physical activity level} = \text{estimated average requirement for energy}$$

A number of terms are used to describe nutrient requirements. These are summarised below:

- **Estimated average requirements (EARs)**: estimated average requirements for food energy or a nutrient recommended by the UK Department of Health. Because the value is an average some individuals will need less and some more.

- **Reference nutrient intake (RNI)**: used for protein, vitamins and minerals. It gives an amount that is enough or more than enough for the needs of 97 per cent of the population. If the average intake of a group of people is at the level of RNI, the risk of deficiency within the group is low.

- **Lower reference nutrient intake (LRNI)**: relates to the small number of people in a group who have only a small requirement for a particular nutrient. It describes an amount that is sufficient for them.

- **Dietary reference value (DRV)**: a value which takes into account EAR, RNI, LRNI and safe intake.

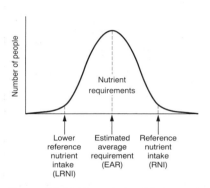

Figure 23.14 The relationship between different nutrient reference values

Measuring human metabolic rate

At the Medical Research Centre's Dunn Nutrition Centre in Cambridge volunteers stay for periods of one to 14 days in order to have their energy expenditure measured. They stay in comfortable hotel rooms called 'whole body calorimeters', which are actually fitted with complex scientific instruments that take round-the-clock measurements. It is possible to see how much energy someone uses doing specific tasks and how this relates to their diet.

The technique used is to give the human 'guinea pigs' water to drink which contains the isotopes heavy hydrogen (^{2}H) and heavy oxygen (^{18}O). The water is absorbed and metabolised and then slowly lost from the body. Much of the heavy oxygen is exhaled in the carbon dioxide breathed out and the heavy hydrogen appears in the water in sweat, urine and faeces. By measuring the rate at which ^{18}O disappears and then subtracting ^{2}H (from the water lost) it is possible to estimate carbon dioxide production. From this metabolic rate can be calculated.

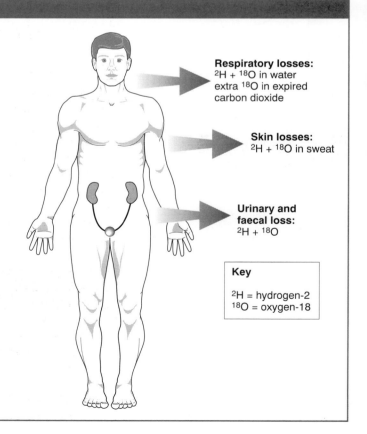

Respiratory losses:
^{2}H + ^{18}O in water extra ^{18}O in expired carbon dioxide

Skin losses:
^{2}H + ^{18}O in sweat

Urinary and faecal loss:
^{2}H + ^{18}O

Key

^{2}H = hydrogen-2
^{18}O = oxygen-18

Figure 23.15 Using water labelled with heavy isotopes of hydrogen and oxygen allows the measurement of energy output from the body

Energy intake and expenditure during an Antarctic expedition

An expedition to cross Antartica on foot was made by Ranulph Fiennes and Dr Mike Stroud over three months in the winter of 1992–3. Lots of scientific data relating to diet and metabolism was collected by the explorers which included measuring energy expenditure using the doubly-labelled water test. It was a great opportunity to test the technique in people pushing themselves to the limits of physical endurance.

In spite of eating food providing almost double the energy intake of a normal person (including nearly four times the recommended daily level of butter) it was not enough, the two men lost nearly 50 kg between them.

What was surprising was that in spite of not having enough energy in their food each man's metabolic rate *rose* significantly, by between 8.8 and 11.2 per cent. This gives strong support for the idea that exercise is the key to effective weight loss. What's more, blood tests showed that the total level of blood cholesterol remained unchanged (in spite of all the butter), and there was an improvement in the level of beneficial high-density lipoprotein (HDL) and a drop in damaging low-density lipoprotein (LDL).

By the end of the expedition the two men were in poor physiological shape. They were less fit than when they began the trek and had lost muscle strength. The effects of not having enough to eat had taken its toll. However, their research added to our understanding of the relationship between diet, body mass, cholesterol and exercise.

Source: *MRC News*, Autumn 1995

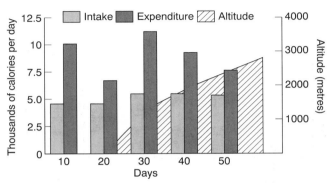

Figure 23.16 At times energy expenditure was nearly double energy intake

23.4 Dietary changes through life

The infant

New born babies are entirely dependent on milk as a source of nutrients for the first few months of life. Boiled water is also offered as a drink. Human milk differs slightly in composition from formula milk that can be made up for bottle fed babies. Human milk contains antibodies that will give protection against infection and babies are able to absorb iron and other minerals more efficiently from human milk, however, it does not contain any vitamin K. Very rarely this deficiency may cause a life-threatening disease in which the baby bleeds spontaneously. To prevent this from happening, drops of vitamin K solution are given to all babies born in the UK 12 hours after birth, and again to breast fed babies at one and six weeks of age.

During the first six months of life, energy requirements are higher in proportion than at any other time. Protein is vital for cell division leading to rapid growth. The skeleton is calcified in the early years and vitamin D is essential to maximise calcium uptake from the gut. Milk is a rich source of calcium for the development of teeth and bones. At birth, the baby has sufficient iron stores for the first six months of life, but after that iron is essential in the diet.

Babies are weaned gradually from around four to five months old, although breast milk is sufficient for a baby's needs for at least six months. Small amounts of different finely mashed foods such as vegetables, cereals,

▶ *Chapter 28.5 describes human milk secretion*

	Human	A modified milk formula* (powder diluted as directed)
energy (kcal)	70	69
protein (total) (g)	1.1	1.5
casein (% protein)	40.0	40.0
carbohydrate (g)	7.4	7.2
fat (total) (g)	4.2	3.6
saturated fat (% fat)	46.0	44.0
linoleic (% fat)	7.0–11.0	17.0
sodium (mmol)	0.6	0.71
calcium (mg)	35	49
phosphorus (mg)	15	30
iron (mg)	0.075	0.9
vitamin C (mg)	3.8	6.9
vitamin D (µg)	0.8	1.1

Table 23.7 A comparison of the composition of human milk and breast milk substitute (values given are per 100 ml)

* Mean of Cow and Gate Premium and SMA-S26.

fruits, fish and poultry are introduced one at a time. These are usually bland in flavour and have no added salt. As the variety and quantity of food that a baby eats increases, the amount of milk it drinks decreases.

The adolescent and young adult

During the ages of ten and 20 years rapid growth and major developmental changes occur in the bodies of males and females. As a result, the requirements for nutrients are modified. During this period the lean body mass and amount of body fat reflect a difference between the sexes, which is much less marked during childhood.

	Age (years)	Male	Female
average lean body mass (kg)	10	25	22
	20	63	42
average fat (kg)	10	7	5
	20	9	14
energy (MJ day^{-1})	11–14	9.27	7.92
	15–18	11.51	8.83
protein (g day^{-1})	11–14	33.8	33.1
	15–18	46.1	37.1
iron (mg day^{-1})	11–18	8.7	11.4

Table 23.8 There is a change in the proportion of muscle to fat in males and females as they mature. Females need more iron than males because menstruation begins. The requirement for calcium (not shown) rises because growth is taking place

At this stage in life young people take on an increasing responsibility for what they eat. Breakfast is often missed and more meals are eaten away from home. Snacks, which are low in nutrients but over-loaded in energy, are common. 'Junk' food is easy, popular and readily available. Its nutrient content varies but can be better balanced than the term 'junk' suggests.

▶ *Chapter 24 covers health problems related to nutrition and the digestive system*

Snacks may replace meals and the overall result may be that some people are not eating a balanced diet. If a balanced diet is not eaten regularly some related health problems will begin to develop.

Figure 23.17 Burgers and chips, a balanced diet?

Pregnancy and lactation

If a pregnancy is planned, a woman is likely to be given some dietary advice about changes she can make to her diet *before* she conceives. A supplement of the vitamin **folic acid** (or **folate**) is started, and is usually taken until three months into the pregnancy. The reason for this is that in a very small proportion of babies the developing neural tube does not close properly and they are born with **spina bifida**. Folic acid is believed to reduce the risk of this happening. Heavy alcohol consumption early in pregnancy may lead to retarded physical and mental development of the fetus, and should therefore be avoided.

Figure 23.18 A pregnant woman needs a well balanced diet – in the last three months of pregnancy she needs some extra nutrients, but 'eating for two' is not good advice

During pregnancy a woman requires extra nutrients for the developing fetus and to provide for the changes taking place in her own body. The placenta has to develop, blood volume is increased and fat deposits are increased around the hips and thighs. Most foods that are usually included in the diet are allowed, with the exception of liver, liver paté, soft cheeses and shellfish. The last three of these all have a slight risk of contamination by bacteria that might harm the fetus.

The extra energy requirement has been calculated to be about 0.8 MJ a day, with a recommended daily intake (RDI) of 10 MJ. In reality many women eat less, on average nearer 9 MJ. The reasons for this may be:

- they reduce exercise;
- weight gain is monitored so that it does not become too high, making a woman aware that over-eating is unnecessary;
- energy metabolism becomes more efficient;
- nutrient absorption (including iron) is more efficient;
- protein metabolism is more efficient;
- discomfort because the baby restricts abdominal organs.

The extra protein required (10 g) brings total daily intake to 60 g. This is covered without difficulty for many women by a normal diet. Calcium requirement increases by a third, i.e. an extra 400 mg each day, and this is usually obtained from milk and/or cheese. (0.5 litres of milk or 60 g of Cheddar cheese both supply about 60 mg calcium.) Absorption of calcium improves during pregnancy.

Iron is a very important nutrient during pregnancy, the daily requirement rising from 15 to 30 mg. It may be given as a supplement, but a healthy woman will probably be able to absorb the extra requirement from her diet.

Haemoglobin levels in the blood are checked during pregnancy and an iron supplement is given if the level falls below 10–10.5 g per 100 ml. The fetus contains about 300 mg iron, and the placenta 50 mg. After the birth there is a normal loss of about 200 mg of iron from the post-natal blood loss. To help balance this, there is no loss of iron from menstruation during pregnancy and absorption of iron through the small intestine increases.

When the baby is born, the mother's nutritional requirements change again. If she is breast-feeding she is likely to secrete around 800 ml milk daily and requires the extra nutrients shown in Table 23.9 (compared with a non-lactating woman).

Nutrient	Extra daily requirement
water	900 ml
energy	2.2 MJ
protein	16.0 g
vitamin A	450 µg
thiamin	0.4 mg
vitamin C	45 mg
zinc	6.0 mg

Table 23.9 The extra dietary needs of a woman breast-feeding her baby

The elderly

The elderly in the UK are the group most at risk of nutritional deficiency. Changes in the body that occur after middle age are:

- reduction in total average body weight;
- lean body mass (males) drops on average from 60 to 50 kg;
- lean body mass (females) drops on average from 40 to 35 kg;
- body fat rises (males) by 20–30 per cent total body weight;
- body fat rises (females) by 27–40 per cent total body weight;
- fat deposits become more central and internal;
- liver mass decreases;
- BMR drops in proportion to the reduction in lean body mass.

After the age of 65 extra care is needed to maintain a balanced diet. Energy intake should be less and fat in particular should be reduced. However, protein requirement does not change. The diet should be high in fibre to help counteract constipation that may arise from reduced exercise. Alcohol intake should be lowered as the reduced liver is less able to metabolise it. Salt in the diet should be reduced as it is known to be positively related to hypertension (raised blood pressure) which tends to rise with age.

23.5 The vegetarian diet

People choose to be vegetarian for many different reasons. They may belong to a culture that has followed this way of life for centuries. As a result they use traditional recipes and are able to prepare varied meals often using legumes (including soya beans) and nuts as good sources of protein. Other reasons have a religious foundation (Seventh Day Adventists) or are based on ethical grounds related to issues such as animal rights.

Different degrees of vegetarianism have been recognised. These are people who:

- do not eat some meat (e.g. veal) or animal organs (brain);
- do not eat meat, but do eat fish and dairy products;
- do not eat meat or fish, but do eat dairy products;
- do not eat any animal products (vegans).

The only group who are at risk are the vegans because they have no source of vitamin B_{12} and lack the richest sources of calcium. It is essential that supplements of vitamin B_{12} are taken during pregnancy and during the first year of life. Babies suffering a B_{12} deficiency are at risk from abnormal cerebral development.

Figure 23.19 A vegetarian meal of stuffed peppers and herb rice might be usefully included in anyone's diet

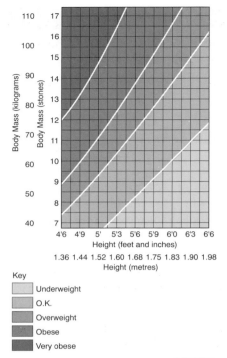

Key

- Underweight
- O.K.
- Overweight
- Obese
- Very obese

Figure 23.20 A chart like this can be used to find your ideal body mass
(See Colour Gallery page 354)

It is important that vegetarian meals are properly planned to provide a substitute for the portion of meat that is being omitted. Merely to leave out meat from the meal and to eat only the accompanying vegetables will not provide a balanced diet for any vegetarian.

23.6 Weight loss diets

It is not always easy to be objective about our body image. We may feel we are overweight when we are not, or vice versa. Calculating body mass index can give a simple objective assessment of body mass. If the body mass index rises above 25, it is sensible to lose the excess.

Body mass index (BMI)

$$\text{body mass index} = \frac{\text{body mass (kg)}}{(\text{height})^2 \; (\text{m}^2)}$$

Body mass index	Interpretation
Below 20	Underweight
20–25	Ideal weight
25.1–30	Overweight
Above 30	Obese

Weight is lost from the body when the intake of energy sources is less than the energy it expends. Fat stores are then used up as the respiratory substrate and mass is reduced. It is generally accepted that a slow steady loss in mass is more likely to achieve permanent lower body mass, than a rapid weight loss resulting from following a 'crash' diet.

The scientific principles behind a diet to reduce body mass are:

- a reduction in energy intake;
- an increase in exercise to raise BMR.

However, some diets have been published which claim that dramatic results are easy to achieve. They may not have a sound scientific basis and there are risks associated with following some extreme diets. In the 1970s over 60 people in the USA who had no previous heart disease died because their hearts stopped beating regularly after using a slimming product called 'Prolinn'. This required them to fast between taking the supplement meals. The product was protein based, but lacked several essential amino acids and was not nutritionally balanced. It has since been shown that prolonged fasting, even in conjunction with a product of sound nutritional value, carries the risk of sudden death.

Other diets that have been in fashion prescribe a very low energy intake. The result is that as weight is rapidly lost the BMR falls, but it stays low even when the diet is stopped. When the person starts eating normally again, but with a lower BMR, their body mass increases again and is very difficult to reduce.

Weight can be lost safely if someone is well motivated to succeed. Reducing the size of portions of food conditions the brain to be satisfied with less. Cutting down on fats and on food and drinks containing added sugars reduces energy intake. Increasing regular exercise, perhaps by taking up a new activity, will help to raise BMR and respire stored energy. If someone needs support joining a *reputable* slimming club may be helpful.

Questions

1 Explain any adjustment a woman should make to her diet when she is pregnant.

2 Look at the following table of percentage clinical obesity in males and females:

	Male	Female
1980	6.0	7.5
1986	7.6	12.0
1991	11.8	15.0

   a) What does the data suggest has happened from 1980–1991?

   b) Suggest reasons for the changes you have noticed.

3 How would you account for the fact that anaemia is more common amongst the Asian population living in the UK than amongst other ethnic groups?

4 What advice would you give to someone deciding to become a vegetarian, to ensure that they maintained a healthy diet?

23.7 The storage of food

All foods or food ingredients were once a living plant or animal. Animals must be killed before being prepared for cooking, and fruit, vegetables and cereals are harvested. Living cells contain enzymes which will destroy cells once the organism has died, causing deterioration in the food unless it is stored correctly. Alternatively, the food may become contaminated by the micro-organisms that grow in it.

The breakdown of tissues in foods by their enzymes is another example of **autolysis**. This may be desirable for a short time; meat that is hung at a cool temperature after killing improves in texture and develops a more mature flavour, and fruits may complete ripening.

Other changes that take place which affect the nutrient content of the food are:

- dehydration;
- loss of vitamin C;
- loss of vitamins A and K due to oxidation;
- fats becoming rancid because the fatty acids are oxidised.

Much of our fresh food is imported from overseas and may have been stored for weeks by the time we buy it. It is essential that the foods are stored under conditions that will limit their deterioration to the minimum. Moderate losses of vitamins are known to occur after harvesting. Even if a carton of fruit juice is opened and kept at room temperature, there will be a loss of vitamins. Vitamins such as riboflavin are destroyed if exposed to sunlight. Cereals such as rice are the only sources of food that can be stored for long periods of time without spoiling because they have a naturally low water content.

23.8 Food preservation

Many foods have to undergo **food preservation** and **processing** in order to keep them in a state fit for consumption for a reasonably long time. Preservation prevents wastage and allows food to be transported to populations long distances away. It makes the food safe to eat by destroying or slowing down the growth of microbes.

Sometimes processing adds to the flavour of food and increases the attractiveness of its appearance. This makes it more appetising, which is especially important for some people such as those who are ill, recovering from illness, and the elderly. Processing also allows convenience foods to be prepared commercially; therefore it is possible to buy complete meals that only have to be heated before eating. Food packaging now lists the contents and nutritional value of the prepared foods.

Table 23.10 Methods of food preservation

Method of preservation	How it works	Notes	Examples of foods treated
Dehydration	removes water so microbes cannot survive		
roller drying		food is passed over heated rollers	potato flakes
spray drying		solution sprayed into heated container at low pressure, water evaporates rapidly	milk powder
freeze drying		food frozen quickly, then warmed slightly, packed in liquid nitrogen to prevent oxidation	coffee
Osmotic	microbes lose water to their surroundings by osmosis, and die		
salting		food is packed in salt or stored in brine	fish, olives
sugar		food has high sugar content or is stored in syrup	jam, fruits
Temperature regulation	at temperatures of 0–5°C bacteria grow very slowly, spores survive	freezers should be −18°C, food must be frozen rapidly, food can be stored for long periods	meat, fish, vegetables, fruit, bread
Sterilisation	food is heated to a high temperature which kills microbes and spores	canning, food is heated to 115°C and then sealed	meat, fish, fruit, milk, vegetables
pasteurisation	partial sterilisation, pathogens killed	milk heated to 72°C for 5 seconds and then cooled rapidly	milk
pH control	microbes grow slowly in an acidic pH	pickling in vinegar	onions, gherkins

Table 23.11 Some common food additives that aid preservation and may add to the appearance and taste of the food

Additive	Function	Notes
Preservatives		
anti-oxidants	act as reducing agents and slow down natural oxidation and spoilage	fats become rancid due to oxidation; vitamins A and K are lost; vitamin E is a natural anti-oxidant in vegetable fats
e.g. sulphur dioxide, sulphites, benzoates	restrict growth of microbes by removing oxygen and creating acid conditions	added to sausages, dried fruits, soft drinks, cold meats; benzoic acid occurs naturally in cranberries
Flavourings	to improve flavour	largest group of additives; natural flavourings e.g. peppermint, orange; synthetic flavourings e.g. caramel added to cola drinks, biscuits, pickled onions
flavour enhancers	added to bring out the natural flavour of food	monosodium glutamate (MSG) is widely used especially in Chinese cooking; some people are allergic to it
Colourings	to improve the colouring of processed food, which may be spoiled during processing	natural colours e.g. cochineal, saffron; synthetic colours are often made from coal tar dyes; colouring may not be added to fresh meat, poultry, fish, baby foods, fresh fruit and vegetables
Texture controllers	alter the texture of foods	
emulsifiers	allow ingredients that do not usually mix to do so, e.g. water and fat to mix to form an emulsion	used in ice-cream, margarine, salad dressings, and desserts; a widely used emulsifier is lecithin
stabilisers	help prevent the components in the emulsion from separating by making the medium more viscous	agar, carob bean gum and alginic acid extracted from seaweed are stabilisers
humectants	keep foods such as cakes or bread moist	e.g. glycerol, sorbitol, mannitol
thickeners	added to soups, puddings	e.g. modified starch
anti-caking agents	to stop lumps forming in powdered foods	e.g. calcium silicate
gelling agents	help jams and desserts to set	e.g. pectin, agar, calcium alginate

23.9 The effect of cooking on the nutritional value of food

When foods are cooked, chemical reactions occurring in the food are speeded up. If the cooking temperature rises above 60°C enzymes in the food will be denatured.

When fruit and vegetables are boiled in water, some of the pectins found in the plant cell walls are hydrolysed and become soluble. This softens the food. In hard water areas the hydrolysed pectins react with calcium ions in the water and there is less likelihood of the vegetables becoming mushy. In soft water areas this reaction does not take place and so there is some loss of calcium from the food being cooked. Vitamins are also leached from the vegetables during soaking or cooking. Some people add sodium hydrogencarbonate (sodium bicarbonate) to vegetables to preserve their green colour, since the pigments naturally decompose on heating. However, this increases the removal of calcium and vitamins from the food.

Vitamin C, folate and thiamin (vitamin B_1) are all unstable on heating. They are highly soluble in water and this is why they are readily lost from the food into the cooking water. The losses are minimised if a small volume of cooking water is used and brought to the boil before the vegetables are added. Vegetables should be cooked for as short a time as possible. If the vegetables are kept warm before serving, there is a significant loss of vitamin C.

Methods of cooking will affect the extent to which vitamin C is lost from food. The vitamin content of freshly picked, uncooked fruit and vegetables is highest but it drops if the food is stored. Tissues that have been bruised or frozen lose vitamins most easily. Cooking in a microwave results in a small loss of vitamins as does steaming, but boiling causes a greater loss. During cooking the loss from leafy vegetables is often as high as 70 per cent, but is lower (40 per cent) from root vegetables.

Nutrient loss during cooking is not confined to vitamins. Minerals are more stable than vitamins but can be lost from vegetables if large volumes of alkaline cooking water are used. Of the essential amino acids, lysine is unstable. Linoleic acid, the essential fatty acid, is destroyed in cooking oils that are re-used for deep-frying.

Cooking method	Vitamin c (mg/100 g)
Garden peas	
raw	24
boiled	16
frozen, boiled	12
canned, reheated	1
Mange-tout peas	
boiled	28
stir-fried	51

Table 23.12 How different methods of treatment affect the vitamin C content of peas

Questions

1 What are (a) the advantages (b) the disadvantages of adding colouring substances to foods?

2 What are anti-oxidants? Give two examples.

3 Why is the vitamin C content of vegetables reduced by boiling, but not vitamin D?

4 What advice would you give about storing and maintaining the quality of fresh vegetables to someone who shopped only once a week?

CHAPTER
24

Diseases Associated with Food and the Gut

24.1 Obesity

Figure 24.1 Some people want to be obese even if it may shorten their life

Obesity occurs when the amount of food that is regularly eaten is in excess of requirement and body mass reaches at least 20 per cent higher than the ideal. Looking back to Figure 23.20 (page 240), obesity is when the BMI exceeds 30. The excess energy consumed cannot be respired by the body and is stored as fat deposits in the adipose tissue under the skin and around internal organs. The problem often starts with a slight excess in weight, which if left uncorrected continues to increase to obesity. There is concern that more than half the total British population is overweight and one third are classed as 'sedentary'. Between 1980 and 1992 the overweight population increased by 15 per cent to 54 per cent of men and 45 per cent of women. The numbers of those who are clinically obese has doubled; 13 per cent of men and 16 per cent of women.

There is no single cause of obesity – rather it is a **syndrome**, or collection of factors. Factors that play a part include:

- genetic predisposition to being overweight;
- low BMR compared to others of similar body form;
- repeated periods on low energy diets causing a lowering of BMR;
- lower glycogen synthesis but more fat synthesis;
- appetite is not well regulated;
- lack of exercise (perhaps because of a dependency on cars);
- increase in alcohol intake.

Causes of secondary obesity are:

- endocrine disorders (uncommon);
- enforced inactivity following an injury or illness, such as arthritis or a stroke;

- following pregnancy and lactation;
- over-eating as a result of a psychological condition such as anxiety or depression ('comfort eating') or a major life change such as unemployment;
- over-eating as a side effect of treatment of drugs that increase the appetite (e.g. steroids).

There are several health risks associated with being overweight. The condition may cause depression and lower self-esteem. Even moderately overweight people may be the victims of prejudice. It can start during childhood and continue into adulthood, where it may affect job opportunities and social status.

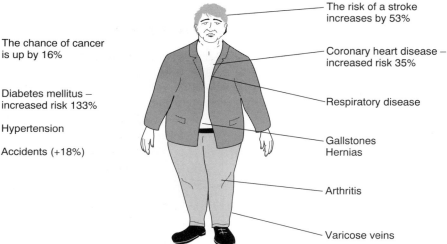

The chance of cancer is up by 16%

Diabetes mellitus – increased risk 133%

Hypertension

Accidents (+18%)

The risk of a stroke increases by 53%

Coronary heart disease – increased risk 35%

Respiratory disease

Gallstones Hernias

Arthritis

Varicose veins

Figure 24.2 Obesity increases the risk of mortality in several serious diseases

There is an increased risk of coronary heart disease and of raised blood pressure (**hypertension**). This in turn increases the chance of a stroke and respiratory disease. Diabetes is more common amongst the overweight, as are gallstones, arthritis and varicose veins.

Fat may harm the fetus

American researchers have recently reported that obese women (defined in this study as women having a BMI of 29 or over) run more than twice the usual risk of giving birth to babies with spina bifida and other neural tube defects, than women of average mass. The risk increased the more obese the mothers were (tripling for a BMI of 32) and did not reduce even if they were otherwise healthy and had taken folic acid supplements. The crucial factor is believed to be the mass of the woman at the time of conception, although why this should be so is not yet known.

Source: *New Scientist*, 20 April 1996

▶ *Chapter 23.4 mentions the use of folic acid during pregnancy*

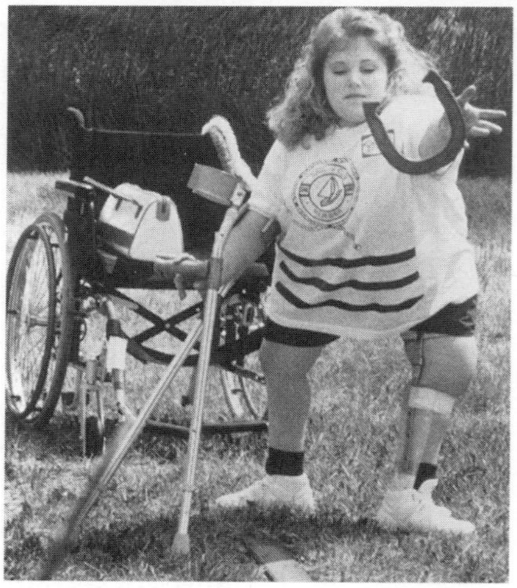

Figure 24.3 A young woman with spina bifida throwing a horseshoe. The causes of spina bifida are not known for certain. Recent research suggests that obesity in the mother at conception may play a part

24.2 Eating distress disorders

Eating distress is a serious psychological problem which needs psychiatric treatment. For these people food becomes an addiction and the centre of their existence; their relationship with food becoming severely damaging. Eating disorders are a collection of conditions that affect individuals, but at the same time the effects can be devastating on their families.

Eating disorders affect 60 000–200 000 people in the UK. The group most likely to be affected are women in their teens and early twenties, but there is an increase in the number of males and children who are being diagnosed. Only about half the people diagnosed as having an eating disorder have recovered five years later.

Anorexia nervosa

Anorexia nervosa is an eating distress disorder which was first described in 1874. As we have said, the group most at risk are adolescent and young adult women. It is a disease which often starts with a person slimming, but the dieting gets out of control. The weight loss drops so that BMI is under 17, yet an anorexic still believes that they are overweight, even fat, and their self-esteem is always low. They deny that they are losing too much weight and exert rigid control over their eating habits so that their loss of body mass continues. The disease is a secretive addiction to controlling the intake of food. It is very difficult and sometimes impossible to treat, and requires specialised psychiatric help.

The physical symptoms that accompany anorexia include:

- amenorrhoea (menstruation stops);
- low blood sugar;
- imbalance of minerals in the body;
- heart, kidney and intestinal damage;
- depression, leading to an increased incidence of suicide attempts;
- anxiety.

Bulimia

Bulimia differs from anorexia in that the symptoms may not be noticed. They can be normal weight and need not look ill. They may be able to live what appears to be a normal life. However, in private they succumb to 'bingeing', that is consuming thousands of units of energy in a short time, often then inducing vomiting to rid themselves of the food. Abuse of laxatives is common and there may also be abuse of diuretics (drugs which reduce the water content of the body).

24.3 Coeliac disease

Coeliac disease affects one person in 1500 in the UK but is rare in Asians and Afro-Caribbeans. It occurs most in early childhood when boys and girls are equally affected, and peaks again between 30 and 50 years of age when twice as many women as men develop the disease.

Coeliac disease is a condition where a protein found in wheat (gluten) and related proteins in barley, rye and oats damage the villi lining the small intestine. This impairs the absorption of nutrients. Once coeliac disease has developed it requires life-long treatment which involves following a strict gluten-free diet in which rice and cornflour are used instead of wheat, rye and oats. There are now a large number of gluten-free products on the market and some gluten-free products are available on prescription.

A little more than gut rot

Julie, a 31-year-old teacher went to her doctor complaining of being underweight. Her colleagues had light-heartedly teased her for being 'skinny' and she was anxious to get her weight up to normal. Apart from slight abdominal pains and loose bowel motions Julie had no other symptoms.

The doctor examined Julie but could find nothing wrong. However, she decided to do some further routine blood tests which detected a mild iron deficiency anaemia and Julie was referred to the gastro-enterology department of the local general hospital.

Here, a procedure called an upper gastro-intestinal endoscopy was performed which allowed the lining of the stomach and duodenum to be examined. Although these appeared normal to the eye, small samples were taken for microscopic examination. These showed that the villi were virtually absent and it was clear to the consultant that Julie was suffering from coeliac disease. Julie was put on to a gluten-free diet, and within a year had recovered her lost weight and her anaemia had disappeared.

24.4 Gastric and duodenal ulcers (peptic ulcers)

You will remember that the content of the duodenum is alkaline, but that of the stomach is strongly acidic. The acid is important in digestion and sterilising the food in the stomach. The secretion of acid is partly under the control of the vagus nerve, part of the para-sympathetic nervous system. However, hydrochloric acid at a pH of around 2 is potentially harmful to human tissue. The lining of the stomach is protected from acid attack by mucus, and in the duodenum acid is rapidly neutralised by strongly alkaline secretions. Sometimes these protective mechanisms fail and acid attacks the epithelium causing inflammation or even ulceration.

Ulceration can cause bleeding or perforation and in the stomach may go on to produce cancer. Apart from stomach acid, smoking is known to increase the risk of peptic ulcers, and some drugs, such as aspirin, and alcohol can also cause erosions (small ulcers) in the stomach.

The history of the treatment of these conditions is interesting. It demonstrates how successive advances in medicine often show us that as knowledge accumulates we discover that the condition is more complex than was at first thought. Initially, surgery was the only treatment available, either removing or sewing up the ulcer. Later, branches of the vagus nerve to the stomach were cut to decrease acid production. Results were disappointing and recurrences of the ulcers were common.

In the 1960s new drugs called H_2 antagonists were developed which significantly reduced acid production in the stomach. The initial results were dramatic and surgery for peptic ulcers was thought to be a thing of the past. However, after a number of years some people were again developing ulcers. More potent drugs have now been developed called proton pump inhibitors.

A drastic experiment

In 1982 at the Royal Perth Hospital Australia, a bacterium called *Helicobacter pylori* was successfully isolated from human stomachs and cultured in the laboratory. The researcher involved, Dr Barry Marshall, was convinced that *H. pylori* was the cause of peptic ulcers. His work was published but the findings were not generally accepted by doctors. Barry Marshall was frustrated and disappointed. He decided to take action to prove his point and asked his technician to prepare a broth of *H. pylori*. Dr Marshall then swallowed the culture in front of his technician! Very soon Marshall became ill with gastritis caused by *H. pylori* and after a few days of worsening illness he took antibiotics and cured himself.

The point had been made. Although *H. pylori* is a difficult organism to grow it is now easy to detect antibodies in a simple test at the doctor's surgery. A drop of blood from a finger prick is used and the results are available within five minutes. This is an example of an ELISA test.

Figure 24.4 (a) This patient is having a blood test to find out whether she is infected with *H. pylori* (b) Two spots show a positive result

▶ **Chapter 30.3** *gives more information on ELISA testing*

ELISA stands for enzyme linked immunosorbent assay and is a method of diagnostic testing.

Following Dr Marshall's work, the *H. pylori* bacterium was subsequently found to be present in the stomachs of all patients with duodenal ulcers and a high proportion of people with gastric ulcers. It was found that such ulcers could be cured by treating patients with simple antibiotics, but only when the stomach acid had been reduced with proton pump inhibitors. By the 1990s it was believed that the cause of peptic ulcers had been found. Infection can be passed from parents to children, by kissing for example, and this was thought to explain the observation that peptic ulcers often run in families.

However, recent experience is showing that infection with *H. pylori* is quite common and not everyone who is infected develops ulcers. Ulcers do sometimes recur due to re-infection in people who appeared to have been treated successfully. So it may be that infection by *H. pylori* is just another piece in what is a complicated puzzle in the search for the causes of peptic ulcers.

24.5 Irritable bowel syndrome

Irritable bowel syndrome (IBS) is a very common condition, but the cause or causes of it are not known. It can come and go suddenly and is made worse be stress or anxiety. IBS is a condition of disordered peristalsis which causes a number of symptoms ranging from diarrhoea to constipation, with associated abdominal pain. More mucus than normal is present in the faeces. Typically, the condition settles at night.

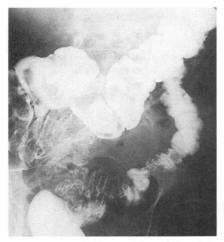

Figure 24.5 Protrusions of the gut wall are characteristic of diverticular disease as this barium enema shows

Treatment may require the use of antispasmodic drugs or traditional remedies such as peppermint oil. Varying the amount of fibre in the diet (either increasing it or decreasing it) may help.

24.6 Diverticular disease

Diverticular disease is a disease which only occurs in developed countries. It happens when people eat a low fibre diet and is common in elderly people. It has been estimated that around 80 per cent of those over 65 years of age have some degree of diverticular disease. As a result of dietary habits and the decreased mobility that is inevitable with ageing, there is an increased incidence of constipation. The faeces become hard and compacted in the colon. In order to move the faecal mass the gut has to contract more forcibly increasing the pressure inside the gut lumen. At weak points in the gut wall small pouches (called diverticula) form and protrude into the abdominal cavity. These may bleed or become the focus for infection. If these areas burst, the abdominal cavity becomes infected (**peritonitis**) which may be fatal.

24.7 Cancer of the colon

Cancer of the colon is sometimes an inherited disease. It is much more common in cultures that have a low fibre diet and eat a fairly high proportion of carcinogens such as saturated fats. Cancer of the colon is more likely to occur in someone who has previously suffered from ulcerative colitis. Ulcerative colitis is a chronic inflammatory disease of the large intestine and rectum.

The chances of surviving cancer of the colon are relatively good because it is often diagnosed early when surgical removal of the tumour is frequently successful.

► **Chapter 5.4 gives more details about cancer**

24.8 Food poisoning

Food poisoning is common and experienced by most people at some time. The symptoms are commonly diarrhoea, accompanied by vomiting and stomach cramps. A telltale feature of food poisoning is that many people who have eaten the same food become unwell at the same time. Most people recover within 72 hours, but the very young and the elderly are at greater risk. This is because they are less able to tolerate the dehydration which commonly occurs. Outbreaks of food poisoning should be reported to the local Environmental Health Officer for investigation.

Food poisoning is caused by microbes such as bacteria, protozoa and viruses that contaminate food. Some are pathogens which having entered the body, multiplied and caused disease. Microbes are almost always ingested with food, and the natural defences of the body are usually able to protect against those that are pathogenic. Illness is most likely to follow when a large number of organisms have been ingested.

Some micro-organisms do not cause infections as such. They secrete toxins into the food which are poisonous to the humans who eat it. The most severe but rare of this type of poisoning is caused by a bacterium called

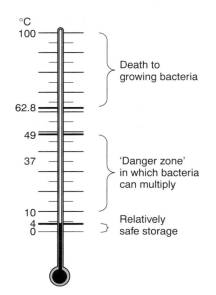

Figure 24.6 Bacteria divide rapidly between 10–49°C and food should be stored below 4°C in a domestic refrigerator to prevent this

Clostridium botulinum. The poison it produces is botulin which is absorbed by the blood and affects the nerves, causing the muscles to become paralysed. *Staphylococcus aureus* is a bacterium which is commonly found in spots and infected wounds. It lives on healthy people causing them no harm, but produces a toxin when it contaminates food.

Bacteria are able to divide every 20 minutes or so at room temperature. This is why it is important to store food at cool temperatures because it limits cell division to a minimum.

Food can become infected in many ways e.g. poultry commonly carry *Salmonella* which may infect the eggs. All pre-cooked dishes must be stored according to the manufacturer's instructions and if they require heating, the food must reach a temperature high enough to kill any pathogens. Other microbes that cause food poisoning include *Listeria, Hepatitis A* and *Escherichia coli.*

Table 24.1 Some microbes that cause food poisoning

Organism	Type	Common symptoms	Examples of food contaminated
Salmonella spp. *Shigella* spp.	bacteria	diarrhoea, vomiting, fever, abdominal pain	under-cooked chicken and eggs; pre-cooked foods not stored below 4°C e.g. cold meats, quiche, sausage rolls
Clostridium perfringens	bacterium	no fever, diarrhoea, nausea, abdominal pain	foods produced in large quantities e.g. in canteens that have not been cooked thoroughly to kill the bacteria
Staphylococcus aureus	bacterium	vomiting, low blood pressure, diarrhoea, abdominal pain	foods contaminated by handlers who are carriers; cream cakes, processed meat and fish, and salads left at room temperature
Bacillus cereus	bacterium	nausea, diarrhoea	fried rice after storage
Escherichia coli	bacterium	diarrhoea/dysentery (severity of illness very variable)	cold meats; cheeses contaminated by food handlers working with raw meat; mince and mince products not thoroughly cooked; also spread person to person
Campylobacter	bacterium	bloody diarrhoea, vomiting	salads/fruit washed in contaminated water; ice cubes made from contaminated water; unpasteurised milk; rarely from poultry
Listeria monocytogenes	bacterium	septicaemia, abortion of fetus	unpasteurised milk and cheese; seafood; raw meat and vegetables
Norwalk agent	virus	fever, debility	shellfish
Cryptosporidium	protoctista	diarrhoea, vomiting	usually water-borne and then contaminates washed fresh fruit or vegetables, ice-cubes, diluted drinks; also found in raw tripe

Keeping food clean

Food becomes contaminated if it is not handled properly. It is therefore very important that strict hygiene is observed wherever food is prepared and served. Precautions include:

- washing hands before food is prepared;
- cuts should be covered;
- hair should be tied back and preferably covered;
- pets should be kept away from food that is being prepared;
- kitchen surfaces should be clean – dishcloths often harbour many microbes and should be regularly disinfected;
- meat should be prepared separately from other foods on a non-wooden board;
- a separate knife should be used to prepare meat and vegetables;
- people who are unwell with food poisoning should not prepare food for others.

E. coli friend or foe?

Escherichia coli, usually known as *E. coli*, is a natural inhabitant of the human bowel and of the large intestines of other animals too. Usually it is harmless, but there are some strains such as *E. coli* 0157:H7 which can cause serious food poisoning. The very young and the elderly are the most vulnerable and may die from the results of dehydration caused by severe vomiting and diarrhoea. The bacteria release powerful toxins that attack the lining of the gut. One particularly dangerous feature of strain 0157:H7 is that it causes kidney failure in some people.

Over the winter of 1996–97 there were several tragic cases of *E. coli* food poisoning. The outbreak in Lanarkshire, which started in November 1996, was the worst that has ever occurred in Britain. Twenty people died and over 400 other cases of the disease were reported, of which 250 were confirmed by laboratory tests. People were not only infected directly by contaminated food, but as the weeks passed some people nursing the sick also became infected.

The initial source of the outbreak was traced to a butcher's shop of good repute. This has led to a political furore about the conditions of hygiene in the country's abattoirs. It has been shown that conditions have made it easy for *E. coli* living in the cow gut to contaminate the meat. If the meat is not thoroughly cooked, *E. coli* can all too easily pass to human hosts.

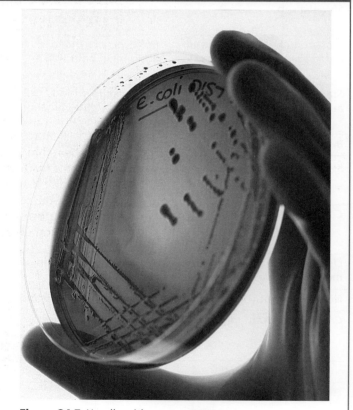

Figure 24.7 Handle with care: a potentially lethal culture of *E. coli* strain 0157:H7 (*See Colour Gallery page 354*)

CHAPTER 25 Aerobic Respiration

In this section we have explored how plants, the principle autotrophic organisms, synthesise organic sugars from the raw materials carbon dioxide and water, using sunlight as the energy source. From these sugars all other food materials in plants are synthesised and then pass through food chains to heterotrophic organisms including humans.

When food molecules are oxidised in the cells of autotrophs and heterotrophs energy is transferred into molecules of ATP, the universal biological energy currency. This process is respiration. Aerobic respiration requires molecular oxygen, but anaerobic respiration does not.

▶ **Chapter 26 covers anaerobic respiration**

25.1 ATP – the biological energy currency

ATP (adenosine triphosphate) is a source of energy which is instantly available for use in metabolism in all living cells. The anabolic reactions in the cell by which new molecules such as proteins and polysaccharides are synthesised require a large amount of energy. These reactions are **endergonic** and they are coupled to **exergonic** reactions which release energy. The importance of ATP is that it is the link between the reactions of metabolism that require energy and those that release it.

ATP is a **nucleotide** which was first isolated in the 1930s from mammalian muscle fibres. It is a stable compound consisting of a molecule of adenine, the pentose sugar ribose and a chain of three inorganic phosphate groups. ATP is a soluble compound which can readily move from the site where it is synthesised, to wherever it is required in the organism.

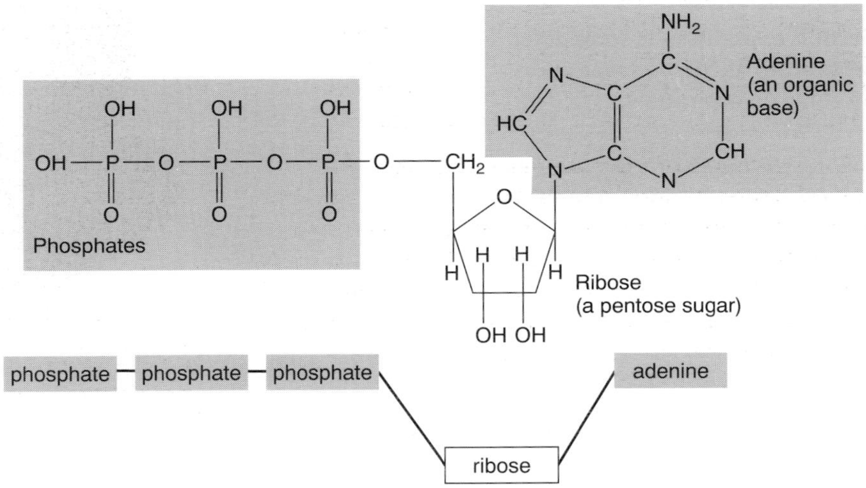

▶ **Chapter 31.3 explains about nucleotides**

Figure 25.1 The chemical structure of ATP

When ATP is hydrolysed in a reaction catalysed by the enzyme ATPase the phosphate group at the end of the molecule is detached and approximately 32 kJ mol^{-1} free energy is released.

The free energy released when a molecule of ATP is hydrolysed to ADP can be represented by ΔG. $\Delta G = -32$ kJ mol^{-1}.

$$ATP + H_2O \xrightarrow{ATPase} ADP + P_i + \Delta G - 32 \text{ kJ}$$
$$\text{inorganic}$$
$$\text{phosphate}$$

If further hydrolysis occurs another phosphate group is detached, a similar amount of energy is yielded and adenosine monophosphate (AMP) is formed.

Figure 25.2 ATP is formed mainly during respiration but also during the first stage of photosynthesis. It provides the energy for cell metabolism, including the active transport of ions and molecules across cell membranes, the synthesis of biological molecules and the contraction of muscle cells.

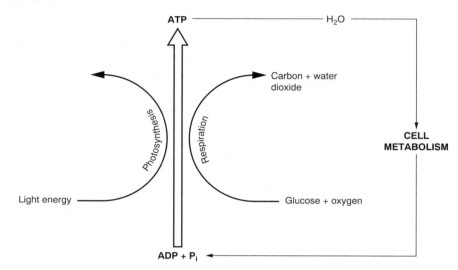

ATP is the universal energy currency because:

- it is an immediate source of energy for all living organisms;
- the quantity of energy released is controlled;
- a single enzyme only is necessary for releasing energy.

Aerobic respiration is sometimes referred to as 'tissue respiration' or 'cellular respiration'.

▶ *Chapter 4.3 describes how ATP is used in active transport*

ATP cannot be stored. In order for the cell to keep endergonic reactions going there has to be a continuous supply of ATP. Since the synthesis of ATP from ADP and P_i is itself a reaction which requires energy, there must be some way of supplying energy to drive it. The oxidation of glucose during aerobic respiration provides one solution. By this process a significant amount of the chemical energy stored in glucose is transferred to ATP; the rest is converted to heat energy.

Questions

1 What is ATP? Why is it important in all living cells?

2 Make a list of three processes in humans that require energy from ATP.

3 Why is ATP well suited to be the energy currency of living organisms?

4 What is the significance of glucose being oxidised during respiration?

5 Is the respiration of glucose an anabolic or a catabolic reaction?

25.2 An overview of aerobic respiration

The glucose which is oxidised during respiration comes from the hydrolysis of cell storage products such as starch and glycogen.

The amount of energy that is contained within a molecule depends on a number of factors including the size of the molecule and its state of oxidation.

- large molecules contain more energy than small ones
- reduced molecules have more energy than oxidised ones

Glucose ($C_6H_{12}O_6$) is a relatively large molecule containing six reduced carbon atoms. Therefore it is a good energy source. Moreover, carbon and hydrogen atoms in a glucose molecule are not in their most stable form.

The oxidation of glucose to carbon dioxide and water with the synthesis of ATP is a metabolic pathway involving many chemical reactions. The main four stages are summarised in Figure 25.3.

The chemical equation which summarises the many reactions involved in aerobic respiration is:

$$C_6H_{12}O_6 + 6O_2 = 6CO_2 + 6H_2O$$

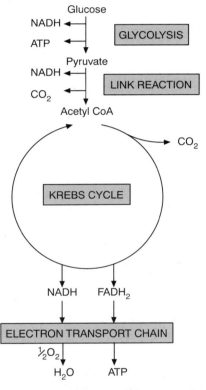

Figure 25.3 A summary of the stages of aerobic respiration in which glucose is oxidised to water and carbon dioxide, and ATP is synthesised

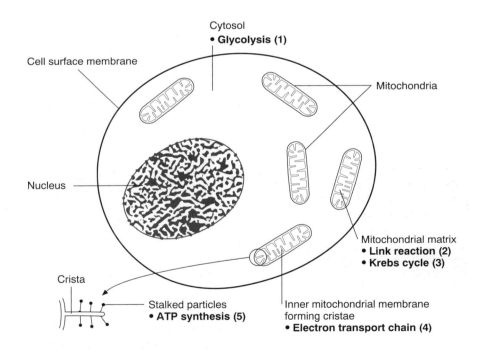

Figure 25.4 Where the main events of aerobic respiration occur in the cell

25.3 Glycolysis

The first stage of aerobic respiration, **glycolysis**, occurs in the cytosol. Glycolysis means 'splitting sugar' and through a series of reactions each hexose glucose molecule is split in to two ions of pyruvic acid called **pyruvate**, each containing three carbon atoms.

In the initial stages of glycolysis, the glucose has to be **phosphorylated** by the addition of two phosphate groups. This raises the energy level of the sugar molecule. The energy and the phosphate groups come from using up two molecules of ATP which are hydrolysed to ADP + P_i.

In the reactions which follow, the phosphorylated hexose (6-carbon) sugar is split in to two molecules of phosphorylated trioses (3-carbon sugars). These molecules now separately enter the pathway leading to the formation of pyruvic acid, but remember that both trioses originated from a single molecule of glucose.

Two atoms of hydrogen are removed from each triose and transferred to the hydrogen carrier NAD^+ reducing it as this equation shows:

$$NAD^+ + 2H \rightarrow NADH + H^+$$

The triose is converted via a series of steps to pyruvic acid. During two of the reactions energy and inorganic phosphate are transferred to a molecule of ADP, converting it to ATP.

> Keeping track of ATP during the aerobic respiration of one molecule of glucose: glycolysis
>
> - two molecules of ATP → ADP when glucose is phosphorylated
> - four molecules of ADP → ATP when two triose sugars from glucose are converted to pyruvate
> - there is a net gain of two molecules of ATP from each molecule of glucose broken down to pyruvate

More ATP is gained by oxidising pyruvate further and this happens in the Krebs cycle (Chapter 25.5).

25.4 The link reaction

Pyruvate now moves from the cytosol into the fluid matrix of the mitochondria. A molecule of carbon dioxide is removed from each pyruvate ion which is now a 2-carbon ion. It reacts with coenzyme A to form acetyl coenzyme A (acetyl CoA). At the same time two hydrogen atoms are transferred to the hydrogen acceptor NAD^+, forming $NADH + H^+$.

25.5 The Krebs cycle

Sir Hans Krebs was Professor of Biochemistry at Sheffield University from 1935–54. During this time he discovered the pathway by which most energy is generated during the process of aerobic respiration. It occurs in the matrix of the mitochondria. Previously called the citric acid cycle, and also sometimes referred to as the tricarboxylic acid (TCA) cycle, it is now named the Krebs cycle after him.

> Ions of NAD (nicotinamide adenine dinucleotide) are present in aqueous solution in the cell as NAD^+.

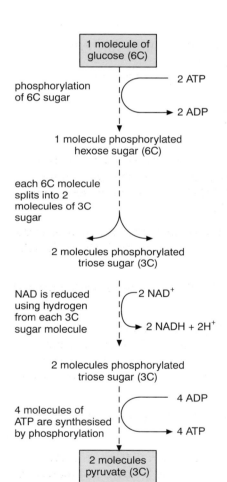

Figure 25.5 A more detailed look at glycolysis

▶ *Chapter 2.5 describes the structure of mitochondria*

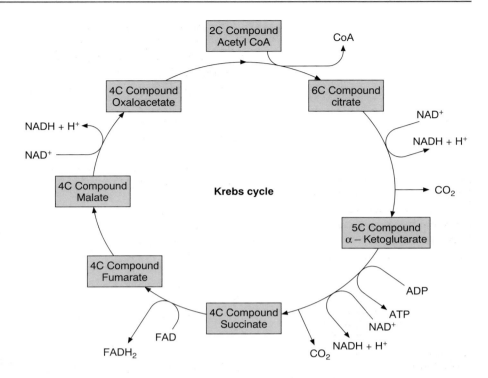

Figure 25.6 The Krebs cycle

The main points of the Krebs cycle are:

1   As each molecule of acetyl CoA containing two carbon atoms feeds into the cycle it combines with a 4-carbon compound, oxaloacetate, to form the 6-carbon compound citrate. (Acetyl CoA has in fact transferred two carbon atoms from pyruvate to citrate.)

2   Citrate (6-carbon) then goes through four redox reactions to complete the Krebs cycle so that oxaloacetate (4-carbon) is regenerated. The cycle will then be repeated.

3   At two points in the cycle a molecule of carbon dioxide (a waste product) is formed.

4   During four steps in the cycle, pairs of hydrogen atoms are removed, by dehydrogenation, to coenzyme hydrogen carriers. The reactions are catalysed by dehydrogenase enzymes. NAD ions receive hydrogen at three steps forming NADH + H$^+$ and FAD (flavine adenine dinucleotide) is reduced to FADH$_2$ from a fourth.

5   A single molecule of ATP is synthesised directly by substrate phosphorylation.

In the final stage of aerobic respiration we shall see how the hydrogen carried by the reduced coenzymes is involved in the formation of molecules of ATP.

Keeping track of ATP during the aerobic respiration of one molecule of glucose: Krebs cycle

The cycle turns *twice* for each molecule of glucose that is respired.

● two molecules of ATP are synthesised

25.6 The electron transport (hydrogen carrier or cytochrome) system

During the final stage in aerobic respiration hydrogen atoms from the reduced coenzymes $NADH + H^+$ and $FADH_2$ are removed and passed along a series of hydrogen carriers at progressively lower energy levels. As NAD or FAD is re-oxidised, the hydrogen acceptor is reduced. The carrier system involves a series of oxidation and reduction (redox) reactions. When hydrogen is passed from $NADH_2$ to flavoprotein (FP), and at the points further along the chain shown in Figure 25.7, the energy released is used to synthesise ATP from ADP and inorganic phosphate, P_i. The formation of ATP here is called **oxidative phosphorylation**.

At this point the hydrogen atoms dissociate. $H \rightarrow H^+ + e^-$.
Only the electrons continue down the respiratory chain

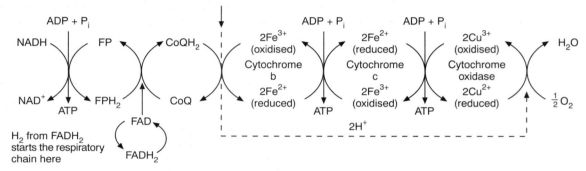

Figure 25.7 The electron transport chain is the final stage of aerobic respiration, and the point at which most energy is released. The carriers and the enzymes that catalyse these redox reactions are arranged in a series along the inner membranes of the cristae in the mitochondria. The carriers include coenzyme Q and different protein pigments called cytochromes, all of which contain iron. The final carrier in the chain is cytochrome oxidase.

Although initially hydrogen atoms pass along the chain, once passed on by FP or $FADH_2$ they split in to *protons* and *electrons*. The protons escape into the matrix between the inner and outer membranes of the mitochondria and only the *electrons* continue to pass along the carrier chain.

When the electrons reach the cytochrome oxidase they recombine with the protons to form hydrogen atoms. The final acceptor in the chain is oxygen which is unable to act as a donor molecule, and is reduced by the hydrogen to water. The electron transport chain can only continue if the molecular oxygen is constantly replenished. In the absence of oxygen, aerobic respiration ceases rapidly.

Keeping track of ATP during the aerobic respiration of one molecule of glucose: electron transport chain

- four molecules of ATP are formed by the oxidative phosphorylation of two molecules of $FADH_2$
- 30 molecules of ATP are formed from the oxidative phosphorylation of ten molecules of NADH

In summary the aerobic respiration of a single molecule of glucose generates a net gain of 38 molecules of ATP

- two molecules of ATP from glycolysis
- two molecules of ATP from the Krebs cycle
- 34 molecules of ATP from the electron transport chain

25.7 The chemiosmotic hypothesis

In 1961 Dr Peter Mitchell proposed his chemiosmotic hypothesis to explain how ATP is synthesised during the last stage of respiration. His ideas were controversial and not accepted at first. However, in 1978 Mitchell was awarded a Nobel Prize in chemistry for this work.

Mitchell proposed that the hydrogen ions formed from hydrogen atoms passing along the electron chain are very significant. As we have said, when they are released from the electron transport chain they move into the space between the inner and outer membranes of the mitochondria. Here the concentration of hydrogen ions builds up and sets up an electrochemical gradient across the inner mitochondrial membrane.

At points along the inner mitochondrial membrane marked by the stalked particles, there are hydrophilic protein channels associated with F_1 protein ATPase. (ATPase is the enzyme that catalyses the synthesis of ATP from ADP and phosphate.) As pairs of hydrogen ions pass through these protein channels enough energy is released for the synthesis of one molecule of ATP.

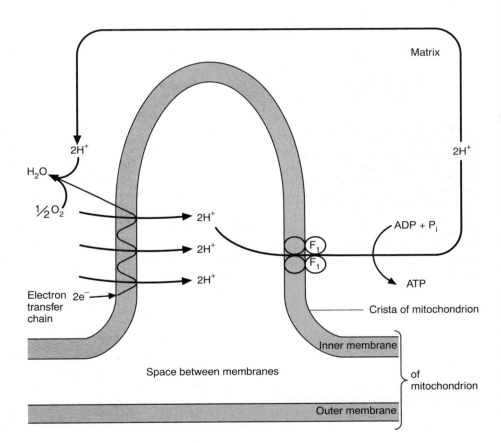

Figure 25.8 The chemiosmotic theory which explains how ATP is synthesised during respiration

The rate of respiration in terms of the synthesis of ATP is controlled by end-product inhibition (negative feedback). An accumulation of ATP inhibits one of the enzymes involved in the phosphorylation of sugar during glycolysis which is allosteric. It is converted to its inactive form in the presence of an excess of ATP.

▶ *Chapter 7.4 covers allosteric enzymes*

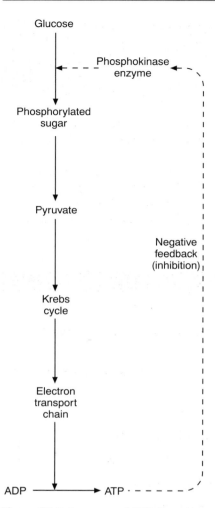

Figure 25.9 An excess of ATP slows down glycolysis and hence the rate of respiration

25.8 The oxidation of fats and proteins to provide energy

We have already come across the idea (Chapter 23.2) that lipids and proteins can, under certain circumstances, be used as substrates and broken down to provide a source of energy, i.e. ATP. They are first converted, by different chemical processes, to acetyl CoA and are then able to feed into the Krebs cycle.

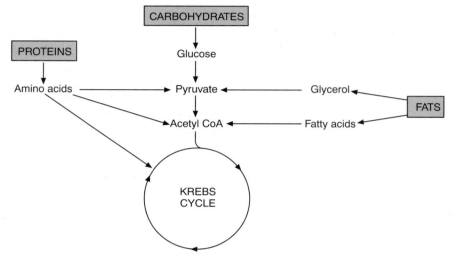

Figure 25.10 The relation between fats, proteins and carbohydrates and the Krebs cycle

The different yields of energy from the complete combustion of the food sources are shown in Table 25.1.

25.9 Respiratory quotient

During aerobic respiration living organisms including humans use up oxygen and give out carbon dioxide. The ratio of the volume of carbon dioxide compared to volume of oxygen is called the **respiratory quotient (RQ)**.

Table 25.1

Food	Maximum energy yield (kJ g⁻¹)
carbohydrate	17.22
lipid	39.06
protein	22.68

$$RQ = \frac{\text{volume carbon dioxide produced}}{\text{volume oxygen used}}$$

The equation for aerobic respiration of glucose is:

$$C_6H_{12}O_6 + 6O_2 = 6CO_2 + 6H_2O$$

From this we can see that the same number of carbon dioxide molecules are produced as the number of molecules of oxygen are used:

$$\text{For glucose RQ} = \frac{6}{6}$$

$$= 1.0$$

The importance of RQ is that it tells us what kind of substrate is being used in respiration. If a pure fat is oxidised in respiration, the RQ is 0.7; if protein is completely respired the RQ is 0.9.

Respiration usually involves a mixture of substrates and oxidation may not be complete, so a person's RQ is around 0.85. A high RQ (above 1.0) is found in tissues that are short of oxygen and have switched over to anaerobic respiration. If the human body is in shock following an accident or severe illness the level of RQ drops.

▶ **Chapter 13.5 gives information on oxygen debt**

Questions

1 What are meant by the terms 'oxidation' and 'reduction'?

2 Where in the cell do (a) glycolysis, (b) the link reaction and (c) oxidative phosphorylation take place?

3 Name two coenzymes which transfer hydrogen atoms along the electron transfer chain.

4 Explain the term 'oxidative phosphorylation'.

5 What is the importance of acetyl CoA to living organisms?

6 The respiration of glycerol is summarised by the equation

$$2C_3H_8O_3 + 7O_2 \rightarrow 6CO_2 + 8H_2O$$

Use the equation to calculate the RQ for glycerol.

7 Complete the following passage using suitable words to fill the blanks.

Aerobic respiration occurs in the presence of _____ . It is a process in which a substrate such as _____ or _____ is oxidised to yield energy in the form of _____ and the waste products _____ and _____ .

The first stage is _____ which occurs in the cell _____ . This results in the breakdown of glucose to _____ . Providing oxygen is present, pyruvate is converted to the 2-carbon compound _____ . This feeds into the Krebs cycle which is completed _____ for each initial molecule of glucose. Each cycle results in the reduction of _____ and _____ , the formation of _____ molecules of carbon dioxide and a single molecule of _____ .

The final stage is called the _____ and involves the oxidation and reduction of a series of _____ . At certain stages energy is freed and is used to convert ADP to _____ . This is called _____ . The mechanism that attempts to explain how this happens is called the _____ hypothesis. The final acceptor in the chain is _____ which is reduced by _____ to _____ .

CHAPTER 26 Anaerobic Respiration

Respiration that takes place in the absence of molecular oxygen is called **anaerobic respiration**. There are very few organisms that are only able to respire to make energy using this method; they are called **obligate anaerobes** and most are species of bacteria. Examples are *Clostridium tetani*, which infects humans causing tetanus, and *Pseudomonas denitrificans*, which lives in infertile waterlogged soil and is important in the nitrogen cycle.

A few organisms are able to respire both aerobically and anaerobically. These are called **facultative anaerobes** and important examples are the common yeast *Saccharomyces cerevisiae*, and *Taenia solium*, the tapeworm which is a parasite that infects the human intestine. The end-product of anaerobic respiration by yeast and other plants is **ethanol**. However, humans and other animals produce **lactic acid** as an end-product of anaerobic respiration. Skeletal muscles in humans can switch temporarily from aerobic to anaerobic respiration during vigorous exercise if oxygen becomes deficient.

As in aerobic respiration the purpose of anaerobic respiration is to synthesise ATP, but as we shall see the anaerobic process yields much less energy than the aerobic pathway from each molecule of glucose respired.

▶ *Chapter 38.5 covers the nitrogen cycle*

26.1 The biochemical pathways of anaerobic respiration

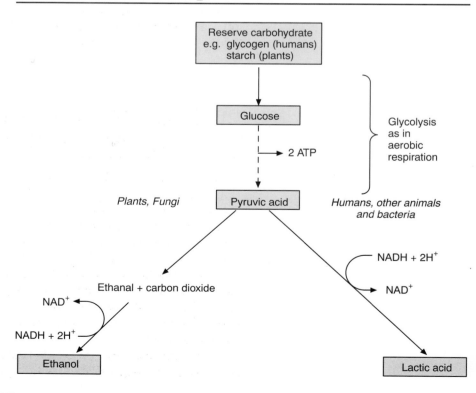

Figure 26.1 A summary of the pathways of anaerobic respiration

The first stage of anaerobic respiration is **glycolysis**. This process does not require oxygen and is *exactly* the same pathway of reactions as occurs in aerobic respiration. Stored food, starch in plants and glycogen in humans, is hydrolysed to glucose to provide the initial substrate for the reactions. During glycolysis the hydrogen atoms that are removed are taken up by the hydrogen carrier (NAD^+) and transferred to pyruvic acid. This is then converted either to lactic acid (in animals and some bacteria) or to ethanol (in plants and yeast).

Notice that there is no Krebs cycle or electron transport chain in anaerobic respiration. We saw in Chapter 25.6 that oxygen is essential for the electron transfer chain to function because it is the way that the cell generates oxidised NAD^+ to accept hydrogen atoms. An alternative way must be found for anaerobic organisms to generate NAD^+ to allow glycolysis to continue. The problem is solved during the conversion of pyruvate ions to lactate or to ethanol as the following equations show:

In humans, animals and some bacteria

$$\text{pyruvate} + NADH + H^+ \rightarrow \text{lactate} + NAD^+$$
$$CH_3COCOO^- + NADH + H^+ \rightarrow CH_3CHOHCOO^- + NAD^+$$

In plants and fungi, including yeasts

$$\text{pyruvate} + NADH + 2H^+ \rightarrow \text{ethanol} + CO_2 + NAD^+$$
$$CH_3COCOO^- + NADH + 2H^+ \rightarrow CH_3CH_2OH + CO_2 + NAD^+$$

The only ATP that is generated during anaerobic respiration are the two molecules formed during the glycolysis of each molecule of glucose. Clearly, this is considerably less than the 38 molecules of ATP generated from the aerobic respiration of a single glucose molecule.

26.2 Lactic acid production and the oxygen debt

During vigorous exercise, the skeletal muscles may use up all the oxygen available for aerobic respiration. In order for the muscles to be able to continue to contract, they switch to anaerobic respiration and build up an **oxygen debt**. This change in metabolic pathway reduces the energy supply and lactate ions accumulate in the muscle tissue. The muscles can only tolerate a certain level of lactate and they then become fatigued and painful. When exercise has stopped the lactate from the muscles is transported by the blood to the liver. Here, some of the lactate is oxidised and some ATP released which allows aerobic respiration to start up again. The oxygen used in oxidising lactate and returning to aerobic respiration is said to 'pay back' the oxygen debt.

Anaerobic respiration in the skeletal muscles (lactic acid fermentation) can be summarised by the following equation:

$$\begin{array}{ccccc}
\text{glucose} & \rightarrow & \text{lactic acid} & + & \text{energy} \\
C_6H_{12}O_6 & & 2CH_3CHOHCOOH & &
\end{array}$$

This is the same reaction which happens in the process of yoghurt making. The bacterium *Lactobacillus* ferments the lactose sugar in milk. As lactic acid concentration rises the pH drops, and this sets the yoghurt.

► *Chapter 13.5 gives more information about oxygen debt*

26.3 Alcoholic fermentation

Yeasts usually respire anaerobically even in the presence of oxygen. Glucose is converted to pyruvic acid by glycolysis as already explained. The pyruvic acid is converted to ethanal and carbon dioxide. Finally, ethanal is reduced to ethanol (alcohol). The overall process can be summarised by the equation:

$$\text{glucose} \rightarrow \text{ethanol} + \text{carbon dioxide}$$

Fermentation was first described by the famous French scientist Louis Pasteur. Yeast has been used by humans for thousands of years in brewing, wine-making and bread-making. It lives naturally on the surface of fruits such as grapes and apples.

Figure 26.2 (a) Scanning electron micrograph of *Saccharomyces cerevisiae* (magnification ×4000). It has single cells which reproduce frequently by asexual budding. (b) Yeast is used to ferment the sugars in fruit juice, converting them to alcohol.

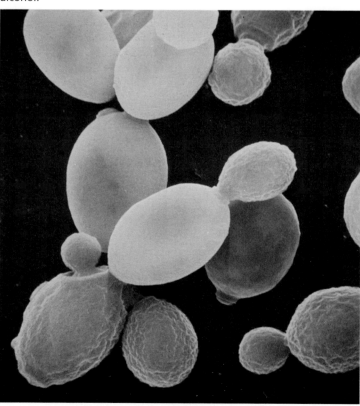

(a)

(b)

26.4 Comparing the energy yields of aerobic and anaerobic respiration

It has been calculated experimentally that the yield of energy from glucose after total oxidation is 2880 kJ mol^{-1}. However, during respiration not all this energy is transferred to ATP. Some is transferred to the surroundings as heat and so is lost from the individual.

When ATP is hydrolysed the free energy liberated is 30.7 kJ mol^{-1}. The maximum efficiency of aerobic and anaerobic respiration can be calculated as follows:

$$\text{Aerobic respiration} = \frac{38 \times 30.7}{2880} \times 100\%$$

$$= \mathbf{40.5\%}$$

$$\text{Anaerobic respiration} = \frac{2 \times 30.7}{2880} \times 100\%$$

$$= \mathbf{2.1\%}$$

A useful comparison is the estimated efficiency of a petrol engine, which is around 25 per cent. It is also important to remember that some of the lactic acid formed during human anaerobic respiration will be respired aerobically, once the oxygen debt has been repaid. This improves the efficiency rating.

Questions

1 Why is it an advantage for a tapeworm to be a facultative anaerobe?

2 a) How many molecules of ATP in total are synthesised during the anaerobic respiration of a molecule of glucose?

   b) What is the net gain in ATP when a molecule of glucose is respired anaerobically?

3 Explain what you understand by the term 'oxygen debt'.

4 Suggest why tapeworms excrete lactate ions into the gut of an infected human.

5 Find out how beer is made commercially.

1 Algae were supplied with a radioactive isotope of carbon, ^{14}C, and allowed to photosynthesise. After a period of time, the light was switched off and the algae left in the dark. Figure 1 shows the relative amounts of some radioactively labelled compounds over the period of the experiment.

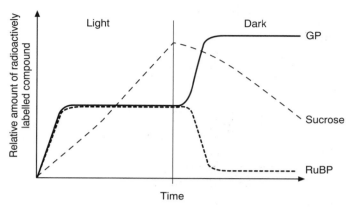

Figure 1

Explain the changes in relative amounts of each of the following substances after the light was switched off:

a) glycerate 3-phosphate (GP) *(2 marks)*

b) ribulose bisphosphate (RuBP) *(2 marks)*

c) sucrose. *(1 mark)*

AEB Specimen Question

2 The epithelial cells of the intestinal villi absorb sodium ions in two different ways. These are shown in Figure 2.

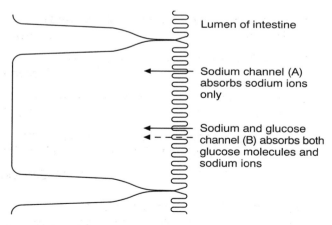

Figure 2

a) Explain how blocking of the sodium channels (A) might lead to diarrhoea. *(2 marks)*

Standard oral rehydration therapy involves giving the patient a mixture of glucose and salts having approximately the same solute concentration as blood.

b) Explain how this treatment benefits the patient. *(2 marks)*

Several ways have been investigated of making oral rehydration therapy more effective.

c) Suggest why:

i) adding extra glucose to the mixture would be unwise. *(1 mark)*

ii) using a mixture of starch and salts reduces the extent and duration of the diarrhoea even more. *(2 marks)*

AEB Specimen Question

3 A female student, of height 1.65 m, decided to try to reduce her mass by restricting her daily energy intake to 5000 kJ. She weighed herself once each week using a standard procedure. The results are shown in Figure 3.

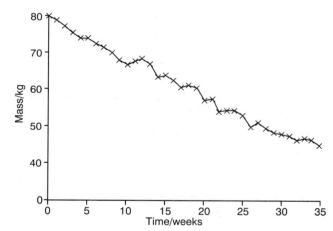

Figure 3 *Adapted from R. B. Stuart, Act Thin Stay Thin (1978)*

a) Suggest a standard procedure which could be used by the student when she weighed herself. *(2 marks)*

b) Comment on the student's loss in mass during the period shown by the graph. *(2 marks)*

c) Body mass index (BMI) is given by the equation

$$BMI = \frac{mass/kg}{(height/m)^2}$$

The minimum recommended body mass index is 20. A BMI below 20 is a sign of being underweight, which can result in ill-health.

After how long should the student have stopped dieting to avoid being underweight? Show how you arrived at your answer. *(3 marks)*

d) Describe the possible harmful effects of being underweight. *(2 marks)*

e) Describe the possible harmful effects of being overweight. *(2 marks)*

Edexcel

4 Figure 4 below shows a calorimeter used to determine the energy content of a sample of food.

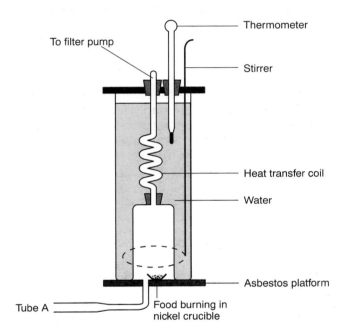

Figure 4

a) State the function of each of the following parts of the apparatus.

   i) The filter pump *(1 mark)*

   ii) The heat transfer coil *(1 mark)*

   iii) The stirrer *(1 mark)*

b) i) Name the gas which enters the apparatus through tube A. *(1 mark)*

   ii) What is the function of this gas? *(1 mark)*

c) Suggest *two* sources of error which may arise when using this apparatus to determine the energy content of food. *(2 marks)*

Edexcel

5 Figure 5 below shows some of the stages in cell respiration.

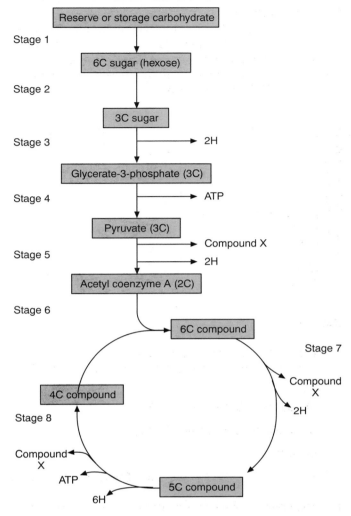

Figure 5

a) What respiratory substrate would be used in a liver cell? *(1 mark)*

b) State in which part of a cell stage 6 occurs. *(1 mark)*

c) Identify compound X, removed at stages 5, 7 and 8. *(1 mark)*

d) Describe what happens to the hydrogen atoms removed at stages 3, 5, 7 and 8. *(2 marks)*

Edexcel

6 Read through the following account of photosynthesis, then write on the lines the most appropriate word or words to complete the account.

Photosynthesis is a type of _____ nutrition, involving the synthesis of organic molecules from inorganic materials. The process involves two types of reactions, light-dependent and light-independent.

In the light-dependent reactions, light energy is absorbed by chlorophyll molecules located on the _____ of the chloroplasts; _____ and _____ are produced and oxygen gas is given off as a by-product.

In the light-independent reactions, _____ accepts molecules of carbon dioxide, which together with the products of the light-dependent reactions, results in the formation of _____ . This compound can be converted to a hexose sugar or used to regenerate the carbon dioxide acceptor molecule.

(6 marks)

Edexcel

7 Figure 6 shows a longitudinal section of part of the ileum wall.

Figure 6

a) Name the structures labelled A, B and C.
(3 marks)

b) Describe *one* way in which the structure of the ileum is adapted to the function it performs.
(2 marks)

Edexcel

8 Complete Table 1 below by writing, in the appropriate boxes, the function of each named nutrient and the name of the disease caused by a deficiency of that nutrient.

Table 1

Nutrient	Function in body	Name of deficiency disease
iron		
	component of rhodopsin (visual purple)	
		scurvy

(6 marks)

Edexcel

9 Figure 7 shows a short peptide. The side chains of the different amino acids are represented by filled shapes. The figure also shows the specific sites at which the peptide chain is broken during digestion in the human gut by three digestive enzymes, trypsin, chymotrypsin and carboxypeptidase.

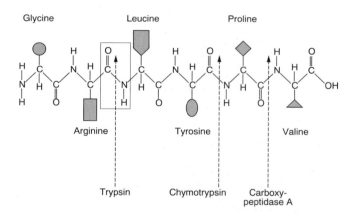

Figure 7

a) i) Name the chemical bond which is broken by the action of these enzymes. *(1 mark)*

ii) Name the type of chemical reaction by which the bonds are broken. *(1 mark)*

iii) Re-draw the part of the chain enclosed in the box marked X to show its appearance after the action of trypsin. *(3 marks)*

b) Trypsin and chymotrypsin are described as *endopeptidases* because they catalyse the breaking of bonds within the peptide chain. Carboxypeptidase A is described as an *exopeptidase* because it catalyses the breaking of a bond at one end of the peptide chain.

i) Comment on the fact that trypsin and chymotrypsin are secreted into the gut anteriorly to carboxypeptidase A. *(3 marks)*

ii) Comment on the fact that trypsin and chymotrypsin break the peptide chain at the sites indicated, but not at other sites. *(3 marks)*

iii) How does the effect of trypsin on peptides and proteins differ from the effect of amylase on starch? *(3 marks)*

Edexcel

10 Figure 8 shows a flow diagram of some of the ways in which pathogens of humans can be transmitted.

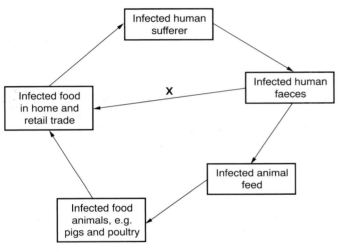

Figure 8

a) Suggest *two* ways in which the transfer of pathogens from human faeces to food, shown by arrow X, is likely to occur. *(2 marks)*

b) State *one* way in which the transmission of pathogens between infected food animals and humans can be prevented. *(1 mark)*

c) i) Explain why socioeconomic factors are often more important in controlling faecal-borne diseases than are antibiotics and vaccination. *(4 marks)*

ii) In what circumstances would treatment with antibiotics be preferable to vaccination in controlling a faecal-borne disease? *(1 mark)*

The cholera vaccine contains heat-killed bacteria and is not very effective, giving partial protection for up to 6 months. However, a recently developed genetically engineered vaccine is expected to give lifelong immunity.

d) Outline, *in principle only*, a method for preparing a vaccine by genetic engineering. *(3 marks)*

Figure 9 shows the annual notifications of food poisoning in England and Wales between 1982 and 1992.

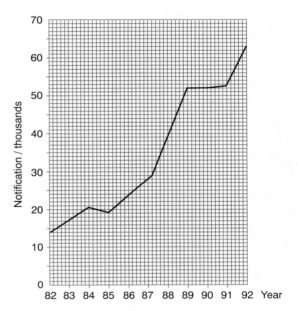

Figure 9
Source: Communicable Disease Surveillance Centre

e) i) Suggest *two* possible reasons to account for the trend shown in Figure 9. *(2 marks)*

ii) Comment on the value of annual notifications as a means of measuring the incidence of food poisoning. *(3 marks)*

UCLES

SECTION 5

The Human Life Cycle

Lifestages

Each individual life physically starts at conception and ends at death. It's a pattern that repeats itself over and over again. Although death does not return life to its starting point, the materials that bodies are made of become available to the ecosystem once again. The life stages begin with the development of the embryo, as tissues are determined and become organised into functional structures such as organs. Birth occurs and both development and growth continue throughout infancy and childhood. A biological milestone is reaching sexual maturity at puberty, during adolescence. For most people adulthood includes a reproductive stage and since the world population is increasing, overall there are more births than deaths. Later there is a decline of physiological effectiveness called senescence, which happens in old age.

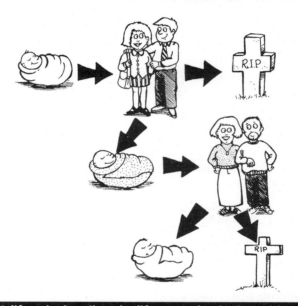

A lifecycle describes the life stages beginning with birth and ending with the death of an individual. However, in terms of the group, reproduction ensures that life is continuous.

Reproduction

Reproduction is essential to perpetuate life and continues the existence of a species. Individuals grow, and later age and die, but reproduction ensures that some of their set of characteristics are inherited through the genetic material which is passed on. Success in biological terms depends on sufficient offspring being produced and a proportion of them reaching reproductive maturity.

Humans are unisexual which means that male and female reproductive systems develop within separate sexes. Therefore humans carry out sexual reproduction, involving the combination of genetic material from two separate parents. Sex cells or gametes contain

Type of mortality*	Number
still births – fetal deaths after 28 weeks of pregnancy	4.3 per 1000 live and still births
perinatal deaths – in the first week of life	7.7 per 1000 live and still births
infant deaths – all ages under one year	7.3 per 1000 live births

*Infant mortality in 1989 (total number of births registered = 501 912)

the genetic material, and bringing them together carries considerable risk in biological terms. Successful fertilisation is by no means guaranteed, since many events may interrupt the journey of the sperm and its contact with an ovum. Yet the advantages outweigh any challenges because sexual reproduction introduces the chance of increasing variety. Genetic variation gives us the expression of new characteristics and in the long-term, the evolution of new lifeforms. This concept is developed in Section 6 Genetics in Action.

Male and female gametes are produced in specialised glands. To give the best chance of fertilisation, male gametes are transferred directly to the female reproductive tract, so that fertilisation is internal. Nevertheless, the vast majority of sperm fail to fertilise an ovum, even though there is a greatly improved chance compared with that offered by external fertilisation. The rate of male gamete production is much greater than ovum production, reflecting the fact that female gametes remain in a protected environment. Chapter 27 describes the formation of gametes and the process of reproduction. Chapter 28 follows the development of an embryo through to birth.

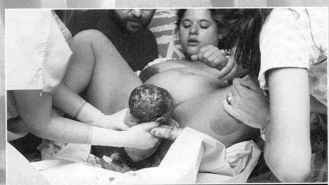

Birth is far safer in some parts of the world than others.

Reproductive technology exists which can either increase the chances of fertilisation for people hoping to have a child, or decrease fertility for those hoping to avoid conception. Alongside our discovery of the human genome and the ability to manipulate genetic information, a host of moral dilemmas arise.

Measuring growth

What is the best approach to measuring growth? The answer to this question may look simple at first glance, since we are familiar with measuring children's height and body mass. But linear measurement is deceptive, since someone can grow taller and thinner, but not heavier. Body mass of living things is not very reliable because of a number of variables, such as water or fecal content. Measuring dry biomass is useful when it is not necessary for the organisms to survive the sampling. But for animals, height and mass are general indicators because there is little alternative. Head size is measured using ultrasound scanning for the fetus, and is measured again after birth. Standard growth charts for British children are shown in Chapter 29.1.

These two 11-year-old children both fall within the normal range of height for their age. As you can see, there is considerable variability. Growth spurts occur at puberty, and boys generally overtake girls in height.

Chapter 30 describes the process of ageing and some theories about why we age. In some societies such as the UK, the proportion of elderly people is increasing, while in other parts of the world the trends are very different. For example in Kenya 50% of the population are under 15 years old. Clearly, demographic trends have implications for society. However, wherever you live in the world, health and disease are all important issues. An aim of medical scientists and technologists is to support our immune systems in maintaining and improving health, and hence the quality of life itself.

CHAPTER 27 Creating New Life

27.1 Meiosis and reproduction

Sexual reproduction is the production of a new individual, brought about by the fusion of two gametes. **Gametes** are male and female sex cells which are produced in specialised glands: the testes and ovaries, respectively. These are the **primary sexual organs** because they produce gametes; the **secondary sexual organs** (described in Chapter 27.2) are other associated tissues and structures needed to bring about the process of reproduction.

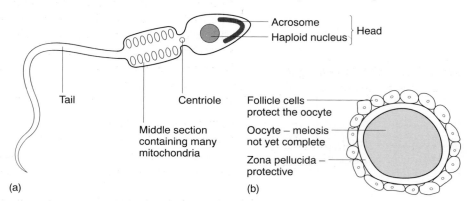

(a)   (b)

Figure 27.1 Human gametes (a) sperm cell (b) ovum

> Gametes are sex cells, which are haploid. Sperm cells are male gametes, produced in the testes. Ova are female sex cells, produced in the ovaries.

▶ *Chapter 33 covers inheritance*

Gametes differ from body tissue cells (called **somatic cells**) in their chromosome number, since they are **haploid (1n)**. This means that their nuclei contain a set of 23 *single* chromosomes, rather than 23 pairs which is normal for all other body cells. It follows then that a new offspring is **diploid (2n)** with chromosomes in pairs, since it gains one set of single chromosomes from the ovum of the mother and one set of single chromosomes from the sperm of the father. **Fertilisation** happens when the nucleus of a male gamete fuses with the nucleus of a female gamete, resulting in a diploid **zygote** which develops as an embryo.

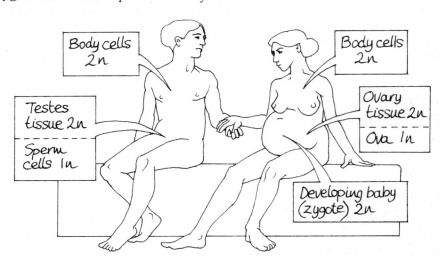

Figure 27.2 Haploid or diploid?

Meiosis produces haploid cells

Mitosis and meiosis are two types of cell division. Mitosis happens when cells divide during growth of body tissues. Meiosis is the type of cell division which occurs when gametes are produced. Meiosis always results in the production of haploid cells which have half the number of chromosomes of the original parent cell.

> Mitosis is the type of cell division that happens during growth; the new nuclei are genetically identical to the parent. Meiosis is the type of cell division which occurs when gametes are produced; the nuclei are genetically different to the parents.

Homologous pairs of chromosomes

An important point to remember is that in any diploid nucleus the chromosomes are in *pairs*. A pair is called **homologous** because the two chromosomes are similar both in structure and in the characteristics they code for. Therefore the two chromosomes in a homologous pair are identical in shape, length and the position of the centromere, which is easy to observe (look at the human karyotype shown in Figure 33.5, page 368). In any homologous pair, both the chromosomes will have genes that code for the same characteristics e.g. eye colour or the ability to produce a particular hormone. This does not mean to say that the two genes are the same, because they may exist in different forms called **alleles**. One chromosome in a homologous pair may have an allele which codes for blue eyes and the other chromosome may have an allele which codes for brown eyes. Therefore the code for a particular characteristic is called a gene and it is located at a particular position on a chromosome. When talking about different forms of a gene, use the word allele.

> ▶ *Chapter 5.3 describes the stages of mitosis*

> ▶ *Chapter 33 discusses how characteristics are inherited*

Events during meiosis

The events that occur in meiosis are continuous but are described in the different phases, some of which are shown in Figure 27.3. These phases show a similar pattern to mitosis (see page 32).

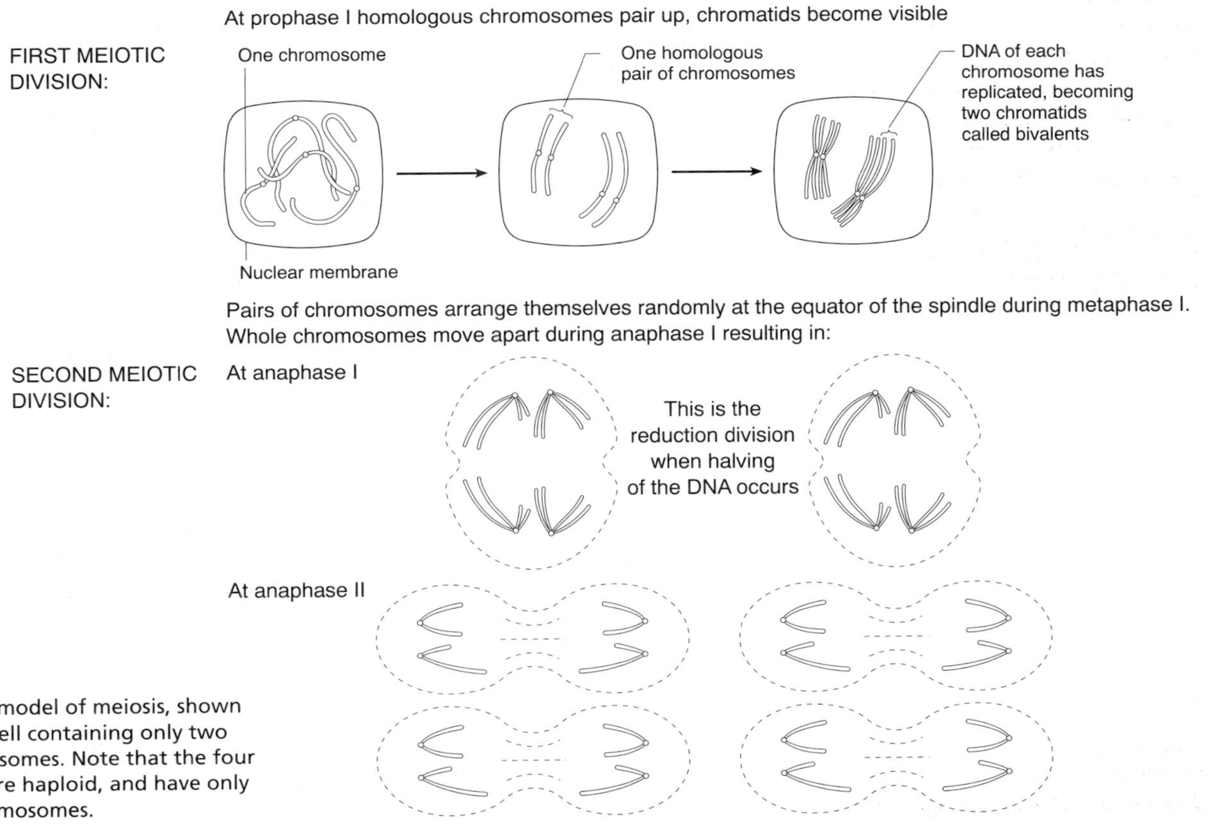

Figure 27.3 A model of meiosis, shown in a simplified cell containing only two pairs of chromosomes. Note that the four resulting cells are haploid, and have only two single chromosomes.

Meiosis is a more complex process than mitosis, and includes *two* divisions. Significant events in meiosis include:

- **Replication** of DNA occurs between one division and the next during interphase just before meiosis starts.
- **Homologous pairs** of chromosomes attract, each appearing as a double thread (two chromatids). **Crossing over** occurs during prophase 1: portions of chromatids exchange at points called chiasma, increasing genetic variation.
- **Independent assortment** of pairs of homologous chromosomes occurs at the centre of the spindle (during metaphase 1): although the chromosomes are in homologous pairs, whether a paternal or maternal chromosome of any pair faces a particular pole of the spindle is completely random, so introducing further genetic variation.
- **Whole chromosomes move** to the poles of the spindle and the cytoplasm begins to divide (during anaphase 1).
- **Nuclear membranes re-form** around the two new nuclei (during telophase 1) and the **cytoplasm begins to divide**, forming two new haploid cells: note that their genetic makeup is *not* identical to the parents; the cytoplasm may not divide completely.
- there is no further replication of DNA, but otherwise the **second division** continues directly in a very similar manner to mitosis.
- **Chromosomes line up** around the equator of the spindle during metaphase 2.
- **Chromatids separate** and move to opposite poles during anaphase 2.
- The spindles disperse, new nuclear membranes form and the cytoplasm begins dividing, to give four new haploid cells. Since a rearrangement of genetic material happened during the first meiotic division, the four daughter cells are all genetically different from the parents and from one another.

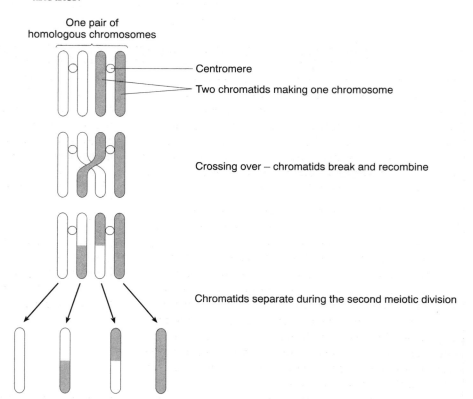

One pair of homologous chromosomes

Centromere

Two chromatids making one chromosome

Crossing over – chromatids break and recombine

Chromatids separate during the second meiotic division

Figure 27.4 Crossing over is an exchange of genetic material which increases variation in the offspring

Distribution of parental genetic material

Imagine a human nucleus containing 23 pairs of chromosomes. A gamete formed from this cell only contains 23 single chromosomes. But which ones are they? The answer is that which chromosome of any homologous pair passes on to the gamete is completely random. In other words, the gamete may receive all maternal chromosomes, all paternal chromosomes or a mixture, the latter arrangement being most common. Figure 27.5 shows this idea with just four pairs of chromosomes.

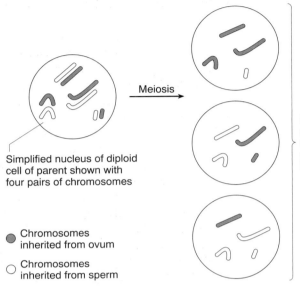

Meiosis

Simplified nucleus of diploid cell of parent shown with four pairs of chromosomes

Examples of haploid nuclei containing different combinations of single maternal and paternal chromosomes which might occur in gametes

● Chromosomes inherited from ovum

○ Chromosomes inherited from sperm

Figure 27.5 The set of single chromosomes in a gamete usually contains a mixture of maternal and paternal chromosomes

Remember also that crossing over occurs while homologous pairs of chromosomes are attracted during prophase 1, before the pairs assort at the centre of the spindle in metaphase. This is why some exchange of genetic material is shown in Figure 27.4.

Genetic tug-of-war?

Meiosis ensures that each parent gives only one chromosome to a gamete and hence to a child. We know that sometimes the process goes wrong, e.g. Down's syndrome occurs because a child inherits an extra chromosome 21, when one homologous pair does not separate. Research has shown that 1 in 100 embryos have an extra copy of chromosome 16, which inevitably leads to natural abortion (miscarriage).

During meiosis, homologous chromosome pairs line up at centre of the spindle, like pairs of shoes lying instep to instep. They are closely linked along their inner edges and they swap sections of DNA when crossing over occurs. Their outer edges attach to the protein fibres of the spindle, and later the chromosome pairs separate and each is drawn to either pole. American scientists who have been studying miscarried embryos think that problems might begin with the crossing over stage. In some cases the rate of crossing over is low in the middle parts of pairs of chromosomes, even though it is normal at the ends of the chromosomes.

The scientists have suggested that if the chromosomes are not linked closely at the middle, they could flop around so that their inner edges may get attached to the protein fibres of the spindle. If a chromosome is attached on its inner and outer edge to the spindle, a 'tug-of-war' could develop with the chromosome being pulled towards both poles at once. Depending on which of the two new daughter cells wins the battle, one could be left without a chromosome and one could have an extra copy.

What might cause the lack of crossing over in the first place? Possibly a problem with the proteins that help to bring homologous pairs of chromosomes together, or which cut and splice the DNA during crossing over. Further research will give more clues.

Source: *New Scientist*, October 1995

Table 27.1 Comparing mitosis with meiosis

Mitosis	Meiosis
the chromosomes replicate once and there is one nuclear division	the chromosomes replicate once and there are two nuclear divisions
the amount of genetic material stays the same	the amount of genetic material halves
homologous pairs do not attract during prophase	homologous pairs attract during prophase 1
no crossing over	crossing over occurs and portions of chromosomes are exchanged
during metaphase single chromosomes (each composed of two chromatids) line up at the centre of the spindle	during metaphase 1 pair of chromosomes (each composed of two chromatids) line up at the centre of the spindle
single chromatids move to the poles in anaphase	whole chromosomes move to the poles in anaphase 1
no second division	a second division occurs and chromatids separate
two new cells are formed – genetically identical	four haploid daughter cells are formed – all genetically different
no genetic variation	genetic variation
occurs during the growth of multicellular organisms, and in asexual reproduction	occurs only in the formation of gametes

27.2 The roles of the male and female reproductive systems

Table 27.2 What do the reproductive systems do?

Male	Female
produce gametes – sperm cells	produce gametes – ova
deliver sperm cells to female reproductive tract	release ova into the oviducts and receive sperm cells into the vagina
	provide a favourable environment for the implantation and development of a zygote
	expel the embryo at birth
produce testosterone	produce oestrogens and progesterone
	produce milk for infant nutrition

The process of ovum production – oogenesis

Even before birth, the ovaries of a female embryo contain the cells which years later, after the onset of puberty,

ovum = singular
ova = plural

may mature into ova. The outer layer of the ovary is a **germinal layer** in which the cells divide repeatedly by mitosis, forming **oogonia**. Both the germinal cells and the oogonia are diploid. The oogonia migrate inwards through the connective tissue. For each germinal cell that produces oogonia, only one oogonium enlarges and becomes a **primary oocyte**, the others degenerate. An oocyte then becomes surrounded by a layer of follicle cells known as the **primary follicle**. There are varying estimates of the number of primary follicles in each ovary at birth, however, of the very large number present, very few of these ever mature into ova.

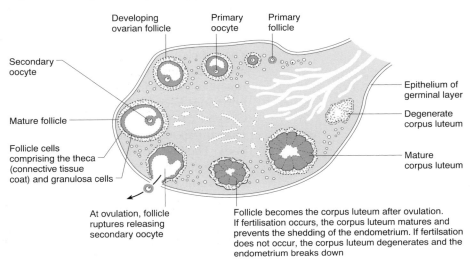

Figure 27.6 The human ovary – shown here with stages in ovum production and release, and the corpus luteum

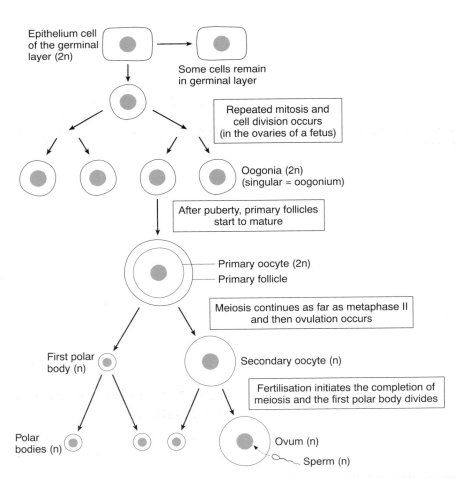

Figure 27.7 How germinal cells become ova

After the onset of puberty, many primary oocytes start the development process each month, but usually only one matures. The follicle continues to enlarge and within it the primary oocyte begins the process of meiosis, however, the first meiotic division produces two haploid cells of different size. The larger one is a **secondary oocyte**, destined to become an ovum. The other is smaller because the cytoplasm divides unevenly, and is known as the **polar body**. The polar body sticks to the secondary oocyte.

The second meiotic division continues as far as metaphase 2, and then the secondary oocyte is released from the ovary – a process called **ovulation**. The secondary oocyte is swept into the funnel-shaped end of the oviduct by cilia and takes two or three days to move along it to the uterus. If the secondary oocyte is not fertilised, it passes out of the body via the vagina. The follicle tissue left behind at the surface of the womb develops into the **corpus luteum**. This is a yellowish mass of cells which has an endocrine function, producing the hormone progesterone. The significance of hormones in controlling the events of the menstrual cycle are explained in Chapter 29. If fertilisation does occur, the secondary oocyte completes the second meiotic division, producing a haploid ovum and another tiny polar body. The first polar body also divides to produce two polar bodies, so that, as expected, four haploid cells result from meiosis: three polar bodies and one ovum. The genetic material of the ovum nucleus and that of the sperm nucleus together form the diploid zygote.

The process of sperm production – spermatogenesis

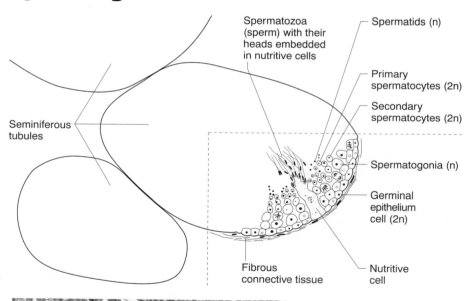

Figure 27.8 Germinal cells in the germinal layer lining the seminiferous tubules divide, first by mitosis and later meiosis, to produce spermatozoa or sperm cells

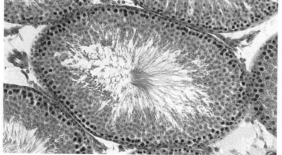

Figure 27.9 Seminiferous tubules in transverse section, as seen using a light microscope

The process of spermatogenesis is similar to that of ovum production in that the first stage is a series of mitotic divisions of diploid cells that make up the germinal layer. Some of these daughter cells remain as part of the germinal layer, but the rest become diploid **spermatogonia**. The spermatogonia divide again by mitosis, some enlarging and becoming **primary spermatocytes**. When the first meiotic division occurs, haploid **secondary spermatocytes** are formed. The completion of the second meiotic division results in four haploid **spermatids**, which develop into spermatozoa or active sperm cells capable of fertilising ova. Sperm cells take about 70 days to develop to maturity.

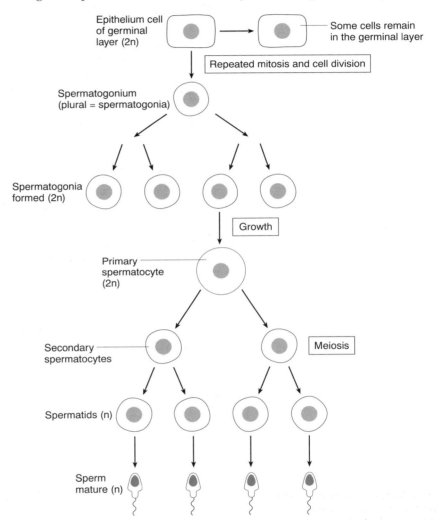

Figure 27.10 Spermatogenesis in outline. Sperm cells are much smaller than ova, and less resources go into producing them. This makes sense biologically, since inevitably the vast majority will not make the journey towards an ovum, and of those that do, very few will survive.

The structure of the female reproductive system

The female reproductive organs include the ovaries, which are located low down in the abdomen but are not directly attached to the oviducts. Instead, the ova they release are swept into the oviducts, passing along them to the uterus. The muscular nature of the uterus allows it to expand many times in size during pregnancy, and contract during labour to expel an embryo. The endometrium lining the uterus has a critical role in the menstrual cycle and in pregnancy, since it provides the set of conditions required for implantation of a fertilised ovum and, along with the placenta, its development into an embryo.

▶ *Chapter 29 has information on the menstrual cycle and pregnancy*

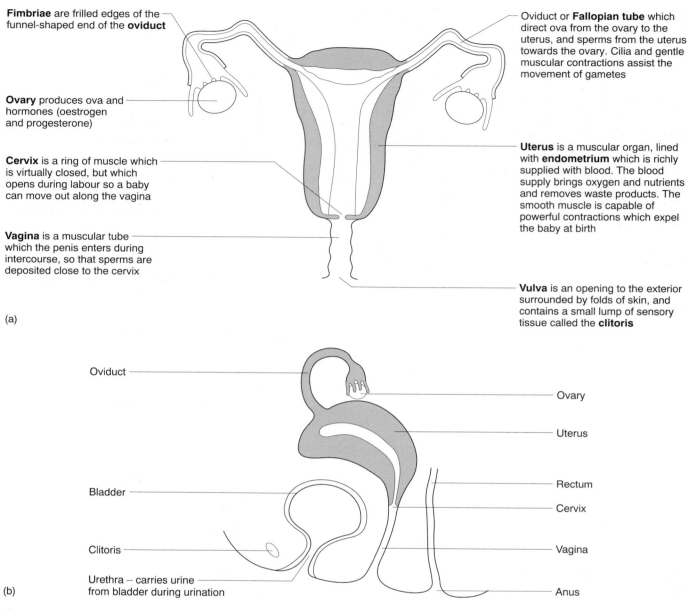

Fimbriae are frilled edges of the funnel-shaped end of the **oviduct**

Ovary produces ova and hormones (oestrogen and progesterone)

Cervix is a ring of muscle which is virtually closed, but which opens during labour so a baby can move out along the vagina

Vagina is a muscular tube which the penis enters during intercourse, so that sperms are deposited close to the cervix

(a)

Oviduct or **Fallopian tube** which direct ova from the ovary to the uterus, and sperms from the uterus towards the ovary. Cilia and gentle muscular contractions assist the movement of gametes

Uterus is a muscular organ, lined with **endometrium** which is richly supplied with blood. The blood supply brings oxygen and nutrients and removes waste products. The smooth muscle is capable of powerful contractions which expel the baby at birth

Vulva is an opening to the exterior surrounded by folds of skin, and contains a small lump of sensory tissue called the **clitoris**

Oviduct

Bladder

Clitoris

Urethra – carries urine from bladder during urination

(b)

Ovary

Uterus

Rectum

Cervix

Vagina

Anus

Figure 27.11 The female reproductive organs (a) ventral view (b) side view

▶ *Chapter 5.4 – Figure 5.6 shows the results of a smear test*

Checking cells of the cervix

The cells of the cervix are continually replaced in response to normal 'wear and tear' of the tissues. At times, cervical cells appear which are abnormal (irregular) in shape. Cells can be taken with a swab from the top of the vagina and examined by microscope for signs of irregularity. This test is called a **smear** and is available as a regular check up every few years. Abnormal cells are not necessarily cancerous, but they are more likely to become so, which is why regular checks are worthwhile.

The structure of the male reproductive system

Spermatozoa are made continuously but at first are not mobile. They take about 2–10 days to make their way to the epididymis, and begin to develop swimming movements. Sperm are stored temporarily in the epididymis, but

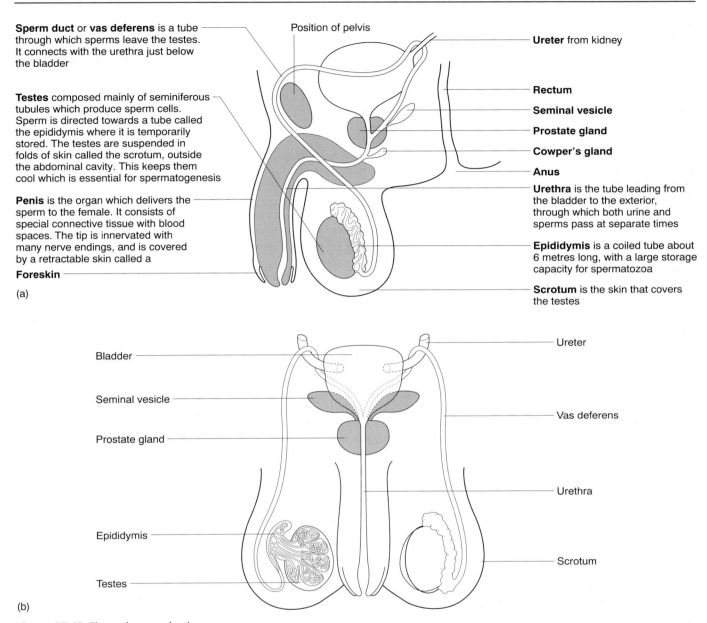

Sperm duct or **vas deferens** is a tube through which sperms leave the testes. It connects with the urethra just below the bladder

Position of pelvis

Ureter from kidney

Rectum

Seminal vesicle

Prostate gland

Cowper's gland

Anus

Testes composed mainly of seminiferous tubules which produce sperm cells. Sperm is directed towards a tube called the epididymis where it is temporarily stored. The testes are suspended in folds of skin called the scrotum, outside the abdominal cavity. This keeps them cool which is essential for spermatogenesis

Penis is the organ which delivers the sperm to the female. It consists of special connective tissue with blood spaces. The tip is innervated with many nerve endings, and is covered by a retractable skin called a

Foreskin

(a)

Urethra is the tube leading from the bladder to the exterior, through which both urine and sperms pass at separate times

Epididymis is a coiled tube about 6 metres long, with a large storage capacity for spermatozoa

Scrotum is the skin that covers the testes

Bladder

Seminal vesicle

Prostate gland

Epididymis

Testes

Ureter

Vas deferens

Urethra

Scrotum

(b)

Figure 27.12 The male reproductive organs (a) side view (b) ventral view

if they have not been ejaculated within a few weeks they are generally reabsorbed. However, sperm which are ejaculated leave the epididymis by way of the sperm duct which connects with the urethra. The prostate gland, Cowper's gland and the seminal vesicle add fluid secretions to the sperm, forming the liquid called **semen**.

Copulation and conception

For most mammals, mating happens when particular hormones reach appropriate levels, linked to seasonal conditions in the environment which give the best possible chance of survival to any offspring. However, humans do not have a 'mating season' as other mammals do. In theory at least, the female is receptive to a male at any time, and so spermatozoa will not necessarily be deposited at a time when ovulation has recently occurred. Sexual arousal causes changes in the male and female reproductive organs which make successful copulation (or intercourse) more likely. In the female, appropriate stimulation of the clitoris gives feelings of sexual pleasure causing more mucus to be secreted in the vagina, facilitating the entry of the penis. In males, the penis becomes erect because of increased blood pressure. This happens under the control of the autonomic nervous system, because the arterial supply to the penis increases greatly in comparison to the venous drainage from it. Friction between the penis and the walls of the vagina stimulate touch receptors in its tip, and bring about a number of autonomic actions. The sphincter muscle at the base of the bladder closes, and smooth muscle in the sperm tubes and associated glands contracts. Ejaculation is brought about by the rhythmic contractions of voluntary muscles in the urethra.

27.3 Fertilisation

Around 300 million sperm are contained in the 3–4 cm^3 of semen from a single ejaculation, which is deposited in the vagina. Muscular contractions of the female tract are probably mostly responsible for moving sperm through the uterus and along the oviducts. The swimming action of the sperm helps to keep them in suspension and to enter the ovum. Despite the millions of sperm deposited, probably only a few thousand ever reach the ovum, although some arrive in the upper parts of the Fallopian tubes within 5–30 minutes. Around the ovum (which is still in the secondary oocyte stage), is a gel-like substance called the **zona pellucida**, along with some follicle cells.

Figure 27.13 A sequence of events called the acrosome reaction triggers the process of fertilisation

1 Changes happen to the membrane covering the acrosome while the sperm is in the female reproductive system

2 As the sperm reaches the oocyte the outer membrane covering the acrosome ruptures and enzymes are released. These digest the zona pellucida and soften the oocyte plasma membrane. Proteins shoot out from the acrosome and pierce the oocyte membrane

3 The remaining sperm plasma membrane and oocyte membrane fuse so the contents of the head enter the oocyte

4 Immediate changes in the electrical properties of the oocyte plasma membrane occur. Cortical granules are then released at the oocyte surface. These cause thickening of the zona pellucida preventing entry of additional sperm

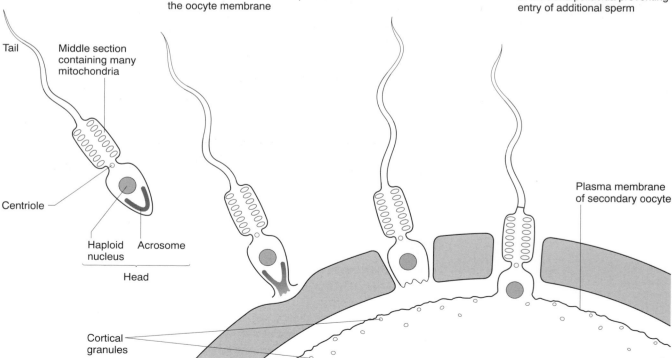

Tail

Middle section containing many mitochondria

Centriole

Haploid nucleus   Acrosome

Head

Cortical granules

Plasma membrane of secondary oocyte

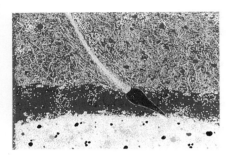

Figure 27.14 Head first into fertilisation, the sperm is seen here embedded in the zona pellucida
(See Colour Gallery page 354)

When the tip of a sperm touches the ovum, the **acrosome reaction** is triggered. Enzymes empty out of the acrosome and begin digesting the zona pellucida – a process which takes the enzyme from more than one sperm cell. Eventually, a sperm cell may get through a weakened point in the zona pellucida, at which point the membrane of the sperm contacts the membrane of the ovum. The membranes fuse and the contents of the head of the sperm becomes integrated with the ovum, causing completion of the second meiotic division. At the same time the polarity of the ovum membrane changes so that no further sperm cells can enter the cell. Much research is still underway to find out more about the exact chain of events occurring during fertilisation; for example it is still uncertain what attracts sperm cells to an ovum.

The explosive origins of life

Professor Michael Whitaker has been studying fertilisation at the University of Newcastle-upon-Tyne. He and his team of scientists have used a laser confocal microscope for their studies, which can focus a laser on any plane or 'slice' through an egg. Fluorescent dyes highlight structures in a plane where the laser is focused. Using this technique the scientists have discovered that immediately after a sperm has fused with an ovum, there is a wave of calcium release which rapidly 'explodes' through the cell, probably via the cytoskeleton of microtubules.

Dr Karl Swann working at University College, London, has identified a protein in the sperm called oscillin. Professor Whitaker suggests that it is this protein which triggers the calcium release, causing the completion of meiosis and the start of a new embryo. Further research may show that levels of oscillin are important in male fertility. What's more, calcium flashes are thought to occur in all dividing cells. Understanding this mechanism may help in discovering what can go wrong with cell division, as in the case of cancer.

Source: *The Daily Telegraph*, 25 June 1996

▶ **Chapter 5.4** *discusses uncontrolled cell division in cancerous cells*

Questions

1 a) What is the name for body tissue cells?

   b) What is meant by the words haploid and diploid?

   c) How are gametes different from other cells in humans?

   d) What is a homologous pair of chromosomes?

   e) Explain the difference between a gene and an allele.

2 a) How do crossing over and independent assortment of chromosomes add to the variation between different generations?

   b) In what ways is internal fertilisation more successful than external fertilisation?

CHAPTER 28 A New Life Develops

28.1 Embryonic development

The zygote is a fertilised egg which divides rapidly as it develops into an embryo.

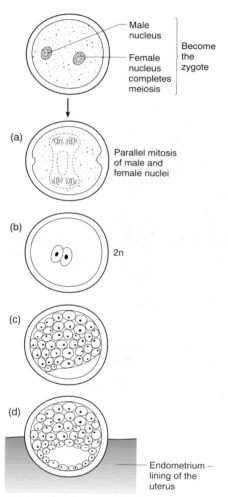

Figure 28.1 Early days in embryo development (a) The fertilised ovum – the ovum nucleus and the sperm nucleus undergo parallel mitosis, and the daughter nuclei become enclosed in nuclear membranes (b) After 12 hours – two diploid cells of the zygote (c) After a few days – a ball of cells, the morula (d) After a week – a hollow ball of cells, the blastocyst

A fertilised egg is called a **zygote**. The zygote passes along the oviduct following fertilisation, reaching the uterus after a few days. During this time it repeatedly divides by mitosis to become ball of cells called the **morula**. The divisions are rapid and interphase is short, so there is little growth occurring. This process, which is known as **cleavage**, results in many small and undifferentiated cells. The ball of cells develops into a **blastocyst**, with a fluid-filled cavity called a **blastocoel**, and may implant into the wall of the uterus within a couple of days. If implantation does not occur, the blastocyst is lost from the body. **Trophoblastic villi** are projections of tissue which grow out from the outer layer of the blastocyst into the wall of the uterus. This is where the placenta will later form from both embryonic and maternal tissue. Implantation is complete by about 11–12 days after fertilisation and the woman is pregnant.

As the embryo develops it requires nutrients and has waste products which need to be removed. At first, the trophoblastic villi which project into the endometrium can cope with these requirements, by diffusion of substances to and from blood spaces called **lacunae**. But as the embryo increases in size so does its requirements. Hence a structure develops which is later called the **placenta**. This is a highly vascular area in which fetal and maternal blood come into very close contact, but do not actually mix. Diffusion across a relatively huge surface area is sufficient to supply the developing fetus with all its needs. Notice in Figure 28.2(a) that there are several **extra-embryonic membranes** surrounding the developing embryo. The amnion forms the **amniotic sac** around the embryo, which becomes filled with **amniotic fluid** and protects the fetus from injury due to physical impact. The **chorion** forms outgrowths which contribute to the development of the placenta, and the **allantois** fuses with the chorion and forms the umbilical cord.

Changes happening within the blastocyst in the early days after fertilisation have a profound effect on the development of the embryo. Initially, the blastocyst develops a three-layered structure: the outer ectoderm, middle mesoderm and inner endoderm. How the cells in these layers will develop becomes determined very early on. Experiments with mice embryos have shown that once this stage is reached, the cells will always develop into specific tissues, even if they are isolated or grafted into a new position on an embryo. The process of tissue determination is called **gastrulation** and in this three-layered stage the embryo is called the **gastrula**. The ectoderm is destined to become the central nervous system, sense organs and epidermis. The mesoderm will become the vertebral column and limb bones, muscle and connective tissues, and also the sex organs and kidneys. The endoderm develops into the intestinal tract and liver, the lungs and glands such as the thyroid, but will also form the primordial germ cells (the germinal layer) in the sex organs. In humans, the main organ systems are in place by around 12 weeks, although they are not fully mature. At this stage the embryo is called the **fetus**.

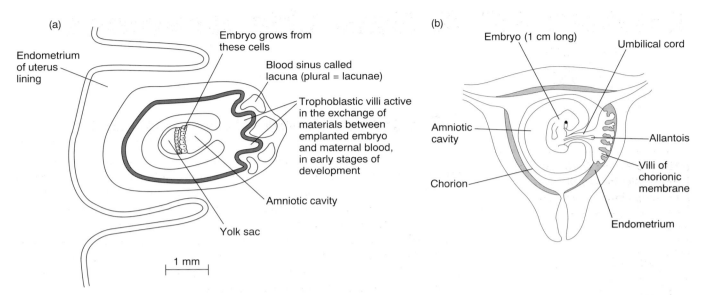

(a)

Endometrium of uterus lining

Embryo grows from these cells

Blood sinus called lacuna (plural = lacunae)

Trophoblastic villi active in the exchange of materials between emplanted embryo and maternal blood, in early stages of development

Amniotic cavity

Yolk sac

1 mm

(b)

Embryo (1 cm long)

Umbilical cord

Amniotic cavity

Chorion

Allantois

Villi of chorionic membrane

Endometrium

Figure 28.2 (a) Around 14 days after fertilisation – the embryo is implanted and trophoblastic villi grow out into the endometrium of the uterus. Blood sinuses between the villi provide nourishment and remove waste products from the embryo (b) 5 weeks after fertilisation – the placenta is developing

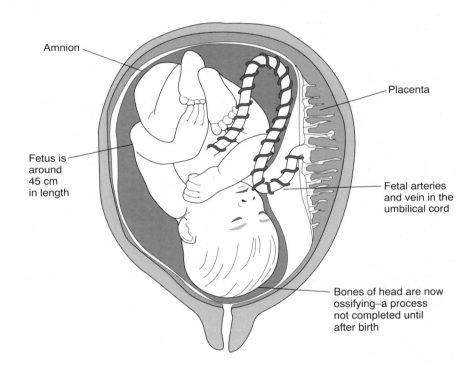

Amnion

Fetus is around 45 cm in length

Placenta

Fetal arteries and vein in the umbilical cord

Bones of head are now ossifying–a process not completed until after birth

Figure 28.3 Development of the fetus at 8 months

The placenta supports the life of the developing fetus by providing many of the conditions needed for life, such as nutrition.

The placenta

In the region between the allantochorion and the endometrium of the uterus, the chorion develops outgrowths called **chorionic villi** into the endometrium. In the area where these are most extensive, the endometrium blood vessel walls break down so that the villi are literally bathed in the mother's blood. The placenta reaches about 20 cm in diameter with a mass of about 650 g when fully developed. The blood system of the mother and the baby are in close contact within the placenta, but are separated by a delicate physical barrier formed by the walls of the fetal blood supply. The separation of the two blood systems is important for several reasons:

- The mother's blood is at a higher pressure than that of the fetus, and this would cause damage.
- The fetus has a different genotype to the mother since it has only inherited some of its genetic material from her.

The villi appear to be coated with special molecules that protect them from being attacked by the mother's immune system as they grow into the endometrium. Without these the surface markers on fetal cells would trigger an immune response in the mother which might potentially kill the fetus.

Table 28.1 Role of the placenta

Respiration	gaseous oxygen exchange between maternal and fetal blood provides oxygen
Nutrition	nutrients such as glucose, amino acids, vitamins and minerals are supplied to the fetus
Excretion	removal of carbon dioxide, urea and other metabolic wastes
Protection	some antibodies supplied by the mother give immunity against infection; barrier stops some bacteria, viruses and toxins (drugs may cross the barrier)
Endocrine	hormones from the chorion and later the placenta help to maintain the corpus luteum and hence prevent the menstrual cycle; lactogen stimulates breast development

Does a fetus feel pain?

There is much debate about whether or not a fetus can feel pain, the answer to which is still uncertain. However, up to 100 years or so ago, people still thought that a fetus was deaf and did not develop hearing until after birth. Yet now it is generally accepted that all types of sound can cause a fetus to wriggle. In fact both advertising and pop music employ rhythms akin to those of the heart and breathing rate because they are pleasing and powerful.

A premature baby has a good chance of survival from as early as 24 weeks, because of scientific and technological advances in intensive care methods. This overlap between the age of a fetus in the womb and survival in premature babies has raised fresh questions. If a premature baby undergoes surgery it is given pain relief, but a fetus of the same age undergoing a similar procedure in the uterus gains only what passes through the placenta. At what stage does the response of the fetal nervous system equate to feeling pain? Activity of the nervous system alone is not evidence, since reflex actions can be observed in people who cannot feel any sensation because of sensory nerve damage.

Nick Fisk and Vivette Glover of Queen Charlotte Hospital and Chelsea Hospital in London have been pioneering the use of pain relief for fetuses of 19 weeks or more, who require life-saving blood transfusions while still in the uterus. The procedure requires a needle to be inserted into the abdomen of the fetus. Glover and Fisk have recorded increased levels of cortisol, endorphin and noradrenaline, all of which are associated with stress or pain in children and adults.

However, these hormone surges are not in themselves firm evidence that a fetus feels pain. In fact at certain stages a fetus has different nerve cell connections and neurotransmitters to adults. Exactly when the nerve fibres that ferry nerve impulses from pain receptors in the tissues to the spinal cord are in place is not known. These nerve fibres seem to be a vital link, although in one post-mortem study on a 19 week fetus they were not found. However, the scientist involved did not rule out the idea that the technology used was not sufficiently sensitive to find the fibres in a tiny fetus.

Data with adults shows that there are several areas of the brain involved in feeling pain in adults: the thalamus and two areas in the cortex. In a fetus the first nerve connections between the cortex and the thalamus occur at 22–24 weeks, with activity in the cortex triggered by sensory impulses around 29 weeks. Electrical activity alone does not necessarily constitute a feeling of pain, and many people would argue that awareness of the sensation comes only through experience.

Whatever the fact of the matter, this is a controversial area because of legal, social and moral implications.

Source: *New Scientist*, 19 October 1996

Does a fetus feel pain? – contd.

Age of fetus (weeks)	Observation
8	reflex response to touch on lips
9	forebrain, midbrain and hindbrain formed; around 250 000 neurones generated per minute
13	electrical activity in brain, above the brain stem (the region when it joins the spinal cord)
14	most of body responds to touch
16	slow eye movements
20	first response to sounds
22	cortex of cerebrum is growing fast
25	fetus has preferred position
28	sounds produce reliable change in heart rate
29	first electrical activity of cortex of cerebrum

Questions

1 How has the increasing survival rate of very premature babies contributed to the debate about when and if a fetus feels pain?

2 Which of the indicators of nervous system development in Table 28.2 do you think suggests that a fetus (or premature baby) may be aware of pain?

3 To what extent do you think that feeling pain is a conditioned response?

4 Suggest what is meant by the 'legal, social and moral implications' mentioned at the end of the article.

Table 28.2 What information can help give answers?

28.2 What determines gender?

The genetic gender of an embryo is determined at fertilisation by the sex chromosome in the sperm nucleus. The nucleus in the ovum contains a sex chromosome called the X chromosome, while the sperm cell can contain either an X chromosome or a Y chromosome. If the zygote contains two X chromosomes it is genetically female and if it contains one X and one Y chromosome it is genetically male. Despite this, however, it seems that up to around six weeks the embryo has both male and female sex organs, although they are at a very simple level of development. It would appear that the presence of an X chromosome in all embryos would direct sexual development along female lines, except for the intervention of a mechanism initiated by the Y chromosome. In embryos with Y chromosomes, this mechanism stimulates the development of the male sex organs and hence differentiates between males and females.

28.3 Being pregnant

When a zygote implants in the wall of the uterus, it begins to produce a hormone that signals to the mother's body the changes which happen during pregnancy. The hormone is called **human chorionic gonadotrophic hormone (HCG)**. HCG stimulates the corpus luteum which was left behind in the ovary after the follicle burst through the surface at ovulation. The corpus luteum keeps producing progesterone, so the lining of uterus is maintained in a suitable condition for the implanted embryo. At 12 weeks, the production of HCG by the embryo falls. This is a critical time, since a drop in progesterone level at this time can trigger miscarriage. In fact the majority of miscarriages happen because of this. However, in successful pregnancies the placenta starts producing sufficient progesterone to maintain the uterus lining. The level of HCG in a woman's urine is used as the basis of a pregnancy test.

A woman's physiology changes during pregnancy. This is really a shift in the homeostatic set-points, which is needed because of the extra demands of pregnancy. For example there is an increased demand on maternal circulation, since the placenta alone requires a supply of 500–800 ml of blood per minute. What's more, a greater blood flow is required to supply sufficient nutrients to the embryo, which is rapidly growing and metabolising. Cardiac output increases, as does blood volume, which helps to maintain blood pressure (see Figure 28.4). Along with active cellular metabolism is the heating effect which causes a slight rise in body temperature.

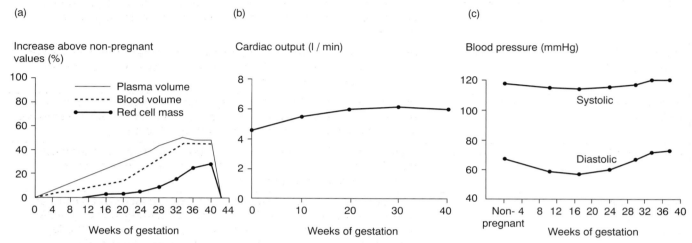

Figure 28.4 Changes in physiology during pregnancy (a) blood volume (b) cardiac output (c) blood pressure

When is a woman like a man?

According to American researchers, pregnancy causes long-lasting biochemical changes in a woman's body. They discovered this by chance while investigating how fast people break down caffeine. Apparently, women who have not been pregnant break down caffeine at only 70 per cent of the rate at which men or women who have been pregnant do. This is due to the level of a particular detoxifying enzyme: women who have been pregnant have a higher level of enzyme than those who have not. The enzyme also breaks down other chemicals such as medical drugs, for example a bronchiodilator used for asthma treatment. The implication is that women who have had pregnancies might require higher doses of medicines if they break them down faster.

College students are often used for the drug studies described and so most of the females have not been pregnant. However, in light of this research it now seems that including previously pregnant women in surveys is important because of the differences in physiology which have been highlighted.

Source: New Scientist, 21 October 1995

Finding out about the fetus

An important part of antenatal care is monitoring the health of the mother as well as the fetus. There are a variety of tests available which give differing types of information. Not all the tests shown in Table 28.3 are routine and new tests are constantly being developed.

Table 28.3 Ante-natal testing

Test	When it's used	Comments
mother's blood pressure	throughout	high blood pressure is dangerous, it is an early sign of pre-eclampsia which if untreated can lead to fetal death and renal failure and fits in the mother which may be fatal
urine	throughout	tested for sugar as an indicator of gestational diabetes (see page 134); also for protein as an indicator of high blood pressure or disfunction
blood tests		for blood group including Rhesus factor (see page 103); for anaemia (see page 231); for syphilis, hepatitis B and HIV (by permission)
ultrasound scan	at intervals	to check fetal size and age, and position with respect to placenta; to detect multiple births; can detect some abnormalities, e.g. skeletal defects
chorionic villus sampling (CVS)	8–11 weeks	definitive diagnosis of Down's syndrome and other conditions such as sickle cell anaemia and thalassaemia; sample taken from chorionic region of developing placenta
alphafetoprotein (AFP) test	16–18 weeks	indicates increased risk of Down's syndrome or spina bifida but is not reliable on its own (the triple test is another blood test which combines AFP with other chemical levels in blood to indicate risk)
amniocentesis	16–18 weeks	used if the results of the AFP or triple test indicate an increased risk; fluid from the amniotic sac is sampled; this is a definitive test for Down's syndrome and spina bifida
fluorescent in-situ hybridisation technique (FISH)		uses molecules labelled with fluorescent dyes to lock onto particular sections of DNA in fetal red blood cells, highlighting known genetic mutations such as that causing Down's syndrome; relies on the fact that a minute amount of fetal blood leaks into the mother's circulation; this test is still being developed

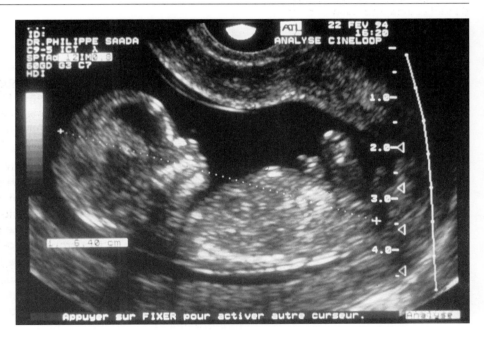

Figure 28.5 A human fetus shortly before birth – note the mother's vertebrae alongside the baby's backbone

Multiple births

Sometimes more than one fetus develops in the uterus at the same time, and this is known as a **multiple birth**. The most common multiple birth is twins – two fetuses – which occurs once in about every 90 births. Natural triplets (three fetuses) or quadruplets (four fetuses) are very rare, but do occasionally occur as a result of fertility treatment which is described in Chapter 29.

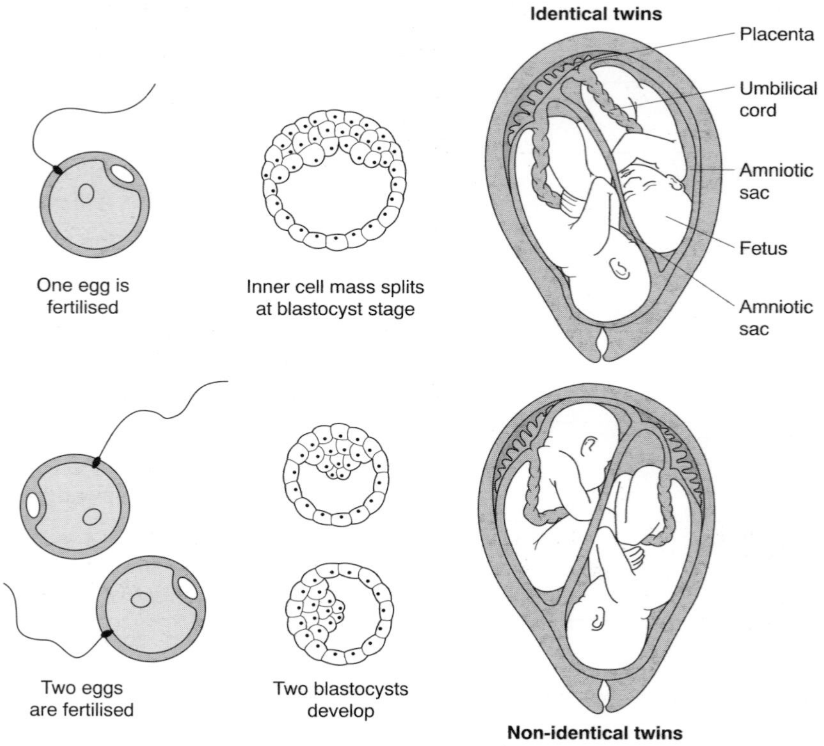

Figure 28.6 Twins can result from the fertilisation of one secondary oocyte or two. In the first case, the zygote divides at the very early blastocyst stage and the two fetuses share a placenta, although they normally each have their own amniotic sac. These twins are genetically identical and are called **monozygotic**. In the second case there are two fertilisations and two zygotes, each developing a separate placenta and their own amniotic sac. These twins are called **dizygotic**. They are not genetically identical and may be different sexes.

28.4 Birth

At the end of a 40 week gestation period the fetus has begun to outgrow the available space in the uterus. What's more, the placenta begins to work less efficiently and so the necessity of birth becomes more urgent. Birth presents dangers for the mother and baby, challenging even modern technologies. However, it seems that the fetus rather than the mother initiates the onset of birth. The pituitary gland of the fetus secretes **adrenocorticotrophic hormone (ACTH)** which stimulates its adrenal glands to produce steroids. These steroids affect the placenta which produces **prostaglandins**, and these cause the uterus muscles to contract. At the same time, the baby's head pressing on the cervix stimulates stretch receptors. They send impulses to the mother's brain and cause the release of **oxytocin** from her hypothalamus. The oxytocin brings on the strong muscular contractions which expel the baby during labour. This process can be lengthy and very painful, although various types of pain relief may be available. Table 28.4 summarises the stages of birth. The heart beat of the fetus can be monitored, either by listening through a stethoscope or ear trumpet, or electronically via a monitor linked to a recording machine.

Many changes happen rapidly after the birth of the baby. The life support system provided by the mother's uterus is no longer available and the baby's body systems have to support life themselves. Firstly, the lungs inflate and the process of gas exchange begins (see pages 75–77); secondly, the blood circulation alters and the liver has an increased work load, particularly in breaking down fetal haemoglobin (see page 141).

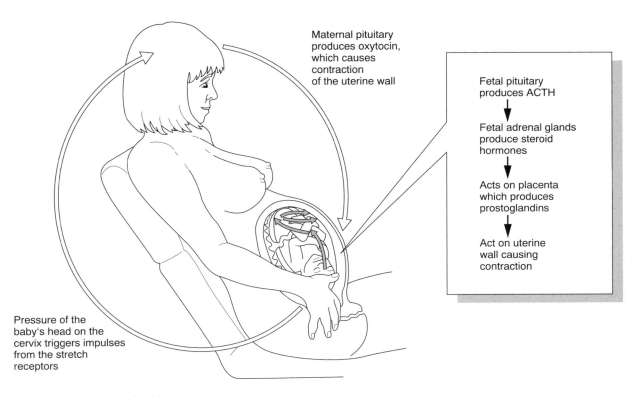

Maternal pituitary produces oxytocin, which causes contraction of the uterine wall

Fetal pituitary produces ACTH

Fetal adrenal glands produce steroid hormones

Acts on placenta which produces prostoglandins

Act on uterine wall causing contraction

Pressure of the baby's head on the cervix triggers impulses from the stretch receptors

Figure 28.7 The hormones involved in birth

Table 28.4 The stages of birth

First stage	dilation of the cervix from 1 mm to 10 cm, a space large enough to let the baby's head through
Second stage	the delivery of the baby – involuntary uterine muscle contractions and voluntary abdominal contractions expel the baby from the uterus and out through the vagina
Third stage	the placenta peels away from the uterus wall and is pushed out in the same way as the baby

28.5 Mammals and milk production

Mammals are the only group of animals that have an almost guaranteed source of food for their offspring, whatever the status of the mother's diet. This is an evolutionary advance in that it gives the best possible chance of survival to offspring and minimises the waste of resources that occurs when many offspring perish. The **mammary glands** or breasts are specially modified glands which produce a secretion called milk in a process which is known as **lactation**. **Oestrogen** and **progesterone** prepare the breasts for milk production throughout pregnancy, but lactation does not start until the level of progesterone drops just before birth. The anterior pituitary gland secretes the hormone prolactin which then controls lactation. Milk comes out of the nipple by a reflex action, stimulated by the suckling of the baby. Sensory receptors in the nipple send impulses to the hypothalamus, stimulating the pituitary gland to produce oxytocin which makes muscle fibres in the epithelial tissue of the breast contract, squeezing milk out.

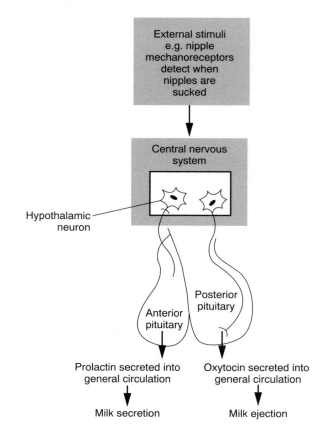

Figure 28.8 Control of lactation

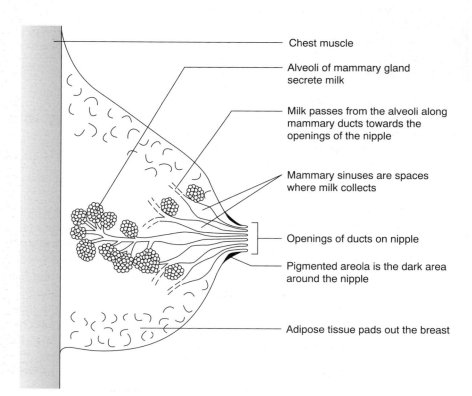

Figure 28.9 The structure of the breast

► *Chapter 23.4 – Table 23.7 gives a comparison of human breast milk and formula milk substitute*

Lactation is an example of exocytosis.

► *Chapter 4.5 describes the process of exocytosis*

There is no doubt that breast-feeding a baby provides it with a uniquely formulated food, tailored exactly to the needs of a human infant. Breast milk is quite sufficient for a baby's needs up to the age of at least six months and in many cultures babies are breast fed for a lot longer than this. Human milk is relatively low in fat and protein in comparison to the milk of other mammals, and the slower growth rate reflects this. Much of the development of a human infant involves learning complex behaviour which is needed later in life. Apart from the fact that breast milk is a perfect food for babies, it provides immunity to many of the diseases which the mother has encountered. The immunological benefits cannot be mimicked in dried milk preparations, which are made from another animal's milk. Bottle feeding is popular with some parents because anyone, not just the mother, can feed the baby. But there is concern about the use of bottle feeding in situations where the water supply may be infected, or there are inadequate resources for sterilising bottles. Also, getting the correct nutrition for the baby does rely on making up the milk formula correctly.

Questions and answers on breast cancer

1 *How common is breast cancer?* It is the most common form of cancer in women, affecting one woman in 12 at some point in their lives.

2 *Why is breast cancer so common?* Oestrogen stimulates mitosis in breast tissue during the menstrual cycle, in preparation for milk production. If pregnancy does not occur, these cells die. This cycle happens regularly over 40 years or so, increasing the possibility of errors accumulating in growth-controlling genes.

3 *How is breast cancer treated?* The main treatments (used singly or in combination) are surgery to remove the tumour; radiotherapy of the local area to kill any tumour cells; chemotherapy to kill epithelial cells; and hormone treatment with anti-oestrogen drugs such as tamoxifen.

4 *What are the risk factors for breast cancer?* Not having a pregnancy at some point in the reproductive phase of life seems to be a risk factor. Two genes (called BRCA1 and BRCA2) increase the risk of a woman having breast cancer.

5 *Is screening effective?* X-ray breast screening is available to women in the UK aged 50–64. This gives a **mammogram**, which is an X-ray photograph that can be analysed (see Figure 28.10).

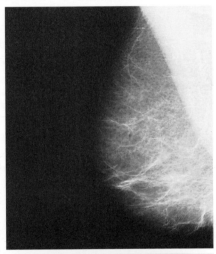
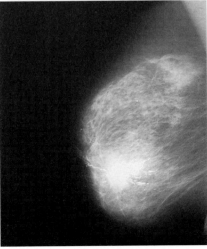

Figure 28.10 These mammograms show a healthy breast (top) and one with cancer (bottom). Tumour tissue which is denser than normal tissues, appears as a whiter area. Around 6000 breast cancers a year are detected by regular screening programmes.

CHAPTER 29

Childhood to Adulthood

29.1 Controlling growth

The hypothalamus in the brain has an initial role in producing releasing and inhibiting factors that influence the pituitary gland. If stimulated, the pituitary gland secretes various hormones which affect tissues and other glands, promoting growth in a variety of ways. The hormones produced by the pituitary gland and their effects, which occur at various stages in life, are summarised as follows:

- Growth hormone (GH or somatotrophin): promotes growth of body tissues generally by increasing protein production.
- Thyroid stimulating hormone (TSH): stimulates the thyroid gland to produce hormones including thyroxine, which increase metabolic rate.
- Follicle stimulating hormone (FSH): promotes production of gametes in the gonads.
- Adrenocorticotrophic hormone (ACTH): stimulates the adrenal cortex to produce glucocorticoids which bring about carbohydrate and protein metabolism, making resources available for cell growth.

29.2 Phases of growth

► *Chapter 5.3 describes mitosis, the type of cell division which happens during growth*

Although they are small and immature, all organs systems are present at birth. Notice in Figure 29.1 that the proportions of the different parts of the body are not the same at birth as in an adult. The head is conspicuously large because it houses the brain, and the liver is also disproportionately large. There is a need for the tissues to grow and to develop. **Growth** is a

Figure 29.1 The size of the head compared with the rest of the human body

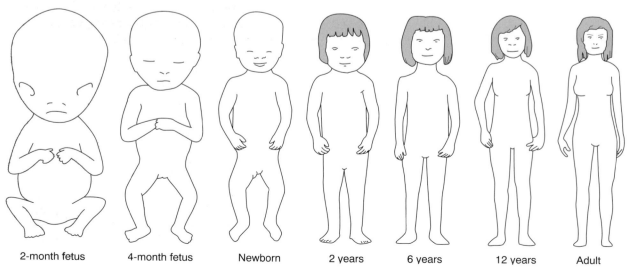

| 2-month fetus | 4-month fetus | Newborn | 2 years | 6 years | 12 years | Adult |

permanent increase in size or mass. This is due to an increase in cell numbers by cell division, an increase of cell contents (which is called the assimilation phase) resulting in cell expansion, and an increase in cell size.

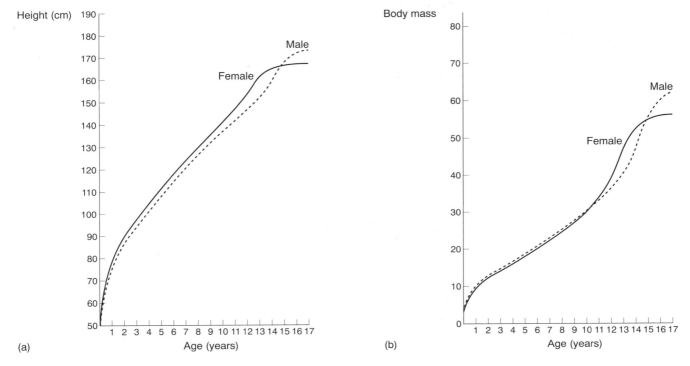

(a)

(b)

Figure 29.2 Growth charts for children in the UK

Physiological events which happen in a newborn child are referred to in Chapter 28.4. This chapter looks at growth and maturation through childhood and adolescence to adulthood, and describes the reproductive phase in detail.

Fetal growth presents the greatest rate of growth, but this stage is not shown in Figure 29.2. After birth, the fastest rate of growth occurs in infancy, slowing during later childhood. There is a further growth spurt during a period coinciding with the onset of sexual maturity, the phase called **puberty**. Until growth stops it is a continuous process, although the rate is not constant. There is a steady replacement of cells in some tissues, particularly the gut, skin and blood, but this does not increase adult size and is not the same as growth. Some tissues such as the liver and thyroid grow only very slowly. However, if an area of the liver is damaged it can suddenly regenerate cells at a faster rate than normal.

29.3 Puberty

> Puberty is a maturing process during adolescence that involves the maturing of reproductive organs and the development of secondary sexual characteristics.

Puberty is a set of changes that happen at adolescence as a child gradually matures into adulthood. The primary sex organs mature and features called the secondary sexual characteristics develop. As previously mentioned, this coincides with a rapid growth phase.

Table 29.1 Changes which occur at puberty

Male	Female
Maturation of primary reproductive organs	
hormone secretion: increased testosterone production by testes	hormone secretion: increased oestrogen production by ovaries
growth of testes and penis	growth of breasts, vagina and uterus
prostate, Cowper's gland and seminal vesicles become functional	onset of menstrual cycle
Development of secondary sexual characteristics	
body hair increases, pubic and facial hair grows	body hair increases, pubic hair grows
shoulders become more muscular	hips broaden, increase in fat layer under the skin
sweat production increases	sweat production increases
testes descend from the abdominal cavity	
voice 'breaks' or deepens due to laryngeal development	

The hormones which promote growth in bone length also cause the ends of the bone to ossify, finally stopping the production of new tissue. The heart increases in mass and size, blood pressure increases and the body's muscle mass increases – all of which allow greater physical performance. The same growth hormones which trigger puberty are released during childhood, but at a much lower level. It is only when a threshold is reached that puberty starts. Obesity tends to promote the onset of puberty, but anorexia delays it.

29.4 The menstrual cycle

Once puberty is established at around 12–13 years of age, the menstrual cycle may repeat continuously until **menopause**, at around 45–55 years of age. An event such as illness or pregnancy interrupts the 28-day cycle. For many women, adult life involves giving birth to a number of children. After the birth of a child, lactation generally prevents ovulation for a period of time by inhibiting gonadotrophin production by the pituitary gland, and so conception may not occur again immediately. Even so, there is an alternating pattern of pregnancy and lactation during the reproductive phase of life. It is only relatively recently that some women have had the option to reduce family size (or not to have children at all) and consequently the time spent in pregnancy and lactation. These women experience menstruation on a more continuous basis than those who have many pregnancies.

It is convenient to call the start of the cycle (day 1) when the bleeding or period occurs, because it is a definite and recognisable point. A period happens when the lining of the uterus is shed. Throughout the cycle the interaction of several hormones bring about control of menstruation (see Figure 29.3).

- Follicle stimulating hormone (FSH) from the pituitary initiates the development of follicles in the ovary.
- Luteinising hormone (LH), also produced by the pituitary, stimulates a mature follicle to make oestrogen. Via a negative feedback loop, oestrogen depresses the production of FSH.
- Oestrogen causes thickening and vascularisation of the endometrium.
- LH and FSH levels peak at day 14 and ovulation occurs, releasing a secondary oocyte from the ovary.
- The empty follicle becomes a corpus luteum, which releases progesterone, maintaining the thickening endometrium. Progesterone prevents the release of FSH and LH, again by means of a negative feedback loop.
- If the oocyte is not fertilised, the corpus luteum begins to degenerate and the level of progesterone falls. Then the lining is shed and levels of LH and FSH begin to rise, starting the cycle again.

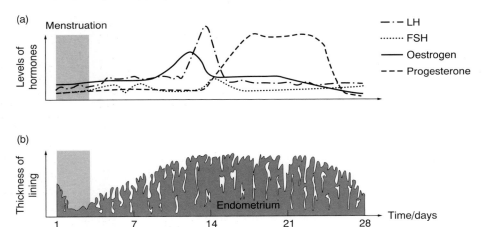

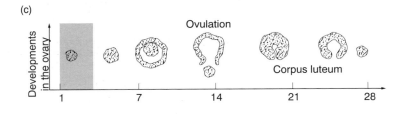

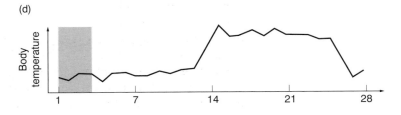

Figure 29.3 The pattern of changes during the menstrual cycle (a) levels of hormones (b) thickness of endometrium in uterus (c) development of follicles in ovary (d) body temperature

During the cycle there is a limited period of female fertility. Fertilisation can only occur at the time the oocyte is moving along the oviduct. This is probably 2–3 days corresponding to days 14–17 in the middle of the cycle. This is not so for males, who produce gametes continuously.

Questions

1 Why does the endometrium thicken during the first half of the menstrual cycle?

2 What is the significance of the negative feedback mechanism involving oestrogen and FSH?

3 What is the role of the corpus luteum after fertilisation?

29.5 Fertility control

Reproductive technology is an expanding area, which includes *reducing* the chances of fertility through contraception as well as *improving* them through a variety of techniques.

Sperm fail to get a grip

Canadian scientists have found a link between male sterility and the lack of a protein on the surface of sperm cells which is needed for the sperm to 'dock' onto the surface of an ovum. The protein is normally added to sperm as they pass through the epididyimis.

All the men studied in the survey had normal sperm counts and their sperm could swim normally. However, nine out of the 16 sperm samples from infertile men contained less than 30 per cent of the docking protein found in the samples from fertile men. The work needs to be repeated with other groups of men, but it seems as if the epidydimis might be causing the problem.

Scientists hope to isolate the gene which codes for the production of the protein, and genetically engineer bacteria to produce large quantities of it. The engineered protein could be mixed with a man's sperm and added to a woman's ova, and the mixture could then be placed in the uterus (as in IVF treatment). The research may even lead to producing a new contraceptive, for example by using an inhibitor for the protein.

Source: *New Scientist*, 8 August 1996

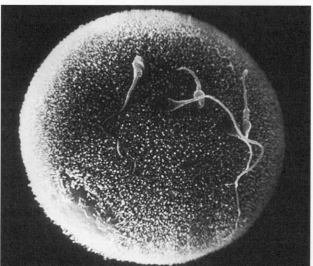

Figure 29.4 Researchers were surprised to find that one particular factor might be the cause of the majority of cases of previously unexplained male sterility
(*See Colour Gallery page 354*)

Decreasing fertility – contraception

Once people reach adolescence they begin to develop a sexual drive which is not directly linked with fertility or seasonal conditions. In theory, a female is receptive to a male at any time, but in practice many factors influence how frequently people have intercourse. Although fertility is limited to a few days during the menstrual cycle, the risk of pregnancy is not desirable for many people. **Contraception** is the term used to describe a variety of methods used to prevent fertilisation (or conception). Contraception is mainly used by people in developed countries, partly because a smaller family size means a better lifestyle, and improved medical facilities mean that fewer children die in infancy. In developing countries contraception other than natural methods is relatively uncommon for a variety of reasons. A large family may have more importance culturally as well as socially, since children care for their parents as they become old. The rate of infant mortality is also higher, due to poorer medical facilities and living conditions. Added to this, there are some religions which condemn the use of artificial contraception and actively encourage large families.

Natural methods of contraception include the rhythm method and withdrawing the penis from the vagina immediately before ejaculation (the withdrawal method). These methods are not particularly reliable. Other methods of contraception include **barrier methods** which physically prevent the gametes coming into contact, and **chemical methods** which stop fertilisation in a number of ways. The IUD (intrauterine device or coil) does not prevent fertilisation but prevents implantation. **Sterilisation** causes complete infertility, and is not easily reversible since it involves surgery. Table 29.2 is a summary of the main methods of contraception.

Table 29.2 The main methods of contraception

Method	How it works	Advantages	Disadvantages
Natural rhythm	intercourse avoided when a change in temperature and mucus production indicate ovulation is occurring	no side effects, free	not reliable
Barrier* condom	male condom covers penis, collects semen, preventing sperm reaching oocyte; female condom fits in vagina locating at rim, collects semen and prevents sperm reaching oocyte	simple to use, no side effects, can give some protection against disease*	may break, more reliable if used with spermicide, interrupts intercourse

Table 29.2 continued overleaf

Table 29.2 continued

Method	How it works	Advantages	Disadvantages
diaphragm or cap	fits inside vagina and covers cervix, prevents sperm entering	no side effects, protects cervix from wear	first fitting is checked medically, more reliable if used with spermicide

Method	How it works	Advantages	Disadvantages
Chemical 'the pill'	chemicals mimic effects of natural hormones; combined oestrogen/progesterone pills prevent ovulation, progesterone only pills do not	very reliable if taken at regular intervals, may reduce the chance of some types of tumour	increases blood pressure and risk of blood clots, may increase the chance of some types of tumour

spermicide	cream, foam, gel or pessary containing a chemical that kills sperm, used alongside barrier methods	increases reliability of barrier methods	not reliable on their own, inconvenient

Other IUD	small device inserted into uterus by a doctor and remains there long-term, prevents implantation	relatively reliable	can cause pain, heavy periods, and infection, can lead to ectopic pregnancy**

sterilisation	in males the vas deferens is cut so sperm remain in body; in females the oviducts are cut so ova cannot reach the uterus	permanent and almost 100% reliable	not easy to reverse, requires anaesthetic (general in female)

*   Diseases such as syphilis and HIV infection can be reduced by using a barrier method e.g. a condom.

** Ectopic pregnancy occurs when a fetus begins developing in the oviduct or in the abdominal cavity.

Figure 29.5 This is a test kit for hormones in urine, which can be bought at pharmacies by women who wish to identify when they are most fertile during each menstrual cycle. Copulation can be avoided during these fertile days or an alternative form of contraception used. The kit stores information and builds up a fertility profile for a woman, claiming to be 93–95% effective.

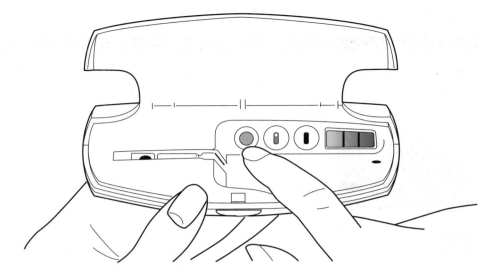

Increasing fertility

For the majority of couples, deciding to conceive a baby is an important and exciting decision which can be fulfilled within a few months. However, about one in ten couples do not conceive a baby after a year or more of trying. For some reason, the combined fertility of some couples is not sufficient to bring about pregnancy. In around 30 per cent of cases, the woman may be infertile and in another 30 per cent the male may be infertile. In the remaining cases, either both partners have lowered fertility, both are infertile, or there is no evident reason for infertility. In the past, many of these couples would have remained childless, but increasingly assisted reproductive technology is being developed to improve fertility. Table 29.3 describes some of the reasons for infertility.

Table 29.3 Reasons for infertility

Male	Female
spermatogenesis produces higher than usual proportion (>20%) of abnormal sperm	in rare cases the ovaries do not contain ova
poor health affects spermatogenesis – low sperm count	ovulation does not occur
hormonal imbalance	hormonal imbalance means that the uterus does not accept a fertilised ovum
blocked vas deferens	blocked oviducts
lack of a protein on the surface of sperm which enables them to bind to the surface of the egg	mucus at neck of cervix does not let sperm enter reproductive tract
genetic disorder: Klinefelter's syndrome (see Chapter 34.4)	genetic disorder: Turner's syndrome (see Chapter 34.4)
temperature increase of testes (e.g. if they are undescended)	woman's antibodies kill sperm

It is now possible to overcome many of the challenges associated with female infertility. **Fertility drugs** are synthetic hormones used to manipulate natural hormonal levels and hence ovulation. Since the technique has been developing over a period of years, multiple births which were once a common feature of this type of treatment are now far less common. **In vitro fertilisation (IVF)** is by far the greatest advance in improving fertility for many childless couples. The technique involves fertilising a woman's ova outside her body (with her partner's sperm if it is viable), allowing the zygotes to undergo a few cell divisions, and then returning them to her uterus, where they implant. Two or three fertilised eggs are returned to the uterus in case implantation is not successful for a particular egg. Naturally, this means that the chance of twins or triplets is increased. Other similar methods exist which are successful in cases of blocked oviducts. It is still necessary to harvest ova (an uncomfortable, expensive and time-consuming process) which are then mixed with sperm outside the body but these are then immediately placed back into the oviducts on the uterine side of a blockage. IVF is, however, expensive and the chances of success are relatively low. There is also a lack of donor eggs, especially for African and Asian women.

Moral dilemmas

The development of assisted reproductive technology has resulted in stores of frozen sperm and 'spare' embryos and means that fertility can be manipulated in many ways. Alongside this, genetic engineering means that the genetic code of a cell is no longer a secret, and that particular genes can be identified. Many embryos are used for research, but in the UK it is illegal to use embryos once they are over 14 days old.

IVF means that it is possible to look at the genome (genetic make-up) of a particular zygote while it is still outside the human body. Clearly, this is useful if you want to look for a particular inherited condition. Traditionally, a couple who are at risk of having children with inherited diseases have to wait for diagnosis from an aminocentesis test. Since this cannot be done until half way through the pregnancy, deciding on an option such as termination is very difficult and distressing. Some inherited diseases are sex-linked in which case males are likely to be affected (see page 376–378). Since the gender of a zygote can be determined, a couple could have the choice of implanting only female embryos if IVF was used.

Genetic engineering which enables the genetic code of a cell to be altered raises further debate. In the UK it is illegal to use gamete cells or embryos in this way, although it might in the future be possible to correct some inherited conditions, for example diabetes might be prevented by supplying a missing gene.

Genetic screening is analysing the genetic make-up of an individual, which is usually done because of a family history of inherited disease. **Genetic counselling** refers to the information and support a couple can be given who are at risk of having children with inherited diseases, because they carry particular genes.

Questions

1 Cystic fibrosis is an inherited disease in which very viscous mucus collects in the lungs and there are digestive problems (see page 366). Even with daily treatment, someone with cystic fibrosis is unlikely to live past young adulthood. If two people are carrying the cystic fibrosis gene, then every time they conceive a child there is a 25 per cent chance of the embryo inheriting the condition. About 1 in 25 people carry a gene for cystic fibrosis.

   a) In terms of planning a family, what are the possible options open to a couple who both carry a cystic fibrosis gene?

   b) How might IVF give the couple another option?

   c) In what ways might the ability to look at the genetic makeup of an embryo be abused by unscrupulous people?

2 Huntington's disease is a condition which only develops once someone reaches around 35 years of age. The symptoms are progressive dementia, involuntary muscle movements, wasting of tissues and finally death. It is caused by a dominant gene, so only one parent has to carry it for there to be a chance of passing it on to children. Unfortunately, people may have already started a family by the time they know. About 1 in 2700 people are carriers, and about 1 in 10 000 suffer from the disease at any time.

   a) What is the advantage of genetic screening to people in whose family there have been previous cases of Huntington's disease?

   b) Should everyone be compulsorily screened for this gene?

   c) Should people who carry the gene be prevented from having children?

CHAPTER 30 Health, Disease and Ageing

30.1 What is health?

Most people find it easy to describe how they feel when they are ill or not feeling well, but describing health can be more difficult. In 1984–5, an extensive health and lifestyle survey (HALS1) of 9000 people took place in Britain. It was a very detailed survey which collected data such as height and body mass, but also information about lifestyle: smoking and drinking habits, exercise and diet. Beliefs about health were questioned too, and a mental health questionnaire was completed on an optional basis. Overall, the survey sought to link lifestyle and circumstances to the physical and mental well-being of the British population. In 1991, 5352 of these same people were surveyed again (HALS2), so that trends over the seven year period could be analysed. Here are some of the comments about what health is from people who were surveyed:

''When you don't hurt anywhere and you're not aware of any part of your body.''
''I call her healthy because she goes jogging and doesn't eat fatty foods.''
''I can walk up the stairs to this flat, without a pause, sixteen flights . . . and I'm not out of breath.''
''I'm at peace with myself. Energetic, outgoing . . .''

In practice, medical professionals tend to define health as *'the condition in which there is an absence of disease or disability'*. Medical practice seeks to improve, sustain or maintain health by reducing disease and disability. The World Health Organisation (WHO) goes further than this, saying that health is *'not the mere absence of disease, but total physical, mental and social well-being'*. Therefore, health is a broad concept which takes into account not only the functioning of the body and mind in clinical terms, but also how happy we feel and how we perceive our own health – our quality of life. The following factors have a great influence on our quality of life:

- Mobility – the ability to get about independently, with or without aid.
- The ability to work – in order to feel self-worth and that we contribute to society.
- The ability to look after ourselves – to feed ourselves adequately, maintain hygiene, and to attend to the basic necessities of life.
- Pain – continual pain is stressful and affects all of life.

Mental health and happiness

Suicide is rarely chosen unless the mind is clouded with depression. Of the people who commit suicide:

- 90% have some form of mental disorder
- 66% have consulted their GP in the previous month
- 40% have consulted their GP the previous week

> Chapter 13.6 is concerned with keeping fit

> Chapter 23 considers diet

Health and disease affect the quality of life.

(a)

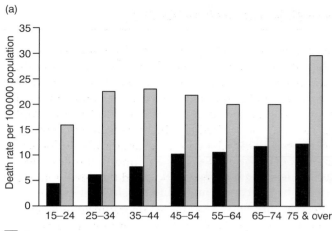

Females

Males

(b)

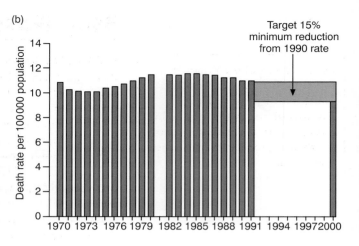

Figure 30.1 A government objective is to reduce the amount of suicide by improving mental health. (a) Suicide related to age (b) Total suicides 1969–1992, including a government target for 2000.

- 33% have expressed clear suicidal intent
- 25% are psychiatric outpatients

Depression is a debilitating illness which affects about 5 per cent of the world's population, influencing their enjoyment of life. The symptoms of depression include sadness, suicidal thoughts, irritability, headaches, fatigue, sleeplessness, loss of sex drive and loss of self esteem. More women suffer from depression than men.

By examining brain tissues of depressed people after their death, it is known that there is a reduced level of a neurotransmitter called 5-HT (5-hydroxytryptamine). Some anti-depressants which are effective in treating depression raise the level of 5-HT in the brain, but at the same time they may interact with other neurotransmitters and cause side effects. The search is still on for more selective medicines which would be effective at low concentrations, but only interact with specific receptors to bring about the desired effect.

Questions

1 Why are both physical and mental health important aspects of a happy lifestyle?

2 a) What are the main trends for the data on suicide shown in Figure 30.1 (a)?

   b) Suggest reasons why occupation might be a factor in the rate of suicide.

3 a) In what ways can we influence how healthy we are?

   b) Suggest some factors which affect health, that are out of an individual's control.

   c) What is the government's role in ensuring a healthy lifestyle for a population?

4 How is the topic of health dealt with by the media? Is it an important social issue?

5 Suggest reasons why people continue to carry on activities, such as smoking, which they know damage their health.

30.2 Patterns in disease

Development of medicines such as antibiotics have reduced infectious diseases globally. Patterns of disease vary globally, but in the UK the main causes of death are coronary heart disease and cancer.

Until a 100 years or so ago, in Britain most people died from infectious diseases. Medical treatments normally took place in a person's home at the bedside, since the hospitals which existed were intended for sick people who lived in poverty. The main method of diagnosis was observation, enhanced by the use of simple tools such as a stethoscope. Chemical testing of samples such as blood or urine was rare and limited. By the mid-twentieth century medical knowledge and technology had increased dramatically, influencing the diagnosis and treatment of disease. Clearly, two important milestones in preventing death from infection were immunisation and the development of antibiotics.

Antibiotics in particular have had a huge impact on modern medicine and the enormous range currently available work in a variety of ways. **Bacteriostatic** antibiotics slow or halt the growth of bacteria, while **bacteriocidal** antibiotics kill bacteria. Antibiotics such as penicillin, cephalosporin and vancomycin inhibit the synthesis of the bonds that strengthen bacterial cell walls: the walls are weak and the bacteria break open. Chloramphenicol, tetracycline, erythromycin and streptomycin all interfere with protein synthesis by binding to bacterial ribosomes, but not to those of human cells. Other types of antibiotics interfere with nucleic acid synthesis in bacterial cells.

Despite these huge advances in the developed world, in developing countries infectious diseases are still important in the pattern of mortality. Nowadays the main causes of death in Britain are non-infectious, such as coronary heart disease and cancers (see *Are heart attacks catching?* on the opposite page). The increased incidence of these diseases may be due to lifestyle changes, but are probably exacerbated by the increase in longevity. The longer people live the more likely it is that toxins accumulate and cause cell damage, leading to the onset of cancer.

Antibodies and disease treatment

Antibodies are used in treatments and in diagnosis of human diseases such as HIV infection. For example, many diagnostic kits contain antibodies linked to other molecules such as enzymes; when the antibody links with its specific antigen, the enzyme brings about a colour change – even in very low concentrations of the antigen. This technique is known as **ELISA (enzyme-linked immunosorbent assay)**. ELISA is a very quick process in comparison to the standard methods of growing micro-organisms from samples taken from a patient. Kits are available for detecting specific microbial antigens, so that results can be back with a patient almost immediately.

Figure 30.2 Pea pods may become a fresh store of medical drugs

Antibodies are currently produced by genetically engineered bacteria in fermentation vats. The bacteria have been given the human genes needed to produce the antibodies, which are proteins that pass out of the bacteria and into the solution within the vat. It is expensive to collect a pure sample of the antibody, which has to be free of the bacteria that produced it as well as from contaminating bacteria.

However a new technique is now being pioneered, which uses plants to produce these valuable products. Plants are genetically engineered to produce an antibody in their seeds, which remains in a usable condition for up to a year. Perhaps this is not surprising since seeds are specially adapted to store substances such as proteins, and to keep them functionally active. The techniques for harvesting the antibodies from seeds are still being researched, but the approach looks promising.

Are heart attacks catching?

Chlamydia pneumoniae is an airborne bacterium that is spread by coughs and sneezes, but it's at the centre of a controversy over heart disease. Some scientists believe that it is somehow linked to coronary heart disease, and the evidence is mounting:

- people with coronary heart disease are likely to have high levels of antibodies to the bacterium;
- DNA and proteins from the bacterium are in the diseased tissue that blocks coronary arteries;
- one team of researchers has grown the bacterium from diseased tissues removed from a patient about to have a heart transplant.

The significance of this research is that if this bacterium is involved in some cases of heart disease, even if not all of them, it could be cured by taking an antibiotic such as tetracycline or erythromycin. *Chlamydia* is notoriously hard to grow, and other scientists have failed to isolate it from diseased heart tissue.

Alongside this research, other studies have added to the debate about why the rate of coronary heart disease has been dropping since around the late 1960s. For example, surveys have shown that a low birth weight in babies and undernourishment in infancy predisposes to heart disease in later life. The suggestion is that the majority of people who were born between the turn of the century and the 1930s were probably undernourished when very young, and therefore suffered a greater risk of heart disease later on in life. But people born after the 1930s benefited from better nutrition and as a consequence were less likely to have heart disease in later life (around the 1970s), which accounts for the drop in coronary heart disease.

The controversy and the research continue: one approach is to investigate heart attack patients by giving some of them medicines to break up blood clots, while others receive both this medicine and an antibiotic to kill any *Chlamydia* infection. The idea is to compare the

survival rate of both groups of patients to see if those with antibiotic treatment have a higher survival rate. This may provide another piece of evidence in the jigsaw.

Source: *New Scientist*, June 1996

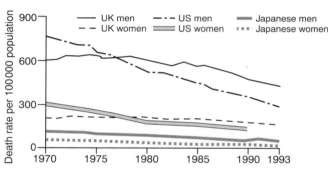

Figure 30.3 The death rate from heart disease has been steadily dropping since the late 1960s, which coincides with the time when 'broad spectrum' antibiotics such as tetracycline were first introduced

Questions

1 Why is the suggestion that bacteria might be the cause of some heart attacks significant medically?

2 Why are some scientists

a) convinced that *Chlamydia* does cause a certain proportion of heart attacks?

b) sceptical of the importance of *Chlamydia* as a causative factor?

3 a) Suggest how an investigation like the one outlined in the passage might be organised. Include your ideas on the nature and size of the sample group to be investigated, and the type of data which might be collected.

b) If a suitable screening test was available, would it be worthwhile (i) medically and (ii) financially?

30.3 Immunity

In brief at the start of Section 2 described the interaction of various body systems, including those involved in the defence against disease. Playing a key part in the body's armoury of defences is the **immune system**, which deals with infection through an **immune response**. This is principally brought about by lymphocytes within the blood system and the lymphatic system. The immune system is able to distinguish between the cells (or some cell components such as proteins) that are part of an individual, and those which are not. In other words, the human body can detect the difference between its own cells and 'non-self' cells. By recognising non-self cells and responding to them, the immune system can kill invading disease-causing organisms.

There are two types of lymphocytes involved in the immune system, **T-cells** and **B-cells**, which respond in different ways to the presence of antigens. Both these types of cells are produced from lymphocyte stem cells in bone marrow. T-cells migrate to lymph nodes via the thymus gland where they are activated in the first few months after birth. The B-cells appear to be activated by bone marrow, the liver and spleen, and migrate to lymph nodes before birth.

> ▶ *Chapter 2 introduces the concept of cell recognition*

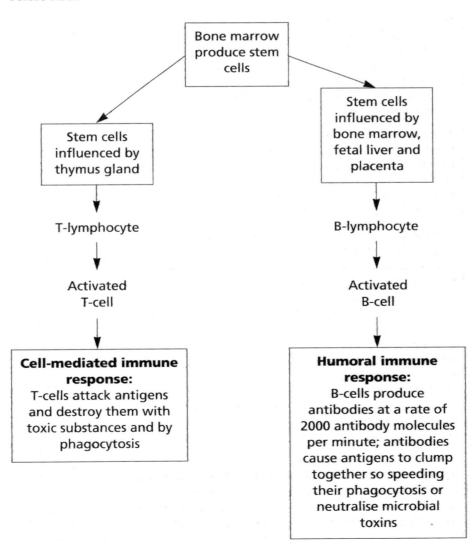

Figure 30.4 Lymphocytes in the blood and lymphatic system defend the body against infection by pathogens

T-cells act at the site of an infection such as a wound, binding to antigens and destroying them. At the same time, some T-cells divide rapidly, producing many more cells which attack the invading antigen. B-cells respond to antigens by dividing to form **plasma clone cells**, and some **memory cells**. In what is known as the **humoral response**, plasma clone cells rapidly produce antibodies and release them into blood plasma. Antibodies are globular proteins known as **immunoglobulins**, which can defend the body in the following ways:

1 antibodies can prevent pathogens entering host cells;
2 antibodies may bind to antigens, causing them to clump together or **agglutinate**, so they cannot infect more host cells;
3 antibodies may bind to antigens and make them more readily engulfed and digested by phagocytes;
4 an antigen–antibody complex may stimulate the destruction of an antigen surface membrane if it has one.

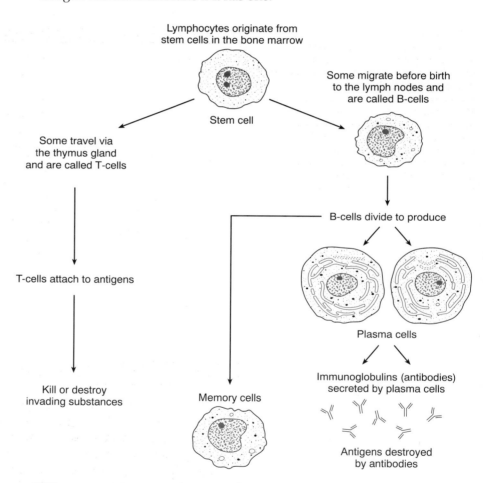

Lymphocytes originate from stem cells in the bone marrow

Stem cell

Some migrate before birth to the lymph nodes and are called B-cells

Some travel via the thymus gland and are called T-cells

T-cells attach to antigens

B-cells divide to produce

Plasma cells

Kill or destroy invading substances

Memory cells

Immunoglobulins (antibodies) secreted by plasma cells

Antigens destroyed by antibodies

Figure 30.5 T-cells and B-cells tackle the problem of destroying antigens in different ways

Different types of immunity

When we come into contact with non-self antigens, the immune system actively produces antibodies to destroy them. This is **natural active immunity**. During the first few days of suckling, a human infant receives ready-made immunoglobulins in the initial flow of the breast milk (called **colostrum**), which gives protection before the baby's own immune system becomes fully active. Since the infant does not produce the antibodies itself, this is **natural passive immunity**.

Acquired active immunity is caused by a vaccine containing a small amount of antigen. The antigen is not normally the living micro-organism itself, as this could prove fatal. Instead, a safe antigen is used which might be:

- a bacterial toxin which has been detoxified;
- dead viruses or bacteria;
- attenuated organisms which have been made harmless by modifying them in some way, although they are still alive.

Acquired active immunity causes the normal immune response, so memory cells are produced and the protection is long-term.

Acquired passive immunity involves supplying ready-made antibodies which are injected directly into the bloodstream. They give short-term protection and might be used in an emergency situation, or where there is a possibility of someone being exposed to a dangerous antigen e.g. tetanus.

Table 30.1 Immunisation protects a child from diseases such as tuberculosis and poliomyelitis, which are usually fatal. But a far-reaching effect is the protection of the whole population, since immunised people do not spread disease. There is no doubt that systematic immunisation programmes are hugely successful in raising the health of a population. The programme of immunisation changes as new vaccines are developed e.g. combined hepatitis A and B, which is soon to be available.

Age	Immunisation against
2 months	diphtheria
3 months	tetanus
4 months	poliomyelitis
	pertussis (whooping cough)
	HIB (one form of meningitis)
13 months	MMR (measles, mumps, rubella)
4½ years (pre-school booster)	diphtheria
	tetanus
	poliomyelitis
	MMR
12 years	BCG – tuberculosis (TB)
14 years	diphtheria
	tetanus
	poliomyelitis

30.4 Medical horizons

Advances in medicine and technology have brought us to the current position, whereby most infections and many clinical conditions can be successfully treated to alleviate symptoms, or provide a cure. Nevertheless, as medical knowledge increases new discoveries and new approaches will be made. What are the frontiers for medical science? Firstly, in the area of drug development, there is the potential to design new medicines which work more effectively than existing ones. This is a necessity rather than just desirable, if organisms become resistant because of repeated exposure to a particular drug (see *Tuberculosis – on the increase*). What's more, to date there are some diseases for which there are no specific drug treatments. Furthermore, in terms of epidemiology, new diseases arise about which we need to collect much information, such as HIV infection and AIDS, and others such as CJD (Creuzfeld–Jacob disease) which are not yet fully understood.

Tuberculosis – on the increase

Tuberculosis or TB is an infection which infects the body through the lungs. In 1995, TB killed almost three million people – the highest death toll from the disease to date. The causative bacterium, *Mycobacterium tuberculosis*, was discovered in the late nineteenth century, but was only tackled with success once antibiotics such as streptomycin were introduced around 50 years ago. Wealthy countries were able to implement large scale and well supervised programmes, but the story in developing countries was very different. Arata Kochi of The World Health Organisation (WHO) believes that in some cases treating people with TB has done more harm than good: patients who were not completely cured but appeared well returned home to infect other people. TB has now reached epidemic proportions, and is not restricted to developing countries. The chairman of the British Lung Foundation suggests that the incidence of TB in East London is higher than in Tanzania, and the incidence in America is rising.

Drug-resistant TB can emerge if the wrong medicines are prescribed or if people do not finish a course of treatment: refugees are at risk because they may not stay in one place long enough. There has been a major outbreak of drug-resistant TB in New York over the past few years and Britain saw its first case in 1995. Clearly, the fight to conquer this particular infectious disease is still on. Scientists are currently working on a new approach: a DNA vaccine. The idea is to use DNA coding for TB antigen in a vaccine. Within a person's body cells, the DNA would instruct cells to make TB antigen, which would then cause an effective immune response.

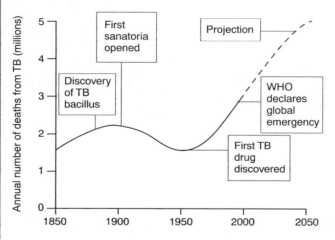

Figure 30.6 The BCG vaccine is no longer effective as a public health measure in developing countries because it protects only 50–80 per cent of infants and does not cure the infectious adult form of the disease

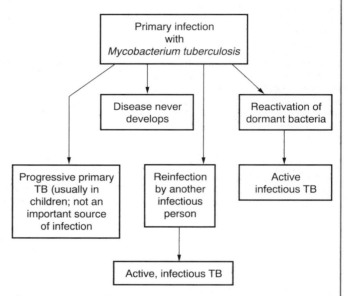

Figure 30.7 *Mycobacterium tuberculosis* is an airborne bacterium, spread by someone who is actually ill with TB through coughs and sneezes. Every second someone is newly infected with TB, but infection is more common than disease. Only 5–10 per cent of people newly infected with TB will go on to develop clinical symptoms straight away. Precisely what happens following primary infection appears to depend greatly on the state of the person's immune system, which may mount an effective and protective immune response.

HIV and AIDS

HIV is the human immunodeficiency virus, which infects a range of body cells, particularly a type of white blood cell called **helper T-cells** or **T4 lymphocytes**. Despite its far-reaching effects in the body, it is very fragile outside it and does not survive in the air. It passes from one person to another through body fluids in these ways:

• during exchange of semen and vaginal fluid during sexual intercourse;

- in blood e.g. when intravenous drug users share syringes;
- in blood products (such as clotting factors used by haemophiliacs) which have not been treated to destroy the virus (in Europe all blood products are treated to kill HIV, and are routinely tested);
- from mother to child during pregnancy (low risk) or during birth.

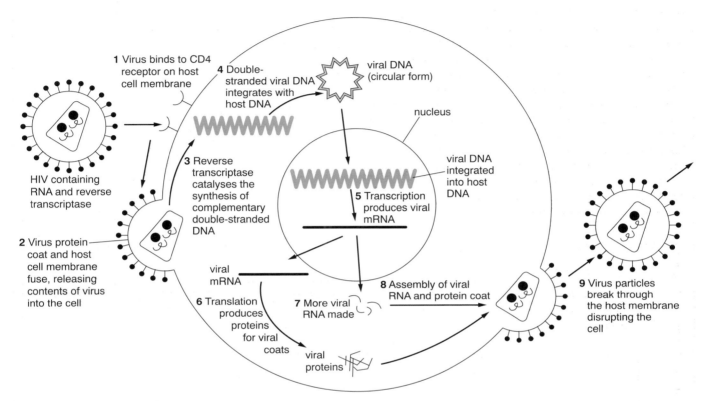

1 Virus binds to CD4 receptor on host cell membrane

4 Double-stranded viral DNA integrates with host DNA

viral DNA (circular form)

nucleus

3 Reverse transcriptase catalyses the synthesis of complementary double-stranded DNA

viral DNA integrated into host DNA

HIV containing RNA and reverse transcriptase

5 Transcription produces viral mRNA

2 Virus protein coat and host cell membrane fuse, releasing contents of virus into the cell

viral mRNA

8 Assembly of viral RNA and protein coat

9 Virus particles break through the host membrane disrupting the cell

6 Translation produces proteins for viral coats

7 More viral RNA made

viral proteins

Figure 30.8 HIV infection of T4 lymphocytes. Helper T-cells appear to be vulnerable to HIV infection because of a specific glycoprotein on the surface membrane. This acts as a receptor for HIV to which they attach.

HIV is a virus particle less than 0.1 μm in diameter, belonging to the group called retroviruses. These viruses contain an enzyme known as reverse transcriptase, which is vital in its infection process. Once inside a helper T-cell, the reverse transcriptase causes the host cell to translate viral RNA to DNA. The DNA enters the nucleus and acts as part of the human DNA. Later, usually after some months or even many years of dormancy, some helper T-cells appear to be triggered into action. The DNA corresponding to the original viral RNA instructs the cell's biochemistry to produce many new RNA molecules and protein coats which assemble as core virus units. As the units break their way out of the helper T-cell they collect plasma membrane from the lysed host cell. The new generations of virus particles spread infection rapidly to other tissues in the body, such as brain tissue and bone marrow.

Altogether the effects of HIV are devastating to the immune system. In attacking the helper T-cells, HIV acts at a key point in the immune system: helper T-cells amplify the responses of other cells within the immune system, and the effectivenss of the system is hugely reduced. As a result, the body is unable to fight off other infections which it normally would. When this stage is reached, a person develops AIDS (acquired immunodeficiency syndrome) and typically presents a collection of symptoms caused by infective organisms, such as pneumonia, as well as a rare form of cancer.

Figure 30.9 The protein core of the HIV particle is antigen p24. Antibody IgM is produced in response to p24 at the onset of HIV infection. At a later stage p24 antibody (IgG) is produced in response to antigen p24 giving longer term protection during the latent phase of HIV infection. gp41 antibody (IgG) is produced in response to gp41, which is a glycoprotein near the surface of the particle.

Testing for HIV

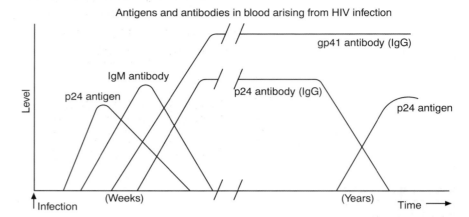

When someone is infected with HIV, the protein coat of the virus particles acts as an antigen, and the immune system responds by making antibodies against the virus. These antibodies can be detected in a sample of blood. It usually takes a few weeks to months for the level of antibodies to accumulate in the person's blood, so during this phase an HIV test may show a negative result indicating that antibodies to HIV have not been found. A positive result means that antibodies to HIV have been found.

HIV subtype E reaches the UK

In Asia, most people who are HIV-positive are heterosexual, while in the West, most people with HIV are homosexual men. For example in the UK around 5000 people are thought to have contracted HIV through heterosexual contact, making up about 19 per cent of the total confirmed cases of HIV infection. The variant of HIV which is most common in eastern countries such as Thailand is known as subtype E, which seems more able to infect the lining of the vagina and the tip of the penis than other subtypes. More evidence may be needed to prove that heterosexuals are at greater risk of infection from subtype E, although it is accepted that different subtypes vary in how effective they are at causing infection. Monitoring the incidence of the different subtypes is vital in monitoring the **epidemiology** of HIV infection, or how the disease spreads through a population.

Source: *New Scientist*, 3 August 1996

Parasites

A **parasite** is an organism that relies on its host for a source of nutrition, metabolic products or other vital conditions for life. Parasites can greatly influence the growth and size of a population because of their damaging or fatal effects. To be successful, a parasite must be able to:

- enter or attach to a host and remain there;
- extract nutritional or metabolic requirements;
- resist the host's immune response;
- remain alive while outside the host;
- find a way of reaching new hosts.

Endoparasites live within the body of a host, while **ectoparasites** live externally. To enter a host, a parasite must be able to penetrate the host's defences. Therefore a cut in the skin is a break in the physical barrier that normally protects us against infection. Mucus membranes such as those in the respiratory system and the reproductive system are also vulnerable to infection by organisms that enter as we breathe. Another infection route is via the gut, when materials enter the mouth and are swallowed, including food and drink. The following examples illustrate some of the general points about the success of parasites.

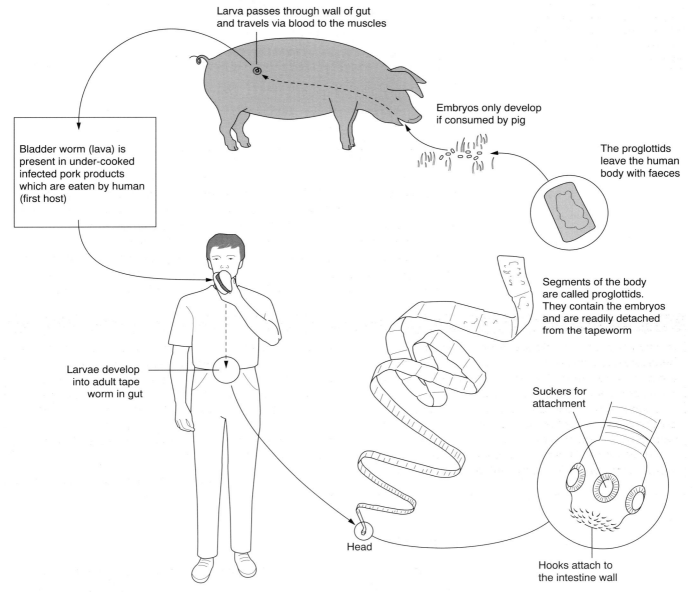

Larva passes through wall of gut and travels via blood to the muscles

Bladder worm (lava) is present in under-cooked infected pork products which are eaten by human (first host)

Embryos only develop if consumed by pig

The proglottids leave the human body with faeces

Segments of the body are called proglottids. They contain the embryos and are readily detached from the tapeworm

Larvae develop into adult tape worm in gut

Suckers for attachment

Head

Hooks attach to the intestine wall

Figure 30.10 The tapeworm is a highly adapted parasite, which may grow to over three metres long. Each proglottid can contain up to 40 000 eggs, which pass out in the host's faeces, ready to infect another host which ingests them.

Salmonella is an opportunist parasite which causes food poisoning in humans if a sufficient number of live bacteria (around ten million at one time) are consumed. *Salmonella* are found in animal intestines, and meat can become contaminated at the time of slaughter. If the meat is not stored properly the bacteria multiply to levels at which they can potentially cause a problem. Both meat which is not properly cooked and eggs are common sources of *Salmonella*, however, these bacteria are killed by thorough cooking. While in the host's intestines, soluble food passes by diffusion into the bacterial cells and is readily metabolised. The symptoms of food poisoning include vomiting and diarrhoea, abdominal pain and fever. The young, elderly or people weakened by other illnesses are most at risk from food poisoning, and since water and electrolytes are lost in large quantities from the body they may become **dehydrated**. Replacing the fluid, or **rehydration,** is the most important aspect of treatment, since the pathogen usually only remains in the gut for a few days and passes out in the faeces or is dealt with by the body's immune system. Other organisms which cause food poisoning include some types of *Escherichia* and *Shigella*, as well as some *Amoeba*.

Parasitic tropical diseases

Parasitic tropical diseases affect many millions of people who live in countries which often do not have the resources to treat people, or to implement preventative methods. For example, around 200 million people in over 70 countries are infected by parasitic flatworms which cause schistosomiasis, a debilitating disease affecting particularly the urinary tract and gut. However, an even more widely spread disease is malaria, affecting probably 300 million people in over 100 countries. Malaria causes a cycle of severe fevers which weaken the body and can result in death. Both schistosomiasis and malaria involve a secondary host known as a **vector**, which transfers the parasite to humans. Mosquitos are the vectors which carry malarial parasites (*Plasmodium*) to humans in their saliva. The saliva becomes mixed with blood when mosquitos pierce the skin to feed. *Plasmodium* has a very complex life cycle which is summarised in Figure 30.11. In common with most parasites, *Plasmodium* can multiply very rapidly, which it does within the liver cells and blood cells of the human host. The final stage of the cycle in humans results in the production of resistant gametes in the blood, which are taken in by the vector when it feeds.

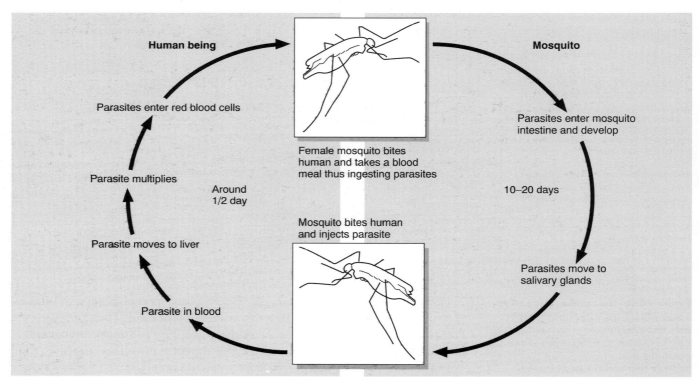

Figure 30.11 Hope is in sight for the future with a promising development in vaccination

Questions

1   Which type of immunity is provided by these events:

   a) immunoglobulins passing to a fetus across the placenta?

   b) recovering from a bout of influenza?

c) injecting with antibodies to prevent symptoms developing in a person who has recently been in contact with an infectious disease?

d) having a vaccination for cholera?

2 a) Suggest reasons why some infectious diseases such as TB, which were once decreasing, are on the increase again.

b) Is immunisation a social responsibility?

3 a) Imagine someone who thinks that they may be at risk of infection from HIV. What issues might they consider before deciding whether to be tested for HIV?

b) Compile a list of pros and cons of being tested.

30.5 Getting old – senescence

What is ageing?

In adulthood by the mid-twenties and up to the age of about 30 years, people reach a peak of physical performance, when their muscle strength, cardiac growth and the functioning of body tissues generally is at a maximum. However, this peak is only maintained for a few years, after which there is a gradual decline in physiological effectiveness – or how well the body works. The changes which result from ageing are known collectively as **senescence**. The rate at which ageing occurs varies between individuals, but the outward signs of ageing are generally noticeable by middle age. For example, the skin develops wrinkles because it becomes less elastic when the cross-linkages between collagen fibres decrease, hair loses coloration and hair loss is common.

Changing with age

People can make positive decisions about maintaining their own optimum health level, for example by choosing a good diet and exercising regularly as well as avoiding known toxins and carcinogens, such as those present in cigarette smoke. The earlier we pay attention to such issues the more likely we are to maximise our potential lifespan. Even so, from around the age of 30 years there is a steady decline in the efficiency of the body, influenced by both genetic and environmental factors. This decline is seen in the major body systems and is partly due to **cell ageing** or a decrease in the rate of cell division. As a result people become less able to withstand infection, and they recover more slowly from injury. There is a reduction in cardiac output and so circulation is not as efficient, which affects both the rate at which cells are supplied with nutrients and the rate toxins are removed from the tissues. The rate of metabolism reduces in general, and people often become less active, requiring less energy supply. Because of this there may be a tendency to put on more body mass, and the ratio of fat to muscle may increase – hence the expression 'middle age spread'. Yet regular and sustained exercise does increase the rate at which lung and heart tissues are replaced, helping to counteract cell ageing, and can also increase the body's metabolic rate. Within the nervous system there is a reduction in the speed at which nerve impulses are transmitted, which slows down response time, including reflex actions.

▶ *Chapter 23.3 gives data on BMR related to age*

Neurological diseases

Brain cells are irreplaceable, and so their loss through injury or disease is permanent. A relatively small number of brain cells die through the natural ageing process on a daily basis. However, **neurodegeneration** is the loss of brain cells on a much larger scale. There are many causes affecting the young as well as elderly. Suffering a stroke is one of the commonest causes of brain damage, affecting about one person in the UK every five minutes. This is an example of an *acute* neurodegeneration, because it happens very rapidly. The effects of a stroke depend on the part of the brain affected. Other types of neurodegeneration, such as Alzheimer's disease, are *chronic* because the loss of mental ability happens gradually.

Table 30.2 Causes of neurodegeneration

Disease	Approximate number of people affected per year in the UK
dementia including Alzheimer's disease	700 000
stroke	130 000
Parkinson's disease	110 000
head injury	13 000
multiple sclerosis	5000

Neurological deterioration which occurs with age is called **senile dementia**, and many thousands of people in the UK are affected by this distressing condition. A five-year study is currently underway to assess more clearly the extent of dementia in the UK. The exact number of people with dementia at any time partly depends on the rate at which it progresses, since in the early stages it is difficult to distinguish from the normal symptoms of ageing. The Medical Research Council are funding a study of 18 500 people in five different centres. Often it is the cerebral functions and conscious thought processes which are particularly affected, so a sufferer has a challenge recognising people, remembering things and understanding what is going on around them. Autonomic functions are not necessarily affected, and body functions such as continence may not deteriorate.

Alzheimer's disease is a form of senile dementia, which in most cases begins to develop in elderly people. Less commonly, younger people develop Alzheimer's disease and there is debate about why this occurs.

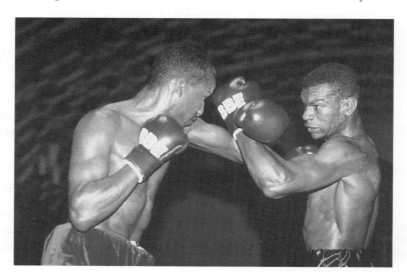

Figure 30.12 Punches score problems for the future, since they cause brain damage

It is likely that some forms of Alzheimer's disease are inherited due to a mutation on chromosome 21, causing an abnormal rate of production and breakdown of a protein, B-amyloid. This collects in solid masses called **plaques**, destroying areas of the brain. The risk of Alzheimer's and related neurodegeneration is increased by brain injury. Similar plaques of amyloid have been found in the brains of boxers (e.g. a 23-year-old boxer who died in the ring as a direct result of a brain haemorrhage), as well as in many older ex-boxers.

Ageing in men – the prostate problem

As sperm are ejaculated they pass the prostate gland which adds secretions to neutralise any traces of urine in the urethra, and also helps sperm mobility. In elderly men it is common for the prostate to enlarge because of infection and inflammation, or because of tumours which may be benign or malignant. If a tumour is **benign** it is non-cancerous, while **malignant** tumours consist of cancerous cells. Clearly the latter type of tumour has the potential to be life-threatening, and in fact prostate cancer is the third commonest cancer death for men after lung and bowel cancer, killing about 34 in every 100 000. As the prostate enlarges it presses on the urethra which it surrounds and narrows or blocks the tube, obstructing the flow of urine. If urine is not emptied from the bladder as regularly as is optimal, infections are more likely to become established and the kidneys may be affected too. At this stage, surgical removal of all or part of the prostate or radiotherapy treatment may be necessary.

Examination of prostate tissue after death suggests that the potential for prostate cancer is common: 30 per cent of men over 50 years of age and more than 50 per cent of men over the age of 80 have tissue evidence of prostate cancer at death, despite having no symptoms during life. Although there may be some cancerous cells present, the condition only advances quickly in some men, leading to premature death. It is possible to test for prostate cancer by measuring levels of PSA (serum prostate specific antigen), as raised levels of this antigen occur with the disease. The aim of a screening programme is to identify early on the cases of prostate cancer which will become invasive and shorten life. Screening all men over a certain age has been suggested as a way of lowering the death rate from this disease. The following points may be considered:

- the test only identifies the presence of cancerous cells, not which cells will advance to cause clinical problems;
- there are adverse physical and psychological effects of the screening process itself;
- the treatment may affect the quality of life and longevity.

The value of screening is still debatable. Some scientists suggest that it may not be a solution, since the evidence of cancer cells alone does not determine who has the type of cancer which advances rapidly and who does not. However, it is true that early diagnosis of the malignant type is an important factor in survival rates.

Ageing in women – the menopause

The menstrual cycle is a regular pattern of changes which happens in a woman's reproductive system throughout the reproductive stage in life, beginning at puberty. At a certain stage, around 45–50 years of age, there is a decline in the level of response of the ovaries to the hormones FSH and

LH. As a result of this, less follicles mature, the production of ova tails off, and oestrogen production by the ovaries falls. Finally, a woman does not have periods any longer, a stage called the **menopause**. These changes take a few years to occur and over that period of time the decreasing level of oestrogen has effects in various tissues, such as the vasomotor nervous system. This sometimes leads to symptoms including flushes and hot sweats, headaches and palpatations. Also, there is a tendancy in the long-term to increasing bone porosity, as calcium withdraws from the deposits in bone. Earlier in life oestrogen protects the body against high blood pressure, as it prevents the formation of cholesterol inside blood vessels. But as the oestrogen level falls after the menopause, there is increased deposition of cholesterol in the blood, a decline in the resilience of blood vessels and therefore increased blood pressure.

Hormone replacement therapy (HRT)

About 85 per cent of women experience some symptoms around menopause, varying from slight to extreme. Depending on how difficult these symptoms are, women may opt for HRT. The basic idea behind this treatment is to replace to a certain extent the oestrogen which the ovaries are producing at a declining and erratic level. Progesterone is included for most women, to counteract the increased incidence of endometrial cancer. There is no doubt that HRT has huge benefits for many women, but despite this there are questions about its use in the long-term (Table 30.3).

Table 30.3 The pros and cons of HRT

Proven benefits	relieves hot flushes and night sweats; reduces bone loss and incidence of broken bones; relieves dryness and discomfort in the vagina
Likely benefits	reduces risk of heart disease (lowering cholesterol); reduces colon cancer; reduces mood swings and memory lapses; keeps the skin in better condition
Proven risks	increase risk of cancer of the lining of the uterus; possible return of menstrual bleeding and pre-menstrual tension symptoms such as fluid retention; may increase benign fibroid growths in the uterus
Likely risks	increased incidence of breast cancer and blood clots (thrombosis); increased body mass; increased headaches; increased risk of gall stones

Why do we age?

Biological ageing is not completely understood. Many studies contributing to what we know point to the idea that there may be a collection of factors or reasons for ageing. The evidence to date is mostly based on studies of cultured cells *in vitro*, and some evidence from observations of whole individuals.

- Cells only undergo about 50 divisions when cultured outside the body, even though they may have sustained optimum growing conditions. What's more, the number of divisions is reduced in cells from ageing individuals, including those of a younger chronological age who have an inherited form of early ageing called Werner's disease. This has led to the idea that ageing is intracellular (Hayflick, 1961).

- There are genetic factors involved since people can inherit the condition of premature ageing. Studies of people who age early suggest that there are genes which promote ageing once they are activated, as if 'ageing genes' act as a genetic clock. However, other people consider that these genes may influence longevity rather than the rate of ageing.

- The thymus gland is responsible for making lymphocytic stem cells immunologically active in the first few months after birth. However, the thymus degenerates by the end of adolescence and becomes less important in the immune response. Overall, the immune system is less effective in fighting infections, and there is more likelihood of autoimmune diseases (such as multiple sclerosis) developing as we age. Could the immune system be a 'clock' which triggers ageing?

- Mitochondrial DNA and the membranes of mitochondria are damaged during a person's lifetime, probably due to free radicals which are very oxidising chemicals present in all cells. The mitochondria become less effective at respiration and so there is a less efficient energy supply for cellular processes (Miguel, 1992).

▶ *Chapter 30.3 describes the immune system*

▶ *Chapter 19 gives details of the endocrine system*

Increasingly, it seems that the accumulation of various chemicals within cells as well as disruption of DNA probably accounts for the lack of cell maintenance and division which contributes to senescence.

Longevity – how long we live

Few humans live to over 100 years, although some people live a lot longer than others despite more difficult living conditions. Most people now expect to live to a 'ripe old age', yet in doing so we are likely to suffer age-associated disability and disease. What scientists aim to do is to understand the risk factors and mechanisms of age-related disease and tackle the causes, so that extending life actually means increasing the time we have a good quality of life. There seems little point in increasing longevity for its own sake.

Table 30.4 Depending on others

Age group at death	Number of years of dependency before death	
	men	women
65–69	3.8	8.9
70–74	3.7	7.9
75–79	3.1	6.1
80–84	3.4	5.0
85+	3.2	4.9

Table 30.4 shows that the older someone is during their independent years, the less time they are likely to be dependent on others before death.

Studying twins is especially useful in exploring the connection between longevity and inheritance, as shown by the data in Table 30.4. **Monozygotic twins** develop from one fertilised egg and so these are identical, whereas **dizygotic twins** develop from two fertilised eggs.

▶ *Chapter 27.3 covers fertilisation*

Table 30.5 The longevity of twins

Age group of the first twin of a pair to die (years)	Average within-pair differences in longevity (months)				
	Single-egg twins		Two-egg twins		
			same sex		opposite sex
	male	female	male	female	
60–75	47.6	24.0	107.9	88.7	109.7
all pairs >60	47.6	29.4	89.1	61.3	126.6

Table 30.6 contains data about the effect of parental age of death on how long their offspring live. This data may add credibility to the idea that there are 'ageing genes' and that genetic factors mostly influence the rate of ageing and longevity.

Table 30.6 Will you live for longer if your parents do?

| Sex of offspring | Average age at death | | | | | |
| | Mother's age at death | | | Father's age at death | | |
	60 or less	61–80	81 or more	60 or less	61–80	81 or more
male	67.6	71.4	73.2	67.0	69.3	70.9
female	73.8	74.1	77.2	73.0	73.5	73.3
average of male/female	70.9	72.8	75.1	69.8	71.4	72.1

Questions

1 a) What are the main effects of ageing?

   b) Does ageing necessarily affect the quality of life?

2 a) What is neurodegeneration?

   b) How does stroke cause neurodegeneration?

3 Screening for disease can provide the early warning needed to give life-saving treatment. Why is screening for prostate cancer not yet routine?

4 a) Why is there still a debate about the usefulness of HRT?

   b) What factors might help a woman decide whether or not HRT was appropriate for her?

   c) Suggest how information about the effects of menopause and HRT might be collected.

5 a) Why is the rate of cell division important to tissue maintenance?

   b) Suggest reasons why the effects of ageing have implications for society as a whole.

6 a) To what extent does the data in Table 30.5 provide evidence in favour of the genetic theory of ageing?

   b) Does the data in Table 30.6 support the idea that long-lived parents give rise to long-lived children? If so, does this agree with the evidence in Table 30.5?

1 Figure 1 shows the responses to *two* identical doses of the same antigen.

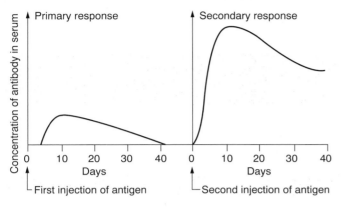

Figure 1

a) i) Identify *two* differences between the responses shown. *(1 mark)*

   ii) Briefly explain the mechanism which accounts for these differences. *(3 marks)*

b) How many days after the first injection should the second injection be given? Explain your answer. *(1 mark)*

AEB Specimen Question

2 An investigation was carried out into the relationship between the birth mass of human babies and concentrations of lead and zinc in the mother's placenta. The results are shown in Figure 2 (a) and (b). Each bar represents the mean of many measurements.

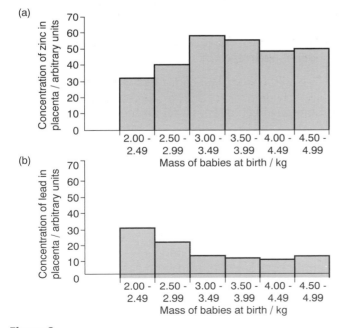

Figure 2

a) Describe the relationship between (i) placental lead and birth mass and (ii) placental zinc and birth mass. Suggest an explanation for each relationship. *(3 marks for each)*

b) Suggest how metal ions such as lead and zinc might pass from the environment to the placenta. *(2 marks)*

c) State *three* other factors that can affect the birth mass of human babies. *(3 marks)*

Edexcel

3 Read through the following account of the hormonal control of the human menstrual cycle and then write on the lines the most appropriate word or words to complete the account.

The release of _____ from the anterior pituitary gland induces the development of primary follicles. Another hormone from the anterior pituitary gland stimulates the thecal cells to produce _____ , which controls the repair of the _____ after menstruation. At ovulation, a _____ is released from the mature follicle. The remaining follicular cells form the _____ which begins to secrete _____ , inhibiting the release of the hormones from the anterior pituitary gland. *(6 marks)*

Edexcel

4 Figure 3 shows a section of a coronary artery made during the post-mortem examination of a person who died of a heart attack.

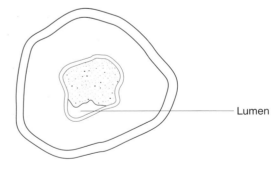

Lumen

Figure 3

a) i) Comment on the appearance of this section in relation to the cause of death. *(3 marks)*

   ii) Suggest *two* dietary factors which might have contributed to this appearance. *(2 marks)*

b) What symptoms might this person have experienced prior to the fatal heart attack? *(2 marks)*

Edexcel

5 Figure 4 shows the structure of a human immunodeficiency virus (HIV).

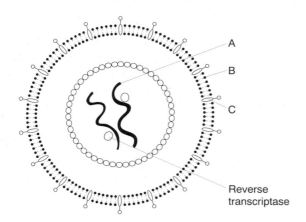

Figure 4

a) Name the parts labelled A, B and C. *(3 marks)*

b) State the function of the reverse transcriptase. *(1 mark)*

c) Explain the meaning of *latency* in the replication cycle of this virus. *(2 marks)*

Edexcel

6 a) Cell A in Figure 5 has two pairs of chromosomes. Cells B, C and D have each arisen from A by cell division.

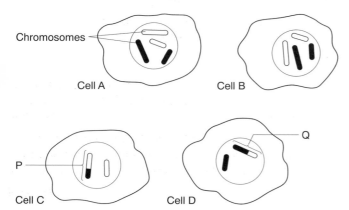

Figure 5

i) For each of the cells labelled B and C, identify the type of cell division which has occurred to produce the cell. In each case give a reason for your answer. *(2 marks)*

ii) Explain the reasons for the difference between the parts labelled P and Q in cells C and D. *(3 marks)*

b) State *one* way in which oogenesis differs from spermatogenesis. *(1 mark)*

c) State *two* ways in which embryo development in flowering plants differs from embryo development in humans. *(2 marks)*

Edexcel

7 In some women, infertility may be treated with the drug clomiphene. Figure 6 shows the blood-oestrogen levels in a woman during and after treatment with clomiphene.

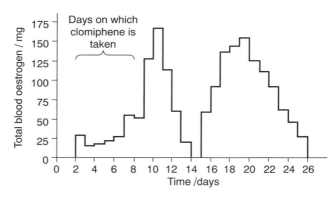

Figure 6

a) Clomiphene stimulates the production of gonadotrophic hormones from the anterior pituitary gland.

i) From the timing of the treatment shown in Figure 6, name the gonadotrophic hormone whose secretion is stimulated by the clomiphene. *(1 mark)*

ii) Explain how stimulation of this hormone brings about the change in oestrogen secretion shown in the graph. *(2 marks)*

b) i) On what day would ovulation be most likely to occur? *(1 mark)*

ii) Give a reason for your answer. *(1 mark)*

AEB Specimen Question

8 Coronary heart disease (CHD) is the leading cause of death in the UK. In 1991 it was responsible for 26% of all deaths in England. Epidemiological studies have identified a series of factors which are associated with CHD and screening for these risk factors has become the accepted method of identifying patients at high risk. A political decision was made in 1989 to include disease prevention and health promotion within the services offered by British doctors. The doctor can earn a fee for organising coronary prevention or health promotion clinics. The Government White Paper 'The Health of the Nation', published in July 1992, included the objective of reducing CHD by 40% by the year 2000 for people aged under 65 years.

Source: Lancet, December 1993

a) Explain how coronary heart disease may cause death. *(4 marks)*

b) Outline the causative link between cigarette smoking and coronary heart disease. *(3 marks)*

c) i) Identify *two* factors, other than cigarette smoking, that an epidemiological study would be likely to find associated with coronary heart disease. *(1 mark)*

ii) Describe briefly how a doctor could screen for the two factors identified in (i). *(1 mark)*

d) Suggest *two* reasons why the British Government has become active in trying to reduce coronary heart disease. *(2 marks)*

e) Suggest *three non-medical* measures which the Government could take to try to reduce the incidence of coronary heart disease. *(3 marks)*

UCLES

9   Table 1 refers to four hormones associated with the human menstrual cycle.

Copy the table and if the statement is correct, place a tick (✔) in the appropriate box and if the statement is incorrect place a cross (✗) in the appropriate box.

Table 1

Hormone	Secreted by ovaries	Reaches highest level in blood before ovulation
Follicle stimulating hormone (FSH)		
Luteinising hormone (LH)		
Oestrogen		
Progesterone		

(4 marks)

Edexcel

10   Read through the following passage, which refers to different types of skelton in various animal groups, then copy it and write on the lines the most appropriate word or words to complete the account.

A _____ skelton is typical of earthworms. Insects have an _____ skeleton, which contains a material called _____. The skeletons of mamals, however, are found _____ their bodies, and are made of bone, which is strengthened with mineral ions such as _____ and _____. *(6 marks)*

Edexcel

11   Figure 7 below shows the structure of part of a mammalian placenta and the umbilical cord, which is attached to a developing fetus.

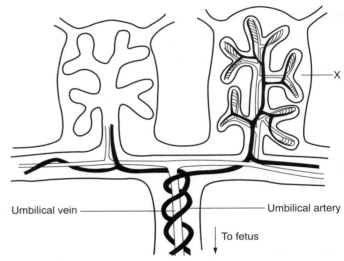

Umbilical vein — — Umbilical artery

To fetus

Figure 7

a) State *two* substances which would be present in a higher concentration in the umbilical vein than in the umbilical artery. *(2 marks)*

b) The cavity labelled X contains maternal blood. Suggest why it is an advantage for this blood to be in a cavity rather than in a vessel. *(2 marks)*

Edexcel

Life has evolved on Earth over millions of years. We cannot yet be sure exactly how it all began, but gradually a picture is being pieced together which one day will lead us to a full understanding of our human origins. In this section we shall begin by looking at DNA (deoxyribonucleic acid) which is the fundamental link between all living organisms.

This remarkable molecule is found in all cells and controls the structure and functioning of the cell. In multicellular organisms such as ourselves it is largely responsible for our individual characteristics. DNA is passed on from one organism to the next generation during sexual reproduction. Because each parent can pass only half their DNA to their offspring, each new individual will differ in detail from its parents due to the expression of its new mix of DNA. The differences are called variation.

The parents have passed half their DNA to both their children; but each received a different mix and so they are each separate individuals.

Modern genetics

Genetics is the study of inheritance. It is a branch of science which has made enormous advances in the twentieth century and has many applications in medicine and industries such as pharmaceuticals, agriculture and food.

Genetic technology may involve the transfer of genes from one organism to another; often bacteria are part of a manufacturing process in which a useful product such as insulin is synthesised.

Genes may be inserted into the DNA of food crops to improve their quality in some way. One of the first such vegetables to reach our shops was a genetically engineered tomato, which does not deteriorate quickly once picked and is said to have improved flavour.

Why is variation important?

Variation is one of the most important factors governing the success of living organisms. The greatest variation comes about through outbreeding, that is when sexual reproduction

A genetically engineered tomato is indistinguishable on sight from one that has not had a gene inserted into its DNA.

occurs between two members of the same species which are not closely related. Variation also occasionally results from mutations which become established in the population as a result of reproduction.

From the diversity within the members of a species at any time, there are some individuals which are better able to adapt to current environmental conditions, whether these conditions are stable or undergoing change. These individuals are the ones most likely to reproduce successfully and compete for resources at the expense of others which are less well adapted. Their advantage leads them to be described as the 'fittest' individuals – meaning those who are best adapted to current environmental conditions. As we shall see, there are selection pressures in the environment which favour the better adapted individuals. This idea formed the basis for 'natural selection', the theory of evolution proposed initially by Charles Darwin and A. Wallace in the middle of the nineteenth century and on which current thinking is based.

In a community which inbreeds, there is less variation, and there is a tendency for unfavourable characteristics within the population to increase. A species with little variation is unable to adapt to its surroundings and will become rare or even extinct.

Artificial selection

Humans have exploited the principles of natural selection in the breeding of plants and animals for their own uses. Individuals with the desired characteristics are allowed to breed to perpetuate the feature, for example a cow may be bred to further improve an already good quality milk. Male animals may be used as studs; the sperm of race horses for example may be collected and used in programmes of artificial insemination to try and breed more winners. Pigs, sheep, poultry and domestic animals such as dogs, cats and fancy birds are amongst other animals subjected to artificial selection of various characteristics. Plants too are bred in programmes using artificial selection to improve yield or resistance to disease.

Champion race horse Lammatarra wins the 1995 Derby. There are high hopes that he will also have a successful career at stud.

CHAPTER 31 Nucleic Acids and Protein Synthesis

Deoxyribonucleic acid (DNA) is the compound in cell nuclei that determines the characteristics of all species of living organisms. DNA is a universal polymer which functions as a code. It allows every single individual plant or animal to have its own unique plan or blue-print (with the possible exception of identical twins). It is DNA which is largely responsible for each of us being different.

31.1 The evidence that DNA is the genetic material

In 1928 Griffith carried out an experiment which was an important step towards establishing that DNA is the genetic material in living organisms. He was attempting to find a vaccine that would protect people against a bacterium called *Pneumococcus* which caused many cases of fatal pneumonia every year. Griffith knew that *Pneumococcus* existed in two forms. One type grew as smooth colonies on agar plates and so was called the S strain. This type caused the disease and the individual cells were recognised because they produced a polysaccharide capsule around themselves to protect them from their host's defence system. The cells of the other type, the R strain, had no capsule and grew as rough colonies on agar plates. The R strain did not cause disease.

> ► *Chapter 3 covers bacterial cells*

Griffith's experiment is shown in Figure 31.1. When he injected heat-killed bacteria of either the S or R strain into mice they did not develop disease. However, when mice were injected with heat-killed S cells and living R cells, some of the mice became ill. What was more surprising was that Griffith was able to isolate *living* S strain bacteria from the sick mice.

It appeared that the genetic instructions needed for the bacteria to cause disease had somehow passed from the dead S cells to the living R cells, so transforming them into pathogens. The phenomenon was called **transformation**, but at that time no one knew what the material carrying the genetic instructions was.

No further progress was made in this direction until 1944 when Avery and his co-workers in the USA published the results of research that they had carried out in an effort to identify the substance. They obtained pure extracts of protein, lipid, polysaccharide and DNA from the S strain of bacteria and wanted to determine which of these could transform R cells into pathogens. From their results they found out that the hereditary material was DNA. However, this was not universally accepted until the late 1950s when the results of further work by Hershey and Chase were published.

Alfred Hershey and Martha Chase were experimenting with the virus bacteriophage T_2 and its host the bacterium *Escherichia coli*, usually known as *E. coli*. They knew that the phage consisted of a protein coat and a core of DNA. They also knew that when the phage infected a host cell, the host very soon began to manufacture new phages. Hershey and Chase wanted to find

> **A bacteriophage is a virus that infects a bacterium.**

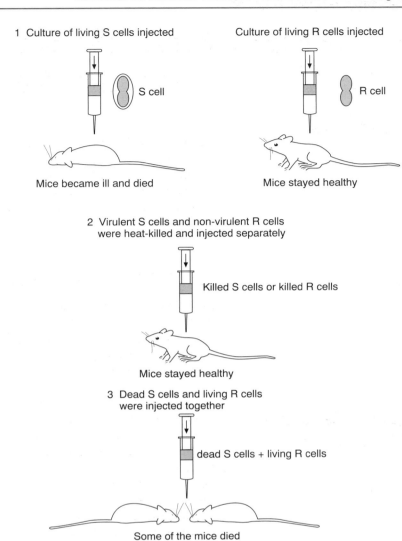

1 Culture of living S cells injected

S cell

Mice became ill and died

Culture of living R cells injected

R cell

Mice stayed healthy

2 Virulent S cells and non-virulent R cells
were heat-killed and injected separately

Killed S cells or killed R cells

Mice stayed healthy

3 Dead S cells and living R cells
were injected together

dead S cells + living R cells

Some of the mice died

From the blood of these dead mice
both living S and R cells were cultured

Figure 31.1 When dead S cells and
living R cells were injected into mice,
living S cells were isolated

▶ *Chapter 3.2 describes how
viruses reproduce in host cells*

out whether the phage protein coat or the DNA in the core carried
instructions to the host.

Hershey and Chase used the technique of **radioactive labelling**. The
experiment depended on the fact that:

- phage DNA contained phosphorus but the protein coat did not;
- the protein coat contained sulphur but DNA does not.

They labelled the DNA in one sample of T_2 phage with radioactive
phosphorus, ^{32}P, and the protein coat of another sample with radioactive
sulphur, ^{35}S. Then, two identical cultures of *E. coli* were infected, one with
the virus carrying radioactive DNA and the other with virus with labelled
protein coat. When the *E. coli* cultures began to manufacture phage particles,
the one that had been infected with labelled DNA produced radioactive
virus particles carrying ^{32}P.

This was conclusive proof that DNA carries the genetic information
needed to instruct host cells to produce viral particles. Since then it has been
universally accepted that DNA is the genetic material.

31.2 DNA – discovering the double helix

The structure of DNA was proposed by Francis Crick and James Watson in a paper in the scientific journal *Nature* in 1953. Watson and Crick worked on a model for the structure at the Cavendish Laboratory in Cambridge. Evidence gathered by Maurice Wilkins and Rosalind Franklin at King's College London was crucial to the final solution. The solving of the structure of DNA was to prove arguably the most exciting and significant biological discovery this century, and has led to immense advancements in our understanding of molecular biology and genetics.

Figure 31.2 Imagine being a scientist who discovered something of huge importance to the human race

It had been known for a while that a molecule of DNA consisted of a sugar, phosphate and four nitrogenous bases, but how these were linked together was not understood.

In 1951 Edwin Chargaff published an analysis of the nitrogen-containing bases found in DNA. His work showed that the number of purine bases (adenine and guanine) is always equal to the number of pyrimidine bases (thymine and cytosine) in any DNA sample. What is more, the number of adenine and thymine bases are equal, as is the number of guanine and cytosine bases. This suggested that adenine pairs with thymine and guanine pairs with cytosine. This information was a vital part of the puzzle that Watson and Crick were trying to solve.

The contribution by Wilkins and Franklin was the important evidence that they obtained from X-ray diffraction studies carried out on DNA. The interpretation of their films led to the idea that the DNA molecule is a helix and also that it consists of two strands.

X-ray crystallography

X-ray crystallography is a technique used to bombard crystals of organic molecules, such as proteins or DNA, with X-rays. It was first used in the 1930s when one of the earliest people to experiment with the technique was the famous scientist Dorothy Hodgkin. Her brilliant work includes discovering the structures of penicillin and vitamin B_{12}.

Rosalind Franklin used X-ray crystallography in her work on DNA. The X-rays are diffracted (spread out) onto a photographic plate or film which is then developed, revealing a pattern of dots and lines. By carefully analysing this image it is possible to work out the three-dimensional shape of the molecule and the arrangement of the atoms it contains.

Figure 31.3 This is the pattern on photographic film obtained when X-rays are diffracted by a DNA crystal – it shows that the DNA molecule has a helical structure

31.3 The structure of DNA

DNA is a nucleic acid. Its molecule is a very long polymer built of units called **nucleotides**. Each nucleotide has three parts: a nitrogen-containing base, a pentose (5-carbon) sugar, and phosphoric acid. There are two types of nitrogenous base: purines and pyrimidines.

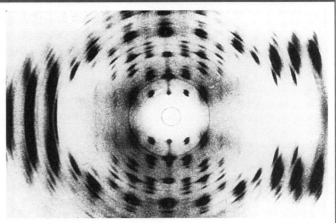

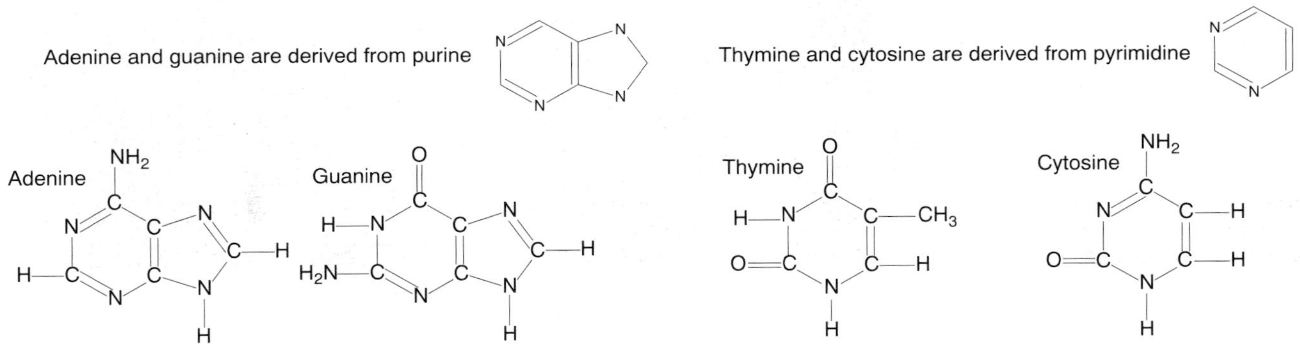

Adenine and guanine are derived from purine

Thymine and cytosine are derived from pyrimidine

Adenine

Guanine

Thymine

Cytosine

Figure 31.4 The four nitrogen-containing bases found in DNA

Notice in Figure 31.4 that a purine molecule is composed of two rings one with six sides and the other with five. In DNA the purine bases are **adenine** (A) and **guanine** (G). The pyrimidines, **thymine** (T) and **cytosine** (C) consist of a single hexagonal ring. It is usual to refer to the bases by their initials.

The sugar in DNA is **deoxyribose**; 'deoxy' means that there is one fewer oxygen atom than in other pentose sugars. Deoxyribose has the chemical formula $C_5H_{10}O_4$ and its structure is a 5-carbon ring. Phosphoric acid has the formula H_3PO_4 and gives the nucleic acid its acidic properties.

Nucleotides are formed when a condensation reaction takes place between a sugar and a nitrogenous base, which then combines with phosphoric acid. One nucleotide joins with another when a covalent bond is formed between the phosphate group of one nucleotide and the sugar of the next.

▶ *Chapter 6 explains about condensation reactions*

Look at Figure 31.5 showing the structure of DNA. The sugar and phosphate groups form a backbone for each strand of the DNA and they are on the outside of the molecule. The nitrogen-containing bases are on the inside. A pyrimidine base on one strand always lies opposite a purine base on the other. These are the **complementary base pairs**. Since adenine pairs with thymine and guanine with cytosine, the bases lying along one strand will determine the order of bases on the other. Hydrogen bonds between each pair of purine–pyrimidine bases hold the two strands of the molecule together. The whole structure then spirals to form a helix.

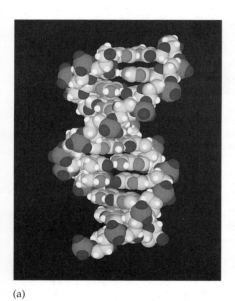

(a)

Figure 31.5 (a) A computer-generated model of the DNA molecule (b) The structure of DNA can be shown simplified like this
(See Colour Gallery page 355)

C30

C31

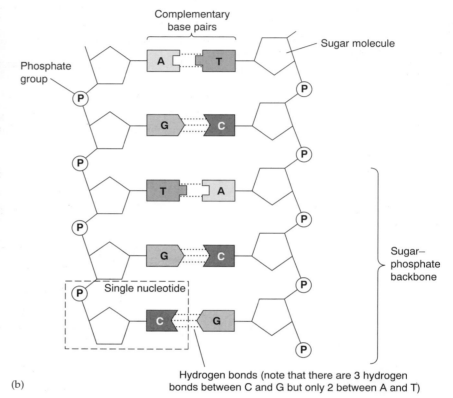

(b)

In 1962 the Nobel Prize for medicine was awarded to Francis Crick, James Watson and Maurice Wilkins in recognition of their work on the structure of DNA. Rosalind Franklin had died of cancer earlier in 1958 and could not be honoured because the prize is not awarded posthumously. It is without question, however, that her contribution was of very great importance.

31.4 Ribonucleic acid – RNA

▶ *Chapter 2.6 describes ribosomes*

The pyrimidines found in DNA are thymine (T) and cytosine (C).

The pyrimidines found in RNA are uracil (U) and cytosine (C).

The other nucleic acid found in cells is RNA (ribonucleic acid). Some RNA occurs in the nucleus but it is mostly found in the cytoplasm, particularly in the ribosomes.

RNA is a single-stranded polymer and, like DNA, is built up of nucleotides. These consist of the pentose sugar ribose, a nitrogenous base and phosphoric acid. There are four nitrogen containing bases. The purines are **adenine** (A) and **guanine** (G) and the pyrimidines are **uracil** (U) and **cytosine** (C). Adenine forms a base pair with uracil, and guanine pairs with cytosine. The sugar ribose has the chemical formula $C_5H_{10}O_5$.

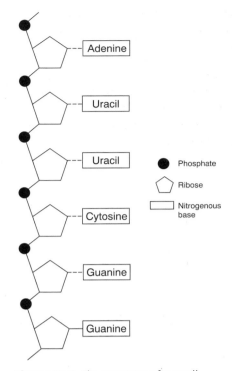

Figure 31.6 The structure of a small section of RNA

There are three types of RNA found in cells and each has a special part to play in protein synthesis as we shall see later in this section.

- Ribosomal RNA (rRNA) is manufactured by the nucleolus. It is found in the ribosomes that lie in the cytoplasm or along the ER (endoplasmic reticulum). rRNA is essential for the assembly of proteins.

- Transfer RNA (tRNA) is found in the cytoplasm. Its molecule has a characteristic clover-leaf shape. The tRNA strand is held in shape by hydrogen bases between base pairs. At one point on the molecule is a sequence of three bases forming the anticodon, which we will return to later. A second sequence of three bases allows the tRNA molecule to dock with an amino acid molecule which will be built into a new polypeptide during protein synthesis.

- Messenger RNA (mRNA) is manufactured in the nucleus. It forms a template of the DNA molecule and transfers the genetic information to the cytoplasm where it is translated and proteins are synthesised. mRNA has a short-lived existence, since it is synthesised when it is needed and then rapidly broken down once it has been used.

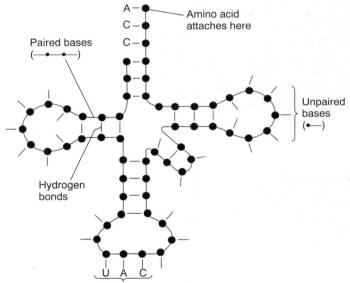

Figure 31.7 The structure of tRNA

RNA	DNA
a single polynucleotide chain	a double polynucleotide chain
three basic forms: t, m, r	one form only
molecular mass smaller	molecular mass greater
nitrogen-containing bases are adenine, guanine, cytosine, thymine	nitrogen-containing bases are adenine, guanine, cytosine, uracil
sugar is ribose	sugar is deoxyribose
occurs in nucleus and cytoplasm	occurs almost entirely in nucleus
may be chemically unstable	always chemically stable
may exist only for a short time	exists permanently

Table 31.1 Some differences between RNA and DNA

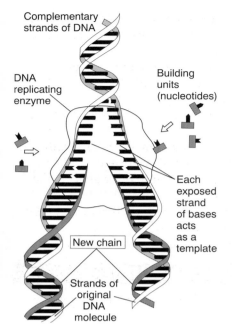

Complementary strands of DNA

DNA replicating enzyme

Building units (nucleotides)

Each exposed strand of bases acts as a template

New chain

Strands of original DNA molecule

Figure 31.8 How DNA replicates itself – semi-conservative replication *(See Colour Gallery page 355)*

C32

Isotopes are atoms of the same element which have the same number of protons and electrons but different numbers of neutrons. Therefore their atomic mass is different.

31.5 The semi-conservative replication of DNA

When Watson and Crick first published their double helix model for DNA they noted that it would be relatively simple for the molecule to replicate itself. An accurate copying mechanism is an essential characteristic of any genetic material. The name of the process by which DNA is copied is **semi-conservative replication**. The way this process works is summarised below:

1 The DNA double helix unwinds at one end and the hydrogen bonds between the base pairs break, so exposing the bases along the two strands.
2 The unpaired bases on each side act as templates for free nucleotides in the nucleoplasm to line up against in the correct position (A against T, G against C).
3 The enzyme DNA polymerase joins each nucleotide to its complementary base on the exposed DNA strands. Then, the nucleotides assemble to form two new DNA strands.

How DNA replicates – the proof

The evidence for semi-conservative replication was provided by the work of Meselsohn and Stahl in 1958. They worked with the bacterium *Escherichia coli* making use of an isotope of nitrogen, ^{15}N, which is slightly heavier than the normal isotope, ^{14}N. Their experiments are summarised in points 1–4 that follow, and in Figure 31.9.

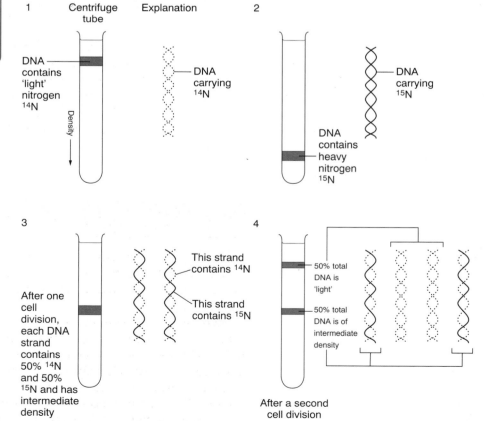

1 Centrifuge tube   Explanation

DNA contains 'light' nitrogen ^{14}N

Density

DNA carrying ^{14}N

2

DNA carrying ^{15}N

DNA contains heavy nitrogen ^{15}N

3

After one cell division, each DNA strand contains 50% ^{14}N and 50% ^{15}N and has intermediate density

This strand contains ^{14}N

This strand contains ^{15}N

4

50% total DNA is 'light'

50% total DNA is of intermediate density

After a second cell division

Figure 31.9 The work of Meselsohn and Stahl

1   *Escherichia coli* was cultured in nutrient medium containing normal light nitrogen, ^{14}N. Some of the cells were extracted and spun in a centrifuge and the DNA fraction was isolated and analysed.

2   The bacteria were then transferred to a medium containing heavy nitrogen, ^{15}N, so that their DNA became labelled with this isotope. The cells were removed and spun in an ultracentrifuge. This time the DNA was denser because it contained heavy nitrogen and it settled at a lower position in the tube.

3   The bacteria were then transferred to a new medium containing only the light nitrogen, ^{14}N. After one generation time cells were extracted and again the DNA was isolated. The DNA was found to be of intermediate density because it was a hybrid of ^{14}N and ^{15}N.

4   When this was repeated after another generation time 50 per cent of the DNA was light and 50 per cent was intermediate.

Questions

1   Why was the evidence of Rosalind Franklin important in discovering the structure of DNA?

2   Look at Figure 31.9. Make drawings of the centrifuge tube to show the results of isolating DNA after another generation time. How can you explain this?

3   Complete the following passage by filling in the blanks with suitable word(s):

A DNA molecule is a polymer of _____ and is found almost entirely in the _____. Tiny amounts occur in the _____ . DNA contains the pentose sugar _____, phosphoric acid and four types of _____. The bases adenine and guanine are examples of molecules called _____ and each has a complementary base pair; adenine pairs with _____ for example. The DNA molecule consists of two strands which twist around one another forming a double _____. Complementary bases on the two strands are held together by _____ bonds. RNA differs from DNA. The sugar molecule is _____ and thymine is replaced by _____. It is a single strand and exists in _____ forms.

31.6 The genetic code

The role of genetic material is to instruct each cell to make specific proteins which are needed for the cell to function. The bases on the DNA in some way code for the amino acids that join in a particular sequence to form each protein.

Since their are 20 common amino acids that may be built into proteins but only four bases (A, T, G, C), it is clear that *one* base cannot code for an amino acid since there would be only four different amino acids. If *two* bases coded for an amino acid only 4^2 or 16 amino acids could be coded for. But if *three* bases formed the code then 4^3 or 64 different combinations of bases are possible. Evidence has shown that three bases do indeed code for an amino acid, and so the code is called a **triplet** code. Each triplet of bases is a **codon**.

Table 31.2 The codons along DNA are transcribed by mRNA and then translated at the ribosomes into the sequence of amino acids to build a particular protein. The codons in this table are those carried by mRNA. The left-hand column gives the first base of the codon, the top row gives the second base and the right-hand row gives the third base.

Second base

First base		U	C	A	G	Third base
U		UUU ⎫ Phe UUC ⎭ UUA ⎫ Leu UUG ⎭	UCU ⎫ UCC ⎪ Ser UCA ⎪ UCG ⎭	UAU ⎫ Tyr UAC ⎭ UAA Stop UAG Stop	UGU ⎫ Cys UGC ⎭ UGA Stop UGG Trp	U C A G
C		CUU ⎫ CUC ⎪ Leu CUA ⎪ CUG ⎭	CCU ⎫ CCC ⎪ Pro CCA ⎪ CCG ⎭	CAU ⎫ His CAC ⎭ CAA ⎫ Gln CAG ⎭	CGU ⎫ CGC ⎪ Arg CGA ⎪ CGG ⎭	U C A G
A		AUU ⎫ AUC ⎪ Ile AUA ⎭ AUG Met	ACU ⎫ ACC ⎪ Thr ACA ⎪ ACG ⎭	AAU ⎫ Asn ACC ⎭ AAA ⎫ Lys AAG ⎭	AGU ⎫ Ser AGC ⎭ AGA ⎫ Arg AGG ⎭	U C A G
G		GUU ⎫ GUC ⎪ Val GUA ⎪ GUG ⎭	GCU ⎫ GCC ⎪ Ala GCA ⎪ GCG ⎭	GAU ⎫ Asp GAC ⎭ GAA ⎫ Glu GAG ⎭	GGU ⎫ GGC ⎪ Gly GGA ⎪ GGG ⎭	U C A G

Key to amino acids

Ala = alanine
Arg = arginine
Asn = asparagine
Asp = aspartic acid
Cys = cysteine
Gln = glutamine
Glu = glutamic acid
Gly = glycine
His = histidine
Ile = isoleucine
Leu = leucine
Lys = lysine
Met = methionine
Phe = phenylalanine
Pro = proline
Ser = serine
Thr = threonine
Try = tryptophan
Tyr = tyrosine
Val = valine

The code was eventually deciphered in 1966 using synthetic RNA and its main features are summarised below:

- It is a **triplet** code, three bases code for one amino acid.
- There is more than one codon for many of the amino acids and the code is therefore described as being **degenerate**.
- It is **non-overlapping**, which means that each codon is read as a separate instruction.
- It is **universal**, that is a codon codes for the same amino acids in all living organisms. The code for methionine (AUG) is often the instruction for starting to build a protein. There are three codons which do not code for an amino acid (UAA, UAG and UGA) but instead give the instruction that a sequence has ended.

31.7 Exons and introns

▶ *Chapter 32.3 explains about introns in more detail*

We know that not all the DNA codes for proteins, and that in some eukaryotic chromosomes, even within the genes (sections of DNA that do code for proteins) are lengths of DNA that do not code for proteins. The useful sequences of DNA which are expressed by the production of proteins are called **exons**, but what the rest of the DNA does has not yet been worked out for certain. Because these non-coding sequences appear to interrupt the exons and to have no obvious function they have been referred to as 'junk DNA' or **introns**.

American geneticists working on fruit flies have suggested that the function of junk DNA may be to help the chromatids stick together before cell division. The highest concentration of junk DNA is found at the centromeres, which during cell division act as anchor points for the spindle fibres that pull the chromatids apart. The researchers believe that the sticky (junk) DNA serves a useful purpose in keeping the chromatids together. It prevents them from becoming separated at random, resulting in daughter cells with either too few or too many chromosomes.

31.8 Protein synthesis

▶ *Chapter 2.6 describes the structure of ribosomes*

A string of codons along the DNA molecule determines the sequence of amino acids which are built up to make a protein. The information is transcribed onto mRNA in the nucleus, and then translated into a polypeptide at a ribosome in the cytoplasm. The amino acids needed to build the proteins come from the pool of organic molecules in the cytoplasm. ATP must be available as a source of energy.

Transcription

The coded information carried on part of the DNA molecule must first be transcribed onto mRNA. This reaction is catalysed by the enzyme **RNA polymerase** which binds to a start signal (the codon for methionine) on the DNA. The DNA unwinds and hydrogen bonds break between the bases in the region where the code is to be copied. One exposed strand of the DNA acts as a template for mRNA. It is called the **sense strand**. Complementary

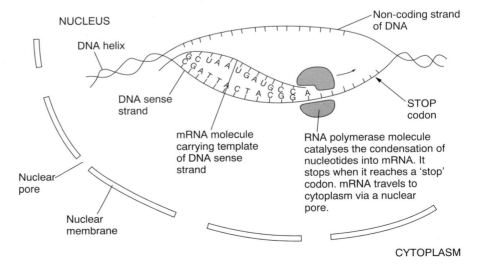

Figure 31.10 Protein synthesis – transcription

bases on free ribonucleotides in the nucleoplasm line up along side the bases on the sense strand. RNA polymerase moves along the DNA catalysing condensation reactions which result in the synthesis of a molecule of mRNA. When the enzyme reaches a stop codon, the mRNA peels off and moves out of the nucleus, through a nuclear pore, to the cytoplasm.

The combination of amino acids with transfer RNA

In the cytoplasm there are over 20 different forms of tRNA, one for each of the twenty amino acids used to build proteins. The amino acids each join to their tRNA in a process which requires energy transferred from ATP. Each tRNA molecule has a specific sequence of three unpaired bases called the **anticodon**, which is complementary to a codon on the mRNA molecule. The tRNA uses the anticodon to line up its amino acid in the correct place in the sequence of amino acids being condensed into a polypeptide.

▶ *Chapter 31.4 describes tRNA*

Translation

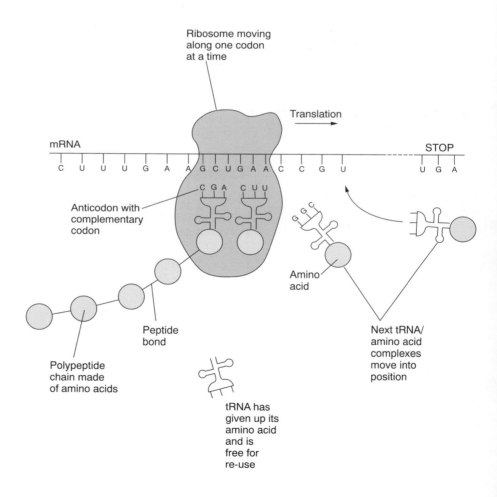

CYTOPLASM

Figure 31.11 The coded message on mRNA is translated into a polypeptide chain

When the mRNA reaches the cytoplasm it binds with a ribosome. tRNA molecules line up in the correct order, each bringing their amino acid to be linked into the polypeptide chain. There are two sites in the ribosome just big enough to occupy two codons. At the first site a tRNA molecule holds the growing peptide chain in position. At the second, a new tRNA molecule and its amino acid attach. The amino acid at the end of the polypeptide chain condenses with the new amino acid forming a peptide bond. The first tRNA molecule detaches and returns to the cytoplasm and can be re-used. The ribosome moves along the mRNA three bases at a time adding further amino acids until it reaches a stop codon. The polypeptide chain is then released into the cytoplasm and will fold itself into a stable tertiary or quaternary structure.

The sequence of codons on mRNA can be read in quick succession by a number of ribosomes, each of which produces a polypeptide chain. These are called **polyribosomes**.

► *Chapter 6.4 covers protein structure*

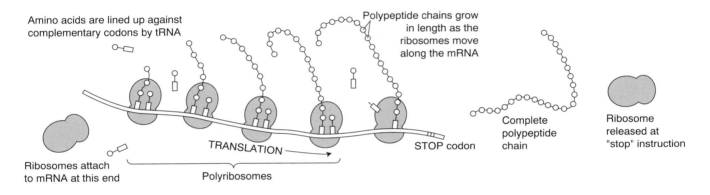

Amino acids are lined up against complementary codons by tRNA

Polypeptide chains grow in length as the ribosomes move along the mRNA

Complete polypeptide chain

Ribosome released at "stop" instruction

TRANSLATION

STOP codon

Ribosomes attach to mRNA at this end

Polyribosomes

∅ tRNA

○ amino acid

Figure 31.12 Polyribosomes are like a conveyer belt, mass-producing polypeptides from a single length of mRNA

CHAPTER 32

Genes and Genetic Engineering

32.1 What is a gene?

A gene is a length of DNA which codes for a specific polypeptide. It is also a hereditary factor which determines a characteristic of an organism.

DNA controls the cell by determining which proteins, including enzymes, it should synthesise. As long ago as 1945 the American geneticists George Beadle and Edward Tatum provided evidence that a gene is the length of DNA that codes for an enzyme. They were working with the bread mould *Neurospora* which they found could be cultured on a minimal medium containing just sucrose, minerals and a vitamin, biotin. The fungus could synthesise all its dietary requirements from these raw materials.

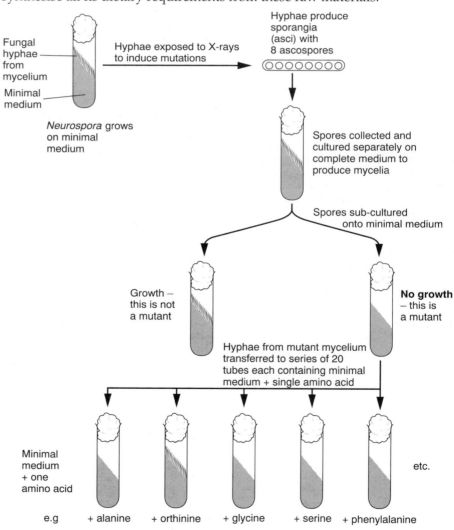

Figure 32.1 Beadle and Tatum's experiment that led to the 'one gene, one enzyme' hypothesis

When *Neurospora* was exposed to X-rays the radiation caused the formation of mutants which failed to grow on the minimal medium, but could grow if a complete medium that provided all essential nutrients was supplied. By systematically transferring spores from the mutants to a series of culture media made up of minimal medium plus a single amino acid, they found that each mutant was deficient only in its ability to synthesise a *single* amino acid.

When a mutant was crossed with a normal strain of the fungus (one able to grow on minimal medium), half the spores the offspring produced were of the normal type and half were mutants. This followed the pattern of inheritance which is to be expected from the laws of genetics. It appeared that the loss of ability to synthesise an amino acid might be due to the mould being unable to synthesise a vital enzyme and, therefore, perhaps a single gene could be responsible for the synthesis of each enzyme. Beadle and Tatum proposed an important idea – the **one gene, one enzyme hypothesis**.

More recent studies have shown that in fact genes control the production of other types of protein in addition to enzymes. We also know that proteins usually contain several polypeptides, each different polypeptide being controlled by a different gene. This means that it is more accurate to re-phrase Beadle and Tatum's hypothesis as the **one gene, one polypeptide hypothesis**.

32.2 How gene action is controlled

All the genes that an organism possesses are present in every cell of the body, in other words every one of our cells contains a complete plan of all our characteristics. However, there is no need for every gene to be expressed in every cell. For example the genes that we carry for tongue rolling are not

Figure 32.2 The Jacob–Monod hypothesis of gene control in *Escherichia coli* (a) When lactose is absent the genes controlling the enzymes for metabolizing lactose are switched off (b) When lactose is present, the genes controlling the synthesis of the enzyme to break down lactose are switched on

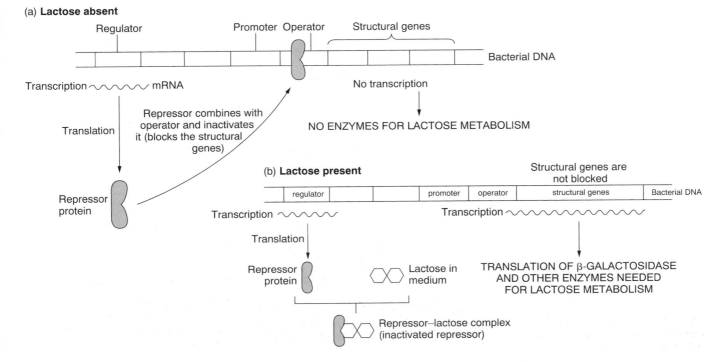

(a) **Lactose absent**

Regulator   Promoter Operator   Structural genes   Bacterial DNA

Transcription ～～～ mRNA   No transcription

Translation

Repressor combines with operator and inactivates it (blocks the structural genes)   NO ENZYMES FOR LACTOSE METABOLISM

Repressor protein

(b) **Lactose present**   Structural genes are not blocked

regulator   promoter operator   structural genes   Bacterial DNA

Transcription ～～～   Transcription ～～～～～

Translation

Repressor protein   Lactose in medium   TRANSLATION OF β-GALACTOSIDASE AND OTHER ENZYMES NEEDED FOR LACTOSE METABOLISM

Repressor–lactose complex (inactivated repressor)

expressed in our striped muscle cells, but the genes that make striped muscle what it is and enable it to contract and to respire will be expressed. How is this achieved?

A model for the regulation of genes was suggested by the French scientists Jacob and Monod in the late 1950s. Their research earned them a Nobel Prize for it led to the understanding of a mechanism that can in effect, switch on and switch off genes as they are required.

Jacob and Monod used a prokaryote, the bacterium *Escherichia coli*, in their experiments and found that it only produced enzymes when they were needed. They studied in detail the synthesis of an enzyme called β-**galactosidase** (lactase) which is necessary for the respiration of lactose to release energy. *Escherichia coli* secretes lactase when lactose is present in the culture medium, but if lactose is absent the bacterium does not synthesise the enzyme.

The length of DNA that codes for the enzyme is called a **structural gene**. Close by on the DNA strand is a region called the **promoter**. Between the two is the **operator** gene, which switches the structural genes off and on. Some distance away on the DNA strand is yet another gene called the **regulator**.

When lactose is absent from the medium, the regulator gene codes for a **repressor protein** to be synthesised. This binds with the operator gene and so blocks transcription of the structural gene. In other words, the genetic sequence that codes for β-galactosidase cannot be transferred to mRNA and so the enzyme cannot be synthesised. However, if lactose is supplied in the culture medium, it combines with the repressor protein and inactivates it. The operator gene is freed so that the structural gene can be transcribed by mRNA. β-Galactosidase is synthesised and the lactose can be respired by the bacterium.

This model applies *only* to prokaryotic cells. We do not yet fully understand the mechanism of gene regulation in eukaryotic cells, which is much more complicated.

32.3 Genetic (DNA) fingerprinting

Almost every individual living organism has their own unique DNA. An exception is the case of identical twins or organisms that have arisen from a parent by asexual reproduction. In the same way that humans have individual fingerprints, a genetic fingerprint can be used to identify individuals or to determine a genetic relationship between two members of the same species, or even between two species. Each human cell may contain up to 100 000 different genes. The genes are separated by lengths of DNA that do not code for proteins and even within individual genes there are introns which are non-coding regions.

It was discovered that these non-coding regions occupying specific locations (loci), contain a particular sequence of nucleotides repeated numerous times, and so produce a pattern which is unique for each individual. The repeating regions are called **minisatellites**. It is these that make up genetic fingerprints.

Multi-locus probing is a genetic fingerprinting technique which relies on detecting several minisatellites simultaneously and produces the familiar bar code pattern on an X-ray plate. This technique was devised in Britain in 1984 at Leicester University and was then developed by the company ICI. It has many uses.

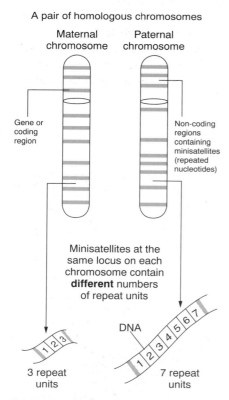

Figure 32.3 Two fragments of DNA with minisatellites of different lengths

Figure 32.4 This scientist is studying autoradiographs (X-ray films) on a light box.

Multi-locus DNA prints are used in paternity cases where there is a dispute as to whether a particular man is the father of a child. In the past, comparison of blood groups was used, but comparing DNA profiles is much more conclusive since the bands in the pattern are inherited, and apart from the odd mutant every bar can be traced back to one of the biological parents. Genetic fingerprinting is also used as a routine measure in immigration cases where people wishing to live in Britain state that they plan to join relations who are already resident. DNA fingerprinting proves or disproves without doubt the genetic relationship of the people involved.

Forensic science is another area in which DNA fingerprinting can be put to use for solving crimes, particularly violent offences such as rape or murder. If traces of biological material such as blood, hairs or semen are left at the scene of the crime they can be analysed and used to develop a genetic fingerprint. Forensic scientists prefer the use of **single-locus probes**, which allows the comparison of *specific* minisatellites.

Figure 32.5 Producing a single-locus probe

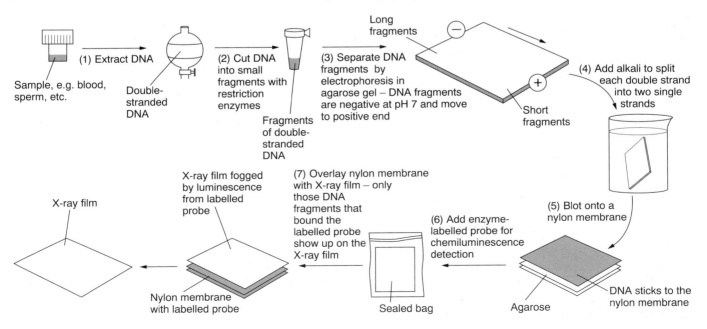

Making a single-locus probe print

1   The DNA must first be extracted. As little as 500 ng of DNA is sufficient to obtain a single probe result.

2   The DNA is then digested with restriction endonuclease enzymes which cut it at specific nucleotide sequences. The fragments obtained will have between 1000 and 20 000 nucleotides each.

3   The DNA fragments are then separated by electrophoresis in agarose gel at room temperature for 20 hours. The DNA sample is placed into a well at one end of the gel which is submersed in a buffer at pH 7.0. An electric current is switched on and the negatively charged fragments of DNA move away from the well towards the positive electrode. Smaller pieces move faster than larger ones and so become separated by size. DNA markers of known molecular mass are also in the mixture being separated to act as controls.

4   The gel is immersed in alkali to separate the two single strands in each DNA fragment.

5   A nylon membrane is laid over the membrane and sheets of blotting paper are put on top. As solution is drawn through the membrane the DNA is carried up and sticks to the membrane. This is a copy of the DNA that separated on the gel during electrophoresis. It is fixed using short wave UV-light.

6   The final stage in the process involves incubating the DNA under strictly controlled conditions of pH, temperature and ionic concentration with a **probe**, which is a special single strand of DNA that contains a complementary nucleotide sequence to the minisatellite region being investigated. The two DNA strands join or **hybridise**. The first probes to be used were radioactive but now chemiluminescent ones such as phosphatase enzymes have been developed, which are safer and give results more quickly.

7   An X-ray film is placed over the nylon membrane and becomes fogged by the probe. This shows the position of the fragments of DNA that have been marked.

8   Once hybridisation is complete and a permanent record has been made, the probe can be removed from the nylon membrane and another added. This allows other specific regions of the DNA to be detected.

The samples are first matched by eye and then confirmed using scanning equipment which compares the separated fragments with the controls. The more probes that are used the more likely that an accurate match will be made.

Be aware . . .

Keep your ears and eyes open and you will often hear or read in the news about DNA fingerprinting being used in criminal investigations.

In Cardiff in late 1996 a man was convicted of the murder of a schoolgirl thirteen months previously. DNA fingerprinting formed part of the evidence against him. Sometimes large scale screening of the people living in an area near to a crime may take place. An innocent person has nothing to fear from taking part in such an exercise because their sample will prove their innocence.

DNA fingerprinting was also used to identify the body of a nine-year-old girl, who was found in March 1997 several weeks after she had gone missing. In the past dental records, when available, were used to identify bodies that had become unrecognisable. A matching DNA print gives absolute and definite proof of a person's identity.

DNA fingerprinting is not confined to humans. It is also used to look for relationships between other species. Increasingly, people are being prosecuted for illegally keeping birds of prey in captivity. The lawful procedure is for the bird to be registered with the Department of the Environment and tagged in the presence of an inspector. There are registration documents and, if necessary, import licences, which must be held. Because it is difficult to breed these birds in captivity, eggs are sometimes stolen from the wild and hatched and the young are passed off as belonging to a licensed bird. Until DNA testing became available late in 1993, it was extremely difficult to prove the parentage of young nestlings. A number of prosecutions have been successful and the illegal possession of these birds will hopefully decline.

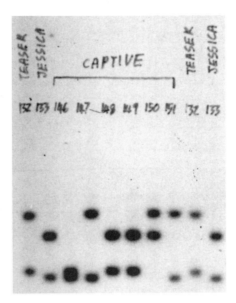

Figure 32.6 A single locus probe applied to a family of peregrine falcons. The parents are Teaser and Jessica and they have six chicks. Notice the matching bands of the offspring and their parents.

32.4 Genetic engineering

For many centuries farmers have carried out **selective breeding**; they have chosen their fittest animals or crop plants and cross-bred them to try and get healthier, higher-yielding animals or plants. We now have a technology that allows us to extend the exchange of genetic material from one species to another.

Recombinant DNA technology (or **genetic engineering**) is very important because it enables us to alter the genetic make-up of an organism. It involves the removal of a gene from one living organism and inserting it into the DNA of another. The gene, which may code for a product useful to humans (e.g. insulin), is often inserted into a bacterial cell and then cultured commercially on a large scale.

Experiments have been carried out to transfer the human gene for milk production into the fertilised ova of sheep. In the future such sheep might be a source of human milk which could be given to bottle-fed babies instead of the powdered formula currently available. Pigs have been given human genes in an attempt to improve the success of future heart transplants from pigs to humans. The idea is that the genetically altered heart would be less likely to be rejected by the human recipient. Any organism that has received a foreign gene is called a **transgenic** organism.

▶ *Chapter 11.3 has more on transgenic pigs*

The first step in the process of recombinant DNA technology is to cut the sequence of bases corresponding to a gene from the DNA of the donor species. This is achieved by using an enzyme belonging to the group called **restriction endonucleases**. These occur naturally in prokaryotic and eukaryotic cells where their function is to attack pathogens such as viruses that invade the cell. Each restriction endonuclease is rather like a pair of molecular scissors, but it can only cut the DNA at a specific site which it recognises by a specific base sequence. The cut is made at two slightly staggered points on each DNA strand leaving a few unpaired bases which are called the **sticky ends**.

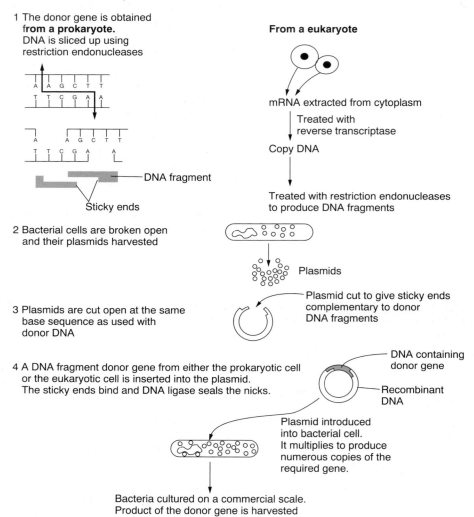

Figure 32.7 The process of recombinant DNA technology

> ▶ *Chapter 3.2 mentions plasmids*

A **vector** is used to carry the gene or gene sequence of interest. Vectors are DNA molecules into which genes may be inserted. They are often circular bacterial **plasmids** or are derived from bacteriophages. Vectors often carry a genetic marker such as a gene for antibiotic resistance. This may be used later to select hosts that are successfully carrying the required gene sequence. The same restriction endonuclease used to cut the DNA of the donor also cuts the vector at a specific site, leaving sticky ends which are complementary to those exposed on the DNA from the original organism. The ends bind together in a process called **annealing** to form recombinant DNA. The structure is made more stable by the enzyme **DNA ligase** which seals 'nicks' in the molecule.

The vector must now be incorporated into a host cell in which it can replicate, usually a bacterium such as *Escherichia coli*. Further transcription and translation of the recombinant gene results in synthesis of the protein that it codes for. By culturing the bacterium on a large scale, the protein can be produced commercially.

There is, however, one complication which means that genetic engineering is not always quite as straight forward as this. In the eukaryotic cell when mRNA copies a section of DNA, it transcribes the introns as well as the useful exons. The introns are removed by enzyme action *before* the mRNA leaves the nucleus and only the exons are translated into protein. If a sequence of eukaryotic DNA is inserted into a bacterial cell, however, the introns are *not* removed. The entire sequence (introns and exons) is translated into a protein, which consequently turns out to be quite different from the intended one.

The solution to this is to use the enzyme **reverse transcriptase**. If mRNA which has copied a DNA sequence for insulin production (for example) is extracted from the cell cytoplasm of a pancreatic islet cell, it will be carrying only exons. In the laboratory **complementary** or **cDNA** can be made from the mRNA using reverse transcriptase. The cDNA will carry only the exons for the required protein. Using a restriction endonuclease and DNA ligase in the way already described, the cDNA is inserted into a plasmid extracted from a bacterial host which acts as the vector. The vector is put back into a bacterial cell free of plasmids and as it multiplies, more cDNA which carries the base sequence required for the protein is formed. The cDNA instructs the bacterial cell to produce the protein e.g. insulin.

> ▶ *Chapter 31.7 covers introns and exons*

Synthesis of insulin and human growth hormone

Both insulin and growth hormones are now routinely synthesised by genetic engineering.

There are about 600 000 diabetes sufferers in Britain today, many of whom require daily injections of insulin. Before it was possible to synthesise insulin using human genes diabetics had to rely on insulin extracted from the pancreases of slaughtered cows or pigs. Some sufferers produced antibodies against the insulin because it did not come from the human body.

During the early 1980s the Danish company Novo Nordisk found a way of converting pig insulin to human insulin and Eli Lilley, the American pharmaceutical company, were granted a licence to manufacture human insulin by genetic engineering. By 1989 it was estimated that 75 per cent of diabetics in Britain were using the human form.

Initially, there were a few problems with the new insulin. In some people the level of sugar in the blood dropped dangerously low without warning symptoms and they suffered 'hypos'. However, these problems have now been overcome and today most diabetics in Britain are treated with human insulin.

The synthesis of growth hormone is another useful application of genetic engineering. Some people have a malfunctioning pituitary gland which produces too little growth hormone. As a result they do not grow fully to their expected height.

The condition can only be treated by growth hormone injections and previously the only source of suitable hormone was the pituitary glands of people who had died. This made the hormone very scarce and extremely expensive. Sadly, a number of people treated with such hormones in the 1970s and 1980s have since died from Creutzfeld Jacob disease because the hormones with which they were treated were contaminated.

Now that it is possible to synthesise growth hormone using genetic engineering, supply is no longer a problem and there is no longer a risk of cross infection.

Synthesis of insulin and human growth hormone – continued

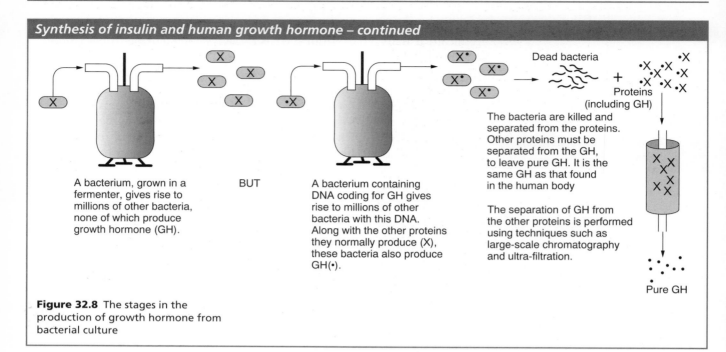

A bacterium, grown in a fermenter, gives rise to millions of other bacteria, none of which produce growth hormone (GH).

BUT

A bacterium containing DNA coding for GH gives rise to millions of other bacteria with this DNA. Along with the other proteins they normally produce (X), these bacteria also produce GH(•).

Dead bacteria

Proteins (including GH)

The bacteria are killed and separated from the proteins. Other proteins must be separated from the GH, to leave pure GH. It is the same GH as that found in the human body

The separation of GH from the other proteins is performed using techniques such as large-scale chromatography and ultra-filtration.

Pure GH

Figure 32.8 The stages in the production of growth hormone from bacterial culture

▶ *Chapter 14.5 covers diabetes in detail*

Questions

1 Why is it not possible to give growth hormone (a protein) orally?

2 It has been suggested that everyone should have their DNA profile stored on a national database. Discuss your views on this in terms of (a) security against terrorism and (b) civil liberties.

3 Explain the function of restriction endonucleases, transcriptases and ligases in recombinant DNA technology.

4 For certain careers such as modelling and the police force certain minimum body heights are specified. Discuss the ethical implications of using growth hormones in short adolescents who wish to follow these careers.

Figure 2.13 Cross section of a tree stump. The vessels have lignin impregnating the cellulose walls which give a very rigid supporting structure and also allows the transport of water through the tree (*See page 16*)

C1

Polypeptide chain 1

Polypeptide chain 2

Polypeptide chain 3

Prosthetic group

Figure 6.13 The quaternary structure a protein (*See page 49*)

C2

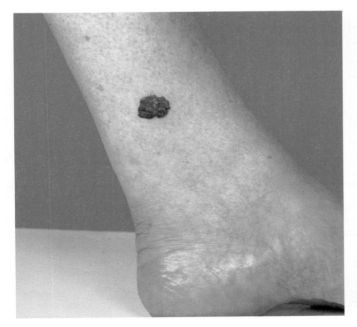

Figure 5.4 (a) Melanoma is a form of skin cancer which readily forms secondary tumours (*See page 35*)

C3

Figure 5.4 (b) Over exposure to the sun increases the risk of skin cancer (*See page 35*)

C4

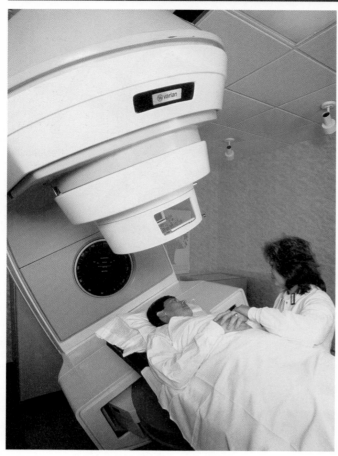

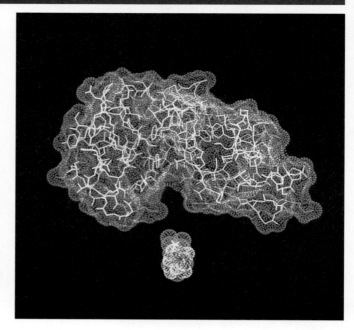

Figure 7.4 The enzyme molecule is considerably larger than the substrate that it reacts with
(See page 52)

Figure 5.7 This patient is receiving radiotherapy for the treatment of a brain tumour
(See page 37)

C5

Figure 7.5 A highly simplified and stylised diagram showing the lock and key hypothesis of enzyme action
(See page 52)

C7

Figure 7.6 Induced fit suggests that enzymes have a more flexible structure than was once thought as shown in this very simplified diagram
(See page 53)

C8

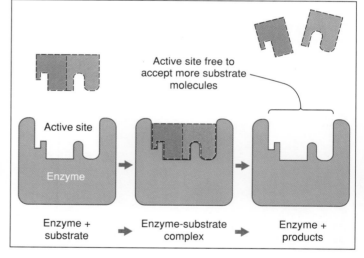

Active site free to accept more substrate molecules

Active site

Enzyme

Enzyme + substrate

Enzyme-substrate complex

Enzyme + products

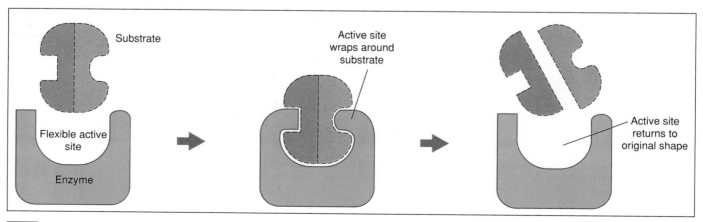

Substrate

Active site wraps around substrate

Flexible active site

Enzyme

Active site returns to original shape

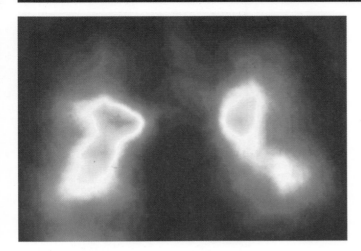

Figure 8.6 This is the coloured gamma camera scan of an asthma patient's lungs. The image followed inhalation of a radioactive gas. The gas penetrates into the airways but not as far as the alveoli. Both lungs show asthmatic obstruction of airways which is indicated by the yellow areas with the right lung more affected and constricted.
(See page 70)

C9

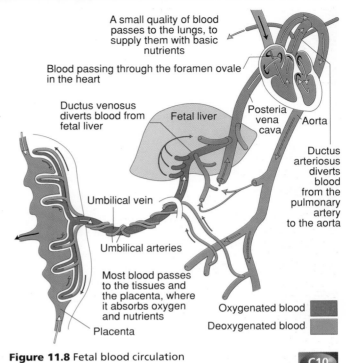

A small quality of blood passes to the lungs, to supply them with basic nutrients

Blood passing through the foramen ovale in the heart

Ductus venosus diverts blood from fetal liver

Fetal liver

Posteria vena cava

Aorta

Ductus arteriosus diverts blood from the pulmonary artery to the aorta

Umbilical vein

Umbilical arteries

Most blood passes to the tissues and the placenta, where it absorbs oxygen and nutrients

Placenta

Oxygenated blood

Deoxygenated blood

Figure 11.8 Fetal blood circulation maximises the flow of oxygenated blood to the fetal tissues
(See page 98)

C10

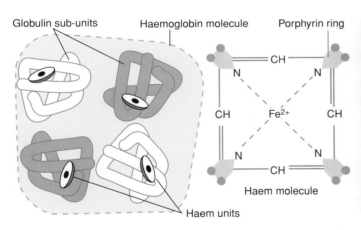

Globulin sub-units

Haemoglobin molecule

Porphyrin ring

CH

N

N

CH

Fe^{2+}

CH

N

N

CH

Haem molecule

Haem units

Figure 10.5 Haemoglobin structure
(See page 83)

C11

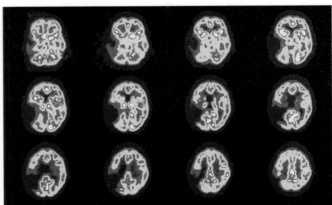

Figure 11.10 A thrombosis in the brain can have an almost instantaneous and often irreversible effect, which is why it is called a stroke. These twelve scans of a stroke patient show different horizontal sections. High brain activity is indicated by white and low activity (areas affected by the stroke) as dark blue
(See page 100)

C12

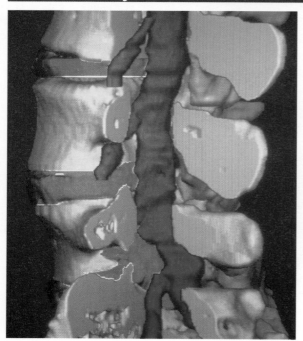

Figure 12.4 This is a three-dimensional computer topography scan. The red areas between the vertebrae are the disks: the lower one has slipped sideways and is pressing on the spinal cord
(See page 108)

C13

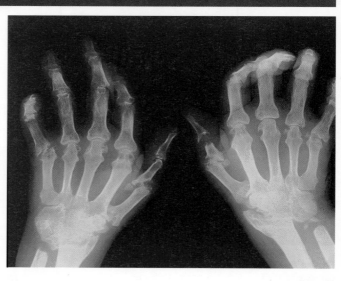

Figure 12.9 Osteoarthritic hands
(See page 112)

C14

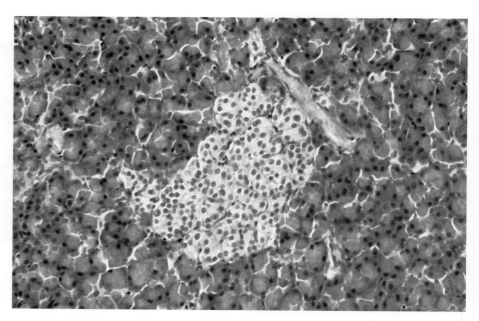

Figure 14.2 The pancreas produces many secretions. It acts as endocrine gland in producing insulin and glucagon which pass directly into blood. It acts as an exocrine gland when digestive secretions are discharged through the pancreatic duct into the duodenum.
(See page 134)

C15

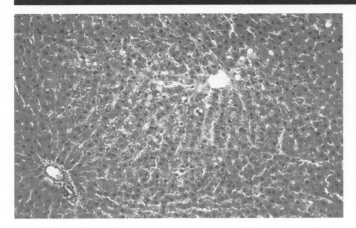

Figure 15.2 Row of hepatocytes within the liver lobules can be seen clearly using a light microscope
(See page 137)

C16

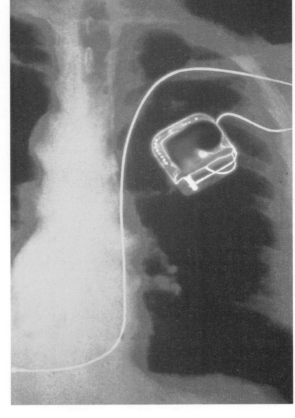

Figure 18.4 False-colour X-ray of a heart pacemaker in position
(See page 162)

C17

Figure 18.2 The nervous system mainly controls the heart rate
(See page 161)

C18

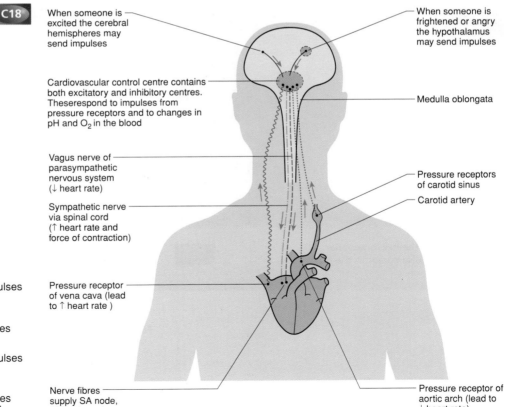

When someone is excited the cerebral hemispheres may send impulses

When someone is frightened or angry the hypothalamus may send impulses

Cardiovascular control centre contains both excitatory and inhibitory centres. These respond to impulses from pressure receptors and to changes in pH and O_2 in the blood

Medulla oblongata

Vagus nerve of parasympathetic nervous system (↓ heart rate)

Sympathetic nerve via spinal cord (↑ heart rate and force of contraction)

Pressure receptors of carotid sinus

Carotid artery

Pressure receptor of vena cava (lead to ↑ heart rate)

Nerve fibres supply SA node, AV node and heart muscle

Pressure receptor of aortic arch (lead to ↓ heart rate)

∼∼∼∼∼∼ Sensory neurone–impulses initiated here have an acceleratory effect

– – – – – – Motor neurone–impulses decrease heart rate

.... Sensory neurone–impulses initiated here have an inhibitory effect

– · – · – · Motor neurone–impulses increase heart rate and the force of contraction

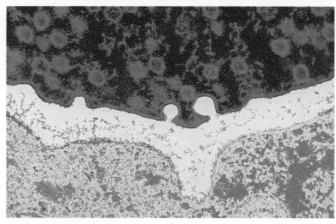

Figure 20.11 The synaptic cleft is around 20nm wide, across which neurotransmitters must pass in order to trigger an action potential in the adjoining neurone
(See page 179)

C19

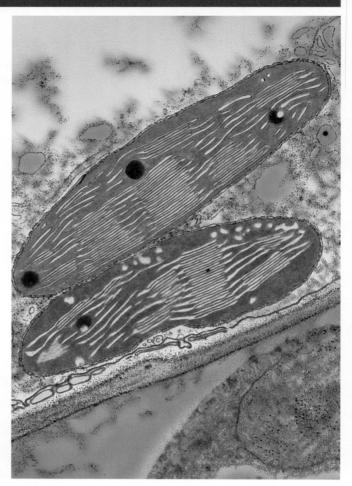

Figure 21.2 Transmission electron micrograph of a chloroplast
(See page 199)

C20

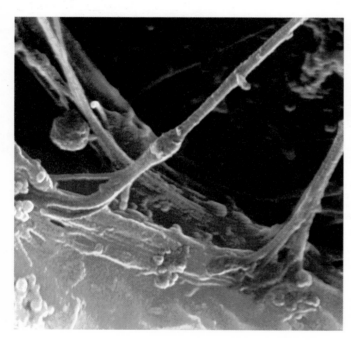

Figure 20.15 At the neuromuscular junction the impulse passes to the muscle causing contraction
(See page 183)

C21

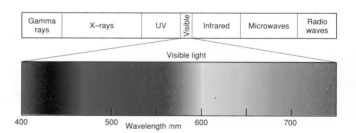

Figure 21.6 Visible light is part of the electromagnetic spectrum
(See page 200)

C22

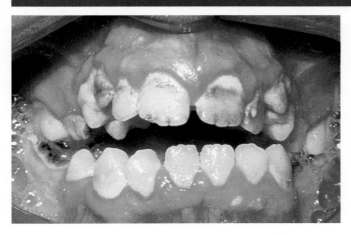

Figure 22.6 This shows cavities caused by decay and reddened patches, the telltale signs of gum disease
(See page 209)

C23

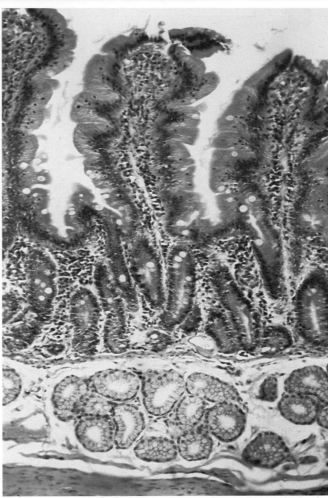

Figure 22.13 Transverse section through the wall of the duodenum
(See page 215)

C24

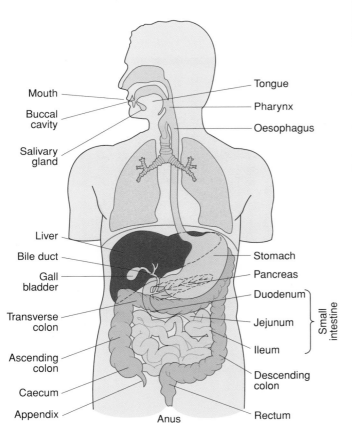

Mouth

Buccal cavity

Salivary gland

Liver

Bile duct

Gall bladder

Transverse colon

Ascending colon

Caecum

Appendix

Tongue

Pharynx

Oesophagus

Stomach

Pancreas

Duodenum

Jejunum

Ileum

Small intestine

Descending colon

Rectum

Anus

Figure 22.7 The human alimentary canal
(See page 210)

C25

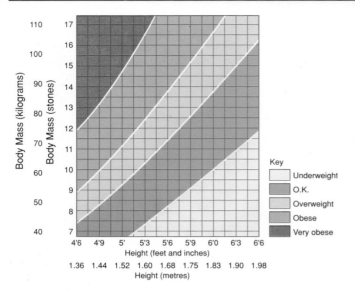

Key

Underweight
O.K.
Overweight
Obese
Very obese

Figure 23.20 A chart like this can be used to find your ideal body mass
(*See page 240*)

C26

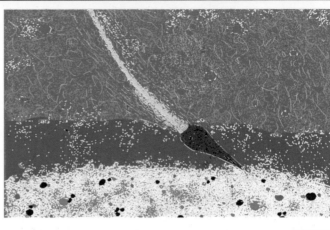

Figure 27.14 Head first into fertilisation, the sperm is seen here embedded in the zona pellucida
(*See page 283*)

C27

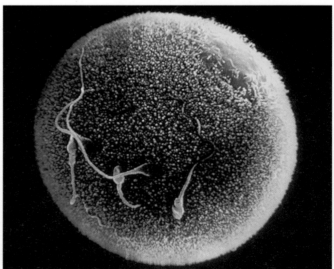

Figure 29.4 Researchers were surprised to find that one particular factor might be the cause of the majority of cases of previously unexplained male sterility
(*See page 298*)

C28

Figure 24.7 Handle with care: a potentially lethal culture of *E. coli* strain 0157:H7
(*See page 252*)

C29

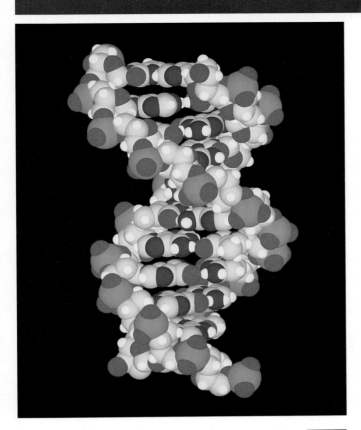

Figure 31.5 (a) A computer-generated model of the DNA molecule
(See page 330)

C30

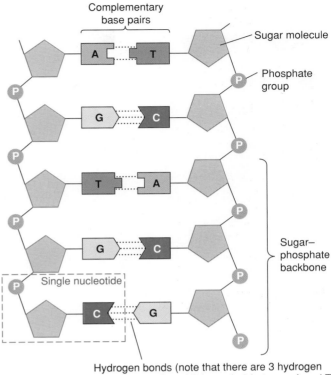

Complementary
base pairs

Sugar molecule

Phosphate group

Sugar–phosphate backbone

Single nucleotide

Hydrogen bonds (note that there are 3 hydrogen bonds between C and G but only 2 between A and T)

Figure 31.5 (b) the structure of DNA can be shown simplified like this
(See page 330)

C31

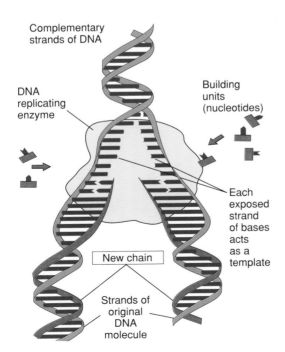

Complementary strands of DNA

DNA replicating enzyme

Building units (nucleotides)

Each exposed strand of bases acts as a template

New chain

Strands of original DNA molecule

Figure 31.8 How DNA replicates itself – semi-conservation replication
(See page 332)

C32

355

Figure 33.7 (a) People of every race can be affected by the albino allele
(See page 369)

C33

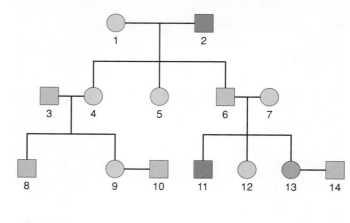

Key to phenotypes

○ Normal female

● Affected female

◻ Normal male

◼ Affected male

Figure 33.7 (b) A family tree where some members have inherited the recessive condition albinism
(See page 369)

C34

Figure 33.13 The wild type *Drosophila* has red eyes, but the mutant has white eyes
(See page 373)

C35

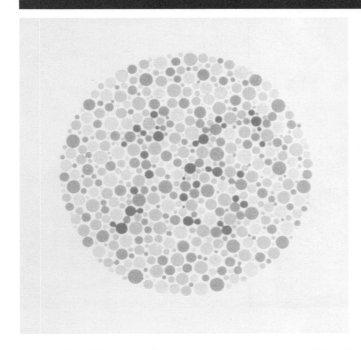

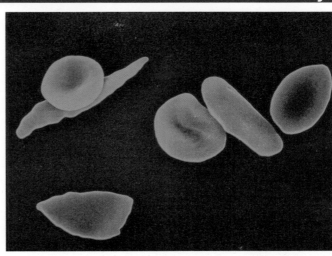

Figure 34.2 A blood smear from someone with the sickle cell trait – both normal and flat, elongated sickled red cells are present
(See page 382)

Figure 33.18 This is one of a set of Ishihara cards used to test for red-green colour blindness. A person with normal colour vision can see the number 16 hidden among the coloured dots. Someone who has red-green colour blindness is unable to see the number
(See page 378)

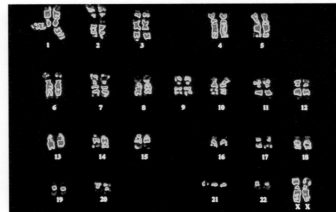

Figure 34.5 The karotype of a person with Down's syndrome showing three copies of the chromosome 21
(See page 384)

Figure 34.13 The colouring on the cat's face and ears is the expression of the Himalayan gene – during winter the points are darker than they are in the summer months
(See page 390)

Figure 35.2 (a) The marine iguana and (b) the saddleback giant tortoise are found only in the Galapagos Islands *(See page 392)*

C40

Figure 35.3 The two morphs of the pepper moth. The light form survives well in unpolluted areas but the dark form is selected against. When conditions are reversed the dark form of the moth is the most successful. *(See page 394)*

C41

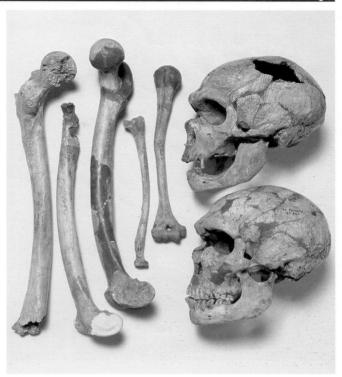

Figure 37.11 Two skulls and bones of Neanderthal man. The upper skull was found in 1908 and the lower skull a year later at different sites in France
(See page 416)

(See page 416)

C43

Figure 37.6 The amazing trail of fossilised footprints discovered in 1978 by Mary Leakey at Laetoli in Tanzania, were those of three hominids (probably two adults and a child) of *Australopithecus afarensis*. The small footprints on the right belonged to hipparion, an extinct three-toed horse
(See page 412)

(See page 412)

C42

Figure 37.10 This is a reconstruction of a hearth used by *Homo erectus*, showing burnt bones and cracked nut shells
(See page 415)

(See page 415)

C44

Figure 37.16 This bison found painted in the Altamira caves in Spain shows how well the anatomy of the animal has been observed
(See page 420) C46

Figure 37.12 A Neanderthal burial site where part of a male skeleton was found – it is about 60 000 years old
(See page 416) C45

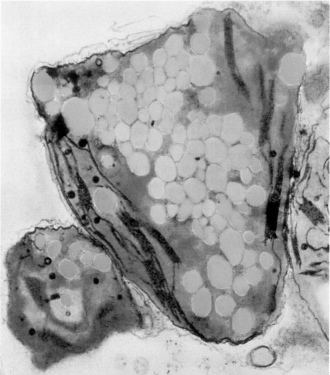

Figure 37.18 Neolithic pots found in Brittany, France
(See page 421) C47

Figure 39.2 Using genetic engineering techniques a thale cress plant (*Arabidopsis*) was given three modified bacterial genes and as a result the cells produced a plastic material called PHB within the chloroplasts. Up to 14 per cent of the dry biomass of the thale cress leaves may be PHB, and the commercial prospects look promising
(See page 450) C48

Figure 38.2 A map of the biomes across the world – notice that the same biome can occur in different regions of the Earth where climatic and soil conditions are similar
(*See page 423*)

C49

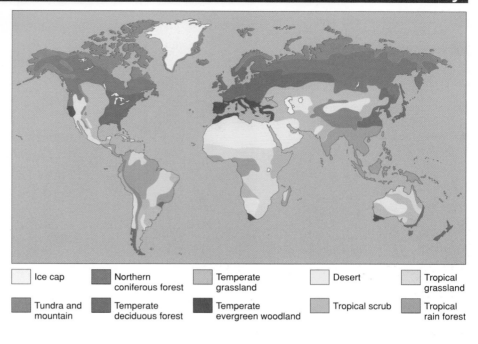

	Ice cap		Northern coniferous forest		Temperate grassland		Desert		Tropical grassland
	Tundra and mountain		Temperate deciduous forest		Temperate evergreen woodland		Tropical scrub		Tropical rain forest

Figure 38.5 A pond such as this is a common ecosystem. It has a community comprising many populations. The other photos show some of the smaller organisms living there (above; protoctists, left: a great diving beetle). It is likely that the pond will be visited by other species of birds, mammals and insects because it is a source of drinking water
(*See page 425*)

C50

Worst cases of sewage and industrial pollution

Worst cases of oil pollution

Major tourist beaches

● Sewage sludge dumping site

■ ▪ Water contaminated with radioactive substances

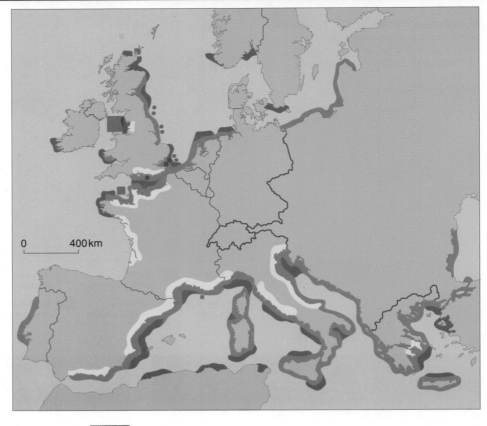

0   400km

Figure 39.8 Pollution around Europe's coastline
(See page 455)

C51

Figure 39.4 Oil is a devastating pollutant along coastlines, killing many fish and seabirds. However studies have shown that natural processes rid an area of petrochemicals faster than might be expected, and that coastlines regenerate in time
(See page 452)

C52

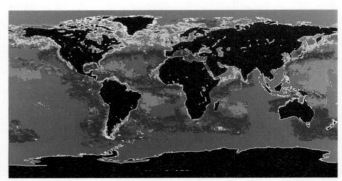

Figure 39.14 The extent of phytoplankton blooms can be seen in this satellite picture. The colours represent varying phytoplankton densities with red the most dense, through yellow, green and blue to violet (least dense)
(See page 459)

C53

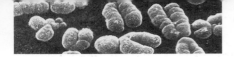

CHAPTER 33 Genetics and Inheritance

Figure 33.1 Gregor Mendel died before the importance of his work was appreciated

> ► *Before you start your study of genetics you should revise the two processes of cell division, mitosis (Chapter 5.3) and meiosis (Chapter 27.1), and their significance*

> ► *Chapter 32.1 answers the question what is a gene?*

Self-fertilisation means that a male gamete fertilises a female gamete of the same flower. Cross-fertilisation occurs when a male gamete fertilises a female gamete of a different flower (of the same species).

Genetics is the branch of science which explains the inheritance of similarities and differences between parents and their offspring. It has many important applications in medicine, agriculture and horticulture. The information which determines a living organism's characteristics is carried by genes located on the chromosomes in the nucleus. Remember that a gene is a sequence of DNA.

The study of modern genetics was begun by Gregor Mendel, a monk and teacher of biology who lived in Brunn, Austria (now Bruno, Czech Republic) in the mid-nineteenth century. In his spare time, Mendel worked on his own carrying out research into the mechanisms of inheritance. His most valuable contribution came from his study of the garden pea, *Pisum sativum*. He carried out many thousands of crosses between different plants following seven particular inherited characteristics. As a result he concluded that characteristics are determined by *factors*. Each parent has two such factors but only one is passed on to each gamete and so to the next generation. When he followed the inheritance of two characteristics that had contrasting forms, he found they showed **independent assortment**, that is either of one pair of characteristics could combine with either of the other pair at random. On the basis of his work Mendel proposed two laws and also published his findings, but sadly during his life their significance was never appreciated. It was not until 1900, 16 years after Mendel had died, that his papers were rediscovered and the importance of his work recognised.

33.1 Monohybrid inheritance

Mendel was without doubt a meticulous scientist. He realised the importance of carrying out his breeding experiments numerous times to eliminate chance results. He was lucky that he chose the garden pea because it shows a number of characteristics (or **traits**) which have two well contrasting forms.

The characteristics that Mendel studied were:

- stem length (tall or short)
- colour of the unripe pea pods (green or yellow)
- form of the ripe seeds (round or wrinkled)
- flower position (terminal or axial)
- form of the pods (inflated or constricted)
- colour of the seed-coat (grey–brown or white)
- colour of the cotyledons (green or yellow)

The pea plant will self-fertilise if it is left undisturbed. It can only be cross-fertilised if it is emasculated, which means that its male stamens are dissected out while immature and before their pollen has been shed. To pollinate the flower artificially as Mendel would have done, pollen from another plant must be dusted onto its stigma. This flower must then be kept covered until its fruits have formed.

Mendel obtained **pure breeding** plants for his experiments. This means that for at least two generations before the experiment the plants had been self-fertilised and had only produced plants showing a particular characteristic, i.e. they bred true. For the first series of experiments Mendel followed a single contrasting pair of characteristics. An experiment to study the inheritance of a single characteristic is a **monohybrid cross**. The results of a monohybrid cross are shown in Figure 33.2.

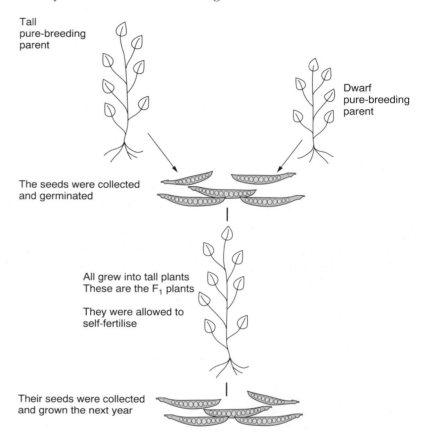

Tall
pure-breeding
parent

Dwarf
pure-breeding
parent

The seeds were collected
and germinated

All grew into tall plants
These are the F₁ plants

They were allowed to
self-fertilise

Their seeds were collected
and grown the next year

The plants in the next generation were 3 tall:1 dwarf

Figure 33.2 Mendel's first experiment, a monohybrid cross. Pure breeding tall and dwarf peas were crossed.

Mendel first took pure breeding tall pea plants and crossed them with pure breeding dwarf plants. These parent plants are called the **P** or **parent generation**. He harvested the seeds and when they were sown they all grew into tall plants (not plants of intermediate height as might have been expected). These were hybrid plants, the F_1 or **first filial generation**. The F_1 plants were allowed to self-fertilise and their seeds collected and sown. In the next generation, F_2, three quarters of the plants grew tall and one quarter were dwarf. The same pattern was found for all seven of the characteristics that Mendel investigated.

Mendel found that in every case, one of the characteristics did not appear in the first generation, but it re-appeared in the next generation. This is called the **recessive characteristic**. There was no blending or mixing of the features of the original parents in the F_1 plants. The characteristic that appeared in the F_1 generation is said to be **dominant**. In the cross described, tall is the dominant characteristic and dwarf is recessive. Mendel concluded from his results that each parent has two *factors* which control characteristics such as tall or dwarf in each cell. Only one factor is passed from a parent to the next generation (in each gamete).

Alleles are different forms of the same gene. Homologous chromosomes carry alleles for the same characteristics. One chromosome has been inherited from the mother and one from the father.

▶ *Chapter 27.1 describes how homologous chromosomes behave during meiosis*

An organism with a pair of identical alleles is a homozygote (noun); or, is described as being homozygous (adjective).

An organism with two different alleles is a heterozygote (noun); or, is described as being heterozygous (adjective).

Mendel knew nothing of genes or of chromosomes, because they had not yet been discovered. This makes his interpretation of the results all the more remarkable. We can now see that Mendel's factors are what we know as genes. Every gene has alternative forms or **alleles**. Alleles occupy the same position on a chromosome. This position is called a **locus**.

Tall and dwarf are alleles of a single gene. Tall is the dominant allele (represented by T) and dwarf is the recessive allele (represented by t) and they will occupy the same locus on homologous chromosomes.

Each true breeding parent has two identical genes, and they are said to be **homozygous**. The tall parent has two dominant genes (TT) and the dwarf parent has two recessive genes (tt). The F_1 plants have received a dominant gene for height (T) from their tall parent, and a recessive gene (t) from their dwarf parent. This means the F_1 plants have two different alleles (Tt) (one allele for being tall and one allele for being dwarf) so they are described as **heterozygous**. All the genes (or alleles) carried by an organism are its **genotype**. The characteristic shown by an organism as a result of the alleles it carries (tall or dwarf) are its **phenotype**. You can see from Figure 33.3 that the recessive alleles are only expressed in the phenotype where the organism has no dominant alleles. Sometimes the phenotype is affected to a degree by environmental factors as we shall see later.

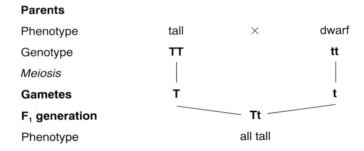

Parents

Phenotype	tall	×	dwarf
Genotype	**TT**		**tt**
Meiosis			
Gametes	T		t

F_1 generation — Tt

Phenotype — all tall

Selfing of the F_1 plants

Phenotype	tall	×	tall
Genotype	**Tt**	×	**Tt**

Meiosis

Gametes (frequency): 0.5T   0.5t   0.5T   0.5t

F_2 generation: 0.25**TT**   0.25**Tt**   0.25**tT**   0.25**tt**

Phenotypes: tall   tall   tall   dwarf

3 tall : 1 dwarf

Alternatively the selfing of the F_1 plants can be shown using a Punnett square:

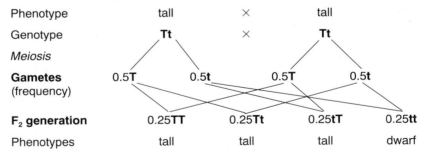

		gametes	
		0.5T	**0.5t**
gametes	**0.5T**	0.25**TT** tall	0.25**Tt** tall
	0.5t	0.25**tT** tall	0.25**tt** dwarf

Figure 33.3 How to summarise a monohybrid cross using a homozygous tall pea plant and a dwarf plant as an example

As a result of Mendel's studies of monohybrid crosses, the **law of segregation** was formulated. It is a statement to the effect that:

'The characteristics of an organism are determined by pairs of factors (alleles). The alleles are separated during meiosis when gametes are formed. Therefore only one allele from each pair is present in a gamete.'

Monohybrid inheritance in humans

A number of characteristics in humans are each coded for by a single gene and so are examples of monohybrid inheritance. These include the Rhesus blood group, tongue rolling, albinism and achondroplasia (dwarfism). Three human genetic diseases caused by the inheritance of a single gene are cystic fibrosis, phenylketonuria and Huntington's disease.

The inheritance of cystic fibrosis

Cystic fibrosis (CF) is a genetic condition affecting 1 in 2000 people in the Caucasian population. It is caused by a recessive gene on chromosome 7. This gene codes for an enzyme that is involved with the regulation of salt and water in epithelial cells. The effect is that abnormal mucus is produced in the lungs and in the gut which is more viscous than normal and does not flow properly so the lungs become congested. The pancreas and its duct becomes blocked and food cannot be digested normally. The disease is treated with drugs and daily physiotherapy to shift the mucus. However, the outlook for sufferers is not good, and many die by the age of 30. Research into the use of gene therapy to cure the symptoms of CF is currently in progress.

Only people who are homozygous for the recessive allele will suffer the disease. It is thought that 1 in 50 people are heterozygous for CF (having one dominant and one recessive allele). They are **carriers** of the disease but have a normal phenotype. If two heterozygous people (carriers) have a child there is a one in four chance that it will have the disease.

When a genetic disease is known to run in a family adults may be given genetic counselling before they try to conceive, so that they understand the probability of the baby being affected by the condition. In early pregnancy genetic screening of the fetus may be offered to the parents.

► *Chapter 29.5 mentions genetic counselling*

In this example the allele for the normal enzyme is **C**. The allele for the CF abnormality is **c**.

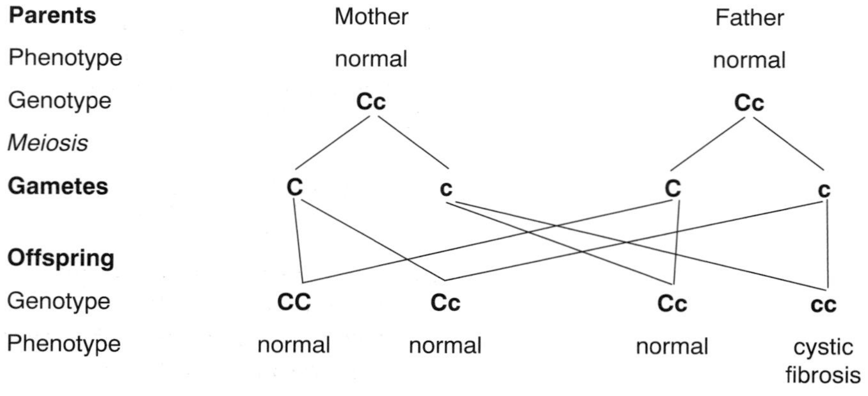

Parents	Mother	Father
Phenotype	normal	normal
Genotype	Cc	Cc
Meiosis		
Gametes	C c	C c
Offspring		
Genotype	CC Cc	Cc cc
Phenotype	normal normal	normal cystic fibrosis

The parents each have a normal phenotype but are in fact carriers, heterozygous for the CF allele. They have a one in four probability of having a child with CF at every pregnancy.

Figure 33.4 The inheritance of cystic fibrosis

Phenylketonuria

Phenylketonuria (PKU) is a genetic disease that occurs in about 1 in every 15 000 births. It is due to a homozygous genotype containing a pair of recessive alleles which prevent the body from secreting an enzyme that catalyses the conversion of phenylalanine to the amino acid tyrosine. In the absence of the enzyme, phenylalanine concentration in the blood rises. This causes irreversible mental retardation, accompanied by restlessness and often epilepsy. There is no cure.

However, if the condition is detected before any damage has been caused, the effects of the disease can be avoided. This is why all babies born in Britain are given a blood test (the **Guthrie test**) which detects PKU when they are two days old. If they are found to have the disease they must be given a diet that is free of phenylalanine, and their development should then be normal. Once puberty has passed it is often possible to introduce a normal diet.

Huntington's disease

Huntington's disease is a rare neurological disease due to a lethal dominant mutant allele gene carried on chromosome 4. It occurs in only 6 in 100 000 of the population in Britain although the incidence is much higher around the Moray Firth area of Scotland. Sufferers are probably heterozygous for the allele. The disease does not show any symptoms until middle age. By this stage in life the sufferer may well have had children and the gene may have been passed on to the next generation.

To begin with affected people have problems with balance and co-ordination. As the symptoms of Huntington's disease progress, mental deterioration and painful involuntary muscular movements, twitching and facial grimaces develop. It becomes impossible for an affected person to care for themselves. The disease lasts for several years, finally ending in death.

33.2 Co-dominance

There are a very few cases where alleles do not cause such a clear cut distinction in phenotype as the dominant/recessive types that are so common. Sometimes both the alleles contribute to the phenotype, that is neither allele is dominant over the other. This is illustrated in humans in the MN blood group system where blood is categorised according to the occurrence of M and/or N antigens found on the surface of the red cells. The gene involved has two alleles M and N. This means that there are three possible genotypes: MM (giving phenotype M), NN (phenotype N) and MN (phenotype MN).

33.3 The human genome

The human **genome** is all the genes that are carried on the 23 pairs of chromosomes found in the nuclei of the somatic (body) cells. The human **karyotype** is the 23 pairs of chromosomes.

An enormous project is being carried out in research centres worldwide to map the position of every human gene, by a process known as transcript mapping. This project is called 'The Human Genome Project'. The map will probably be completed during the first five years of the twenty-first century.

This knowledge is very important for people who have genetic diseases in their family. In fact we all carry mutant genes but they only cause a

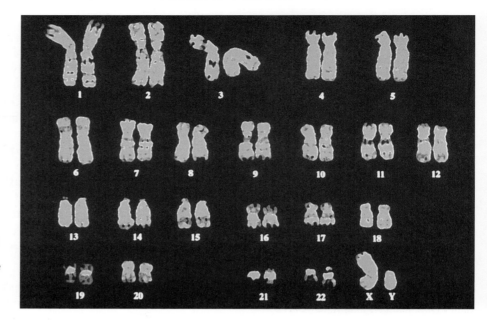

Figure 33.5 The 23 pairs of homologous chromosomes that make up the human karyotype. Each pair carries alleles for the same characteristics except the 23rd pair which are the sex chromosomes XX or XY.

genetic defect in children if both partners carrying the same mutant recessive allele pass it on in the gametes. In theory, it will be possible to screen people to find out which defective genes they are carrying. An ethical code will have to be put in place to decide how this information can be managed for the benefit of the individual.

Questions

1 Discuss whether you think it should be compulsory for everyone to undergo screening for defective genes.

2 What would be the advantages to the individual if screening were to become statutory?

3 How might an individual find themselves disadvantaged if they knew that they carried defective genes?

33.4 Human pedigrees

Human family trees are useful for showing how an inherited characteristic (or **trait**) has passed through a family and whether it is due to a dominant or a recessive allele. By convention males are shown by squares and females by circles. Shading indicates that the individual has the trait being followed. Members of the same generation are shown at the same level across the page and successive generations appear down the page. Figure 5.5 in Chapter 5 (page 35) is a family tree showing how breast cancer runs in families.

By studying family pedigrees we can see that in some conditions most generations are affected. This indicates that the trait is due to a dominant gene. For other characteristics we find that the trait frequently skips generations which is the pattern for a trait due to a recessive allele. When first cousins marry, or a small population inbreeds, a genetic defect due to a recessive gene arises more often than would be the case if the couple were not genetically related.

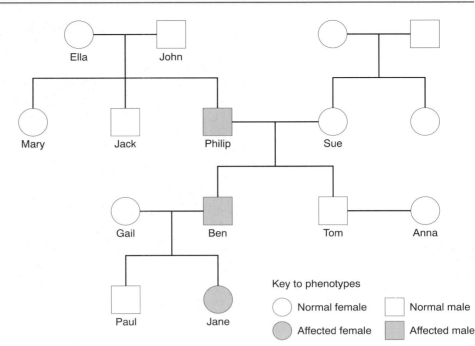

Figure 33.6 The human pedigree of a family with members inheriting dwarfism shows the pattern typical of a condition due to a single dominant gene

(a)

Figure 33.7 (a) People of every race can be affected by the albino allele (b) A family tree where some members have inherited the recessive condition albinism
(See Colour Gallery page 356)

C33

C34

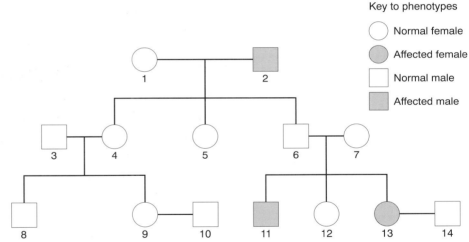

(b)

Questions

1 Look again at Figure 33.6

   a) In whose cells might the mutation causing dwarfism have occurred?

   b) Name the carriers of the dwarfism allele shown in the pedigree.

2 From the family tree shown in Figure 33.7, which members:

   a) are certainly carrying the recessive allele for albinism?

   b) may carry the allele for albinism?

3 If person 14 in Figure 33.7 is a carrier, what is the chance of 13–14 having albino children?

33.5 Dihybrid inheritance

Mendel extended his early experiments by breeding peas and following the inheritance of two traits. These were Mendel's **dihybrid crosses**. Again, he started with parents breeding true for two contrasting characteristics. For example in one experiment he used peas which grew from wrinkled green seeds. He already knew from the monohybrid crosses that round was dominant to wrinkled and yellow was dominant to green. The plants in the F_1 generation all produced seeds that were round and yellow.

Mendel collected the seeds from the F_1 plants and germinated them and allowed the F_2 plants to self-pollinate (self). Altogether there were 556 F_2 plants. They had the combinations of seed type shown in Table 33.1.

This shows that the largest group of plants had the two dominant characteristics and the smallest group had the two recessive characteristics. The rest of the plants were new types with one dominant and one recessive characteristic – round (dominant), green (recessive); or wrinkled (recessive), yellow (dominant). The ratio of the numbers of different types of seed was 315 : 108 : 101 : 32. We can simplify this to approximately 9 : 3 : 3 : 1. Mendel continued his investigation and found that exactly the same pattern appeared in three other dihybrid crosses involving different pairs of contrasting characteristics.

Mendel concluded from the appearance of new combinations of characteristics in the F_2 plants, that the factors for seed colour and shape must be inherited independently of one another. The F_1 plants must be heterozygous and carry the factors RrYy, where R is the dominant allele for

Table 33.1

Seed type	Numbers
round, yellow	315
round, green	108
wrinkled, yellow	101
wrinkled, green	32

The F_1 plant has diploid cells with pairs of homologous chromosomes carrying the alleles R, r, Y and y

 During prophase 1 the chromatids become visible

During anaphase 1 of meiosis, the homologous chromosomes separate at random

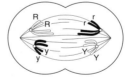 or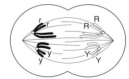

At anaphase 2 chromatids separate

  or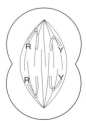

There is an **equal probability** of each type of gamete RY, Ry, rY and ry being produced

Ry   rY   ry   RY

Figure 33.8 During meiosis the homologous chromosomes separate independently – as a result four types of gametes form in approximately equal numbers

form (round) and r the recessive allele (wrinkled), and Y is the dominant allele for colour (yellow) and y the recessive allele (green). When the plants self, they must produce equal numbers of gametes each with one allele for seed shape and one for seed colour, that is RY, Ry, rY and ry.

Look at Figure 33.9 to see how the random fertilisation of gametes gives rise to the 9 : 3 : 3 : 1 ratio of phenotypes in the F_2 generation. As a consequence of the results from dihybrid crosses, Mendel's second law, the **law of independent assortment**, was derived. In modern language it means that: *there is an equal chance that either one of a pair of alleles of a gene may be inherited with either of the two alleles of another gene.*

Let the alleles be shown by: **R** = round, **r** = wrinkled, **Y** = yellow, **y** = green.

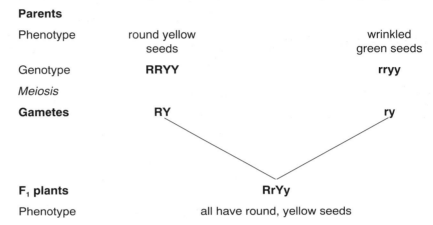

Parents

Phenotype	round yellow seeds		wrinkled green seeds
Genotype	**RRYY**		**rryy**

Meiosis

Gametes   RY   ry

F_1 plants   **RrYy**

Phenotype   all have round, yellow seeds

When the F_1 plants are selfed, each type of gamete is produced in equal numbers. A Punnett square is used to find the genotypes of the F_2 progeny. The phenotypes have also been added:

Gametes	$\frac{1}{4}$**RY**	$\frac{1}{4}$**Ry**	$\frac{1}{4}$**rY**	$\frac{1}{4}$**ry**
$\frac{1}{4}$**RY**	$\frac{1}{16}$**RRYY** round yellow	$\frac{1}{16}$**RRYy** round yellow	$\frac{1}{16}$**RrYY** round yellow	$\frac{1}{16}$**RrYy** round yellow
$\frac{1}{4}$**Ry**	$\frac{1}{16}$**RRYy** round yellow	$\frac{1}{16}$**RRyy** round green	$\frac{1}{16}$**RrYy** round yellow	$\frac{1}{16}$**Rryy** round green
$\frac{1}{4}$**rY**	$\frac{1}{16}$**RrYY** round yellow	$\frac{1}{16}$**RrYy** round yellow	$\frac{1}{16}$**rrYY** wrinkled yellow	$\frac{1}{16}$**rrYy** wrinkled yellow
$\frac{1}{4}$**ry**	$\frac{1}{16}$**RrYy** round yellow	$\frac{1}{16}$**Rryy** round green	$\frac{1}{16}$**rrYy** wrinkled yellow	$\frac{1}{16}$**rryy** wrinkled green

This shows that F_2 plants (the result of selfing the F_1 generation) are:

9	:	3	:	3	:	1
round yellow		round green		wrinkled yellow		wrinkled green

Figure 33.9 Dihybrid inheritance – the result of crossing pea plants from round yellow seeds with plants produced from wrinkled green seeds

33.6 Test crosses

Monohybrid and dihybrid crosses tell us that the majority of organisms have the dominant phenotype. They contain at least one dominant gene for the

> The genes carried by an organism are its genotype. The appearance of the organism expressed by its genes (alleles) are its phenotype. An organism with a dominant phenotype may have a homozygous genotype (2 dominant alleles), or a heterozygous genotype (1 dominant, 1 recessive allele). Both will look the same.

characteristic(s). However, the genotypes of the organisms may be different, in other words the organism may be homozygous or heterozygous for the characteristic. The easiest way of establishing the genotype of the plant or animal is to cross it with one which is homozygous recessive for the characteristic. This is called a **test cross** or **back cross**.

The alleles for height in a pea plant are T = tall and t = dwarf. If we consider a tall pea plant it could have the genotype TT (homozygous) or Tt (heterozygous); either way it has the tall phenotype. If the plant is crossed with a dwarf plant (homozygous recessive, tt) we can look at the offspring and deduce the genotype of the parent. If they are all tall plants, the parent must have the genotype TT; if there is a mixture of tall and dwarf plants the tall parent must have the genotype Tt. This is explained in Figure 33.10.

True breeding (homozygous) tall pea plants look identical to heterozygous plants. The way to determine their actual *genotype* is to cross the tall plants with dwarf peas (homozygous recessive). There are two outcomes.

Parents	(1)	tall × dwarf	or	(2)	tall × dwarf
F₁ progeny		1 tall : 1 dwarf			all tall

Explanation

T is the allele for tall and **t** the allele for dwarf.

Cross 1
- The F₁ progeny showed a mixture of phenotypes (half of each type). They could receive only the recessive **t** allele from their dwarf parent.
- Some of the offspring also received **t** from the other (tall) parent and so were dwarf plants (**tt**).
- The rest of the offspring received the dominant allele (**T**) from the tall parent and are tall (**Tt**).
- This tall parent must be **heterozygous** (**Tt**).

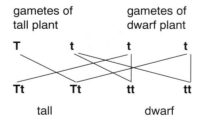

Cross 2
- All F₁ were tall.
- They could receive only **t** from the dwarf parent.
- They were all tall and so must have received **T** from the tall parent.
- This tall parent must be **homozygous** (**TT**).

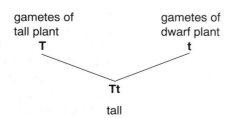

Figure 33.10 The monohybrid test cross

Genetic experiments using the fruit fly *Drosophila melanogaster*

The fruit fly, *Drosophila melanogaster*, is an excellent organism for genetic research. It is small, cheap to culture and has a short life cycle (10 days at 25°C), producing large numbers of offspring which quickly mature. The males and females are easily distinguished and the fly has genetic features which are distinctive and easily observed with a microscope while the fly is under a light anaesthetic. The female flies used in the crosses must be virgin flies for once a female has mated she may continue to store sperm. The fruit fly has four chromosomes. In the wild *Drosophila* lives in temperate and tropical regions often being found around rotting fruit.

Drosophila was first used in genetics experiments by the American geneticist and Nobel Prize winner Thomas Morgan at the beginning of the twentieth century. Morgan's research confirmed that Mendel's interpretation of his work was correct. Morgan proposed the **chromosome theory of heredity**, that Mendel's factors are genes, arranged in sequence along

chromosomes. Morgan used the wild type fly (i.e. the common form) and crossed it with mutants. There are a number of such mutants that are found fairly commonly as shown in Table 33.2.

Wild type	Genotype	Mutant	Genotype
grey body	GG	ebony body	gg
long wing	WW	vestigial wing	ww
red eye	RR	white eye	rr

Table 33.2

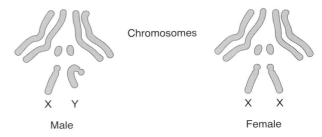

Chromosomes

X Y

Male

X X

Female

Figure 33.12 *Drosophila* – the karyotype of *Drosophila* is four chromosomes

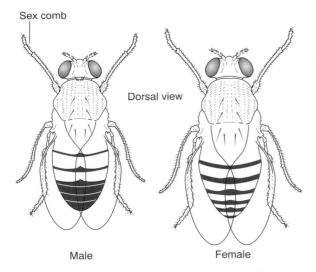

Sex comb

Dorsal view

Male

Female

Figure 33.11 *Drosophila* – male and female fruit flies

Figure 33.13 The wild type *Drosophila* has red eyes, but the mutant has white
(*See Colour Gallery page 356*)

33.7 Autosomal linkage

In 1906 a cross was made between sweet pea plants with purple flowers and long pollen grains, and other sweet pea plants with red flowers and round pollen grains. The F$_1$ plants had purple flowers and long pollen grains showing that these were the dominant alleles. When the F$_1$ seeds were grown and selfed, the four expected combinations of phenotype (9 purple flowered–long pollen, 3 red flowered–long pollen, 3 purple flowered–round pollen, 1 red flowered–round pollen) were not obtained. Instead there were many more plants like the original parents and very few of the new combinations. In the sweet pea, flower colour and shape of pollen grain did not follow the Mendelian pattern.

The reason for this is now known. The alleles for flower colour and pollen shape are carried on the *same* chromosome. This means that they are likely to be inherited together in a block and do not undergo independent assortment. Such genes are said to be **linked**. However, there were a few new combinations of characteristics (red flowers–round pollen and purple flowers–long pollen). There must have been an exchange of genetic material during 'crossing over' of the chromatids of homologous chromosomes, while meiosis was taking place and the gametes were being formed.

▶ *Chapter 27.1 describes crossing over*

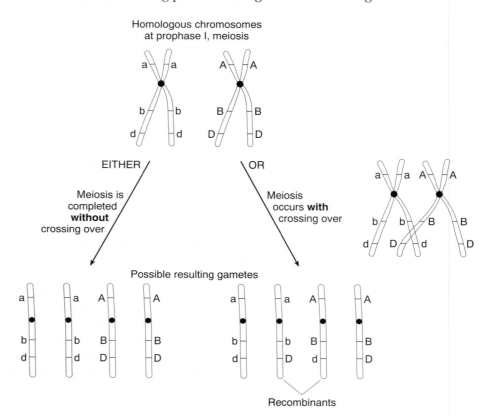

Figure 33.14 Linked genes tend to be inherited together. New combinations of alleles arise during meiosis if crossing over occurs.

Cross over value

If linked genes are close together on a chromosome, the frequency of a chiasma forming between them and alleles being exchanged with the partner homologous chromosome is much less likely than if the genes are further apart. The frequency with which recombinants (individuals with a new combination of alleles) are formed is called the **cross over value** (**COV**). It is calculated using the following expression:

$$\text{COV} = \frac{\text{number of recombinant individuals}}{\text{total number of offspring}} \times 100\%$$

Each one per cent is equivalent to one unit of length on the chromosome. For organisms such as *Drosophila* that have been extensively researched, it is known which genes occur on the same chromosome, and it is possible to use COV to draw gene maps. For example if we know that COV for genes W and X is five per cent and COV for W and Y is 20 per cent, the possible maps would be:

(a)
$$W\text{--------}X\text{-----------------------------------}Y$$
$$\quad\quad\quad\quad\quad\quad\quad\quad\quad\quad\quad\text{20}$$
$$\quad\quad\quad\quad\quad 5$$

or

(b)
$$X\text{---------}W\text{--------------------------------------}Y$$
$$\quad\quad\quad 5\quad\quad\quad\quad\quad\quad 20$$

To confirm which map is correct we need to know the COV for X and Y. If the COV for X and Y is 15 per cent we can be sure that map (a) is the correct one but if it is 25 per cent then (b) is correct.

Maps have been produced for the chromosomes of *Drosophila*, maize, some fungi, bacteria and viruses. Mapping the human genome is far more complicated.

▶ **Chapter 33.4 covers mapping of the human genome**

33.8 The inheritance of sex

We have seen that the human karyotype consists of 23 pairs of chromosomes. The first 22 pairs are called **autosomal** chromosomes and the 23rd pair are the **sex** chromosomes. In humans, females have two X chromosomes and males have an X and a Y chromosome. The sex chromosomes are transmitted in the same way as other homologous chromosomes. The Y chromosome determines maleness by bringing about the development of the embryonic gonads to testes. This happens because of a gene on the Y chromosome that codes for a testis determining factor. The gene is absent from the X chromosome and in females the embryonic gonads develop into ovaries.

homo = same
hetero = different

Females will produce gametes carrying an X chromosome and males will produce equal numbers of gametes carrying X or Y chromosomes. Females are thus called the **homogametic** sex and males are the **heterogametic** sex. However, this is not the situation in all species. In birds the homogametic sex is the male (XX) and the heterogametic sex is the female (XY). In butterflies and moths the males have only a single sex chromosome (XO) and the females have two sex chromosomes (XX).

Parents	Mother	Father
Parental sex chromosomes	XX	XY
Gametes	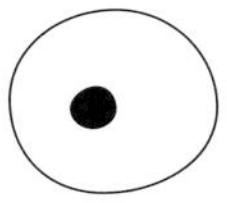 1.0 X	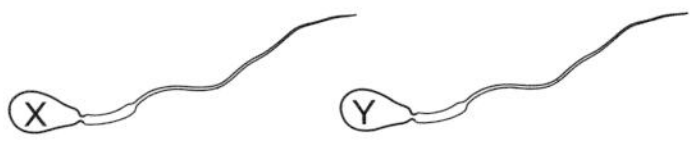 0.5 X 0.5 Y
Children	0.5 XX Female	0.5 XY Male

Figure 33.15 The inheritance of sex in humans

Since all female gametes carry the X chromosome and half male gametes carry X and half Y, a fertilised egg has a 50 per cent chance of being male or of being female. However, there seem to be slightly more males born than females (106 males : 100 females). This may mean that sperm carrying the Y chromosome survive better than those carrying X, or are more successful at fertilising the ovum.

► *Chapter 34.4 describes mutations affecting the sex chromosomes*

Barr bodies

The female human zygote carries two X chromosomes. Once the embryo has divided to a size of around 2000 cells one of the pair of X chromosomes in each cell becomes inactivated. The X chromosome that has 'shutdown' forms a darkly stained body inside the nuclear membrane called a **Barr body**. The event is random in each cell and means that a female has a mosaic of maternal and paternal X chromosomes expressing themselves.

Usually, this is not obvious to see, but tortoise-shell cats provide an exception. These cats are always female and are heterozygous for coat colour (XBXb). They carry the alleles on their X chromosomes. The tortoise-shell coat phenotype shows a random distibution of red (Xb) and black (XB) hairs which reflects the active chromosomes.

33.9 Sex linkage

There are a number of traits that have a special pattern of inheritance because their alleles are carried by the sex chromosomes. This is another example of a discovery made as a result of breeding experiments using *Drosophila*. In human males the small size of the Y chromosome means that a number of alleles cannot be carried. Therefore whatever alleles are present on the male X chromosome will be expressed. If the X chromosome is carrying a mutant allele it will show in the phenotype, even if it is recessive.

Haemophilia

► *Chapter 10.4 also mentions haemophilia*

Haemophilia is an example of a sex-linked disease. It is a condition where the blood is unable to clot properly due to a deficiency in a blood clotting factor. Untreated it leads to painful internal bleeding into joints and severe internal haemorrhages.

The disease is caused by a recessive gene carried on the X chromosome. A male carrying the recessive gene who has no allele on his Y chromosome will be a haemophiliac. The chance of this happening is about 1 in 25 000. The genotype of a haemophiliac male can be shown as X^hY and of a normal male as X^HY. X and Y are the sex chromosomes and H or h the alleles for the blood clotting factor.

Females are less likely to be haemophiliacs because they carry a blood clotting allele on each of their X chromosomes. Providing that they have at least one dominant allele (H) they will have normal blood clotting. The possible genotypes and phenotypes for females in respect to the blood clotting allele are: X^HX^H (normal) X^HX^h (normal phenotype but carrying a recessive allele) and X^hX^h (haemophiliac).

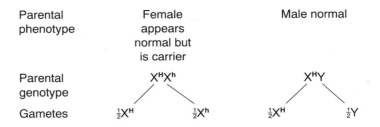

Possible genotypes and phenotypes of children:

	$\frac{1}{2}X^H$	$\frac{1}{2}X^h$
$\frac{1}{2}X^H$	$\frac{1}{4}X^HX^H$ normal female	$\frac{1}{4}X^HX^h$ carrier female
$\frac{1}{2}Y$	$\frac{1}{4}X^HY$ normal male	$\frac{1}{4}X^hY$ haemophiliac male

Figure 33.16 The inheritance of haemophilia in the offspring of a carrier female and normal male

Haemophilia was passed by Queen Victoria, who was a carrier, to some of her descendents. The family pedigree is shown in Figure 33.17. It is possible that Victoria received the recessive gene from her mother. The present British Royal Family, although descended from Queen Victoria, are not affected by the recessive gene.

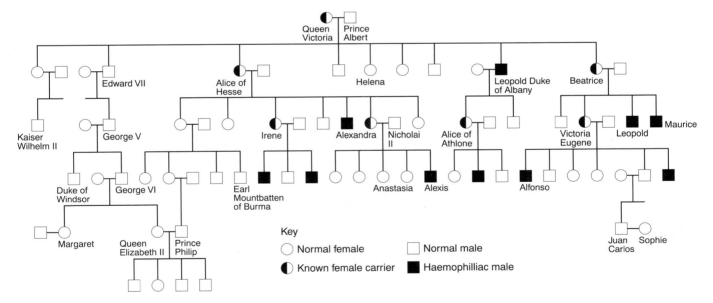

Figure 33.17 The pedigree of the Royal Family descended from Queen Victoria showing haemophilia

Red–green colour blindness

An allele carried on the X chromosome is responsible for the proper functioning of the cones found in the retina of the eye. About 8 per cent of males carry a recessive allele which causes them to be red–green colour blind. Only 0.4 per cent females are affected although some have normal sight but are carriers of the recessive gene. Again, the pattern is that a mother is the carrier and passes the recessive gene to a son who is then affected by colour blindness. He cannot pass this to his sons but there is a 50 per cent chance that he may pass the recessive gene to any daughters.

The family pedigree where some members are colour blind:

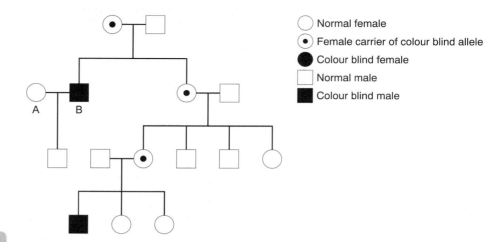

○ Normal female
⊙ Female carrier of colour blind allele
● Colour blind female
□ Normal male
■ Colour blind male

Figure 33.19 The inheritance of colour blindness

► **Chapter 20.6 covers the eye in detail**

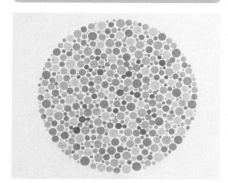

Figure 33.18 This is one of a set of Ishihara cards used in testing for colour blindness. A person with normal colour vision can see the number 16 hidden among the coloured dots. Someone who has red–green colour blindness is unable to see the number.
(See Colour Gallery page 357)

If A and B had a daughter she would be a carrier of the colour blind allele as we can show. Let the allele for normal colour sight be **C** and the allele for colour blindness be **c**.

Parents	A	B
Phenotype	Normal sight female	Colour blind male
Genotype	$X^C X^C$	$X^c Y$
Gametes	X^C	X^c Y

Children's phenotypes and genotypes:

	X^c	Y
X^C	$X^C X^c$ female carrier	$X^C Y$ male normal sight

33.10 Multiple alleles

So far we have looked at a number of genetically determined features where the gene has either a dominant or a recessive form, that is the gene has two alleles. However, there are genes which have more than two alleles. The gene controlling the ABO blood group in humans is an example. The gene has three alleles but each person has only two of them in their genotype. The gene involved is represented as I and its three alleles are I^A, I^B and I^O. Alleles I^A and I^B are co-dominant, and both are dominant to I^O (which is recessive).

The difference between the blood groups lies in the glycoprotein antigens found on the cell membrane of the red blood cells. Blood group A cells have antigen A, group B have antigen B, group AB have both antigens A and B and group O have no antigens on the red cells. Allele I^A and I^B code for antigens A and B, and I^O for no known antigen.

► **Chapter 33.2 explains co-dominance**

Table 33.3

Blood group	Alleles
O	$I^O I^O$
A	$I^A I^A$
	$I^A I^O$
B	$I^B I^B$
	$I^B I^O$
AB	$I^A I^B$

33.11 Gene interaction – polygenes

The characteristics that we have looked at so far have all been due to the inheritance of alleles of single genes. They are also examples of **discontinuous variation**. That is there is a definite distinction between phenotypes expressing the dominant or recessive gene. For example people are albino or they are not; they suffer from cystic fibrosis or they do not. Sex is also an example of discontinuous variation for we are either male or female.

There are, however, a number of characteristics that are controlled by more than one gene, in some cases by several genes (**polygenes**). This leads to a range in phenotype in the population, or **continuous variation**. Human skin colour is determined by eight alleles and height, shoe size and eye colour are all continuously variable. If measurements of a trait such as height are sampled in a population, it will be found that they follow a normal distribution: a few people will be small and a few will be tall, but most will fall between the two extremes.

It should be noted that some continuously variable traits are influenced by the environment. Body mass in humans is an example. The genotype will code for a certain body mass for any individual. However, if the individual lives where food is short it is unlikely that the body mass will reach its potential. Conversely, if someone regularly consumes more food than they need, they are likely to exceed their genetically determined body mass.

▶ *Chapter 11.4 covers blood groups*

▶ *Basics in Brief explains about normal distribution*

CHAPTER 34 Variation

34.1 The significance of genetic variation

The existence of genetic variation between individuals of the same species means that each has a unique set of characteristics. These differences are important because they result in some individuals being better able to adapt to prevailing environmental conditions than others. These individuals are the ones who will survive longer to reproduce, pass on their characteristics and contribute to the evolutionary process.

There are several causes of genetic variation. Firstly, meiosis allows for different combinations of genes to be passed on in the gametes. The formation of chiasmata during the first prophase results in new combinations of alleles on the chromosomes. This is followed by the independent assortment of homologous chromosomes during the first metaphase. Fertilisation, when two gametes fuse, also contributes to variation since which sperm of the many surrounding an oocyte actually fertilises it, depends completely on chance.

However, perhaps the most significant changes occur as a result of **mutation**, a sudden, permanent change in structure or amount of DNA. A mutation varies from a tiny change in the DNA structure involving a single nucleotide, to a larger change in chromosome type or number. An individual carrying the mutation is called a **mutant**. The rate of natural (chance) mutation at any one locus on a chromosome is low, there being between 1 and 30 mutations per million gametes. Most mutations occur in the somatic (body) cells and so are not passed on. Only mutations carried by gametes will be inherited by the next generation. The majority of mutations are disadvantageous to the individual, beneficial mutations are extremely rare.

34.2 The causes of mutations

The natural mutation rate is increased by the action of a **mutagen**, a factor which brings about a mutation. Most forms of high energy radiation can cause mutations, e.g. X-rays, α- and β-particles and γ-rays are mutagenic since they damage DNA. The number of mutations is proportional to the dose of radiation received. The effect is also cumulative, so continuous exposure to low level radiation can be harmful over a long period of time. Non-ionising radiation such as UV light is also known to be mutagenic. The increase in UV radiation reaching the surface of the Earth through the damaged ozone layer is believed to be the cause of mutations leading to types of skin cancer. Some chemicals are also mutagenic, for example mustard gas, colchicine and cyclamate (an artifical sweetener that is now banned).

▶ *Chapter 17.2 describes the effect of ultraviolet light on human skin*

▶ *Chapter 5.4 covers cancer and mutations*

34.3 Gene or point mutations

A mutation which occurs at a single locus is called a **gene** or **point mutation**. The mutation in some way affects the sequence of nucleotide bases on the DNA at the locus, i.e. it changes the genetic code. This results in the incorrect sequence of amino acids being assembled to build the protein controlled by that gene, and so the wrong protein is formed or no protein at all. If the protein is an enzyme it may well be unable to function as it may not have the correct conformation (shape). This may be fatal because it brings about the failure of a vital metabolic pathway. Sometimes the mutation causes inaccurate information to be transcribed from the DNA. This may result in a defect in the individual, but not cause death.

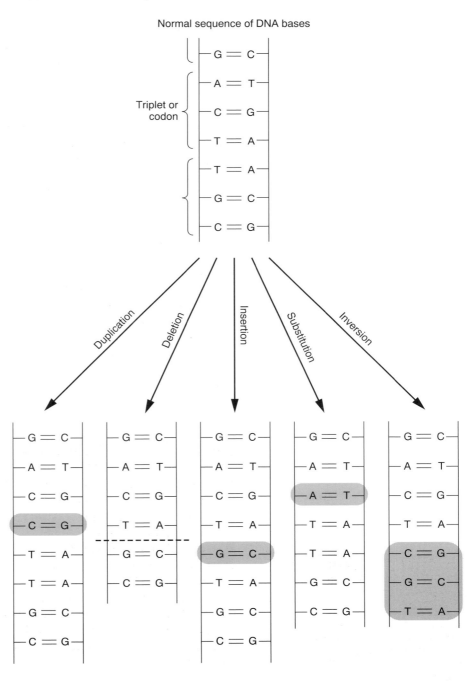

Figure 34.1 Point mutations are the result of changes to the genetic code – they are thought to be very important in bringing about evolutionary change

There are several different types of gene mutation. Consider this message and see how its sense is changed or made nonsense by slight alterations in one or more letters.

The intended message is: the old cat saw the big rat

- **Duplication:** part of the sequence of nucleotides on the DNA chain is repeated.
   The message becomes: the old cat <u>tsa wth ebi gra t</u>

- **Deletion:** one or more of the nucleotide bases are removed from the DNA.
   The message becomes: the <u>odc ats awt heb igr at</u>

- **Insertion:** extra nucleotide bases are added to the DNA chain.
   The message becomes: the old cat sa<u>a</u> wth <u>h</u>eb igrat

- **Substitution:** a nucleotide is replaced by one that has a different nitrogen-containing base.
   The message becomes: the old cat saw the big <u>c</u>at

- **Inversion:** a nucleotide sequence separates from the DNA chain but then rejoins in reverse order.
   The message becomes: the old cat <u>was</u> the big rat

Duplications, insertions and deletions are called **frameshift mutations** because once the mutation has occurred the rest of the DNA code following it will be misread. A major change in metabolism is likely to result. Substitutions and inversions can change the sense of the code.

Sickle cell anaemia

> ► *Chapter 10.3 describes the structure of haemoglobin*

In humans the condition called sickle cell anaemia is due to the inheritance of a mutated gene responsible for producing β-haemoglobin. A substitution occurs in the code for the sixth amino acid so that it is changed from CTT to CAT. The effect is that at this point in the amino acid chain, thymine is replaced by adenine. As a result in β-haemoglobin the sixth amino acid is valine instead of glutamic acid. The allele for normal haemoglobin is HbH and for the mutant allele is HbS.

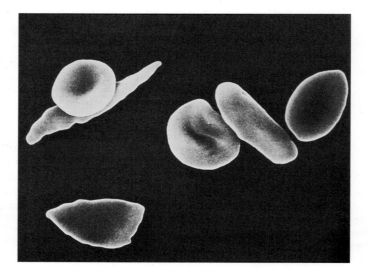

Figure 34.2 A blood smear from someone with the sickle cell trait – both normal and flat, elongated sickled red cells are present *(See Colour Gallery page 357)*   C37

The sickle cell haemoglobin, haemoglobin S, crystallises at the low concentrations of oxygen that may be found in the blood capillaries. The growing crystals distort the red blood cells so they become the shape of a sickle or half moon. The sickle cells are less efficient at carrying oxygen than normal cells and they can block capillaries. When oxygen then fails to reach parts of the body severe pain is experienced – this is called a crisis.

Sickle cell anaemia occurs in people who are homozygous for the mutant gene (HbSHbS). It is a severe and debilitating disease, heart and kidney failure are common and many sufferers die when quite young. People who are heterozygous for the gene (HbHHbS) are said to have sickle cell trait. Slightly over half of their red blood cells are normal and the rest carry haemoglobin S. Health is generally good although they may suffer from slight anaemia. This situation, where both alleles contribute to the phenotype of the heterozygote, is an example of **co-dominance**.

There is an advantage in having the sickle cell trait for people living in parts of the world where malaria is endemic. The parasite *Plasmodium* that causes malaria lives for an important part of its life cycle in the red blood cells. People who have the sickle cell trait can get malaria but the disease is not as severe as in those with normal haemoglobin, who may die during a severe outbreak.

▶ *Chapter 30.4 has information on parasites*

(a) Frequency of sickle-cell allele

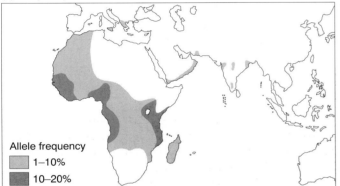

Allele frequency
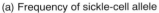 1–10%
▮ 10–20%

(b) Distribution of malaria

Figure 34.3 The first map (a) shows the distribution of the sickle allele. The second map (b) shows how malaria occurs in the region. Notice the correlation between the two.

34.4 Chromosome mutations

There are two types of mutation that can occur in chromosomes, aneuploidy and euploidy. **Aneuploidy** involves changes to part of a chromosome or sometimes the duplication of a single chromosome; **polyploidy** (**euploidy**) involves altering the number of whole sets of chromosomes.

Aneuploidy

We have already said that during meiosis, chiasmata form between homologous chromosomes. Two chromatids (one from each chromosome) pull apart, but may break under strain in places and then rejoin to the other chromosome in the pair. This can lead to a variety of structural changes in the chromosome. **Deletions** occur when a fragment of the chromosome breaks off but fails to join up again and so is lost. Alternatively, the fragment may join up with another homologous chromosome (**translocation**) or may invert before rejoining the same chromosome (**inversion**).

(a) Deletion

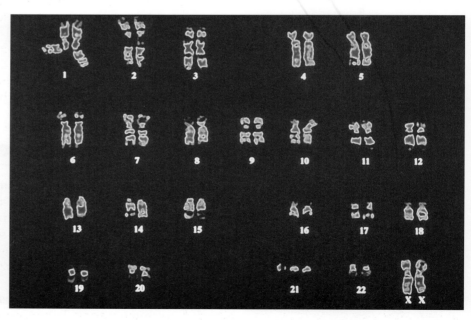

Figure 34.4 Some types of mutation that bring about structural changes of chromosomes

In some instances in humans there may be the addition or deletion of a whole chromosome. This changes the chromosome number to either 46 + 1 or to 46 − 1 and usually has severe consequences. Many fetuses with an abnormal chromosome number will naturally abort. Down's syndrome is due to an extra chromosome number 21 in the karyotype (47 chromosomes in total). Three copies of a chromosome are called **trisomy**.

Figure 34.5 The karyotype of a person with Down's syndrome showing three copies of chromosome 21 (See Colour Gallery page 357)

Figure 34.6 This seven year old boy with Down's syndrome is doing a puzzle with his mother

The features of a person with Down's syndrome are characteristic. Growth may be retarded to some degree and due to skeletal abnormality the face tends to be flat with the eyes slanting slightly outwards. There may also be associated congenital heart defects, an increased incidence of respiratory disease and learning difficulties. However, with the improvements in medical care of the past 50 years and more educational opportunities, the future for children born with Down's syndrome is now much brighter. Life expectancy has increased and many people with Down's syndrome are able to work and live with some degree of independence within a sheltered environment.

Scientists are unsure why Down's syndrome happens. It is probably due to the failure of either pairs of chromosome 21 or the chromatids of chromosome 21 to separate during meiosis. Therefore some gametes are formed carrying two copies of chromosome 21 and others without a copy of the chromosome. If these gametes achieve fertilisation, most of the fetuses will be aborted (miscarried) naturally.

The incidence of babies born with Down's syndrome is about 1 in 650 births, but is significantly higher in women over 40 years old. Pre-natal testing is available to pregnant women which assesses their risk of carrying a fetus with Down's syndrome. A further test, amniocentesis, can confirm this.

▶ *Chapter 29.5 covers amniocentesis and genetic counselling*

Aneuploid conditions of the sex chromosomes

Aneuploidy involving a change in the number of the sex chromosomes has been observed in many species including humans. It probably happens because of failure of the X and Y chromosomes to pair properly during the first meiotic prophase or because the X and Y chromosomes fail to separate during the first anaphase. The consequence is that the individual does not have the normal XX or XY chromosomes. In Turner's syndrome, which affects about 1 in 3500 females, the somatic cells have only a single X chromosome, the second one is missing. The ovaries do not develop and so the woman is infertile. Secondary sexual characteristics do not develop naturally, but hormone treatment can be given to stimulate secondary sexual development.

Klinefelter's syndrome affects people who have XXY chromosomes. Their phenotype is male, however the testes are small and do not produce sperm. The secondary sexual characteristics develop to varying degrees and there is commonly little development of facial hair. The karyotype of people with Turner's syndrome is 45 chromosomes and for Klinefelter's syndrome is 47 chromosomes. Cases are also known of people who are XXX or XYY.

Polyploidy

Polyploidy is the type of chromosome mutation that results in more than two sets of chromosomes and can arise from faults in mitosis. For example the chromatids may fail to separate during anaphase; there may be a failure of the spindle to form. The most common polyploids are triploids (three sets of chromosomes) and tetraploids (four sets). Polyploidy occurs quite commonly in plants, the polyploids tend to be larger and more vigorous than the diploid form. However, it is virtually unknown in animals, although post-mortem studies on naturally aborted human fetuses have shown that some are triploid. Some polyploid plants are fertile but many are not. Reproduction can only then occur asexually or by artificial propagation such as taking cuttings.

Polyploidy can occur in hybrids of two different species. The hybrid itself may be sterile, but should there be a doubling of the chromosome number to produce a polyploid, meiosis may be possible and gametes may be formed.

Figure 34.7 The fruits of the cultivated blackberry (tetraploid plant) are much larger than those of the wild (diploid) relative

► *Chapter 37.10 covers farming by Neolithic man*

This is believed to have happened to wheat over thousands of years, bringing about our modern bread wheat which is a hexaploid (six sets of chromosomes). A wild variety of wheat (*Triticum monococcum*), a diploid plant, was cultivated in Neolithic times around 8000 BC. Its yield must have been small and it had other disadvantages; the heads were easily broken off by wind and so were wasted. Evolution has been brought about by hybridisation of *T. monococcum* with other diploid wheats, followed by later chromosome doubling, giving rise to the tetraploid emmer wheat used for pasta. Hybridisation of the emmer wheat with another wild wheat (einkhorn) and further chromosome doubling has taken place so that we now have modern wheat (*Triticum aestivum*) which is a high-yielding plant.

Figure 34.8 Heads of wild wheat *Triticum monococcum* and modern wheat *Triticum aestivum* (right)

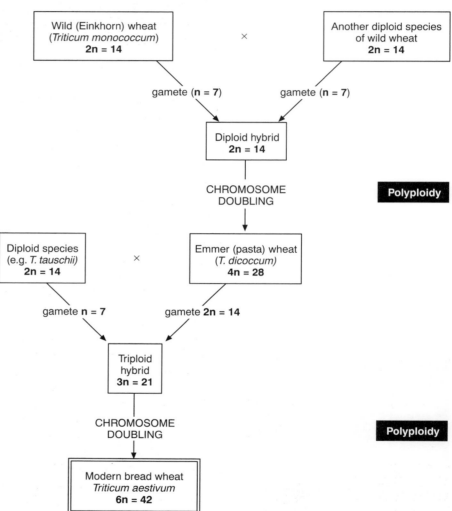

Figure 34.9 The evolution of bread wheat

34.5 Conserving genes

Many of the old species of wheat are no longer cultivated. Some species have been lost but many are conserved in **gene banks**. The total genes of a species together constitute the **gene pool**. At present, many species are rapidly becoming extinct and the gene pool is shrinking. This means that the **diversity** of different species is also being reduced. There is less opportunity for new varieties to arise and it is less likely that species will evolve that are better adapted to the current environment.

Figure 34.10 Red kite scavenging

Genes are conserved in botanical gardens, zoos, seed banks and sperm banks. Rare species can be protected and may be encouraged to breed. There has, however, been a problem with breeding in zoos because **inbreeding** has become common and the offspring have had reduced viability. This happens because the animals tend to be related, having been bred in a very small gene pool. In the wild most species show **outbreeding**. By using DNA fingerprinting on animals being bred in different British zoos, it has been possible to identify which ones are closely related. Breeding programmes can then be devised which increase the gene pool by mating unrelated animals from different zoos.

Organisations interested in conserving threatened plants and animals organise breeding programmes in protected environments followed by release into the wild. The number of species of birds in Britain is under constant scrutiny. The red kite was a common scavenger on the streets of London during the nineteenth century. By the 1980s, however, it could only be found in small numbers in the more remote parts of central Wales. It had become virtually extinct through changes in land use and because it was hunted and eggs were stolen from nests.

A project organised by the Royal Society for the Protection of Birds is actively seeking to increase the numbers of red kites and to introduce them back into England. The birds are now protected by law. Nests of known breeding pairs are guarded by volunteers while the eggs are being incubated and the young reared. Red kites have also been reared in captivity and were first released into England in 1989.

The increasing world population and demand for timber and other plant products by the developed world all contribute to the loss of plant species. Wakehurst Place in Sussex is the home of the seed bank of the Royal Botanical Gardens at Kew. Originally, the seed bank was set up to preserve seeds from the collection of plants in Kew Gardens, but it now concentrates on storing seeds from much further afield. The seed bank is currently being expanded as part of the activities to mark the millennium, and aims to hold seeds from 10 per cent of all plant species in the world by the year 2010. This huge operation involves locating some 25 000 different species of plant in the wild and then collecting from them 20 000 seeds from as many different individuals as possible, in order to ensure that there is a diversity of genes stored. The seeds are treated before storage and may remain viable for as long as 200 years.

Figure 34.11 This woman is working in a seed bank. Why do you think that the seeds are stored at a low temperature?

34.6 The Hardy–Weinberg principle

The frequency of alleles in a gene pool and the phenotypes of a population remains constant providing that sexual reproduction is random and there are no selection factors acting on the population.

In 1908 two mathematicians, Hardy and Weinberg, independently published a mathematical model which allowed the frequency of genotypes in a population to be calculated from the frequency of the phenotypes.

It works only if certain assumptions are true. These are:

- the population consists of diploid, sexually reproducing organisms;
- the population size is large;
- allele frequencies do not change over time;
- mating is random within the population, but not between generations;
- there is no immigration into or emigration from the population.

If we consider two alleles, A and a, the three possible genotypes that may exist are AA, Aa and aa. Let the frequency of allele A be p and the frequency of allele a be q. The frequency of alleles in the population is 100 per cent or 1, therefore:

$$p + q = 1$$

Table 34.1

Gametes	A	a
Frequency	p	q
A	AA	Aa
p	p^2	pq
a	Aa	aa
q	pq	q^2

We can construct a Punnett square (Table 34.1) to see how the gametes carrying the A and a alleles combine at fertilisation.

This shows that the frequency of the genotype AA is p^2, of Aa is 2pq and of aa is q^2. In other words we have a relationship between the allele frequency and the frequency of the genotypes.

If we know that A is dominant to a we can work out the frequency of phenotypes in the population from the table. Those with the dominant phenotype will be $p^2 + 2pq$ and those with the recessive phenotype will be q^2.

The frequency of all phenotypes in the population must be 100 per cent or 1, therefore:

$$p^2 + 2pq + q^2 = 1$$

This is the Hardy–Weinberg formula.

Using the Hardy–Weinberg formula

We can show how the Hardy–Weinberg formula is used by considering the inheritance of tongue rolling in humans. Some people can readily roll their tongue into a U-shape while others cannot. This ability is due to a single gene, R. The allele for rolling is dominant to the allele r, the inability to roll the tongue. People who can roll their tongues have either the genotype RR or Rr and the non-rollers have rr.

Figure 34.12 Tongue roller and . . .

non-roller

In an imaginary population, the frequency of tongue rollers is known to be 80 per cent and of non-rollers, 20 per cent. From the Hardy–Weinberg formula $p^2 + 2pq + q^2 = 1$ the frequency of genotypes is:

$$RR = p^2$$
$$Rr = 2pq$$
$$rr = q^2$$

20 per cent of the population are non-rollers and have the genotype rr. So:

$$q^2 = 0.2$$
$$q = \sqrt{0.2}$$
$$= 0.447$$

We have seen that $p + q = 1$, therefore:

$$p = 1 - 0.447$$
$$= 0.553$$

To find the proportion of the population for the other two genotypes:

$$(RR) \quad p^2 = 0.553 \times 0.553$$
$$= 0.31$$

$$(Rr) \quad 2pq = 2 \times 0.553 \times 0.447$$
$$= 0.49$$

and as we know $(rr) = 0.20$

Hint: In order to check the answer return to the formula $p^2 + 2pq + q^2 = 1$, and substitute your calculated figures into it: $0.31 + 0.49 + 0.20 = 1$.

This shows us that the genotypes of the original population consists of 31 per cent homozygous tongue rollers (RR), 49 per cent heterozygous tongue rollers (Rr) and 20 per cent homozygous non-rollers (rr).

34.7 The effect of genotype and the environment on phenotype

Although the DNA is a copy of the instructions for the development and functioning of an organism, there is evidence that shows that the extent to which the genotype is expressed is sometimes controlled by environmental factors. A well documented example is that of cats and rabbits that carry the Himalayan gene. The animal has a light coloured coat with dark points at the extremities of the body, particularly over the face and ears. As the weather becomes cooler and day length shortens in autumn, the animal's points darken, only to lighten again when the warm weather returns. It is thought that the points darken to increase heat absorption, so reducing heat loss from the body. Dark patches of hair can be induced artificially by keeping a cold pad over part of the light fur.

Figure 34.13 The colouring on the cat's face and ears is the expression of the Himalayan gene – during winter the points are darker than they are in the summer months
(See Colour Gallery page 357)

C38

Many human characteristics are influenced by the environment. We have already mentioned body mass as being very sensitive to food availability. The development of other characteristics, such as intelligence, artistic, sporting and technical skills, depends on our inherited ability but also upon our experiences. Mannerisms are genetically determined, but also learned from our parents during our upbringing. Interesting studies involving identical twins that have been separated at birth and raised in different environments have provided evidence to support the importance of environmental influences in development.

▶ *Chapter 30.5 includes examples of twin studies*

CHAPTER Evolution
35

35.1 Early theories of evolution

Before the nineteenth century, creation was the most commonly held belief to explain how species arose. Many religions taught that a God created life when the Earth began and people who hold this view are called 'creationists'. It is not possible to test these ideas by scientific investigation.

In the early part of the nineteenth century John Baptiste Lamarck, a French biologist, proposed the idea of inheritance by **acquired characteristics**. He believed that during life an organism might increase the use of part of its body and in some way alter its characteristics. The change could be passed on to future offspring. Lamarck quoted the example of the giraffe that he suggested had to stretch its neck in order to reach the high branches for leaves to feed on. The effect was that over a number of generations the neck grew longer. When the giraffe reproduced, future generations would have the advantage of a longer neck. Conversely, if part of the body ceased to be used it would, in time, disappear.

Lamarck's views were not seriously accepted at the time; the creationists' view prevailed. His ideas were not, however, rejected on scientific grounds and today they are considered to be useful because they directed people's thoughts towards the subject of evolution and encouraged the progression of ideas.

35.2 Natural selection

Charles Darwin and Alfred Wallace both published papers in 1858 to propose the theory of evolution by natural selection. They had not researched the problem together but had come to the same conclusion at the same time.

Both were aware of the doctrine proposed by Thomas Malthus at the end of the eighteenth century. Malthus had realised that in time the number of humans alive would exceed food supply and that famine, disease and war would be inevitable. Darwin saw that these principles could be applied to all living organisms, and the ideas formed the basis of the Theory of Natural Selection.

It is important to remember that Darwin and Wallace had no knowledge of genetics or of the mechanisms of inheritance. The modern version of Darwin's theory, expressed taking this knowledge into account, is called Neo-Darwinism.

Natural selection is thought to be the most important process that brings about evolution in a population. It causes a change in the frequency of alleles in the gene pool.

The theory can be summarised by the following four statements which must hold true, and so allow two conclusions to be drawn.

1 Individuals differ from each other.
2 Offspring usually resemble their parents.
3 More offspring are produced than will reach maturity and reproduce.
4 There is a struggle to survive and only those well adapted to their environment will survive.

The conclusions that can be drawn from this are:

1 The individuals that successfully reproduce will pass the characteristics that have allowed them to be well adapted on to their offspring.
2 Over a period of time some members of a species may change their characteristics and become sufficiently distinct as to be considered a separate species.

Charles Darwin and his voyage on HMS Beagle

Charles Darwin (1809–82) was a keen and talented naturalist. He studied first at Edinburgh and then at Cambridge University and in 1831 was offered the opportunity to join a voyage on HMS Beagle. The purpose of the expedition was to chart maps of the southern hemisphere. The ship was away for five years.

Darwin's most important work was studying the reptiles and birds of the Galapagos Islands some 500 hundred miles from the coast of South America. The ship only spent a few weeks there but Darwin had the opportunity to observe close at hand many animals and plants that had never before been documented, and he realised the significance of what he was able to see.

The Galapagos Islands are volcanic in origin and so there would have been no life there to start with. The animals living on these remote islands were species that had originally arrived from the mainland. In the absence of competition from predators they had adapted to the new conditions and developed into new races. Darwin was able to observe finches, giant tortoises and the now famous giant iguana lizards. He could see differences between the populations on the different islands.

Darwin was the first scientist to collect observations to support the idea that evolution had occurred. When he returned home he spent many years collecting his ideas together, meticulously supporting them with evidence that he gleaned from other branches of science such as embryology, comparative anatomy and palaentology (the study of fossils). His findings were published in his book *The Origin of the Species by means of Natural Selection or the Preservation of Favoured Races in the Struggle for Life* in 1859.

Figure 35.1 Charles Darwin

(a)

(b)

Figure 35.2 (a) The marine iguana and (b) the saddleback giant tortoise are found only in the Galapagos Islands.
(See Colour Gallery page 358)

35.3 Selection pressures

Natural selection takes place because the organism is subject to a selection pressure exerted on it by the environment that it is living in. We recognise three types of selection that can operate on a population.

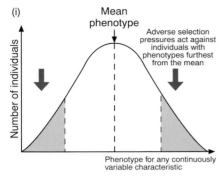

(i)

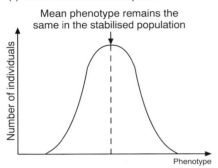

(ii) When selection is complete

Figure 35.3 To begin with there is a wide range of phenotypes – as a result of selection pressures the phenotypes at the extremes of the normal range are eliminated

Stabilising selection

This occurs in all populations and works to eliminate the extreme phenotypes in the population. As a result there is then less variation within the population and so there is less likelihood of evolutionary change. It is possible that stabilising selection might explain the increased incidence of the sickle cell trait in areas where malaria is endemic. In a prehistoric population some individuals carried the sickle cell allele. Homozygotes for the sickle cell allele would probably have died in childhood. Many of the homozygotes for the normal allele would have died from malaria. The group which were best adapted to the environmental conditions would have been those who were heterozygotes. These would be the group most likely to reproduce and with the best chance of survival. There would be an increase in the frequency of the heterozygous genotype amongst the population.

Another example of stabilizing selection is that of mortality in human infants. Babies which are very light or very heavy at birth show a higher death rate than those of average birth weight. Advances in neo-natal paediatric medicine increase the chances of survival for the babies being selected against.

Directional selection

This occurs when there is a change in environmental conditions. Selection pressure will act on the species and the members of the population with the phenotype best adapted to the new conditions will increase in number at the expense of those individuals that are least well adapted. There will be a shift in the optimum phenotype of the population in response to the selection pressure.

The evolution of populations of bacteria resistant to antibiotics illustrates directional selection. If exposed to an antibiotic some of the bacteria will die. Others that carry a mutation conferring resistance upon them will survive and reproduce.

Another famous example of directional selection is that of the peppered moth, *Biston betularia*. Before the industrial revolution, the most common peppered moth was *B. betularia typica*, a pale, speckled moth that is well camouflaged against tree trunks. Its predators are various species of birds. In Manchester in the mid 1850s a dark mutant of the moth occurred. The type was easily visible against tree trunks and therefore readily preyed upon. However, by the end of the nineteenth century 98 per cent of the peppered

Figure 35.4 When there is a change in environmental conditions, directional selection pressures are set up and there is a shift in the mean of the phenotype, to the one which is best adapted to the new conditions

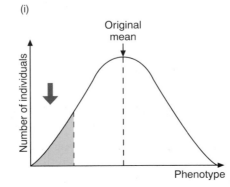

Figure 35.5 The two morphs of the peppered moth. The light form survives well in unpolluted areas but the dark form is selected against. When conditions are reversed the dark form of the moth is the most successful.
(See Colour Gallery page 358)

Figure 35.6 The effect of disruptive selection is to produce two populations

▶ *Chapter 37 covers the evolution of modern humans*

An organism's ecological niche is its role within the ecosystem that it inhabits.

moths in Manchester were the dark type named *B. betularia carbonifera*. As the surroundings had become polluted the tree trunks had blackened and the dark moths were less visible and better able to escape capture than the light moths. Since in recent years efforts have been made to reduce pollution the number of light moths has increased again. When two or more phenotypes exist like this in a population it is called **polymorphism**, each type is a **morph**.

Disruptive selection

This is the most unusual kind of selection pressure, however, it is important in bringing about an evolutionary change. It occurs when selection pressures favour the extreme types of phenotype. Those in the middle are eliminated and *two* populations result. Each has a distinct appearance and is a morph of that species.

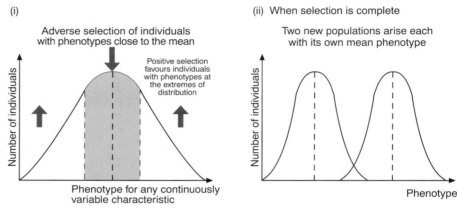

35.4 Speciation

Speciation is the forming of new species of organism. A **species** is a group of organisms that share a gene pool and can reproduce to produce *fertile* offspring. A species usually consists of a number of populations. If a population becomes isolated in some way or another so that the members form a breeding group they are called a **deme**. Selection pressures can work on the demes and coupled with variation will result in different phenotypes and genotypes arising from the original population.

Geographical isolation

A physical barrier such as a mountain range, sea or desert can prevent members from two populations of the same species from breeding. This is called geographical isolation. As a result, each separate population inbreeds and slowly adapts to the environmental conditions that occur. This is **allopatric speciation**.

Darwin's finches are a superb example of allopatric speciation. On his travels Darwin observed 14 species of finch. Their anatomy and breeding habits were similar but they varied in the shapes of their beaks and in their feeding habits. He reasoned that when the birds from the South American mainland first reached the Galapagos Islands there was no competition from other species for food and other resources. As the finches adapted to the new conditions selection would have occurred and new varieties of finch would have arisen, each occupying its own ecological niche.

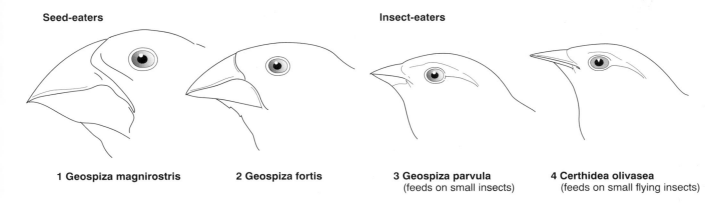

Seed-eaters   Insect-eaters

1 Geospiza magnirostris   **2 Geospiza fortis**   **3 Geospiza parvula**
(feeds on small insects)   **4 Certhidea olivasea**
(feeds on small flying insects)

Figure 35.7 Darwin's finches – notice how the shape of the beak is adapted to the bird's food

The differences in the birds shown in Figure 35.7 are due to **adaptive radiation**. Over time the finches would have dispersed to other islands in the group and would have inbred, giving rise to new species. Where the breeding of a single species results in one or more new species it is called **intraspecific speciation**. A species arising from reproduction between members of two species is hybridisation or **interspecific speciation**.

It is recognised that many islands widely separated from land masses, such as the Falklands, Hawaii and the Seychelles, have their own endemic species. Some islands off the British coast, probably formed after the last Ice Age, have distinct populations of various plants or animals that differ from mainland forms. These are not yet distinct species. St Kilda in the Outer Hebrides which is now uninhabited by humans has its own variety of long-tailed field mouse. Also, the St Kilda wren has a longer tail than the variety found on the mainland.

Reproductive isolation

If a species inhabiting an area becomes separated into two or more reproductively isolated groups, new species may arise by **sympatric speciation**. A number of factors may prevent the two populations from breeding successfully. If the two populations have come to differ in their karyotype, for example if polyploidy has arisen, the hybrids could be sterile.

Mechanical isolation

Mechanical isolation can be the result of a physical problem, for example in an animal species it may be impossible for the male penis to penetrate the female vagina. Alternatively, there may be chemical incompatability so that sperm cannot survive within the female to fertilise the egg, or pollen grains may not germinate on the stigma of the flower that they have reached. The male gametes may reach the female gametes but fail to fertilise them or the offspring may be infertile, as is the mule, which is the product from a mating between a donkey and a horse.

Behavioural isolation

Behavioural isolation is also a recognised barrier to successful reproduction. Some animals go through a complicated courtship ritual before they mate. They may perform complex dances, specific behaviour patterns, sing, develop bright colours and so forth. If any detail of the courtship ritual is different from usual, it can prevent mating.

CHAPTER 36

The Classification of Living Organisms

36.1 Taxonomy

There are several million different species of organisms living on our planet now, but there have been numerous others which are now extinct.

Are there any species we still have to find?

The answer to this question is without doubt 'yes'! What is more exciting is that these organisms may not be very far from urban areas.

A population of 40 pine trees of a previously unknown species, was recently discovered growing at the bottom of a 600 m gorge in the Wollemi National Park, 200 km from Sydney. David Noble who found them was not a member of a scientific expedition but was abseiling in the gorge. He recognised that the trees, which were about 40 m tall, were unusual and took a branch back to Sydney for examination.

There, the scientists who examined the leaves thought that they had come from a fern. However, having compared them with a fossil of an extinct species of pine, they concluded that the branch had come from a species which belongs to the same family as the Chilean monkey puzzle tree. This small group of ancient pine trees are probably the only remaining members of a species that was common millions of year ago.

Figure 36.1 This ancient species of pine has only recently been discovered – how it fits into the evolution of pines is not yet known

Clearly, it is important to have a system of classifying and naming organisms which is international, so that scientists can communicate effectively about particular organisms. The study of biological classification is called **systematics** and the study of the different ways of sorting organisms into groups is **taxonomy**. Taxonomy can be approached from three points of view:

- **Phylogenetics** (the orthodox approach) – which recognises the evolutionary relationships between organisms.
- **Phenetics** – basing the grouping of organisms according to many similar characteristics, although the group may not share a common ancestor.
- **Cladistics** – a method which tries to trace the descent of a group of species from a common ancestor. Cladistics is a relatively new method of taxonomy, which was developed during the 1970s. It is the focus for a good deal of controversy, particularly between cladists and orthodox taxonomists.

The opposite of homologous structures are analogous structures. They have a similar function in the adults of two types of organism which have no common ancestor. An example is the wings in butterflies and birds.

Carl Linnaeus, a Swedish botanist in the eighteenth century, was the first person to succeed in devising an acceptable system for classifying living things. He used **morphology** (form) and **anatomy** to group organisms according to their **homologous structures**. These are characteristics which are related in *origin* and *structure*, but may have a different *function* in the adult of the organism. An example is the arms of humans and the wings of birds. The arms are used to help maintain balance and for swimming and hands have evolved which allow lifting and grasping, pushing and pulling. Birds use their wings for flying, but wings are related to human arms because both evolved from the pentadactyl forelimb of a common ancestor.

Linnaeus' classification is described as a **natural** classification because it separates species according to their total similarities and differences. This is unlike an **artificial** classification which selects a single distinct characteristic on which to base groupings. (For example a system which is used to classify flowers simply on their colour would be artificial.)

Today, many branches of science such as genetics, biochemistry, physiology and ecology can provide evidence for the evolutionary relationships between living organisms.

▶ *Chapter 35.4 explains the concept of a species*

36.2 The naming of living organisms

Every different species that has been identified has been given two latin names which are universal and unique to that species. This system is called a **binomial system**. Many species also have a common name, but these may vary from one region of the country to another. The first latin name describes the group that the plant or animal belongs to, and is its **genus**. For example the animals belonging to the dog family all have the genus name *Canis*. The second latin name is the **species** name and tells us which individual of the genus we are dealing with. So *Canis familiaris* is the dalmation, *Canis latrans* the coyote and *Canis lupus* the timber wolf. Humans and their ancestors share the genus *Homo*.

genus = singular
genera = plural

The genus always starts with a capital letter and the species name with a lower case letter.

(a)

(b)

(c)

Figure 36.2 Three members of the genus *Canis* are (a) the dalmation (*Canis familiaris*), (b) the coyote (*Canis latrans*) and (c) the timber wolf (*Canis lupus*)

36.3 The five kingdoms of living organisms

The current method of classifying living organisms divides them into five large groups called **kingdoms**. This was worked out in the 1960s by Lynn Margulis and Karen Schwartz who modified a system proposed a few years earlier to replace the traditional two kingdoms of plants and animals. The kingdom is the largest taxonomic group.

Table 36.1 The five kingdoms, the groups of organisms they contain and major characteristics

Kingdom	Organisms included	Characteristics
Prokaryotes	bacteria, blue-green bacteria	no true nucleus; very simple cells
Protoctista	algae, protozoa, slime moulds	single eukaryotic cells; multicellular algae
Fungi	Zygomycota e.g. breadmould, Ascomycota e.g. *Neurospora*, Basidiomycota e.g. mushroom	all made of microscopic strands called hyphae; hyphae are multinucleate; non-photosynthetic; heterotrophic
Plants	mosses, ferns, conifers, angiosperms (flowering plants)	multicellular; cells are eukaryotic; photosynthetic; cellulose cell walls
Animals	Cnidaria (jellyfish), flatworms, roundworms, annelids, arthropods, molluscs, starfish, Chordata	multicellular; cells are eukaryotic; heterotrophic; have nervous co-ordination

Figure 36.3 These organisms (a) the moss, (b) the mollusc and (c) the fish belong to three of the five different kingdoms we now recognise

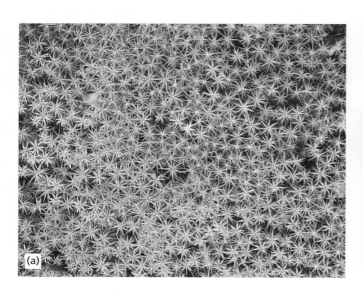

phylum = singular
phyla = plural

Each kingdom is divided into a number of smaller groups, each one called a **phylum**. The organisms in a phylum all share basic common features.

Humans belong to the phylum **Chordata** (the chordates), along with fish, amphibians, reptiles, birds and the other mammals. They all have a vertebral column and a hollow dorsal spinal cord and the group is commonly known as the **vertebrates**. However, there are other less obvious features, some of which are present only early in the animals' development, that link the members of the chordates together including a **notochord**, **gill slits** and a **post-anal tail**.

The phyla are divided into smaller groups called **classes**. The classes of the phylum Chordata are:

- Chondrichthyes – the cartilagenous fish e.g. shark
- Osteichthyes – bony fish e.g. carp, pike
- Amphibia – amphibians e.g. frogs, toads, newts
- Reptilia – reptiles e.g. snakes, turtles, lizards
- Aves – birds e.g. eagle, blackbird
- Mammalia – mammals e.g. humans, apes, cats, whales, bats

Table 36.2 The classification of humans, *Homo sapiens* – each successively larger group makes up the taxonomic hierarchy

Taxonomic rank	Classification
Kingdom	animal
Phylum	chordates
Class	mammals
Order	primates
Family	hominidae
Genus	*Homo*
Species	*sapiens*

The members of a class share more easily observed features of structure, function and behaviour. We see that mammals have skin and are hairy. They have a diaphragm muscle separating the thorax and abdomen. Mammals mostly give birth to their offspring and suckle them on milk while they are young. They have two sets of teeth, they are endothermic and gaseous exchange occurs at the lungs.

Classes are sub-divided into orders, which are made up of smaller groups called **families**. Each family consists of one or more genera. Each genus is identified as one or more species.

Each type of group of organisms within a taxonomic system is called a **taxon**. The succession of groups in a system of classification is called the **taxonomic hierarchy**. Every organism is assigned to a kingdom and then to progressively smaller units of classification, a phylum, class, order, family, genus and species. The species is the basic unit of classification. The human species is *Homo sapiens*.

Questions

1 Write a short explanation of what taxonomy is, and why it is important.

2 What is the difference between (a) phylogenetics and cladistics and (b) natural and an artificial classification.

3 a) Classify, as fully as you can, the chimpanzee.

b) What makes a bat a mammal?

1 In some genetic engineering processes a synthetic gene is inserted into a bacterial host. This process is shown in Figure 1.

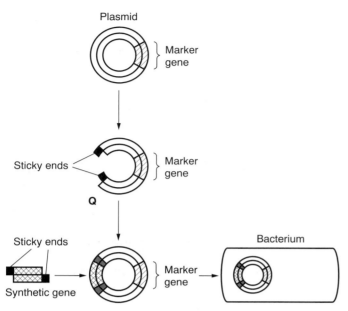

Figure 1

a) i) What term is used to describe the function of the plasmid in this process? *(1 mark)*

   ii) Name the type of enzyme used at Q to cleave (cut) the DNA. *(1 mark)*

b) Genetically engineered human insulin is now used in the treatment of diabetes. State *three* advantages of the use of this type of insulin.

(3 marks)

Edexcel

2 Table 1 shows the percentages of the bases in samples of DNA from different sources.

Table 1

Source of DNA	Percentage of base present in sample			
	adenine (A)	guanine (GA)	cytosine (C)	thymine (T)
yeast	31.3	18.7	17.1	32.9
wheat	27.3	22.7	22.8	27.1
broad bean	29.7	20.6	20.1	29.6
ox thymus gland	28.2	21.5	22.5	27.8
ox spleen	27.9	22.7	22.1	27.3
ox sperm	28.7	22.2	22.2	27.2

a) Describe and explain the relation between:

   i) the total amount of adenine and the total amount of thymine in any one organism. *(2 marks)*

   ii) the total amount of adenine + guanine and the total amount of cytosine + thymine in any one organism. *(2 marks)*

b) Explain how it is possible to have two very different organisms such as ox and wheat with very similar proportions of bases in their respective DNA.

(1 mark)

Table 2 shows the genetic code. The position of each base in an mRNA triplet may be read from the table to give the abbreviated amino acid name.

Table 2

1st position	2nd position				3rd position
	U	C	A	G	
U	Phe	Ser	Tyr	Cys	U
	Phe	Ser	Tyr	Cys	C
	Leu	Ser	STOP	STOP	A
	Leu	Ser	STOP	Trp	G
C	Leu	Pro	His	Arg	U
	Leu	Pro	His	Arg	C
	Leu	Pro	Gln	Arg	A
	Leu	Pro	Gln	Arg	G
A	Ile	Thr	Asn	Ser	U
	Ile	Thr	Asn	Ser	C
	Ile	Thr	Lys	Arg	A
	Met	Thr	Lys	Arg	G
G	Val	Ala	Asp	Gly	U
	Val	Ala	Asp	Gly	C
	Val	Ala	Glu	Gly	A
	Val	Ala	Glu	Gly	G

c) Give the sequence of amino acids forming the polypeptide represented by the length of mRNA below. Read the mRNA from left to right.

   U C C C C A C C G G U C U A A *(1 mark)*

d) Using examples from Table 2, explain what is meant by:

   i) a degenerate code *(2 marks)*

   ii) a codon *(2 marks)*

   iii) its corresponding anticodon. *(2 marks)*

e) Errors may occur in copying DNA. Suggest one explanation for the fact that many of these have little or no effect on the polypeptide for which they code. *(1 mark)*

Figure 2 shows the amounts of DNA in a number of individual nuclei from a mouse testis.

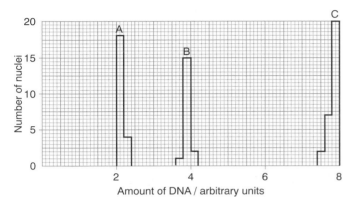

Figure 2

f) i) Which of the three groups of nuclei, A, B, or C represents mature sperm cells? Give a reason for your answer. *(2 marks)*

   ii) Explain, in terms of cell division, why there are three groups of nuclei. *(3 marks)*

g) Suggest *two* reasons why more valid results can be obtained from an investigation of this type if it is carried out on a testis rather than an ovary. *(2 marks)*

AEB Specimen Question

3 Read through the following passage on gene technology (genetic engineering), then write on the lines the most appropriate word or words to complete the passage.

The isolation of specific genes during a genetic engineering process involves forming eukaryotic DNA fragments. These fragments are formed using _____ enzymes which make staggered cuts in the DNA within specific base sequences. This leaves single-stranded 'sticky ends' at each end. The same enzyme is used to open up a circular loop of bacterial DNA which acts as a _____ for the eukaryotic DNA. The complementary sticky ends of the bacterial DNA are joined to the DNA fragment using another enzyme called _____ . DNA fragments can also be made from _____ template. Reverse transcriptase is used to produce a single strand of DNA and the enzyme _____ catalyses the formation of a double helix. Finally new DNA is introduced into the host _____ cells. These can then be cloned on an

industrial scale and large amounts of protein harvested. An example of a protein currently manufactured using this technique is _____ .

(7 marks)

Edexcel

4 Figure 3 shows part of a family tree in which the inherited condition of phenylketonuria occurs.

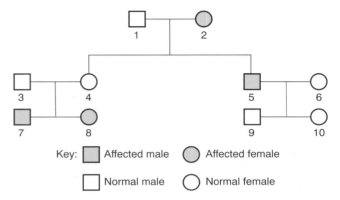

Key: ■ Affected male ● Affected female
     □ Normal male   ○ Normal female

Figure 3

a) Identify and explain *one* piece of evidence from this family tree to show that the allele for phenylketonuria is recessive to the allele for the normal condition. *(2 marks)*

b) Giving a reason for your answer in each case, identify *one* individual who must be:

   i) heterozygous *(1 mark)*

   ii) homozygous. *(1 mark)*

c) If individual 10 married a man who was heterozygous for the gene, what is the probability that their first child would be affected? *(1 mark)*

AEB Specimen Question

5 The main function of a chromosome is to act as a template for the synthesis of RNA molecules, since only in this way does the genetic information stored in chromosomes become directly useful to the cell. RNA synthesis is a highly selective process. In most mammalian cells only about 1% of the genetic information is transcribed into functional RNA sequences.

Before a cell can divide it must produce a new copy of each of its chromosomes. Thus cell division is preceded by a special 'DNA-synthesis phase', during which each chromosome is replicated to produce two chromatids. These remain joined together at the centromere until mitosis that soon follows.

a) Explain what is meant by the term *template*.
(3 marks)

b) Suggest why only about 1% of genetic information is transcribed into functional RNA sequences in most mammalian cells. (3 marks)

c) List *four* ways in which replication *differs* from transcription. (4 marks)

UCLES

6 Figure 4 below shows the sequence of amino acids in part of a molecule of haemoglobin. This sequence of amino acids was determined by the sequence of codons shown on the adjacent messenger RNA during the process of translation. The codon sequence on the messenger RNA was determined by the base sequence on the adjacent DNA strand during the process of transcription. The bases on this DNA strand have not been specified.

Chain of haemoglobin	Val	His	Leu	Thr	Pro	Glu	Glu
mRNA	GUA	CAU	UUA	ACU	CCU	GÅA	GAG

DNA single strand

Key
Val = valine   Thr = threonine
His = histidine Pro = proline
Leu = leucine   Glu = glutamic acid

Figure 4

a) Write in the complementary base sequence on the DNA strand in Figure 4. (2 marks)

b) Comment on the fact that glutamic acid has two different codons. (2 marks)

c) i) If the base U was substituted for the base marked *, how would the haemoglobin chain be different? (1 mark)

ii) This substitution produces an abnormal form of haemoglobin called haemoglobin S. What condition is associated with this abnormal haemoglobin? (1 mark)

d) Substitution of this type is an example of a 'point mutation of a gene'. Name *two* other ways in which a point mutation may occur in genes. (2 marks)

Edexcel

7 The karyotype in Figure 5 was obtained from a person suffering from a genetic disorder.

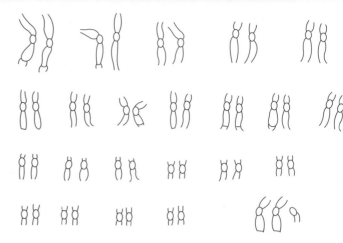

Figure 5

a) i) How many chromosomes are shown in this karyotype? (1 mark)

ii) Which is the Y chromosome in the karyotype. (1 mark)

b) Briefly describe the chromosomal events which may have led to this disorder (2 marks)

c) Give *two* ways in which the karyotype of a person with Down's syndrome would differ from the karyotype shown above. (2 marks)

Edexcel

8 Sickle-cell anaemia is an autosomal recessive genetic defect.

Figure 6 below shows the pedigree of a family affected by sickle-cell anaemia. (Individuals are numbered 1, 2, 3 etc. to 12.)

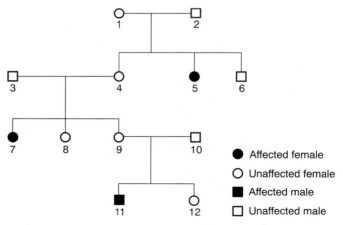

● Affected female
○ Unaffected female
■ Affected male
□ Unaffected male

Figure 6

a) State the numbers of all the individuals in the pedigree that are certain to be heterozygous for this gene. (3 marks)

b) What is the probability that individual 6 is heterozygous for this gene? *(1 mark)*

c) The parasite which causes malaria digests haemoglobin in the red blood cells (erythrocytes). Suggest why individuals heterozygous for this gene may show increased resistance to malaria. *(2 marks)*

Edexcel

9 a) Distinguish between the terms *gene* and *allele*. *(3 marks)*

b) Figure 7 below shows a family tree in which the blood group phenotypes are shown for some individuals.

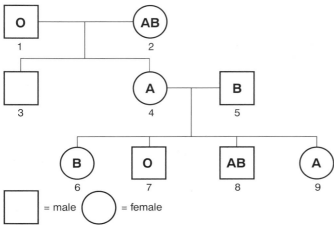

Figure 7

i) Using the symbols I^A, I^B and I^O to represent the alleles, indicate the genotypes of the people numbered 1–6. *(5 marks)*

ii) State the possible blood groups of person 3. Explain your answer. *(3 marks)*

Edexcel

10 a) Explain what is meant by the term *sex linkage*. *(2 marks)*

b) One of the genes which controls coat colour in cats has its locus on the X chromosome. This sex-linked gene has two alleles, **Q** and **B**. Female cats have two X chromosomes (XX), male cats have one X and one Y chromosome (XY).

In female cats, possible genotypes and phenotypes are shown in Table 3.

Table 3

Genotype	Phenotype
X^OX^O	Orange
X^OX^B	Orange and black (tortoiseshell)
X^BX^B	Black

State the *two*, possible genotypes for a male cat and, in each case, indicate the phenotype. *(4 marks)*

c) An orange and black (tortoiseshell) female cat was mated with a black male cat. Draw a genetic diagram to show the possible genotypes and phenotypes of the kittens resulting from this cross. *(5 marks)*

Edexcel

11 Figure 8 shows how bread wheat *(Triticum aestivum)* has arisen by polyploidy.

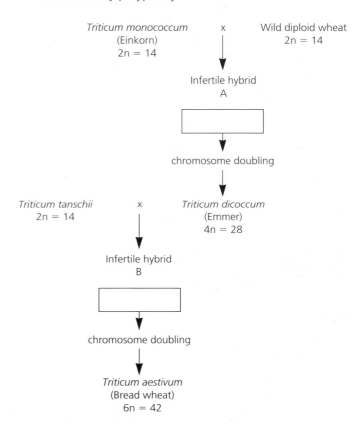

Figure 8

a) Copy the figure and in the boxes, write in the chromosome numbers of the infertile hybrid A and the infertile hybrid B. *(2 marks)*

b) i) Why are hybrids A and B infertile? *(1 mark)*

ii) Explain how doubling of the chromosomes results in infertile hybrids becoming fertile. *(2 marks)*

c) *Triticum durum* is another species of modern wheat. Why is it important that more than one species of wheat should be cultivated nowadays? *(1 mark)*

Edexcel

SECTION 7

Humans in Their Ecosystem

in brief — **Naive custodians of the planet?**

Over the vast timescale since Earth first formed there have been continuous changes to the matter making up the planet itself and to the lifeforms which later appeared on it. Section 6 describes the concept of evolution: the gradual process of change in the characteristics of living things, due to alterations to their genetic material. These genetic changes are potentially successful or unsuccessful in helping organisms survive and adapt to their environment. Successful changes tend to be perpetuated because they increase survival. So in the evolutionary sense, human development is steered by the ecosystem of which we are part. Ecology is the study of environments useful to us because the knowledge we gain can help us to survive *and* thrive. Even so, at times humans have been reckless with their world and unthinking about the future.

Searching for our ancestors

The puzzle of human evolution is by no means unravelled, although the events lead us from our close primate relatives, the chimpanzees, to the earliest hominids and, later, modern humans, the species *Homo sapiens*. This fascinating trail is outlined in Chapter 37.

The story of Cheddar Man highlights how chance plays a part in the challenges facing scientists investigating human evolution. Using material extracted from inside the pulp cavity of one of Cheddar Man's molar teeth, DNA was separated and analysed. In this case, the mitochondrial DNA, which is mainly inherited from the mother within the mitochondria of her ovum, was what the scientists were looking at most closely. The sperm's small contribution of mitochondrial DNA is thought to be lost during uneven partitioning of cells as the embryo develops. This means that maternal mitochondrial DNA may not change from generation to generation, therefore providing evidence of a direct line of inheritance.

Cheddar Man's DNA was compared with DNA from 20 local people whose families were known to have lived in Somerset for many generations. By chance, one man joined the sample 'just to make up the numbers'. The DNA match was unequivocal: the two men have a common maternal ancestor. However, Cheddar Man and the man shown in the picture are about 300 generations apart.

Cheddar Man is the oldest complete skeleton ever found in Britain. His Paleolithic remains were discovered in a cave near Cheddar in Somerset.

Examining ecosystems

The major ecosystems of the biosphere and the methods used for studying them are described in Chapter 38, and *Basics in Brief* gives some ideas for developing your own investigations. However, we do not need to look further than our own bodies to learn about ecology as the following summary of athlete's foot shows.

The ecology of athlete's foot

There is no doubt that fungi cause athlete's foot, but this simple statement does not begin to explain the complexity of the lesions or how the fungi and bacteria living on our feet interact. Like organisms in any ecosystem, these microbes compete for resources.

A simple summary like that given in the table would suggest that in the succession of organisms within the ecosystem, fungi are the pioneers. They first digest the keratin and penetrate the dead skin cells, while producing antibiotics to eliminate many of the competing bacteria. The surviving bacteria develop resistance to the fungal antibiotics and increase in numbers, thriving on the nutrients released by the breakdown of skin cells by the fungi. At this stage the skin begins to break down, and further bacterial infection can develop within the wounds.

The impact of human activities

It is easy to focus on environmental tragedies and mishaps, but nevertheless we do need to use our environment. Chapter 39 considers how we might take a balanced view of some human activities and how they affect the Earth.

Mismanagement of the environment can result in devastation. This forest clearance in Western Australia has caused salt to rise to surface soil layers, making it impossible for many plants to survive.

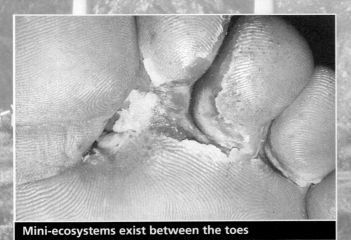

Mini-ecosystems exist between the toes

Profile of the ecosystem	
Abiotic factors	body surface temperature: 31–35 °C, reaching 37 °C in a fur-lined boot, favours spore production by fungi pH: 5.5–6.5, favouring fungal growth humidity: 100% depending on footwear oxygen availability: lower than optimum for fungal growth food source: amino acids, other organic acids, vitamins and salts in sweat, as well as dead skin cells which fungi can attack
Biotic factors	the human host: who might use antifungal foot cream or wash their feet fungi: principally two species of *Trichophyton* and one of *Epidermophyton* bacteria: >2 million cm^{-2}

CHAPTER 37 The Evolution of Modern Humans

37.1 How did humans evolve?

Evolution is an on-going process in which all living organisms including humans are involved. We do not know exactly when life began, but it is likely that the first simple life forms appeared between 3000 and 4000 million years ago. The human species, *Homo sapiens*, is one of the most recent, emerging probably only 100 000–200 000 years ago. In what is a relatively short period on the geological time scale, the evolution of *H. sapiens* has been rapid. Humans are just one species of animal evolving along side thousands of other living organisms.

Table 37.1 The main events in geological time are represented here as though they had taken place over a single year – notice how recently modern humans appeared

Date	Event
January 1	the Earth is formed
May 18	most of the Earth's land masses are created
August 8	purple bacteria appear that can metabolise oxygen
November 26	jawed fish evolve; plants colonise the land
December 5	reptiles evolve
December 18	birds evolve
December 21	egg-laying mammals and flowering plants appear
December 26	last dinosaurs roam the Earth; earliest primates appear
December 27	(before dawn) America and Europe separate (late afternoon) lemurs, horses and bats appear
December 29	(before dawn) monkeys, penguins, rhinos and true cats evolve (early afternoon) whalebone whales appear
December 30	(early morning) first apes appear; grasslands spread
December 31	(mid-morning) origin of hominids (11.56 pm) modern humans appear

As humans, many of us tend to regard ourselves as superior to other animal species because we have developed many complex skills. These cover a wide range of disciplines including communication, arts, science, medicine, law and philosophy, and industrial and technological processes. However, it is becoming clear that some of these human activities are causing harmful long-term changes to our environment. These are discussed further in Chapter 39.

▶ *Section 6 explains variation, natural selection and types of isolation, which all play a part in the evolutionary process*

An artefact is an object of archaeological interest, such as a tool, possession or a work of art. Sometimes artefacts are found buried in a grave with the body.

The details of how humans evolved are becoming clearer all the time and much has been discovered in the last 30 years. Evidence from several different areas of science contribute to understanding our origins. For many years anthropologists and archaeologists have been searching for fossil evidence relating to our ancestors. However, fossils and artefacts alone will not reveal the whole picture and other scientific evidence such as psychology, comparative physiology, biochemistry and DNA studies must be linked to these finds.

37.2 Our closest relations in the animal kingdom

A good place to start reviewing the evidence for human evolution is to take a look at our closest living relatives. Humans belong to the order of mammals called **primates**. The origins of living primates are very ancient and by looking at changes in the environment over time and the related changes in anatomy and culture we can get some idea of how humans have evolved to the present.

The first primates appeared around 75 million years ago and were insectivores. This was the time when insects and insect-pollinated flowers were evolving too and both provided important foods for the primates. It is thought that the insectivorous tree shrews which live in the Far East today are probably like the very first primates.

Figure 37.1 Tree shrews are insectivorous and are believed to be very similar to the first ever primates

As the earliest primates were small some of them were able to move into the smaller branches of trees where they were safe from larger predators. Here they could also gather an abundance of foods – leaves, flowers, fruits, insects and bird's eggs – without having to wait for them to fall to the ground. Those that were successful were the animals able to move with agility and to develop near automatic responses to the new environment. Successful reproduction allowed selection of the types best adapted to the prevailing conditions.

Modern primates that have evolved from these early ancestors include lemurs, tarsiers, New World monkeys such as the marmosets, Old World monkeys including baboons, mandrills and the rhesus monkey and, finally, apes such as gorillas, gibbons and chimpanzees. The chimpanzee is the most closely related to humans, indeed 98 per cent of DNA is common to both species.

Chimpanzees

The link between chimpanzees and modern humans is not direct as was once thought. At some time, probably between 5.5 and 8 million years ago, the evolutionary line from chimpanzees separated and from those animals modern humans evolved. The identity of our first ancestors is one of the great puzzles that has yet to be solved.

One of the aspects of chimpanzees that has been extensively studied is their behaviour. The work of Jane Goodall in this area is famous. Chimps are social animals living in communities of up to 50 animals, although they are usually found in sub-groups, couples and their young for example. Over time the families may join with others, and later break up again with members swapping groups. There is a hierarchy within any group which is dominated by males.

There is no fixed breeding season. Once a female is pregnant she will not again be sexually receptive until her offspring is fully weaned, about four years later. A close bond between the mother and infant continues after this and they may remain together for life. Males share parental care and protect their offspring against other aggressive animals.

Chimpanzees show a remarkable degree of learned behaviour. They learn by observation, imitation, trial and error, and practice. They also learn to make and use tools. For example they are known to strip leaves from twigs up to three feet long. The twig is then stuck into a termite nest and pulled out after a few minutes covered with insects which are eaten. Tools are also used to get water out from hollows, and as missiles in aggressive displays.

The chimpanzees' diet is mainly fruits and invertebrate animals. Sometimes they will work in groups to hunt and kill small animals. The meat is then shared amongst the group. This shows that the chimpanzee has a degree of intelligence and conceptual thought, which was previously not credited to any non-human primate.

Figure 37.2 A chimpanzee using a simple tool to dig out food

The main features of primates

- Primates have primitive mammalian features.
- They are **arboreal**, i.e. they live for much of the time in the canopy layer of trees and are adapted for life in the forests. They must have the ability to react quickly as conditions in the tree tops may be mechanically unsafe. They spend some time on the floor of the woodland.
- They have five digits on each limb. At the tips of the digits are sensitive pads protected by nails which replace the claws of earlier animals and allow the primate to grasp. Infants cling to their mothers from birth.
- A large **clavicle** (collar bone) means that the arms hang at the sides of the body rather than the front. This is particularly well developed in the apes and increases the mobility of the forelimb. Primates are able to swing through the branches in which they live.
- They have **stereoscopic (three-dimensional) vision** which allows a finer judgement of distance and depth. This is only possible because the eyes are set next to one another in the same plane so that the visual fields of

each eye overlap. The tarsiers, monkeys, apes and humans have colour vision. As the primates' sight developed, their sense of smell declined.

- The brain is relatively large in comparison to other mammals. The cerebral hemispheres (regions of conscious thought) are very well developed. This is directly related to improved vision.
- The neck is mobile so that the primate can turn its head in all directions, increasing its field of vision.
- The diet is mixed and the teeth relatively unspecialised.
- Primates give birth to only one, or at the most two young at a time. Non-human primates will continue to give birth throughout life.

37.3 A very important climatic change

It is generally believed that apes evolved in Africa. Up until about six million years ago the African continent was covered in lush tropical forest. However, the climate became cooler and drier, as the Earth entered an ice age, which caused significant changes in the vegetation. The area of tropical forests was reduced so that it remained around the Equator, but otherwise was replaced by scrubland, small woods and vast areas of grassland called **savannah**.

At the same time a huge rift valley opened up along the eastern side of the African continent and so populations of apes became geographically isolated from one another. Since the populations did not come into contact with one another they interbred amongst themselves. Ape speciation was taking place on a grand scale. Unfortunately, there are very few fossils known that can be dated as surviving from this period but it seems it was during this time that one of our ancestors diverged from the line of evolution of the chimpanzees. These animals were the very earliest **hominids**, i.e. they belong to the human family.

37.4 Bipedalism – moving around on two legs

Reports of the earliest and most recently discovered remains of hominids to be discovered in northern Ethiopia were published in 1994 by Tim White of the University of California at Berkeley, and by Meave Leakey the following year. Leakey declared her find to be a new species, *Australopithecus anamensis*. White named his discovery *Australopithecus ramidus* but renamed it and gave it a new genus, *Ardipithecus ramidus*, shortly after. Their relative positions in the evolution of later hominids is still the subject of much controversy.

These animals lived about 4.4 million years ago, and there is very little fossil evidence from this time. We do not know for certain if these hominids were **bipedal**, that is whether they walked upright on two legs. It is likely, however, that as they left the forests, where they would have swung through the trees, they would have started to walk on their hind legs when they reached the plains.

The position of the **foramen magnum**, the opening in the base of the skull through which the spinal cord passes to the brain, is important

Figure 37.3 This orang-utan shows the ability of arboreal primates to grasp branches strongly and judge distances while moving through the tree canopy

Hominids – all animals including humans, which arose at the point in evolution where there was a split between chimpanzees and the line to modern humans.
Hominoids – all apes and hominids.

Chapter 35.4 covers speciation and geographical isolation

evidence here. In dogs and other quadrupedal (four-legged) mammals the opening faces directly backwards, but in primates the opening is found to have moved forwards towards the centre of the skull. This arrangement allows the head to balance on the vertebral column, which is far better suited to an upright posture. The position of the opening in the skull of *Australopithecus* suggests that it was at least at times bipedal.

Bipedalism is of special significance because it allowed the hominids to adapt successfully to life in the grasslands. Bipedalism was associated with a change in the shape of the pelvis which became more shallow and more basket-shaped. The advantages of life on two legs far outweigh the disadvantages.

The main disadvantage is:

- away from the cover of trees the risk of predation by large cats increases.

The advantages of bipedalism are:

- the area of skin exposed to the Sun is much reduced (from about 20 per cent to 6 per cent; if an animal is able to walk on two feet, heat absorption is reduced.
- the body is exposed to air that is cooler than the air close to the ground.
- heat generated by muscles is reduced by up to 50 per cent and so it is possible to forage for food during the hot periods of the day away from the forests; longer distances can be covered without tiring.
- food can be carried to places where it can be eaten in relative safety; weapons and tools can also be carried.
- the range of vision is increased for spotting food and predators.

As well as becoming upright, hominids have become less hairy than other animals living in the savannah. In the tropics hair reflects heat away from the body and protects skin from the strong Sun. However if a hominid is upright it is standing in its own shadow and so only the skin on the top of its head needs hair for protection. This exposes a large area of hairless skin from which heat can be transferred directly to the surroundings.

37.5 The first hominids

The first examples of hominids belonging to the genus *Australopithecus* which lived about 4–2 million years ago were discovered in the 1970s. There appear to have been two forms: the lightly built or gracile type, and a heavier robust species with massive jaws and a relatively small cranium. Both were discovered in Africa. The robust group evolved separately from the line that gave rise to the genus *Homo*, and became extinct only about one million years ago.

So it is the gracile hominids which are thought to have belonged to the evolutionary line leading to *Homo*. An almost complete skeleton of such a female hominid was discovered in 1974 in Hadar in Ethiopia by the American anthropologist Donald Johanson. She was named 'Lucy' because the Beatles' song *Lucy in the Sky with Diamonds* was playing at the camp when her skeleton was brought back. Johanson realised that the structure of Lucy's lower jaw was different from any other known hominid, so he called this new species *Australopithecus afarensis*, after Afar, the region of Ethiopia where she was discovered. Dating of the rocks where Lucy was found showed her to be about three million years old.

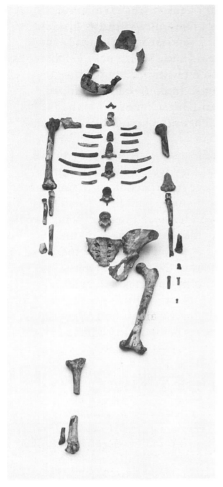

(a)

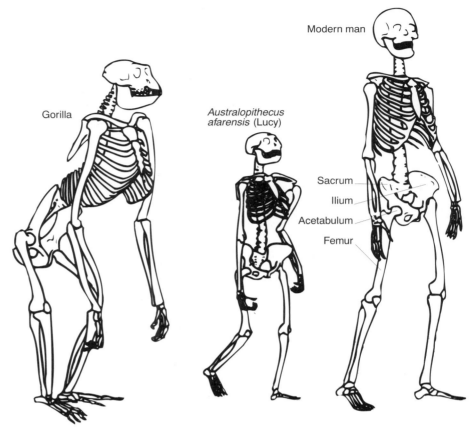

(b)

Figure 37.4 (a) The remains of the skeleton of Lucy found by Johanson. Her hip and leg bones suggest that she was bipedal, but above the waist she was more like an ape with long arms which may have been used for moving through the trees. (b) The skeletons of the ape and modern human are useful for comparison.

These early hominids were smaller than modern people, being only 1–1.5 m in height, and they were relatively more muscular with a body mass of 30–70 kg. The males appear to have been about double the size of the females which has led some scientists to suggest that *A. afarensis* is actually two species, rather than one. The arrangement of their teeth was more like that found in modern humans than in gorillas, as you can see in Figure 37.5, although the lower jaw still protruded forwards. The canines were reduced in size and careful examination of these teeth suggests that these hominids had learnt to chew their food.

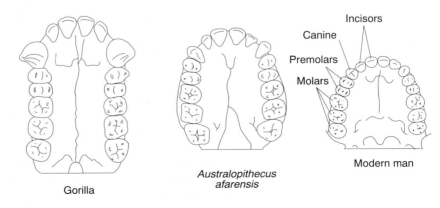

Figure 37.5 Notice that *A. afarensis* had smaller canines than the gorilla, but there was still a small gap between the canines and incisors. The arch of teeth was more rounded, as we find in modern humans.

Figure 37.6 The amazing trail of fossilised footprints discovered in 1978 by Mary Leakey at Laetoli in Tanzania, were those of three hominids (probably two adults and a child) of *Australopithecus afarensis*. The small footprints on the right belonged to hipparion, an extinct three-toed horse.
(See Colour Gallery page 359)

Figure 37.7 This skull of an early species of *Homo*, *Homo habilis*, was found in Kenya in the 1970s. It was reconstructed from 150 bone fragments.

> The Paleolithic Era was the Old Stone Age, when chipped stone tools were used.

Four years after the discovery of Lucy, Mary Leakey was excavating at Laetoli in Tanzania. She uncovered a trail of hominid footprints that had been preserved in a local volcanic ash which sets hard, like cement when damp. These date back some 3.6 million years and show that bipedalism was well developed by then. The prints are extremely important because they proved that the walking mechanism unique to humans had developed earlier than had previously been recognised. The arch of the foot had evolved. It works by acting as a spring so that as the hominid lands on its heel it is able to rise again on its toes.

Although Australopithecines were bipedal it seems from the evidence from their arm, hand and foot skeletons that they were still adept at tree climbing. Here, they would have found refuge from predators, mainly large cats, and a rich source of food. The females ate more fruit than the males, who tended to eat on the ground and at lower levels in the trees. It is possible that they used simple tools in the same way that chimpanzees do today; perhaps sticks to poke into termite mounds or to dig up roots, or rocks to open up fruit. Their brains were small, similar to the size of an ape's, and we know nothing about the way that these hominids organised their social groups. *Australopithecus* was a successful genus, probably living in Africa for around a million years, but it is important to realise that it had a tiny brain (see Figure 37.9) and had evolved only as far as being an upright ape.

37.6 The evolution of Homo habilis

The earliest species of *Homo* was *Homo habilis*. It is believed to have evolved from *Australopithecus* around 2.3 million years ago. Significantly, it had a larger brain (800 cm^3 in volume) than *Australopithecus*, a higher skull and a more vertical face. The molar teeth were smaller and more rounded and the spinal cord joined the brain at a more forward position.

How the first species of *Homo* evolved is the subject of controversy. Some people believe that a change in diet from the mainly vegetarian diet of *Australopithecus* to one that contained more meat was important. It is agreed that a cold, dry period occurred 2.3–2.6 million years ago. During that time plant food sources may have become scarcer and the hominids are likely to have adapted to the change by including more animal foods in their diet. Initially, they probably scavenged or even stole food from other predators for they did not hunt and kill their own prey. Since their teeth were not well adapted for meat eating the hominids needed tools for butchering the meat. Evidence for such scavenging is found in the marks of stone tools on animal bones, overlying the tooth marks of carnivores that had presumably discarded their prey.

The oldest stone tools which first appeared 2.5 million years ago are called **Oldowan** tools. They marked the beginning of the Paleolithic Era. These pebble tools were made by striking flakes off the surface of rocks to produce a crude implement that could cut into animal skin and remove meat. However, over a million years there was no significant advance in the design of tools.

The combination of meat-eating and the ability to make stone tools was nevertheless important. The extra protein in the diet aided the development of larger brains. Also, meat eaters do not have to eat as often as animals that live on plant foods and so *Homo* had more time to explore and exploit the

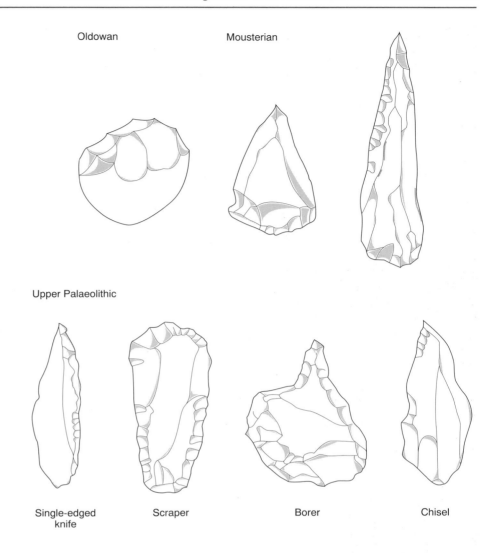

Oldowan   Mousterian

Upper Palaeolithic

Single-edged knife   Scraper   Borer   Chisel

Figure 37.8 Oldowan tools are the earliest identifiable stone tools, Mousterian tools were made by Neanderthal man and the Upper Paleolithic tools by the earliest modern human

environment. There would have been more time to hunt for the carcasses of dead animals and the development of bipedalism would have been advantageous. It is probable that the distances the animals ranged over when looking for food were as great as 20 square miles. Since *H. habilis* was small in size, it was at a considerable physical disadvantage and would have relied on its wits to find a way of getting meat from a carcass without being attacked by predators or other larger scavengers.

It is likely that the males were the scavengers. Sexually mature females would have probably been pregnant or have infants to feed and care for. Scavenging for meat was a dangerous pursuit, and in terms of evolution and reproductive success it is more risky to lose females than males; a population can maintain its numbers with fewer males, since each can impregnate many females. The females would have gathered fruits, leaves and other plant foods as their ancestors had always done. However, they needed to collect more than was required for their own consumption, so that there would be enough over to share with the males, who would in turn give them meat. This required planning: the food had to be gathered in suitable quantities and then stored without spoiling, and it would also have to be produced at a known location for sharing. Therefore increasing demands were also being made on the female brain.

37.7 The species Homo erectus

Homo erectus was the next hominid species appearing about 1.75 million years ago. More fossils have been found of this animal than of its ancestors and they show that *H. erectus* migrated out of Africa to southeast Asia where Java man was discovered in 1890. (At the time Java man was thought by some scientists to be the missing link between humans and apes, but we now know this is not the case.) By 700 000 years ago *H. erectus* had reached China and Europe. This was a large animal, the males being 1.8 m in size. The capacity of the brain had increased to about 1200 cm^3 and there was far less difference in body size between the males and females compared with earlier species of *Homo*.

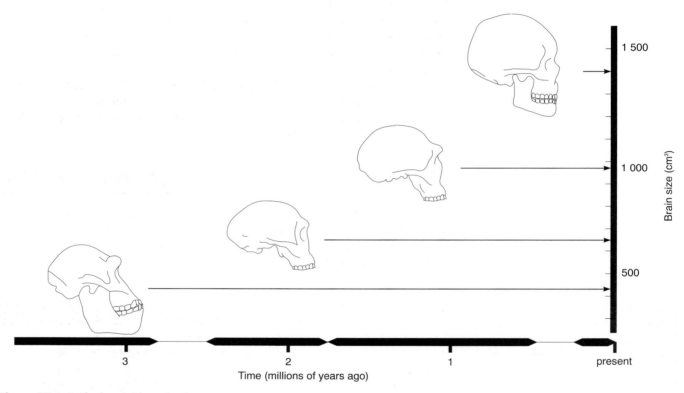

Figure 37.9 As the hominids evolved their brain capacity increased dramatically

As might be expected, the larger brain enabled *H. erectus* to make more sophisticated tools so that implements for different jobs were invented. So appeared the hand axe, cleavers for killing and butchering animals and a variety of scrapers for cleaning animal hides, making them supple and suitable for clothing and bedding. Tools that have been found in different regions vary in type, illustrating that *H. erectus* was able to make implements suited to the region it was living in.

Homo erectus is known to have discovered fire and how to control it. Exactly when this happened is difficult to judge, but in the late 1980s some bones that appeared to have been cooked deliberately were found during the excavation of a site in South Africa. The bones date back almost 1.25 million years. The ability to cook food was a significant step forwards in human culture and so with improving technology and the ability to keep warm, *H. erectus* could migrate to any area where there was meat. So it was with fire and tools that *H. erectus* reached China and Europe.

Figure 37.10 This is a reconstruction of a hearth as used by *Homo erectus*, showing burnt bones and cracked nut shells (*See Colour Gallery page 359*)

C44

Learning to control fire meant that:

- *Homo erectus* was able to cook food, making it more digestible and killing harmful bacteria.
- Over time, eating food that was less tough led to a reduction in the size of teeth.
- Migration to cooler climates was possible.
- Light could be provided during hours of darkness.
- Relationships between hominids and their predators changed. The early hominids were preyed upon by the large cats of the African savannah and lived a very dangerous existence. Predators are, however, afraid of fire, and so fire gave *H. erectus* a means of protection and perhaps even led to a position of dominance.

While *H. erectus* evolved, the method of obtaining meat started to change from scavenging to hunting. This was in part possible because of the more sophisticated tools that were being made, but also because of the more complex social interaction that was developing. There was more organisation and planning and hunting took place in teams so that a large amount of game was caught. Food gathering would still have taken place. It is certain that improvements in communication and language occurred, the latter being possible partly because of the reduction in the size of the teeth and change in the shape of the jaw.

37.8 The arrival of Homo sapiens

There is a wealth of fossil evidence to show that *H. erectus* spread out of Africa. However, what happened next in the story of the origin of modern man is currently the subject of a very important debate amongst evolutionary scientists.

Whatever happened next?

The questions being asked are these:
- Has modern *H. sapiens* evolved directly from the diverse populations of *H. erectus* that lived around the world? For example have Asians existing today evolved from early populations of *H. erectus* that lived in Asia?
- Is *H. sapiens* a totally new and much more recent species that came from somewhere else and replaced *H. erectus*?

Answers to these questions from two opposing views (although some people have opinions that lie between the extremes) can be summarised as follows:
1 Modern humans have evolved in different regions of the world from the populations of *H. erectus* that once lived there. Other populations probably migrated through at various times and then there would have been some interbreeding and consequent mixing of genetic material between the groups.

Evidence to support this view comes from archaeology, the appearance of fossils found in different parts of the world, and from genetics.
2 The 'Out of Africa' view is held by other people who think that a new species, *H. sapiens*, developed in Africa between 100 000 and 200 000 years ago. It was so readily able to adapt to prevailing environmental conditions that it replaced *H. erectus* and went on to populate all parts of the globe.
Support for this idea comes mainly from comparisons of mitochondrial DNA taken from people in different regions of the world, but evidence from the fossil record is also taken into account. The DNA evidence appears at present to favour the Out of Africa hypothesis.

Following the arguments of each side is fascinating, but beyond the scope of this book. One very readable reference where you can learn more is *Ape Man – The Story of Human Evolution* by Rod Caird (1994).

▶ *Chapter 37.9 explains that another controversy exists over the appearance of modern humans*

Whatever its origin, *H. sapiens* first appeared around 200 000 years ago. Two sub-species are of particular interest, the earlier was the archaic human *H. sapiens neanderthalensis*, or Neanderthal man, and the one that appeared later is Cro-Magnon man, *H. sapiens sapiens*, who was very similar to modern day humans. Remains of Neanderthal people have been found in many parts of the world. They were common in Europe, Asia and Africa where they lived from about 130 000–35 000 years ago.

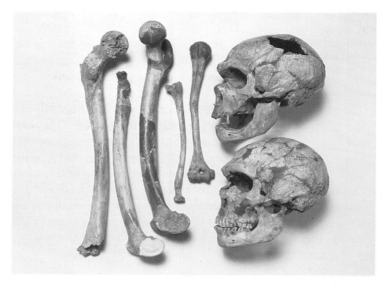

Figure 37.11 Two skulls and bones of Neanderthal man. The upper skull was found in 1908 and the lower skull a year later at different sites in France
(See Colour Gallery page 359)

The average life span of the Neanderthals was about 30 years although some lived to be between 40 and 50. They were heavily built and had large brains with an average capacity of 1530 cm^3 (larger than modern humans). The males were about 1.8 m tall and the females 15 cm shorter. Their build was heavy and they were very strong. Their stout skulls are recognised by the heavy brow ridges and the long and low shape behind. It is not clear whether the Neanderthals had developed speech although they must have had a well developed means of communication. They had big jaws and teeth that were larger than those of modern humans and could have been used to supplement their tools.

The Neanderthals improved the technology of making weapons and tools. Their flint tools are called **Mousterian** after Le Mousier in France, one site where many have been found. They are lighter, smaller and more refined than previous tools and of greater variety. Borers and notched flakes are included which could be attached to wooden shafts to make spears. Clearly, the development in tool design led to more successful hunting and permitted improved clothing and shelters to be built. The Neanderthals hunted with spears which they thrust into animals at close quarters. This would have required a great deal of strength and stamina. They used and controlled fire on a larger scale than *H. erectus*, for cooking and to provide warmth in colder climates.

Figure 37.12 A Neanderthal burial site where part of a male skeleton was found – it is about 60 000 years old
(See Colour Gallery page 360)

Neanderthal people lived under rock ledges or, where the climate was less favourable, in caves, as small bands or as single family groups. Remains have been found in France of an arthritic man and in Iraq of an amputee, suggesting that the Neanderthals cared for their disabled and had developed a high degree of caring and social concern. They were the first people to deliberately bury their dead but this may have been simply for reasons of hygiene rather than because they had evolved a belief in some form of after life. Evidence exists that they exhibited some rituals and religious behaviour.

Figure 37.13 This is the skull of a Cro-Magnon which is thought to be about 30 000 years old – notice how similar it is to the skull of a modern human

The Upper Paleolithic Era is the late Old Stone Age which began about 35 000 years ago. Cro-Magnons were the Upper Paleolithic people of Europe who lived at the end of the late Stone Age and were of modern appearance.

► *Chapter 37.8 looks at the possible origins of archaic Homo sapiens*

The last Ice Age in Europe lasted from about 75 000 to 10 000 years ago.

A significant find made in Bulgaria was of animal teeth in which a hole had been pierced. The teeth were around 40 000 years old and are thought to have been part of a necklace or decoration for clothing. This is perhaps the earliest form of art but it did not develop until the arrival of the Cro-Magnons which is discussed in Chapter 37.9. It was a considerable innovation for the archaic humans to have created something which was not functional, but was made to be enjoyed and appreciated. From these early beginnings a wealth of creativity was born. Tools and weapons were decorated with carvings and sculptures were made. Neanderthals were certainly not savage and ape-like as early archaeologists had thought. They eventually become extinct about 35 000 years ago.

37.9 Cro-Magnons – the Europeans of the late Old Stone Age

From around 45 000 years ago another sub-species of *Homo* co-existed with the Neanderthals in Europe. These were the **Cro-Magnon** people, *Homo sapiens sapiens*, named after the rock shelter in France where the first discovery of their bones was made. They were longer limbed and built more lightly than the Neanderthals and very similar in structure to modern humans. The Cro-Magnons and the people of the Upper Paleolithic Age were more intelligent than their predecessors and this led to more social co-operation and cultural development which was regional and highly specific. New areas of the world such as Australia and South America were colonised.

What was the fate of the Neanderthals?

Recent discoveries in Spain and Portugal of Neanderthal remains have been dated at 26 000 years old. The Neanderthals appear to have disappeared (apparently quite suddenly) while the Cro-Magnons survived and flourished. To date scientists cannot be sure why this was. There are two views which attempt to explain the disappearance of the Neanderthals:

1 The Neanderthals interbred with the new species *H. sapiens sapiens* whose genes became dominant over a number of generations so that the Neanderthal features died out.
2 The Neanderthals had a slower birth rate than the new *H. sapiens* sub-species. They were less able to adapt and compete with the more advanced technology of the Cro-Magnons and so they became extinct.

Clearly, the Neanderthals had survived for a very long time, about 4000 generations. However, there was little advance in their technology until the Cro-Magnons first appeared. These people made superior weapons and shelters. They were able to keep fires going for longer and construct them so as to radiate heat more effectively. This was important because the Cro-Magnons appeared during the last Ice Age when Europe, as far south as London, was covered with a thick sheet of ice. In fact the climate varied from time to time and was accompanied by changes in the vegetation. The animal populations, reindeer, ibex, horses, bison and **aurochs** (ancestors of modern cattle), fluctuated too. In the north and east woolly mammoths and rhinoceroses were found at times.

Developments in the late Old Stone Age

Tool making

- An improved method of making blades from flints called the **pressure-flaking** technique was developed. The piece of flint was broken to create a striking platform and then a piece of bone, antler or wood was used to break off flakes from the flint core. The advantage of this was to allow the toolmaker more control over the shape of the tool than had been possible previously.
- The **burin**, an invention of the Mousterian toolmakers, became common. It was rather like a stone chisel and could be used for carving antler or bone into fishing hooks, harpoon heads and needles.
- The **atlatl**, a piece of wood with a groove in it for throwing a spear with increased force, was devised.
- The **bow and arrow** allowed the arrow to travel even further and with more force.

Figure 37.14 Tools from the Upper Paleolithic Era including a harpoon carved from antler

Cultural development

As was mentioned previously, it was not until Cro-Magnon man was living along side the Neanderthals that decorative objects were made. The stimulus for this innovation can only be guessed at. Possibly, it was directly connected with one population meeting another. Some form of social identity had to be communicated by the members of each group and personal decoration is one way of doing this. It is possible that social hierarchies began to develop. For whatever reason, pendants, beads and the like were created from teeth, bones and ivory.

The effort required to make even a single bead would have needed great patience and concentration. Early on, ivory from the tusks of mammoths was the preferred material to work with although teeth and seashells were also used. It has been estimated that it would take between one and three hours to break off a small piece of ivory tusk to work with before the bead could be shaped, a hole bored through and finally polished. The beads were strung on sinew to make necklaces or possibly also sewn individually onto clothing. Since hundreds of beads were made by each group, there must have been a good reason.

Many sculptures particularly of animals and of the human female form have also been found. These were all enduring personal items that could have been passed from one generation to the next. This custom is related to a settled rather than a nomadic lifestyle and these people were probably living in more permanent camp-sites.

Perhaps a fertility rite?

Female statuettes appeared from about 30 000 years ago. One very famous one called the Venus of Willendorf was discovered in Austria. The statuette was made from a type of limestone which is not found anywhere in Austria, so either she was not made there or the limestone must have been brought to Austria from elsewhere. There are traces of red ochre on the sculpture, indicating that she was originally coloured.

The purpose of such statuettes is unknown. Some of them have been deliberately broken in two and the pieces buried separately. This suggests that the objects formed some part of a ritual, an idea which in turn leads on to the possibility that complex beliefs and ideas had evolved. It is also thought that the figures may have been part of fertility rituals, but in hunting and gathering societies, population control might have been more important than increasing the size of the community.

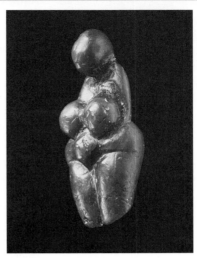

Figure 37.15 A female statuette sculptured by people during the Upper Paleolithic Era

Cave art

The ability to create images in two dimensions was not developed until thousands of years after the first beads or sculptures were created. Many of the most famous cave paintings have been found in southwest France and Spain and other parts of Europe, but there are also examples in South America and Australia. They are between 24 000 and 10 000 years old.

The earliest technique was to engrave shapes, usually animals such as aurochs, deer and bison, in the clay with the fingers and at the same time incorporate the natural features of the wall. Another common subject was children's and female's hands. There was no background to the paintings and the animals were not painted to scale. By studying the images in a large number of caves it has become clear, however, that the art was not created in a haphazard way. There was planning and relationships between different animals that were repeated many times.

The technology involved in creating the paintings was complex. While studying the famous paintings in the caves at Lascaux, 12 different pigments were discovered, of which only four were natural. The rest would have been made by mixing and heating natural pigments to 1000°C. Scaffolding would have had to have been erected since some of the painting is on walls two to four metres high. Light similar to candle light was created in the cave by burning animal fat in the middle of small stone slabs.

The painted caves were not inhabited but they were visited by children and adults. Some of the paintings have been found deep in dark caves. They may have been places of sanctuary, or have served some kind of magical or religious function, or they may have been places where young people learnt about the animals that they would rely on for life. It is likely that we shall never know what the purpose of these very special places actually was.

By the end of the Old Stone Age about 10 000 years ago, the Cro-Magnons had developed a complexity of tools and culture in a complex social structure which may have had religious cults. The Ice Age was over and the climate became warmer. This time was called the Mesolithic Age. Gradually, forests became established and there were changes in the animal

Figure 37.16 This bison found painted in the Altamira caves in Spain shows how well the anatomy of the animal had been observed
(*See Colour Gallery page 360*)

C46

> Agriculture is one, if not *the* most important development that has ever been made.

populations. Deer, beavers, wild pigs and bears became common while other species such as the mammoths became extinct because they could not adapt to the new environmental conditions. Wood was used to make tools and implements and even simple canoes.

The large human brain was being used to invent ways of surviving. The bow and arrow became the chosen weapon and replaced the spear. Dogs were also used in hunting to help sniff out the game, but there was not always enough meat to be found and fish and wild birds were added to the diet. Fruits and seeds were also still important foods.

Throughout this time, groups of people migrated through Europe reaching as far as parts of Asia and Africa. Although the Mesolithic people were making these advances, they had no sure means that the food supplies they relied on would last.

37.10 The Neolithic Era

Some time between 8000 and 5000 BC a new way of life was slowly evolving in the Near East. In Turkey, Iraq and Iran humans were learning to farm. The time when humans became farmers is called the **Neolithic** or New Stone Age. The land was being tilled, seeds of crops, such as wild wheat and barley, were sown, reaped and some stored for the next year's crop. The two crops were high in food value and the stubble left after harvesting could feed animals. This required *planning*.

As well as farming crops, these people learnt to tame sheep, wild cattle, pigs and goats. The animals became domesticated and provided a reliable source of milk, meat and hides. They bred in captivity ensuring the continuation of the flock. The Neolithic farmers learnt that they did not have to kill all the animals at once, as early humans would have done. Artificial selection began so that the animals with the best characteristics were allowed to breed. Since the first farmers did not have to spend their time following wild cattle any longer and they were cultivating crops, their food supply was reliable except in times of drought or other natural disasters. Their family groups could live in permanent settlements.

The farmers gradually spread west from the Near East but did not reach Europe until about 5000 years ago. By this time they had learned to build simple but permanent homes. Each was a rectangular hut with a single door,

Figure 37.17 This is part of the neolithic settlement of Skara Brae in Orkney. It is believed to be around 5000 years old. A dresser, fireplace and beds are shown here.

Figure 37.18 Neolithic pots found in Brittany, France *(See Colour Gallery page 360)*

C47

walls made of mud and stone, and a roof thatched with reeds or straw, held up by central timber posts. At one end was a fire and a hole in the roof to allow smoke to escape. The materials used to build the dwellings varied from one location to another, depending on what was available.

Settlements were established which were like small villages. There was co-operation between the family groups and the work was shared. The women carried out the cultivation of some plants and collected wild ones, cooked, made pots and wove fabric, besides caring for the smallest children. The men cleared ground for farming, farmed, looked after the animals, hunted and fished. They also made tools and built the dwellings. Children would have helped with some tasks from an early age. Each settlement lasted for several years, but when the land became impoverished the population would move on, clear more land and build new homes.

It was the cultivation of wheat and barley that led to the use of simple corn mills and of pottery. The early type of mill was made from a slightly hollowed rough stone in which the grain was placed. It was then ground into a rough flour by a second stone. The teeth of skeletons from this time are often badly worn down due to the coarseness of the flour and the grit it contained.

Pots were needed to hold the stored grain and for cooking the food. Once a suitable clay had been found a small amount of 'temper', sand or straw was added to hold its shape and prevent it from cracking. The Neolithic pots were coil pots, made from clay rolled into coils which were placed one on top of another and then smoothed. The pots were placed in the Sun to dry and then finally baked in a fire, converting the clay to pottery. The discovery of pottery meant that Neolithic man was no longer limited in the shape and size of the vessel, as had previously been the case when only natural materials could be used. Neolithic man was inventive and went on to discover how to weave flax into linen cloth and to make fabric from sheep's wool.

Questions

1 Make a list of major changes to the environment that human activities have caused in the past two centuries?

2 The most important features of primates relate to their ability to grasp and to highly developed vision. Explain why this is so.

3 Why is the development of a bipedal gait so important in the evolution of hominids?

4 In what ways is *Homo habilis* considered to be more highly evolved than *Australopithecus afarensis*?

5 Turkana boy was discovered in northern Kenya in 1984. He was a member of the species *Homo erectus* and his skeleton is a particularly interesting specimen. Use the resources available to you to find out why. Write a short report on your findings.

6 The Neanderthal people had very large noses (about four times larger than modern humans). It has been suggested that the size of the nose may have been involved in thermoregulation. Propose a simple hypothesis in support of this idea.

7 Explain the importance of the discovery of farming.

CHAPTER 38

Ecology – the Scientific Study of the Environment

Ever since humans appeared on Earth, they have changed their environment and used its resources. Two of the most fundamental life processes, breathing and feeding, impose immediate changes on the surroundings. But more important than this are the ways in which humans behave in exploiting their environment. The human intellect is unique, in that it gives us the power of logic and problem solving, of planning and inventing and therefore using the Earth's resources to the full. Humans are part of the biosphere composed of its complex inter-relationships between biotic (living) and abiotic (non-living) factors and we are now learning to manage our dynamic planet and its atmosphere. Scientists study how the living and non-living elements interact and affect the environment both locally and on a global scale. Changes are monitored and where possible action is taken when things are found to be going wrong. This is explored further in Chapter 39.

The Gaia hypothesis

The Gaia hypothesis was first proposed by James Lovelock in 1972. Lovelock is a distinguished British scientist who formulated his hypothesis while he was working for NASA on life-detection experiments for other planets. He developed his ideas with the American Lynn Margulis, one of the most eminent scientists of the late twentieth century. Their work was, at least initially, criticised and not well received. Lovelock proposed the hypothesis that the Earth is a self-regulating planet – a living organism that evolves and maintains its own temperature and chemistry through natural feedback mechanisms. He named his hypothesis 'Gaia' after the Greek Earth goddess.

Every living organism on Earth is involved in the cycling of energy and nutrients between the seas, land and atmosphere. Genetic information is passed from one generation to the next during reproduction. There is communication between individuals and all these together allow change, diversity and specialisation to occur at all levels. For around 3.6 billion years the activities of living organisms have kept conditions on the planet favourable. However, Lovelock is greatly concerned that we are not looking after our Gaia, planet Earth. If any species adversely affects the environment, it will become less favourable for their offspring who may fail to adapt to changes and so will become extinct. Should we destroy our planet, we are unlikely to escape and find another Gaia.

Figure 38.1 From space the enormity of the Earth's biosphere can be seen

38.1 The basics of ecology

Ecology is the huge branch of biology that studies the relationships between living organisms and their environment. Ecological research may range from an investigation of the distribution of a single species (**autecology**), to the study of the inhabitants of a particular habitat, or of the factors operating in an ecosystem or even a biome. A study of a community and its surroundings is called **synecology**. Applied ecology is the basis of environmental science and conservation. In order to understand the principles of ecology it is first necessary to explain some basic terms more fully.

Biome

The part of the Earth and its atmosphere which is inhabited by living organisms is called the **biosphere**. The surface of the Earth is covered by approximately 71 per cent ocean and 29 per cent land. It is made up of a series of **biomes**, areas of similar climatic type (temperature, rainfall and humidity) each with a characteristic pattern of vegetation and fauna. Biomes that we recognise include tropical rain forest, temperate deciduous woodland, savannah grassland, desert and tundra.

► *Chapter 39.3* **includes information on a tropical forest in Malaysia**

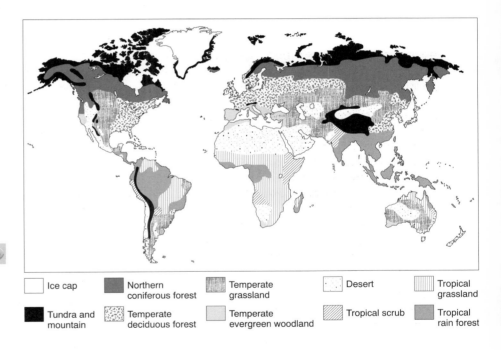

Figure 38.2 A map of the biomes across the world – notice that the same biome can occur in different regions of the Earth where climatic and soil conditions are similar
(*See Colour Gallery page 361*)

☐ Ice cap	▨ Temperate grassland
■ Tundra and mountain	▨ Temperate deciduous forest
■ Northern coniferous forest	☐ Temperate evergreen woodland
⬚ Desert	▨ Tropical scrub
▥ Tropical grassland	▨ Tropical rain forest

Although biomes can be clearly defined it should be realised that usually there are no clear boundaries between one biome and the next, more often there is a gradual transition.

Habitat

A **habitat** is where a species lives. It is a more precise description than a biome, because it is an actual place. We know that certain species may be expected to live in a particular type of habitat e.g. a pond, a sand dune, a playing field or a mixed woodland. There are different habitats everywhere – in towns as well as in the countryside. *Anywhere* that is inhabited by at

(a)

(b)

Figure 38.3 (a) Taiga is the biome of northern coniferous forest found at about 60°N latitude. It occurs in Russia, Scandinavia, Scotland and Canada. The vegetation consists of a few species of coniferous trees. (b) Savannah grassland in Kenya. In spite of seasonal rains, a dry season and high temperatures prevent the growth of trees and the predominant vegetation is grass and scrub. The animals living here are diverse and include wildebeest, antelopes, lions and other big cats.

least *one* living species is a habitat. Within most habitats are smaller areas with their own local conditions. These are called **microhabitats**; an example might be a fallen tree or log in a wood. The log itself starts to rot as woodlice and other animals move in to feed there, mosses and sometimes ferns grow on the log.

Animals can be the habitat of other animals. Human skin is the habitat of the house dust mite which is responsible for some forms of asthma.

Communities and populations

Community is the word which describes all the organisms living in a habitat. There are relationships between the members of the community which may be of mutual benefit. The plants in a deciduous woodland support many molluscs and insects, which provide food for the birds. Other birds feed on seeds and fruits from plants in the wood. Since birds travel large areas they disperse the seeds. Trees give shelter to birds. Clearly many of these interactions are concerned with feeding and will be discussed more fully in Chapters 38.3 and 38.4. Each distinct species in a community is called a **population**.

Ecosystem

An **ecosystem** is a community of organisms living in a habitat together with all the environmental factors present. These include the relationships just mentioned and all the non-living factors such as temperature, rainfall, light intensity, soil type and nutrients, and atmospheric concentrations of oxygen and carbon dioxide. Within each ecosystem a species is said to occupy an **ecological niche** which is the term used to describe its position in the food web for that community.

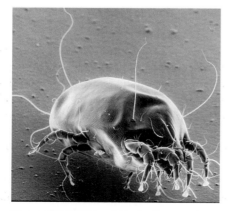

Figure 38.4 A house dust mite scavenging on the surface of human skin

Figure 38.5 A pond such as this one above is a common ecosystem. It has a community comprising many populations. The photos on the right show some of the smaller organisms living there. It is likely that the pond will be visited by other species of birds, mammals and insects because it is a source of drinking water. *(See Colour Gallery page 361)*

If left undisturbed ecosystems develop to a point where they are stable. Within the ecosystem nutrients are recycled and the system is therefore self-contained or closed.

If an ecosystem has no plants or autotrophs to provide the input of energy, it is described as open. Open ecosystems are rare, an example is the bat caves of Borneo. The bats must leave their ecosystem (the cave) to feed on insects from other ecosystems. Within the cave the bats excrement and dead bodies provide nutriment for centipedes, spiders, fungi and bacteria.

Figure 38.6 The bat cave is an extraordinary ecosystem. It is not self-supporting because in these dark conditions plants cannot survive and photosynthesise; in other words there are no autotrophs here to support the heterotrophic feeders.

Succession

If a community such as a meadow is left undisturbed for a period of a year or more, noticeable changes will take place. The grass will grow taller; new plants will establish themselves. If the meadow was left indefinitely in a temperate climate such as the British Isles, the grass would be replaced by scrub and shrubs and eventually woodland would be established. This natural progression which occurs in all terrestrial and aquatic habitats and in microhabitats is called **succession**. It occurs all the time, indeed it begins every time the lawn is mown!

Primary succession occurs when bare rock, sand or areas of burnt ground are colonised by plants for the first time to establish a new habitat. The first coloniser is called the **pioneer species**. For example on bare rock the pioneer species is often a lichen. Lichens actually consist of an alga and a fungus living in a mutualistic relationship (i.e. one which is to the advantage of both partners). Lichens can withstand the harsh conditions on the rock face and may trap particles there from the rock. These and the decomposed remains of dead lichens form enough nutrients to support the next colonising plant, often a species of moss. Small animals will migrate in as the habitat becomes established. The succession continues as rock is eroded and organic matter accumulates. Ferns grow followed by species of grass and other small flowering plants. Over many years the depth of soil increases and small shrubs and eventually trees are established. Deciduous oak woodland is the final stage in succession in all but the highest parts of Britain. It is called the **climax community**. The climax community is determined by climate; it is stable and characterised by one or more dominant species, in our example the oak, *Quercus robur*.

Succession that takes place where there are already some established plants, or where a previously colonised area has been cleared or burnt is called **secondary succession**.

Each stage in a succession is called a **sere**. This is well illustrated when succession occurs in freshwater, as you can see in Figure 38.7.

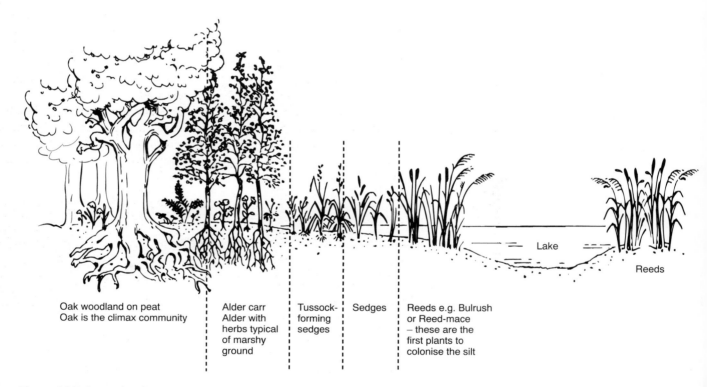

Oak woodland on peat
Oak is the climax community

Alder carr
Alder with herbs typical of marshy ground

Tussock-forming sedges

Sedges

Reeds e.g. Bulrush or Reed-mace – these are the first plants to colonise the silt

Lake

Reeds

Figure 38.7 Succession from water to land in a hydrosere. The lake becomes silted up as a stream flows through. The silt builds up and becomes colonised first by reeds. This is very interesting to see because all the stages in the succession, the seres, are present together, culminating in oak woodland.

Questions

1 Which biome do the Inuits live in. Find out about their traditional way of life. Why is it now under threat?

2 Name a habitat that you have studied. Make a table to give the phylum, a characteristic feature and the common name for each of five different species living there.

3 Explain the difference between

   a) an ecosystem and a community

   b) a community and a population

   c) a biome and an ecosystem

4 Look at Figure 38.7 of succession from water to land, an example of a hydrosere. Describe what is happening in your own words.

38.2 Practical methods for sampling organisms

One of the questions that ecologists often need to answer is whether the number of organisms in a population is changing, or whether the number differs in one area from another. You might for example be set an exercise to collect data to compare the numbers of a particular plant species growing in an area of mown grass with the number in the same field where the grass was unmown. It would be quite unrealistic in terms of time and effort to count literally every plant, and in addition might well damage the habitat. This is why ecologists rely on methods of sampling in order to estimate population size. For the sample to give the most accurate estimate, a method designed to sample at random must be employed.

Different techniques are used for sampling plants and animals. Plants being static are usually easier to work with; animals may need to be marked in some way and trapped temporarily as part of the procedure. A quick and easy method for estimating numbers of a species within a defined area is to use the ACORN scale:

> A = abundant
> C = common
> O = occasional
> R = rare
> N = never (i.e. absent)

This is a subjective method where an estimate is made of frequency or cover. It is necessary to define each term for the exercise, for example, abundant >50 per cent, common 15–50 per cent, occasional 5–15 per cent, rare <5 per cent. A major disadvantage is that the size of a specimen tends to interfere with judgement, so that large specimens tend to be over-rated while small ones are under-rated. It is a useful method for estimating the frequency of sessile animals, such as limpets on a rocky beach.

Quadrats

Quadrats are frames commonly used to sample plant communities. The most commonly used sizes are 1×1 m (1 m^2) and 0.5×0.5 m (0.25 m^2) and they may be sub-divided into smaller squares. If the area to be sampled is large, as might be the case when sampling woodland, a quadrat can be pegged out with rope or tapes.

> A sample is a small number which represents a whole population. A sample is collected at random to eliminate bias in the sample, which would lead to inaccurate results.

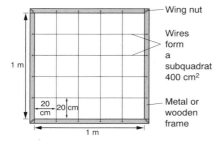

Figure 38.8 A typical frame quadrat commonly used in ecology

It is important to decide where the quadrats should be placed. Spinning round with your eyes closed and throwing the quadrat over your shoulder does not mean random – and could be dangerous! Decide on the total grid to be sampled and mark out two axes x and y at right angles with 50 m tapes. Use a random numbers table or scientific calculator to define a co-ordinate at which you should place the bottom left-hand corner of your quadrat. For example if the first pair of numbers is 13,29 pace to 13 m along the x axis and then 29 m along the y axis; at this point you place your quadrat. Generate another pair of numbers and repeat the process until sufficient data has been collected.

The measurements that can be obtained by using quadrats are as follows:

- **Species density:** used to find the mean number of members of a particular species per unit area. This can be a laborious method if the number of sampling units is large.
- **Frequency:** the chance or probability of finding a particular species in any single throw of the quadrat. It is a rapid method of assessing the dispersion of a species within the sampling area. The presence of a species or number of different species is recorded in each quadrat. If a species occurs in two out of ten quadrats, its frequency will be

$$\frac{2}{10} \times 100\% = 20\%$$

- **Cover:** the percentage of the ground covered by the species in each quadrat is estimated. This is a useful method for species such as mosses or grasses where it is difficult to distinguish and count individual plants.

Point quadrats

Figure 38.9 shows a point quadrat which is used in dense vegetation. The pin is moved along from one hole to the next and the species that it touches are recorded. The percentage cover is then calculated by:

$$\text{percentage cover} = \frac{\text{number of touches}}{\text{total pins dropped}} \times 100$$

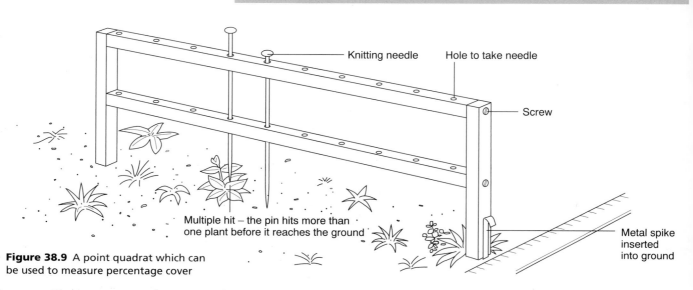

Figure 38.9 A point quadrat which can be used to measure percentage cover

Transects

A **transect** is a line along which organisms can be sampled at regular intervals. The length of a transect may be quite long (e.g. 200 m) and this is a particularly useful technique where there is a noticeable change in the flora or fauna, for example as is found across a rocky shore, from the sand across sand dunes to salt marsh, or from the inside to the outside of a wood.

Over short distances, such as from one bank of a stream to another, the profile of the land can be measured using 2 m rules as is shown in Figure 38.10. For longer distances, surveying poles and a spirit level are needed to record data for drawing the profile of the transect.

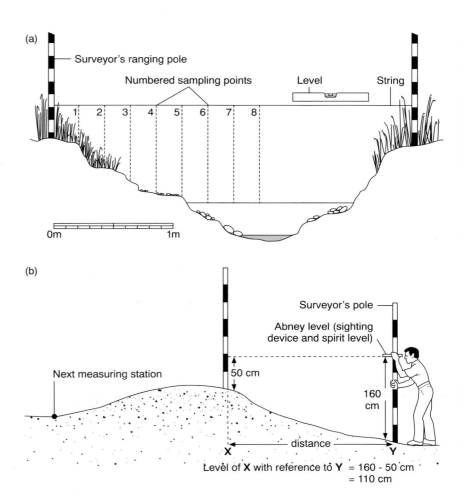

Figure 38.10 (a) Sampling the profile of a short transect. (b) A long transect where there is a change in elevation requires more equipment

A **belt transect** consists of two tapes running parallel a metre apart. The same effect is achieved by placing a frame quadrat alongside the tape. The vegetation is then recorded as a band.

Sampling animals by capture – mark – recapture

Capture–mark–recapture is a useful method of estimating the members of a mobile animal population. Specimens are collected by a suitable method, counted (C) and marked in such a way as to not knowingly harm them.

They are then released back to the area in which they were captured. After a suitable time the population is sampled again using as similar a method as possible to the first occasion. The total number of animals in the second catch is counted (N) and the number of marked individuals (M) is noted. The size of the population is then calculated as $\dfrac{C \times N}{M}$. This is called the **Lincoln Index**.

The assumption behind this procedure is that the proportion of marked individuals in the second sample is the same as the proportion of marked individuals in the population as a whole. This will only be true if:

- the marked individuals had sufficient time between the two sampling sessions to distribute themselves evenly between the rest of the population;
- there is no disadvantage to individuals in being marked e.g. they are not more conspicuous to predators (which would cause them to be under-represented in the second sample);
- there are no births or deaths in the population between the two samples being taken;
- the marks do not come off between capture and recapture.

How to practise capture–mark–recapture

A simple demonstration of capture–mark–recapture can be carried out with beads. Only your teacher or laboratory technician should know the size of the 'population' of beads which should be recorded in a sealed envelope.

With your eyes closed remove about a third of the beads and count them (C). Mark the beads in a way that can be cleaned off for future use, count them and return them to the container. Then shake the beads. Remove a second sample (of similar size to the first). Count and note the number of unmarked beads (N) and marked

beads (M) that the sample contains. Apply the formula $\dfrac{C \times N}{M}$ to calculate the size of the population of beads, and compare your answer with the figure provided in the sealed envelope.

Question

What, in your opinion, are the limitations of this model in demonstrating capture–mark–recapture?

Calculating species diversity index

We have already considered the importance of biodiversity in relation to the long-term survival of living organisms. The diversity of species is usually proportional to the stability of the ecosystem and this is why it is so important to conserve complete ecosystems. If a species becomes endangered then it should be conserved, but if its ecosystem is preserved the species will have less chance of becoming endangered in the first place.

The bittern, a bird recognised most readily by the booming call of the male, used to be fairly common in parts of the country where reed beds were established. During the twentieth century the number of reed beds has decreased, farming practices have changed and in some areas, such as the Norfolk Broads, tourism has been encouraged. These together with other factors have changed the ecosystem in which the bittern thrived. As we approach the end of the twentieth century, there are now only 20 booming bitterns, hopefully with mates, left in Britain.

▶ *Chapters 34.5 and 39.1 cover the importance of biodiversity*

A straight forward method of describing the diversity of species in a habitat is to make a list of the organisms found there. However, this data gives only a limited picture of the situation. It is far more useful to count the numbers of organisms in the populations of interest in the habitat, and from this an index of diversity can be calculated. A simple formula that can be used is:

$$d = \frac{N(N-1)}{\Sigma n(n-1)}$$

where   d = species diversity index
N = total number of all members of all species
n = total number of organisms of a particular species
Σ = the sum of

> The higher the value of d, the greater the index of species diversity of the habitat being studied.

Reminder: $\Sigma n(n-1)$ means that $n(n-1)$ is worked out for every species counted, and these are then added together.

Worked example

Species	A	B	C	D	E	F	G	H	I	J
Number	97	4	16	14	55	28	2	84	11	16

Total number counted = 327

$$d = \frac{327(327-1)}{97(97-1) + 4(4-1) + 16(16-1) + 14(14-1) + \ldots 16(16-1)}$$

$$= \frac{106\ 602}{20\ 794}$$

$$= 5.13$$

38.3 Where plants and animals live depends on environmental factors

The physical environment of the ecosystem is crucial in defining the distribution of species there. The factors which give an ecosystem its particular characteristics can be divided into two types:

- **Abiotic** (non-living) factors include soil type, salinity (salt concentration), water, temperature, light intensity, humidity, wind, fire, aspect and altitude.
- **Biotic** factors which are living organisms that affect the distribution of organisms within the ecosystem. This is explained in terms of relationships between organisms such as competition. Prey/predator, pathogen/host and parasite/host relationships are also important. Humans are sometimes said to be the most important biotic factor, since the impact that we have made on our planet is incalculable.

Abiotic factors

Soil

Soils are present in most ecosystems, for even aquatic habitats have soil underlying them. Factors that affect the ecosystem as a result of the soil type are called **edaphic** factors.

A soil consists of a mixture of mineral particles that originate from the weathering of rocks, **humus**, which is a complex colloidal substance originating from decaying organic matter, air (between the particles), water and dissolved minerals. Soil is frequently inhabited by large numbers of animals, micro-organisms, fungi and plant roots. There may be a layer of leaf litter covering the soil.

Table 38.1 Mineral particles in a soil are defined by their size

Particle type	Diameter (mm)	Observed using
gravel	>2.0	naked eye
coarse sand	2.0–0.2	naked eye
fine sand	0.2–0.02	naked eye
silt	0.02–0.002	light microscope
clay	<0.002	electron microscope

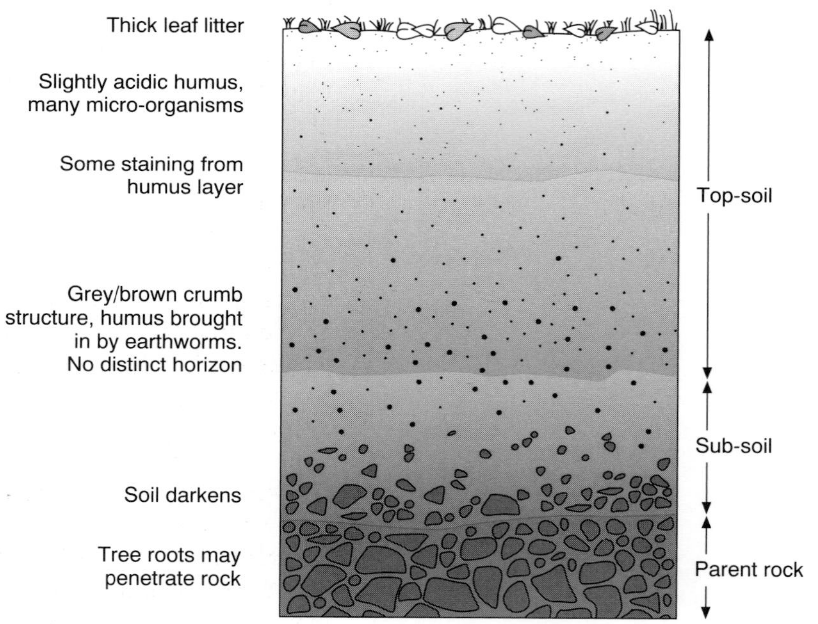

Thick leaf litter

Slightly acidic humus, many micro-organisms

Some staining from humus layer

Grey/brown crumb structure, humus brought in by earthworms. No distinct horizon

Soil darkens

Tree roots may penetrate rock

Top-soil

Sub-soil

Parent rock

Figure 38.11 A typical soil profile under deciduous topsoil. The top-soil is the most fertile area. It is rich in organic matter although this may be lost by leaching to lower levels. The sub-soil underlies it and is low in humus. Below this is the underlying rock. You can often see the soil profile of your local area if you look at places being excavated for new buildings or where road works are underway.

Soils are usually described according to the commonest type of mineral particle that they contain. These particles are important because they give the soil its properties. Table 38.2 summarises the properties of sand and clay, two very different soil types.

Table 38.2 A comparison of clay and sand

Property	Sand	Clay
particle size	large	very small
texture	coarse	smooth
aeration	good	poor
water retention	not good	good (but may get water-logged)
drainage	good	poor
nutrient content	low	high – clay particles have a negative charge and attract cations (which are not leached)
general	light, easy to work	heavy, difficult to work

The most fertile of soils is **loam** which contains about the same amounts of sand and silt, and slightly less clay. Loam has a good crumb structure, meaning that the soil particles are bound together by humus with the effect that drainage, water retention and aeration are all good. The clay content provides nutrients. Both sandy and clay soils can have their structure and consequently their fertility improved by the addition of organic matter. This is why manure is added to soils.

pH is an important characteristic of a soil and may have a direct effect on the plants able to grow in it. Soils which are particularly acid or alkaline have characteristic species which grow on them. The most fertile soils have a pH close to neutral.

The pH of a soil solution can be tested with a broad range indicator, but a pH meter (that has been calibrated before use) can give a quantitative reading. Measurement of pH can be useful when studying the distribution of species.

Climate

The biomes on Earth are defined by the soil type and climate in different regions. Climate describes the seasonal patterns of temperature, rainfall and light that are based on long-term records. The term **microclimate** can be applied to local areas of a habitat that may be different from other parts. An example might be a rocky gully on a steep exposed hillside. The gully might be damp, humid and darker than the hillside, sheltered from wind and have a smaller temperature range. Plants such as ferns might be found there, although ferns would not be able to grow on the hillside.

Temperature is an abiotic factor which can be easily measured in investigations relating species to their habitats. The mercury thermometer is the traditional instrument for measuring temperature, but it can be tedious and time consuming if a large number of readings are required. A maximum–minimum thermometer can be useful for readings taken over a long period, however, the use of data-logging equipment is ideal since it can be set up and left, and the temperature data can be run through a computer at a later and more convenient time. Moreover, the readings are not subject to human error.

Water is vital for all living organisms. Therefore rainfall is especially important for terrestrial organisms. Those that live in parts of the planet where rainfall is low have special adaptations to aid their survival. Plants in

Figure 38.12 Data-logging equipment is extremely useful for collecting temperature readings, pH, light intensity and so on during ecological investigations. Some data-logger can be left set up for 24 hours or longer. Back in the lab they can be downloaded to a computer which will quickly produce a graph from the readings.

warm, dry habitats are called **xerophytes** and are adapted to conserve water. They are often succulent and may be hairy to create a humid microclimate around themselves; spines sometimes replace leaves to reduce water loss by transpiration.

Aquatic organisms are affected by the water that they live in. Temperature, pH, oxygen concentration, nutrients and light intensity are all significant. Plants are limited to depths that light can penetrate and provide enough energy for photosynthesis. In streams and rivers the rate of current flow is important and the morphology (shape or form) of most plants protects them from being damaged. On the coast there are extra factors to consider, such as the tides which cover and expose the shores every 24 hours. The seaweeds and animals that inhabit the tidal zone have extreme conditions to adapt to. Many animals (e.g. lugworms) are able to burrow under the sand when the tide is out, while limpets for example are protected by their tough shells. In addition, the currents and wave action are important.

Light varies in intensity and wavelength, and with daylength (apart from the Equator). It is necessary for photosynthesis, and to enable many animals to see. Where there are seasons it is the pattern of daylight and night that is critical in stimulating plants to flower.

Figure 38.13 A wood (a) immediately after coppicing and (b) In the fourth Summer after coppicing the woodland is regenerating and other species have established themselves

(a)

(b)

Light intensity is measured with a light meter or with data-logging equipment as described earlier. It is often a significant factor in plant and animal distribution. For example if part of a wood is managed by coppicing, more light will penetrate to the ground. As a result more plants can establish themselves on the floor of the wood and a greater number of animal species will migrate there. This can be shown experimentally by sampling the organisms and measuring light intensity in the coppiced and uncoppiced areas of the wood.

> Coppicing is a technique used in forest management. It means cutting down shrubs and young trees such as hazel, almost to ground level. After 5–15 years several tall straight stems grow up and are then cut again.

Biotic factors

Biotic factors are the effects that the activities of one living organism have on another. These often relate to feeding: herbivores graze on plants and carnivores consume other animals. Some organisms are decomposers or detritivores and their activities are explained in Chapter 38.5. Competition is also a biotic factor, either being between the members of a single species or between two species.

> ▶ *Chapter 30.3 describes the parasite–host relationship and infectious diseases (the pathogen–host relationship)*

> ▶ *Chapter 39 explains the effects that humans have had on the biosphere*

Predation

Predators are species that kill another species (their prey) for food. The relationship is actually more complex than it might at first appear. The immediate benefit to the predator is clear, although the important benefits to the prey are not. It is likely that most of the predated species that are actually caught are the weaker members of the population. By removing them, the predators are improving the genetic pool of the prey species. In addition, the size of the prey population is being regulated so that it does not exceed the number that the habitat can sustain.

If a predator is specialised for feeding on one particular type of prey their respective population sizes show a characteristic cyclical pattern. This is demonstrated by ladybirds (predators) and greenfly (their prey). During some summers there are many greenfly and very few ladybirds. However, those that are around have plenty of food and so breed and increase the population size. The following year there are more predators which continue to increase their numbers and as they do so the numbers of greenfly drop. If the ladybird population increases in size too rapidly, there will be insufficient food and their numbers will crash, allowing the population of greenfly to recover.

Competition

Living organisms compete for basic essential resources: food and water, shelter, a mate and space. Plants, in addition, compete for light and nutrient ions. If the resource being competed for is in short supply, there will be a reduction in the growth rates of the competitors.

- Competition between members of two species is **interspecific** competition. Predation is an example of interspecific competition. The advantage of periodic crashes of the population is that only individuals best adapted to current environmental conditions will survive to produce the next generation.
- Competition between members of the same species is called **intraspecific** competition.

Red and grey squirrels

The red squirrel is a native mammal of the British Isles and until the end of the nineteenth century was common, living in both deciduous and coniferous woodland. An adult has an average body mass of 300 g.

The larger grey squirrel (average mass 550 g) is a native of North America. The Victorians were keen to introduce it to Britain and between 1876 and 1929 it was established in 30 sites. The populations of grey squirrels increased slowly and in areas where they had been established for 15 years, the reds disappeared. The red squirrel has become more rare and is now found only in dense isolated coniferous woods and in the most northerly parts of England and Scotland. They are nimble and able to feed on the cones always available in the canopy. Grey squirrels do better in deciduous or mixed woodlands.

The grey squirrel does not usually physically attack the red squirrel. It seems that the two squirrels occupy the same ecological niche since there are reports of them being seen feeding in the same tree. The competitive advantage of the grey squirrel may be in part due to its ability to digest acorns better than red squirrels. Conservationists have encouraged the planting of mixed woodlands in recent years, but others fear that this might tip the balance once and for all against the red squirrel. If its coniferous strongholds are destroyed, we may lose the red squirrel permanently.

This may be an example of Gause's **competitive exclusion principle** which states that two species cannot co-exist unless their ecology is different. This means that the two species cannot exist in the same habitat if they occupy the same ecological niche. Since the two variants of squirrel occupy the same ecological niche, the population of the stronger competitor, the grey squirrel, has increased at the expense of the populations of the red squirrel.

▶ *Chapter 38.1 explains about ecological niches*

The growth of a population

The growth of a population shows the same pattern in *all* living organisms. It can most readily be observed in the laboratory using bacteria because they are relatively easy to culture and have a short life cycle so they can complete many generations in only a few days.

Look at Figure 38.14 which shows a typical growth curve. It is called a **sigmoid curve** because of its characteristic S-shape.

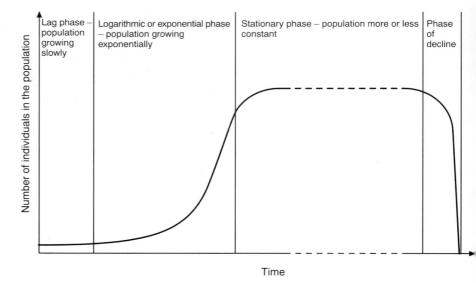

Figure 38.14 This shows the growth of a population of living organisms – it is widely applicable although the time scale will vary enormously from one organism to another

The first phase is called the **lag phase** when there is a very slow increase in numbers. It is the time needed for the organisms to settle into the environment. As reproduction increases and there are more births than deaths, the numbers in the population start to rise. This is the **exponential** or **log phase** during which there is little competition for resources. Expansion of the population rises at an ever increasing rate until eventually, due to external factors (which constitute **environmental resistance** and slow down fertility and survival), numbers become stationary. The main external factors which limit the size of a population include:

- a shortage or lack of water or food;
- a lack of light (plants);
- a shortage of oxygen;
- a build up of toxic pollutants in the habitat;
- predators;
- pathogens, especially highly infectious species;
- catastrophic natural phenomena, e.g. floods, earthquakes.

At this point, equilibrium or the **stationary phase** is reached and the number of births and deaths balance one another. At this size the population has reached the maximum capacity which the environment can sustain, this is called the **carrying capacity**.

To return to the bacteria being cultured in a closed environment such as a flask, the stationary phase will come to an end as resources are used up and the surroundings become contaminated by waste metabolites. The numbers in the population then fall and deaths exceed births. This is known as the **phase of decline**.

However, besides births and deaths, the size of a population will vary according to the number of individuals of the same species joining the population (immigration) and the numbers of individuals that leave (emigration). The change in size of a population can be expressed by:

$$B + I - D - E$$

where B = births, I = immigration, D = deaths and E = emigration. Sometimes immigration and emigration are important factors.

Human populations

The human population curve is unusual because numbers grew only very slowly for many years until the Middle Ages. One estimate is that before 1600 AD the population had taken 2000 years to double. The next doubling took 150 years and the next only 80 years. The population has doubled again in the past 50 years. This shows that we are in a phase of exponential growth which is unchecked.

The increase in the population has been brought about by improvements in agriculture, food production, technology and medicine. These advantages are not evenly shared by all the people on this planet, and millions die through disease and starvation. Nevertheless, the population continues to increase at a huge rate. Unless humans take more responsibility to reduce the increase in numbers there will inevitably be

disaster, bringing a natural check on a population that is getting beyond a size the environment can sustain.

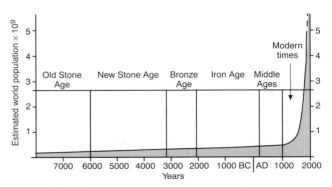

Figure 38.15 The human population growth curve

Questions

1 What is the difference between climate and weather?

2 Design an investigation to study the distribution of a species, plant X, along a transect running from 50 m inside a mixed woodland to 20 m into a meadow bordering the wood. What abiotic factors might be measured to account for any difference that might be found. How would you do this?

3 Draw a flow diagram to show how environmental resistance is a process of negative feedback, exerting homeostatic control on the size of a population.

38.4 Energy flow through an ecosystem

Before you study this chapter you should refer to Chapter 21 to remind yourself of the main points about photosynthesis.

Food chains and webs

Photosynthesis is the process by which autotrophs manufacture hexose sugars such as glucose which can then be converted to many different food constituents. The most important group of autotrophs in any ecosystem are the green plants and photosynthetic algae. As they synthesise the food that will directly or indirectly feed the rest of the community, the autotrophs are called **producers**.

The animals that feed directly on plants, herbivores, are the **primary consumers** of the community. They are preyed upon by carnivores called **secondary consumers**. In turn, these animals are the food of the **tertiary consumers**, which may form the food of the **top carnivore**. The top carnivore does not have any predators and eventually dies through injury, disease or old age. Dead organisms and egested waste are broken down by decomposers.

The sequence of living organisms from producer to top carnivore is a **food chain**, which shows the passage of organic food from one organism to the next. Each consumer derives nutrients from the organism it feeds on and energy is transferred from food to ATP to supply the energy needs of the organism. In turn it provides a source of food and energy for the next animal in the chain. Each level in the food chain is called a **trophic level** (trophic meaning feeding).

▶ *Chapter 38.5* ***explains about decomposers***

Figure 38.16 A generalised food chain. Remember that the first trophic level is always occupied by an autotroph since it transfers some of the energy in sunlight to food, so making an energy source available to animals at higher trophic levels.

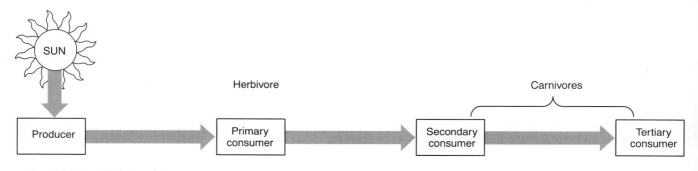

In any ecosystem there are actually many different feeding interactions between the populations in the community. It is an over-simplification to imagine that there are just a few simple food chains in operation. Many species have more than one source of food and a more accurate representation of the relationships that exist can be shown by drawing up a **food web**.

Figure 38.17 A simplified grazing food web for the short-eared owl

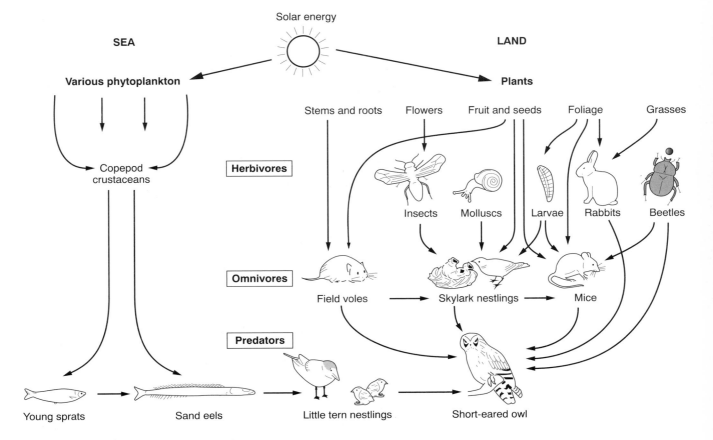

Besides the grazing food web already described, ecologists also recognise that ecosystems contain a **detritus food web** occupied by decomposers, and usually one or more **parasitic food webs**.

> **Detritus is fragments of dead organic matter.**

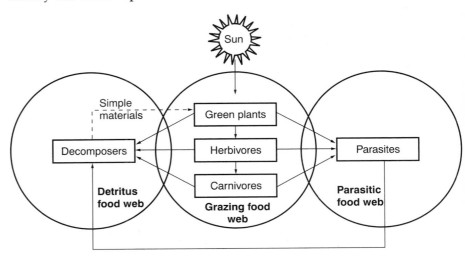

Figure 38.18 This shows the different kinds of food web that are found in an ecosystem

Ecological pyramids

Pyramids of numbers

Food chains and webs are qualitative: they tell us which organisms feed on which, but they give no indication of the numbers of different organisms in the ecosystem. It was noticed in the 1920s that there appears to be a drop in the numbers at each trophic level of a food chain as you move towards the top carnivore.

By sampling and estimating the size of populations at each different trophic level, pyramids of numbers were constructed. A bar is drawn for each level, starting with the producers, to show to scale the number of organisms present in that population (each individual is equal to one unit of length). The original observation was shown to hold true in some ecosystems, but in others the shape of the pyramid was inverted. Pyramids of numbers are of limited value because they give no indication of the size (mass) of the organism. A huge producer such as a beech tree will be shown on a pyramid of numbers by the same sized unit as a single grass plant.

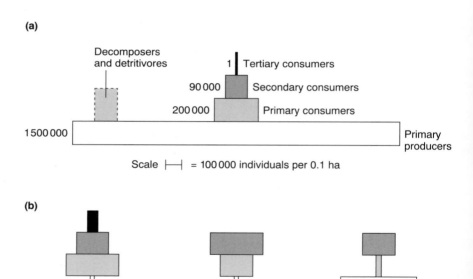

Figure 38.19 (a) A pyramid of numbers for a grassland ecosystem that shows the predicted pyramidal shape (b) These pyramids of numbers are inverted. Notice the reasons why this may happen.

(i) Producer is a single plant such as a tree

(ii) Producer is a single plant which is infected with parasites (primary consumers) and they in turn are parasitised by further parasites

(iii) A large number of producers are eaten by a single primary consumer which is infected with parasites (secondary consumers)

Pyramids of biomass

A second type of ecological pyramid is a pyramid of biomass. Biomass is mass of organic matter, and these pyramids are constructed by collecting the organisms in a food chain and finding their mass at each trophic level. Pyramids of biomass often show a pyramidal shape, the greatest mass being found at producer level, supporting a lesser mass of herbivores which in turn support progressively smaller masses of carnivores at the upper trophic levels.

There are few circumstances when pyramids of biomass do not show the expected form. It is known that at certain times of the year in lakes and oceans, the mass of producers, microscopic organisms called phytoplankton, have a lower biomass than the primary consumers, zooplankton, that they support. This might at first glance seem odd, but what has to be understood is that the phytoplankton has a short life cycle and so the phytoplankton biomass is rapidly being replaced. This is what sustains the zooplankton. The measurements made for the purpose of constructing a pyramid of biomass are like a snap-shot showing one moment in time and do not take into account the tremendous turnover of phytoplankton.

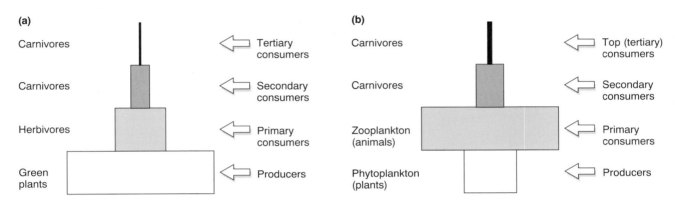

Figure 38.20 (a) A typical pyramid of biomass for a pond (b) An inverted pyramid of biomass from the English Channel in winter

Pyramids of energy

A pyramid of energy represents the total energy at each trophic level in the food chain. Pyramids of energy are expressed in units of energy per area per time, e.g. kilojoules m^{-2} yr^{-1}. Energy decreases as food is passed to successive levels in the food chain, or in other words more energy is passed from producers to herbivores than is passed from herbivores to the primary carnivores. This is because at each trophic level the organism respires and some energy is effectively lost from the ecosystem because it is transferred to the surroundings as heat; other energy may be transferred to decomposers. There must be a continual input of energy to keep the system going. This is an example of the laws of thermodynamics which are explained in the introduction to Section 4 (page 196).

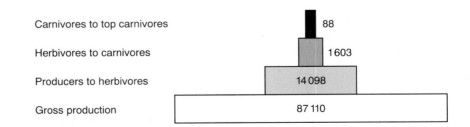

Figure 38.21 A pyramid of energy for Silver Springs, Florida. The numbers show energy flow measured in kJ m^{-2} yr^{-1}.

The advantages of pyramids of energy are:

- they take into account the rate of production over a period of time;
- they can show whether two species with the same biomass have a different energy content;
- inverted pyramids are not obtained.

The efficiency of energy flow

Since humans depend on photosynthesis for food and other products such as timber, rope, fossil fuels and textiles, it is important to understand how the maximum yield can be obtained.

Radiation from the Sun falls onto leaves and is used in photosynthesis. The amount of light intercepted varies according to local vegetation cover and latitude. It has been estimated that the energy reaching leaves in Britain is 1×10^6 kJ m^{-2} yr^{-1}. Of this as much as 95–99 per cent is reflected away from the leaf surface, conducted or transferred by convection. The tiny amount of energy left is all that is available for photosynthesis. Nevertheless, it is enough to synthesise organic compounds which accumulate in plants and can be used as food sources. The rate at which chemical energy is stored by plants is called **gross primary productivity (GPP)**. Some of the GPP is used by the plant during metabolism (**R**). What is left over is called **net primary production (NPP)**. NPP is the energy available to the next trophic level and is measured as kJ m^{-2} yr^{-1}. NPP is calculated using the following expression:

$$NPP = GPP - R$$

When consumers feed there is a transfer of energy and organic materials to the next trophic level. Energy is transferred away from each trophic level of the food chain due to respiration and egestion and excretion. Any energy that is left may be used by the heterotroph for growth, reproduction and the repair or replacement of tissues. These make up the **secondary production** of the heterotroph.

Figure 38.22 This shows the energy flow through a grazing food chain. Notice the loss of energy at each stage. On average 10 per cent energy is transferred from plants to herbivores, while animals transfer 10–20 per cent energy to the following trophic level.

The energy consumed by an animal (at any trophic level) is:

growth + respiration + egestion + excretion

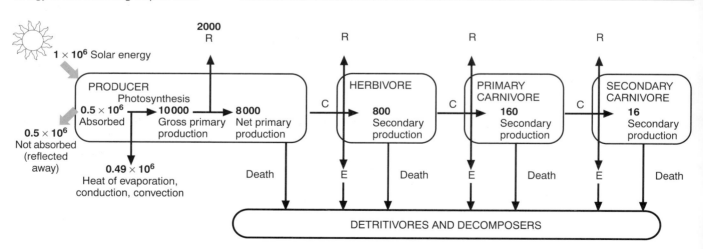

R = energy loss through respiration
E = energy lost from grazing food chain to detritivores and decomposers through excretion (e.g. urine) and egestion (e.g. faeces)
C = consumption by organisms at the higher trophic level

Questions

1 Study Figure 38.17 on page 439 carefully and make a table of the occupants of each of the *five* trophic levels shown. Which organisms occupy more than one trophic level? Is there any advantage in this?

2 Suggest why herbivores make less efficient use of their food than carnivores.

3 Is the energy transferred from the food chain via egesta or excreta lost to the ecosystem?

4 What is likely to happen to most of the net primary production of (a) a forest and (b) an ocean?

38.5 Recycling to keep a balance

The ability of an ecosystem to survive successfully depends on stability. If there are changes in either biotic or abiotic factors operating in the environment the delicate balance of the ecosystem is upset and the consequences may be serious. The natural way in which balance is maintained in the ecosystem is by recycling natural resources. When plants or animals die they remain in the ecosystem but must be removed. Detritivores, animals such as vultures and carrion crows, and dung beetles feed on dead tissues. Other decomposers, mainly saprophytic bacteria and fungi play an important role too as they secrete enzymes to break down organic matter and absorb soluble products, but return minerals to the soil. These activities are part of the detritus food web which, as we have seen in Figure 38.18 (page 439), is linked to the grazing food web. This part of the chapter examines some of the ways in which balance is maintained in the ecosystem.

> A saprophyte digests dead organic matter and excreted and egested waste, bringing about its decomposition.

Carbon cycle

Carbon makes up less than one per cent of our planet and yet it is one of the most important elements for living organisms because it is central to the composition of the biochemical molecules of which their structure and metabolism are based.

There is much concern that mainly due to our over use of fossil fuels in the past 150 years the carbon cycle is no longer balanced. Carbon dioxide, methane (CH_4) and carbon monoxide levels in the atmosphere are all rising and contributing to the Greenhouse Effect and subsequent global warming. The development of an industrialised society has produced a need for fuels as an energy source. However, fossil fuels are a finite resource and will not last indefinitely. This is why it is vital to conserve our fossil fuels and to develop alternative and viable sources of renewable energy.

> ▶ Chapter 39.5 covers the Greenhouse Effect and global warming

The carbon cycle has three pools called **sinks** or **sources** (providers) in which carbon is stored for different periods of time. Carbon moves between the pools as it is cycled.

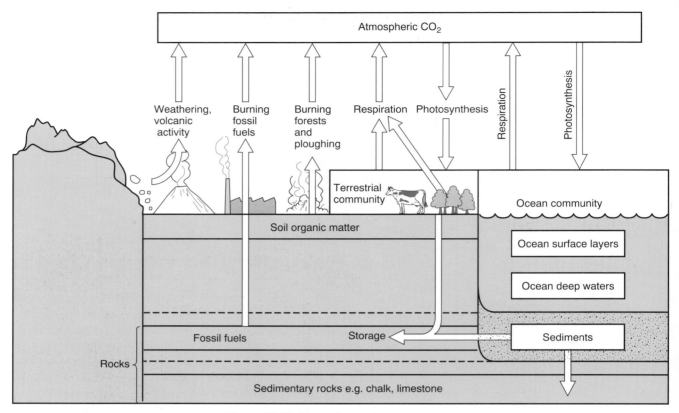

Figure 38.23 The carbon cycle

Figure 38.24 This man was found preserved in a peat bog in Denmark in 1950. He is thought to have been dead for about 2000 years, yet it was still possible to see his finger prints! Most bog people from about this time were human sacrifices who died violent deaths and were then left in the peat bog. Before the killing they were given a last meal of some kind of grain porridge. We know this because when bodies are found, forensic scientists analyse the stomach contents.

1 Carbon is stored for the shortest time in the *biological* part of the cycle, where most of the carbon is present in plants, the atmosphere and the surface layers of oceans. A much smaller proportion of carbon is stored in animals.

2 Carbon is present in the *soil* where it is stable. This carbon does not move so readily between the carbon pools.

3 Carbon is stored for the longest time in the *geochemical* part of the cycle, in rocks and in the deepest parts of oceans. By natural processes such as volcanic activity, weathering of rocks and movements in the Earth's crust, carbon is moved to the surface. Fossil fuels are mined and burnt to release carbon dioxide to the biological pool.

The processes of photosynthesis in green plants and respiration in all aerobic organisms are vital to the biological part of the cycle because they balance the level of carbon dioxide in the atmosphere, soil and in aquatic habitats. Once plants and animals die they usually decay and any carbon stored in their remains is released to the atmosphere by the action of decomposers.

However, when living things die they do not always decompose. The shells and skeletons of animals that die in the sea fall to the bottom and eventually become chalk or limestone. If a dead plant or animal lies in anaerobic and acidic conditions, such as those found in peat or acidic lakes, decomposition does not occur because the decomposers cannot survive there. Organic compounds which build up over millions of years are converted into fossil fuels such as coal, oil and gas. In this way carbon moves from the biological pool to the geochemical sink.

Nitrogen cycle

Nitrogen is needed by living organisms because it is an essential constituent of proteins. The atmosphere is almost 80 per cent nitrogen but this is not readily available to plants and animals for direct use. The most useful nitrogen sources for plants are nitrate ions (NO_3^-) and for animals are amino acids.

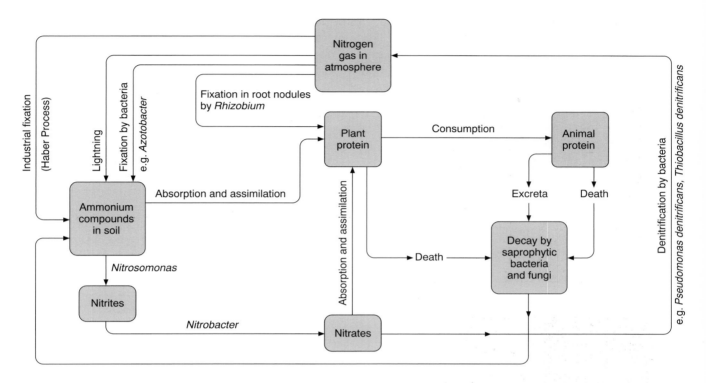

Figure 38.25 The nitrogen cycle

Three main processes allow the flow of nitrogen through the ecosystem. Nitrogen fixation, nitrification and denitrification.

Nitrogen fixation

Nitrogen fixation allows nitrogen gas from the atmosphere to become fixed into nitrogen compounds such as nitrates, nitrites and ammonia. This occurs during thunder storms when lightning acts as a source of energy for the combination of nitrogen with oxygen, so forming nitrogen oxide:

$$N_2 \quad + \quad O_2 \quad \rightarrow 2NO$$
$$\text{nitrogen} \quad \text{oxygen} \quad \text{nitrogen oxide}$$

Nitrogen oxide may be further oxidised to nitrogen dioxide:

$$2NO \quad + \quad O_2 \quad \rightarrow 2NO_2$$
$$\text{nitrogen} \quad \text{oxygen} \quad \text{nitrogen dioxide}$$

The nitrogen dioxide may dissolve in rainwater and form nitric acid which is a source of nitrate ions.

Figure 38.26 The nodules on the roots of a leguminous plant

The Haber–Bosch process is an industrial process which produces ammonia that is used in the manufacture of fertilisers. Nitrogen from the atmosphere reacts with hydrogen at high temperature in the presence of a catalyst.

However, the most efficient way in which atmospheric nitrogen is fixed is by prokaryotes capable of metabolising the gas directly using ATP and nitrogenase enzymes. The bacteria *Azotobacter* and *Clostridium* and some species of blue–green bacteria living freely in the soil are capable of nitrogen fixation. Other species such as *Rhizobium* infect the roots of plants belonging to the Papilioniaceae (the legumes or pea family). Soya, peas, beans, clover and many other plants belong to this family. The infection causes nodules to form on the roots which are inhabited by *Rhizobium. Rhizobium* incorporates nitrogen from the air into ammonia which is used to synthesise proteins, nucleic acids and vitamins. These may be used by the legumes, which in turn provide shelter and nutrients (e.g. carbohydrates) for the bacteria.

The *approximate* relative fixation of atmospheric nitrogen is: lightning 7%, industrial processes 30%, and bacterial fixation 60%.

Nitrification

Nitrification involves the oxidation of ammonium compounds and nitrites to produce nitrates which are used by plants. The ammonium compounds are the result of the action of decomposers on organic waste products and dead organisms. Nitrification is brought about by nitrifying bacteria which are examples of **chemoautotrophs**. This means that they derive energy from chemical reactions which is used to synthesise their food. Two important nitrifying bacteria are

1 *Nitrosomonas* which oxidises ammonium to nitrites:

$$\underset{\text{ammonium}}{NH^{4+}} \xrightarrow{\text{oxygen}} \underset{\text{nitrite}}{NO^{2-}} + \text{energy}$$

2 *Nitrobacter* which oxidises nitrites to nitrates:

$$\underset{\text{nitrite}}{NO^{2-}} \rightarrow \underset{\text{nitrate}}{NO^{3-}} + \text{energy}$$

Some of the nitrogen compounds formed during nitrification are not used directly by living organisms. Nitrates may be leached out of the soil as they are very soluble and accumulate in rivers and lakes; some compounds become part of sediment and are eventually incorporated into rocks.

Denitrification

Denitrification is a process in which nitrogen is returned to the atmosphere due to the action of denitrifying bacteria, so reducing the fertility of the soil. The species involved include *Thiobacillus denitrificans* and *Pseudomonas denitrificans* which inhabit wet, cold and infertile soils that are low in oxygen. During respiration they use the nitrate ions (which are reduced) as an oxidising agent for the oxidation of organic compounds. The energy yield is higher than for anaerobic respiration, which these bacteria can switch to should such conditions prevail.

CHAPTER 39 Humans and Their Environment

39.1 The human population

The human population is increasing very rapidly and human activities have long-term and far-reaching effects on the environment.

The far-reaching and mainly permanent nature of the changes brought about by human activities means that we need to consider our actions very carefully, and to take responsibility for them both in a personal and global context. This is particularly true because the human population has increased and is continuing to increase so rapidly. Since there are more people alive, the effects of their activities on the environment are amplified. Since humans manipulate their environment, they are to a certain extent exempt from the natural checks and balances which would control population size for any other species.

Table 39.1 Population data.

Country	Population estimate mid-1990s (millions)	Natural increase (annual %)	Population aged under 15/over 65 (%)
Poland	37.8	0.6	26/10
UK	57.4	0.2	16/15
West Germany	63.2	0.0	15/15
USSR	291.0	0.9	25/9
Kenya	24.6	3.8	50/2
Nigeria	118.8	2.9	45/2
Burkina Faso	9.1	3.2	48/4
Botswana	1.2	2.9	46/3
China	1119.9	1.4	27/6
Japan	123.6	0.4	20/11
Pakistan	114.6	3.0	44/4
India	853.4	2.1	39/3
Indonesia	189.4	1.8	38/3
Saudi Arabia	15.0	3.4	45/3
USA	251.4	0.8	22/12
Jamaica	2.4	1.7	37/6
Mexico	88.6	2.4	42/4
Peru	21.9	2.4	38/4
Brazil	150.4	1.9	36/4
Australia	17.1	0.8	22/11
World	5321.0	1.8	33/6

Source: Population Concern

Are we reaching the situation where the biosphere will no longer be able to support the population? Already there is an enormous strain on the Earth to produce sufficient food and many people do not have enough, although this is partly a problem of distribution. In some countries there is excess food, including meat, eggs and grain, while in other countries people are dying of starvation. A long-term solution is more complex than merely taking food from one area of the world to another.

The need to increase food production has brought about differences in the way that we use land. For example large fields are easier to farm using machinery than by hand, so many kilometres of hedges have been removed to make way for mechanisation. Hedges provide habitats and food supplies for many small mammals, birds and invertebrates, and their loss has affected both the total amount and the diversity of species living there. **Deforestation** is the clearing of established forest, usually to provide further land area for farming or horticulture. Although in some areas the existing forest is replaced with other tree species (e.g. conifers) the nature of the forest as a habitat has changed, becoming much less varied in terms of the resources it offers for other species. Adding to the loss of habitats are new farming methods which have introduced large areas of **monoculture**. This means that for many hectares only one species, such as wheat, might be the dominant plant. Fewer types of other plant species survive alongside the wheat than would be found in an unfarmed meadow, which again has an effect on the animal life or the **fauna** of an area. These examples describe the concept of **biodiversity**, or the number of different species within an ecosystem, which many people are concerned to protect.

Modern farming methods focus on the need to increase the production of food from a particular area, and because of this chemicals, generally known as **agrochemicals**, are used. For example the use of fertilisers has improved the mineral content of soil so maximising crop yields, while pesticides are used to control pests and diseases in crop plants. Similarly, intensive farming methods have been employed for animal farming. In the case of egg production this requires giving animals premium food supplies to raise their productivity and using antibiotics to control diseases in flocks. The use of agrochemicals must be closely monitored, because the mechanisms and effects of the movement of these materials through an ecosystem are often unknown, and are potentially hazardous.

There is also pressure for land to be used for housing and consequently a spread of **urbanisation**, many more people live in towns nowadays than used to be the case. It is estimated that by the end of the turn of the century around 50 per cent of people will live in towns and cities. This causes enormous challenges in terms of sanitation and the supply of basic services such as domestic energy supplies. Extensive road systems have been built to service modern transport needs and there is a sharp increase in road traffic and the pollution arising from it.

Figure 39.1 Living space for humans intrudes on the natural environment of other species

It is obvious that many human activities result in pollution and the effects of pollutants are often inter-related. For example, carbon dioxide contributes to acidity in rainwater, damaging soil conditions and waterways, as well as being a 'greenhouse gas' and contributing to global warming (explained further on in this chapter). The scale and speed of the impact on our world is the reason for concern, and what leads to potential conflict between using the environment and conserving it. Even though many of the long-term effects of human activities will never be felt by the people who are alive today, humans as the dominant animal species must take responsibility for the environmental heritage of their descendants.

Questions

1 Suggest reasons why the human population has increased so rapidly in such a relatively short time?

2 How might the success of the human population be limited by the effects of their activities on the environment?

39.2 Balancing exploitation and conservation

The biosphere is an ecosystem within which the activities of all species are inter-related, so that the consequences of the actions of one species may affect many other living things. If humans continue to use the environment with a lack of respect, there will be further damaging changes which will ultimately threaten our existence. We need resources from our environment and protecting it is in our own best interests.

For many people, the word 'conservation' probably sums up an image of someone in green gum boots, making a fuss about an environmental issue, or perhaps a marine scientist diving with dolphins in an exotic location. However, beyond these media-generated and superficial images lies the real meaning of **conservation**: the application of the principles of ecology to manage an environment, so that despite human activities it remains in balance. Conservation is active in that it seeks to sensitively protect the environment for all species, while safeguarding sustainable yields of resources. In other words, conservation is not merely keeping things as they are, but managing changes sensibly. Management techniques include:

- Setting aside land, for example a Site of Special Scientific Interest (SSSI) in which sensitive environments are maintained; keeping Areas of Outstanding Natural Beauty and National Parks for the enjoyment of all.
- Mowing to increase species diversity by preventing communities reaching climax.
- Protecting and re-establishing hedgerows.
- Controlling water levels of estuarine marshes and bogs to prevent the water table dropping, and conditions drying out.
- Providing recreational facilities such as footpaths and bridlepaths, viewpoints and picnic spots to minimise damage by trampling.
- Developing and implementing policies for sustainable timber production and fish catches.

- Establishing national and international guidelines on pollution control, and on the release of genetically engineered organisms into the wild.

39.3 The loss of forests – deforestation

> Deforestation damages ecosystems, reduces biodiversity and is a cause of desertification.

Trees are the Earth's dominant plant species, forming climax communities across more land area than another other type of plant (see Figure 38.2 on pages 361 and 423). Tropical rainforest is the most complex of all biomes and is a dynamic system which can vary quite substantially over a relatively small distance, depending on factors such as altitude, slope, bedrock and humidity. About 40 per cent of the world's rainforests had been destroyed by 1980, and the destruction continues, threatening the future of these unique ecosystems. These forests are important in the biosphere because:

- they help to maintain climate conditions by:
  - net production of oxygen in daylight, replenishing our atmosphere;
  - absorption of carbon dioxide, helping to reduce the effects of global warming;
  - acting as a thermal buffer, dampening changes in temperature at the Earth's surface;
  - acting as a reservoir of water, by retaining water in the root and leaf litter layers, and helping to prevent flooding;

  - loss of water into the atmosphere, helping to maintain the water cycle.
- They contain up to 90 per cent of the world's biodiversity.
- They prevent the loss of soil through soil erosion and the subsequent development of deserts (**desertification**) because the plant root systems bind the soil structure, which is otherwise vulnerable to wind erosion, and during tropical thunderstorms.
- They are important economically, particularly in timber production.

Why is biodiversity important?

The genetic material in living things is a gene pool or a stock of fresh genes which may be useful for breeding new species or developing new products in the future. Many plants are useful sources of chemicals for making medicines, for example aspirin (a painkiller or **analgesic**) was originally extracted from willow bark and quinine (an anti-malarial drug) was extracted from the chinchona plant. Living things are also useful resources of food and all types of materials such as rubber, cotton and leather. **Biotechnology** is an expanding area for scientific and technological research, which involves products from living things and the genetic manipulation of living cells themselves.

Rainforests and nutrient cycling

Leaf litter forms continuously in rainforests and in large amounts – up to 10 tonnes per hectare per year. Fungi and invertebrates such as termites are important in the rapid breakdown of this dead organic matter, releasing nutrients for the production of fresh biomass. Soil provides the physical structure within which efficient recycling of these nutrients occurs, and there is very little movement of nutrients to lower soil levels. Loss of minerals by leaching is relatively slow despite the fierce rainstorms, because the canopy

Figure 39.2 Using genetic engineering techniques a thale cress plant (*Arabidopsis*) was given three modified bacterial genes and as a result the cells produced a plastic material called PHB within the chloroplasts. Up to 14 per cent of the dry biomass of the thale cress leaves may be PHB, and the commercial prospects look promising.
(*See Colour Gallery page 360*)

C48

and the thick layer of leaf litter are protective barriers. The rainforest acts as a reservoir of minerals which are mainly contained in the leaf litter and in the biomass itself (up to 75 per cent in the large leaves common for rainforest plants). Some of the main ways in which a rainforest discourages nutrient loss include:

- root systems are shallow and spread widely;
- mycorrhiza (fungal filaments associated with the roots) digest leaf litter and transport the nutrients directly into roots so minerals are not lost by leaching;
- aerial roots collect nutrients from the atmosphere;
- plants produce relatively few seeds, so not many nutrients are locked up in them;
- large leaves form a protective canopy during thunderstorms, reducing loss by leaching.

The Pasoh rainforest, Malaysia

The Pasoh Forest is located in the central lowland area of Malaysia, covering an area of around 600 hectares. The types of trees vary across the area with a change in altitude, which increases towards the east. In the lowland area on the west, the canopy is taller and larger, and supports a greater biodiversity than on the east. The core zone of undisturbed forest is too small to support animals that roam over a large area such as tigers or elephants. However, there are many smaller mammals, birds and invertebrates. Part of the forest was logged commercially over 40 years ago and has been left to regenerate. Figure 39.3 shows the effects of logging and regeneration on the biodiversity of birds surveyed in the area. Table 39.2 shows how the soil characteristics were altered by logging.

These are some of the points contained in the Malaysian National Forestry policy, which is aimed at achieving sustainable forestry:

- an inventory of trees is made before felling, to assess what is there;
- only trees over 50 cm diameter are tagged for felling;
- the company which fells the trees must assess how to do this with minimal damage to the rest of the forest, for example by controlling the direction in which felled trees fall;

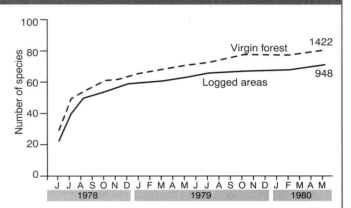

Figure 39.3 The impact of logging and subsequent regeneration on the biodiversity of birds in Pasoh Forest

- a company must have a felling licence;
- after felling forestry staff must survey the forest;
- illegal felling can result in prosecution;
- 5–10 years after felling, there is regeneration management by forest staff, e.g. the removal of creepers from young trees, planting of other tree species;
- the next felling cycle may start after 30 years.

(This article was based on 'Tropical rainforests in Malaysia' from *Geography Review*, September 1996.)

Table 39.2 The impact of logging and subsequent regeneration on soil characteristics in Pasoh Forest

Soil characteristic	Undisturbed forest soils	Recently disturbed (compacted) forest soils	Change (%)
bulk density (g cm^{-1})	0.52	1.44	+276
moisture content (%)	28.80	19.70	−32
organic carbon (%)	2.70	1.27	−53
total nitrogen (%)	0.23	0.07	−70

Questions

1 To what extent does felling of rainforest trees affect:

   a) biodiversity? (Suggest reasons for the changes which occurred at Pasoh, based on Figure 39.3.)

   b) soil characteristics? (Suggest reasons for the changes which occurred at Pasoh, based on Table 39.2.)

   c) the cycling of minerals generally?

   d) the economy of a country?

2 a) What further points might be added to a policy for sustainable forestry, such as that set out by the Malaysian Government?

   b) What factors determine whether a sustainable forestry policy is likely to succeed?

   c) What might be the effect of a boycott by Western countries on rainforest timber?

3 Why does selective logging have a far lower impact on the ecology of an area than replanting a natural forest with plantation trees, such as rubber or conifers?

39.4 Water pollution

What causes water pollution?

Figure 39.4 Oil is a devastating pollutant along coastlines, killing many fish and seabirds. However, studies have shown that natural processes rid an area of petrochemicals faster than might be expected, and that coastlines regenerate in time.
(See Colour Gallery page 362)

Water pollution can harm aquatic organisms and may be hazardous to human health as well as reduce the enjoyment of using waterways for recreation. The main cause of water pollution is the discharge of organic materials into waterways, from industries (such as food processing), domestic sewage and farms (such as manure slurry). These materials are broken down by bacteria, which require dissolved oxygen from the water to respire. Inorganic fertilisers cause pollution because they are soluble and are easily leached out of soil, increasing the content of minerals in water, particularly phosphate and nitrate. High mineral levels cause rapid growth of algae which form blankets of growth on the surface of a waterway. When the minerals are depleted the algae die and drop to the bottom, adding to the organic load in the water. Blue–green cyanobacteria cause blooms too, which block the light and effectively kill other aquatic plants. Whatever the cause, this oxygen depletion kills animal life which relies on dissolved oxygen in water, an effect called **eutrophication**.

    Acidification is the lowering of pH in waterways, usually as a result of rainwater which is acidic running off the land and draining into rivers and lakes. It has serious consequences since many fish cannot live below pH 5, but also because the acidic rainwater can leach minerals (e.g. aluminium) out of the soil, which can be toxic in themselves. The causes and effects of acidity in water are discussed in more detail further on in this section. Detergents cause foaming where water is running fast, which is unsightly, but the detergent also increases the levels of minerals such as phosphate and nitrate in water.

    Water quality in England and Wales is monitored by the Environment Agency (formerly the National Rivers Authority), and by the Scottish Environment Protection Agency in Scotland. Water quality can be assessed using chemical and physical tests, as well as investigating bioindicators such as species with a low tolerance to pollution. The dissolved oxygen test is literally a measure of the quantity of dissolved oxygen. The **biochemical oxygen demand (BOD)** is the oxygen demanded by the breakdown of

> Water pollution can lead to loss of dissolved oxygen by eutrophication. Acidification is the lowering of pH, leading to the death of pH sensitive organisms.

► *Chapter 38.2 describes some practical ways of investigating an ecosystem*

organic materials in mg dm^{-3}: the less oxygen needed, the lower the BOD and the higher the water quality. The suspended solids test is a measure of the amount of solids which can be filtered out of water and weighed dry, reflecting the clarity or turbidity of a water sample.

Figure 39.5 These freshwater animals are useful bioindicators of pollution – they are listed in the order in which they disappear as oxygen levels fall

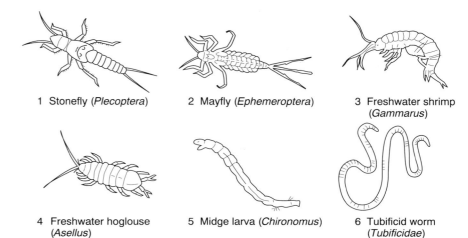

1 Stonefly (*Plecoptera*)   2 Mayfly (*Ephemeroptera*)   3 Freshwater shrimp (*Gammarus*)

4 Freshwater hoglouse (*Asellus*)   5 Midge larva (*Chironomus*)   6 Tubificid worm (*Tubificidae*)

Table 39.3 Since 1970, waterways in England and Wales have been assessed for quality every five years, using this scale.

River class	Chemical factor	Biological factor	Potential uses
Class 1	dissolved oxygen >80% BOD <2.5	non-toxic to fish	drinking water, game and coarse fishing; high amenity value
Class 2	dissolved oxygen >70% BOD <4	non-toxic to fish; may include rivers containing high-quality effluent	
Class 3	dissolved oxygen >60% BOD <6	non-toxic to fish; water not showing visible signs of pollution, except some humic discoloration or foaming below weirs	water suitable for drinking after advanced treatment; coarse fishing; moderate amenity value
Class 4	dissolved oxygen >50% BOD <8		
Class 5	dissolved oxygen >20% BOD <15	fish absent or sporadically present	suitable for low-grade industrial use

Figure 39.6 Many industries rely on large amounts of water for processing, such as the paper-making industry. In some countries such as Finland, effluent from paper mills is a major water pollutant, although the amount of water needed to process one tonne of paper pulp has dropped from 200 to 50 m³ over the last 50 years. What's more, the industry has successfully made cleaner effluent an issue, as shown by this data.

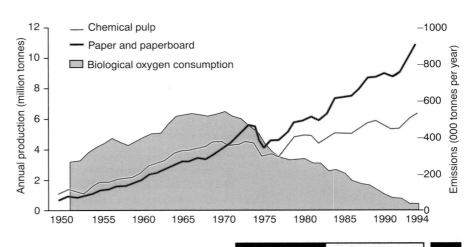

Sampling the River Perry

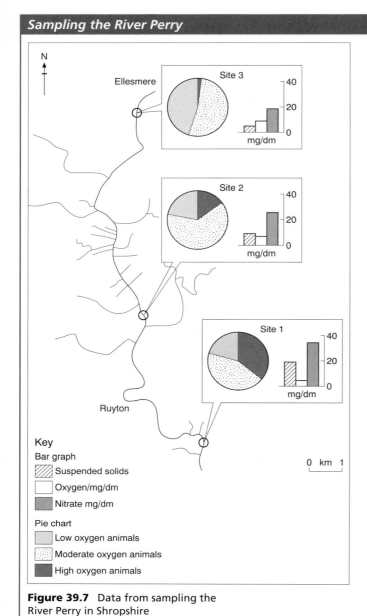

Figure 39.7 Data from sampling the River Perry in Shropshire

Table 39.4 Data collected from the River Perry

Organism	Site 1	Site 2	Site 3
stonefly	16	1	0
mayfly	46	23	4
freshwater shrimp	39	58	8
freshwater hoglouse	3	7	14
midge larva	14	19	45
tubificid worm	21	17	62
total high demanders	62	24	4
total moderate demanders	77	101	129
total low tolerators	35	36	107
grand total	174	161	240
nitrate (mg dm^{-3})	34	26	18
oxygen (mg dm^{-3})	4.5	6.6	8.2
suspended solids (mg dm^{-3})	19	9	5

Source: Geography Review, January 1997

Use the data presented in Figure 39.7 and Table 39.4 to answer the following questions.

Questions

1 a) Which of the sites provided the most polluted water?

  b) Explain the reasons for your choice in terms of physical and chemical tests and biological indicators.

  c) Suggest possible sources of the water pollution at this site.

2 The other two sites sampled are less polluted. Suggest how these factors might contribute to the difference in pollution between the less polluted sites and the most polluted site:

  a) the flow of water from other areas into the River Perry.

  b) the presence of bacteria which degrade organic materials.

3 In what ways is the amenity value of waterways reduced by pollution?

How healthy is our coastline?

There are numerous forms of pollution contributing to the condition of coastal waters. For example, pollution comes from ships, in river water carrying industrial and farm wastes, as well as from the discharge of sewage. Apart from being a health hazard for humans, pollution may contribute to disease and death in other animal species such as seals.

> Water pollution originating from sewage, farms and industry can be a hazard to human health.

Questions

1 In which areas is there a match between the worst cases of pollution and tourist beaches?

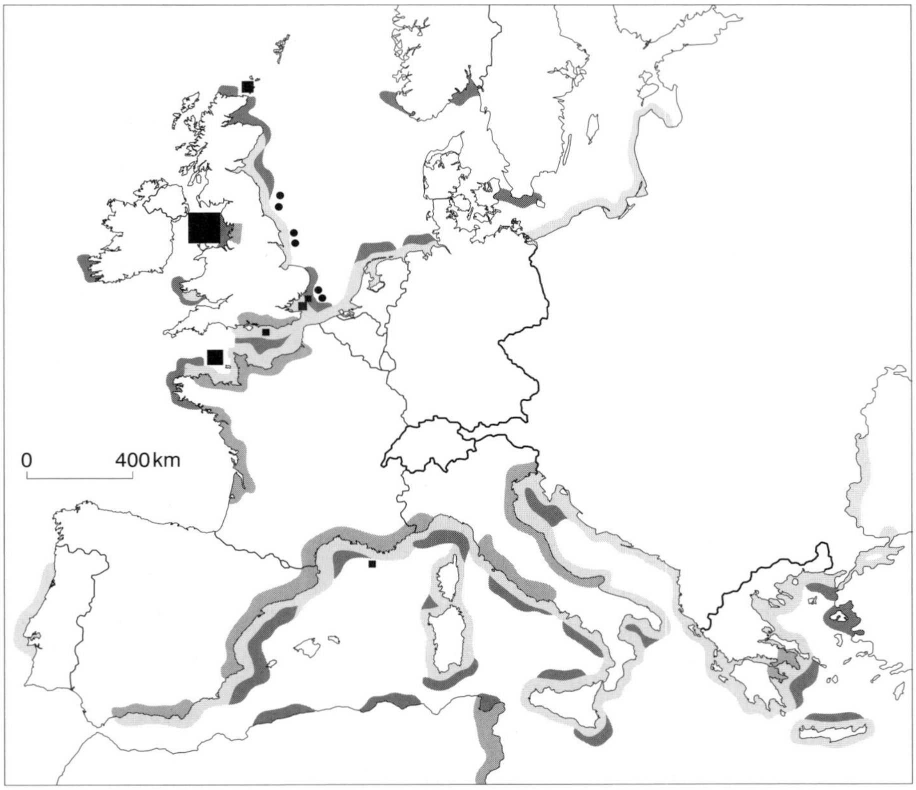

Worst cases of sewage and industrial pollution

Worst cases of oil pollution

Major tourist beaches

• Sewage sludge dumping site

■ • Water contaminated with radioactive substances

Figure 39.8 Pollution around Europe's coastlines
(See Colour Gallery page 362)

0   400km

2 a) Seawater is tested for coliform bacteria, faecal streptococci and *Salmonella*, all of which may be found in sewage. Why are these organisms a health hazard?

b) Sewage is diluted and discharged into the sea through long pipelines that reach far out to sea, and yet there is still sewage contamination on beaches. Suggest reasons why this is so.

c) Suggest a reason why coastal fisheries are affected by pollution.

39.5 Using fuels

In the Western world we are highly reliant on fuels to sustain our lifestyle and standard of living: for transport, powering machinery and all types of electrical appliances, heating and lighting. Figure 39.9 shows the sources of energy in the UK, including the significant share contributed by fossil fuels. **Fossil fuels** include gas and oil, and coal which formed millions of years ago over a long period of time. Neither the conditions nor the species which brought about the formation of these fuels exist on Earth today, and so fossil fuels are not currently forming in the same way. This means that fossil fuels are finite sources of stored energy and will run out if we continue to use them. However, here we are more concerned with the effects of burning fossil fuels, either directly to gain heat, or in power stations to generate electricity, or to power vehicles. Fossil fuels are organic since they originate from living things. Other organic fuels which can be burned are peat, timber, condensed straw, dried manure and algal biomass.

Key

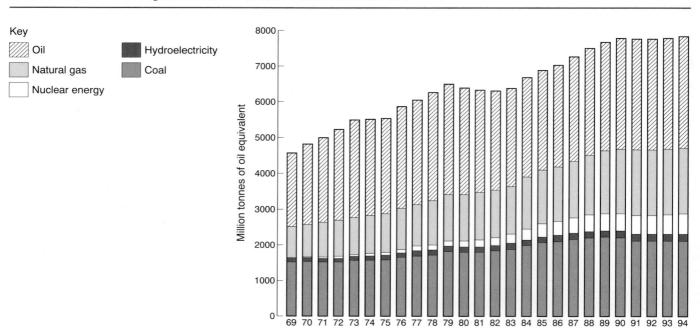

Figure 39.9 World primary energy consumption

Source: BP Statistics of World Energy 1996

Sulphur dioxide and oxides of nitrogen are the main causes of acid rain. Acidification of soil and water damages wildlife.

Combustion causes pollution

Fossil fuels are mostly made of carbon and hydrogen, with some other elements such as nitrogen or sulphur. Combustion is an oxidation process, producing oxides of non-metal elements: carbon dioxide (CO_2), water (H_2O), sulphur dioxide (SO_2) and nitrogen oxides (collectively NO_x). These non-metal oxides are acidic and to varying degrees soluble, making their emission into the atmosphere serious because they dissolve in rainwater, lowering the pH and causing **acid rain**. Clean rainwater is naturally very slightly acidic (around pH 5.6) because of the carbon dioxide which has

Figure 39.10 In the 1980s, many acres of softwood forests were destroyed in Norway and Sweden by acid rain, much of which had drifted eastwards from Britain and other Western European countries. This project uses purified water to keep the soil wet and stops rain from penetrating it

dissolved in it. At this pH some minerals such as calcium, magnesium and trace elements begin to be lost by leaching. However, acid rain is more acidic than this (around pH 4.0–4.5) and as a consequence it affects soil conditions by lowering the soil pH and further altering the mineral balance. This can affect the growth of plant roots and alter their tolerance to drought. Therefore the more gaseous acidic oxides (particularly sulphur dioxide) which we generate by burning fuels, the greater the effect on rainwater, soil water and waterways.

It is worth noting that there are natural processes which cause the formation of carbon dioxide and methane, for example the process of decay, and the action of micro-organisms in water-logged conditions such as those occurring in rice-growing areas. Therefore the balance of gases in the atmosphere varies locally according to the particular conditions, both those caused naturally and by human activities. Gaseous acidic oxides are only some of the culprits in the reduction of air quality. Vapours from volatile organic solvents, petrochemicals such as diesel fumes, and other industrial chemicals, as well as ozone (O_3) at low levels in the atmosphere, all contribute to air pollution. Air pollution is linked to increased levels of respiratory conditions such as asthma and bronchitis.

▶ *Chapter 8.4 describes the causes, effects and treatment of asthma*

Ozone high in the atmosphere protects human health by absorbing UV radiation.

Ozone and human health

Atmospheric oxygen (O_2) is vital for the process of respiration and hence for life itself for most living things. But oxygen can also exist as ozone (O_3) in which form it can have both advantages and disadvantages for human health.

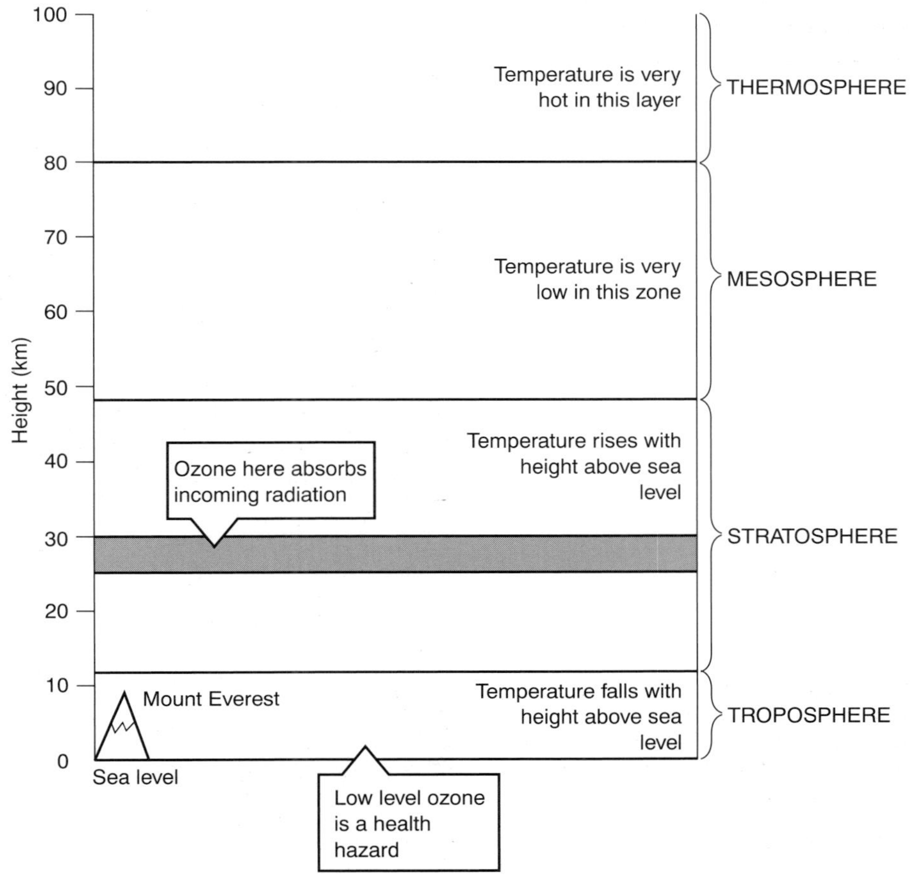

Figure 39.11 At higher levels in the atmosphere where ozone is a benefit to human health, pollutants destroy ozone. But close to the Earth's surface, pollutants cause the production of ozone which is a hazard to human health.

▶ *Chapter 17.2 mentions skin cancer, which can be caused by UV radiation*

At ground level (up to 1 km above the ground) ozone is a health hazard because it is highly reactive. It is capable of oxidising phospholipids in cell membranes as well as attacking cysteine, an amino acid component. The amount of ozone in the boundary layer and at ground level is worse during the summer months since its formation relies on sunlight, and also in rural areas because, ironically, the pollutant nitric oxide (NO) combines with ozone forming oxygen and nitrogen dioxide.

Greenhouse gases and global warming

The way in which carbon cycles within the biosphere is shown in Chapter 38, Figure 38.23. You notice that the form in which carbon occurs can vary, for example as inorganic carbon dioxide and organic carbohydrates (such as glucose, glycogen and starch). Many of the processes which bring about a change in carbon compounds, such as photosynthesis, are natural. Others, such as combustion, are due to human activities and in this sense are interfering with the balance of the carbon cycle. One piece of evidence of our disturbance of this balance is the accurate measurement of the concentration of atmospheric carbon dioxide since the late 1950s. Other evidence includes the analysis of trapped air bubbles in cores of polar ice. The significance of this increase in concentration is that carbon dioxide is a **greenhouse gas**, which means that it absorbs infrared radiation and warms up. Some of the infrared energy it absorbs is radiated into space, and some of it radiates back towards Earth, causing a heating effect at the surface. This heating effect is called **global warming**. Other greenhouse gases are methane, nitrous oxide (N_2O) and ozone.

Carbon dioxide, methane and ozone are the main greenhouse gases. These gases cause global warming.

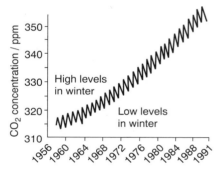

Figure 39.12 Carbon dioxide levels fluctuate seasonally during the year but are rising overall

Figure 39.13 The greenhouse effect

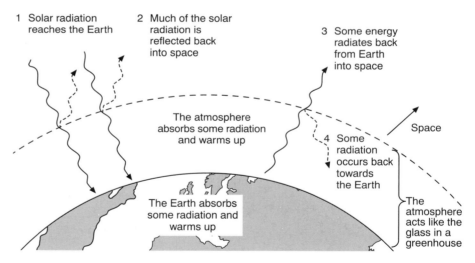

1 Solar radiation reaches the Earth

2 Much of the solar radiation is reflected back into space

3 Some energy radiates back from Earth into space

The atmosphere absorbs some radiation and warms up

Space

4 Some radiation occurs back towards the Earth

The Earth absorbs some radiation and warms up

The atmosphere acts like the glass in a greenhouse

Not all of the carbon dioxide released by burning fossil fuels or the decomposition of organic material remains in the atmosphere. Much of it dissolves in freshwater and seawater, or becomes incorporated into biomass or energy sources for living things. The rainforests are of major importance in this respect, because their rate of carbon dioxide fixation during photosynthesis is high. Blooms of marine phytoplankton are also important, and have been recorded in temperate and high-latitude waters. When nutrients are brought to the surface layers of water by storms, sudden blooms of phytoplankton grow, fixing carbon dioxide. Later they die and sink down deep to the ocean floor.

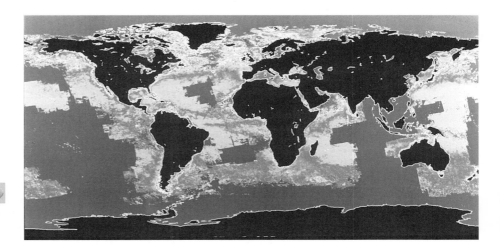

Figure 39.14 The extent of phytoplankton blooms can be seen in this satellite picture, as the light coloured areas *(See Colour Gallery page 362)*

C53

No one knows for sure what the extent or effects of global warming will be. Computer models of existing data can be used to predict what will happen if any of the data variables (such as carbon dioxide concentration in the atmosphere) changes. However, the challenge with this approach is that there is not enough accurate data to develop a foolproof model. Most scientists are seriously concerned about the potential effects of global warming, partly because they are so unpredictable. Certainly, it will take many decades for the levels of greenhouse gases to diminish, even after we stop being irresponsible about releasing so much into our atmosphere. These are some of the possible effects of global warming:

- By around the year 2040, the average temperature at the Earth's surface could have risen by 2–5°C.
- The ocean waters may expand and some of the polar ice caps might melt, raising sea level probably by up to 30 cm.
- Climate changes may include higher winds and rainfall nearer the polar caps and drier conditions elsewhere.
- A change in the distribution of diseases, such as malaria, might occur. For example the vector for the malarial parasite may be able to survive in areas other than those it currently exists in.
- The seeds of some plant species might become non-viable, if they require a frosting period to begin germination but frost no longer occurs in the locality of the species.

Renewable resources of fuel

One answer to the problem of fuels running out is to look for a source which can be replaced over and over again. These sources are often gained from living things as is shown by the following two examples.

Example 1 – Gasohol from sugar

Sugar cane grows in tropical and sub-tropical zones around the world, where the warm and wet climate is ideal for rapid growth. The cane has a high photosynthetic efficiency compared to other plants, storing a high yield of sucrose. The cane is processed soon after harvesting to extract the raw sugar juice separate to the fibre. The sugar juice is further purified and can be used:

- in the food industry;

- to make molasses for animal feed;
- to make ethanol, by yeasts fermenting the sugar and subsequent distillation of the solution – the ethanol can be used to run vehicles, which can be powered by a 95 per cent solution.

Even the fibre can be burned to generate electricity for powering the processing plant. This scheme was first pioneered in Brazil, where the vast majority of vehicles are run on ethanol or a mixture of ethanol and petrol.

Example 2 – Biogas from fermenting domestic and agricultural waste

Organic waste such as animal dung is naturally degraded by micro-organisms in anaerobic conditions, generating methane. On a small scale, the fermentation of animal dung to produce **biogas** is important, particularly in countries where electricity production does not occur on a large scale in rural areas. Pakistan, India and China have widely distributed biogas fermenters which are useful for village communities. In developed countries, much of the huge amount of domestic waste produced each year is dumped underground at land-fill sites. Here again, natural processes produce methane gas which can be effectively harnessed as a fuel for electricity generation. What's more, using the methane prevents a dangerous build up and escape of this flammable gas, which would contribute to the greenhouse gases in the atmosphere.

Alternative fuels

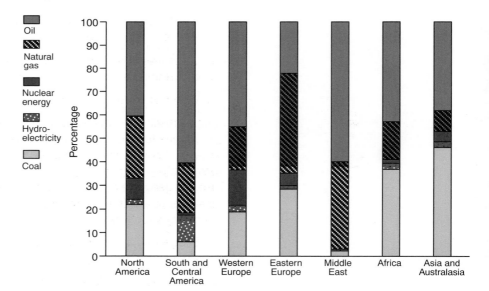

Figure 39.15 Are alternative sources of energy to fossil fuels poised to take a greater market share?

Further choices of fuel source include the transfer of solar and kinetic energy (wind and hydroelectric) and nuclear power. Each of these options has its own impact on the environment, and has advantages and disadvantages economically, but a full discussion of these considerations is beyond the scope of this text. The most controversial of these options is probably nuclear power, because of the health and safety risks surrounding its production and the disposal of the radioactive waste produced.

Questions

1 a) List pollutants which:

   i) form from the combustion of fossil fuels

   ii) form due to natural processes.

   b) Explain why pollutants have a bad effect on the environment in terms of:

   i) acid rain and acidification

   ii) ozone at different levels in the atmosphere

   iii) global warming.

2 a) Explain how bioindicators might be used to monitor the water quality in a river over a period of time.

   b) How is seawater quality monitored?

3 In what ways might human activities be changed to protect the environment from the effects of pollution?

4 Draw up a table of information about greenhouse gases, such as the types and sources.

5 a) Suggest some advantages of renewable fuels.

   b) Why are renewable fuel sources not used more widely?

   c) What factors might encourage a greater use of renewable fuel sources in the future?

6 a) What are the advantages of a country being able to produce its own fuel source?

   b) Why has the gasohol programme not been developed for the UK?

7 In a pilot scheme, algae are grown in a closed vessel in optimum conditions for their growth. The algae are regularly harvested from the growth medium, dried and used as a combustible fuel. During its combustion, some energy is transferred to boil water, and the steam used to generate electricity. Energy is also supplied to heat the growth chamber to a suitable temperature. Some of the carbon dioxide produced by combustion is bubbled back through the growth chamber.

   a) Suggest what conditions might best encourage the rapid growth of algae.

   b) How might the algae be harvested from the culture medium?

   c) Suggest a reason why some carbon dioxide is fed back through the growth chamber.

   d) What is the energy source for the growth of algae?

   e) In what way is this process almost self-sustaining?

8 Ionising radiation which is emitted by radioactive waste is damaging to DNA. What is the significance of DNA damage

   a) to cellular function?

   b) in inheritance?

39.6 Controlling pests in food production

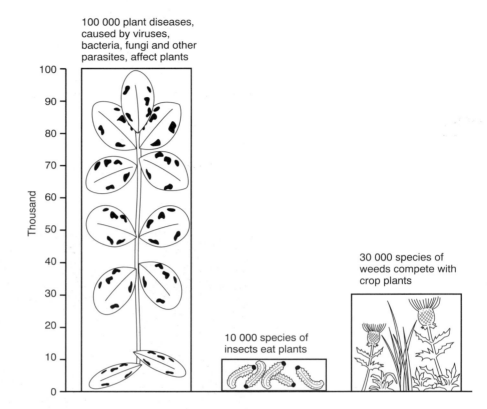

Figure 39.16 Micro-organisms cause diseases of crops, invertebrates damage crop plants and weed plants compete with them, all contributing to a reduction in crop yields

100 000 plant diseases, caused by viruses, bacteria, fungi and other parasites, affect plants

30 000 species of weeds compete with crop plants

10 000 species of insects eat plants

We depend on plants for food and use them to feed farm animals, as well as using them to produce materials such as rubber and many medicines. Preventing pests from damaging crops is economically sound, because despite the cost of using pest control, less crops are lost and so the cost of production is reduced. Even with crop protection methods, about a third of the world's crops are destroyed by pests annually. A variety of methods are used to counteract pests, such as cultural, biological and chemical controls.

Cultural methods

Cultural methods involve how a crop is farmed, such as leaving fields free of crops for a year, leaving bigger spaces between crop rows, or inter-planting different species.

Biological control

Biological control involves using a natural enemy of a pest to control its numbers. Overall, there are many advantages of using biological control because it is generally low cost, not damaging to the environment and self-perpetuating once established. However, one limitation is that the pest does remain in reduced numbers, so some crop damage is inevitable, and biological control alone is not sufficient if crops have a long transport time before reaching their market place.

Figure 39.17 This parasitic wasp is a natural enemy of aphids

Figure 39.17 shows a natural enemy of aphids which can used in the biological control of this pest. Aphids are small sap-sucking insects which get their nutrition from plants by piercing the cells with needle-like mouthparts until they reach the phloem tissue, and then sucking out the sap. Apart from taking nutrition from the plant, they are vectors for plant diseases, for example transferring pathogenic virus particles or fungal spores. Parasitic wasps help to destroy these pests, because they lay their eggs inside aphids. The egg develops within the aphid, finally killing it.

There may, however, be some undesirable and unpredictable effects of introducing a natural enemy into an area, particularly if it is not one that normally lives there, i.e. it is introduced from elsewhere. This was the case with the cane toad, which was introduced to Queensland, Australia, from South America to deal with pests such as rats that live in sugar cane plantations. Unfortunately, these toads turned out to be very general in their appetites and began to destroy native populations of other animals, such as the pygmy possum.

Figure 39.18 The cane toad is a killer

Figure 39.19 This diagram shows how the populations of a pest and its natural enemy fluctuate. When the number of pests is high, the enemies have a greater food source and their numbers rise. However, an increase in enemy population means that they kill more of the pest population, so depleting their own food supply. Using a broad spectrum insecticide kills both the pest and its natural enemies, and so surviving members of the pest population reproduce rapidly, virtually unchecked by the reduced enemy population.

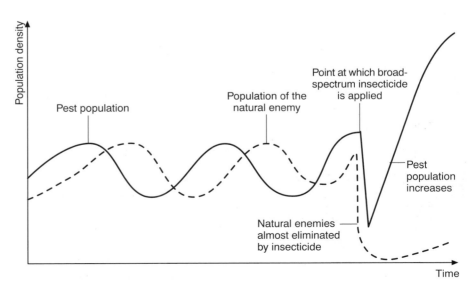

Chemical control

Chemical control involves using pesticides, which are usually grouped according to their target pest (Table 39.5). A well designed pesticide is specifically toxic to a pest or particular type of plant so it does not damage any other species, although in some cases a **non-selective** pesticide is used to clear land of all plant life. Chemical control methods are rapid and initially effective. However, it is becoming clear that in the long-term there are problems associated with using pesticides because pests often re-appear later, having developed resistance to the pesticide which was used. Also, there are environmental risks because pesticides are very stable compounds that do not to break down easily, so they may accumulate in soils as well as in living things. The effects of pesticides which accumulate in the ecosystem are often unpredictable until the level of pesticide is significant, at which point a long break down period is a disadvantage. Some pesticides mimic the effects of reproductive hormones, and this may be to blame for some unusual patterns of reproductive behaviour and reduced fertility in seabirds. Added to this, the cost of using chemical control is increasing as new compounds constantly need to be developed to cope with pest resistance.

Table 39.5 Chemicals used to kill pests

Pesticide	Target	Features
fungicide	fungi	systemic fungicides spread within the water transport system of a plant, e.g. organic compounds such as thiocarbamates
		non-systemic fungicides remain on the plant surface, e.g. sulphur dust
insecticide	insects	organic compounds, e.g. pyrethroids, based on natural insecticide found in some Chrysanthemum flowers; many insecticides such as pyrethroid work by interfering with nerve impulse transmission in insects
herbicide	plants (weeds)	non-selective herbicides kill nearly all plants they come into contact with and are used for clearing land or after a crop has been harvested, e.g. paraquat
		selective herbicides only affect one type of plant, so might be used to control broad-leaved plants such as dandelions in a wheat crop

The accumulation of pesticides

At the start of the 1940s, the organochlorine pesticide DDT (1,1-diphenyl-2,2,2-trichloroethane) was recognised for its effectiveness, even at low concentrations. DDT affects the sensory neurones of insects and was used with great success, particularly in controlling the mosquitoes which spread malaria. The use of DDT was widespread, since there did not seem to be a problem with toxicity in humans. Later, scientists discovered that because DDT is fat soluble, it tends to accumulate in fatty tissues within the bodies of animals further up the food chain; in these higher concentrations it is very toxic to invertebrates, fish and birds. This is called **bioaccumulation** and is illustrated by the data given in Table 39.6.

DDT and another pesticide called dieldrin are known to have affected populations of golden eagles in Scotland. The eagles fed on sheep carcasses which had been dipped in insecticides to control ticks and other parasites. The chemicals accumulated in the eagles' body tissues and affected reproduction and egg shell strength.

DDT is now banned in many countries, although it is still used in some developing countries because of its effectiveness in controlling malaria.

Table 39.6 DDT in the food chain

Animal	DDT (ppm)
zooplankton	0.04
small fish	0.5
large fish	2
fish-eating bird	25
water	3×10^{-6}

Integrated pest management

> Cultural, biological and chemical methods can be used to control pests. IPM uses a variety of these methods.

Often a variety of pest control methods will be used in a pest control programme called **integrated pest management (IPM)**. Growing and harvesting crops is a dynamic process, and the aim of an integrated programme is to use whatever method is optimum at a particular stage during the life cycle of crop plants. The method is selected by balancing a number of considerations, for example how effective the method is and the cost and ease of implementing the method. Figure 39.20 outlines how IPM might work for a crop of sugar beet, protecting it from diseases such as 'yellows disease' which is spread by aphids. The combination of more than one method of control may be more effective than using each method separately.

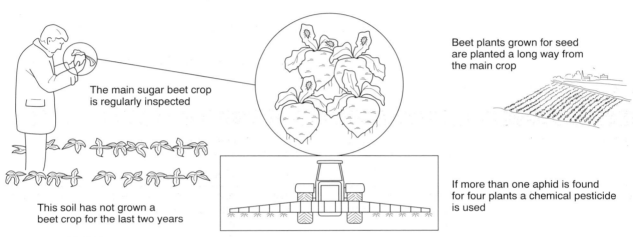

The main sugar beet crop is regularly inspected

Beet plants grown for seed are planted a long way from the main crop

This soil has not grown a beet crop for the last two years

If more than one aphid is found for four plants a chemical pesticide is used

Figure 39.20 In this IPM programme, several methods of crop protection are employed. Firstly, cultural methods include growing crops in widely spaced fields, and not growing the same crop in the same plot two years running. The crop is inspected regularly, and if more than one aphid is found for every four plants, chemical pest control in the form of spraying insecticide is introduced. *Source:* Zeneca *Food for thought* crop protection project briefing sheets for science students

Questions

1 a) List some reasons why crop protection is important.

   b) Suggest why crop protection methods vary in different countries.

   c) What are some of the disadvantages and advantages of

   i)   cultural control?

   ii) biological control?

   iii) chemical control?

   d) The use of pesticides is more likely to be necessary if cash crops for export are being produced, than if the goods are for home consumption. Suggest a reason why.

2 a) Which natural substances in some chrysanthemum species have pesticidal properties?

   b) Suggest why plants such as chrysanthemums produce compounds which have pesticidal properties.

3 The leaf-roller caterpillar and the red spider mite are both pests in apple orchards in Pennsylvania. Figure 39.21 shows the relationship of control methods in an IPM programme for these two pests:

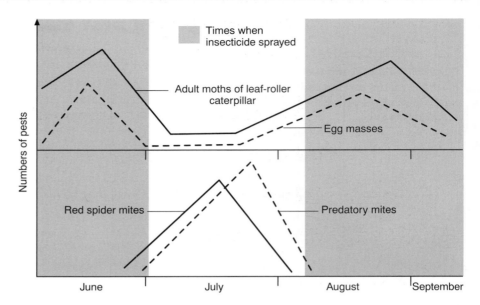

Figure 39.21 Pest control on apples

a) Which control method is involved in preventing damage from
(i) leaf-roller caterpillars (ii) red spider mites?

b) Which pest is a greater problem (i) at the start of the summer
(ii) midsummer?

c) Why is the timing of insecticide sprays for the leaf-roller caterpillar
critical in the overall programme?

d) What effects might a non-selective (broad spectrum) insecticide have
on the insect populations?

4 a) DDT is usually applied in very low concentrations for pest control, yet
it can cause death to animals further up the food chain. Explain why
this can happen.

b) The latest pesticides are less stable in the soil than the older style
pesticides. How does this affect the rate at which they break down?
Why is this feature useful?

c) Make a list of the ideal properties for a pesticide.

d) Suggest how people who work with pesticides might be at risk from
these compounds.

1 Figure 1 summarises data collected during a field trip. It shows a profile through some sand dunes and the percentage cover of four different species of flowering plant along a transect through these dunes.

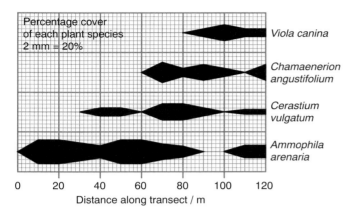

Figure 1

a) With the aid of the information in this diagram, explain what is meant by a succession. *(1 mark)*

b) Which of the four species named is best described as a pioneer species? Give evidence for your answer. *(2 marks)*

c) Table 1 shows the total number of plants of each species found in a 1 m² quadrat placed 40 m from the start of the transect.

Table 1

Species	Number of plants
Ammophila arenaria	35
Cerastium vulgatum	6

i) Calculate the index of diversity from the formula

$$\text{Index of diversity} = \frac{N(N-1)}{\sum n(n-1)}$$

Show your working. *(2 marks)*

ii) How would you expect the value of the index to change with distance along the transect? *(1 mark)*

AEB Specimen Question

2 Figure 2 represents the energy flow in kJ m⁻² year⁻¹ through the community in one area of sea in the English Channel.

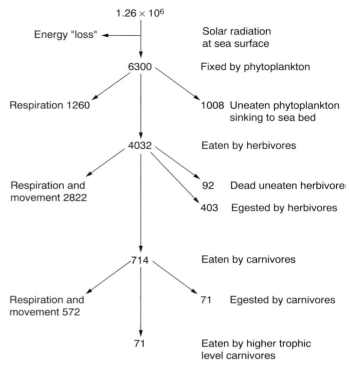

Figure 2

a) i) What percentage of the energy at the sea surface is fixed by the phytoplankton? *(1 mark)*

ii) Give *two* reasons for the 'loss' of energy at this stage. *(2 marks)*

b) Calculate:

i) the net primary production *(1 mark)*

ii) the total energy available to decomposers. *(1 mark)*

AEB Specimen Question

3 Figure 3 shows the lower jaws and teeth of three primates.

Figure 3

a) Give *two* differences between the teeth in jaw B and those in jaw A which may be used to identify jaw B as coming from a hominid. *(2 marks)*

b) i) In what way does the dentition in jaw B differ from that in jaw C? *(1 mark)*

   ii) How might this difference be related to diet? *(1 mark)*

AEB Specimen Question

4 Figure 4 shows the energy flow through a freshwater ecosystem. All units are kJ m^{-2} year^{-1}.

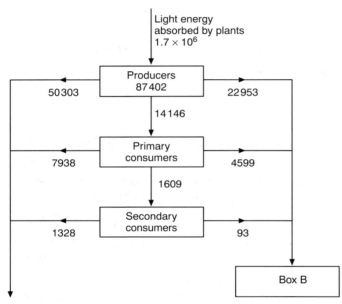

Figure 4

b) Name:

   i) process A *(1 mark)*

   ii) the group of organisms represented by Box B. *(1 mark)*

b) Showing your working in each case, calculate:

   i) the percentage efficiency with which light energy is converted into energy in producers; *(2 marks)*

   ii) the amount of energy which goes to tertiary consumers. *(2 marks)*

AEB Specimen Question

5 a) Give *two* differences between the members of each of the following pairs.

   i) Old World and New World monkeys *(2 marks)*

   ii) Old World monkeys and apes *(2 marks)*

b) Figure 5 shows the skeletons of a gibbon (anthropoid ape) and a human drawn to the same scale.

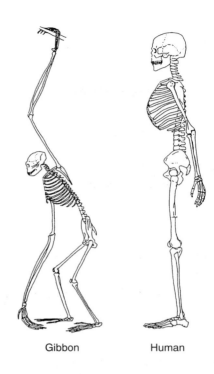

Gibbon   Human

Figure 5

The lengths of the forelimb and backbone of each organism, measured from the diagram, are given in Table 2.

Table 2

Organism	Length of forelimb (mm)	Length of backbone (mm)
gibbon	72	37
human	54	51

i) The ratio of the length of the forelimb to the length of the backbone is 1.95:1 in the gibbon. Calculate the ratio of the length of the forelimb to the length of the backbone for the human. Show your working. *(2 marks)*

ii) Suggest a reason for the different relative lengths of the forelimb in gibbons and humans. *(2 marks)*

c) Comment on differences, shown in Figure 5, in the skeletons of gibbons and humans with respect to:

i) the pelvis *(2 marks)*

ii) the hind limb. *(2 marks)*

Edexcel

6 a) Figure 6 shows the side views and rear views of the skulls of two subspecies of *Homo sapiens*.

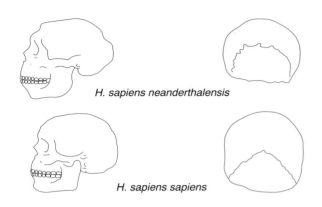

H. sapiens neanderthalensis

H. sapiens sapiens

Figure 6

State *three* visible differences shown by the skulls of these two subspecies. *(3 marks)*

b) Describe *one* method by which fossilised skeletons can be dated. *(2 marks)*

Edexcel

7 One method of sampling populations in an ecological study is to use a quadrat. A quadrat is an area of known size. Individuals of a population are not distributed uniformly, so if an estimate of density is to be made, a system of *random sampling* must be adopted.

a) i) Describe how random sampling can be carried out. *(2 marks)*

ii) Suggest *one* limitation of random sampling methods. *(1 mark)*

b) i) Describe how you could use a quadrat to estimate the percentage frequency of plants in a habitat. *(3 marks)*

ii) Suggest *one* way in which quadrats could be used to study changes in plant populations. *(3 marks)*

c) Describe *one* method you could use for sampling the animals present in a *named* habitat. *(2 marks)*

Edexcel

8 In an investigation to find the effect of applying a nitrogen fertiliser to a cereal crop, four fields were treated with different quantities of the fertiliser. One field was left untreated. The grain yield and the quantity of nitrogen leached from the soil in each field were measured. The results of this investigation are shown in Figure 7.

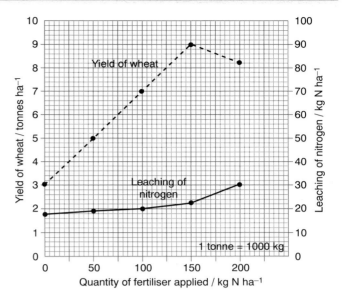

Figure 7

a) Explain why nitrogen fertiliser is applied to most crops. *(3 marks)*

b) With reference to Figure 7, comment on the effect of increasing the quantity of nitrogen fertiliser on

i) grain yield *(2 marks)*

ii) quantity of nitrogen leached from the soil. *(2 marks)*

c) i) Complete Table 3 below by calculating the quantity of nitrogen leached in grams per kg grain yield. *(2 marks)*

ii) Plot the figures from Table 3 on graph paper with quantity of fertiliser applied (kg N ha^{-1}) on the *x*-axis and quantity of nitrogen leached (g kg^{-1} grain yield) on the *y*-axis. *(2 marks)*

d) Explain the importance of this type of investigation to farmers. *(3 marks)*

UCLES

Table 3

Quantity of nitrogen fertiliser applied (kg N ha^{-1}	Quantity of nitrogen leached (g kg^{-1} grain yield)
0	6.0
50	
100	2.8
150	
200	3.7

9 A student noticed that the density of some plant species appeared to differ depending on how far the plants were from a main road.

The mean density (plants per m²) of three plant species A, B and C was measured at different distances from the main road. The mean density of the same three plant species was also determined at the side of a narrower secondary road in the same locality.

The results of the investigations are shown in Figure 8.

a) Describe a procedure the student could have used to determine the mean density of the three plant species. *(4 marks)*

b) i) Comment on the relationships between plant density and the distance from the main and secondary road for species A and B. *(4 marks)*

ii) Comment on the ways in which the distribution of plant species C differs from that of plant species A. *(2 marks)*

c) In addition to determining the plant densities, the student measured the pH of soil samples taken at the same distance from each of the roads. The results are shown in Figure 9.

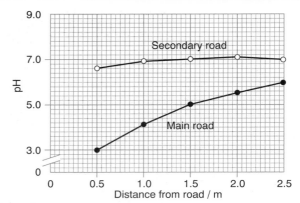

Figure 9

i) Suggest an explanation for the differences between the pH of the soil at the side of the main road and the pH at the side of the secondary road. *(2 marks)*

ii) Using the data given for pH, suggest an explanation for the distribution of the three species A, B and C. *(2 marks)*

iii) Suggest *one* factor, other than pH, which could account for the differences in density distribution of the plant species at the side of the main road. *(1 mark)*

Edexcel

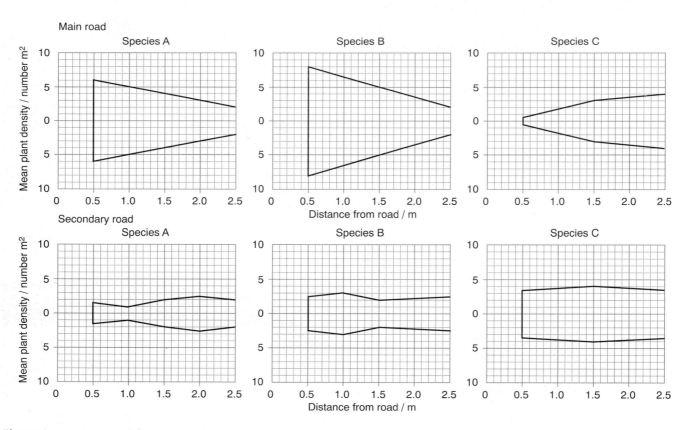

Figure 8

Basics in Brief

Skills with numbers

Statistics

In this book, the term **statistics** is used to mean the science of collecting and analysing data, and the word **data** is used for numerical or non-numerical information. In any investigation, scientists can usually only collect a relatively small amount of data from a sample of living things, and there is bound to be some experimental error however careful they are. The idea of using statistics (or statistical techniques) is to assess how certain they can be that their data is typical of a much larger sample. This is a basis from which to make predictions about trends and patterns.

Statistics is significant

Collecting the data is one thing, but understanding what it means and what it tells you is another. Cases of BSE and the number of people eating beef. Significant risk? Probably not, yet decisions of huge economic and social relevance may depend on the significance.

Some basic terms

- **arithmetic mean:** the sum of measurements divided by the number of measurements
- **categorical data:** does not have a numerical value e.g. blue or brown eyes
- **continuous data:** any value in a given range e.g. the height of a person
- **discrete data:** can only take distinct values in a certain range e.g. number of siblings
- **interval data:** data measured in quantified units e.g. mass, linear height
- **matched pairs:** data is collected from the same or closely related subject for each condition e.g. bubbles of oxygen emerging from the cut stems of two lengths of pondweed are counted at different temperatures, where both stems are taken from the same plant
- **median:** middle value when all the values are ranked in order of magnitude; useful when some of the sample values are very different from the majority of the values, in which case the sample mean is altered by them
- **mode:** the value that occurs most frequently; generally used for categorical data
- **normal distribution:** evenly distributed data around a central cluster giving a bell-shaped curve
- **ordinal data:** arrangement of data in order (where size is not known) e.g. not sour, slightly sour, very sour

- **probability (p):** the likelihood of an event occurring by chance
- **range:** the difference between the highest and lowest measurement
- **significance level:** the probability of an event occurring by chance shown as a decimal fraction or percentage e.g. the probability of an event occurring by chance is 0.05 or 5%
- **standard deviation:** a way of measuring the spread around a sample mean
- **unmatched pairs:** data is collected from sources which vary in more than one respect, making it less reliable to compare them e.g. heart rate of two people after different amounts of exercise, where the people differ in age or gender

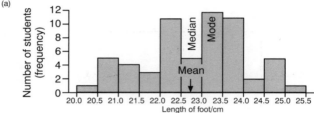

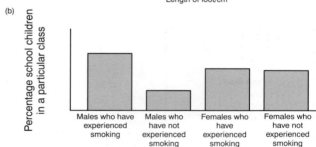

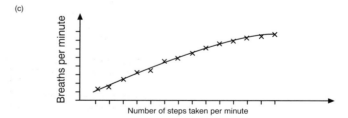

Figure 1 Data is presented in a variety of ways
(a) A histogram showing frequency of foot length in a group of students: all lengths are possible within the measured range for the independent variable, which is foot size.
(b) A barchart showing school children who have experienced cigarette smoking by the age of 13 years: there are distinct categories of students, who have either tried smoking or who have not (this is the independent variable).
(c) A line graph of breathing rate (recorded at the same time after starting exercise) plotted against number of steps taken per minute. Where the independent variable is chosen by the experimenter (number of steps per minute) and the dependent variable changes according to the independent variable (breathing rate depends on the amount of exercise).

Calculating the arithmetic mean

$$\bar{x} = \frac{(\Sigma x)}{n}$$

n = the number of measurements
x = the measurement
$\bar{x}$ = the arithmetic mean (called $\bar{x}$ bar)
Σ = the sign for sum or add up

Choose your statistics carefully

Before starting an experiment or investigation it is important to think about how the data will be analysed. In other words, deciding on statistical tests should happen at the planning stage, to make sure that useful data is collected. Figure 2 shows a flow chart on how to choose a statistical test from a small selection, and therefore the type of data required.

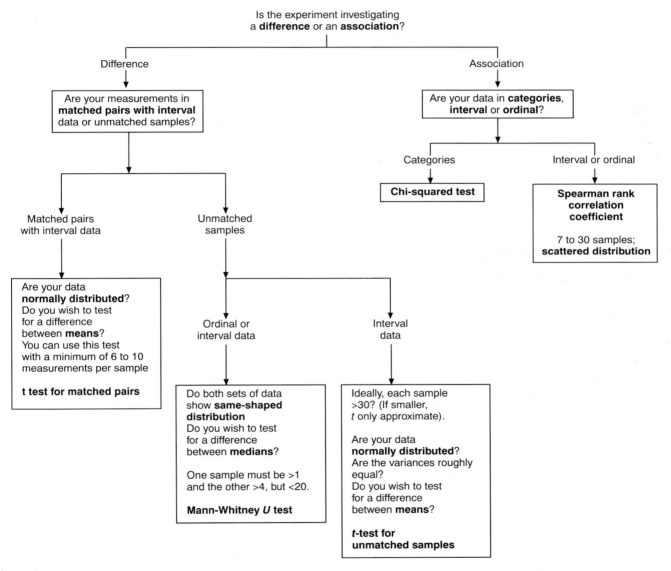

Figure 2

Using IT

Information technology (IT) is about all aspects of collecting, storing, retrieving, analysing, interpreting and presenting data or other information. How much use you make of IT during your studies depends to a certain extent on the availability of facilities, the nature of the course and personal preference. However, IT skills are useful for any sort of coursework

investigation or assignment. To illustrate this point, Figure 3 shows how IT might be used in fieldwork, however, the ideas are transferable to other types of projects.

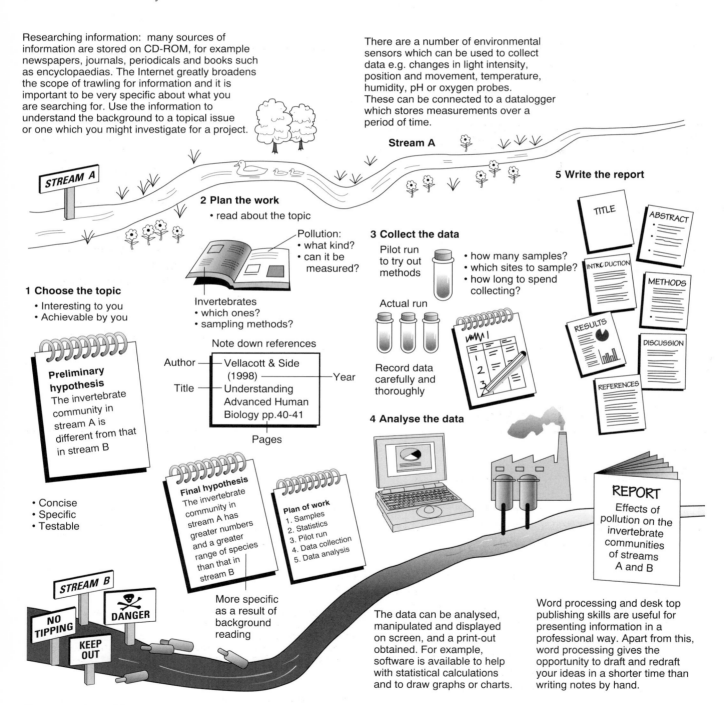

Researching information: many sources of information are stored on CD-ROM, for example newspapers, journals, periodicals and books such as encyclopaedias. The Internet greatly broadens the scope of trawling for information and it is important to be very specific about what you are searching for. Use the information to understand the background to a topical issue or one which you might investigate for a project.

There are a number of environmental sensors which can be used to collect data e.g. changes in light intensity, position and movement, temperature, humidity, pH or oxygen probes. These can be connected to a datalogger which stores measurements over a period of time.

Stream A

5 Write the report

TITLE
ABSTRACT
INTRODUCTION
METHODS
RESULTS
DISCUSSION
REFERENCES

2 Plan the work
• read about the topic

Pollution:
• what kind?
• can it be measured?

3 Collect the data

Pilot run to try out methods

• how many samples?
• which sites to sample?
• how long to spend collecting?

Actual run

Invertebrates
• which ones?
• sampling methods?

1 Choose the topic
• Interesting to you
• Achievable by you

Note down references

Author — Vellacott & Side (1998) — Year
Title — Understanding Advanced Human Biology pp.40-41
Pages

Record data carefully and thoroughly

Preliminary hypothesis
The invertebrate community in stream A is different from that in stream B

4 Analyse the data

• Concise
• Specific
• Testable

Final hypothesis
The invertebrate community in stream A has greater numbers and a greater range of species than that in stream B

Plan of work
1. Samples
2. Statistics
3. Pilot run
4. Data collection
5. Data analysis

REPORT
Effects of pollution on the invertebrate communities of streams A and B

STREAM B
NO TIPPING
DANGER
KEEP OUT

More specific as a result of background reading

The data can be analysed, manipulated and displayed on screen, and a print-out obtained. For example, software is available to help with statistical calculations and to draw graphs or charts.

Word processing and desk top publishing skills are useful for presenting information in a professional way. Apart from this, word processing gives the opportunity to draft and redraft your ideas in a shorter time than writing notes by hand.

Figure 3 Adapted from an article in *Biological Science Review*, May 1996.

SI (Standard International) units

SI units are used universally in scientific work. They allow the measurements made in all studies to be compared. Table 1 shows some examples of SI units and Table 2 gives the different SI units for length.

Table 1

Physical quantity	Name of SI unit	Symbol
length	metre	m
mass	kilogram	kg
time	second	s

Table 2 SI units for length

Name	Symbol	Decimal fraction of a metre
kilometre	km	$10^3 = 1000$ m
metre	m	$1 = 1000$ mm
millimetre	mm	$10^{-3} = 1000$ µm
micrometre (micron)	µm	$10^{-6} = 1000$ nm
nanometre	nm	$10^{-9} = 1000$ pm
picometre	pm	10^{-12}

Other units that you are likely to use:

- Mass   kilogram (kg)
  gram (g) = 0.001 kg (that is 1000 g = 1 kg)

- Volume   decimetre dm^3 (previously the litre)
  cubic centimetre (1 cc) = millimetre (ml) or $1\ dm^{-3}$
- Area   hectare (ha)   1 ha = 10^4 m
- Pressure   Pascal (Pa)   1 Pa = 1 newton m^{-2}
- Energy   joule (J)
  kilojoule (kJ) = 10^3 J or 1000 J
  megajoule (mJ) = 10^3 kJ or 10^6 J

Rules for writing SI units

1 The symbol is not an abbreviation and so it is only followed by a full stop at the end of a sentence.
2 The units are never written as plurals (2 kg and 3 m are correct but 2 kgs and 3 ms are wrong).
3 Symbols that are combined to show for example the number of a particular species (say 30) found per square metre are written in full as 30 per square metre, or in short as 30 m^{-2}. The stroke (/) is used only for showing the unit of a variable (as on the axis of a graph) such as temperature/°C.
4 When writing decimal numbers the decimal point should be in line with the base of the numerals e.g. 2.345. Large numbers should be written with a space (not a comma) separating groups of three digits e.g. 200 000.

Full information can be found in *Biological Nomenclature: Recommendations on Terms, Units and Symbols* published by the Institute of Biology (1989).

Revise basic chemistry

Atom

- The atom is the smallest particle of matter. All matter is made of atoms.
- Each atom has a central nucleus containing *positively* charged **protons** and **neutrons** which have *no charge*.
- Around the nucleus *negatively* charged **electrons** orbit in shells.
- The innermost shell carries up to two electrons and the next three, a maximum of eight. The shells fill up in order. An incompletely filled shell is *unstable*.
- The number of protons and electrons are the same and so an atom has no charge.
- An atom may gain an extra neutron. This will make it heavier, but will not alter its charge. If an atom has two forms like this, they are called **isotopes**.

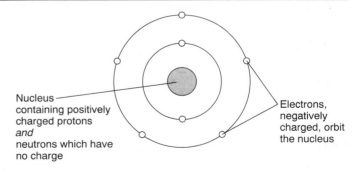

Nucleus containing positively charged protons *and* neutrons which have no charge

Electrons, negatively charged, orbit the nucleus

- There are always the same number of protons (+ve) as electrons (–ve) and so the atom is not charged
- Each electron shell (orbit) has a maximum number of electrons that it can hold. For the first (innermost) shell this number is 2, and for the second shell it is 8. When a shell is 'full' the atom is unreactive.

Figure 4 This shows the nucleus of an atom with the shells of electrons orbiting around it

Element

- An element is a pure substance which contains identical atoms, e.g. calcium, carbon, hydrogen, oxygen, nitrogen.
- The **Periodic Table** displays all the elements.
- All elements have a *symbol* by which they are internationally recognised. Some of the symbols that are commonly found in biology are shown in Table 3.

Table 3 Some chemical elements of biological importance

Element	Symbol
carbon	C
hydrogen	H
oxygen	O
nitrogen	N
phosphorus	P
sodium	Na
potassium	K
sulphur	S
calcium	Ca
iron	Fe
chlorine	Cl

Compound

- A compound is a substance made of more than one type of atom which cannot be separated except by a chemical reaction, e.g. carbon dioxide (CO_2) contains one atom of carbon (C) and two atoms of oxygen (O).

Molecule

- Molecules are groups of atoms joined together by chemical bonds. They have a stable arrangement of electrons in their outer shell.
- A molecule of an *element* will contain just one type of atom chemically combined, e.g. oxygen (O_2) is two oxygen atoms combined.
- A molecule of a *compound* will have more than one type of atom chemically combined, e.g. a molecule of sodium chloride or salt (NaCl) contains one sodium atom (Na) and one chlorine atom (Cl).

Ion

- An ion is a charged particle.
- If an atom *loses* an electron it becomes an ion which has a *positive* charge (or **cation**), e.g. Na^+ is a sodium ion.
- If an atom *gains* an electron, it has a *negative* charge (and is called an **anion**), e.g. Cl^- is a chloride ion.
- Groups of atoms may be charged, e.g. CO_3^{2-} is the carbonate ion.
- Ions often form when compounds are in solution.

Chemical bonds

- Chemical bonds are forces holding the atoms combined in a molecule in place (Figure 5).
- **Covalent bonds** form when two atoms *share* electrons from their outer shells and so in effect fill and stabilise the shells. If a single electron is required to complete a shell, the atom has a **valency** (combining power) of one. The valency of an atom can be two (e.g. oxygen), three (e.g. nitrogen) or four (e.g. carbon).
- **Ionic bonds** occur when atoms gain or lose electrons and become ions. For example a sodium atom (Na) may lose an electron from its outer shell to a chlorine atom (Cl). The result is that a positive sodium ion (Na^+) and a negative chloride ion (Cl^-) are formed. The ionic bond is the **electrostatic force** that attracts the two ions in the sodium chloride compound (NaCl).
- **Hydrogen bonds** are *weak* electrostatic forces between a slightly positive hydrogen atom and a slightly negative oxygen atom. They are important in attracting water molecules, in large numbers they hold organic molecules together and they also link the two strands of the DNA helix.

Oxidation and reduction (or redox reactions)

Redox reactions are important chemical reactions because they are the basic reactions of metabolism.

Reminder: Metabolism involves two types of process:

1 **Catabolism** in which molecules are broken down using oxidation reactions which are exergonic (energy is transferred away from the original molecules).
   Example: aerobic respiration.
2 **Anabolism** in which molecules are synthesised using reduction reactions which are endergonic (and require an input of energy into the system).
   Example: photosynthesis.

The changes that can occur in molecules during oxidation and reduction reactions are shown in Table 4.

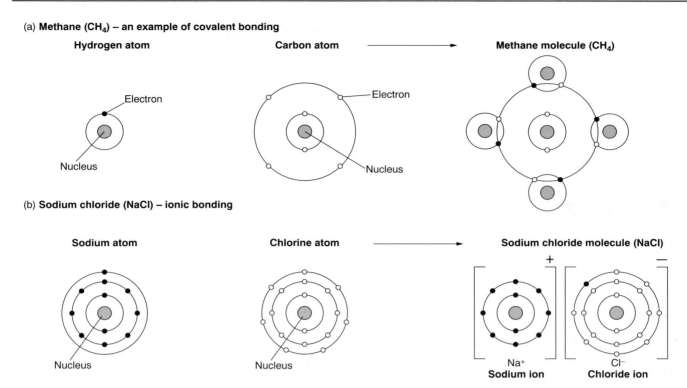

(a) Methane (CH₄) – an example of covalent bonding

Hydrogen atom Carbon atom Methane molecule (CH₄)

Electron
Nucleus
Electron
Nucleus

(b) Sodium chloride (NaCl) – ionic bonding

Sodium atom Chlorine atom Sodium chloride molecule (NaCl)

Nucleus Nucleus

Na⁺
Sodium ion

Cl⁻
Chloride ion

Figure 5 (a) Methane has the chemical formula CH₄. There are covalent bonds between the carbon and four hydrogen atoms. Each hydrogen atom shares its single electron with the carbon atom, so filling the outer shell of the carbon atom (eight electrons). At the same time the structure of the hydrogen atoms is stabilised because each now has a full outer shell.
(b) An ionic bond holds the positive and negative ions together, as in a molecule of sodium chloride, NaCl.

Table 4

	Oxidation reaction	**Reduction reaction**
hydrogen	is lost	is gained
oxygen	is gained	is lost
electrons	are lost	are gained
energy	output	input

So in other words:

- a molecule which has lost hydrogen and/or electrons or has gained oxygen has been **oxidised**;
- a molecule which has gained hydrogen and/or electrons or has lost oxygen has been **reduced**.

pH

pH is a scale which measures the acidity of a solution. The pH scale runs from 0–14. The lower half of the scale pH <7.0 is acid, pH 7.0 is neutral and pH >7.0 is alkaline (or basic).

Acidity is due to hydrogen ions (H^+) in solution:

- for a pH lower than 7.0 there are *more* hydrogen ions than hydroxyl ions (OH^-);
- at pH 7.0 there are *equal* concentrations of hydrogen ions and hydroxyl ions;
- for a pH higher than 7.0 there are *fewer* hydrogen ions than hydroxyl ions.

The pH scale is **logarithmic** which means that for every change in one unit on the pH scale there is a ten-fold (×10) change in concentration in hydrogen ions.

How do we find the pH?

1 pH can be determined using an **indicator** such as Universal Indicator which changes colour on contact with the test solution. Indicator is available both in paper form or as a solution.
2 pH can also be measured with a **pH meter** connected to a probe which is sensitive to hydrogen ions. Some meters must be standardised with a solution of known pH before being used.

Why is pH important?

- The pH of the internal environment of a living organism is critical and *must* remain within narrowly defined limits.
- The pH of the external environment is an important ecological factor.
- pH changes affect the functioning of proteins, including enzymes, by changing the shape of the protein molecule.

INDEX